P9-DVP-981

In the Stream of History

Shaping Foreign Policy for a New Era

In the Stream of History

Shaping Foreign Policy for a New Era

Warren Christopher

Stanford University Press
Stanford, California
1998

E.C.C.C. LIBRARY

Stanford University Press
Stanford, California
© 1998 by Warren Christopher. All rights reserved.

No part of this book may be reproduced
or utilized in any form or by any means, electronic
or mechanical, including photocopying and recording,
or by any information storage and retrieval system,
without permission in writing from the publisher.

Printed in the United States of America

CIP data are at the end of the book

JX
1417
.C48
1998

To Marie, with love

Preface

I have long been intrigued by the vital role that speeches play in state-craft. This interest goes back to 1959, when I took a leave from my law firm, O'Melveny & Myers, to go to Sacramento as Special Counsel to newly elected California Governor Edmund G. (Pat) Brown. As a speech-writer for the Governor, I drafted his inaugural address, coining the phrase "responsible liberalism" to describe his approach (the word "liberal" was not yet politically taboo). I also worked on his major messages on education (supporting expansion of California's renowned system of higher education), on water (leading to enactment of the historic California Water Plan), on smog (foreshadowing the first major assault on air pollution), and on employment discrimination (supporting the controversial Fair Employment Practices Commission). The initiatives launched in these messages became the foundation for California's extraordinary progress during the Governor's two terms in the Statehouse.

Although I remained in Sacramento only a year, Governor Brown became a lifelong friend and supporter. Almost until he died in 1996 at age 90, the Governor spoke about my work on his inaugural address and other speeches. He enjoyed telling how Clark Clifford put skillful finishing touches on my draft of his remarks at the annual Washington Gridiron Club dinner in 1959, and how the success of those remarks contributed to a brief boomlet of support for him as the 1960 Democratic presidential nominee.

As the years passed, I observed many instances in which the drafting and delivery of a speech produced an innovation or policy change that might not otherwise have occurred. In particular, for the Secretary of State, speeches are a primary means of setting and articulating U.S. foreign policy. As I worked on my farewell remarks prior to leaving that office in January 1997, I had the chance to reflect on the role of speeches in shaping my major themes and initiatives as Secretary. These musings led to discussions with Norris Pope, the Director of Stanford University Press, about a book organized around speeches I had delivered during my four years in office.

The speeches selected for inclusion in this book identify the major foreign policy challenges faced and decisions made during President Clinton's first term. The essays that introduce the speeches illuminate policy-making in the Clinton Administration. They describe the circumstances in which the speeches were delivered, reveal their broader purposes and the ways they were used as instruments of diplomacy, and establish the contexts in which major policy decisions were made. They are intended not only to give the who, what, when, and where behind these events, but most important, to explain the why and how. The Prologue sets the scene for the whole group of speeches, describing how I came to be appointed Secretary, the importance of speeches as a tool of diplomacy, and my assessment of the opportunities and challenges facing American foreign policy. To gather the strands together at the end of the book, the Epilogue recounts my decision to return to private life and offers some thoughts on objectives for the United States in the years ahead.

The book is intended to give the reader a window into our diplomacy from 1993 to 1997. I hope it will be interesting and useful, especially for students of contemporary American foreign policy and scholars of diplomatic history, here and abroad. It does not purport to be a comprehensive history of American foreign policy in this four-year period. Because the subjects of my speeches were dictated in part by exigencies we did not control, the book may give disproportionate emphasis to certain topics, and it no doubt slights or even overlooks others of importance.

This book, like other endeavors in my life, is the product of teamwork. To the other members of the team, I am deeply grateful.

Derek Chollet was the principal researcher and helped with the drafting. To our collaboration, he brought insight, energy, cheerfulness, and wisdom beyond his age.

Former colleagues at the State Department provided invaluable assistance. Strobe Talbott was a constant source of wise advice, encouragement, and sensitive revisions that could not have come from anyone else. Peter Tarnoff read the entire book at a crucial moment, and provided many thoughtful suggestions. Tom Donilon watched over the entire project with his customary wisdom and tough-mindedness. Winston Lord and Dennis Ross generously provided advice and expert editing on the portions relating to Asia and the Middle East, respectively. Bennett Freeman helped me with the concept for the book, for which there seems to be no close precedent, and then skillfully reviewed the scene-setting essays. Nick Burns, Lynn Davis, Meg Donovan, Robert Einhorn, Robert Gallucci, Les Gelb, James Gibney, John Hannah, Richard Holbrooke, Heather Hurlburt, Craig Johnstone, Barbara Larkin, Tom Malinowski, George Moose, Jeremy Rosner, Wendy Sherman, Joan Spero, James Steinberg, Alec Watson, and Andrew Weiss generously provided their memories and insights to help me piece together the scene-setters and other material.

The State Department graciously allowed me to refresh my memory from my papers and other documents from my time in office. Bill Burns ensured that the Department's resources were made available to me, and Scott Zeiss and Ken Rossman were also most helpful. Jim O'Brien shepherded the manuscript of this book through the customary Department review process.

The Stanford University Press made the publishing experience an entirely pleasurable one. Director Norris Pope was a model of helpfulness from beginning to end, encouraging me to undertake this unusual project and then supporting its expansion. Not the least of his contributions was the selection of Lynn Stewart as my copy editor. Since I make no claims to writing as a vocation, I relied on her talented and keen eyes to edit, hone, and tighten the manuscript. I am grateful to Janet Wood for the design of the book, to Stacey Lynn for overseeing production, and to Executive Editor Muriel Bell for her help in the process. Stanford's Provost, Condoleezza Rice, somehow found the time to read and support my proposal for the book, and to offer suggestions.

O'Melveny & Myers provided the kind of nurturing support that could only come from a firm with which I have been happily connected, on and off, for 47 years. My secretary, Kerin Holmes, not only typed and managed the flood of drafts and revisions, but straightened out my grammar, found missing facts, and finished my sentences. My Executive Assistant, Kathleen Osborne, organized my life and fended off intrusions so that I could find time for the book. Our librarian, Pat Smith, ensured that my requests for library help were always complied with and often exceeded. My partner Richard Ross provided wise advice on contractual issues, and Mark Steinberg, another partner, brought his sharp eye for photographic images to the selection of the pictures and also provided sensitive comments on the text.

With all of the excellent help I had, the book should have been perfect. Alas, it is not. When the errors are discovered and interpretations challenged, it will be good to remember that I alone am responsible.

Note to the Reader

The speeches in this book are reprinted verbatim from State Department sources, except for the correction of obvious typographical errors.

The Department of State has reviewed the manuscript of this book to ensure that its contents do not compromise national security. This review should not be construed as concurrence with the text. Opinions and characterizations are those of the author and do not necessarily represent official positions of the United States Government.

Contents

Photographs follow p. 270. All photographs are from State Department archives unless otherwise indicated.

Get out in the stream of history, and swim as fast as you can.

—*Advice given by*
United States Supreme Court Justice
William O. Douglas to his law clerk
Warren Christopher, 1949 Term

Prologue

When 1992 began, I was starting to think about new directions. Ten intense years as Chairman of O'Melveny & Myers, an international law firm headquartered in Los Angeles, were drawing to a close. During that period, the firm had grown from 254 to 550 attorneys and had steadily improved its financial performance. Also ending was my work as Chairman of the Independent Commission on the Los Angeles Police Department, which had been established in the wake of the videotaped beating of Rodney King. Although I planned to remain an active partner in the law firm, at age 66 I was anticipating a greater emphasis on public affairs and pro bono activities, such as my chairmanship of the Carnegie Corporation of New York, a foundation that supports innovative programs in international dispute resolution and child development.

My involvement with Arkansas Governor Bill Clinton's campaign for the presidency developed unexpectedly. Mickey Kantor, a longtime friend, fellow Los Angeles attorney, and member of the Independent Commission, was Clinton's national campaign manager. I had been interested in Clinton since he had briefly considered running in 1988, and had met him at Kantor's home. In the summer of 1991, Clinton came to my office in downtown Los Angeles to exchange views with me on police issues. His extensive knowledge of law enforcement matters, especially the emerging concept of community-based policing, impressed me. Although I did not know him well, I became convinced by the end of 1991 that he was the best candidate for the presidency. At Kantor's request, I agreed to introduce the Governor at a fund-raising dinner in Beverly Hills on Feb-

1

ruary 28, 1992, not long after the New Hampshire primary. Clinton had revived his fortunes by finishing a strong second there despite scurrilous tabloid charges, but it remained a perilous time for his campaign.

Clinton arrived in Los Angeles late in the afternoon after a demanding campaign stop in Seattle, and his staff was anxious for him to get an hour's rest before the evening events. My instructions were to greet him at the hotel, walk him up to his suite, and leave him to nap. However, he had other plans; as was often the case, he preferred talking to sleeping. He ordered some fruit from room service and plied me with questions about the Presidents I had served, especially Lyndon Johnson. He roared with laughter when I told him about the time I broke a toe rushing to answer a 2:00 A.M. telephone call from Johnson and had a long conversation with him without letting on.

Soon it was time for us to go to the dinner. As I walked through the hotel with him, I had my first chance to observe the Clinton treatment. He dispensed smiles and hugs, and charmed all those who were lined up in the passageways to greet him. When he stopped to shake hands or say hello, he displayed the "locked-on" eye contact that is his special gift. He had the kind of raw appeal that I had not seen since President Kennedy.

The campaign staff had offered to help me with the introduction, but instead I had written it myself, and it happened to click. The audience especially liked my comment that in the face of the tabloid attacks in New Hampshire, Governor Clinton had "avoided the paralysis of self-pity, and he didn't whine." Many people have asked me how Clinton can carry on despite harsh and unremitting attacks, both political and personal. The answer lies in his unusual ability to start anew and undaunted each day, no matter what has gone before.

The Vice Presidential Search

Not long after the Beverly Hills event, the Governor asked me to head up the effort to help him select a running mate. Washington lawyer Vernon Jordan, who was a close friend of both Mr. and Mrs. Clinton, and Vermont Governor Madeleine Kunin joined me on a three-person search committee.

My first meeting with Governor Clinton on the vice presidential selection accurately foreshadowed our subsequent working relationship. Kantor and I flew overnight to meet him at a campaign stop in Tallahassee, Florida, on April 25. When we arrived at his hotel suite at about 8:00 A.M., he was out running. After returning and showering, he joined us for breakfast. His healthy appetite was on full display after his long run, but it did not keep us from getting down to business. In 90 minutes, we covered a lot of ground. Speaking from an outline that Kantor and I had prepared, I described the qualifications for the vice presidency and the proposed ground rules for the search. Clinton listened intently, with few interruptions, and in subsequent weeks he frequently referred back to points I had made.

Although we discussed a long list of factors to be considered, I emphasized that in this age of instant communications, a running mate's basic ability and achievements are more important than the geographical or ideological balance he or she brings to the ticket. Clinton agreed and later said publicly that the most important criterion for a Vice President was the ability to assume the presidency if necessary. He also agreed that the search should begin with interviews that would simultaneously seek advice on the search itself, evaluate those being interviewed, and gauge their levels of interest in the position.

Kantor and I had prepared a list of possible running mates, and the Governor went over it carefully, adding some names, removing others, and imploring us to be imaginative and not limit ourselves to those who were already government leaders. This process resulted in a "long list" of 38 people on whom we would prepare first-stage background memoranda based upon public sources. The Governor said he would expect periodic reports from us and would later quietly interview a "short list," but agreed that there should be no demeaning public parade of candidates. I left the meeting with the sense of authority and flexibility that I would feel many times in the next four years. Clinton had laid down a broad set of parameters, but within them, he was open to suggestions and willing for me to proceed in my own way. I could tell that he read everything I sent him, but he did not micromanage.

That spring, the Governor was, of course, campaigning vigorously all over the country. During this period I delivered to him the first-stage memoranda on potential running mates; after he studied them, we reviewed the results of my interviews at some length. I consulted closely with Vernon Jordan and Governor Kunin as the process moved along.

On June 7, Governor Clinton told Kantor and me that he wanted to move to the "second stage" on a short list consisting of Governor Mario Cuomo of New York, Senator Al Gore of Tennessee, Congressman Lee Hamilton of Indiana, former Senator Paul Tsongas of Massachusetts, and Senator Harris Wofford of Pennsylvania. Subsequently, he added Senators Bob Kerrey of Nebraska and Bob Graham of Florida to this list. He resisted pressure from party officials to add a woman and an African American for purposes of diversity. I commented that doing so would depart from the principled process he had set in motion. He agreed, adding that it would be misleading to those involved and that "people don't like to be used."

The second stage required the individuals being considered to complete a detailed questionnaire and allow the examination of their tax returns and medical records. Governor Cuomo and former Senator Tsongas declined to proceed to this stage, the latter in part for reasons of health. During June and early July, Governor Clinton interviewed those remaining on the short list, and I reviewed with him the results of the second-stage investigations. I traveled to Little Rock on July 8 to give him the answers to some last-minute inquiries regarding various candidates.

Earlier that day, I had met with Senator and Mrs. Gore at their farm in Carthage, Tennessee. I was impressed that as a young Congressman, Gore had devoted the necessary time and effort to make himself an expert on arms control, and that as a new Senator, he had had the discipline to research and write a major book on the environment. I thought that these areas of expertise would complement Governor Clinton's own background. Beyond Gore's public record, I was taken with his high personal standards. Although not authorized to make a proposal, I wanted to get a sense of how he was likely to respond if asked to join the ticket; his demeanor in this regard was reassuring.

At about 11:00 that night, after some conversation and deliberation, Governor Clinton said he was ready to invite Senator Gore to be his running mate. First, however, he honored a commitment to call Senator Graham in time for him to meet a midnight deadline to file for reelection. At about midnight, Clinton talked to Gore, who accepted his invitation without hesitation, and the two immediately began discussing the strategy for making the announcement. Thus began the most extraordinary partnership of its kind in our history, with the Vice President's influence especially strong in foreign affairs.

The Offer I Couldn't Refuse

A few days after the election, President-elect Clinton asked me to serve as his Transition Director. He had been pleased with the process that resulted in his choice of Senator Gore as his running mate, and he wanted me to adapt it to the selection of his first cabinet. As a result, in the heady atmosphere of victory, the President-elect, the Vice President–elect, and a group of key advisers gathered daily in the den of the Governor's Mansion in Little Rock to consider the departments, one by one. We started with those responsible for economic issues, which had been so dominant in the campaign.[1]

When we came to the Department of State, however, Clinton short-circuited the process. As the other participants left the room after a two-hour discussion of the Department and the leading candidates for the position of Secretary, he asked me to stay behind. We should not waste any more time, he said; I was his choice to be Secretary, and Gore agreed with him. That came as a surprise, because when I had been appointed Transition Director, I had publicly taken myself out of the running for any cabinet position. But the President-elect said that he didn't feel bound by my recusal.

This was the one offer that could have made me change my mind about staying in Los Angeles. I had a lifelong interest in diplomacy and foreign affairs. Born in 1925, I grew up in Scranton, North Dakota, a classic small prairie town of 300 people in the southwestern corner of the state. Until

---

[1]The economic team assembled by President Clinton was strong and deep, and it was instrumental in achieving a record-breaking period of sustained prosperity. It included the Treasury Secretary, Lloyd Bentsen, formerly Chairman of the Senate Finance Committee; the Chairman of the new White House National Economic Council, Robert Rubin, previously co-Chairman of the investment banking firm Goldman, Sachs; the Director of the Office of Management and Budget, Leon Panetta, formerly Chairman of the House of Representatives Budget Committee; and the Chairman of the Council of Economic Advisers, Laura Tyson, formerly a professor of economics at the University of California at Berkeley.

my father, who ran the local bank, had a massive cerebral hemorrhage when I was 11, Scranton was a wonderful place for me to grow up, but from an early age, I was anxious to look beyond the prairie horizon. Up-to-date periodicals were scarce in Scranton, and I eagerly awaited each arrival of *National Geographic* and *Time* (which then had an extensive foreign section). A move to Los Angeles in a vain attempt to restore my father's health, high school and college in California, and naval service in the Pacific put me in direct touch with the broader world.

At Stanford Law School in 1946, my dean, Carl B. Spaeth, had just come from a State Department position, and it was he who first sparked my interest in public service. He talked to me about Dean Acheson, who had been named Secretary of State in 1948, and gave me his early speeches. Thereafter, I followed Acheson's career as a lawyer-diplomat with great interest. After law school, I clerked for Supreme Court Justice William O. Douglas, who traveled the world whenever his Court duties permitted and wrote fascinating books about his trips. As I was completing my clerkship, I asked his advice about my future, and he responded, "Get out in the stream of history, and swim as fast as you can."

In 1961, I had my first chance to get involved in foreign affairs, in a rather unusual role. Friends from law-clerking days recommended to George W. Ball, then the Under Secretary of State for Economic Affairs, that I head up an interagency team on international textile negotiations that he was supervising. The team's goal was to provide some relief for the domestic textile industry without succumbing to protectionism—a very tall order.[2] Before the year was out, I had joined Ball in representing the United States in an international conference in Geneva and headed up bilateral textile negotiations in Tokyo. Over the next four years, I took several brief leaves from law practice to lead the U.S. delegation in follow-up negotiations. From 1967 to 1969, I served as Deputy Attorney General of the United States under President Lyndon Johnson.

Not long after President Carter was elected in 1976, his Secretary of State–designate, Cyrus Vance, called out of the blue to ask me to take the recently created number-two position in the Department, that of Deputy Secretary of State. Vance and I had become well acquainted in

---

[2]Ball, *The Past Has Another Pattern: Memoirs*, pp. 190–93 (New York: Norton, 1982); James A. Bill, *George Ball*, p. 66 (New Haven, Conn.: Yale University Press, 1997).

1967, when he was called back from civilian life to be President Johnson's special representative during the Detroit riots, and I served as his deputy. Then, in 1974, when he was President of the bar association of New York City and I held the comparable position in Los Angeles, we had shared ideas and exchanged visits.

At the State Department, Vance was a superb leader, mentor, and friend. When he resigned in April 1980 over the ill-fated hostage rescue mission in Iran, it was widely rumored that I would succeed him. However, President Carter chose Senator Edmund Muskie instead, and swallowing my disappointment, I continued to serve as Deputy Secretary. During the last eight months of the Administration, I led the negotiations to free the 52 American hostages in Iran. As the nation hoped and prayed for their release, President Carter awarded me the Medal of Freedom on January 16, 1981—while I was still in Algiers in round-the-clock negotiations, and just four days before the hostages were freed on the very day his term ended. After leaving the Department, from 1981 to 1993 I kept my hand in foreign policy by serving as a board member and Vice Chairman of the Council on Foreign Relations.

So as I pondered President Clinton's offer, I reflected on my background. Despite my prior work in foreign policy, my life had primarily been in the law, and for the last decade, I had focused on law practice, law firm management, and local government issues. At the same time, I had a strong interest in diplomacy and some qualifying history. I also had a long-standing conviction that broad experience in American public life is valuable to high-level makers of foreign policy.

After discussing the offer with my family and spending a sleepless night, I said yes. My appointment was announced on December 22, 1992. With the President's agreement, I began to shift gears to preparing to assume leadership of the State Department. Almost immediately, I launched into planning the first of the statements and speeches that form the body of this book.

Speeches and Statecraft

Throughout history, speeches have consistently been a crucial component of diplomacy. In the last five decades, such speeches as George Marshall's announcement of American assistance for war-ravaged Europe, John Kennedy's statements concerning Soviet missiles in Cuba, and Ronald Reagan's call in Berlin for Mikhail Gorbachev to "tear down this wall" have played dramatic roles in the foreign policy theater. Given this legacy, some have lamented that in an age of instant electronic communication and overnight opinion polling, speech-making has become devalued. Some claim that the making of speeches, like the making of policy, has become dangerously ad hoc, motivated not by any principle or purpose but by public whims and the lure of the sound bite. During the eight years that I spent in the State Department, I saw little evidence to support such claims. As this book demonstrates, I believe speeches continue to be prime vehicles for articulating and developing coherent foreign policy.

As I prepared to lead the Department, I was aware that my speeches would receive considerable attention. When a Secretary of State makes a speech, he or she speaks for the United States of America. The press flashes the words around the world; countless media outlets will report on them, and the entire speech will be broadcast on C-SPAN and available on the Internet. Almost 200 embassies in Washington are listening, analyzing, and reporting to their home capitals. Dozens of columnists, many of whom write exclusively on foreign affairs, are poised to exercise their critical skills. Conscious that my speeches would appear in various media and would be evaluated and reevaluated over time, I viewed them less as orations than as spoken essays, written for the eye as much as the ear.

In diplomacy, speeches are given for four general purposes: strategic, conceptual, tactical, and bureaucratic. Many speeches have multiple purposes, but one of them is usually primary. For example, the main goal of three of my speeches on China was *strategic*. They established the broad outlines of our policy. Whether reiterating the three U.S.-China communiques, pressing the Chinese on human rights, or warning them not to take aggressive actions against Taiwan, I sought to reaffirm the fundamental underpinning of America's approach toward Beijing, while explaining our interests and signaling our intentions. I quickly learned that the Chinese also recognized the strategic purpose of speeches and followed my remarks very closely. (See Chapters 10, 20, and 29.) The speeches on Russia, supporting democracy and market reform but recognizing the differences between our nations, were also primarily strategic in character. (See Chapters 2, 5, and 18.)

Speeches are used *conceptually* to frame problems and set policy agendas. They aim to influence people's thinking about how they should consider certain challenges or interests. By laying out road maps for future policy, such speeches are instruments of leadership. My statements on the future of European security (Chapter 27), on reform of the United Nations (Chapter 23), and on environmental protection (Chapter 28) are prime examples. The last of these is notable for marking a departure in policy and setting a new agenda for the future. As often happened, the decision to make this speech forced me to think through and articulate my own views—in this case, on the relationship between protection of the environment and national security.

Foreign policy speeches are often deployed *tactically* to send messages about U.S. policy on particular issues of the day. For example, my March 1994 speech in Tokyo (Chapter 9) candidly addressed a specific set of problems with our close ally, Japan, and my September 1993 speech at Columbia University (Chapter 4) outlined the next steps in the Middle East peace process in the wake of the Oslo breakthrough. These speeches were valuable tools of day-to-day diplomacy, and statements made on the public record were often more effective and credible than private ones.

Almost every speech is also used *bureaucratically*, to force decisions within our government. Henry Kissinger once observed that while public speeches are ostensibly directed to outsiders, perhaps their more important role is to lay down guidelines for the bureaucracy and settle internal debates.[3] The drafting of a speech almost always reveals the differences among the bureaus of the Department, and the clearance process outside the Department frequently involves sharp and illuminating clashes with other elements of the government—especially the White House, the National Security Council (NSC), the Office of Management and Budget (OMB), Treasury, and the Department of Defense. Sometimes the President himself becomes involved.

Of course, policy debates such as these are the lifeblood of government. In any given week as Secretary, I received dozens of memoranda advocating various particular policy directions. However persuasive their contents, they did not constitute U.S. policy unless they were incorporated into a speech, public statement, or formal government document.

[3]See Henry Kissinger, *American Foreign Policy*, pp. 22–23 (New York: Norton, 1969).

The challenge of articulating a position publicly compels leaders to make policy choices. Often decisions on what to do and what to say publicly are made simultaneously. The process of speech preparation is one of the most overlooked aspects of foreign policy decision-making.

Examples of speeches used as bureaucratic tools are those I made at NATO meetings about expanding the Alliance (Chapters 8, 16, and 19). The calendar for these meetings forced the Administration to make decisions. Once we had done so, I used the speeches to chart a course for our Alliance partners, such as by setting time lines for future decisions.

Just as many speeches have multiple goals, many are aimed at multiple audiences. In our democracy, maintaining public support for foreign policy is vital. To sustain American leadership, the State Department has to do all it can to justify its policies and to defend its budget to the American people. Thus, beginning with my confirmation statement, in which I proposed an "America Desk" at the State Department, I was determined to engage my domestic audience actively. I was always conscious of how my speeches would be received both on Capitol Hill and beyond the Beltway, and attempted to calibrate every sentence to take into account several domestic as well as several foreign audiences.

The entire speech process needs to be managed at a high level. Whether to make a speech on a given subject at a given moment is itself a policy decision of some significance, and choosing the right forum is also important. Typically, I would make these decisions only after discussing them with my Chief of Staff, Tom Donilon, who had in turn consulted with many others. We would then consider the general thrust of the speech and sometimes rough out an outline. Next, one of the speechwriters, usually working with one or more of the substantive bureaus, would prepare a draft. In the later part of my term, the able and articulate Policy Planning head, Jim Steinberg, played an increasingly significant role at all stages of speech preparation. All of these efforts were brought into focus in lengthy speech conferences in Donilon's office, which had a connecting door to my study on the Department's seventh floor. As soon as new drafts became available, I would begin reviewing and editing them. When I began using a TelePrompTer to improve my delivery, the TelePrompTer practices inevitably turned into final editing sessions.

I relied heavily on Tom Donilon's judgment on speech matters, and found that his unusually deep experience in American politics for a person so young translated easily into the nuances of diplomacy. Although he chose not to be the on-camera spokesman for the Department, he nevertheless shaped our public message by collaborating on speeches, conducting background interviews with the press, and working with our official spokesmen, Mike McCurry and later Nick Burns.

The day-to-day manager of the speech preparation process was Bennett Freeman, a talented and committed Deputy Assistant Secretary, who headed up a team of capable young speechwriters. The longest-serving of these were Tom Malinowski, a Polish-born Rhodes Scholar who specialized in European security, and James Gibney, a Foreign Service Officer with experience in Asia. Others who served me ably were David Frank, Vinca Showalter, Heather Hurlburt, Eric Liu, Janet Bogue, and David Yang. A tribute to the quality of this team was the fact that three of them—Showalter, Liu, and Gibney—were later hired away by the White House to write speeches for the President.

The World as We Found It

As I prepared to take office, I felt that the Bush Administration had left us a solid policy foundation, although we planned to make many course adjustments (placing greater emphasis on issues that transcended the interests of individual nations, such as international economics, human rights, and environmental degradation). Before President Clinton's inauguration, I met with both former Secretary of State James Baker and the current Secretary, Lawrence Eagleburger, to discuss their experiences and the challenges ahead. These discussions further impressed me with the foreign policy achievements of President Bush and his team.

With the disappearance of the Soviet Union and the collapse of the Warsaw Pact, the Bush Administration had skillfully begun the opening of political and economic relations with Central Europe and the former Soviet states. Enabling a unified Germany to remain in NATO was a remarkable diplomatic achievement. In the Middle East, they had effectively marshaled and led an international coalition against Iraq, and Secretary Baker had ably organized the Madrid Peace Conference, which opened the way for direct negotiations between Israel and its Arab neighbors. Finally, in our hemisphere, the Bush team had made important strides toward free trade by negotiating the core provisions of NAFTA and had reached an accommodation with the Democratic Congress on the sulfurous issues of rebel movements and government repression in Central America.

While each of these achievements was a valuable building block, we spent much of our time, especially in the first two years, handling the more difficult legacies of the Bush Administration. Every new government must confront its inheritance from its predecessors, and we were no exception. For example, though relations with Russia were relatively good, we believed that the Bush team had not done enough to embrace either political or economic reform efforts there. In the Persian Gulf, despite its impressive performance in the 1991 war, that Administration left an Iraq that, while defeated, was far from vanquished; Saddam Hussein openly defied UN resolutions even before President Bush left office, and proved to be a continuing menace to his neighbors over the next four years. Somalia was another complicated inheritance. One of President Bush's last initiatives after his 1992 defeat had been to introduce U.S. troops into that war-torn country to curb the humanitarian crisis there. While the cause was noble, the Administration had greatly underestimated the difficulty of the task and the length of the U.S. troop deployment.

We also faced festering crises in Bosnia and Haiti. The Bush team had concluded that our national interests were not sufficiently engaged to justify U.S. military action in either case, but that premise became increasingly unsustainable. Most troublesome, perhaps, the Bush Administration had done little to curb North Korea's ambitious nuclear program, which appeared on the verge of producing deliverable nuclear weapons. This ugly situation presented one of the greatest diplomatic challenges of the first term.

Thus, I entered office at a moment characterized both by a general confidence in the fundamental underpinnings of U.S. foreign policy, and by anxiety about many specific policy challenges. Moreover, as the first post–Cold War Administration, we were responsible for defining and shaping foreign policy for a new era.

The President-elect planned to announce my selection as Secretary of State on December 22, 1992, and as I sat down to draft my statement for that occasion, the concerns described above provided the context. The timing of the announcement and the hectic atmosphere of Little Rock did not allow for reflection or the full discussion of ideas that would soon become standard operating procedure at the State Department. I also knew that I would have an opportunity to make a more carefully prepared and extensive statement at my confirmation hearing. Nevertheless, the following excerpt from the comments I made on December 22 accurately foreshadows many of the themes of the next four years.

In my law school days, I was inspired to public service by the examples of General George Marshall and Dean Acheson, but it was beyond imagining that I would someday be asked to serve in the office they had held. Marshall and Acheson were present at the creation of the Cold War era. Then, we were being challenged by a formidable adversary, and an alien ideology. America measured its success by how well it contained Soviet expansion and halted the spread of communism.

Today, we face a new and more complicated era. As Governor Clinton said, we are "the inheritors of a new world." That world is still a dangerous place. While the risk of nuclear war has diminished, the new era has produced a new set of dangers—ethnic and religious conflicts threaten to ignite widespread hostilities in Central and Eastern Europe; weapons of mass destruction may reach the hands of untested and unstable powers; new threats spring from old rivalries in the Middle East, Europe and Asia. At the same time, we face a world where borders matter less and less; a world that demands that we join other nations to face challenges that range from overpopulation to AIDS to the very destruction of our planet's life support system.

In this new era, the Clinton/Gore Administration will be confronted again and again by whether and how to use U.S. power and U.S. resources. We will need bold new thinking to guide us in this new era. In contrast to the well-understood goals of the Cold War era, it will be difficult to measure success as we deal with these new challenges. No doubt our surest test will be the well-being of the American people and their unfailing concern for others. In confronting these challenges we must remain cognizant that a great power requires not only military might but a powerful economy at home—an economy prepared for global competition. In today's world, that means that foreign policy and domestic policy must be addressed simultaneously, not sequentially—or else neither will be successful for very long.

Every four years, the voters have an opportunity to reset our course in foreign policy. This year they embraced Governor Clinton's concept that the strength of our economy is the foundation of our foreign policy, that our force structure needs to be revamped, and that democracy must be promoted on a worldwide basis. But our administration will pursue these goals with an appreciation of history, both recent and ancient. American foreign policy is a continuum. It is at its best when it reflects a bipartisan consensus, as with the Marshall Plan or the quest for arms control. Politics may not stop at the water's edge, but its intensity should yield to the national interest.

Getting Started

Within a few days after my nomination was announced on December 22, 1992, I began to prepare for my confirmation hearing before the Senate Foreign Relations Committee. To avoid any gap between my predecessor, Lawrence Eagleburger, and myself, Senator Claiborne Pell, the Committee Chairman, had set an early hearing date at my request. By appearing on January 13, a week before Inauguration Day, I would be the first nominee of the new Administration to go before Congress.

Claiborne Pell, who was in his sixth term as Senator from Rhode Island, gave me support and friendship during my entire tenure, first in his role as Committee Chairman in 1993–94 and then as Ranking Member when the Republicans took over the Senate in 1995. He was a committed internationalist who took great pride in his early diplomatic career as a consular officer and who could always be counted on to be sensitive to the needs of the foreign service. He had attended the 1945 San Francisco conference at which the United Nations was founded and half a century later still carried a copy of the UN Charter in his jacket pocket for ready reference. A New England aristocrat, Pell had a magic touch with Rhode Island voters, campaigning in a gentlemanly fashion, eschewing personal attacks on his opponents, and winning by wide margins. He retired at the end of 1996.

The confirmation hearing was the vehicle for the Senate to fulfill its constitutional "advise and consent" responsibility. Senators have never taken this duty lightly, particularly in foreign affairs, where the rivalry between the branches of government has become famous. When it came to foreign policy prerogatives, the constitutional Framers intentionally created an ambiguous arrangement. Each branch has found parts of the Constitution that support its claim of primacy. This arrangement is truly, in the words of one prominent constitutional scholar, an "invitation to struggle."[1]

Despite this inherent rivalry, authority in foreign affairs has gravitated toward the presidency, particularly since the Second World War. Although Watergate and the Vietnam War temporarily moved the pendulum back toward Congress, the long-term trend has been toward executive primacy in foreign affairs. I firmly support this trend. Only the Executive can provide a clear, coherent definition of our national interests and make the quick policy adjustments often required in foreign affairs. Congress will always have an opportunity to assert its views and help shape the policy agenda. Indeed, President Carter's Secretary of State Cyrus Vance and I estimated that in the late 1970s, when I served as his Deputy, we spent at least a quarter of our time engaged in relations with Congress, whether testifying, preparing to testify, or hearing from or consulting with individual Members. Using its power of the purse, Congress has sought to seize control and micromanage foreign policy, but the executive branch has fought back, relying on the President's constitutional authority to conduct foreign relations.

Shortly after leaving the State Department in 1981, I spoke and wrote about creating a "compact" between the Executive and Congress in foreign affairs, stressing bipartisanship and the complementary decision-making roles of the branches. The key to an effective foreign policy, I wrote in 1982 and still believe today, would be to have each branch "respect and defer to the unique capabilities of the other, so that instead of magnifying the weaknesses of each, we would embrace the strength of the whole. . . . The Presidency and the Congress were not designed to mirror each other or to compete over the same functions but to complement each other, bringing unique qualities to bear on the decisions they were expected to share."[2]

I had been through two confirmation hearings before—in 1967, when President Johnson nominated me to be Deputy Attorney General under

---

[1]Edward S. Corwin, *The President: Office and Powers, 1787–1957*, p. 171 (New York: New York University Press, 1957).

[2]"Ceasefire Between the Branches: A Compact in Foreign Affairs," *Foreign Affairs* 60, no. 5 (summer 1982): 999.

Ramsey Clark, and in 1977, when President Carter nominated me as Vance's Deputy—and had testified before Congress numerous times throughout my government career. But this confirmation hearing would be much different, much more important. As the senior foreign policy spokesperson, it would be up to me to lay out the new Administration's approach, both conceptually and substantively. The Democratic Party had been out of power for 12 years, and mine would be one of the first official statements to address the international agenda in the new era.

The President-elect had just won an election dominated by domestic concerns, especially the economy, and many expected the new Administration's attention to turn to problems at home. My statement had to show why and how foreign policy still mattered, and how we would deal with our campaign promises. We knew that several audiences would be watching closely: international leaders, whether friends or foes; Members of Congress, to see how the new Administration would address their particular concerns; and the American people, to see how this new and largely unfamiliar team would operate.

Although I anticipated being on the Hill for at least two days fielding questions from the members of the committee, my opening statement would be a critical part of my performance. It had to be a comprehensive tour of the international scene, not only setting forth the broad conceptual outlines of our approach, but detailing priorities on specific issues—whether Russia or the Middle East, Bosnia or China.

We were entering a new world of enormous opportunity and challenge. The end of the Cold War had caused many mushrooms to sprout that had been suppressed by the superpower rivalry, and it was up to us to lay out a vision for the future. Our task, I thought, was not unlike that which President Truman, General George Marshall, and Dean Acheson faced after 1945. In this sense, my opening statement would be more than my personal introduction as the Secretary-designate; it would be the first step in shaping America's post–Cold War foreign policy.

Even before I returned to Washington, I had lengthy telephone conversations with my staff to discuss the broad themes and outlines of my statement. The drafting process got under way in earnest when I traveled to Washington in early January. With five years' hindsight, it seems to me that the final statement we produced was an accurate road map, presenting many of the themes we emphasized throughout the President's first term.

In the statement, I wanted to stress four core ideas as guiding principles of our foreign policy. The first was the multi-dimensionality of "security." This recognition that economic security mattered as much as military security required that we not only revitalize our economy at home, but appreciate the value of economic statecraft—for example, support of free trade, promotion of U.S. business abroad, and discriminating use of economic sanctions to influence others.

Second, I believed that we had to reaffirm our commitment to use military power when necessary, to harness force to diplomacy. A credible threat of military action is often essential to diplomacy, and sometimes the threat must be carried out. Particularly since the Democratic Party had been out of office for over a decade (and had been unfairly labeled by some opponents as skittish about using force), I believed that I had to send an unambiguous signal in this regard.[3]

The third core principle I wanted to outline was that of adapting our foreign policy, both conceptually and organizationally, to the new threats and challenges that lay ahead. Perhaps the most widely quoted sentence from the testimony was, "We cannot afford to careen from crisis to crisis." This meant emphasizing a "preventive diplomacy"—one capable of anticipating crises rather than simply managing them. This could be done by actively supporting democracy and human rights in order to stem political conflict before it started, as well as by focusing on global environmental threats and sustainable development to avert humanitarian crises that might require later intervention. The State Department itself had to be reorganized to deal with this new agenda, and I proposed creating a new Under Secretary of State for Global Affairs to deal with such transnational issues as narcotics, international crime, environmental degradation, refugees, and human rights. I was also determined to achieve a cultural change by making the Department more business-friendly, with the aim being "to improve the international competitiveness of American business."

Finally, I felt that in the absence of the Soviet threat, we had to shore up domestic support for our diplomacy. To blunt neo-isolationist sentiments that seemed to be reemerging, the new Administration had to show that, more than ever, events abroad mattered to the American peo-

---

[3]By coincidence, at the very time of my confirmation hearing, the Bush Administration launched limited air attacks on Iraq in response to its violations of UN resolutions. President-elect Clinton supported the attacks, saying, "It was the right decision, done in the right way."

ple. For this reason, I believed that the State Department needed a symbolic "America Desk" to show the American people that in this new era, foreign policy is not necessarily foreign, and that we will always strive to protect American interests.

The day-to-day management of the Department would be in the capable hands of Under Secretary Richard Moose, but I also wanted to use my statement to signal the need for adequate resources for the task. My brief exposure to the Department during the transition period had made me concerned about the obsolescence of our information systems and the cutbacks in our representation abroad. I would return to this subject many times during my tenure, and it became a central theme of several of my last speeches.

Under the direction of Chief of Staff Tom Donilon, Jeremy Rosner and Will Marshall, two talented analysts at Washington's Progressive Policy Institute, packaged these ideas in a rough draft.[4] At a January 4 luncheon meeting in the Secretary's eighth-floor dining room (which Secretary Eagleburger had been gracious enough to offer), my top transition advisers and I discussed and edited the draft. All agreed that the core ideas had been well presented, so our focus was sharpening and fine-tuning it. We also worked to make the point that in this new era, strategy could not be defined by a single, overarching doctrine like "containment." We wanted to reject abstract conceptualization in favor of concrete goals. The thought, which both the Senators and the media picked up on, was that our strategy would be measured "not by its theoretical elegance but by its results."

Producing an opening statement, while undoubtedly arduous, is not the most difficult aspect of preparing for congressional testimony. The toughest part is getting ready for the question-and-answer period, during which each committee member can inquire about any subject he or she

---

[4]In 1993–94 Jeremy Rosner joined the White House and became President Clinton's top foreign policy speechwriter. He had an important hand in many eloquent presidential speeches, notably those commemorating the Allied landing in Normandy in 1944. It is worth adding that the President's major speeches carry his own strong imprint. Much to the consternation of his staff, he often kept rewriting up to the very last minute. When he made changes in the car on the way to giving a speech, which he often did, it was no small technical challenge for Rosner and the other speechwriters to get them cranked into the TelePrompTer.

desires—whether it be Russia, East Timor, trade policy, or even, as I soon learned, issues deriving from my tenure in the Johnson and Carter Administrations, or anything else in my personal career. Preparing for this interrogation feels like cramming for the entire bar exam in one week.

To train for the onslaught, I submitted myself to the notorious State Department "murder board" process for four days, during which my key advisers shot questions at me until I begged for mercy. The driving logic of those four days was, "The tougher the murder board, the easier the actual hearing." This process was enhanced by excellent intelligence about each committee member's special concerns. Led by Meg Donovan, a longtime committee aide who had joined my transition team, we made sure that I had answers to what my staff playfully called the "pet rock" questions. I also talked to most of the committee members, in person or by phone, to seek their advice or hear their concerns. During my term I developed the practice of always calling the Chairman, and often the Ranking Member, the day before I was to give testimony to ask their advice and pick up any last-minute hints as to what was on the committee's mind. This habit paid dividends time after time.

There is nothing quite like a major congressional hearing. Before nine o'clock on the morning of January 13, Room 628, the cavernous hearing room in the Dirksen Senate Office Building teemed with people—many members of the press, but also many well-wishers and onlookers. This was the first Capitol Hill event to signal that a new Administration was coming to town. With 19 Senators perched high above, and the television cameras trained on me, I assumed my lonely seat at the front of the room. At the outset, happily, I was joined by the two Senators from my home state of California, Dianne Feinstein and Barbara Boxer, who formally presented me to the committee. It was the first time in history that two female members of the U.S. Senate introduced a cabinet appointee.

After presenting my opening statement, I received many friendly comments from committee members, both Democrats and Republicans. Their own statements, which many Senators read before the question period began, were informed and thoughtful; I was happy to hear that we often shared the same concerns. The Senators liked my statement on marrying force and diplomacy, and they agreed with the importance of revitalizing foreign policy here at home with the America Desk concept and of making it more business-friendly abroad.

For the next eight hours of the hearing, extending over two days, I answered questions. Most of them concerned critical issues of the day—whether the deteriorating situation in Bosnia, our position on NAFTA or GATT, or Tibet. But issues related to my past government service and my professional life at O'Melveny & Myers were not ignored. The first round of questions from Senator Jesse Helms, the ranking Republican member of the committee, concentrated solely on my negotiations for the release of American hostages in Iran in 1980–81. Other Senators questioned me about any knowledge I had concerning the U.S. Army's use of covert surveillance to gather information about civil rights and antiwar activists in the late 1960s.[5]

This hearing was my first public exposure to Jesse Helms in my new role. Although we later developed a satisfactory rapport, our initial relationship was frosty. After launching an attack on my service during the Carter Administration, he turned to ethical issues. Probing such issues, particularly possible conflicts of interest, had become a tradition of the Senate confirmation process. Almost every modern Secretary of State, from Henry Stimson and Dean Acheson to George Shultz, had been pressed about the possibility that past business relationships would bias his foreign policy decisions.

After a long and active career at O'Melveny & Myers, I certainly expected to be questioned on these issues, and I had already instituted a rigorous policy to recuse myself from any cases that might present even the perception of a conflict of interest. At the hearing, Helms displayed large, telegenic charts showing that O'Melveny & Myers had a considerable Japanese client base, and intimated that I would be easily wooed by the Japanese. I noted my prior experience in representing the United States in contentious textile negotiations with the Japanese, and emphasized my strict policy of recusal, which had been praised by other Senators. Nevertheless, Helms remained skeptical. He also insisted that I reply in writing to over 400 additional questions prior to confirmation.

---

[5]This issue, about which I had testified before Congress in 1977, resurfaced only days before my 1993 hearing. In responding to these questions, I was ably assisted by Joel Klein, a Washington lawyer who is now head of the Department of Justice Antitrust Division and who helped me review my files for this period, which are deposited at the Johnson Library. My recollection, which these written records confirmed, was that I had no knowledge of such covert activities. Had I known about them while Deputy Attorney General, I would have been strongly and actively opposed to them.

When Senator Helms took over as Committee Chairman following the Republican victory in the 1994 mid-term elections, the first signs were ominous. He initially suggested that President Clinton would be in danger if he visited a U.S. military base in North Carolina, but after some counseling from the Republican leadership, he backed off and tried to be on his best behavior. I made a special effort to ensure that we could work together, and he was often helpful in ensuring that the routine business of foreign policy could go forward. He and his Chief of Staff, Admiral James W. ("Bud") Nance, a boyhood friend of his from Raleigh, North Carolina, once came down to the Department for lunch, which helped to smooth our relationship. In my last appearance before the Committee, when I introduced Secretary-designate Madeleine Albright, he emphasized that our differences were never personal. Nevertheless, our positions on matters of substance were at such variance that it placed severe limitations on our relationship.

The hearings finally ran out of steam and recessed after two days. The committee sent my nomination forward, and on Inauguration Day, the Senate confirmed unanimously my appointment as the 63d Secretary of State. To ensure continuity of foreign policy leadership, I was sworn in at a private ceremony in Blair House only hours after President Clinton's inauguration, with only my wife, Marie, and protocol officials in attendance. After weeks of preparation, I was anxious to get to work and never scheduled a large swearing-in ceremony.

Statement at Senate Confirmation Hearing

Statement Before the Senate Foreign Relations Committee,

Washington, D.C., January 13, 1993

Mr. Chairman: It is a great honor to appear before you as President-elect Clinton's nominee for Secretary of State. This hearing room is a long way from Scranton, North Dakota, population 300, where I was born and raised, and I am deeply moved by being here in these circumstances.

You and the members of this committee have contributed much leadership and wisdom to our nation's foreign policy over the past decade. Let me say at the outset that I look forward to a close and cooperative relationship with you. I also look forward to your questions and will try to answer them with the ruthless candor for which diplomats are famous.

In the 3 weeks since President-elect Clinton asked me to serve as his Secretary of State, I have received about as much commiseration as congratulation. Friends point to this new world's raw conflicts and stress our own limited resources. They tell me I have drawn an important but unpleasant assignment.

I appreciate their concern. But I dispute their assessment. I believe we have arrived at a uniquely promising moment. The signature of this era is change, and I believe many of the changes work in our favor. The Cold War is over. Forty years of sustained effort on behalf of collective security and human dignity have been rewarded. Millions who lived under the stultifying yoke of communism are free. The tide of democratic aspirations is rising from Tibet to Central America. Freer markets are expanding the reach of prosperity. The nuclear nightmare is receding, and I want to congratulate President Bush and [Russian] President Yeltsin on their successful negotiation of the START II Treaty [Strategic Arms Reduction Treaty]. We now have the opportunity to create a new strategy that directs America's resources at something other than superpower confrontation.

Perils of the New Era

Neither President-elect Clinton nor I have any illusions about the perils that lurk in many of this era's changes. The end of the Cold War has lifted the lid on many cauldrons of long-simmering conflict. The bloody results are evident in the former Yugoslavia and elsewhere. Nor will this era lack for ruthless and expansionist despots; [Iraqi President] Saddam Hussein confirmed that fact. Yet it is also true that we are now relatively more powerful and physically more secure. So while we are alert to this era's dangers, we nonetheless approach it with an underlying sense of optimism.

Not since the late 1940s has our nation faced the challenge of shaping an entirely new foreign policy for a world that has fundamentally changed.

Like our counterparts then, we need to design a new strategy for protecting American interests by laying the foundations for a more just and stable world. That strategy must reflect the fundamental changes that characterize this era:

The surfacing of long-suppressed ethnic, religious, and sectional conflicts, especially in the former Soviet bloc;

The globalization of commerce and capital;

A worldwide democratic revolution, fueled by new information technologies that amplify the power of ideas;

New and old human rights challenges, including protecting ethnic minorities as well as political dissidents;

The rise of new security threats, especially terrorism and the spread of advanced weaponry and weapons of mass destruction; and

Global challenges including overpopulation, famine, drought, refugees, AIDS [acquired immuno-deficiency syndrome], drug-trafficking, and threats to the earth's environment.

To adapt our foreign policy goals and institutions to these changes, President-elect Clinton has stressed that our effort must rest on three pillars:

First, we must elevate America's economic security as a primary goal of our foreign policy.

Second, we must preserve our military strength as we adapt our forces to new security challenges.

Third, we must organize our foreign policy around the goal of promoting the spread of democracy and markets abroad.

As we adapt to new conditions, it is worth underscoring the essential continuity in American foreign policy. Despite a change in administrations, our policy in many specific instances will remain constant and will seek to build upon the accomplishments of our predecessors. Examples include the Middle East peace process, firm enforcement of the UN sanctions against Iraq, ratification and implementation of the START II

Treaty, and the continuing need for U.S. power to play a role in promoting stability in Europe and the Pacific.

Nevertheless, our Administration inherits the task of defining a strategy for U.S. leadership after the Cold War. We cannot afford to careen from crisis to crisis. We must have a new diplomacy that seeks to anticipate and prevent crises, like those in Iraq, Bosnia, and Somalia, rather than simply to manage them. Our support for democratic institutions and human rights can help defuse political conflicts. And our support for sustainable development and global environmental protection can help prevent human suffering on a scale that demands our intervention. We cannot foresee every crisis. But preventive diplomacy can free us to devote more time and effort to problems facing us at home.

It is not enough to articulate a new strategy; we must also justify it to the American people. Today, foreign policy makers cannot afford to ignore the public, for there is a real danger that the public will ignore foreign policy. The unitary goal of containing Soviet power will have to be replaced by more complex justifications to fit the new era. We need to show that, in this era, foreign policy is no longer foreign.

Practitioners of statecraft sometimes forget [that] their ultimate purpose is to improve the daily lives of the American people. They assume foreign policy is too complex for the public to be involved in its formation. That is a costly conceit. From Vietnam to Iran-contra, we have too often witnessed the disastrous effects of foreign policies hatched by the experts without proper candor or consultation with the public and their representatives in Congress.

More than ever before, the State Department cannot afford to have "clientitis," a malady characterized by undue deference to the potential reactions of other countries. I have long thought the State Department needs an "America Desk." This Administration will have one—and I'll be sitting behind it.

Guiding Principles for Foreign Policy

I will not attempt today to fit the foreign policy of the next 4 years into the straightjacket of some neatly tailored doctrine. Yet, America's actions in the world must be guided by consistent principles. As I have noted, I believe there are three that should guide foreign policy in this new era.

First, we must advance America's economic security with the same energy and resourcefulness we devoted to waging the Cold War. The new Administration will shortly propose an economic program to empower American firms and workers to win in world markets, reduce our reliance on foreign borrowing, and increase our ability to sustain foreign commitments. Despite our economic woes, we remain the world's greatest trading nation, its largest market, and its leading exporter. That is why we must utilize all the tools at our disposal, including a new GATT [General Agreement on Tariffs and Trade] agreement and a North American Free Trade Agreement that serves the interests of American firms, workers, and communities.

In an era in which economic competition is eclipsing ideological rivalry, it is time for diplomacy that seeks to assure access for U.S. businesses to expanding global markets. This does not mean that our commercial goals will trump other important concerns, such as non-proliferation, human rights, and sustainable development in the Third World. But for too long, we have made economics the poor cousin of our foreign policy. For example, in nearly all the countries of the former Eastern bloc—nations whose economies and markets are on the threshold of growth—we have for years assigned only one Foreign Service officer to assist U.S. companies. In the case of Russia, that means one commercial officer for a nation of 150 million people. Other economic powers, such as Germany and Japan, devote far more personnel to promoting their firms, industries, and economic concerns.

The Clinton Administration intends to harness our diplomacy to the needs and opportunities of American industries and workers. We will not be bashful about linking our high diplomacy with our economic goals. We will ask our foreign missions to do more to gather crucial information about market opportunities and barriers and actively assist American companies seeking to do business abroad.

Second, we must maintain a strong defense as we adapt our forces to new and enduring security challenges. As a result of efforts begun in the late 1970s by President Carter and continued under Presidents Reagan and Bush, our Administration inherits the best fighting force in the world. But the world has changed.

We face a paradox. The collapse of the Soviet Union enables us to reduce our Cold War military forces. But it also leaves American power as the main ballast for an unstable world. Our ability to manage the transition to a more stable system of international relations will depend on tenacious diplomacy backed by credible strength. The President-elect and Secretary [of Defense]-designate Aspin have described how we must adapt our armed forces to new missions. And I agree with President-elect Clinton's statement that we will resolve constantly to deter, sometimes to fight, and always to win.

I have spent a good portion of my life practicing various forms of diplomacy, negotiation, and problem solving—from the effort to secure the release of the American hostages in Iran, to responses to urban unrest and police brutality, to the practice of law over 4 decades. I have argued and still believe that diplomacy is a neglected imperative. I believe we must apply new dispute resolution techniques and forms of international arbitration to the conflicts that plague the world.

I also know from experience that nations do not negotiate on the basis of goodwill alone; they negotiate on the basis of interests and, therefore, on calculations of power. As I reflect on our experience in the Cold War, it is clear that our success flowed from our ability to harness diplomacy and power together—both the modernization of our forces and negotiations for arms control; both advocacy for human rights and covert and overt opposition to Soviet expansionism.

In the years to come, Americans will be confronted with vexing questions about the use of force—decisions about whether to intervene in border disputes, civil wars, outright invasions, and in cases of possible genocide, about whether to intervene for purposes that are quite different from the traditional missions of our armed forces—purposes such as peace-keeping, peace-making, humanitarian assistance, evacuation of Americans abroad, and efforts to combat drug smuggling and terrorism. While there is no magic formula to guide such decisions, I do believe that the discreet and careful use of force in certain circumstances—and its credible threat in general—will be essential to the success of our diplomacy and foreign policy. Although there will always be differences at the margin, I believe we can—and must—craft a bipartisan consensus in which these questions concerning the use of force will no longer divide our nation as they once did.

However, we cannot respond to every alarm. I want to assure the American people that we will not turn their blood and treasure into an open account for use by the rest of the world. We cannot let every crisis become a choice between inaction or American intervention. It will be this Administration's policy to encourage other nations and the institutions of collective security, especially the United Nations, to do more of the world's work to deter aggression, relieve suffering, and keep the peace. In that regard, we will work with [UN] Secretary General Boutros-Ghali and the members of the Security Council to ensure [that] the United Nations has the means to carry out such tasks.

The United Nations has recently shown great promise in mediating disputes and fulfilling its promise of collective security—in Namibia, Cambodia, El Salvador, and elsewhere. But the United Nations cannot be an effective instrument for sharing our global burdens unless we share the burden of supporting it. I will work to ensure that we pay our outstanding obligations.

Ultimately, when our vital interests are at stake, we will always reserve our option to act alone. As the President-elect has said, our motto in this era should be: Together where we can; on our own where we must.

One of the main security problems of this era will be the proliferation of very deadly weapons—nuclear, chemical, biological, and enhanced conventional weapons—as well as their delivery systems. The [Persian] Gulf war highlighted the problem of a fanatical aggressor developing or using weapons of mass destruction. We must work assiduously with other nations to discourage proliferation through improved intelligence, export controls, incentives, sanctions, and even force when necessary. Overall, this Administration will give high priority to the prevention of proliferation as we enter a new and exceedingly dangerous period.

Third, our new diplomacy will encourage the global revolution for democracy that is transforming our world. Promoting democracy does not imply a crusade to remake the world in our image. Rather, support for democracy and human rights abroad can and should be a central strategic tenet in improving our own security. Democratic movements and governments are not only more likely to protect human and minority rights, they are also more likely to resolve ethnic, religious, and territorial disputes in a peaceful manner and to be reliable partners in diplomacy, trade, arms accords, and global environmental protection.

A strategic approach to promoting democracy requires that we coordinate all of our leverage, including trade, economic and security assistance, and debt relief. By enlisting international and regional institutions in the work of promoting democracy, the United States can leverage our own limited resources and avoid the appearance of trying to dominate others. In the information age, public diplomacy takes on special importance—and that is why we will support the creation of a Radio Free Asia to ensure that the people of all Asian nations have access to uncensored information about their societies and about the world.

Democracy cannot be imposed from the top down but must be built from the bottom up. Our policy should encourage patient, sustained efforts to help others build the institutions that make democracy possible: political parties, free media, laws that protect property and individual rights, an impartial judiciary, labor unions, and voluntary associations that stand between the individual and the state. American private and civic groups are particularly well suited to help. In this regard, we will move swiftly to establish the Democracy Corps, to put experienced Americans in contact with foreign grassroots democratic leaders, and to strengthen the bipartisan National Endowment for Democracy.

We most also improve our institutional capacity to provide timely and effective aid to people struggling to establish democracy and free markets. To that end, we need to overhaul the U.S. Agency for International Development [USAID]. The agency needs to take on fewer missions, narrow the scope of its operations, and make itself less bureaucratic. As a matter of enlightened self-interest as well as compassion, we need to extract lessons from USAID's past successes and failures to make its future efforts stronger.

In all this work, we must ensure that the people who carry out our nation's foreign policy have the resources they need to do the job. I want to work with you to ensure they have adequate facilities, training, information systems, and security. We also need to take a new look at the way our State Department is organized and our policy is formulated. In the coming weeks, I intend to streamline the Department of State to enhance our capabilities to deal with issues that transcend national boundaries and to improve the international competitiveness of American business.

The Clinton Administration will put America back in the forefront of global efforts to achieve sustainable development and, in the process, leave our children a better world. We believe that sound environmental policies are a precondition of economic growth, not a brake on it.

These three pillars for our foreign policy—economic growth, military strength, and support for democracy—are mutually re-enforcing. A vibrant economy will strengthen America's hand abroad, while permitting us to maintain a strong military without sacrificing domestic needs. And by helping others to forge democracy out of the ruins of dictatorship, we can pacify old threats, prevent new ones, and create new markets for U.S. trade and investment.

Principal Challenges to U.S. Security

Let me take a few moments to consider how this strategic approach applies to the principal security challenges that America faces in the 1990s. None is more important than helping Russia demilitarize, privatize, invigorate its economy, and develop representative political institutions. President Yeltsin's courageous economic and political reforms stand as our best hope for reducing the still-formidable arsenal of nuclear and conventional arms in Russia and other states of the former Soviet Union, and this, in turn, permits reductions in our own defense spending. A collapse of the Russian economy, which contracted by 20% last year, could fatally discredit democracy, not only in the eyes of the Russians but in the eyes of their neighbors as well. Our Administration will join with our G-7 [Group of Seven leading industrialized nations] partners to increase support for Russia's economic reforms. That aid must be conditioned on the willingness of Russia to continue the difficult but essential steps necessary to move from a command economy to a more market-oriented one.

We shall also place high priority on direct and technical assistance for Russia's efforts to dismantle its weapons and properly dispose of its nuclear materials, to provide civilian employment for defense technicians, and to house its demobilized forces. We must say to the democratic reformers in Russia that the democratic nations stand with them and that the world's experience in coping with similar problems is available to them. We should also orchestrate similar international action to help Ukraine, the other Commonwealth [of Independent] States, the Baltics, and the nations of Eastern and Central Europe.

In Europe, we remain committed to NATO, history's most successful military and political alliance, even as we support the evolution of new security arrangements that incorporate the emerging democracies to the east. Our Administration will support efforts by the Conference on Security and Cooperation in Europe to promote human rights, democracy, free elections, and the historic re-integration of the nations of Eastern and Western Europe. I can also assure you that this Administration will vigorously pursue concerted action with our European allies and international bodies to end the slaughter in Bosnia—a slaughter that has claimed tens of thousands of lives and that threatens to spread throughout the Balkans. Europe and the world community in general must bring real pressures, economic and military, to bear on the Serbian leadership to halt its savage policy of ethnic cleansing.

In Asia, we confront many challenges and opportunities. In particular, as President-elect Clinton stressed during the campaign, a complex blend of new and old forces requires us to rethink our policy toward China. On the one hand, there is a booming economy based increasingly on free market principles, which is giving hundreds of millions of Chinese citizens an unprecedented degree of prosperity and a thirst for economic as well as political reform. On the other hand, we cannot ignore continuing reports of Chinese exports of sensitive military technology to troubled areas, widespread violations of human rights, or abusive practices that have contributed to a $17-billion trade imbalance between our two nations. Our policy will seek to facilitate a peaceful evolution of China from communism to democracy by encouraging the forces of economic and political liberalization in that great country.

Elsewhere in Asia, the countries of the Pacific Rim are becoming a global center of economic dynamism. In 1991, our trans-Pacific trade exceeded $316 billion, dwarfing our $221-billion trade with Western Europe. We must devote particular attention to Japan. Japan has recently taken important steps to meet more of its international security responsibilities, such as assisting in peace-keeping efforts from Cambodia to Somalia. Now it must do more to meet its economic responsibilities as well—to lower trade barriers more quickly and to open its economy to competition. Together, Japan and the United States account for a third or more of the global economy. That obligates us both to steer clear of the reefs of recrimination and the rise of regional trading blocs that could sink prospects for global growth. But we also have an obligation to America's firms and workers to ensure [that] they are able to benefit from the growth of Japan's economy, just as the strength and openness of the U.S. economy has helped fuel Japan's prosperity over many decades.

In South Korea, we will continue to maintain our military presence as long as North Korea poses a threat to that nation. And on Asia's subcontinent, our interests include combating nuclear proliferation; restoring peace to Afghanistan; seeing an end to communal strife that threatens India's democracy; and promoting human rights and free elections in Burma, Pakistan, and elsewhere.

In the Middle East, we must maintain the momentum behind the current negotiations over peace and regional issues. President Bush and [former] Secretary of State Baker deserve great credit for bringing Arabs and Israelis to the bargaining table, and the Clinton Administration is committed to building on that historic breakthrough. Our democracy-centered policy underscores our special relationship with Israel, the region's only democracy, with whom we are committed to maintaining a strong and vibrant strategic relationship. We also believe that America's unswerving commitment to Israel's right to exist behind secure borders is essential to a just and lasting peace. We will continue our efforts with both Israel and our Arab friends to address the full range of that region's challenges.

Throughout the Middle East and the Persian Gulf, we will work toward new arms control agreements, particularly concerning weapons of mass destruction. We will assume a vigilant stance toward both Iraq and Iran, which seem determined to sow violence and disorder throughout the region and even beyond. In this region, as well, we will champion economic reform, more accountable governance, and increased respect for human rights. And following a decade during which over 1,000 Americans were killed, injured, or kidnaped by perpetrators of international terrorism, we will give no quarter to terrorists or the states that sponsor their crimes against humanity.

Nowhere has the march against dictators and toward democracy been more dramatic than in our own hemisphere. It is in our self-interest to help Latin America consolidate a decade of hard-won progress. In the past several years, as democracy has spread in the region and market economies have been liberalized, our exports to Latin America have doubled. In close partnership with our hemispheric partners, Canada and Mexico, we should explore ways to extend free trade agreements to Latin American nations that are opening their economies and political systems. At the same time, we expect to complete understandings regarding the North American Free Trade Agreement as outlined by President-elect

Clinton. We also need to make the Organization of American States [OAS] a more effective forum for addressing our region's problems. In Haiti, we strongly support the international effort by the UN and the OAS to restore democracy. In Cuba, we will maintain the embargo to keep pressure on the Castro regime. We will strongly support national reconciliation and the full implementation of peace accords in El Salvador and Nicaragua. And in the Andean countries, the power of the drug lords must be broken to free their people and ours from the corrupting influence of the narcotics trade.

In Africa, as well, a new generation is demanding the opportunities that flow from multi-party democracy and open economies. They deserve our understanding and support. We need to assist their efforts to build institutions that can empower Africa's people to husband and benefit from the continent's vast resources; deal with its economic, social, and environmental problems; and address its underlying causes of political instability. We will be equally committed to working with Congress to redirect our foreign assistance programs to promote sustainable development and private enterprise in Africa. In South Africa, we shall work actively to support those, black and white, who are striving to dismantle the hateful machinery of apartheid and working with determination to build a multi-racial democracy.

The Triumph of Freedom

As I said on the day President-elect Clinton nominated me to be Secretary of State, back when I was in law school, two of my heroes were [former Secretaries of State] Gen. George Marshall and Dean Acheson. And I am enormously honored by the opportunity to occupy the post held by them and by many of the most revered names in our nation's history. Marshall and Acheson were visionaries who recognized at the dawn of the Cold War that America could not remain safe by standing aloof from the world. And the triumph of freedom in that great struggle is the legacy of the activist foreign policy they shaped to project our values and protect our interests.

Now, as in their day, we face a new era and the challenge of developing a new foreign policy. Its activism must be grounded in America's enduring interests. It must be informed by a realistic estimate of the dangers we face. It must be shaped by the democratic convictions we share. And, to command respect abroad, it must rest on a sturdy, bipartisan consensus here at home.

The ultimate test of the security strategy I have outlined today will be in the benefits it delivers to the American people. Its worth will be measured not by its theoretical elegance but by its results. If it makes our people more prosperous and increases their safety abroad; if it helps expand the stabilizing and ennobling reach of democratic institutions and freer markets; if it helps protect the global environment for our children—if it achieves these kinds of benefits, then we will have discharged our responsibilities to our generation as Marshall, Acheson, and the other architects of the post-war world discharged theirs.

They have given us a high standard to emulate as we define anew the requirements of U.S. global leadership. I look forward to working with both parties in Congress to construct a new framework for that leadership, a framework within which healthy debate will occur but within which we can also build a strong consensus that will help us cooperatively pursue the national interest at home and abroad.

Supporting Russian Reform

Russia made a surprise appearance as an issue in the 1992 presidential campaign. Earlier in his term, President Bush had approached Russian political and economic reform in a supportive manner that appeared to leave little room for us to disagree. As time passed, however, his Administration's early enthusiasm for providing financial assistance for Russian reform lagged. The Administration did continue to work with Russia on critical security issues; these efforts included negotiating a protocol to extend arms control agreements to Kazakhstan, Belarus, and Ukraine, as well as opening discussions on a START III agreement.[1] But with the campaign focused on the Republican failure to cope with the faltering U.S. economy, Bush seemed to shy away from vigorous support for economic aid for Russia.

Former President Richard M. Nixon gave the Democrats a welcome if unusual assist in making the case for supporting Russia. Throughout 1992, Nixon lobbied the Bush Administration to provide Russia with large-scale economic assistance, and when it was not forthcoming, he openly criticized the Bush team's hesitant approach. In a heavily publicized March 1992 speech in Washington, Nixon argued that supporting Russian reform was the great global challenge of our time and lamented that the

[1]This agreement would be the third stage of the Strategic Arms Reduction Talks; the previous stages, START I and START II, had been finalized in 1991 and 1993, respectively. START II was ratified by the U.S. Senate in 1996, but the Russian parliament has not yet acted on it.

Bush Administration had shown a lack of resolve in meeting it. Under such pressure, the Bush White House the following month sent to Congress a broad $24 billion assistance package known as the FREEDOM Support Act, but the advocacy seemed halfhearted. Governor Clinton, who had developed an interest in Russia in his student days at Oxford, seized the issue, arguing that Russia should be a top foreign policy priority and pressing for bipartisan support for a large aid package. He argued that the Bush Administration was squandering a historic opportunity to help shape the future of Russia, a theme that he stressed in the fall in a campaign speech in Milwaukee.[2]

Upon his election, President Clinton decided that we should make an early, all-out effort to engage Russia's reformers and support their efforts. Russian hard-liners, most of them former members of the Soviet elite, were resisting market reforms and posing a direct political threat to President Boris Yeltsin. Our assessment was that America's national interest lay squarely in supporting the process of reform—that this was a key payoff of the end of the Cold War. Moreover, we were determined to avoid repeating the Bush Administration's slow start; in 1989, its policy toward the then–Soviet Union had become bogged down for months in a "strategic review," resulting in delays that produced early tensions with the Soviets. The Russian economy was now in dire straits, and the President believed that it needed and deserved our support without delay. He gave this support his highest priority in the foreign policy arena.

Our challenge was to convince the American people that assisting Russia, both politically and economically, was a strategic imperative for the United States. A week and a half prior to the first summit between Presidents Clinton and Yeltsin in Vancouver, British Columbia, I gave a speech in Chicago that was designed to make that argument. The midwestern venue was chosen intentionally because that region, long hostile to foreign aid, was likely to be the most skeptical about assistance to Russia. I felt that we needed to make our case directly to the people in places like Chicago (and Minneapolis, where I gave my next major speech on this topic). My goal in the Chicago speech was not to announce a specific

---

[2]When Boris Yeltsin came to the United States in June 1992, Clinton took a redeye flight from Las Vegas to Washington so that he could have a short meeting with him at Blair House. When introduced to Clinton, Yeltsin said, "My, what a young man you are," and it was plain that he did not regard him as a serious challenger to Bush. Clinton noticed the attitude and laughed about it later.

program to support Russia, but to address the issue in terms of broader U.S. interests and to lay the groundwork for public support for the initiative the President would announce in Vancouver.

The Chicago speech was also intended to send an important signal to the Russians. A few days before the speech, the struggle between Yeltsin and opponents of reform came to a head. In an effort to end the constitutional crisis that had paralyzed Russian politics for several months, Yeltsin called for a national referendum to decide the course of reform. Clinton called several meetings to discuss how we could encourage the reforms. He felt that Yeltsin was handling the situation with a combination of deftness and toughness, and he wanted to support him personally.

In endorsing Yeltsin's move to let the Russian people decide, the President and I wanted to stress that as long as reform moved in the direction of democracy, civil liberties, and free markets, we would be there to help. My speech emphasized that "we must have no illusions about the situation in Russia" and that we must be realistic in our approach. The sentence "We should extend to the Russian people not a hand of pity but a hand of partnership" encapsulated the basic concept of the speech. Helping Russia consolidate democracy was "not a matter of charity but a security concern of the highest order," I said. It was "no less important to our well-being than the need to contain a hostile Soviet Union was at an earlier day."

Perhaps the most important of the messages I intended to convey in the speech was that "Russia's transformation will take a great deal of hard work—probably a generation to complete." I stressed the importance of maintaining a long-term perspective and emphasized that "our commitment to Russia's democracy must be for the duration."

The April 2–3 summit between Clinton and Yeltsin in Vancouver, the President's first meeting abroad, set the tone for their future relationship. This was the first time I had seen Yeltsin in a diplomatic setting, and I was impressed. Physically, he was a formidable figure who, like Clinton, seemed taller than he actually was because of his large shoulders and arms and his assertive presence. When his health is good, he is a powerful personality who can go through a complex agenda with lightning speed. In Vancouver, he came on strong with Clinton, hoping to buffalo him.

Clinton had been thoroughly briefed by Strobe Talbott, his longtime friend and the Administration's key Russia expert, and by the National

Security Council staff, and he dealt with Yeltsin with self-confidence and charm. Yeltsin soon recognized that he had met his match and became less blustery. In retrospect, the personal rapport the two Presidents established at Vancouver proved critical as U.S.-Russian relations evolved during Clinton's first term. Their conversations were typically characterized by friendly, often colorful banter, and they could iron out areas of disagreement that could not be resolved by their ministers or aides. I believe their warm relationship was crucial to two important later developments: Russian participation in the multinational force in Bosnia, and an agreement between Russia and NATO.

Clinton wanted to use Vancouver not only to get the FREEDOM Support Act back on track (which he did), but to launch new initiatives, such as resuming grain sales to ease chronic food shortages and establishing an enterprise fund to assist privatization. The President's announcement of an economic assistance program totaling $1.6 billion was a dramatic signal that he would fulfill his campaign pledge to make Russian reform a top priority. The summit also became an important building block for the President's leadership at the G-7 summit in Tokyo two months later, when he mobilized massive international support for Russia and Ukraine.

The Vancouver meeting also gave me an opportunity to develop my working relationship with Russian Foreign Minister Andrei Kozyrev. A young diplomat who had served at the UN and had a strong command of English, Kozyrev was one of the key internationalists in the Yeltsin government. From our earliest encounter in Geneva in February 1993, he was nervous that he would be among the first members of Yeltsin's cabinet to be sacked because of his high "pro-American" profile. His concerns were so great that he even asked for our help in keeping his job. This request foreshadowed his increasingly perilous position on the Russian scene, but he hung on until he was forced out in January 1996. In his later years in office, his tenuous status limited his effectiveness in the Russian bureaucracy and caused him to take some frustrating stances, but we never had reason to doubt his commitment to good relations with the United States.

The themes from the Chicago speech were repeated two months later in Minneapolis as support for Russia moved to the top of the congressional agenda. The site at the University of Minnesota's Hubert H. Humphrey Institute for Public Policy was nostalgic for me. As a native North Dakotan, I was returning to my home country of the northern plains; I had practically grown up on Minnesota sports and newspapers. Moreover, my public life had been significantly influenced by two of Minnesota's most prominent sons—Vice Presidents Hubert Humphrey and Walter Mondale. Humphrey had been Vice President during my stint in the Johnson Administration, Mondale during my four years with President Carter. Mondale, who was soon named our Ambassador to Japan, spent the entire day of the speech with me; this included a visit to the city's International Center for Victims of Torture, where we heard vivid accounts of the horror of the war in Bosnia.

We and our G-7 counterparts had made explicit commitments for Russian aid at the cabinet-level meeting in Tokyo in April, and my Minneapolis speech was the occasion for a detailed explanation of our rationale for asking the American people to support this proposed assistance. As a result, the speech had a rather complex and substantive flavor. Our case was bolstered by the April 25 referendum in which the Russian people had voted by a large majority to support Yeltsin's reform efforts.

Our effort to articulate American leadership was complicated by an incident that, with several years' hindsight, causes one to sigh, "Only in Washington." The problem stemmed from a comment made by Peter Tarnoff, the Under Secretary for Political Affairs, in an off-the-record talk to the Washington press corps a few days before the Minneapolis speech.[3] Discussing the importance of balancing current economic realities with the role of the United States abroad, Tarnoff stressed the Administration's oft-cited theme that "economic priorities are paramount." This statement alone offered nothing new. What caught reporters' attention were his next thoughts: the United States had "to make commitment[s] commensurate with [economic] realities. This may on occasion fall short of what Americans would like and others would hope for."

In retrospect, Tarnoff's statement was quite unremarkable—the United States should only expend resources commensurate with the interests at stake. However, some in the press interpreted his remarks as signaling a coming retreat from the American role abroad. Since the briefing was not "on the record," Tarnoff could properly be referred to only as a "senior administration official." However, the *New York Times*

---

[3]Peter Tarnoff, a longtime friend, served with great ability and dedication throughout my four years as Secretary. He skillfully handled some of the most delicate and difficult diplomatic assignments for the President and the State Department.

soon "outed" Tarnoff as the source of the comments, which led to yet more media commentary.[4]

Tom Donilon and I decided to use the Minneapolis speech to correct these misinterpretations of Tarnoff's statements. This effort seemed to have the intended effect: most of the press coverage focused on my comments about U.S. leadership, quoting extensively from the speech. Indeed, the *Washington Post* counted over 20 references to the words "lead" and "leadership" in the speech. Even at the expense of rhetorical overkill, we were determined to dispel any suggestion at home or abroad that the first Democratic Administration in a dozen years was sounding retreat.

The Three Pillars of U.S. Foreign Policy and Support for Reform in Russia

Address Before the Chicago Council on Foreign Relations, the

Executives' Club of Chicago, and the Mid-America Committee,

Chicago, Illinois, March 22, 1993

It is a pleasure for me to be here today. This might surprise you, but I am happy to be here on a white and snowy morning. It reminds me of growing up in North Dakota—walking home from school and having my mother greet me with a cup of hot chocolate. You can see I have happy memories of the Midwest, so I'm especially happy to be here.

I'm particularly pleased to be speaking to this very audience. Secretaries of State spend probably too much of their time explaining American foreign policy to foreign diplomats, and they might tend to take for granted audiences such as this, the audiences that really count: the American people.

I want to say a special welcome today to the students that are here

---

[4]Since no *New York Times* reporter had been present at the initial briefing, the *Times* claimed that the standard rule of non-attribution did not apply. Apart from any foreign policy implications, the entire incident touched off quite a debate within the press about the ethics and ground rules of identifying the source of a "background" comment.

from the congressional districts of Congressmen Reynolds and Rush. You students have a tremendous stake in our foreign policy. After all, you are the ones that will have to live with the consequences of all that we do. So it's critical that your voice be heard, and I am particularly glad that you're here today.

My trip today is only the first of many that I hope to be making to the cities and towns of the United States. My mission is quite a simple one: to begin an ongoing conversation with the people here in America about the world we live in and our country's proper role in it.

It is fitting that I launch this process, I think, here in Chicago. Your city is a city that symbolizes America in so many ways—by its location here in the country's heartland, by its fighting spirit, by its broad shoulders, and most of all by its good common sense. Yet at the same time, Chicago is very much at the center of the world—with its mighty industries exporting goods around the globe, with its commodity markets linking international investors near and far.

Chicagoans and all Americans have a right to a foreign policy that serves their interests in very concrete ways. They want a foreign policy that will build a safer world, a more prosperous world, and a world where their values can be secure. That is exactly the kind of foreign policy that Governor—that President Clinton—I still call him Governor Clinton sometimes—has charged me to carry out.

At the State Department, we have a desk responsible for every foreign country, or virtually every foreign country—the China desk, an Argentine desk, a Russia desk. As Secretary of State, I am determined that the State Department will also have an "American desk"—and I want to be sitting behind that desk. My foremost mission is to advance the vital interests of the citizens of the United States. Today, and over the coming weeks and months, I want to outline how the Clinton Administration plans to pursue that objective—pursue the objective of furthering the interests of the American people.

America in a New World

As you all know, our world has changed fundamentally in recent years. Walls have come down. Empires have collapsed. Most important, the

Cold War is over, and the Soviet Union is no more. Soviet communism is dead. But with it so is the reference point that guided our policies for over 40 years. It was easy when we could simply point to the Soviet Union and say that what we had to do was to contain Soviet expansion. That reference point explained why our international leadership was so necessary, why our defense burden was so heavy, and why assistance to other countries was so critical.

Today, we face a vastly more complicated world. It is a world of breathtaking opportunities to expand democracy and free markets. But it is also a world of grave new perils. Long-simmering ethnic conflicts have flared up anew in the former Yugoslavia and elsewhere. Weapons of mass destruction are falling into the hands of very dangerous dictators. And new global challenges cry out for attention around our entire world—challenges like the environment, over population, drug-trafficking, and AIDS.

Like the last generation's great leaders who met the challenges of the Cold War, we need a new strategy for protecting and promoting American interests in this new era. We need a strategy that will face the questions that Americans are asking, and most understandably asking: Why, they say, with the threat of Soviet expansionism gone, do we need to be active on the international front? Why must America continue to carry the heavy burdens of leadership? Why, when we so urgently need renewal here at home, should we continue to dedicate large resources abroad?

The Three Pillars: Renewing America's Foreign Policy

President Clinton has responded to these challenges by laying out an American foreign policy based upon three pillars:

First, building American prosperity;

Second, modernizing America's armed services; and

Third, promoting democracy and human rights abroad.

This policy's fundamental premise is that in today's world foreign and domestic policy are inseparable. If we fail to maintain our strength at home, we will be, certainly, unable to lead abroad. If we retreat into isolationism, it will be impossible to revitalize our domestic strength. America cannot thrive in a world of economic recession or violent conflicts or a world which is riven with dictatorships.

It is no accident that President Clinton has identified promotion of America's economic security as the first pillar of our foreign policy. We've entered an era where economic competitiveness is vital to our ability to succeed abroad. As an essential first step, as you know, the President has put forward a bold, new program to get America's own economic house in order. It's a comprehensive strategy that will invest in the needs of our people, reduce our deficits, and lay the foundation for long-term economic growth. The single most important step that we can take to strengthen our foreign policy, to strengthen our position in the world, is to enact the President's economic program—and to do so just as soon as possible.

But steps at home cannot ensure America's prosperity. Today, we are irreversibly linked to the global economy. Our lives are constantly touched by huge flows of trade and finance that cross many borders. To take another example, over 7 million Americans are now employed in export-related jobs—many of them here, of course, right in the Chicago area.

Our ability to prosper in this global economy depends upon our ability to compete. That means harnessing our diplomacy to serve our economic goals. We must ensure that foreign markets are open to U.S. goods and U.S. investments. We must fight unfair competition against U.S. business and labor. And we must press the world's other financial powers to enact responsible policies that foster growth.

The second pillar of our foreign policy will be to modernize our armed forces to meet new needs around the world and to meet continuing threats. The collapse of the Soviet Union enables us to significantly scale back our military establishment. But, nevertheless, our power must always be sufficient to counter any threat to our vital interests. We must be able to deter and, when necessary, to defeat any potential foe. That's why we are taking steps to make our military more agile, mobile, flexible, and smart. Let me emphasize that President Clinton is determined to have the best-equipped and best fighting force in America to defend America.

As we talk about our armed forces, I think it's important for me to say that America cannot be the world's policeman. We cannot be responsible for settling every dispute or answering every alarm. We are indispensable, but we certainly must not be indiscriminate. America's leadership will require that we wisely marshal the West's collective strength.

Ethnic conflicts—and the humanitarian disasters they generate—deeply offend our conscience. In many cases, they also pose a serious risk to international peace. And they produce thousands of refugees, so often, that strain the political and economic stability of an entire region. Our imperative is to develop international means to contain and, more important, to prevent these conflicts before they erupt. Here, it is critical that we use the United Nations in the manner its founders intended, and there is high, new hope that this may take place. UN peace-keeping capabilities must be strengthened so as to allow prompt, preventive action. Our other instruments of collective security, such as our NATO alliance, must be adapted in this new era to support the UN efforts.

One of the most promising areas for preventive diplomacy is in the Middle East. Here, fortunately, the end of the Cold War has not unleashed conflict; but, rather, it has created new opportunities, new chances for ending conflict. I recently returned from a 7-day trip to the region, where I held extensive talks with all the top leaders of the Arab and Israeli Governments. I came back absolutely convinced that there is a historic opportunity to take new strides toward peace in this troubled region.

Now it's imperative that all sides to this long-simmering conflict seize this opportunity to return to the negotiating table in Washington on April 20, as we have invited them to do. If they return and enter negotiations, the United States is ready to act as a full partner in their efforts. If they do not, however—if they allow this unique chance to slip away—another generation in the Middle East could be lost to an endless cycle of confrontation and, eventually, to renewed conflict.

Let me now turn to the third pillar of this Administration's foreign policy: encouraging the global revolution for democracy and human rights that is transforming the world. By helping promote democracy, we do more than honor our deepest values. We are also making a strategic investment in our nation's security. History has shown that a world of more democracies is a safer world. It is a world that will devote more to human development and less to human destruction. And it is a world that will promote what all people have in common rather than what tears them apart.

The Challenge of Our Time: Helping Russian Democracy

These three pillars of American foreign policy—building America's prosperity, modernizing America's armed forces, and promoting democratic values—form the core of the Clinton Administration's new diplomacy. Now I would like to tell you how these three pillars converge and form the basis for one of our highest foreign policy priorities—and that is helping the Russian people to build a free society and a market economy. This, in my judgment, is the greatest strategic challenge of our time. Bringing Russia—one of history's most powerful nations—into the family of peaceful nations will serve our highest security, economic, and moral interests.

For America and the world, the stakes are just monumental. If we succeed, we will have established the foundation for our lasting security into the next century. But if Russia falls into anarchy or lurches back to despotism, the price that we pay could be frightening. Nothing less is involved than the possibility of renewed nuclear threat, higher defense budgets, spreading instability, the loss of new markets, and a devastating setback for the worldwide democratic movement. This circumstance deserves the attention of each and every American.

Over the days and weeks ahead, the Clinton Administration will set forth a comprehensive strategy to support Russia's democracy and its efforts to build a market economy. My intention today is not to announce a detailed program of new initiatives; rather, what I would like to do is to try to provide a strategic context for the approach that we will follow. I want to explain the tremendous interest we have in doing everything we can to help Russia's democracy succeed.

Let me stress here today that by focusing on Russia, I do not mean to neglect the other new independent states. The well-being of Ukraine, of Kazakhstan, of Belarus, of Armenia, and, indeed, of each of the former republics, is a matter of utmost importance to America. We are committed to developing strong bilateral relations with each of these countries. We will support their independence and do everything we can to assist in their integration into the world community. Indeed, it is partly out of concern for their welfare that I want to concentrate on Russia today. For the fact is that the future security of each of these neighbors of Russia depends so heavily on Russia's own democratic revolution.

Let me step back for just a moment and analyze with you the breathtaking benefits that the end of the Cold War has brought to the United States and the world. To mention just a few of the results:

Historic agreements have been reached to slash the nuclear arsenals that threatened our country with annihilation.

The nations of the former Warsaw Pact are now free of Soviet domination and of the burden of communism.

The possibility of a superpower conflict on the European continent has now all but vanished, allowing us to bring home thousands of troops and to reduce our defense budgets.

Around the globe, totalitarian regimes that looked to the Soviet Union for help and support are now isolated and on the defensive.

And from Vilnius on the Baltic to Vladivostok on the Pacific, vast new markets are opening—opening slowly but nonetheless opening—to Western business.

With a reforming Russia, all of these historic achievements were possible. But without it, many will not be sustainable.

So we stand again at a historic crossroads. It is very reminiscent of the crossroads that we faced in 1918 and 1945. Then, we were summoned after conflicts to lead the world by building a new peace. After World War I, we chose to retreat, and the consequences were disastrous. However, after World War II, our leaders had the wisdom to answer the call. We fostered institutions that rebuilt the free world's prosperity. And we helped to lead a democratic alliance that contained and, ultimately, drained Soviet communism.

Today, for the third time this century, we have a historic opportunity to build a more secure world. We must redouble our efforts to help the Russian people as they struggle in an effort that has no historical precedent. With great courage, they are attempting to carry out three simultaneous revolutions: first, transforming a totalitarian system into a democracy; second, transforming a command economy into one based upon free markets; and third, transforming an aggressive, expansionist empire into a peaceful, modern nation-state. If they succeed in this tremendous experiment, we all will succeed.

Now it appears that another turning point has been reached in Russia's transition. For months, a constitutional crisis between President Yeltsin and the parliament has paralyzed Russian politics. That crisis came—as you all know—came to a head over the weekend. President Yeltsin has called for a national plebiscite to resolve the constitutional impasse. In doing so, he has again demonstrated his faith that the only force that can guarantee reform is the people—the Russian people.

We welcome President Yeltsin's assurance that civil liberties, including freedom of speech and of the press, will be respected at this difficult moment. We also welcome his firm rejection of imperial and Cold War policies. The most important point is that Russia must remain a democracy during this period, moving toward a market economy. This is the basis, the only basis, for the U.S.-Russian partnership.

The United States has strongly supported Russia's efforts to build a democracy. Under President Yeltsin's leadership, historic progress has been made toward a free society. We urge that this progress continue and that the Russian people be allowed to determine their future through peaceful means and with full respect for civil liberties. On that basis, Russia can be assured of our full support in the days ahead.

Now, today's crisis in Russia results from one indisputable fact: The pain of building a new system virtually from scratch is exacting a tremendous toll. The patience of the Russian people is wearing thin, a fact that is reflected in Russia's current political stalemate. Nevertheless, we should notice that over the last year, President Yeltsin and Russia's other democrats have demonstrated their commitment to reform in many ways. Civil liberties have been dramatically expanded. The military budget has been significantly cut. Prices have been freed in most sectors, and the result has been [that] the once-long lines that formed outside Russia's stores have come to an end. Tens of thousands of shops, restaurants, and other firms have been put into private hands, and a real start has been made on the most difficult process of even privatizing the large enterprises. As a result of these steps, the share of the work force engaged in private commerce has more than doubled over the last 2 years.

I'm glad to say that over the weekend, President Yeltsin recommitted his government to economic reform. He laid out in clear and strong language the key elements of such a program: continued privatization of firms, selling land to farmers, stopping inflation, and stabilizing the ruble. If this program is implemented, our capacity to help will be greatly enhanced.

Russia's reformers are now looking to the West for support at this moment of extreme difficulty. The United States has a deep self-interest in responding to this historic challenge. We should extend to the Russian people not a hand of pity but a hand of partnership. We must lead a long-term Western strategy of engagement for democracy.

Here in America, it is very important that we not create a false choice between what is required to renew our economy at home and what is necessary to protect our interests abroad. We can and must do both. During the long struggle of the Cold War, we kept the American dream alive for all people here at home. At the same time, we made great sacrifices to protect our national security, and today we can and must meet the same challenge. To succeed, we must first change our mindsets. We must understand that helping consolidate democracy in Russia is not a matter of charity but a security concern of the highest order. It is no less important to our well-being than the need to contain a hostile Soviet Union was at an earlier day.

Tomorrow and the next day, in Washington [DC], President Clinton and I will meet with the Russian Foreign Minister, Andrei Kozyrev. We will communicate to him our support for Russia's continued democratic development. And we will reiterate that the current situation in Moscow must be resolved peacefully and in a way consistent with civil liberties. At his meeting with President Yeltsin next month in Vancouver [Canada], President Clinton intends to spell out the tangible steps we will take to assist Russian reform. The President is still considering the specific measures he will announce. But our bottom line is that we will be increasing and accelerating our support for Russia's democracy. We cannot do it alone, but we must be prepared to do our part and to do it fully. The United States favors a meeting later in April where the foreign and finance ministers of the leading industrial democracies will coordinate their joint efforts to assist in Russia's historic transformation.

As I said earlier in my remarks, my task today is not to spell out specific initiatives. Nevertheless, I would like to offer just a few thoughts on the central issue of Western aid to Russia in general terms. Clearly, our assistance must be better targeted and better coordinated than it's been in the past. It must focus on areas and constituencies in Russia that have the greatest impact on their long-term reform. It must not and cannot be limited solely to public funds. Rather, it must catalyze our private sectors to take a leading role in Russia's transformation through trade, investment, and training. And our aid must be felt at the grassroots, to ease the pain of the Russian children, workers, and senior citizens who are suffering through this transformation.

Despite all of its current economic difficulties, it is worth remembering that Russia is inherently a rich country. Its people are well-educated. Its natural resource base exceeds that of any other country in the world. For example, Russia's oil reserves are huge and, if properly exploited, could probably finance much of Russia's economic reform. But today, thousands of aging oil wells and pipelines in Russia stand idle, decaying and desperately in need of critical spare parts. If Russia could find the means to repair them, perhaps with our help, the oil sold would be a lucrative source of foreign exchange that could do a great deal to stabilize their economy.

One area of possible assistance where America's vital interests are directly engaged is our effort to dismantle the nuclear weapons of the former Soviet Union. The $800-million program established through the leadership of Senators Nunn and Lugar to destroy these weapons is a direct investment in our own security. Unfortunately, some bottlenecks, both here and in Russia, have allowed only a small fraction of the $800 million to be spent up to this point. Part of it has been caused by bureaucratic delays in Washington, and we are fully determined to remove these obstacles. We want to see these weapons dismantled in the very shortest possible time.

Another important goal we should have is strengthening the groups in Russia that will form the bulwark of a thriving democracy. There are public opinion polls in Russia, too, as you know, and time after time they show one thing: By large margins, it's the younger generation that expresses the greatest sympathy for democracy. The younger people are the ones who are pushing for more economic freedom and closer contacts with the West. Ultimately, whatever the result of today's political turmoil, this is the group that will carry the day for Russia's successful transition to democracy.

Through exchange programs, many young Russians can be brought to the West and exposed to the workings of democracy and our free market. Russian students, public officials, scientists, and businessmen are hungry for such experiences. Upon their return home, they can adapt their knowledge to best suit Russia's conditions. And, perhaps most important of all, we can win long-term friends and partners for freedom.

The existence, to take another example, of a strong, independent media is also essential for a democratic society. While Russia's free press has experienced tremendous growth in recent years, there is still a real need for professional training of reporters, editors, and news managers. Here, technical assistance can make a real difference.

Another area that deserves strong support is Russia's privatization effort, which, as I said, has made some progress. This process has continued across many of Russia's regions despite the political problems in Moscow. Putting private property into the hands of the Russian people is a critical step in building a free market economy. It will create millions of property owners and private entrepreneurs—a genuine middle class with a powerful stake in continued reform.

Of course, at the end of the day, Russia's progress toward the market and democracy cannot occur without an overhaul of the general ground rules of the Russian economy. It will be vital to reduce their budget deficit, control the money supply, stabilize the ruble, and close down inefficient factories. Unfortunately, these are also steps that will cause the greatest pain and political risk. Here again, Russia needs our help. The West must find a way to respond, and the response can't be limited to big promises and little delivery. We are now engaged in intensive consultations with our partners from the leading industrial democracies to develop a program of joint assistance to Russia in these areas.

Helping Russia's Democracy: A Long-Term Commitment

Let me close by making two points. First, we must have no illusions about the situation in Russia. Even with our help, the road ahead is rocky. Setbacks will be inevitable. Russia's transformation will take a great deal of hard work—probably a generation to complete. As we meet, a great struggle is underway, as you know, to determine the kind of nation that Russia will be. However, as we focus on today's drama, it's important that we maintain a long-term perspective. Just as our vigilance in the Cold War took more than 4 decades to pay off, our commitment to Russia's democracy must be for the duration. Our engagement with the reformers must be for the long haul—whether they're "out" as well as when they're "in," whether they're "down" as well as when they're "up." However difficult things may be in the short run, we should have faith that the strategic course we have set—supporting democracy's triumph—is the correct one.

Second, we should know that any realistic program to assist Russia won't be cheap. But there's no question that our nation can afford its fair share of the international effort. We can't afford, indeed, to do otherwise. Together with President Clinton, I am determined to work with the Congress to find the funding. I am confident that the necessary resources can be found as we restructure our defense budget. But it will require bipartisanship, leadership, and vision, and, vitally, it will take a Russian partner committed to democratic values and to market reform.

At a time of great domestic challenge, some would say that we should delay bold action in the foreign realm. But history will not wait. As Abraham Lincoln advised his countrymen, "We cannot escape history. We . . . will be remembered in spite of ourselves." Today, history is calling again for our nation to decide whether we will lead or defer, whether we will shape this new era or be shaped by it. How will history remember us? I, for one, am confident that we will make the right choice—that we will be bold and brave in revitalizing our nation here at home, while continuing to promote our interests and ideals abroad.

U.S. Support for Russian Reform: An Investment in America's Security

Address at the Hubert H. Humphrey Institute of Public Affairs at the University of Minnesota, Minneapolis, May 27, 1993

Fritz Mondale suggested that I come here today, and I am delighted to be back in the Upper Midwest. Scranton, North Dakota, where I grew up, was much too small to have a daily paper, and I depended upon the *Minneapolis Tribune*, which was brought only one day late on the Milwaukee railroad. I grew up on Gopher football, and probably could still name some of the members of the 1935 team.

In those Depression years, I learned that politics should be about helping people. Through my life and in my career, no single state has produced more caring politicians than Minnesota—notable among them Fritz Mondale.

Fritz Mondale is a man I have been proud to work with and stand by for nearly thirty years. We worked together to advance justice at home and human rights abroad. In the Carter Administration, we worked together to win approval of the Panama Canal Treaties and the Taiwan Relations Act, two of the signature endeavors of the Carter Administration. We also worked together on behalf of Southeast Asian refugees and against the proliferation of weapons of mass destruction.

In recent years, in private life, Fritz Mondale has worked to promote democracy and human rights around the world as Chairman of the National Democratic Institute. Wherever he has gone, Fritz has shown America's most decent face to the world, and reminded Americans of our most inspiring values.

I am especially pleased to be speaking to you today at a great state university that honors the memory of Hubert Humphrey. His achievements on the domestic front were so imaginative and so important—from civil rights to Medicare—that we sometimes forget the lasting contribution he made in the field of international affairs.

Like many of his contemporaries, Hubert Humphrey knew what he was against: communism and repression. But like few others, he was also just as passionate about what he stood for and what America ought to stand for in the world: peace and freedom. He knew where America should go—and as much as anyone of his generation, he knew how to get there. The Arms Control and Disarmament Agency; the Nuclear Test Ban Treaty; the Peace Corps and the Food for Peace program: these are all part of Hubert's legacy. Hubert's ideas made the world better, by bringing out the best in America.

This is one in a series of speeches I will be giving around the United States. I want to make sure that foreign policy isn't foreign to the American people.

At the State Department, we have a desk for virtually every foreign country: a China desk; a Brazil desk; a Russia desk. As Secretary of State, I am determined that we will also have an American desk—and that I will sit behind it. My principal mission is to advance the vital interests and values of the citizens of the United States. That's my job.

I want to help American businesses succeed in the global economy. That is why I visited Honeywell earlier today to discuss their investments in Russia. It was an inspiring visit to a very great company.

I want to underscore our unshakable commitment to human rights. That is why I am visiting later today the Center for Victims of Torture here in Minneapolis.

And I want America to make essential investments in our national security. That is why I have come here to talk to you about America's policy toward Russia. No relationship is more important to the long-term security of the United States than our strategic relationship with Russia.

Today's students are the first generation of Americans to have come of age in the post–Cold War era. It is your generation that will define America's destiny in the next century. It is your generation that will decide to what purpose America's leadership and power will be put.

Today, I want to talk about our new opportunity to make a new democratic world. As we meet, the people of Russia are struggling heroically to build a free society and a market economy. If they succeed, the payoffs for America promise to be profound: in the reduced threat of nuclear war; in lower defense budgets; and in the vast new markets that can fuel global prosperity and create jobs for Americans.

But if reform fails, and if Russia reverts to dictatorship or collapses into anarchy, the consequences would be appalling. The shadow of nuclear confrontation could return. Our "peace dividend" would be cancelled. Cooperation in foreign policy would vanish. And the worldwide movement toward democracy would suffer a devastating setback.

America faces a choice. Either we do all we can now to help Russia's reformers succeed—or we stand aside, take our chances, and just watch events unfold. If we stand aside, we will forfeit a rare chance to shape a more peaceful world.

Some believe that with the end of the Cold War, America ought to step back from the world stage. What a disservice that would be to all Americans, especially to young Americans. You deserve the same chance my generation had to fulfill America's unique destiny to promote freedom and democracy around the world.

Some say that our nation is on a course of decline, that we can no longer afford to lead. It is true that the United States faces many challenges today unlike any in the nation's history. But to me, that means we must be more engaged internationally, not less; more ardent in our promotion of democracy, not less; more inspired in our leadership, not less.

America must lead because the need for American leadership is undiminished. We are a blessed and a powerful nation. We must shoulder the responsibility of world leadership.

We stand prepared to act decisively to protect our interests wherever and whenever necessary. When it is necessary, we will act unilaterally to protect our interests. Where collective responses are appropriate, we will lead in mobilizing such collective responses. But let me make it clear today. Make no mistake: The United States will lead.

At two other points in this century, America faced a choice similar to the one we face today.

The first defining moment for American leadership came in 1918 in the aftermath of World War I. After that terrible conflict, Europe lay devastated and demoralized. Empires that had stood for centuries collapsed overnight. Violent revolution and revenge erupted.

Amid the chaos, the world looked to the United States for the strength and moral vision to ensure a lasting peace. That was the dream of President Wilson. He was a visionary in his grasp of a profound truth of this bloody century: American leadership is the linchpin of a more just international system.

But Wilson's plan to join the League of Nations was defeated in Congress. Instead of deciding to lead, the United States chose to retreat. For America and the world, the consequences were tragic.

Within a decade, the storm clouds gathered. Hitler became Germany's chancellor, and, six years later, Germany marched into Czechoslovakia. A militarist Japan invaded Manchuria. Fascist Italy conquered Ethiopia. And the systematic persecution and destruction of Europe's Jews commenced. All the while, America reclined in isolationism. Then the infamous attack on Pearl Harbor shattered a false peace. And nearly 300,000 Americans gave their lives on the battlefields of Europe and the Pacific to help win World War II.

Then came the second defining moment for American leadership. Americans saw European democracies teetering on the edge, economies lying in ruin, communist dictatorships consolidating their hold in Eastern Europe, the Iron Curtain descending, and a Cold War chilling the new peace.

Once again, the world looked to America's strength and moral force to build peace from the ruins of war. But this time, America responded positively.

It took principled presidential leadership—and bipartisan statesmanship—to win congressional approval and lasting public support. Fortunately, we were blessed with leaders—Truman, Marshall, Acheson, Vandenberg—who had learned the bitter lessons of 1918.

Together, Democrats and Republicans put the pillars of peace and security in place—at Bretton Woods, with the Marshall Plan, and through NATO. And those pillars still stood as the Berlin Wall fell.

Put simply, Communism was defeated. Freedom was defended. Our values triumphed.

In the late 1940s, I had returned from service in the Pacific during the Second World War and was attending law school. I remember the atmosphere when, as Averell Harriman once said, most Americans wanted nothing more than to "go to the movies and drink a Coke."

Yet when the American people saw what was at stake, they exercised their common sense. They accepted the necessity for American leadership of the post-war world. They understood it was right, it was necessary, and it was in America's interest.

We spent literally trillions of dollars to deter the communist threat. And we put the lives of our finest young Americans on the line to preserve freedom.

The sacrifices were great, but the payoffs were even greater. My generation enjoyed security and unparalleled prosperity. And we helped to turn our former wartime adversaries—Germany and Japan—into peacetime allies and leading partners in the democratic community.

Certainly, there are differences between the situations we faced after two world wars and the situation today. But there are also important parallels that ought to guide us. We must recognize the need for American leadership; the need for bipartisanship in our foreign policy; the need to make investments now to avoid far larger expenditures and a much more dangerous world later; the need to talk sense to the American people.

Even as we make the tough choices at home to put our economy in order, we must extend a hand of cooperation to the peoples of the former Soviet Union, not out of charity, but out of responsibility to ourselves— to secure our own interests and to defend our own values. Helping democracy succeed in Russia is probably the wisest—and least expensive—investment that we can make today in America's security.

A democratic Russia creates a new global political landscape. Today, Russia is showing a willingness to work with the United States and other nations to prevent the spread of the conflict in Bosnia and to exert pressure for a political outcome. Our new relationship with Russia gives us the chance to work together on the world's problems, and to carry out preventive diplomacy and solve conflicts.

The need for American action is reinforced by the results of Russia's April 25 referendum. In a great expression of democratic faith, the Russian people reaffirmed their commitment to political and economic reform. While the experts insisted that Russians had grown cynical about democracy and apathetic toward politics, nearly two-thirds of voters came to the polls.

Even more remarkable was the outcome of the referendum itself. After almost 18 months of painful economic reforms, a strong majority of the Russian people expressed their support for President Yeltsin and for more reform. And they did so with the backing of President Clinton, whose support of Yeltsin and reform in Russia has been strong and unflinching.

President Clinton is determined to meet the challenge of leadership—to tip the global balance in favor of freedom. This is why he has led America into an alliance with Russian reform.

Working closely with Russia's democrats and our Western allies, the President has developed a two-part strategy to support the new Russian revolution: First, a focused program of U.S. initiatives to help the development of Russian democracy and free enterprise; second, a large-scale package of measures to support a transformation of the Russian economy, a package jointly sponsored by the world's major industrial democracies and major financial institutions.

President Clinton is delivering on the commitments that he made to President Yeltsin at Vancouver in early April—commitments that were important to the outcome of the referendum.

He pledged concessional loans for agricultural products. Very soon, Russia will sign a $700 million Food for Progress concessional loan agreement, an agreement that will provide aid for Russia. That will also help wheat, corn, and soybean farmers here in the Midwest.

He pledged support for privatization in Russia. U.S. teams are now in Russia helping establish capital markets, including a fledgling stock market, and an Enterprise Fund to invest in start-up small businesses in Russia.

He pledged support for student exchange programs as part of a Democracy Corps. More than 2,000 Russian students will come to America in the coming weeks as part of "Democracy Summer."

Other parts of the Vancouver program are also moving ahead. We are working to revive Russia's energy sector—to provide hard currency for Russia—and lessen U.S. dependence on Persian Gulf oil. We are also helping to resettle recently demobilized Russian soldiers. That action will support the withdrawal of Russian troops from neighboring countries.

President Clinton's initiative is guided by several basic principles.

First, we want to deliver quick and tangible benefits to the Russian people. If the faith demonstrated in last month's referendum is to be sustained, they must see that they are the beneficiaries of reform and not its unintentional victims. And if Americans are to support this initiative, we must—and we will—make sure that the aid is not just well-intentioned but also well-spent.

A Congressional delegation, led by House Majority Leader Richard Gephardt, recently saw first-hand how the United States is helping to make privatization work in Russia. They observed auction centers in Moscow and Nizhny Novgorod both funded by USAID and operated by Price Waterhouse, to carry out the sale of state-run enterprises.

Second, we need to assist Russia's conversion to a market economy. Ultimately, increased interaction with the world economy—far more than aid—will transform Russia. For its part, Russia needs to establish the necessary legal and political conditions to attract foreign trade and investment—which we hope will include businesses that will create American jobs.

For our part, President Clinton has ordered a full review of Cold War laws and regulations. They were meant to restrict trade with a communist Soviet Union, but they now only impede our relations with a democratic Russia. To the maximum extent possible, consistent with America's interests, U.S. markets should be open to competitive Russian products. Similarly, Americans should be allowed to export our goods and technology to Russia.

Third, we want to dramatically expand efforts to send American business and trade union leaders, farmers, and community organizers to Russia. We want to increase contact and cooperation between our armed forces and the Russian military. We want to bring tens of thousands of Russians to the United States, where they can experience the sights, sounds, and practices of a thriving democracy and a market economy.

Our exchange programs will place a special emphasis on the younger generation of Russians and Americans. I hope each of you consider taking part at some point.

Fourth, our assistance to Russia must also reinforce U.S. security. This approach means helping Russia and its neighbors dismantle their dangerous nuclear arsenals. This is simply the best security that our money can buy.

Fifth and finally, our assistance efforts must not take place in isolation, but must be part of a larger partnership between Russia and the international community. That is why President Clinton's strategy to support Russia's democracy is tied to a larger-scale multilateral initiative with our principal industrial partners around the world.

This multilateral program was announced last month in Tokyo at an extraordinary meeting of foreign and finance ministers from the seven major industrialized countries and Russia. At that meeting, Russia's representatives outlined a bold new plan to control Russia's money supply, to cut its budget deficits, and to undertake even more fundamental economic reform.

In response to such actions, the world's leading democracies—working through the International Monetary Fund and the World Bank—announced their readiness to provide Russia with financial support. Fifteen billion dollars of Russia's foreign debt has recently been rescheduled. The multilateral package announced at Tokyo amounts to more than $28 billion to help Russia stabilize its currency, finance critical imports, and divest itself of inefficient state enterprises.

The disbursement of these resources will be closely linked to Russia's progress in economic reform. In contrast to previous assistance efforts, the Tokyo program sets realistic standards for Russian performance. We plan to match Russia's progress with a prompt infusion of resources that will reinforce reform and will benefit Russian people at the grass-roots level.

At the G-7 meeting in Tokyo in April, the United States committed to going beyond the pledges made in Vancouver. We put forth a $1.8 billion additional proposal to build upon our efforts in support of reform.

I am pleased that just yesterday, the funding for that proposal was approved by the House subcommittee that oversees these matters, chaired very effectively by Congressman Dave Obey from your neighboring state of Wisconsin. And I am also pleased that the package drew strong bipartisan support.

We have made important progress since Vancouver. I am confident that we will sustain that progress until the July summit meeting in Tokyo, when we hope for another burst of enthusiasm and commitment to support free markets and democracy in Russia.

Our closest allies clearly recognize that helping Russia is in their interest, too. Canada, Germany, Japan, and Britain have each announced substantial new aid packages during the last two months. We hope that by the July summit in Tokyo, we will be able to announce agreement with our allies on the creation of a new special privatization fund. We will work closely in this effort with Japan and Germany. And we hope that Japan fully recognizes the leading role it can play not only in Tokyo this summer, but thereafter in helping deliver the kind of total package that will secure Russia's place in the community of democratic nations.

I think that all of us in Washington realize that asking American taxpayers to help support Russia is not easy, especially when we face important challenges here at home. But I disagree with those who think it's wrong or politically unwise to ask the American people to support a program that is so clearly in our interests.

That's why we are *asking*—and that's why we're asking *now*. I urge you to support the President's plan to help Russia's democracy proceed. I am convinced that this investment in Russia's democracy is essential to America's future security.

I am especially asking the young people here today to make your choice. I am not among those who think that your generation is disengaged, or cynical, or apathetic about what happens in the world around you. Don't let those critics sell you short. I believe you deserve more credit, and I ask you today to help prove me right. I ask you to tell your parents, your peers, your representatives in Congress, that you understand the vital link between the success of Russian democracy and America's long-term security.

You understand that freedom abroad means opportunity in America. You understand that assistance to our friends in Russia is insurance against having enemies in Russia.

If we do not act today, your generation may inherit an America of few choices and many burdens. You may inherit an America of lost opportunities. We may never build a national service program. We may never fully fund Head Start for poor children. We may never be able to afford the technologies we need to clean up our environment. Unless we help Russian democracy now, we will pay the price. And my responsibility, together with you, is not to let that happen.

We have come so far. We have spent so much. We have earned the promise of a safer, freer, and better world. To retreat now would be to walk away from nearly a half century of American leadership, sacrifice, and commitment.

Our purpose over the last half century was to arrive right where we are today: to be able to ask the American people to form a partnership with Russia because it is in America's most fundamental interest. That is why we ask—and that is why we are confident that the Congress and the American people will respond affirmatively when we make this request to measure up to our mutual responsibilities.

THREE

America's Commitment to Human Rights

This speech, delivered before the first World Conference on Human Rights in 25 years, was a statement of personal conviction as well as foreign policy strategy. The pursuit of human and civil rights has been at the heart of my own work in public life. As Deputy Attorney General in the Johnson Administration, I was actively involved in the passage of the historic 1968 Civil Rights Bill. As President Carter's Deputy Secretary of State, I led the Administration's effort to determine how diplomatic leverage (such as foreign aid) could be deployed to promote human rights, and oversaw the preparation of early State Department Human Rights Reports. In my home city of Los Angeles, I served as Vice Chairman of the Governor's Commission on the 1965 Los Angeles riots (the McCone Commission), and in 1991 as Chairman of the Independent Commission on the Los Angeles Police Department (the Christopher Commission), which investigated police brutality in the wake of the Rodney King beating incident. The latter commission proposed sweeping charter reforms that were later approved overwhelmingly by a public referendum.

The work of reconciliation and tolerance in America is far from finished. But we have the mechanisms to address the remaining problems, and we will not rest until we overcome them. Our commitment to basic human rights is one of the major reasons that people from around the world look to America for leadership. Although such statesmen as Woodrow Wilson and Harry Truman were among the first to advocate human rights on a global scale, not until President Carter's Administration were these issues conceptualized as a fundamental component of U.S. foreign policy. His efforts gave human rights a permanent place on the American foreign policy agenda. At his direction, we reminded the world leaders with whom we met, whether friendly or otherwise, that whether they acted to provide basic, fundamental rights to their citizens would have a significant influence on our relations with them.

After the Carter Administration left office in 1981, the place of human rights became bogged down in controversy. The Reagan and Bush Administrations did not challenge the importance of human rights principles, but many of their officials felt those principles were primarily useful in the struggle against communism, rather than being universally applicable standards. They were particularly reluctant to criticize some Cold War allies who were strategically important but had serious shortcomings in the human rights area.

Bringing human rights back to the center of foreign policy was a strong commitment of the new Clinton Administration. From my experience in the Carter years, I believed that promoting human rights should complement, not compete with, other objectives. Inside the State Department, I wanted a human rights bureau that would work in close harmony with other regional and functional bureaus, so as to emphasize human rights as a critical component of our broader foreign policy agenda. As an important first step in this effort, I asked John Shattuck, who was Vice President of Harvard University and a former Executive Director of the ACLU and Amnesty International board member, to head the human rights bureau. Shattuck did an excellent job of working closely with other Assistant Secretaries to integrate human rights into other foreign policy initiatives. As an example, his efforts in 1995 to investigate human rights abuses in Bosnia provided strategic leverage in our pursuit of peace, and he played a vital role in negotiating the human rights components of the Dayton accords.

The June 1993 conference in Vienna provided an excellent opportunity to revitalize American commitment to human rights as an integral part of our foreign policy. For 12 days, representatives from over 160 nations and 2,000 non-governmental groups debated and discussed specific human rights causes as well as general principles, and concluded by signing an international declaration modeled on the 1948 United Nations Universal Declaration of Human Rights. By addressing the conference's opening session, I wanted to signal the new Administration's commitment and help set the agenda for the upcoming discussions.[1]

My speech in Vienna made the point that the relevant issue is how to address human rights most effectively. Preparation of this speech involved a lively tug-of-war between two camps—one that wanted to stress the traditional human rights approach, which focuses on protecting individuals from torture, oppression, and other invasions of personal freedom, and one that wanted to emphasize guaranteeing human rights through promoting democracy. The point of the democracy-centered argument was that in the post–Cold War era, we have an opportunity to move beyond an individually aimed human rights policy to an approach that takes on the issue at a more fundamental level. If democracy takes hold, the argument runs, human rights will follow.[2] This emphasis on democracy, some argued, was a broader, more strategic approach than that taken by me and others in the Carter Administration.

In the original drafts of the speech, the democracy argument was made but not heavily stressed. As successive drafts were exchanged with the White House, as well as with outside advisers, the emphasis on the role of democracy in promoting human rights increased. Several advisers recommended that the speech focus largely on building democracy.

Although sympathetic to that overarching theme, I was not comfortable presenting democracy as the be-all and end-all for human rights. I believed that the traditional human rights agenda still needed to be pursued. It was true that the collapse of communism had made the potential for democratic expansion greater than ever before, but nevertheless we needed to be sure that our human rights policy could address problems in many countries that were unlikely to become democratic anytime soon. Moreover, there were several functioning democracies that had less-than-adequate human rights records. I strongly believe that while democracy is necessary for securing human rights, it is not, in itself, sufficient for doing so. Bennett Freeman helped me crystallize this view as we worked on the final draft of the speech in Istanbul before flying to Vienna.

[1]Former President Carter attended the Vienna conference as a special guest of the UN Secretary General and was in the audience during my speech.

[2]During the 1992 campaign, President Clinton asserted that promoting democracy would be a core tenet of his foreign policy. He made the case most thoroughly in an October 1, 1992, speech in Milwaukee.

In addressing one of the hot topics at the conference, the speech firmly upheld the view that human rights are universal. In April 1993, 34 Arab and Asian nations had joined together to issue the Bangkok Declaration, which asserts that notions of human rights are linked to nations' social, cultural, and historical diversity. Arguing that such fundamental differences do not allow universal human rights standards, the Bangkok statement demanded respect for national sovereignty and an end to the use of human rights as an instrument of political leverage. As a response, I wanted to send an unambiguous message to states like China, Iran, and Burma that they could not hide behind such claims of cultural exceptionalism. "That *each* of us comes from different cultures absolves *none* of us from our obligation to comply with the Universal Declaration," I said. Then, in the most widely quoted line of the speech, I bluntly explained, "We respect the religious, social, and cultural characteristics that make each country unique. But we cannot let cultural relativism become the last refuge of repression."

I also used my remarks to outline some specific steps to improve human rights abroad. Describing an action plan for the UN, I called for that body to establish two new posts, a High Commissioner for Human Rights and a Special Rapporteur on Violence Against Women. Foreshadowing the First Lady's crucial participation in the Beijing Women's Conference later in the Administration, I stressed the need to work to advance women's rights on a global basis and promised that the United States would lead that effort. Finally, I pledged that we would push the U.S. Senate to ratify four treaties that had been negotiated during the Carter years.[3]

Coming early in the Administration, the Vienna speech laid the foundation for a strong emphasis on human rights throughout my four years in office. While recognizing that a vigorous human rights policy was only one part of our broader global strategy, I believed that it deserved to be given more prominence than it had received in the prior 12 years. In this sense, the decision to go to Vienna, and the speech itself, proved to

---

[3]Calling for immediate ratification of The International Convention on the Elimination of All Forms of Racial Discrimination, I said that we would soon urge Senate approval of The Convention on the Elimination of all Forms of Discrimination Against Women; The American Convention on Human Rights; and The International Covenant on Economic, Social and Cultural Rights.

be symbolic. A profound concern for human rights was an important ingredient in many of our policy decisions.

Democracy and Human Rights: Where America Stands

Address at the World Conference on Human Rights,

Vienna, Austria, June 14, 1993

Thank you, Mr. Chairman. And thanks to Secretary General Fall and the Preparatory Conference Chair Warzazi.

Ladies and gentlemen, I speak to you as the representative of a nation "conceived in liberty." America's identity as a nation derives from our dedication to the proposition "that all Men are created equal and endowed by their Creator with certain unalienable rights." Over the course of two centuries, Americans have found that advancing democratic values and human rights serves our deepest values as well as our practical interests.

That is why the United States stands with the men and women everywhere who are standing up for these principles. And that is why President Clinton has made reinforcing democracy and protecting human rights a pillar of our foreign policy—and a major focus of our foreign assistance programs.

Democracy is the moral and strategic imperative for the 1990s. Democracy will build safeguards for human rights in every nation. Democracy is the best way to advance lasting peace and prosperity in the world.

The cause of freedom is a fundamental commitment for my country. It is also a matter of deep personal conviction for me. I am proud to have headed the U.S. Government's first interagency group on human rights under President Carter, who is with us today. President Carter will be remembered as the first American President to put human rights on the international agenda. He has helped to lift the lives of people in every part of the world. Today, we build upon his achievements—and those of the human rights movement since its inception.

In this post–Cold War era, we are at a new moment. Our agenda for freedom must embrace every prisoner of conscience, every victim of torture, every individual denied basic human rights. It must also encompass the democratic movements that have changed the political map of our globe.

The great new focus of our agenda for freedom is this: expanding, consolidating and defending democratic progress around the world. It is democracy that establishes the civil institutions that replace the power of oppressive regimes. Democracy is the best means not just to gain—but to guarantee—human rights.

In the battle for democracy and human rights, words matter, but what we *do* matters much more. What all of our citizens and governments do in the days ahead will count far more than any discussions held or documents produced here.

I cannot predict the outcome of this Conference. But I can tell you this: The worldwide movement for democracy and human rights will prevail. My delegation will support the forces of freedom—of tolerance, of respect for the rights of the individual—not only in the next few weeks in Vienna, but every day in the conduct of our foreign policy throughout the world. The United States will never join those who would undermine the Universal Declaration and the movement toward democracy and human rights.

Securing Freedom After the Cold War

The Universal Declaration enshrines a timeless truth for all people and all nations: "Respect for human rights and fundamental freedoms *is* the foundation of freedom, justice and peace" on this earth. The Declaration's drafters met the challenge of respecting the world's diversity, while reflecting values that are universal.

Even before the Declaration was adopted, the Cold War had begun to cast a chilling shadow between word and deed. But the framers of the Declaration hoped that each successive generation would strengthen the Declaration through its own struggles. It is for each generation to redeem the promise of the framers' work.

Time and time again since the adoption of the Universal Declaration, human rights activism has unlocked prison cells and carved out pockets of freedom for individuals living under repression. Today, the global movement from despotism to democracy is transforming entire political systems and opening freedom's door to whole societies.

The end of the Cold War is the most uplifting event for human rights since the first World Conference met. Not only were the Havels and the Sakharovs set free, in large measure by their own inspiring examples, but hundreds of millions of ordinary men and women were also released from the hold of oppressive governments that controlled their lives. Now, in country after country, they are turning toward democracy to secure their newly won freedoms, guarantee their human rights, and hold their governments accountable.

Nowhere is this great drama playing out on a more central stage than in the former Soviet Union. Ensuring the success of democracy in Russia, Ukraine and the other New Independent States is the strategic challenge of our time. President Clinton is determined to meet that challenge of leadership—to tip the world balance in favor of freedom. That is why he has led America into an alliance with Russian reform spearheaded by President Yeltsin.

The promotion of democracy is the front line of global security. A world of democracies would be a safer world. Such a world would dedicate more to human development and less to human destruction. It would promote what all people have in common rather than what tears them apart. It would be a world of hope, not a world of despair.

Democracy and Diversity

In 1993 alone, in addition to a massive turnout for democracy in Russia, we have seen unprecedented free elections in Cambodia, Yemen, Burundi, and Paraguay. The Truth Commission in El Salvador has completed its healing work. And the people of South Africa have made dramatic progress toward non-racial democracy.

Around the world, people are doing the hard, sometimes painful work of building democracies from the bottom up. They are making democracy work not just on election day, but every day. They are promoting civil societies that respect the rule of law and make governments accountable.

Citizens' groups are pressing for social justice and establishing non-governmental human rights organizations. Women's groups are advocating equal treatment and fighting the widespread practice of gender-based violence. Workers are forming free trade unions. Independent media are giving pluralism its voice. All are creating counterweights to repression by affirming and asserting fundamental freedoms of expression, association, and movement.

American support for democracy is an enduring commitment. We know that establishing and sustaining democracy is not a linear proposition. The world democratic movement will encounter setbacks along the way. But with constant vigilance and hard work, democracy will succeed.

Look at the recent example given us by the people of Guatemala. Two weeks ago, they overcame a coup that had dissolved democratic institutions. They showed that democracy has a new resilience in the Americas, with roots extending deep into civil society. The resolve of the Guatemalan public, backed by the United States and the OAS-led international community, has resulted in the election of a respected human rights defender as President of Guatemala.

To those who say democracy is a Western contrivance, I say, you forgot to tell the people of Cambodia. Ninety percent of them summoned up courage, in the face of real threats, to re-claim their country by voting in last month's UN-monitored elections. In what was once a killing field, democracy is taking root.

Democratic aspirations are rising from Central Asia to Central America. No circumstances of birth, of culture, or of geography can limit the yearning of the human spirit and the right to live in freedom and dignity. Martin Luther King, Mohandas Gandhi, Fang Lizhi, Natan Sharansky—all came from different cultures and countries. Yet each shaped the destiny of his own nation and the world by insisting on the observance of the same universal rights.

That *each* of us comes from different cultures absolves *none* of us from our obligation to comply with the Universal Declaration. Torture, rape, racism, anti-Semitism, arbitrary detention, ethnic cleansing, and politically motivated disappearances—none of these is tolerated by any faith, creed, or culture that respects humanity. Nor can they be justified by the demands of economic development or political expediency.

We respect the religious, social, and cultural characteristics that make each country unique. But we cannot let cultural relativism become the last refuge of repression.

Ladies and gentlemen, the universal principles of the UN Declaration put *all* people first. We reject any attempt by any state to relegate its citizens to a lesser standard of human dignity. There is no contradiction between the universal principles of the UN Declaration and the cultures that enrich our international community. The real chasm lies between the cynical excuses of oppressive regimes and the sincere aspirations of their people.

No nation can claim perfection—not the United States nor any other nation. In 1968, when the U.S. Delegation arrived at the first World Conference on Human Rights, my country was reeling from the assassination of Martin Luther King. The murder of Robert Kennedy soon followed. King and Kennedy were deeply committed to building a more just society for all Americans. Their valiant work and their violent deaths left deep imprints on an entire generation of Americans—among them, a university student named Bill Clinton.

Democracy Can Deliver

Many young democracies contend with the vast problems of grinding poverty, illiteracy, rapid population growth, and malnutrition. The survival of these democracies may ultimately depend on their ability to show their citizens that democracy can deliver—that the difficult political and economic choices will pay off soon and not just in some distant, radiant future.

Nations that free human potential—that invest in human capital and defend human rights—have a better chance to develop and grow. Nations that enforce the right to seek and obtain employment without discrimination will become more just societies—and more productive economies. And nations that are committed to democratic values create conditions in which the private sector is free to thrive and to provide work for their people.

States that respect human rights and operate on democratic principles tend to be the world's most peaceful and stable. On the other hand, the worst violators of human rights tend to be the world's aggressors and proliferators. These states export threats to global security, whether in the shape of terrorism, massive refugee flows, or environmental pollution. Denying human rights not only lays waste to human lives; it creates instability that travels across borders.

The Future Lies with Free People

The worldwide prospects for human rights, democracy, and economic development have never been better. But sadly, the end of the Cold War has not brought an end to aggression, repression, and inhumanity.

Fresh horrors abound around the world. We have only to think of the enormous human costs of regional conflict, ethnic hatred, and despotic rule. We have only to think of Bosnia—just a few hundred miles away from this meeting hall, but worlds away from the peaceful and tolerant international community envisioned in the Universal Declaration.

A lasting peace in the Balkans depends on ensuring that all are prepared to respect fundamental human rights, especially those of minorities. Those who desecrate these rights must know that they will be ostracized. They will face sanctions. They will be brought before tribunals of international justice. They will not gain access to investment or assistance. And they will not gain acceptance by the community of civilized nations.

The future lies in a different direction: not with repressive governments but with free people. It belongs to the men and women who find inspiration in the words of the Universal Declaration; who act upon their principles even at great personal risk; who dodge bullets and defy threats to cast their ballots; who work selflessly for justice, tolerance, democracy, and peace. These people can be found everywhere—ordinary men and women doing extraordinary things—even in places where hate, fear, war, and chaos rule the hour.

We must keep the spotlight of world opinion trained on the darkest corners of abuse. We must confront the abusers. We must sharpen the tools of human rights diplomacy to address problems before they escalate into violence and create new pariah states.

Today, on behalf of the United States, I officially present to the world community an ambitious action plan that represents our commitment to pursue human rights, regardless of the outcome of this Conference. This plan will build on the UN's capacity to practice preventive diplomacy, safeguard human rights, and assist fledgling democracies. We seek to strengthen the UN Human Rights Center and its advisory and rapporteurial functions. We support the establishment of a UN High Commissioner for Human Rights.

Advancing Women's Rights

The United States will also act to integrate our concerns over the inhumane treatment of women into the global human rights agenda. We will press for the appointment of a UN Special Rapporteur on Violence Against Women. We will also urge the UN to sharpen the focus and strengthen the coordination of its women's rights activities.

Eleanor Roosevelt and the other drafters of the Declaration wanted to write a document that would live and last. They were determined to write a document that would protect and empower women as well as men. But that remains an unfulfilled vision in too many parts of the world, where women are subjected to discrimination and bias based solely upon gender.

Violence and discrimination against women don't just victimize individuals; they hold back whole societies by confining the human potential of half the population. Guaranteeing human rights is a moral imperative with respect to both women and men. It is also an investment in making whole nations stronger, fairer, and better.

Women's rights must be advanced on a global basis. But the crucial work is at the national level. It is in the self interest of every nation to terminate unequal treatment of women.

Next Steps of Our Own

Beyond our support for multilateral efforts, the United States recognizes that we have a solemn duty to take steps of our own.

In that spirit, I am pleased to announce that the United States will move promptly to obtain the consent of our Senate to ratify The International Convention on the Elimination of All Forms of Racial Discrimination. We strongly support the general goals of the other treaties that we have signed but not yet ratified. The Convention on the Elimination of all Forms of Discrimination Against Women; The American Convention on Human Rights; and The International Covenant on Economic, Social and Cultural Rights: All of these will constitute important advances, and our Administration will turn to them as soon as the Senate has acted on the racism Convention. We also expect soon to pass implementing legislation on the Convention Against Torture in furtherance of the worldwide goal of eliminating torture by the year 2000. To us, these far-reaching documents are not parchment promises to be held up for propaganda effect, but solemn commitments to be enforced.

My country will pursue human rights in our bilateral relations with *all* governments—large and small, developed and developing. America's commitment to human rights is global, just as the UN Declaration is universal.

As we advance these goals, American foreign policy will both reflect our fundamental values and promote our national interests. It must take into account our national security and economic needs at the same time that we pursue democracy and human rights. We will maintain our ties with our allies and friends. We will act to deter aggressors. And we will cooperate with like-minded nations to ensure the survival of freedom when it is threatened.

The United States will promote democracy and protect our security. We must do both—and we will. We will insist that our diplomats continue to report accurately and fully on human rights conditions around the world. Respect for human rights and the commitment to democracy-building will be major considerations as we determine how to spend our resources on foreign assistance. And we will weigh human rights considerations in trade policy, as President Clinton demonstrated last month.

We will help new democracies make a smooth transition to civilian control of the military. And we will assist militaries in finding constructive new roles in pursuit of peace and security—roles that respect human rights and contribute to international peace.

Working with the UN and other international organizations, we will help to develop the public and private institutions essential to a working democracy and the rule of law. And we will continue to support America's own National Endowment for Democracy in its mission to help nourish democracy where it is struggling to grow.

A Place to Stand Upon

The international debate now turns less on *whether* human rights are appropriate for discussion—and more on *how* to address them most effectively. The debate turns less on *whether* democracy best serves the needs of people everywhere—and more on *how soon* their democratic aspirations will be met.

Two hundred years ago, in his famous *Rights of Man*, the political philosopher Thomas Paine wrote this concerning Archimedes' image of the incomparable force of leverage: "Had we a place to stand upon, we might raise the world."

Ladies and gentlemen, the nations of the world do have a place to stand upon: If we stand upon the bedrock principles of the Universal Declaration of Human Rights, if we support the democratic movement on a worldwide basis, we shall speed the day when all the world's peoples are raised up into lives of freedom, dignity, prosperity, and peace.

That is where this Conference *should* stand.

That is where America stands.

Thank you very much.

Building Peace in the Middle East

With the Madrid conference in October 1991, President Bush and Secretary of State James Baker had taken the landmark step of providing a basis for face-to-face negotiations between Israel and its neighbors.[1] Indeed, they had established a foundation for the peace process that was to be the basis of many of our accomplishments during the first Clinton term. Nevertheless, negotiations between the parties had been stalled since August 1992, when Secretary Baker resigned to head the Bush re-election campaign. The United States has long recognized its vital interests in preventing conflict in the Middle East, in avoiding the disruption of oil supplies from that region, and in helping defend the security of Israel. Accordingly, the President and I made the strategic decision that the Middle East peace process would be one of our highest priorities.[2]

When I took office, the immediate impasse stemmed from Israel's deportation to a no-man's-land in Lebanon of hundreds of Palestinians sus-

---

[1] The Madrid conference, co-chaired by the United States and the Soviet Union, brought together Israeli, Syrian, Lebanese, Egyptian, and joint Jordanian-Palestinian delegations, among others, for a dramatic opening plenary meeting followed by the start of bilateral negotiations between Israel and each of the other four nations.

[2] In light of subsequent events, it is ironic that in the weeks before my confirmation some Jewish groups raised questions about my commitment to Israeli security. There were no specific allegations, only suspicions based upon my high position in the Carter Administration, which they viewed with skepticism. Several Jewish leaders in California rallied to my defense, pointing out my record of friendship for Jewish causes. I talked to Senator Joseph Lieberman of Connecticut, who took the generous

pected of terrorism. None of Israel's four negotiating tracks—with Syria, Lebanon, Jordan, or the Palestinians—would budge until this issue was resolved. We opposed the deportations, believing that they contravened international law, but the Israelis felt they were justified by security concerns. I at once initiated a series of telephone conversations with Prime Minister Yitzhak Rabin, who recognized that something had to be done but wasn't prepared to accept a wholesale return of the deportees.

The deportee negotiations marked the beginning of my official relationship with Rabin, whom I had known only slightly when I was in private life. On the telephone, as in person, he was reserved and gruff, but I was immediately drawn to his strength and honesty. I saw him dozens of times between these first contacts and his assassination on November 4, 1995. We developed a close working relationship, often involving a late supper at his residence in Jerusalem after a long day for both of us. He was tough and direct, and I was never confused about his position. I came to have not only great respect for him, but also a full appreciation of how he had earned the confidence of the Israeli people when others could not gain it. With Rabin in office, there was an unprecedented opportunity for peace, and we were prepared to give him our enthusiastic support. The President and I embraced Rabin's vision of what the realistic goals were for rapprochement in the Middle East and how the peace negotiations should proceed.

Three years later, I was with President Clinton at the White House when he received word of the assassination. I have never seen any public event affect him so much. He was silent for a long, long time and finally gave instructions to prepare for his attendance at the funeral on the other side of the world, a most unusual step. My own personal sadness was matched by my sense that the peace process had lost an indispensable leader.

---

step of inviting about a dozen national Jewish leaders to his office to meet me. Among them was Lester Pollock, President of the Conference of Presidents of Major American Jewish Organizations, with whom I formed a lasting friendship. I told the Jewish leaders that the President and I were prepared to provide unstinting support for those who took risks for peace and that while they might not always agree with me, they would have access to me on a regular basis. The issue was never pressed at my confirmation hearing, and over the next four years, I met on a regular basis with the American Jewish leadership.

To try to unlock the deportee issue and restart peace negotiations, President Clinton sent me to the region in mid-February 1993, less than three weeks after his inauguration. This trip was my first abroad as Secretary, which underscored the importance we placed on bringing peace to the region. It laid the groundwork for a resolution of the deportee problem later in the spring, when Rabin announced that some of the deportees could return immediately and the rest within a year. More generally, my conversations throughout the region led me to believe that if the deportee issue were resolved, the parties would be prepared to resume negotiations.

Two months later, we sought to seize this opportunity by inviting Arab, Israeli, and Palestinian representatives to Washington. The ensuing meetings between the parties were the first face-to-face negotiations under the Madrid framework since the deportee issue had erupted five months before. The talks were followed by several rounds of shuttle diplomacy, which at this time were the main component of our involvement in the Israeli-Palestinian track.

In late August 1993, Marie and I returned to California for our first vacation since I had become Secretary of State. After seven exciting yet grueling months in office, I looked forward to a period of rest and reflection. However, shortly after we had arrived at our beach house near Santa Barbara, I received an urgent call from Rabin. He explained that there had been a breakthrough between Israelis and Palestinians during secret negotiations in Oslo, and he asked if his Foreign Minister, Shimon Peres, could come to see me in California.

Although political partners in the Labor government, Rabin and Peres were longtime rivals, suspicious of each other and a study in contrasts. Where Rabin was taciturn and practical, Peres was expansive and visionary. At one time or another, Peres had held virtually all of the major portfolios in Israel. He was a gifted author and produced brilliant phrases and aphorisms, seemingly off the top of his head. In the conclusion to the speech reprinted below, I quoted an eloquent tribute that he had paid to America.

Rabin seemed unsure about the kind of agreement Peres would deliver from Oslo, and he wanted to withhold judgment until we had time to react to it. "I'd like to know what you think about this," he said. I told him I would see Peres and immediately phoned Washington to find a site for a secret meeting. Remembering a visit I had made in 1946 as a Navy ensign, I suggested Point Mugu, a small naval air station in Oxnard, California, about an hour's drive from Santa Barbara.

I had been aware of secret discussions between Israelis and Palestinians in Oslo and other venues, and received occasional reports about their progress. Because of Rabin's open skepticism—expressed as recently as earlier that month—I had never looked for much to come out of these discussions. Thus, when Peres and Norwegian Foreign Minister Johan Jorgen Holst[3] arrived at Point Mugu, I hardly expected the dramatic news they brought. They reported that the Israelis and Palestinians had reached agreement on a Declaration of Principles for the future of the West Bank and the Gaza Strip and had created a document providing for mutual recognition.

After outlining the proposed agreement, Peres and Holst asked what I thought. I asked for a few private minutes with Dennis Ross, my top adviser on the peace process, who had joined me at Point Mugu. There was no doubt that we should bless this breakthrough. It fundamentally changed the dynamic of the peace process. The Israelis and the Palestinians finally agreed to mutual recognition, eliminating one of the most intractable aspects of the negotiations thus far. Nevertheless, the agreement struck me as very general, and both Ross and I saw immediately how much it left to be done. It set goals for certain components of the peace (such as Israeli withdrawal from the occupied territories and Palestinian autonomy, broadly defined), but it was silent on any specific steps to accomplish them.

We knew, as did the parties, that the United States would have to play a major role in implementing the agreement. To signal their appreciation of the American role, the Israelis asked if we would host a signing ceremony. I immediately agreed. I called the President, and we began making

---

[3]Holst, who deserves great credit for hosting and mediating the successful negotiations in Oslo, tragically died in January 1994 at 56. I traveled to Oslo and spoke at his funeral. During my visit, I had my first opportunity to meet with Dr. Gro Brundtland, the youngest person to date—and the first woman—to be Prime Minister of Norway, and I was immediately impressed with her vision and pragmatism. After voluntarily stepping down as Prime Minister, she was named to head the World Health Organization, an important UN agency, in early 1998. Also on this trip, one of the Norwegian newspapers—with the help of our embassy—surprised me by presenting me with a picture of the farmhouse about 60 miles from Oslo where my forebears had lived before emigrating to the United States in 1853.

arrangements for a White House event in the second week of September. Rabin initially hesitated to attend, but when I conveyed an invitation from the President, he characteristically replied, "I will come; I have no choice." When PLO leader Yassir Arafat also agreed to attend, the stage was set for the reluctant but historic handshake. In the minutes before the ceremony, Rabin and Arafat circled the Blue Room in the White House to avoid contact, but Rabin assured us that when the time came, "I will do what I have to do." And, as all the world could see, he did.

The ceremony on the White House lawn on September 13, 1993, was the kind of golden moment that comes rarely in public life. After poignant opening remarks by Clinton, Rabin made the most moving speech of the day. It is impossible to capture on paper the full emotion of his remarks. In a deep, gravelly voice, struggling to control his feelings, he began, "This signing . . . today, it's not so easy, neither for myself as a soldier in Israel's war, nor for the people of Israel." Continuing, he said, "Let me say to you, the Palestinians, we are destined to live together on the same soil, in the same land. . . . We who have fought against you, the Palestinians, we say to you today in a loud and a clear voice, enough of blood and tears. Enough!" He added, "We, like you, are people—people who want to build a home, to plant a tree, to love, to live side by side with you in dignity, in empathy, as human beings, as free men."

Rabin's eloquent words were followed by speeches by Arafat, Peres, Palestinian adviser Abu Mazen, Russian Foreign Minister Kozyrev, and me. The ceremony symbolized how rapidly relationships were changing, and how former enemies had become mutually dependent partners almost overnight. When Arafat joined other honored guests for lunch at the State Department, I could only marvel at the pace of change.

Arafat, who was making his first visit to the White House, is a fascinating person by any measure. There are very few people in the world whose clothing makes them so instantly recognizable. For many years, the kaffiyeh—the Arab headgear he wears—not only served as an emblem for his fellow Palestinians but also turned a rather homely man into a colorful figure. Until the 1990s, Arafat was one of the most feared people in the world, and U.S. officials refused to negotiate with him. He led a revolutionary movement and was denounced as a terrorist. Much of that perception was changed by the agreement he signed at the White House and the Nobel Peace Prize he received with Rabin and Peres.

In my first private meeting with Arafat in Jordan in December 1993, he opened with a highly emotional tirade and followed up with a withering series of complaints that must have been his stock-in-trade in earlier years. I stood my ground and told him that we could have a relationship, but not by shouting at each other. In later meetings, we moved to a more practical level. Once, when I reached him by telephone in Gaza while his longtime adversary King Hussein of Jordan was visiting, he interrupted our conversation to say, "Let me put the King on and you can hear his views firsthand." They handed the telephone back and forth as we worked out the final details of the Hebron agreement, which provided for Israeli redeployment from much of the city. While he is a highly intelligent person, Arafat retains the instincts of a guerrilla leader and has some frustrating habits as a negotiator. He never seems willing to come to closure; it is always "just one more thing." However, just as Yitzhak Rabin did, I came to respect him for his devotion to the Palestinian cause. As Rabin said to me one night, "He is indispensable. I don't know who we would talk to if we didn't have him."

The signing ceremony on the White House lawn fit well into plans the Administration had to launch a major public campaign on foreign policy in late September. Within a four-day period, National Security Adviser Anthony Lake, UN Ambassador Madeleine Albright, and I would deliver speeches focusing on different aspects of our foreign policy, leading up to a comprehensive speech the President would deliver before the UN General Assembly. Traditionally, U.S. Presidents use their annual opportunity to address the General Assembly—known informally as UNGA—to survey the international scene as well as launch initiatives or make commitments to particular policies.

The Oslo breakthrough gave a new focus to my speech, which was delivered at Columbia University. I set out to provide the strategic context for the "Framework Agreement," explaining its historical significance as well as the tremendous psychological threshold that had been passed. We also had to show that the United States would lead the effort to assist the parties in implementing it. Although the speech was decidedly upbeat, it emphasized that everyone—the parties in the region, our allies abroad, the American people—should recognize that great gaps remained to be filled before a lasting peace could be realized.

Two issues stood out in the Columbia speech. First, I made the point that for the agreement to succeed, the international community needed to support the peace process not only politically, but economically. During the Point Mugu meeting, Peres had stressed the importance of promoting development in the occupied territories, which were then in horrible economic shape. As a first step, I used the speech to announce that the United States would soon host an international donors' conference to mobilize resources needed to make the agreement work. "The international community must move immediately to see that the agreement produces tangible improvements in the security and daily lives of the Palestinians and the Israelis," I explained. The first donors' conference took place in early October, and we obtained over $2 billion in commitments from other governments for assistance for the territories.

Second, the speech was significant in what I did *not* say about Syria. During my last round of shuttle diplomacy in August 1993, both Rabin and Syrian President Hafiz al-Assad had hinted that they were ready to engage in meaningful discussions about the Israeli-occupied Golan Heights. However, once the Framework Agreement with the Palestinians became reality, Rabin told us that immediately moving forward with Syria would simply be too much for the traffic to bear. Israelis first had to digest the profound psychological shift of Oslo. In carefully crafted language, I signaled Assad subtly by listing Syria along with Jordan and Lebanon as elements of the larger task of nurturing a comprehensive peace. By not singling it out for special attention, we sent the message that engaging Syria could not be the immediate priority.

The penultimate portion of the speech, under the heading "Reflections on America's Role," was the remnant of the broader speech that I had been laboring over since mid-summer, before the Israeli-Palestinian accord changed my focus. Reiterating my mantra of the importance of maintaining U.S. leadership, this section reflected two broad themes: the lingering debate between isolationism and engagement, and the current questions about whether America should use its power alone or with others—multilateralism versus unilateralism, to use the jargon. I argued that the Rabin-Arafat handshake on the White House lawn symbolized the importance of asserting, not abdicating, American leadership in the world. On the largely tactical multilateralism-unilateralism debate, I made a strong case for thinking about multilateralism not as an end, but as a means of reducing the burden on the United States. However, if necessary to protect vital interests, America would go it alone. In a widely quoted line, I stressed that the United States would never "subcontract its foreign policy to another power or another person." This directly addressed many critics, mostly on the Republican side, who claimed that we were willing to let the United Nations or its Secretary General, Boutros Boutros-Ghali,[4] take the lead in diplomacy. Yet I also stressed the value of working with others to advance our interests.

Building Peace in the Middle East

Address at Columbia University, Co-sponsored by the Council on

Foreign Relations, New York City, September 20, 1993

President Rupp, ladies and gentlemen: Thank you, Les Gelb, for that generous and insightful introduction. The Council on Foreign Relations is very fortunate to have Les Gelb as its new president. As many of you know, I had the pleasure of working with Les during our last tour in government. He is one of the nation's leading foreign policy thinkers and writers. His advice is valued by me, in New York, and around the world.

Thank you, also, President Rupp, for co-sponsoring our get-together today in this very elegant setting. Columbia University is one of this country's oldest and most prestigious institutions of learning. From the schoolroom on Lower Broadway where Samuel Johnson taught eight students in 1754 to this magnificent campus on Morningside Heights, Columbia has represented the spirit of inquiry and intellectual freedom that has made America strong.

Columbia has certainly contributed to the strength of the State Department. In addition to Madeleine Albright, two of our Under Secretaries, Joan Spero and Lynn Davis, have studied here and taught here. They carry on Columbia's great tradition of sending women and men into public life with a strongly internationalist outlook. My visit here today is one of several I have made and plan to make around the country to

---

[4]Our differences with Boutros-Ghali, which eventually led to our veto of his second term, are discussed in Chapter 23.

talk about our foreign policy. It happens to be my view that Secretaries of State should spend more time explaining foreign policy to the audience that really counts—the American people. And I intend to do so.

A week ago, from a small platform on the south lawn of the White House, the world took a very big step toward a peaceful future. That simple hand-shake between implacable foes extends a mighty, redemptive power that can help heal the wounds of this too-often-violent century.

Like the collapse of communism before it, the beginning of the historic reconciliation between the Israelis and the Palestinians confirms our belief that hope can eventually replace despair, cooperation can overcome conflict, and peace and freedom can triumph over war and tyranny. Today, I will share with you my thoughts on last week's historic developments in the Arab-Israeli peace process. I will try to place the events of last Monday in historical context and describe to you the steps we must take to ensure that this chance for peace does not slip from our grasp.

For more than 45 years, Democratic and Republican administrations have worked tirelessly to break the cycle of violence between Israel and its Arab neighbors. They did so because they understood that the United States has enduring interests in this strategic and historic crossroads; enduring interests in a region where conflict always seems to threaten world peace; enduring interests in the security and well-being of Israel and in cooperative relations with the Arab world from one end to the other; and enduring interests in the region's oil resources, which serve as the lifeblood of so much of the world's economy.

These durable interests have made Middle East peace a constant and essential goal of U.S. foreign policy. For decades, that goal eluded us. The region remained a tinderbox, threatening to embroil us and the rest of the world in its deadly wars. This volatility was due in no small part to the existence of a Soviet Union determined to fuel the forces of radicalism and conflict. While the Soviets were by no means the only cause of the Arab-Israeli dispute, they did everything in their power to see that the region remained at a constant boil. Their policies emboldened radicals, intimidated moderates, and left Israel—save for its friendship with the United States—in a lonely state of siege. Throughout the long struggle of the Cold War, only one Arab country—Egypt—managed to breach the wall of conflict that Moscow had helped to erect. Egypt braved ostracism to make peace with Israel. For 14 long years, that heroic achievement stood strong. It also stood alone—until last Monday.

The Israeli-Palestinian agreement—in which Egypt's President Mubarak played such a strong, critical role—is a powerful vindication of that nation's courage and vision.

It was not until the Cold War began to wane that new opportunities arose to combat rejectionism in the Middle East and to promote peace. This was most dramatically demonstrated during the Gulf War. With the United States and the Soviet Union working together, Saddam Hussein's radical challenge was decisively turned back. Without Moscow's patronage, Saddam's "war option" proved to be no option at all for him. America's overwhelming display of power, principle, and leadership helped to tilt the Middle East's balance of power toward moderation and toward the opportunity for reconciliation that has been seized.

Had the United States let it rest there—had we left to others the job of turning opportunity into reality—last Monday's dramatic event might never have taken place. Only America could have provided the Arabs and the Israelis with the assurances they needed to go to Madrid and risk breaking the taboo on direct negotiations. Upon his election, President Clinton immediately reaffirmed America's historic role and enduring strategic interest in the Middle East and in Arab-Israeli peace. President Clinton saw the opportunity for a historic breakthrough. On the morning after his election, he vowed to make the pursuit of Middle East peace a top priority. That is why he moved so quickly to gain the trust of key regional parties and to reaffirm America's unstinting support for Israel's security. And that is why, for my first official trip abroad, he sent me to the Middle East. His message was clear: The United States was irrevocably committed to advancing the peace-making process, to reinvigorating the negotiations, and to elevating America's role to that of full partner.

The President's efforts built upon the hard work of his predecessors. Our victories in the Cold War and in the Gulf created an environment in which peace-making became possible. Our Administration's intervention at key moments this year, to resolve crises over Palestinian deportees and over the violence in Lebanon, salvaged the peace process when it teetered on the brink of collapse. Throughout the last 22 months, under both Republican and Democratic Presidents, America's sustained political involvement—whether in presenting a draft declaration of principles or in constantly pushing to define the parameters of the possible—set the stage for decision-making in the secret Oslo channel, for which we owe so much to the Norwegians and, particularly, to Foreign Minister Holst.

In the end, of course, last Monday's triumph belongs to the parties themselves—to the Israeli and the Palestinian people—who reached out to each other. And that is exactly as it should be. Indeed, the basic premise of the Madrid process has been that face-to-face negotiation between the parties is essential. From the beginning, the United States has encouraged communications in as many different channels as possible—both formal and informal, public and private—with the understanding that the most durable solution would be one forged in direct negotiations. It certainly would be a great mistake if the United States were now to withdraw or shrink from its full and long-standing partnership that it has undertaken in the peace process. Our leadership is essential if this historic agreement is to realize its full potential.

Today, on behalf of President Clinton, I announce our intention to lead a wide-ranging effort not simply to give peace a chance but to ensure that it will not fail. Just as the United States organized a successful international coalition to wage war in the Gulf, we will now organize a new coalition—a coalition to breathe life into the Israeli-Palestinian Declaration.

As a first step, the United States will convene the Conference to Support Middle East Peace, building on the Madrid framework. Secretary Bentsen and I, together with our Russian counterparts, will invite foreign and finance ministers representing the European countries, Japan, Saudi Arabia and the Gulf states, Canada, the Nordic countries, and many others—and, of course, the Israelis and the Palestinians. The World Bank will also be present, and it will play a major role in coordinating and providing this assistance.

The purpose of this Conference will be to mobilize resources needed to make the agreement work. The international community must move immediately to see that the agreement produces tangible improvements in the security and daily lives of the Palestinians and the Israelis. If peace is to be achieved, the agreement must be translated into results quickly and vividly.

There are varying estimates of the resources required to start building an economic base in Gaza and the West Bank. The World Bank's initial estimate is that $3 billion will be needed over the next 10 years. An important portion of this sum will be needed for a quick-start effort over the next year, beginning in the next few months. All agree that we must take immediate steps to address the high rate of unemployment that robs families of hope and fuels extremism. Housing, roads, and other permanent improvements must be developed quickly. We must also act now to provide assistance in public administration, tax collection, and social services. Given the number and the commitment of our international partners, we are confident these needs can be met. And we will stimulate these supporters by our own example. Working with the Congress, we expect to assemble an initial 2-year package worth $250 million to dedicate to this cause.

In this vital effort, we must also involve the private sector. A significant part of the initial U.S. package will include OPIC loans and guarantees to spur private sector involvement and economic growth in the region.

There is another resource that America can and should provide for this effort. At the White House last Monday, immediately after the signing ceremony, the President, the Vice President, and I met with a group of Jewish- and Arab-Americans. This was truly a unique and special event, the first time in my experience that they have met jointly at the White House. We were moved by their shared sense of hope and by their spirit of reconciliation from that magnificent day. The President decided that we must draw on their talent, ingenuity, and goodwill. In that spirit, the President will appoint a task force of Jewish- and Arab-Americans to help us develop joint projects and private investment in the region. The United States will name a senior coordinator for U.S. assistance—much as we have done in the case of the former Soviet Union.

Ladies and gentlemen: The real barrier to peace between the Israelis and Palestinians—the psychological barrier—has already been breached. Compared to that obstacle, the resource challenge we face can surely be met. I am convinced that, working with our international partners, we can and will succeed.

The implementation of the Israeli-Palestinian agreement represents only part of a larger task in the Middle East. We must nurture a comprehensive reconciliation between Israel and the rest of the Arab world. We must achieve a peace between the people of Israel and the peoples of Jordan, Syria, and Lebanon. In the recent round of bilateral negotiations between their governments in Washington, the discussions—I'm glad to say—were serious and constructive. Later this month, at the UN General Assembly, I will meet with my counterparts from Syria, Jordan,

Lebanon, and Israel to try to keep these negotiations moving and to discuss further steps ahead. We will work tirelessly to ensure that all the children of the region can come to know, in President Clinton's words, "a season of peace."

Another aspect of our effort to promote comprehensive reconciliation is working to encourage other Arab friends to act boldly in support of peace. The core antagonists in this conflict have courageously opted for mutual recognition and an end to their state of war. This bold step demands an equally bold response from their regional counterparts. There have been some good signs already. Jordan's decision to sign a substantive agenda with Israel last Tuesday is a prime example. Another good example is the meeting that same day in Morocco between Prime Minister Rabin and King Hassan, which was also a promising first step that the United States applauds. Other nations must also seize this vital moment for reconciliation. Now that Israelis and Palestinians have agreed to work together to promote their economic well-being, it is certainly illogical for Arab nations to continue their boycott of Israel. Every moment the boycott remains in force, those responsible are punishing Palestinians as well as Israelis. The boycott is a relic of the past. It should be relegated to history—right now. There is more to peace than the signing of agreements and the gathering of resources. There is a need for a fundamental change in the hearts of the former antagonists. The leaders of the region must exhort those who have used violence as a political tool to renounce it without reservation or exception.

It is also imperative that quick action be taken to remove other vestiges of a bygone era. This means revoking, at the upcoming session of the UN General Assembly, those UN resolutions that challenge Israel's very right to exist. It also means acting to approve, unanimously this time, Israel's credentials at this year's UN General Assembly. And it also means, in the U.S. Congress, amending statutes that inhibit dealing with the PLO.

I reiterate a simple but profound truth: Only an Israel that is strong, confident, and secure can make peace. Only an Israel that is certain of its strategic partnership with the United States can take the necessary risks. On behalf of President Clinton and the American people, I restate a long-standing pledge to the Israeli public: As you and your leaders continue down the courageous path you have chosen, you should know that America's commitment to Israel's security and well-being will remain unshakable. It is quite revealing that at this time of great hope, when the entire world is praising last Monday's events, they are being denounced in places like Tehran, Baghdad, and Tripoli. In response to such intemperate words, let me make clear that we are committed to seeing that the forces of moderation in the region are stronger than the forces of extremism. To all who are prepared to work with us in building a new Middle East of peace, security, and prosperity, I say: You have a reliable and committed partner in the United States. To those who would sow dissension, intolerance, and violence, I say this: The United States, its friends, and its allies will take the necessary steps to ensure that you fail.

Reflections on America's Role

This remarkable week for peace in the Middle East reminds us of the necessity for, and the importance of, American leadership in the world—especially in regions of vital interest to us.

My colleague Tony Lake will speak tomorrow at the Johns Hopkins School of Advanced International Studies. He will address the broad outlines of our foreign policy. His speech will reflect broad policy discussions within our Administration, and I commend it to your attention.

Before concluding today, I want to comment briefly on two issues that have been the subject of a good deal of public debate. The first is whether America should pursue an activist foreign policy. The second is whether America should act alone or together with other nations to protect our vital interests abroad.

The first issue is really the latest round in a century-old debate between engagement and isolationism. I want to assure you that the United States chooses engagement. The alternative—neo-isolationism—can be reduced to a simple syllogism: The Cold War is over; we won; let's go home and attend to our problems. We must reject isolationism for the dangerous argument that it is. We must renew our commitment to internationalism, which has served us so well for the last 50 years. The pied pipers of isolationism misread the history of this century. They mistake the future of our economy. They minimize the threats to our security. And they misjudge the character of our people.

The end of the Cold War has not ended history. Nor has it severed the links between America and the world. But it has left the United States with a continuing responsibility—and a unique capacity—to provide leadership. Why, you may ask, should we remain engaged? First, because it is strongly in our economic interest to do so. We live in a technologically interconnected age. Vast amounts of information and vast numbers of dollars can be transmitted around the world at the speed of light. In such a world, how will we enhance our prosperity if we do not work to open up and expand international markets? How will we possibly promote the global growth that is necessary to our prosperity if we do not successfully complete the Uruguay Round negotiations of the GATT? And how will we create high-paying jobs for Americans if we are not willing to create export opportunities through international agreements such as NAFTA? Second, we must remain active and assertive for the sake of our security. Were it not for sustained American involvement over the last four decades, we would not be on the road to peace in the Middle East. American engagement is also essential in other regions where our vital interests are at stake. Indeed, in key regions, the United States is the fulcrum on which peace and security rest.

If democracy reverts to dictatorship in the former Soviet Union, Americans are likely to pay a very severe price in a revived nuclear threat and increased defense budgets. If ethnic conflict in Europe widens, if our security is threatened again in Asia, if terrorism spreads, if the proliferation of weapons of mass destruction is not checked—if any of these things comes to pass—then our own security and our ability to focus on domestic renewal will be directly put at risk. In short, we must remain engaged not out of altruism, not out of what one scholar has called the "imperial temptation" but because there are real American interests that will suffer if we are seduced by the isolationist myth.

The second issue under recent debate is whether America should exercise its power alone or with others—to use the customary jargon, unilaterally or multilaterally. That issue, as framed, creates a false polarity. It is not an "either-or" proposition.

The central purpose of our foreign policy is to ensure the security of our nation and to ensure its economic prosperity as well—and to promote democratic values.

In protecting those interests, the United States must maintain its military strength and reinvigorate its economy so that we can retain the option to act alone when that is best for us. Let no one doubt the resolve of the United States to protect its vital interests.

Yet in protecting our vital interests, we should not ignore the value of working with other nations. From the Gulf War to the international campaign to aid democracy in Russia, we have seen how collective action can advance American foreign policy interests. It can bolster our efforts to stem the proliferation of weapons of mass destruction, to knock down barriers to global trade, and to protect the environment. We have also seen that collective action requires—and cannot replace—American leadership. No other nation possesses our military might, economic strength, or moral authority. These assets give us the ability to act alone when necessary. When appropriate, though, we can also leverage our might by sharing the burden with other nations. But we should remember that our ability to generate effective multilateral responses will often depend upon our willingness to act alone.

Let me be clear: Multilateralism is a means, not an end. It is one of the many foreign policy tools at our disposal. And it is warranted only when it serves the central purpose of American foreign policy: to protect American interests. This country will never subcontract its foreign policy to another power or another person. While this largely tactical debate on the means of American engagement has proceeded, President Clinton has been meeting the key foreign policy tests and challenges: recognizing that domestic economic renewal is fundamental to America's foreign policy interests, mobilizing critical and timely support for Russian democracy as an essential investment in our national security, calling for a NATO summit to adapt the alliance to meet the new security challenges of a vastly changed Europe, advancing a New Pacific Community while negotiating a new framework for our economic and trade relations with Japan, and leading the global effort to curb the proliferation of weapons of mass destruction.

Conclusion

In concluding, I will suggest to you another and different measure of our leadership—and that is how the world sees us. Last week in Washington,

Israeli Foreign Minister Shimon Peres paid our country an unusual tribute. In the history books, he said:

> Nobody will understand the United States, really: You have so much force, and you didn't conquer the land of anybody; you have so much power, and you didn't dominate another people; you have problems of your own, and you have never turned your back on the problems of others.

And Shimon Peres then turned and said: "Thank you so much for being what you are."

To those who question the need for American engagement, I say, ask Shimon Peres.

Let these indelible events of the last few years—the handshake at the White House; the Berlin Wall falling; the Soviet Union crumbling; Nelson Mandela walking out of prison to build a new South Africa—let all these point us toward asserting and not abdicating our international role.

Let that shining moment last week on the White House lawn light the way for a just and lasting peace in the Middle East—and illuminate the need for America's continued leadership in the world.

Thank you very much.

A Partnership with Russia

As my motorcade sped through central Moscow on the morning of October 22, 1993, we passed the charred, hulking structure that had once been the White House, the home of the Russian parliament (the Duma). The building stood on the bank of the Moscow River, just a few blocks from the U.S. Embassy. Less than three weeks before, when hard-line forces led by Alexandr Rutskoi and Ruslan Khasbulatov had occupied the White House, President Yeltsin had ordered the Russian military to counterattack. Tanks had shelled the building, which was finally retaken by elite Russian troops.

In the United States, we had watched these dramatic events unfold on television. Gathered in the Oval Office, we had recognized that America's reaction would send an important signal to other nations. Despite our concern about the violence, President Clinton made a firm decision to support Yeltsin. We were aware of the parallels between this situation and the abortive Soviet coup in August 1991, and Clinton did not want to repeat the performance of the Bush Administration, which many criticized for being too tepid in denouncing that coup. Clinton wanted to make it clear that the United States continued to stand behind the forces of democratic reform, which he believed Yeltsin represented. Now, as I drove past the blackened building, my thoughts were dominated by the image of the latest coup's incredible end, with the Russian White House in flames and the plotters in custody.

These stunning events on the weekend of October 2–3 had heightened the significance of my trip to Moscow. In prior planning for the visit, we had tentatively decided to focus on advancing one key element in our policy—denuclearization. I would also be traveling to the three other "nuclear" former Soviet states—Ukraine, Kazakhstan, and Belarus[1]—to push them to implement the 1992 Lisbon Protocol and remove nuclear weapons from their soil.[2] Although denuclearization continued to be a major focus of my trip—and an area in which we achieved tangible results—after the attempted coup much of our attention turned to how we would handle the political turmoil in Moscow.

The moment was critical for political and economic reform in Russia. Parliamentary elections were scheduled for December 12. Yeltsin had won an important constitutional referendum in April, weathered the summer, and then faced down his hard-line opponents. It seemed to us that recent events had reinforced his position and consolidated the forces of reform. I hoped that my meetings in Russia, culminating with my speech before the Academy of the National Economy in Moscow, would make it clear that President Clinton's commitment to Russian reform would remain firm in the days ahead.

After productive morning visits with Russian Prime Minister Viktor Chernomyrdin and Foreign Minister Kozyrev, I hoped to meet with Yeltsin late that afternoon. Since my arrival the night before, it had remained uncertain whether I would be able to see the Russian President, who had reportedly left Moscow to deal with health problems and recuperate generally from recent events. Kozyrev was plainly nervous about the situation, but he pledged to do all he could to see that I met with Yeltsin.

When we received word that the President could see me, I immediately departed from Moscow via helicopter for the 45-minute ride to Zavidovo, a hunting lodge nestled in a dense forest, where Yeltsin was convalescing. When he greeted me at the door, it was clear that his back was bothering him greatly; his movements were stiff and almost robotic. Ac-

---

[1]I also visited the beautiful Hanseatic port of Riga, Latvia, to give U.S. reassurance to the leaders of Latvia, Estonia, and Lithuania.

[2]The Lisbon Protocol called for the four former Soviet states with nuclear weapons to sign and ratify the START I Treaty and to accede to the Nuclear Non-Proliferation Treaty as non-nuclear states.

companied only by Strobe Talbott, Ambassador to Russia Tom Pickering, and a translator, I entered a rather bizarre room filled with tropical
plants and stuffed game to begin the meeting.

Yeltsin thanked me for our support during the Duma crisis. He spoke
of that episode quite somberly, but reassured me that things had calmed
down appreciably since October 3 and that the "dual authority" problem
no longer existed. He detailed the process then under way to prepare for
the December parliamentary elections, explaining that for the first time,
political parties were forming on a democratic basis. Only those parties
involved in the armed insurrection could not participate. "This will be
the first free and fair election for the parliament since 1917," he said.
"Communism is dead, and the only thing left for me to bury is Lenin."

After discussing plans for Clinton to visit Moscow in January,[3] I
turned the conversation to what I described as the most substantive issue to be addressed—the future of NATO. Shortly before my departure
for Russia, we had met at the highest levels in Washington to agree on
a plan offering the former Soviet bloc states, including Russia, a form
of partnership with NATO that would fall short of full membership in
it. Rather than expand NATO immediately, we sought to build relationships with those countries that might join it at a later date. This
proposal, entitled the Partnership for Peace, would be formally presented by the United States at the January 1994 NATO summit (see
Chapter 8).

Yeltsin became quite animated when I described the Partnership proposal. The Russians had been very nervous about the NATO issue in the
run-up to our visit. Yeltsin had feared that we might try to bring some of
the Central European states into NATO immediately, while working to
keep Russia out. He called the Partnership idea a "stroke of genius," saying it would dissipate Russian tensions regarding the East Europeans and
their aspirations toward NATO. I explained that we would explore possibilities for adding members to NATO in due course, but that any expansion would be long-term and evolutionary. "This really is a great idea,
really great," Yeltsin said enthusiastically. "Tell Bill that I am thrilled by
this brilliant stroke." In retrospect, it is clear that his enthusiasm was

[3]Yeltsin remarked to me, "I have a very large interest in making this visit a full
success. . . . The people of Russia will welcome President Clinton with enthusiasm."
I announced the plans for the visit later that day.

based upon his mistaken assumption that the Partnership for Peace would not lead to eventual NATO expansion.

In my speech the next morning before the Academy of the National Economy, I intended to send a message directly to the Russian people that reform was in their best interest, and to convey publicly the same support I expressed to Yeltsin, Chernomyrdin, and Kozyrev privately. The Academy, which was strongly identified with Yegor Gaidar, Russia's First Deputy Prime Minister and a leading economic reformer, seemed the ideal venue for such a speech. Further, I hoped to pitch my remarks directly to those who had the greatest stake in Russia's democratic transformation—its younger generation. To accent this "youth" angle, I had asked Eric Liu, a promising speechwriter and self-described "Gen X" spokesman, to help draft a few sections.[4]

My remarks amounted to a ringing endorsement of Yeltsin. I explained that while the United States doesn't easily support dissolving—or shelling—democratic institutions, President Yeltsin had taken these steps under "exceptional circumstances." Emphasizing the importance of reform, I asked the audience not to let their "healthy skepticism" of politics spiral into "cynicism"; explicitly playing on the language of the Soviet revolution, I explained that they were the vanguard of a new revolution of political freedom, social justice, and economic opportunity.

The speech also outlined the logic and purpose behind what we had begun to call our "strategic partnership" with Russia—our cooperation on global and regional issues that once divided the two superpowers. I wanted to show that such terms as "partnership" and "cooperation" were not simply euphemisms for U.S. aid and charity to Russia, but had real meaning as we moved toward shared goals. Perhaps the most critical area of mutual advantage, I stressed, was preventing the proliferation of nuclear and other weapons of mass destruction. This section of the speech

---

[4]In an effort to connect with a young audience, Bennett Freeman and Liu had added several references from popular youth culture, mentioning the rock band R.E.M. and *Rolling Stone* magazine. Unfortunately, when I took the stage that morning, the audience looked more like a collection of weary members of the former communist power elite than the next generation of Russian leaders. There was but a sprinkling of young people. Given this, some of the references in my speech must have left many in the audience quite perplexed. Frankly, I myself had never heard of R.E.M., and I later received some ribbing from the traveling press asking what my favorite R.E.M. song was.

was important for my upcoming discussions in Belarus, Kazakhstan, and Ukraine, particularly my talks two days later in Kiev with President Leonid Kravchuk and leaders of the Rada, Ukraine's parliament.[5]

The initial reaction to my Moscow remarks was quite good: the U.S. press characterized them as the Administration's clearest explanation to date for its decision to side with Yeltsin during the October coup, and as a plain message of support and encouragement for reform. In a private meeting with me after the speech, Yegor Gaidar commented that while international speakers often seem out of sync with Russian sensibilities, my remarks hit the right balance by laying out the need for reform without lecturing the audience. Such an approach "could only improve U.S.-Russian relations," he said.

Unfortunately, the hopeful vision portrayed in my speech soon became tarnished. Seven weeks later, reform in Russia suffered a serious blow. In the December 12 parliamentary elections, former communists and hard-liners hostile to Yeltsin scored major victories, rebuffing key reformers like Gaidar (who resigned from Yeltsin's cabinet in January 1994) and winning a majority of seats. Vladimir Zhirinovsky, a truly frightening character with a history of anti-Semitism and militarism, emerged as the big winner and now seemed poised to challenge Yeltsin. Like many other experts, we were surprised by the extent of the hard-line breakthrough, resulting primarily from the trauma of economic reform. In the wake of these elections, our Russian policy generally, and this speech specifically, came under criticism from commentators.

[5]Ukrainian leaders had been making noises about holding on to their nuclear weapons; in Moscow, Kozyrev had told me that Ukraine's "real intention" was to keep its nukes and that this position could not be changed "without further pressure." Because of such foot-dragging, the United States had withheld $155 million in economic aid from Ukraine. When I raised the issue in Kiev, Kravchuk reassured me that he had every intention of making Ukraine a nuclear-free state and wanted to adhere to the Lisbon Protocol, but that his country had to receive compensation for such actions. "It is impossible to convince the Rada that weapons should be returned to Russia free of charge," he said. The problem had become so acute, Kravchuk explained, that it could only be solved through a Russia-U.S.-Ukraine trilateral framework. We believed this idea had merit and began to lay the groundwork for some sort of three-way negotiation. This meeting was the forerunner of the later Trilateral Agreement for the complete denuclearization of Ukraine. In retrospect, it seems that our decision to condition the $155 million in assistance on Ukrainian cooperation in denuclearization talks was *the* critical factor in shaping Kiev's behavior.

In retrospect, this address does appear too sanguine—we did overestimate the popularity and strength of reform in Russia. Nevertheless, even with the benefit of several years' hindsight, while I might change some of the tone of the speech, I would not alter its substance. Put simply, Yeltsin and his allies were the best choices we had in Russia. They were democratically elected and committed to liberalizing their country economically and politically as well as to building a security partnership with us. The prospects for reform were indeed tenuous—but this was all the more reason why Russia needed U.S. support, both rhetorical and substantive.

After the December elections, the President and Vice President decided that despite the setback, we would continue to support Yeltsin and reform. When the Vice President went to Moscow in the immediate aftermath of the election to attend a meeting of the Gore-Chernomyrdin Commission, he denounced Zhirinovsky's views and renewed our support for Russian reform.[6] Although there have surely been bumps in the road, I believe history has already shown we made the right choice. Zhirinovsky has now all but disappeared from the scene, and Yeltsin achieved a comeback victory to win a second term as President in the hotly contested 1996 elections.

A New Generation of Russian Democrats

Address at the Academy of the National Economy,

Moscow, October 23, 1993

Thank you very much, ladies and gentlemen, Mr. Aganbegyan, Deputy Prime Minister Gaidar. It is a great pleasure and a distinct honor to be at

[6]These periodic meetings between Vice President Gore and Russian Prime Minister Chernomyrdin—held formally under the aegis of the bilateral Gore-Chernomyrdin Commission on Economic, Security and Scientific Issues—became a valuable channel through which we could address our mutual agenda. In addition to handling such immediate concerns as nuclear non-proliferation and Russian economic reform, Gore and Chernomyrdin worked to develop common approaches on other issues, including technology investment and space exploration.

the Academy of the National Economy today. For five years, this institute has fed the Russian hunger for reform and economic renewal. It is shaping a generation of leaders who will contribute richly to the future of this great country. The openness to new ideas, the search for a better life—these are the impulses that inspired Yegor Gaidar to apply his exceptional talents in economics in the service of your nation. They are the impulses that brought you here to learn and to forge careers in a growing private sector. And they are impulses that will serve you well in this challenging, new era.

Academies and institutes such as yours are symbols of a new attitude in Russia. You who are here today do not fear openness; you welcome it. You do not shun the clash of ideas; you relish it. And you do not shrink from the uncertainty that reform brings; instead, you celebrate its promise. I grew up in the 1930s during what we call in America the Great Depression, in a small farming town on the North Dakota prairie along the northern border of the United States. Our house was at the western edge of town, and it faced the fury of the northwest wind. As a result, we endured icy blizzards in the winter and prairie fires and tumbleweeds in the fall. Crop failures and dust storms combined to impoverish many farm families. It was the kind of adversity that the Russian people know so well.

Today, as Russia faces its future, you, too, are enduring some very difficult times. Your character is being tested. But you are showing that with courage, such adversity can be conquered. On October 3–4, the world witnessed what we all hope was the last gasp of the old order in Russia. The political crisis was a struggle of the sort well known to students of Russian history—a battle between reform and reaction. As the crisis unfolded, we in America knew what we had to do: We stood firmly behind reform. Let me be clear about our decision to support your President during this crisis. The United States does not easily support the suspension of parliaments. But these are extraordinary times. The steps taken by President Yeltsin were in response to exceptional circumstances. The parliament and the constitution were vestiges of the Soviet communist past, blocking movement to democratic reform. By calling elections, President Yeltsin was once again taking matters to the Russian people to secure their participation in the transformation of Russia.

Time and again in recent years, the Russian people have demonstrated their commitment to freedom. In August 1991, President Yeltsin stood on top of that tank—and faced down the forces of reaction. In April of this year, the people of Russia cast a resounding vote in favor of reform. And just three weeks ago, the defenders of the old order were defeated in their violent, desperate attempt to reverse the progress that you have made.

I know that some of you may be tired of politics. But I will ask of you what Bill Clinton asked of young Americans when he ran for President last year: Do not let your healthy skepticism harden into cynicism—and do not let the promise of change wilt into apathy. As you work to improve your own life, do not stifle your willingness to work for the common good.

The possibilities for you are immense. Like no previous generation in history, you are aware of the cultural and political changes in the world around you. From R.E.M. to CNN, from rap music to Rolling Stone magazine, you know the outside world better than your parents or grandparents—or, indeed, better than I did when I was growing up. You know that people your age can make a difference. You are the new generation of democrats in Russia. You are at the vanguard of a revolution of rising expectations: for a decent standard of living; for a humane society; for an environment that is clean and workplaces that are safe; for a greater voice in shaping your future. That is why you are starting your own businesses, your own political organizations, your own magazines. More than any recent generation of Russians, you have control over your own destiny. And the choices you make—in December, in June, and in the coming years—will change Russia and the world.

As you make these choices, please know this: The American people are with you. When our President spoke to your President on the telephone September 21, he said, "History is on your side." Bill Clinton was speaking to Boris Yeltsin. But in a very real sense, he was speaking to each of you. History is on your side—the side of democracy—and so are we.

When those demagogues at your White House waved the hammer and sickle in the name of democracy, you saw the hypocrisy. When you heard the defenders of the old system calling for "renewal," you knew that they meant a renewal of stagnation and a betrayal of Russia's youth. And you had the nerve to chase away both the gaunt specter of the Soviet past and the new extremists who want to win with bullets what they cannot win with ballots.

But now you face a different challenge: national reconciliation. Having been "scorched by the deadly breath of fratricide," as President Yeltsin said, you are returning now to the heroic task of building an inclusive, self-confident democracy.

We are truly proud to stand with you and to call Russia our friend and partner. That spirit of friendship animates every student exchange program that links you with your counterparts in America. That same commitment inspired the great Rostropovich to proceed with a concert of our National Symphony Orchestra in Red Square last month, even as the political crisis reached its climax. And that same spirit brought to Russia a young American just out of law school named Terry Duncan. Trying to help a wounded American photographer during the violence of October 3, he lost his life, and the new generation of democrats in Russia and America lost a true friend.

But what America and Russia share is not merely friendship. What our two nations are building together is a strategic partnership. This is a phrase that President Clinton and I have repeatedly used in our dialogue with Congress and the American people. Let me tell you why we use this phrase "strategic partnership"—and what we mean by it.

With the sweeping changes of the last several years, Russia remains a very great power. This is guaranteed by your proud civilization, your rich culture, your great resources, your scientific achievements, and your resilient character. But with the end of the Cold War, we have an opportunity to be not only great powers but partners in the joint pursuit of a safer, freer, more prosperous world. For decades, our two nations eyed each other with suspicion, living in fear of mutually assured destruction. Now we can pursue mutually reinforcing interests. Today, we are cooperating on the global and regional issues that once divided us. Where there was once contention, there is now common cause. This agenda for cooperation is firmly in our shared interest. And that is why I have confidence that we will work together.

It is in our shared interest to prevent the proliferation of nuclear weapons within the former Soviet Union. Proliferation would increase both the risks and the costs of conflict among the new independent states. That is why we welcomed the 1992 commitment of Ukraine, Belarus, and Kazakhstan to sign and ratify the START I Treaty and to accede to the Nuclear Non-Proliferation Treaty as non-nuclear weapons states. We welcome the fact that Belarus has fulfilled these commitments.

And we are encouraged that Kazakhstan and Ukraine have reiterated their determination to do the same. I will be visiting these three states over the next few days, and I will be working to ensure that those obligations, taken at Lisbon, are fulfilled.

It is also in our shared interest to help curb the spread of weapons of mass destruction outside the former Soviet Union as well. Non-proliferation is our arms control agenda for the 1990s. Many of the world's potential proliferators are Russia's neighbors, not ours. We share a common threat—and that is why we must work together. Acting alone, we are unlikely to stem the growing tide of proliferation. But working together, we stand a much better chance of succeeding in this absolutely vital effort.

Let me give you some examples. Last month, President Clinton proposed an international ban on the production of plutonium and uranium for nuclear weapons purposes. Last week, President Yeltsin expressed his readiness to work together toward that end. Russia's views are also similar to ours with respect to completing a comprehensive test ban treaty—and urging others not to test—a very high priority for both of us. And we are launching cooperative efforts in the exploration of space.

It is also in our shared interest to promote peace in the Middle East and in other volatile regions around the globe. Last month in Washington, my colleague Foreign Minister Kozyrev and I had the privilege of witnessing, on the lawn of our White House, the handshake between Yitzhak Rabin and Yasir Arafat. But Russia and America did not merely witness that historic moment; our cooperation helped to make it possible. Our work together as co-sponsors of the Middle East peace process is a wise investment in our common security. And it is a testament to our uncommon ability to turn mistrust into trust and confrontation into collaboration.

A democratic, productive Russia—a Russia fully engaged in preserving global peace and fully integrated into the global economy—that kind of Russia will be a strong partner in international diplomacy and trade. That is the course you have wisely chosen for Russia. And that is why we support your epic struggle to make reform work.

You are embarking on an unprecedented journey. There is no map, no blueprint for what you are doing. As you chart this new course in Russian history, let me share some basic, simple convictions drawn from our experience: Democracy works. Free markets work. And moreover, they work together. They reinforce each other. And together they will strengthen your nation's security and your prosperity. Your movement to greater freedom is not meant to empower any single party; it will empower all of the Russian people. By the same token, the object of American support is not one group of leaders. Instead, it is a revolutionary process, the process of reform. By "reform," I mean the transformation of the political system from dictatorship to democracy, the conversion of a command economy into a market economy, and the development of a system that meets the genuine needs of people. This reform also means the success of a foreign policy that fully respects the sovereignty, independence, and territorial integrity of all states—even as it protects Russia's legitimate interests. In seven weeks, you will give fresh meaning to the idea of reform when you vote in your elections. You have already begun preparing for this most fundamental civic responsibility by practicing the forms and expressions of self-government: articulating, organizing, and dissenting.

Let me stress that dissent and open debate are not just noisy, sometimes bothersome consequences of democracy; rather, they are vital elements of a democratic and civil society. These freedoms are a refutation of—and an antidote to—totalitarianism and dictatorship.

We recognize that governments have a responsibility to preserve civil order which is, among other things, a precondition for civil rights. But even in times of intense political struggle, the imperative of civil order must be reconciled with free expression. Even when battling the forces of reaction, true democrats have nothing to fear from a free press. As President Yeltsin said on Thursday, "We can be sure democracy will survive as long as there is a free press." Foreign Minister Kozyrev repeatedly stressed during our talks yesterday his personal commitment to a free press as Russia proceeds with your elections in December.

Russia is being reborn as a democracy, as a nation brave enough to break with the past and wise enough to plan for the future. America celebrates this rebirth with you. We know that you, the Russian people, will be making the critical decisions. But we stand ready to help you achieve the free and fair elections you have earned.

The United States has offered assistance around the world to many countries to support democratic election processes. We are prepared to provide, if asked, immediate technical assistance for the upcoming parliamentary elections that you will have in December. Our efforts would focus on the nuts and bolts of free elections, from voter education to poll-watching. As in all countries where we support the election process, any assistance we would mobilize here would be politically neutral, non-partisan, and available to all participating parties and groups.

In the longer term, U.S. efforts are focused on helping Russia strengthen its democratic institutions and the rule of law. Through judicial reform activities with the American Bar Association, through people-to-people exchanges, through training programs in public administration, through efforts to develop political parties, we want to help you lay a solid foundation for democratic government.

Russia, like America, is a vast and multiethnic nation. Americans draw strength from our diversity, because we are united by a creed of freedom, individual rights, and equal opportunity. Those same ideals can now be a durable thread that weaves together the sprawling social fabric of Russia. While democratic reform is necessary for the empowerment of the Russian people, it is not sufficient. Economic reform is just as vital—and its success lies just as much in your generation's hands, the hands of students like you at institutions like these.

The transition from a command economy to a market economy can be, as you know so well, extremely painful. It can cause insecurity. It can disrupt communities. And it is often accompanied by corruption and crime.

But the majority of the Russian people understand that this transition is essential. They demonstrated that in April. For Russia to play her full role in the world, for Russia to build a 21st century economy, for Russia to sustain and develop its immense resources, there is no other way.

One of Russia's most challenging economic priorities is to control inflation. Economic history teaches us that hyperinflation corrodes living standards—and can crack democracies. President Yeltsin and the Finance Ministry are making serious efforts to address this problem and to lift the standard of living of each and every Russian. The move to sound fiscal and monetary policies is absolutely essential.

Wherever communism is being replaced by markets, privatization is an important key to economic reform. It means slashing subsidies and credits to centralized enterprises. It means developing the financial infrastructure to support more foreign investment. And privatization depends upon, and in turn reinforces, democratic reform. Indeed, the two work together: The more that people work in and own private enterprises, the more likely they are to participate in the democratic process and reinforce reform. I'm glad to say that Russia's privatization effort is a continuing success story—and America's assistance programs are designed to support it. Today the private sector here, I'm told, accounts for a once-inconceivable 25% of Russian GDP. More than 4,000 medium and large businesses have been privatized at the rate of almost 600 a month. Fifty-seven percent of small shops and restaurants—some 70,000—have been privatized.

In short, countless Russians are becoming their own bosses. Rather than taking orders from bureaucrats, you are filling orders for your own businesses. Your nation is moving from vested interests for the few to investment opportunities for the many. Like the rise of democracy, the transition to an open economy involves a revolution of attitudes and skills. You are learning how to be managers in a profit-driven world, how to be employees in a competitive economy, and how to be consumers in an open market. You are, in short, learning the ways and means of economic freedom. This is a great challenge—and an enormous opportunity—for young people. You can change the economic landscape of Russia—while preserving the bedrock sense of community that is the enduring source of Russia's strength.

And the United States is ready to help. Hundreds of American businesses, from Ben and Jerry's to Honeywell, from Pratt & Whitney to PepsiCo, are investing in the future of Russia. Americans have initiated banking and legal reform efforts, small business training programs, agribusiness and energy sector projects, and high-technology ventures.

Our commitment is a real one. This year alone, the United States pledged $1.6 billion in bilateral assistance programs. In Tokyo last July, we proposed a $3-billion privatization and restructuring program for Russia, which our G-7 partners have joined. And just last month, the U.S. Congress approved the Clinton Administration's request for an additional $2.5 billion in technical and humanitarian assistance. How the Russian people shape and carry out their reforms is, of course, for you to decide. America is willing to provide support to that effort. And we want to ensure that this assistance—whether private or public—is coordinated with the pace of reform and delivered effectively to the people of Russia.

As you approach the December elections, I am struck by the immensity of the stakes. Rarely in the history of democratic government will single votes, cast by young people in particular, carry such momentous weight. I have every confidence in the outcome. Every time the Russian people have had a chance to choose, they have chosen reform over retrenchment, hope over fear, and the future over the past. I know most of you are probably tired of foreigners coming here and quoting to you the famous lines of the poet Fyodor Tyutchev. But I cannot resist, because they allow me to make perhaps my most important point. Tyutchev once wrote that:

> Russia is understood not by the mind, Nor by a common rule. She has a special stature of her own: In Russia one can only believe.

My friends, Bill Clinton and I believe in Russia. So do your many American friends. We believe that the new Russia will not only survive, it will thrive. And we believe the new generation of democrats here today will seize the opportunities and secure the gains made possible by reform.

Let me conclude with a personal observation about one of my heroes in public life—one of my predecessors as Secretary of State—Dean Acheson. The telling title of Acheson's memoirs was Present at the Creation, a phrase that referred to his substantial role in shaping the Marshall Plan and the policies of containment at the beginning of the Cold War.

Forty-five years later, we are also present at the creation—the creation of a new Russia. Our mission is fundamentally positive: not to contain communism but to enlarge freedom, not to engage in strategic deterrence but to advance a strategic alliance with reform in Russia and throughout the former Soviet Union.

President Clinton and the people of my country are proud to join with you in this endeavor for the next generation. Our two great nations, in this age of Russian rebirth, have been liberated to share interests, ideals, and aspirations. Now let us share our strength to build a future worthy of the youth of your country and mine.

Thank you very much.

NAFTA and American Interests

One of the crucial duties of all cabinet officers is to help the President on Capitol Hill. For the Secretary of State, this responsibility is at its zenith during the approval process for treaties and trade agreements.[1] A Secretary's support for a presidential initiative can take many forms—testimony before congressional committees, contacts with individual Members, press conferences, and speeches. A speech I gave in Los Angeles on the North American Free Trade Agreement (NAFTA) fit into that pattern.

Gaining congressional approval for NAFTA emerged as one of the first tests of the President's commitment to structuring the post–Cold War international economy to America's advantage. If approved, NAFTA would create a powerful hemispheric free trade zone comparable with the European Community. While NAFTA had been negotiated and signed by the Bush Administration, it was up to us to win congressional approval of it.

This proved to be a tall order. Although NAFTA enjoyed wide support among Republicans, our own party was bitterly divided over it. The debate pitted those who shared the President's "New Democrat" philosophy—which recognized the link between opening the global marketplace and revitalizing American prosperity—against the more traditional

---

[1]Formal treaties require ratification by two-thirds of the Senate, whereas trade agreements can be approved by a majority vote in both the Senate and the House of Representatives.

union-oriented wing of the party, which feared that NAFTA would send American jobs south of the border. Given this divide, NAFTA was a tough issue for the President. During the 1992 presidential primaries he had been dogged with criticism for supporting it, and he had responded during the fall campaign by proposing that it should be accompanied by "side agreements" to condition free trade on protection of labor and the environment.

Beginning in the summer of 1993, the Administration started to push vigorously for NAFTA's approval. An economic summit with Asian leaders was scheduled for November, and the Uruguay Round of negotiations under the General Agreement on Tariffs and Trade (GATT) was reaching the endgame. In this context, early approval of NAFTA would provide significant momentum for our broader strategy of opening up the world economy. We wanted to achieve what we later referred to as a "triple play," including success at the Asian summit and in the Uruguay Round, as well as approval of NAFTA. Despite the considerable domestic political risks, the President made the decision that we had to go all out to obtain congressional approval. William Daley of Chicago, now Secretary of Commerce, was brought to the White House to coordinate the Administration's efforts, and he did an outstanding job.

To me, NAFTA was both good economic policy and good foreign policy. It exemplified a theme that I had stressed since my confirmation hearing: there was no longer a bright line between our foreign and domestic policy interests. To be strong abroad, we had to be strong at home. The Deficit Reduction Act, passed in August 1993, signaled a determined effort to deal with the mounting federal deficit and strengthened our standing around the world. By expanding our trade with Mexico and creating higher-wage jobs for American workers, NAFTA would help build on this strength.

NAFTA's approval also became an issue of American leadership in the hemisphere and the world; it had been my objective from the beginning to cast it as such. We had to show that we were ready to compete in the international economy, not retreat from it. I was absolutely convinced— and made the case privately in numerous White House meetings—that failure to approve NAFTA would not only traumatize our relations with Mexico and undermine our credibility throughout Latin America, but have a profound ripple effect on our ability to lead in *all* areas of foreign policy. It would signal across the globe a retreat from our usual strong

NAFTA AND AMERICAN INTERESTS • **107**

advocacy for opening markets and expanding trade. Put in these terms, NAFTA was a fight we simply could not afford to lose.

My November 2 speech before a joint meeting of the Los Angeles World Affairs Council and the Town Hall of California, the only formal speech I gave in my home city during my four years as Secretary, was part of the Administration's final push for NAFTA. The speech followed numerous other high-profile efforts, such as the Vice President's crushing debate with Ross Perot on *Larry King Live* and an event in which President Clinton and I joined all the living former Secretaries of State at the White House in an unusual display of bipartisan support.[2] Since early September, I had also made several public statements on NAFTA's importance, both in print and in testimony before Congress.[3] Coming little more than two weeks before the scheduled November 17 vote in the House of Representatives (where NAFTA's support was much more tenuous than in the Senate), the Los Angeles address was my most important intervention on NAFTA.

The speech set forth the argument for NAFTA in its most basic form. Much of what I said about NAFTA's benefits related specifically to the California venue: with nearly 90,000 jobs supported by exports to Mexico, and with a high-tech industry that would certainly expand under the agreement, California had a unique stake in expanding trade southward. Yet, as I pointed out, Californians also had legitimate concerns about NAFTA, particularly regarding illegal immigration, detrimental side effects on the environment, and drug trafficking. Rather than exacerbate such problems, I argued, NAFTA and its side agreements would actually empower us to solve them.

To me, the positive case for NAFTA was clear. Equally, the consequences of its rejection would be quite profound and could not be ignored. As Secretary of State, it fell primarily to me to frame the debate

---

[2]In a similar event, when the environmental and labor side agreements to NAFTA were signed on September 14, President Clinton and I joined former Presidents Ford, Carter, and Bush in a White House ceremony to signal support for the main agreement.

[3]See, for example, "NAFTA Promotes Prosperity," *Philadelphia Inquirer*, Sept. 6, 1993, and the testimony by me, Treasury Secretary Lloyd Bentsen, and U.S. Trade Representative Mickey Kantor before the Senate Finance Committee, "NAFTA: A Bridge to a Better Future for the United States and the Hemisphere," Sept. 15, 1993.

as a foreign policy issue and explain how failing to approve NAFTA would harm our overall ability to lead globally. Particularly on the eve of the final GATT negotiations, I explained, a defeat of NAFTA would critically injure presidential leadership at precisely the wrong moment. NAFTA was more than a measure of America's pre-eminent role in the world; the vote presented a critical test of the President's personal ability to lead, and would be a defining moment for him.

The speech closed with some rhetoric aimed at my primary audience: Congress. Like my Russia speeches that spring, this address and the NAFTA effort overall highlighted that diplomacy is often as much about domestic politics as foreign relations. The NAFTA vote, like the SALT II effort I had witnessed during the Carter Administration, exemplified the critical role that Congress plays in shaping U.S. foreign policy through the approval or rejection of international agreements.[4] With SALT II, President Carter fought unsuccessfully to get congressional approval for an agreement he believed had great strategic value. In my view, the stakes of NAFTA were at least as great—nothing less than America's role in the post–Cold War world.

On November 17, the House passed NAFTA by a vote of 234–200. Three days later, the Senate followed with a vote of 61–38. The comprehensive two-month lobbying effort, capped by a furiously paced final two weeks, had succeeded. While some have criticized our delay in launching the campaign for NAFTA approval, there is no dispute that, once under way, we were effective in explaining the stakes to the American people and shepherding the agreement through Congress.

Although my speech and similar efforts by other senior officials were certainly important, NAFTA's success showcased the power of President Clinton's formidable political skills. I believe that the passage of NAFTA can be credited primarily to his efforts, public and private. Once he focused on the issue, he personally carried the day in articulating and persuading the American people of the importance of NAFTA. Happily for America's long-term strategic interests, Congress heard this message.

---

[4]SALT II is an acronym for the Strategic Arms Limitation Treaty capping the Soviet and U.S. nuclear arsenals. President Carter's effort to obtain Senate ratification was sidetracked by the adverse reaction to the 1979 Soviet invasion of Afghanistan.

With NAFTA's ratification, we had taken a major step in building a new global economic architecture.

NAFTA: In the Overriding Interest of the United States

Address to the Los Angeles World Affairs Council and Town Hall of California, Los Angeles, November 2, 1993

It is wonderful to return to the City of Angels from the City of Angles. It is even better to be back home and among friends.

The last time I spoke to an audience at this hotel was June 2, 1992, the night the voters of Los Angeles approved the reform measures recommended by the Independent Commission on the Los Angeles Police Department. What has happened in the life of America in the intervening 17 months has been quite remarkable. The country has elected a new President, has seen him craft a striking new domestic agenda, and has watched as he helped orchestrate one of the most wished-for handshakes in recent history. Certainly this has been a time of dramatic change in my life as well. My journey over these 17 months has not been calm, but it has given me challenges and an opportunity to serve, for which I am deeply grateful.

It is a great pleasure to serve as the catalyst for a joint meeting of two strong and independent forces in the Los Angeles community. The World Affairs Council makes a vital educational link between the people of Southern California and the practitioners of our foreign policy. Town Hall and its thousands of members have been sharing food for body and food for thought for more than 50 years, and I am honored to stand before the members of these two groups today.

My presence here is intended to underscore that there is no longer a bright line separating our foreign and domestic policy interests. For America to be strong abroad, we must be strong at home. And to be strong at home, to achieve the domestic renewal that our nation needs, we must reject the voices of isolationism; we must be engaged internationally.

No issue more clearly illustrates the links between foreign and domestic policy than the North American Free Trade Agreement. Winning approval of NAFTA is among the Administration's highest priorities. In fact, just a week ago at a Cabinet meeting, our Treasury Secretary, Lloyd Bentsen, turned to me and said, "Young man, you're going to have to go out on the road for NAFTA." So here I am. Today, I want to speak both as Secretary of State and as someone from this community who cares deeply about its future.

NAFTA is in the best interest of California and Los Angeles—and it is in the overriding interest of the United States of America. That is the message today. And that is the message the President and a distinguished group of Americans are underscoring today at the White House.

NAFTA is an essential part of the Administration's strategy to promote prosperity through trade expansion. That strategy has other elements crucial to America's economic renewal: first, concluding the GATT Uruguay Round negotiations by December 15; second, negotiating a new economic framework with Japan to correct our trade imbalance; and third, developing the Asia-Pacific Economic Cooperation forum as an important mechanism for spurring growth and creating jobs around the dynamic Pacific Rim. A vote for NAFTA on November 17 in the Congress will move this entire strategy forward.

This agreement will allow us to take command of our economic future and strengthen our security. It will give our exporters the opportunity to sell without barriers in what will be the world's largest free trade area, a unified market of 370 million consumers. Mexico is America's fastest-growing major export market, and we have a vital stake in its future growth and openness. NAFTA will enhance the trade opportunities that have lifted our exports to Mexico more than 200% since 1986, creating more than 400,000 American jobs in the process. NAFTA will create even more high-wage, high-skill American jobs—and it will boost our ability to compete globally.

The European nations and Japan leave no stone unturned to compete in their regional markets, where they have a natural geographic advantage. America's economic self-interest demands that we compete in every region around the world. But, like the European Community and Japan, we must have a trade strategy tailored to our region—and NAFTA is absolutely crucial to that strategy.

Almost 90,000 jobs in this state are supported by exports to Mexico.

NAFTA will prove particularly beneficial to California. For example, California's high-tech firms will see their sales rise dramatically. Our vast agricultural industry also stands to gain substantially from NAFTA. For California, increased trade offers a logical avenue to economic recovery and renewed prosperity.

I have not forgotten that border states like California endure burdens even as they enjoy benefits. But I am convinced that NAFTA gives us the chance to multiply the benefits and to better manage the burdens.

For the United States and Mexico, NAFTA is about much more than tariffs and trade, growth and jobs. It is the symbol of a new relationship and a new structure of cooperation. Approval of NAFTA and the side agreements accompanying it will increase Mexico's capacity to cooperate with us on a wide range of vital issues that affect our security in direct and tangible ways. Let me discuss three of them: illegal immigration, the environment, and narcotics.

California and all of America will continue to find strength in diversity. Indeed, one reason Los Angeles is a world-class city is that people from all over the world have chosen to live here and to contribute to its enormous vitality. At the same time, the Clinton Administration is committed to reducing illegal immigration, and NAFTA is critical to that effort. My colleague, Attorney General Janet Reno, said in San Diego a few weeks ago that the passage of NAFTA will help her protect our borders. She said, "NAFTA is the best hope for reducing illegal immigration in the long haul." And she warned that if NAFTA fails, "stopping the flow of illegal immigrants will be much, much more difficult, if not impossible."

NAFTA also addresses another issue that transcends political boundaries—the problem of pollution. This Administration has made the environment a foreign policy priority because we can address environmental concerns only with the cooperation from other countries, especially our neighbors.

Mexico recognizes its pollution problems and is addressing them, both on its own and in cooperation with the United States. NAFTA reinforces that cooperation. Unlike any previous trade agreement, NAFTA explicitly links trade with the environment. With the NAFTA side agreement on the environment, and with our efforts to find innovative and reliable funding for border environmental cleanup, we are taking steps to fight pollution along the border.

NAFTA will also help us make progress in combating narcotics. Mexico recognizes that illegal narcotics is a shared problem that can be solved only through cross-border cooperation. President Salinas has tripled Mexico's counter-narcotics budget and has shown real resolve to attack corrupt government officials and drug barons. Some of Mexico's most notorious drug traffickers are now behind bars. This is breakthrough progress—and it must be sustained.

As you well know, the United States and Mexico for many years were, as one observer put it, "distant neighbors." Until recent times, Mexicans saw the United States as a source of pressure and even danger, while Americans saw Mexican poverty as a source of instability and concern.

But Mexico has been growing and changing, modernizing and developing a middle class. In the last few years, Mexico has made unprecedented efforts to open its economy and reform its political institutions, including the judiciary and its electoral system. Mexico's attitudes about the United States and the world have also changed dramatically for the better.

Now, with NAFTA, we can move beyond old suspicions and outdated assumptions. NAFTA will mark a turning point in the history of our relations throughout Latin America. It will encourage democratic governments throughout the hemisphere that have opened their economies to American trade and investment.

In many respects, Latin America is pointing the way toward a new and better future in the post–Cold War era. In this hemisphere, democracy is ascendant. Markets are opening. Conflicts are being resolved peacefully. By approving NAFTA, the United States sends a powerful signal that we support these favorable developments throughout our hemisphere.

For more than half a century, every American President—Democrat and Republican—has stood for closer cooperation with Mexico. NAFTA represents a bipartisan commitment to widening and improving America's ties to our Latin American neighbors, beginning with Mexico. Today, NAFTA has the support of all five living former Presidents of the United States—an unusual display of bipartisan unity.

I believe that the vote on NAFTA on the 17th of November will be one of the most vital decisions that the Members of Congress will make in this decade. To recognize fully what is at stake, we have to consider not only the economic and diplomatic gains we will realize if NAFTA goes into effect, but what America—and Americans—stand to lose if it is defeated.

One of my most important duties as Secretary of State is to consider the downside of alternate courses of action—and I can tell you that the downside of rejecting NAFTA could be enormous.

First, defeat of NAFTA would seriously damage our relations with Mexico. Our carefully nurtured efforts to improve relations would be scuttled as a sense of rejection sets in across the border. For the United States, that would be a self-inflicted setback of historic proportions. The defeat of NAFTA would undermine Mexico's capacity to cooperate with us on the vital cross-border issues such as illegal immigration and pollution that affect millions of Americans.

Second, rejection of NAFTA would hand our major economic competitors in Europe and East Asia a gilt-edged invitation to go after what should be a natural market for our goods and services. If we reject NAFTA, investors and merchants from Japan, Taiwan, and Germany will be on the phone—or on the next plane—to Mexico City immediately after the vote. They will not hesitate to gain a foothold where we feared to tread.

Third, a defeat of NAFTA would send a chilling signal about our willingness to engage in Latin America at a time when so many of our neighbors are genuinely receptive to closer cooperation with the United States. It would complicate our efforts to find diplomatic solutions to regional crises that threaten peace and stability in the hemisphere.

Fourth, there is no good time—but there could not be a worse time than now—to turn our backs on NAFTA. The Uruguay Round of the GATT negotiations is in its climactic stage. Between now and December 15, the President must be in a position to exercise maximum leverage to conclude that Round successfully. Rejecting NAFTA would create the perception that America is not prepared to act on behalf of its global economic interests at a time when those interests are so clearly at stake.

Fifth and finally, NAFTA's rejection would undermine our commitment to open markets and a liberal world trading order. Opposing an agreement that eliminates tariff barriers is really an argument for protectionism. It is only a short intellectual walk from opposing the lowering of tariffs to favoring the erection of even higher trade barriers.

That very simply is the wrong course. We have seen the consequences of protectionism once in this century, in the late 1920s and the early 1930s—and once was certainly enough for those of us who grew up in the Depression. Make no mistake about it: To oppose NAFTA is to reject the principles of free trade that have helped to make the last half century in America the most prosperous time in our history.

Beyond all the specific points that can be marshaled for NAFTA, a broader, more overriding principle is at stake. America cannot and will not thrive if we withdraw from the world.

The defeat of NAFTA would not only forfeit an opportunity to strengthen our economy. It would also constitute a profoundly disturbing move toward isolationism—toward the abdication of the role America must assert to protect our interests and promote our values. It would weaken our position not only on international economic issues but on foreign policy issues as a whole. The vote on NAFTA will determine whether we choose to engage or retreat from the global economy; whether we will enable our workers, the most productive in the world, to compete and win or whether we will try in vain to insulate ourselves from rapid worldwide economic change.

NAFTA is a once-in-a-generation opportunity that must not be lost. It is nothing less than a test of American leadership and America's sense of purpose in the post–Cold War world.

Whether we like it or not, the vote on NAFTA will reveal how we see ourselves and will be reflected in how the world sees us.

I do not believe that Congress will choose to shrink from a natural and growing market for our goods and services. I do not believe that Congress will decide to undercut the President at a time when negotiations on the Uruguay Round are at the critical stage. I do not believe that Congress will endorse the kind of economic isolation that squanders the chance to create American jobs and surrenders a part of America's global leadership.

Let me tell you what I do believe. I believe that Congress will vote to approve NAFTA—and I believe that vote for American engagement will echo throughout the hemisphere and across the world. I believe that Congress will choose a course that expands political freedom and free markets throughout our hemisphere and extends cooperation between the United States and the countries of Latin America. I believe that Congress will reinforce the foundation of free trade that will be a platform for global prosperity in the next century. I believe that the vote to approve NAFTA will represent a defining moment for American principle and power.

I believe—in fact, I know—that approval of NAFTA will signal our confidence in ourselves at home and strengthen our credibility abroad. With NAFTA, we are building an economic future and a foreign policy worthy of our great nation.

Thank you very much.

SEVEN

The New Pacific Community

In my confirmation statement, I had stressed that the "countries of the Pacific Rim are becoming a global center of economic dynamism." Influenced by a life and career in California, I had long believed that American foreign policy was too Eurocentric. This is not to downplay Europe's importance to our vital interests, for as I explained time and again in public statements throughout 1993, Europe remains at the core of our foreign policy, and we would continue to be engaged there. However, with the Cold War's end, I believed that the United States needed a foreign policy that looked across the Pacific as much as the Atlantic. I was convinced that we should strengthen our efforts to seize economic and diplomatic opportunities in the Pacific.

Preserving peace continues to be central to America's role in the Asia-Pacific region. Even though Cold War tensions have subsided, regional security threats remain. The possibility of renewed fighting on the Korean Peninsula or a conflict between China and Taiwan cannot be discounted. Moreover, stemming the proliferation of weapons of mass destruction in the area is a vital security interest. The core of our military commitment to the region lies in our bilateral security alliances with Japan, South Korea, Australia, Thailand, and the Philippines, together with the maintenance of our forward military presence.

At the same time, America's economic stake in Asia is enormous. In my view, no other region better demonstrates the importance of the economic dimension of diplomacy. The countries of Asia have been transformed from "dominoes to dynamos," as my senior adviser for the region, Winston Lord, cogently observed. In three decades, Asia's share of the world's GDP went from 8% to 25%. Asia is our largest trading partner, as both a customer for U.S. exports and a supplier of our imports. American exports to the region totaled over $120 billion in 1992, accounting for over 2.4 million American jobs.

Given these realities, we set out to engage Asia actively during President Clinton's first year in office. By November I had visited the area three times. In addition, we used two scheduled events to highlight the region for the American public and signal our engagement to the nations there. It was fortunate that Clinton's first trip overseas was to Asia, to attend the G-7 summit in Tokyo. There the President laid out his vision of a Pacific Community and our economic strategy; he then went on to Seoul, where he articulated our regional security approach.

The calendar did us another favor by giving us the opportunity to host the fifth Asia-Pacific Economic Cooperation (APEC) Ministerial Meeting in Seattle. Composed of both Asian and Western Hemisphere nations, APEC was established in 1989 as a way to manage economic interdependence and facilitate cooperation among them.[1] Compared with other international forums, APEC was developing slowly, with little visibility. Its secretariat in Singapore was tiny by EU standards, and its 10 working groups (focusing on such issues as energy cooperation, telecommunications, tourism, and marine resource conservation) garnered little attention. If Europe had too many multilateral institutions—and too many meetings—Asia seemed to have too few.

In establishing our goals for Asia and APEC, we had historical precedents upon which to draw. After World War II, the United States led the effort to create multilateral institutions that sparked European recovery and helped sustain prosperity. Such institutions as NATO, the World Bank, the International Monetary Fund, and the GATT defined our

[1]APEC began as an informal grouping of 12 Asia-Pacific economies: Australia, Brunei, Canada, Indonesia, Japan, South Korea, Malaysia, New Zealand, the Philippines, Singapore, Thailand, and the United States. In 1991, the so-called "three Chinas"—China, Hong Kong, and Taiwan—joined the forum. At the 1993 Seattle meeting, Mexico, Chile, and Papua New Guinea were invited to join, bringing APEC membership to 18. At the 1997 meeting, APEC invited Vietnam, Peru, and Russia to join in 1998, after which there will be a 10-year moratorium on new members.

leadership role and bound us to the region. In this new era, we wanted to bring the same approach to engaging our Asian partners. Strengthening APEC fit squarely into that vision.

In the summer of 1993, we decided to use the November APEC meeting to elevate the organization's credibility and stature. Up to that point, the annual ministerial meeting had been APEC's most public function, and it had often gone unnoticed. After intense discussion within the Administration of the risks and rewards involved, the President decided to invite the leaders of the APEC members to Seattle for an unprecedented Leaders' Meeting. By raising the APEC gathering to the summit level, the President permanently changed its character from a low-visibility bureaucratic endeavor to a high-profile meeting involving the Asia-Pacific economic giants. This was the first time all of these leaders would meet together. From that point on, the annual APEC meetings became the principal forum in which the Asia-Pacific leaders would meet.

To help create a sense of personal camaraderie and political community among these 15 leaders, the President wanted the meeting to be an informal, collegial affair. He hoped that the leaders would speak candidly about common problems and goals. Eschewing the rather formal surroundings that usually constrain such events, the President hosted the meeting on Blake Island, a beautiful resort a few miles off Seattle in Puget Sound. The President urged the leaders to come without their Foreign Ministers or a large retinue of aides—and without ties. News reports later indicated that Japanese Prime Minister Morihiro Hosokawa had set the style by arriving in a trendy black leather jacket.

The Administration also decided to use the occasion to outline its Pacific agenda for the American people. Both the President and I had touched on the themes of this agenda several times earlier in the year, but we hoped that the intense media coverage of the summit would focus public attention on our message. The remarks I made during the ministerial meeting were intended to lay the groundwork for the Leaders' Meeting and the President's address to it two days later. My speech was a focused exposition of U.S. strategy and objectives regarding Asia generally and APEC specifically; it placed our efforts with APEC in context and established a road map for the future. The President himself touched on many of the same points, but, appropriately, he did so in a much more sweeping and general manner.

My speech was based on three themes that anchored our Asia policy—

strengthening regional economic relationships; ensuring peace and stability; and enlarging democracy. These were the core goals of what President Clinton referred to as the New Pacific Community. The first section of the speech framed APEC within our broader regional economic interests, stressing the need to strengthen APEC as an institution. The section also emphasized the importance of improving bilateral trade ties, particularly with states like Japan and China. To further accent the importance of Pacific trade, on this trip I visited the Boeing plant to see the production of the new state-of-the-art 777 aircraft, and I also made remarks one evening at the Air and Space Museum.

Frequently, of course, what is said in a speech about the hot topic of the day attracts the most public attention. This was the case with the message I sent to North Korea in the middle section of the speech, which concerned our continuing security interests in the region. When President Clinton took office, evidence had already begun to accumulate that North Korea was close to producing a small nuclear weapon, or indeed had done so, in violation of its commitments under the Nuclear Non-Proliferation Treaty. This issue came to a head when North Korea refused to allow inspectors from the International Atomic Energy Agency (IAEA) full access to its nuclear sites. The speech stressed that the United States and the nations of the region insisted that North Korea "set aside its nuclear ambitions" and not "be allowed to pose a nuclear threat" to its neighbors. If North Korea's belligerence continued, I warned, the United States was prepared to push for more punitive options, such as imposing UN sanctions. We knew this threat contained certain risks; North Korea claimed that any move toward sanctions would be considered an act of war. We continued to wrestle with the issue for the better part of the next year, conducting intensive negotiations (and threatening sanctions and reinforcement of our forces in South Korea) until we reached the Agreed Framework under which North Korea committed to freezing and ultimately dismantling its nuclear weapons program. (See Chapter 15.)

The third major section of the speech, focused on democracy as the foundation of our policy, replayed many of the themes I had stressed during my human rights speech in Vienna (Chapter 3). I reviewed the basic conceptual underpinnings of our democracy-building approach, repeating that "culture" cannot be used as an excuse to violate basic human rights, that aspirations for freedom are universal, and that expanding liberty in the world also serves our security and economic interests. I signaled to the Chinese regime—a signal both the President and I also conveyed in our private bilateral talks with Chinese leaders in Seattle—that our goal was to achieve a deeper engagement and build a comprehensive relationship that would permit resolution of our differences in many areas, including human rights.

Finally, this speech explicitly declared that strengthening APEC was an important part of our broader international economic agenda. Along with attaining congressional approval of NAFTA and concluding GATT's Uruguay Round by December 15, a successful APEC meeting was a critical part of the economic "triple play" for which we aimed. In my speech, I called on our Asian partners to push for concluding GATT, and I made a final strong pitch for NAFTA. In retrospect, it is amazing how closely the timing of these important events dovetailed. The House of Representatives approved NAFTA by a close vote of 234–200 on the very evening of my APEC speech. With NAFTA's approval by the Senate assured, the President came to Seattle emboldened, ready to translate this new confidence into making APEC stronger.

America's Pacific Future

Address at the University of Washington,

Seattle, November 17, 1993

Thank you for that introduction, Professor Lardy. I want to thank the World Affairs Council and the Jackson School for having me here today. Scoop Jackson believed that America derived strength from its willingness to engage abroad, and he would be proud of the work being done here in his name.

One hundred and thirty-two years ago, the University of Washington was carved out of Seattle's emerald wilderness by a band of hardy and intellectually hungry pioneers. The first faculty consisted of one professor; the first graduating class, one student. From those simple origins on that rugged frontier, the University of Washington has become one of America's great public universities. I want to acknowledge, in that regard, my longtime friend Bill Gerberding, President of this university.

Today, another frontier beckons. And Seattle stands not at the end of the trail but at the beginning. As we approach the next century, America must once again look west—west to Asia, west to our Pacific future. In the 19th century, American visionaries connected the coasts with great iron railroads. Now, with the ethereal reach of satellites and the blinding speed of fiber optics, we are traversing the Pacific. With the same determination that brought trains to Washington State, we are building bonds of communication, commerce, and culture with Asia.

Signs of our Pacific future are sprouting here like espresso stands. Trade with Asia accounts for 95% of the volume of Seattle's bustling ports. A quarter of the city's schoolchildren are Asian-Americans. Pike Place Market overflows with the scents, flavors, and dialects of the Pacific Rim. And in every sector—from aircraft to software to real estate—Seattle's economy is increasingly tied to Asia's. My message today is simple: As Seattle goes, so must the nation. As Asia advances, so must we. For, today, no region in the world is more important to the United States than Asia. America has fought three wars in Asia during the past half-century. We have abiding security interests there. As to our economic interests, 40% of our trade is with Asia, half again as much as with Europe. And every day, immigrants from Asia and their descendants are fulfilling the American dream, enriching our culture and maintaining tangible ties across an ocean of opportunity.

Just over a generation ago, when many of these immigrants were first arriving on American shores, Asia seemed mired in a cycle of epic suffering. But a new determinism pervades Asia now. Despair about decay has given way to faith in progress. In southern China, towns that were once agrarian backwaters are leaping forward into the industrial age. In Singapore's gleaming harbor, where laborers once carried sacks of rice on their backs, enormous cranes now swivel and stretch to unload high-technology cargo. And in the towering skyscrapers of Jakarta, Indonesians born in bamboo huts are making fortunes in Asian commodity markets. Like Mount Rainier, Asia's astounding revival and the challenges it presents are best viewed from a panoramic perspective. Asia is likely to account for half the growth in world trade between now and the year 2000. It includes the world's fastest-growing economies and most promising terrain for American exports. But at the same time, we are running unacceptable trade deficits with some of our Asian trading partners.

In security terms, Asia is more stable—and, if you will, more pacific—than at any other time since the turn of the century. But at the same time, we need to meet new security challenges that cloud the horizon.

Across the region, the rising tide of democracy is watering some of freedom's most parched terrain. But at the same time, some of the world's least open regimes can also be found in Asia. As we look ahead, then, we must remove the peril and realize the promise of wider engagement with the Pacific. That is why President Clinton has called for a New Pacific Community, built on three core elements: shared prosperity, shared strength, and a shared commitment to democratic values.

I. Prosperity

Let me turn first to the economic dimension. In Asia, we see most clearly that economic policy stands at the center of our foreign policy. Last year, our exports to the region totaled $128 billion and created 2.4 million American jobs.

This Administration is working to widen trade and investment in Asia on three levels: globally, through the GATT; regionally, through the APEC forum; and bilaterally, with individual nations.

No region has more at stake than Asia in the removal of barriers to global trade and investment. Asia has asked us to remain engaged in the region, and we will do so. But for the American people to appreciate the benefits of such engagement, Asia's markets must be open to our goods and services.

Today I urge the leaders of the Asian economies to join us in pushing for a successful conclusion of the GATT Uruguay Round. If the round succeeds, it will open markets and create jobs around the world. If it fails, however, we will all suffer from the punishing effects of rising protectionism. While we work to open global trade, we must also strengthen our regional trading ties. Today's historic vote on NAFTA is a test of our willingness to do that. It is a test of our desire to compete rather than retreat. NAFTA, as the President and I have been saying, is in our overriding national interest. It takes down barriers to prosperity. It demonstrates that as we enter the next century, America is looking outward, not turning inward. That is why the President has put so much on the line for NAFTA's passage. And that is why I believe the House of Representatives will approve NAFTA today.

APEC, the forum for Asia-Pacific Economic Cooperation, is another vital part of our strategy to strengthen regional trading ties. APEC was created only four years ago—not to micromanage trade but to get bureaucracy out of the way of business and to promote cooperation among diverse economies.

This year's meeting here in Seattle, to be followed by President Clinton's historic gathering of APEC leaders, is dedicated to expanding Pacific trade and investment. We will begin to bring greater harmony to the trade policies of APEC members. We will work to facilitate the entry of American businesses into Asian markets. And we will work to strengthen APEC as an institution.

In the software business today, "open architecture" is the coin of the realm. That, in essence, is what my colleagues and I are developing: an open environment in which we can increase by many times the $500 billion in trade among APEC members. But let me be clear: APEC is a building block, not a trading bloc. The United States views APEC as the cornerstone of regional economic cooperation. These regional efforts, in turn, are a catalyst for global trade cooperation.

At the same time, the Clinton Administration is working to strengthen some of our most important bilateral economic relationships in Asia. China, one of America's largest trading partners, has a trade surplus with the United States that reached nearly $20 billion last year. To address this problem, we are working with the Chinese to achieve full implementation of our market access agreements. In South Korea, we have launched a new dialogue that will improve the trade and investment climate for U.S. businesses. And with Japan, we are negotiating a new economic framework. The security and political dimensions of our partnership with Japan are in sound condition. But the economic pillar is urgently in need of repair. This Administration attaches as high a priority to improving our economic ties with Japan as it does to maintaining our security and political links. That is why we are working to correct our persistent trade imbalance. We are determined to forge a more equitable and mutually beneficial partnership.

II. Security

Ultimately, all our efforts to advance American prosperity in Asia depend on the peace and security of the region. America's continued security engagement is, therefore, the second core component of our New Pacific Community. I was a 20-year-old Navy ensign—the same age as many of you here today—when World War II and its aftermath first linked America to the security of the Pacific. Today, the reasons for us to stay anchored in Asia have changed. But they are still compelling. For it remains in our unambiguous national interest to deter regional aggression and to sustain Asia-Pacific economic growth. While the tensions of the Cold War have subsided, many Asian nations harbor apprehensions about their closest neighbors. An American withdrawal would magnify those concerns. And so America must stay engaged.

Our security role in Asia begins with our treaty alliances with Japan, South Korea, Australia, Thailand, and the Philippines. We will honor these obligations and maintain our forward military presence throughout the Pacific.

At the same time, we are working in Asia to prevent the proliferation of weapons of mass destruction. Nowhere is the threat of nuclear proliferation more serious today than in North Korea.

North Korea is caught in a kind of time warp. It is the most isolated country in the world, unmoved by the winds of change that have swept across the region. It has buried the economic dreams of its people to raise a million-man army, most of which is deployed at South Korea's doorstep.

The other nations of the region share President Clinton's firm view that North Korea must set aside its nuclear ambitions. It must not be allowed to pose a nuclear threat to South Korea or its other neighbors. North Korea has refused to grant international inspectors full access to its nuclear sites. The United States is committed to a diplomatic solution as the best means of resolving the nuclear issue. At the same time, we insist on North Korea's full compliance with all of its international commitments, including the Nuclear Non-Proliferation Treaty. North Korea must fulfill its full-scope safeguards obligations and permit the inspections required by the International Atomic Energy Agency. North Korea must also fulfill its denuclearization agreement with South Korea.

These are not only the views of the United States; they are the views of the world community. We are not approaching this on a unilateral basis. We are working with others in the region.

If North Korea refuses the necessary inspections—and refuses to resume a dialogue with South Korea on nuclear issues—then we are prepared to recommend that the UN Security Council consider options other than negotiation. This need not be the outcome of this impasse. We urge North Korea to join the community of responsible nations by responding positively to the comments I have made here today.

As we work to resolve the impasse with North Korea, we must also develop new regional approaches to prevent conflicts. That is why at the ASEAN Post-Ministerial Conference last July, my fellow ministers and I established the ASEAN Regional Security Forum. This forum will supplement, but not replace, our treaty alliances. These security discussions will ease tensions and discourage arms races. It will include the ASEAN nations, the United States, Japan, Canada, South Korea, Australia, and others. It will also include—mark this—China, Russia, and Vietnam. Ten years ago, or even five, such an array of countries would have been unthinkable. Next year, it will be a reality.

III. Democracy

Just as security is the bedrock for the pursuit of prosperity, so democracy is the foundation for security. More open societies make for a more stable region. Democratic nations make better neighbors and better trading partners. That is why the support of democracy and human rights is the third core element of our New Pacific Community. President Clinton has said that "free markets not only enrich people; they empower them." As more Asians enter the middle class, they will seek a greater voice in their communities. As factories bloom across China, political power will come increasingly from the end of an assembly line.

Greater openness will also help sustain modernization in Asia. After all, how can countries attract investment without the rule of law? How can they combat corruption without a free press? How can they generate prosperity without constant currents of information?

There are those who say that democracy is somehow unsuited for

Asia, that our emphasis on human rights is a cloak for cultural imperialism. But there is no cloak over the city of Phnom Penh, where Cambodians voted this spring in their first free election. There is no cloak over Seoul, where former dissident Kim Young Sam is now Korea's President. Nor, indeed, is there a cloak over Shanghai, where a talk show called "Radio Orient" receives thousands of calls and letters every day.

To be sure, great areas of Asia lag behind the march of history. But the yearnings for freedom are not a Western export. They are a human instinct. All across Asia, the United States is working to respond to those yearnings. We are, in short, aligning ourselves with the future.

Human rights is a key issue in our relations with several Asian countries, including Burma, Vietnam, Indonesia, and China. The Clinton Administration has developed a policy toward China that reflects both our values and our interests. China is a great nation and an influential member of the world community. A stable, prosperous China is in the long-term interest of the United States.

Recent problems have created the risk of a downward spiral in our relationship. On human rights, unless there is overall, significant progress, the President will not be able to renew China's most-favored-nation status. We are encouraged by Beijing's recent offer to open its prisons to the International Red Cross. We hope that is a harbinger of sustained progress on human rights in China. On trade, we continue to have concerns about market access, textiles, and intellectual property protection. And on non-proliferation, we have imposed sanctions on China for its shipment of M-11 missile components to Pakistan. At the same time, we have made clear that we are willing to negotiate the necessary conditions for a waiver of those sanctions. And so we have launched a process of deeper engagement with China to make progress in these key areas. Our goal, I emphasize, is to build a comprehensive relationship that permits the resolution of our differences.

Conclusion

Many of the issues that can bring together the New Pacific Community are global issues—challenges that cut across political borders. Consider, for example, the environmental problems that Asia, with its huge appetite for energy sources, will face in the next century. Consider that 20 years from now, 1 billion more people will live in Asia alone.

Problems like these demand transnational solutions. That is why this Administration has brought global issues into the mainstream of our foreign policy.

Recently, I passed by Red Square—the one in Moscow, that is—to give a speech to Russian students. They, like many of you, are wary of sweeping proclamations about "our moment in history." But your generation—whether in Moscow or Seattle or Beijing—truly stands at a pivotal point, between the Cold War and a new millennium. For Russia's youth, the question is whether to believe in free markets and democratic reform. For you, the question is simpler: whether to believe in yourselves.

Over the last several years, some Americans have worried that Asia's success spells trouble for the United States. They look at Japan's performance, or China's incredible growth, or the ferocious development of Asia's "four tigers," and they have feared that America's best days are behind us. I see it altogether differently. Asia's success is ours, too—because Asia's dynamism creates enormous new markets for our products; because for a half-century our engagement has supported regional stability; and because Asia's drive toward freedom echoes the enduring strength of our values.

I look at the flower of Asian prosperity, and I see the seeds of American renewal. The virtues that have made America great—thrift, diligence, optimism, resilience—must guide us again as we rebuild America's economy and engage ever more vigorously with Asia.

Can we summon the confidence to do that? Can we muster the courage to seize this opportunity? From Lewis and Clark's expedition to the first flight of a Boeing airplane, everything in our history suggests that we can. And everything in our future—our Pacific future—says that we must.

Thank you very much.

EIGHT

A New NATO: The Partnership for Peace

When our Administration came into office, one of its toughest challenges was to deal with the future of NATO. The Alliance was a creature
of the Cold War, and its paramount mission was defense against the Soviet Union. With the collapse of the Warsaw Pact, NATO was facing a
crisis of purpose and confidence—it had to redefine its mission and establish a new identity. I felt that the United States, as NATO's dominant
power, had to take the lead in enhancing NATO's relations with the East
and in integrating all of the nations of Europe.[1]

During the summer of 1993, I asked the Department to conduct a pol-
icy review in order to produce a plan for NATO's future. The capable
Under Secretary for International Security Affairs, Lynn Davis, joined
Stephen Flanagan, a knowledgeable European security specialist on my
Policy Planning staff, to lead this effort. We had three basic options: (1)
to conclude that NATO's purpose had been fulfilled and disband it; (2)

---

[1]Enlargement of NATO would help accomplish this important mission of integration. But enlargement was not the only new direction for the Alliance. After the
July 1997 NATO summit, when Poland, Hungary, and the Czech Republic were invited to start negotiations to join NATO, former Secretary of Defense William
Perry and I wrote in the *New York Times* that the primary threat to NATO members
is not now to their collective territory but "to their collective interests beyond their
territory." Therefore, the Alliance's emphasis should shift to defense against these
common threats, which include proliferation of weapons of mass destruction, terrorism, genocidal violence, and disruption of the flow of oil. "NATO's True Mission,"
New York Times, Oct. 21, 1997.

to preserve the status quo without any change in membership or purpose; or (3) to reach out to the East and expand that membership and purpose. I concluded that the only viable option was the third one. Both security and diplomatic objectives drove the logic behind expansion. Militarily, including new nations in the Alliance would help to solidify a zone of stability in Central Europe. Diplomatically, we could use NATO membership as an incentive to foster democratic reform. We could condition membership on criteria such as respecting minority rights, renouncing territorial claims, accelerating democratization, and instituting civil-military reforms.[2]

In moving forward on expansion, we had to weigh the risks of aggravating Russian anxieties and undermining President Yeltsin. Particularly with the Duma elections scheduled for December 1993, we needed to allay any Russian perception that expanding NATO was anti-Russian. The wall dividing Europe had just come down; we did not want NATO expansion to erect another. While some observers preferred accelerated expansion, Strobe Talbott believed it should occur gradually and in parallel with the development of a cooperative relationship between NATO and Russia—and between NATO and Ukraine. His judgment was influential throughout the process, and continues to be so.

We recognized that the conditions were not yet ripe for precipitous action. Neither our Allies, our Russian partners, nor the prospective new members themselves were ready for immediate enlargement of NATO. Indeed, many in our own government remained concerned about expansion. The Pentagon pointed out the difficulty of integrating outdated militaries into NATO structures and stressed that the United States should be cautious about taking on any new defense commitments in Europe.

The Administration's internal debate crested in October 1993, shortly before my trip to Russia. At a White House Principals Committee meeting,[3] we decided to recommend the general concept of expanding

[2]As we deliberated about NATO's future within the Administration, academic specialists carried on a lively debate publicly. For a useful article that influenced my thinking, see Ronald Asmus, Richard Kugler, and F. Stephen Larrabee, "Building a New NATO," *Foreign Affairs* 72, no. 4 (Sept.–Oct. 1993): 28–40. Asmus is now a Deputy Assistant Secretary of State in the Bureau of European and Canadian Affairs, concentrating on NATO matters.

[3]Almost all major foreign policy issues were taken up by the Principals Committee, a consultative group chaired by the National Security Adviser and composed of

NATO, but to follow a sequential approach. The President accepted our recommendation. He believed that NATO expansion could be a driving force to integrate and unify Europe for the first time in modern history. This, he felt, could eliminate or reduce the risk of another war in Europe that might once again draw the United States into a deadly and costly conflagration, as had happened twice this century.

As the first step, we endorsed a proposal sculpted principally by General John Shalikashvili, Chairman of the Joint Chiefs of Staff. "General Shali," as he is affectionately known, is a magnificent officer whose prior assignment had been as Supreme Commander of NATO. His idea, known as the Partnership for Peace, would provide a means for building cooperation between NATO and all the former Warsaw Pact states, including Russia, that wished to participate. Each state would develop its own Partnership with NATO, participating in training exercises and consulting with the Alliance about military tactics and strategy. Participants would develop the standard operating procedures, habits of cooperation, and routines of consultation that are the core of an effective military alliance. The Partnership would be a way to enhance military-to-military relations between these nations without undertaking a commitment under Article V of the NATO Treaty to defend each nation's borders. Over time, the most successful Partnership members would be the prime candidates for NATO membership. The Partnership was seen as a way to begin integrating the most capable states into Alliance structures, as well as to provide a process by which the other prospective members could develop and modernize. The proposal struck the right balance, setting forth a gradual, transparent process of offering reform-minded nations a chance to develop a Partnership with NATO, holding out the prospect of full NATO membership, and not confronting Russia with an immediate fait accompli.[4]

As it developed, the Partnership exceeded even our most hopeful ex-

---

the Secretaries of State and Defense, the Director of the CIA, the Chairman of the Joint Chiefs, the U.S. Ambassador to the UN, and several other senior officials. Its meetings were held in the Situation Room, in the basement of the White House. Sometimes the President and Vice President attended. The usual formal product of a meeting was a set of recommendations to the President.

[4]For details of my initial discussions with Yeltsin on the idea, see Chapter 5. Thus far, the best account of this process is James Goldgeier's "NATO Enlargement: Anatomy of a Decision," *Washington Quarterly* 21, no. 1 (winter 1998): 85–102.

pectations. By creating links between NATO and non-member nations, it helped to prepare the way for expansion, providing participants with an incentive to modernize their armed forces and pursue democratic reforms. Ultimately, 26 non-NATO countries participated vigorously and made the program a success.

At the NATO ministerial meeting in Athens in June 1993, I had proposed a NATO summit, to be held in January 1994, which would bring the heads of government together for the first time since 1991. The decision for the President to travel abroad always involves questions of high policy and intricate scheduling, but after some last-minute telephone calls to the White House, I had obtained authority to make this summit proposal. I felt that President Clinton needed to put his imprint on NATO and European policy, and that the summit would provide the right forum for doing so.

My remarks at the NATO ministerial meeting in Brussels in December 1993 were a critical part of our strategy to make the summit successful.[5] I had to make the case that the program for the summit would measure up to the tasks of demonstrating NATO's relevance and of intensifying its nascent security relationship with the East. Moreover, since America had focused so much recent attention on such non-European issues as NAFTA and APEC, I felt it important to reaffirm publicly the importance of Europe to American foreign policy.

The themes I laid out in Brussels provided the foundation for the President's announcement of NATO expansion at the January 1994 summit meeting and established the outlines of our NATO policy during the next year. I posed the alternatives to my colleagues starkly: the Alliance had to choose whether to "embrace innovation or risk irrelevance." Stating that we needed to use the summit to "signal that we envision an evolutionary expansion of the Alliance," I outlined the details and attributes of the Partnership program.[6] I stressed that the Partnership was the be-

---

[5]Technically, this was a ministerial meeting of the North Atlantic Council (NAC), NATO's political governing council and the forum in which Alliance partners deliberate about NATO's policy direction. In the regular weekly meetings of the NAC, we were represented effectively by our Ambassador to NATO, Robert Hunter.

[6]The initial reaction from our NATO Allies about the program was positive. Hungary, the Czech Republic, Slovakia, and Poland—the so-called Visegrad states—

ginning of the process to expand NATO's membership. In two key sentences, I said, "Partnership is an important step in its own right. But it can also be a key step toward NATO membership."

This speech was also significant for something that was not directly involved with NATO but had much to do with U.S.-European relations. In the final section, I deliberately changed the subject to discuss the importance of successfully concluding the Uruguay Round of the GATT negotiations by the December 15 deadline. These negotiations were then under way across town at the European Community's offices. The day before the ministerial meeting, I had discussed the issue with Jacques Delors, the President of the EU Commission, and I had also stayed in regular contact with my friend Mickey Kantor, who as the President's Trade Representative was the lead U.S. negotiator on GATT. As I hinted in my statement, NATO and GATT were really two sides of the same coin—that coin being transatlantic security *and* prosperity. We could not compartmentalize these issues; how we handled our relations in one area would influence the other. I knew that this was an unusual if not unprecedented subject to raise at a NATO meeting, but I wanted our Alliance partners to know that we had no less interest in concluding the Uruguay Round than in reshaping the military Alliance.

The GATT negotiations were finished by the deadline, completing the "triple play" that included the NAFTA vote and the APEC summit meeting. Although Mickey Kantor deserves the lion's share of the credit for his skillful bargaining on GATT, he later generously credited me with "upping the ante" through my NATO intervention. By stressing GATT's importance in the NATO setting, we sent a signal as to how serious the United States was about completing GATT. We also sent a broader message that while our security commitments would remain unshakable, the United States would elevate the priority it attached to its economic interests. That priority would continue to be a hallmark of the Clinton presidency.

---

were disappointed that we had decided to delay expansion, but I was able to counter their disappointment by describing the benefits of the Partnership. Yeltsin strongly supported the Partnership idea, likely on the theory that it would obviate or at least delay NATO expansion. Support also came from other leaders in the former Soviet Union, as well as in Bulgaria, Romania, Albania, and the Baltics.

Strengthening the Atlantic Alliance Through a Partnership for Peace

Remarks at the North Atlantic Council Ministerial Meeting,

NATO Headquarters, Brussels, December 2, 1993

I am delighted to be with you for this very important meeting of the North Atlantic Council. First, let me pay tribute to our Secretary General. Manfred Woerner deserves tremendous credit for his leadership, determination and dedication. We are all in his debt. Let me add that I have valued the exchanges that I've had in recent weeks with many of my colleagues here today as we have approached this ministerial. Last June in Athens, on behalf of President Clinton, I proposed a NATO summit. Today, we must ensure that the Brussels summit that is just six weeks away is successful for our Alliance and for each of our member nations.

At the summit, President Clinton will articulate his vision of transatlantic security and prosperity—and the strong and unbreakable link between the United States and Europe. The President recognizes that American leadership remains indispensable. And he is determined that the United States will continue to provide that leadership because it is profoundly in the interest of both the United States and Europe to do so.

The security of our Alliance depends not only on our military capability. Security also depends fundamentally on our ability to consolidate democratic institutions, ensure respect for human rights, and sustain the hard march of economic reform to eventual prosperity. Each of these post–Cold War elements of security must advance—or none of them will. Western leaders in the late 1940s created the institutions that enabled Western Europe to rebuild and renew itself after the Second World War. Their foresight and fortitude and the steadfastness of their successors enabled our values to prevail in a long and bitter Cold War. And millions of people, for the first time in their lives, have the chance to enjoy political freedom and economic opportunity. We must resolve to secure and expand the blessings of peace that our predecessors did so much to achieve. We must help to fill the vacuum of insecurity and instability that has come with the demise of the Soviet empire. We must build the structures and the patterns of cooperation that will help to ensure the success of democracy and free markets in the East. We must move decisively beyond the age of confrontation in Europe when the balance of power was a poor substitute for a concert of free peoples. We must infuse this Alliance with the new vision and vitality that earned many of our distinguished predecessors the mantle of statesmanship.

We have many issues to decide. But the Alliance must also make an historic choice. That choice is whether to embrace innovation or risk irrelevance. We must adapt this Alliance to the new security challenges that confront Europe today. At the same time, we must strengthen the core political cooperation, security commitments and military capabilities that have kept the 16 strong and free. We must act to revitalize the Alliance's continued central role in European security and in the transatlantic partnership.

We all recognize that our most important summit task is to decide how the Atlantic Alliance will reach out to the East. Two years ago, we created the North Atlantic Cooperation Council—the NACC. With the Partnership for Peace, we can now deepen NATO's engagement with the East. We must demonstrate that the West is committed to helping Europe's new democracies address some of their most immediate security problems. At the same time, we should signal that we envision an evolutionary expansion of the Alliance. We should make it clear that, as a matter of principles, NATO is open to the admission of new members. We should extend an invitation to join the Partnership for Peace to all NACC states and other nations on whom we agree. Those who join will enter a much fuller relationship with NATO. The Partnership for Peace will provide a means for each state to develop a practical working relationship to NATO and determine what resources it wants to commit to that relationship. We envision defense cooperation developing in a broad range of fields.

The Partnership will be a military relationship but, like all of NATO's activities, it will have a strong political dimension. The Allies should provide all participants in the Partnership with a pledge of consultation in the event of threats to their security. And for partners once part of the communist world, this cooperation will help adapt defense structures to civilian control.

The Partnership will enhance regional stability. It will develop capabilities to meet contingencies, including crisis management, humanitar-

ian missions and peace-keeping. It will develop useful habits of cooperation. It will enable us to develop common military standards and procedures. Peace partners will train side-by-side with NATO members and
take part in joint exercises. To ensure operational effectiveness, the Partnership should have a planning group in Mons and should make full use
of the political and military institutions of NATO here in Brussels. Active partners will have permanent representatives to take part in the work
of these organizations when dealing with Partnership matters.

Our new partners should finance their own involvement, but some new
NATO resources will be necessary. There will be costs, but of a manage-
able size. The United States stands ready to contribute its share, and it is
essential that all Allies do the same. Let me be clear with respect to a very
important issue that the Partnership raises. The Partnership is an important step in its own right, but it can also be a key step toward NATO
membership. While many factors will enter into decisions about expanding NATO membership, active participation in Partnership activities will
help prepare countries to meet the obligations of membership.

NATO is not an alliance of convenience, but an alliance of commitment. Expanded membership must strengthen, not weaken the ability of
the Alliance to act.

The Partnership will maintain NATO's core purpose and capabilities.
The current military and political processes of the Alliance will continue
undiluted, but the Partnership will multiply the ability of the Alliance to
meet security needs.

I am pleased that the Partnership for Peace has received the active
support—and reflects the constructive suggestions—of every NATO
ally. The Alliance must understand that this Partnership represents a decisive commitment to become more fully engaged in security to the East.
This is an historic commitment that our leaders should be prepared to
make at the January summit. Today, we should continue our work to
make sure that next month NATO will take this decisive step to deepen
our security cooperation with our new Partners. We want the Partnership to begin functioning next year. Turning former adversaries into
partners is in the fundamental interest of every member of this Alliance.
We must seize this extraordinary opportunity—the opportunity that this
Alliance has worked so successfully to create.

A second summit objective I want to address is the need to strengthen
the evolving relationship between NATO and the Western European

Union. Previous American administrations were ambivalent about the development of a distinct European security capability. Today, the United States fully supports efforts to create a strong and effective European Security and Defense Identity. Such an identity is a natural element of European integration. It will make the European Union a more capable partner in the pursuit of our mutual interests.

The relationship between NATO and the WEU must be based on mutual trust and transparency. To work effectively and to avoid a costly duplication of defense resources, NATO should be prepared to offer the WEU the use of common NATO assets in the conduct of its operations. This would make WEU capabilities separable but not separate from the Atlantic Alliance. At the same time, as we have agreed, we would expect that the North Atlantic Council would consult on issues that affect the security of the Allies. And NATO should have full opportunity in those consultations to consider the appropriate response.

These NATO deliberations would not contemplate an Alliance veto over WEU actions. But the use of NATO common assets to support a WEU operation would clearly require a decision by the NAC. This approach would safeguard collective Alliance capabilities while supporting the development of the European Union.

A third summit objective should be adapting Allied military capabilities. We have made important progress in enabling NATO to support the international community's efforts to achieve a peaceful settlement in Bosnia. Building on this model, the United States has proposed the creation of Combined Joint Task Forces. We believe CJTF strikes the right balance. It would allow new flexibility for organizing peace-keeping and other tasks. It would enable NATO to take effective action in contingencies that do not evoke Article V of the North Atlantic Treaty. It would also enable the WEU to take autonomous actions with NATO support, when appropriate. And it would do all this while preserving the unique capabilities of the integrated command for collective defense requirements under Article V. The task force would be tailored in size, force mix and nationality for both NATO and non-NATO missions. The CJTF concept will strengthen existing command arrangements and make them more flexible. It will allow maximum use of limited resources. It will demonstrate that each of our countries is bearing its fair share of common responsibilities. And it will help ensure that NATO and WEU work as partners, not rivals, as their relationship evolves.

Finally, between now and the summit, we must also prepare the Alliance to meet other new challenges that have come in the wake of the Cold War. Most urgent is curbing the spread of weapons of mass destruction and the means of delivering them. This threat constitutes the arms control agenda of the 1990s. At the summit, we must make a fundamental Alliance commitment to combat proliferation. The most immediate task is to develop the overall policy framework to NATO efforts against proliferation. We envision a senior group at 16, with representatives of both foreign and defense ministers. NATO supports, but should not duplicate, non-proliferation efforts underway through other institutions and negotiations.

Our non-proliferation agenda should be consistent with our essential mission of protecting the security of our members. We must adapt Alliance military strategy and capabilities to deter the use of weapons of mass destruction and protect against their use. We must intensify our individual and collective efforts to isolate states that actively pose proliferation threats. I also want to comment on Bosnia, particularly the humanitarian situation. While we welcome the resumption of the peace negotiations, the most pressing fact is that winter has descended. The United States has therefore announced an additional contribution of $150 million to increase the food, winterization supplies, refugee assistance and medical aid reaching the people of Bosnia. We are prepared as part of this effort to double the number of U.S. flights in the Sarajevo airlift, double the amount of relief provided by air drops and begin airlifting supplies into Tuzla Airport if it can be opened. We call upon other governments and regional organizations to increase their commitments to help the people of Bosnia survive this winter.

Let me raise one final issue that is not on our agenda today but that each of our nations must also address. Last June at our Athens ministerial, I made a statement in this forum with respect to the Uruguay Round. Let me repeat that advancing transatlantic security requires us to focus not only on renewing the NATO Alliance but also on successfully concluding the GATT negotiations.

Our publics and parliaments understand that transatlantic relations cannot be overly compartmentalized—either substantively or institutionally. As great Allies and great powers, Europe and the United States share great responsibilities. We are partners in a community of shared values and interests. Our values and interests converge in this Alliance—

and they converge in a successful conclusion to the Uruguay Round. Through NATO and through GATT, we can reinforce transatlantic security and prosperity—and reaffirm the transatlantic partnership. We have the chance to construct the architecture of a better world. Since the end of the Second World War, together we have created and sustained a successful liberal trading order. That system has allowed our economies to grow and our people to prosper. Now we have an historic opportunity to open markets further, to the benefit of our nations on both sides of the Atlantic.

These are momentous weeks for the West. By December 15, we have the responsibility to come together and lift the global economy. On January 10, we have the responsibility to come together and renew the most successful Alliance in history. The United States and Europe share these responsibilities—and we must meet them.

Straight Talk with Japan

Japan has played an important role in my life at several points. As a young naval ensign, I was aboard ship in the Pacific when the atomic bombs were dropped on Hiroshima and Nagasaki in August 1945, bringing the war to a swift conclusion. Our ship rode out the typhoon that swept Tokyo Bay in September 1945, while on another ship in the bay, the historic peace treaty was signed by General Douglas MacArthur, to end World War II. When I went ashore, I was overwhelmed by the immense destruction in Tokyo and by the sad faces of the Japanese people, most of them too frightened to respond to our awkward attempts to show compassion.

Fast-forward to August 1961, when Japan was the site of my first diplomatic experience as I headed the U.S. team negotiating for a cotton textile agreement. Under Secretary of State George Ball had reached out to Los Angeles and brought me to Washington for a crash course in international trade and dealing with the textile lobby. Aided by the scholarly U.S. Ambassador to Japan, Edwin Reischauer, who had been a distinguished professor of Japanese studies at Harvard, I spent about a month in Tokyo engaged in intense, but eventually successful, negotiations. Follow-on assignments continued sporadically until 1965. In the 1980s, as Japan recovered to become the world's second-strongest economic power, I recruited a premier Japanese-practice group for our law firm, traveled several times to Japan, and represented a major American corporation as it tried to adapt its products and sales strategy to a rigidly structured Japanese market.

All of these experiences were important to me as Secretary of State. I was not a Japan expert in an academic or formal sense, but neither was I a complete novice.

With our new emphasis on economic statecraft, President Clinton was determined from the very beginning to improve our trading relationship with the Japanese. This not only was right for America's economy—whose businesses and workers suffered from tight Japanese markets—but was consistent with our overall foreign policy agenda of expanding economic relationships outside Europe. Our efforts to retool our relationship with Japan were plagued by the unusual instability of its government. During his first four years, President Clinton had to deal with five Prime Ministers (Kiichi Miyazawa, Morihiro Hosokawa, Tsutomu Hata, Tomiichi Murayama, and Ryutaro Hashimoto), while I had five different counterparts (Foreign Ministers Kabun Muto, Tsutomu Hata, Koji Kakizawa, Yohei Kono, and Yukihiko Ikeda). We repeatedly had the frustration of developing a good rapport with one official only to have a new face appear.

Although we immediately focused on trade concerns, we never lost sight of the broader stakes in this crucial bilateral relationship. Our security and political ties with Japan were basically sound, but we were worried that failure to address trade issues could lead over time to an erosion of U.S. domestic support for the relationship, including our security links. For that reason, we had to try to open Japan's markets and reduce its trade surplus. We knew that this effort would lead to some friction with Japan, and throughout the period of trade tensions—which dominated our relationship during the first two years of the Administration—we worked hard to bolster our other ties by pursuing security dialogues, cooperating on regional concerns, and promoting a common agenda on global issues.

In early 1993, President Clinton and Prime Minister Miyazawa were off to an excellent start when a somewhat embarrassing incident occurred. In a dinner meeting with Russian President Boris Yeltsin in Vancouver in April, Clinton made an offhand comment that the Japanese sometimes meant "no" when they said "yes." After the dinner, Yeltsin's translator left his notes on the table, and they found their way to the press. When this comment was reported, it created a mild uproar. However, with a skillful touch, Miyazawa deflated the flap by declaring that one of the favorite American songs in Japan was "Yes, We Have No Bananas." The issue promptly disappeared.

Miyazawa was soon ousted in a cabinet shake-up, and in the summer of 1993 his successor, reform Prime Minister Hosokawa, and President Clinton agreed to establish a formal dialogue to discuss areas of mutual cooperation. They entered into a Framework Agreement that called for both sides to address three areas: global issues (such as population, the environment, and disease), macroeconomic issues, and trade relations in certain sectors (such as telecommunications, auto parts, and medical equipment). The Clinton Administration committed to reducing the ballooning U.S. budget deficit and improving American competitiveness. Japan promised to reduce its massive trade surplus by boosting domestic demand and to open specified areas of its economy to more imports and greater foreign investment. Both governments also acknowledged a commitment to promote an open world trading system.

We had high hopes that the Framework Agreement was a major step in creating a U.S.-Japan relationship characterized by cooperation rather than competition. By early 1994, however, judging from Japan's conduct, the agreement might as well not have been signed. Japan's markets remained as closed as ever, and no serious attempt had been made to open them. Our frustrations with Japan's foot-dragging came to a head in February 1994, when Hosokawa visited Washington to meet with Clinton. In an intense day of discussions, while the rest of Washington remained paralyzed by a snowstorm, the two leaders spoke frankly about our differences but fell well short of resolution. In an unusual display of public candor, particularly for two close allies, the President and the Prime Minister announced that they could not agree. As things stood after these unproductive meetings, the Framework Agreement was a dying letter.

The month after the Hosokawa visit, I made my third trip to Japan in just over a year as Secretary of State. Quite clearly, our relationship was reeling. In both public and private meetings in Tokyo, I needed to deliver a firm statement about Japan's responsibilities under the Framework and to plan the next steps in the bilateral trade relationship. But my mandate also had to be a bit wider. As Secretary of State, it fell to me to frame our economic differences in the context of our broader strategic interests. Unlike an official concerned solely with economic or trade issues, such as the U.S. Trade Representative, I had to keep an eye on every aspect of our relationship with Japan.

That relationship is like a three-legged stool; our economic interaction, security partnership, and political cooperation on global matters should play mutually supportive roles. During the Cold War, however, the United States went out of its way to let each leg stand on its own, citing, for example, the need to maintain security and political ties even if economic differences lingered. Now, in an era in which the line between economic and military security has blurred, compartmentalizing these interests has become far more difficult.

Nevertheless, before tackling the economic issues, I wanted to use my trip to demonstrate publicly that our security ties with Japan remained strong. To that end, I led the first cabinet-level, or "2 + 2," meeting of the U.S.-Japan Security Consultative Committee (SCC). The SCC was designed to bring senior defense and diplomatic officials together to discuss military cooperation and regional security issues.[1] In this two-hour meeting, we had a wide-ranging and friendly discussion about many vital issues, including containing the North Korean threat, designing a theater defense system, and renewing Japanese Host Nation Support for U.S. military bases and personnel. In the Pacific theater, Japan played a pivotal role in providing support for American forces, which numbered about 100,000 (approximately as many as were stationed in Europe).

When it came time for me to meet with Hosokawa, I spoke frankly about economic issues. I told him that Japanese non-compliance with the Framework Agreement transcended the question of economic fairness, and had become one of trust. "This erosion of trust and confidence is more important than number, statistic, or percentage," I said. Buffeted by political infighting and probably knowing his days were numbered, Hosokawa was amazingly candid. "The Japanese political system is not

---

[1]The SCC was originally created by the 1960 U.S.-Japan Mutual Security Treaty, but until 1994, it only met below the cabinet level. We decided to raise the level of representation to convey the importance that both sides placed on maintaining close security ties. At the 2 + 2 level, the meetings would usually be led on the U.S. side by the Secretaries of State and Defense, and on the Japanese side by their counterparts. The Japanese Foreign Minister and I attended this first meeting, and the senior Defense representatives were Frank Wisner, then the Under Secretary of Defense for Policy, and General Aichi, the Japanese Defense Agency Director. The discussions begun here were instrumental in improving military cooperation between the United States and Japan. The SCC also helped to lay the groundwork for a September 1997 agreement on new mutual security guidelines that described arrangements for minesweeping in international waters, enforcing economic blockades, and sharing intelligence.

functioning as it should," he said. He conceded the need to reduce Japan's massive trade surplus, agreeing that the nation must demonstrate visible progress. Yet, he explained, there was considerable political resistance to reform: "In the economic area, there is a wall of bureaucrats resisting change that needs to be broken through. This will take great energy." Not long thereafter, Hosokawa was replaced by Socialist Party leader Murayama, the head of a weak coalition.

Given the stubborn resistance Hosokawa described, I used my March 11 speech before Keizai Doyukai, an association of Japanese business leaders, to send an unambiguous signal about the stakes of non-compliance with the Framework Agreement. In early drafts of the speech, we had somewhat danced around the disagreements at hand, implying differences rather than directly addressing them. I wanted to make our case explicitly rather than implicitly, reaching out to a wider Japanese audience, over the heads of the Tokyo bureaucracy. After some standard rhetoric stressing the importance of our bilateral ties, I moved directly to the economic issue, forthrightly explaining that our differences required "urgent repair" and that "we must not allow a situation to persist that might eventually erode public and political support for our overall relationship."

The heart of this speech was a point-by-point explication of Japan's failure to live up to its commitments. Intentionally written like a lawyer's brief, the middle section detailed the pledges that the Clinton Administration had fulfilled and flatly pointed out that Japanese commitments had not been, and must be, met. This was the same point I made privately with the Japanese leaders: they needed to take credible and concrete actions, and take them immediately.

The message was as blunt as any I delivered as Secretary of State. In a particularly tough section, I placed Japan's consistent reluctance to reform in a broader historical context: if Japan truly expected to be one of the world's leaders in the 21st century, I explained, it had to live up to its responsibilities. The speech stands out as unique not only because of its unvarnished message to a key ally, but also because the Secretary of State was venturing into territory often considered more appropriate for the Treasury Secretary or the U.S. Trade Representative. In doing so, I was reflecting one of the Administration's core principles, namely, the paramount importance of economic security to American foreign policy in the post–Cold War era.

The subsequent years of the President's first term saw great progress in U.S.-Japan relations. We not only reduced Japan's trade surplus but strengthened our security bonds and our overall bilateral relationship. Under the strong leadership of U.S. Trade Representative Mickey Kantor, we entered into more than 20 market access arrangements pursuant to the Framework Agreement, arrangements that included the difficult automotive, insurance, and semiconductor sectors. Foreign Ministers Kono and Ikeda joined me in taking responsibility for the overall relationship and intervening constructively in the trade talks at crucial points. And in 1996 we successfully updated the U.S.-Japan security treaties. However, the speech that follows came at a low point in the relationship, which explains its stern tone.

The U.S.-Japan Relationship: The Responsibility to Change

Address to the Japan Association of Corporate

Executives, Tokyo, March 11, 1994

Chairman Hayami, ladies and gentlemen: It is a great honor to address a group as distinguished as the Japan Association of Corporate Executives. I admire the creative role that your members played in making Japan one of the great economic success stories in history. I am personally familiar with Japan's remarkable economic accomplishments. I have been coming to Japan since 1961 when President Kennedy asked me, as a young lawyer, to represent the United States in trade negotiations. I have been an appreciative visitor many times since.

When I am abroad now, I spend most of my time meeting other diplomats. In those sessions, we often resort to specialized language. But on this visit, I wanted to address a different audience and to deliver a message that is straightforward and clear. I am here today to speak to you as business leaders and as citizens of Japan. As President Clinton told Prime Minister Hosokawa last month in Washington, "no relationship in the world is more important today" than the one between the United States and Japan. At a time of global and domestic change, it is a relationship that endures because of political, security, and cultural bonds that are unbreakable. The United States and Japan have the two largest economies in the world. We are bound by a solemn treaty alliance. We are a force for security and stability in the Pacific. We defend democracy and support sustainable development around the world. In each of these arenas, we are called upon to lead. The character of our leadership will help to determine how secure, how free, and how prosperous the world will be.

In his address at Waseda University last July, President Clinton called on Japan to join the United States in building a "New Pacific Community" based on "shared strength, shared prosperity, and a shared commitment to democratic values." Constructing that Community will require a vigorous partnership between the United States and Japan. And, as the President said, it also will require "both our nations to lead and both our nations to change." It is with a clear understanding of how much is at stake that I will address the future of the U.S.-Japan partnership. I will focus on economics and trade first because it is our economic relationship that requires urgent repair.

One month ago today, President Clinton and Prime Minister Hosokawa met in Washington. Their discussions underscored the strength of the security and political ties between us. But the impasse in the Framework negotiations that our governments launched last year also revealed that we still need a better balance in our overall relationship. The United States is determined to put its economic relationship with Japan on the same constructive and responsible foundation on which our diplomatic and security partnership rests.

The outcome on February 11 was without precedent. For the first time, an American President and a Japanese Prime Minister said in public that they could not agree in private. Both the President and the Prime Minister made a deliberate decision not to paper over our differences. The acknowledgment of that outcome was a welcome sign of a new candor in our relationship. But that outcome also represented a failure to carry out the Framework Agreement that our two nations had reached last July.

For the world's two largest economies, agreeing to disagree is not good enough. Acknowledging our economic differences must be a starting point for finally resolving them.

Our relationship has always been more than the sum of its parts. Last month, we pledged not to let our disagreements over the Framework interfere with our continued cooperation in other vital areas. But we must not allow a situation to persist that might eventually erode public and political support for our overall relationship. When we signed the Framework Agreement last July, we saw it as a major step toward change. The Agreement represents a common understanding of our shared responsibilities and the commitments we made to the world. We pledged jointly "to promote global growth, open markets, and a vital world trading system." Each government also made individual commitments.

For its part, the United States promised to reduce its budget deficits and improve its competitiveness. And we pledged to keep our markets open. It is beyond argument that the United States has kept these commitments, and the result has been strong growth and new jobs.

For more than a decade, Japan and the other G-7 countries urged America to exercise greater fiscal discipline. You were right. The American people elected President Clinton, in part, to cut the budget deficit—and he has. After a tough fight in Congress last summer, we passed a bold deficit-reduction program. Our deficit is projected to shrink for the third year in a row, the first time that has happened in more than four decades.

We are also honoring our commitment to improve American competitiveness. We are working to cut health care costs, encourage new technology, and improve education and training. In industry after industry—from autos to steel to computers—our private sector is becoming more productive and competitive. Quality is unquestionably up; costs are down. We are taking responsibility for our economic problems. We are not blaming others.

For its part in the Framework, the Government of Japan also made significant commitments. Japan promised to give a strong and sustained boost to its domestic demand in order to significantly reduce its current account surplus. Japan also committed to increase market access for foreign goods and services and to open specified sectors of its economy to more imports and greater foreign investment. These commitments have not been met.

First, Japan's trade surplus with the United States is increasing, reaching a record $59 billion in 1993. Moreover, Japan's imbalances span the globe. Japan's surpluses with the European Union and with its Asian trading partners have nearly doubled since 1990. Given Japan's present policies, few are forecasting "the highly significant decrease" in Japan's current account surplus called for in the Framework.

Second, a reduction in Japan's current account surplus and a sustained, significant increase in Japan's global imports will depend in large part on macroeconomic policies that stimulate demand in Japan. The recent stimulus packages, including the new budget announced last month, are insufficient to produce sustained, demand-led growth.

Third, Japan has pledged sectoral agreements that will produce "tangible results" in certain areas. But Japan has been unwilling to reach agreements on specific steps to open markets in the priority sectors of insurance, government procurement, and autos and auto parts. Our two governments agreed in the Framework to use "objective criteria" to evaluate progress in order to determine if the agreements are succeeding in opening markets. But Japan has declined to provide realistic ways to measure progress to ensure that any such agreements are working. I came to Japan to make sure our message is understood: Your government needs to take firm action to honor the commitments it made in the Framework Agreement. The agreement represents commitments made voluntarily by Japan to its most important partner and ally. Trust and confidence are important between good friends.

We do not seek new agreements for their own sake. We have had a decade of agreements—and still many Japanese markets remain closed to American products and services that are popular and competitive around the globe.

Our objectives are simple: to open markets and to promote global growth. To advance those objectives, Japan needs to take concrete and credible actions, and to take them now. The United States continues to champion free trade. In his first year in office, President Clinton has registered the most significant accomplishments on behalf of free trade and global growth of any U.S. President in nearly half a century.

President Clinton pushed to conclude the Uruguay Round, the most far-reaching trade agreement in history. Against the odds, and at great political risk, he won passage of the North American Free Trade Agreement. And he took an important initiative to deepen our engagement in this dynamic region when he hosted, in Seattle, the first-ever meeting of leaders from the Asia-Pacific Economic Cooperation forum.

As the President has said, America wants to compete in the world, not retreat from it. The United States remains firmly committed to free trade in theory and in practice. And we expect the same of other nations. President Clinton's decision last week to reinstate the Super 301 provision of our trade law must be seen in this light. The President's purpose was to provide a basis to open foreign markets, not to close ours. Super 301 is meant to supplement, not supplant, our bilateral trade negotiations and our commitment to multilateral remedies. It is a flexible, orderly, and transparent process that helps to identify unfair trade practices and eliminate them in ways consistent with the GATT. Nobody wants a trade war. We want trade opportunities—for the United States, for Japan, and for the world.

Last July's Framework commitments were made for Japan's benefit as well as that of the United States and other nations. By boosting domestic demand, opening markets, welcoming foreign investment, and deregulating its economy, Japan would create business opportunities for Japanese as well as foreign companies. It would spur innovation and improve productivity. Fulfilling the Framework commitments would expand choices and lower prices for Japanese consumers and businesses. Joint American and Japanese studies show that consumers in Japan spend, on average, 40% more than Americans for the goods they buy. For example, I am sure that you have noticed prices for personal and office computers in Japan are coming down as competitive American firms are able to enter the Japanese market. Open markets not only help lower prices, they also fuel growth. Ultimately, only Japanese consumers, not the rest of the world, can pull Japan out of recession. Meeting the Framework commitments also would allow Japan's people to enjoy more fully the benefits of their hard work in an even more innovative and vibrant society. The aspirations of the Japanese people are converging with those of people in other advanced industrial nations. Amid all the initiatives, all the negotiations, and all the agreements, let us be clear about the benefits we seek: more choices for our citizens, better jobs, and greater rewards for our workers.

Almost eight years ago, the ground-breaking Maekawa Report called for a more open economy and a smaller trade surplus. Since that report was issued, the world has seen remarkable change. The Berlin Wall fell; the Soviet Union disintegrated; South Africa abolished apartheid; Israel and the Palestinians made an historic breakthrough for peace. We also have seen your nation assume ever-greater responsibilities for promoting security and development around the globe.

Still, Japan's unbalanced economic relationship with the world persists. Japan's surpluses with the United States, Europe, and Asia are now a major asymmetry in the global economy. At the same time, the share of income in Japan devoted to consumption has actually fallen.

In addition, Japan still has the lowest rate of foreign direct investment among the world's advanced economies. While the United States has 29% of the world's foreign direct investment and the European Union has 39%, Japan has less than 1%. This shows that, despite its spectacular export performance, Japan has a long way to go to become fully integrated into the global economy.

Your organization has been a pioneering advocate for economic reform. As Mr. Hayami has said, Japan's economic challenge today remains fundamentally the same as that described in the Maekawa Report. The study you issued last November concluded that such a course would boost Japan's economy and lift its living standards. Earlier this week, Mr. Hayami conveyed to the Prime Minister a new report calling for open markets and expanded domestic demand. I expect that your report will be taken very seriously.

Today, many Japanese are voicing a desire for reform. Whether business leaders such as yourselves, or political leaders, or consumers, they are supporting change. The demand for reform has inspired—and elected—a new generation of leaders. Prime Minister Hosokawa has shown a commitment and determination to change by reforming Japan's political system, opening its construction and rice markets, and seeking to deregulate the economy. We know he is committed to further economic change and openness. We commend him, and we encourage him to push ahead.

As Japan assumes the global leadership role it has earned, we can begin to build a new Pacific future in which open societies are linked by shared values and open markets. To widen the circle of democracy and prosperity in the region, we also must strengthen the circle of security and stability. Whatever the economic challenges we must overcome— and they are great—our security alliance will remain a solid anchor of our relationship.

President Clinton is reinforcing America's security engagement in the region. During his trip to Asia last July, he outlined four priorities for Asia-Pacific security. Our first priority is a continued American military commitment, based upon our treaty alliances with Japan, South Korea, Australia, Thailand, and the Philippines. We will maintain a substantial forward-deployed presence in the Asia-Pacific as the linchpin of that commitment. We will soon have as many military personnel stationed in East Asia as in Europe.

Yesterday, the Under Secretary of Defense and I met with your Prime Minister and Foreign Minister to discuss bilateral and regional security issues. This morning, we convened a meeting of the Security Consultative Committee, the first ever at this level, to consider ways of further strengthening our security partnership.

Another priority is to curb the proliferation of weapons of mass destruction. North Korea's nuclear program is a threat to regional stability and our common goal of non-proliferation. With Japan's support, and working closely with the Republic of Korea, we have begun discussions with the North Koreans to help resolve the nuclear issue. Although we have made some progress, the challenge ahead remains very great.

We recognize that the promotion of democracy enhances our security because democratic nations rarely start wars or threaten their neighbors. The United States and Japan have worked together to help the people of one of Asia's most tortured countries, Cambodia, shape a free society. Yesterday, I joined your Foreign Minister at the International Conference on the Reconstruction of Cambodia as we reaffirmed our commitment to help Cambodia rebuild. Our joint efforts demonstrate that even the most bitter conflicts can be resolved by patient diplomacy and determined peacemaking. The Cambodian people demonstrated another truth when they voted last May: The demand for liberty is a human instinct, not a Western export. Tonight I travel to Beijing, where I will reiterate that overall significant progress on human rights remains necessary if I am to recommend the renewal of most-favored-nation trade status for China. What we seek in China should not be regarded as extraordinary. What we seek is no more than the recognition of the most basic, universally recognized human rights. And human rights is a key issue in our relations with several other Asian countries, including Vietnam and Burma. We look forward to joining Japan, East Asia's largest democracy, in a constructive approach toward each of these nations.

Our cooperation on global issues such as the environment and population is also strong and growing. We are working together to develop advanced transportation and environmental technologies. Last month, President Clinton and Prime Minister Hosokawa agreed, as part of the common global agenda of the Framework, to coordinate a $12 billion assistance program to stem population growth and to prevent AIDS in developing countries. Yesterday I recommended to your government that we continue and expand these efforts.

These many examples of our diplomatic and security cooperation point to the deep and abiding strength of our bilateral relationship. They demonstrate our shared determination to promote global peace and prosperity. Japan should continue to assume greater responsibilities in the post–Cold War world. That is why the United States strongly supports a permanent seat for Japan on the UN Security Council.

I was born in 1925, just before the start of the Showa Era. I have seen Japan prosper. I have seen the relationship between our nations mature. As we approach the next century, in the early years of the Heisei Era, I am confident that we will continue to prosper and mature. But I hope my years give me the perspective to say this: For our overall relationship to improve, we must change. The vitality of our partnership depends on our capacity to adapt to a changing world. Our security and diplomatic partnership is already evolving to meet new challenges. Now our economic partnership must adapt as well.

I have assumed that I could speak openly today about our economic differences precisely because our broader relationship continues to be so secure. We cannot realize the full potential of our relationship unless we have harmony and strength among all its elements. We must make our economic and trade links as mutually beneficial as our political and security bonds.

I acknowledge that there are some who are pessimistic about the future of our partnership. I want you to know that I am not one of them. I am optimistic that we will meet our responsibility to change.

As we move ahead, I am confident we will sustain the maturity that has developed in our relations. But that maturity also means taking responsibility for our respective parts of the problem and taking action to repair them. We cannot let political deadlock, or bureaucratic inertia, or outdated thinking stand in the way. If together we meet this test of history, our two nations will be far better placed to meet the regional and global challenges of the 21st century. The world looks to us for leadership. As the world's two largest economies, we share great responsibilities: to build a better future for the Japanese people, for the American people, and for the world. We must accept these responsibilities.

Thank you very much.

China: A Decision to Engage

In its first 16 months in office, the Clinton Administration had moved on several fronts to bring Asia to the center of American foreign policy, heading in the direction of what President Clinton referred to as the New Pacific Community. With the 1993 U.S.-Japan Framework Agreement, we had laid plans to improve bilateral economic relations, even as we worked to strengthen our other, positive ties. Although the initial Japanese performance under the Agreement was disappointing, I still felt that overall things were moving in the right direction. We had also continued to strengthen relations with South Korea and worked intensively to handle the most immediate regional security threat, North Korea. And, with the historic November 1993 APEC summit in Seattle, the President had set a bold course for regional integration and American engagement.

Notwithstanding such progress, another important challenge we faced in Asia proved daunting: China. During the 1992 presidential campaign, Governor Clinton had sharply criticized the Bush Administration for being too "soft" on the Chinese by refusing to use American leverage to improve China's sordid human rights record. Most-favored-nation (MFN) status, the core of U.S. trade relations with China, had remained in place despite the Tiananmen Square debacle, the repression of Tibet, and the continued jailing of dissidents. In perhaps the toughest foreign policy rhetoric of the campaign, Clinton had chastised Bush for dealing far too lightly with the "butchers of Beijing."

Such campaign statements colored our early decision-making toward

China. Given the bright line candidate Clinton had drawn, we were, to a certain extent, boxed in on the issue. To maintain credibility, we had to get tougher with Beijing. This was an important consideration during the first half of 1993, when we began to evaluate whether to renew MFN, which can be more accurately described as the normal trading relations that we have with virtually all nations in the world.

After much deliberation, we decided that rather than revoke MFN outright—which many in the Administration and on Capitol Hill were prepared to do—we should structure our policy to provide China with an incentive to improve human rights. In a May 1993 executive order, the President set specific terms for future MFN renewal that reflected his campaign commitments, explicitly linking U.S. trade relations to human rights progress. The order called for China to loosen emigration restrictions and curb the use of prison labor. It also stressed that China should make "overall, significant progress" in such areas as adhering to the Universal Declaration of Human Rights, releasing political prisoners, protecting Tibet's distinctive religious and cultural heritage, ensuring humane treatment of prisoners, and permitting international radio and television broadcasts into its territory. With these conditions, we believed we had set the bar high enough to maintain credibility but low enough to make realistic progress. We sought, in brief, to bring about some genuine improvement, but in a way that would not force us to revoke MFN in June 1994, when we would reassess our policy.

Although we continued to develop other areas of the U.S.-Chinese relationship and opened a dialogue with the senior Chinese leadership, it was impossible to step out of the shadow cast by MFN and human rights. As the June 1994 deadline approached, this shadow only darkened. The Chinese were making some modest progress—releasing a few dissidents, proceeding with minor prison reform, and opening talks with the Red Cross—but not nearly enough to meet the standards we had announced. The pivotal point in developing my own position on these issues was the trip I made to Beijing on March 12–14, 1994. This visit proved as frustrating as any I made as Secretary of State.

"My first day in Beijing mirrored the mood of the week preceding my arrival—rough, somber, sometimes bordering on the insolent." This statement, the first sentence of my first report to the President from Beijing, efficiently summarizes the tense atmosphere surrounding the trip.

Just days before, the Chinese leadership had "welcomed" me with a new crackdown, rounding up several prominent dissidents. The Chinese were particularly angry that John Shattuck, our Assistant Secretary for Human Rights, had met with the dissident Wei Jingsheng a short time earlier.[1] We interpreted the latest crackdown as a direct response to that meeting. At a stopover in Australia en route to Beijing, my top advisers and I discussed canceling my trip in protest. We decided it would be more effective to tell the Chinese face-to-face that we disapproved of their actions and to seek to move ahead with our overall relationship. Even before reaching Beijing, I signaled my displeasure to both the Chinese and our domestic audience, remarking to the press that I was concerned that China was "going in the wrong direction."

The Chinese leadership heard this message and registered their own displeasure in response. On the eve of my arrival, they arrested two more Shanghai activists, and detained two American journalists for six hours of interrogation. They also abruptly delayed my scheduled meeting with President Jiang Zemin and intensified their tough public rhetoric.

Of my private meetings, the first day was undoubtedly the worst. I reported to President Clinton that it was a "rocky, foreboding beginning," and that unless there was improvement soon, I might have to consider cutting short my trip. In meetings with Premier Li Peng and Foreign Minister Qian Qichen, I gave a detailed presentation outlining our mutual interests, goals, and concerns. I didn't pull any punches on human rights, explaining that the President and I were "deeply disturbed" by the latest events. Given these problems, I told them, MFN was in serious jeopardy. The Chinese were not impressed, sardonically pointing to our own domestic "rights" problems (Li Peng explicitly referred to the 1991 Los Angeles riots, presumably for my benefit) and explaining that they were fully prepared for MFN revocation. Li Peng told me at one point that while President Nixon and his Secretary of State Henry Kissinger were credited for opening U.S.-Chinese relations, President Clinton and I could be blamed for "losing" China.

The atmosphere improved a bit the next day, although there was still no substantive movement on any issue. When I was received by President Jiang Zemin, he gave one of his classic diplomatic performances,

[1]Wei Jingsheng was incarcerated again in 1994. In late 1997, he was released to travel for medical treatment in the United States, where he remains.

which combined Chinese poetry, Confucian sayings, aphorisms, and comments on American speeches and personalities. In this monologue, Jiang elliptically signaled a willingness to move beyond our recent disputes ("Without fighting, two people cannot become friends") and stressed that we should seek to improve relations gradually ("If one tries to eat too much one cannot digest it"). Overall, I found the Chinese President somewhat upbeat; as I told President Clinton, "after having been roughed up on the first day by the 'bad cop' Premier Li Peng, I was given amiable treatment by the 'good cop.'"

The trip ended on a more hopeful note. In my final meeting on March 14, Foreign Minister Qian abandoned the rather hostile pose he had struck two days before. In many ways, the trip followed the plot of a three-act play, one that diplomats often encountered in the Middle Kingdom. The first act featured a rough atmosphere and stern exchanges with the Premier and Foreign Minister, while the second found President Jiang emitting a friendlier tone, albeit without specifics. The third and final act, capped by my session with Qian, offered some substantive concessions (such as the signing of a new agreement on prison labor), with some reason to expect more.[2]

Despite this relatively positive finale, I boarded the plane for home with the distinct impression that our policy of influencing Chinese behavior through MFN conditions would be difficult to sustain. While I still hoped to find a way to use economic leverage to improve human rights enforcement, it was clear that the threat to revoke MFN was not having its desired effect, at least in the short term. Moreover, within the Administration, the consensus for using MFN as a tool had frayed. The key economic agencies—Treasury, Commerce, the Trade Representative, Agriculture—were openly unhappy with our policy, and it was clear they would fight against using MFN in this way. Even the President's own enthusiasm had waned in light of widespread business opposition.[3] There was no doubt

---

[2]This trip was the subject of negative reviews in the U.S. press. Many commentators argued that given the results, I never should have gone to Beijing. I firmly stood by my decision to proceed with the visit; in my view, it is much better to engage than to isolate, and publicly snubbing Beijing would have been a grave error. I responded to the critics in a *Washington Post* op-ed piece, "My Trip to Beijing Was Necessary," Mar. 22, 1994.

[3]I also had experienced firsthand the business community's firm opposition to revoking MFN. In Beijing I had had breakfast with about 150 members of the

that the costs of revoking MFN would be high. In addition to chilling the vital relationship with China, revocation would hurt innocent bystanders like Hong Kong. Undoubtedly the Chinese would find satisfaction in our failure to follow through on our threats to revoke, but this was not a sufficient reason to pursue a policy that had proved futile. Adding it all up, I reluctantly concluded that it had become necessary to change our policy. I recommended to the President that the United States renew MFN.

My May 27 speech before the Asia Society in New York City was framed by the MFN renewal, which President Clinton had announced the day before. The main purpose of the speech was to explain this decision, stressing the theme of engaging China to promote change. This engagement theme targeted not only China, but all of our interests in Asia. On this latter point, I sought to build on past statements—such as my addresses in Seattle in November 1993 and in Tokyo in March 1994 (Chapters 7 and 9)—to paint the future of U.S.-Asian relations as the New Pacific Community. I also referred to our continuing efforts to build regional architecture as part of this community—the Association of Southeast Asian Nations (ASEAN) Regional Forum on the security side and APEC on the economic front.

For obvious reasons, we labored over the MFN section of the speech intensely; in many ways, what I said about MFN was a speech within a speech. I wanted to take this opportunity to expand on the President's announcement, placing the decision in its broader strategic context and setting a course for future policy. Human rights remained important to this Administration, and I needed to explain how a more comprehensive, finely nuanced strategy of engagement would be more likely to produce results than the blunt instrument of MFN revocation.

My intention was not to sugarcoat our change of direction. We had shifted our policy, and we needed to be frank about that decision. Although China had made limited progress in some areas of human rights, I said, I could "neither invent nor inflate China's performance." Pretending there was much progress where there was little—which sometimes happens in diplomatic discourse—was untenable given the circumstances. Any attempt at doing this would have undermined our credibil-

---

American Chamber of Commerce, which subsequently issued a statement criticizing our MFN–human rights linkage as "well-intentioned but ill-considered."

ity, not only at home, but in Beijing and Asia more generally. The main point was that our earlier approach of using economic pressure to improve human rights had proved insufficient: "Linking human rights to MFN has taken us as far as it can," I said.

However candid my remarks were about our own policy shift, I did not let the Chinese off the hook. I stressed that we would continue to focus intensely on their human rights problems, highlighting areas in which they needed reform. In a carefully planned remark, I quoted Chinese dissident Wei Jingsheng in saying that political democracy—China's "Fifth Modernization"—must accompany economic liberalization. I knew that citing a figure like Wei would send an unmistakable signal to the Chinese that they would not like—and frankly, that was my intention.

The speech also focused briefly on our two other critical regional concerns: Japan and North Korea. On Japan, I reiterated the importance of improving economic relations along the lines of the Framework Agreement. Negotiations had proceeded since my visit to Tokyo in March, although Japan still had to do more to widen market access and increase domestic demand. On North Korea, the most urgent regional security problem, I set forth very clearly a carrot-and-stick approach. I renewed my call for negotiations, along with stressing our firm resolve to take "sterner measures" if North Korea refused to cooperate.

China MFN, Japan, and North Korea were the most immediate concerns we had in Asia. In this sense, the speech established a road map for our regional policy during the months ahead. In the context of these specific problems, it highlighted our overarching strategy of asserting leadership through engagement with the key powers.

●

America and the Asia-Pacific Future

Address to the Asia Society, New York City, May 27, 1994

It is a privilege to speak to America's preeminent organization dedicated to forging links across the Pacific.

We are joined in a common endeavor: to help build, with our partners and friends, a New Pacific Community. Our engagement in Asia is essential to the security and well-being of the American people, as well as our friends in the region. Over the last 16 months, we have moved the Asia-Pacific region to the center of America's foreign policy agenda. And we have demonstrated to our Asian partners that the United States will exercise its pivotal leadership role in the Asia-Pacific region. The President has articulated a broad vision and backed it up with important initiatives: hosting the APEC leaders meeting last November in Seattle; promoting regional security dialogues including Vietnam, Russia, and China for the first time; launching a set of framework talks with Japan to revitalize our economic relationship; and staunchly supporting the emergence of a democratic Cambodia. We have also maintained our forward-deployed military presence—a key to the region's strategic stability and a foundation for its continued economic success.

This week's headlines dramatically illustrate our commitment to comprehensive engagement in Asia and the building of a New Pacific Community. We have agreed with Japan to move forward with negotiations on the Framework Agreement. We have proposed a third round of negotiations on the nuclear issue with North Korea. We agreed with Vietnam to establish liaison offices in Hanoi and Washington, creating a stronger foundation to pursue the fullest possible accounting for Americans missing in action. And yesterday, of course, the President made a crucial decision concerning our policy toward China.

Each of the week's developments is significant in its own right, but they should not be viewed in isolation. The confluence of these major developments reflects the multiple strands of our broad engagement in Asia. Our approach is attuned to the complexities of this dynamic region.

The stability of the Asia-Pacific region is a vital American interest. For 50 years, we have understood that the emergence of a dominant hostile power in Asia would threaten important U.S. allies and, ultimately, America itself. Instability and conflict in Asia would undermine prospects for global economic growth, threaten democracies, and encourage proliferation of weapons of mass destruction.

In the last half century, tens of thousands of Americans have died in defense of our interests in Asia. We have built strong alliances with Japan, South Korea, Australia, the Philippines, and Thailand—a democratic core that provides a firm basis for deterring aggression. Thirty-seven thousand U.S. troops bravely stand watch at Korea's 38th parallel—the world's most dangerous fault line.

America's long-standing security ties to the region are matched by our exploding economic and cultural links. Asia has the world's fastest-growing economies. More than 40% of American trade is with Asia, supporting almost 2.5 million U.S. jobs. And millions of Asian-Americans retain a special interest in their ancestral homelands.

All Americans also have a stake in supporting democracy and human rights in Asia. We do so because it is consistent with our values as a people and our interests as a nation. States that respect the rule of law at home are more likely to observe the rule of international law abroad, and they are less likely to practice terrorism or to push refugees across borders.

Our commitment to democracy and human rights is neither occidental nor accidental. We are not imposing an American model; we are supporting a universal impulse for freedom. Last year, that impulse inspired the people of Cambodia, where farmers, monks, and former soldiers risked violence to vote. These authentic voices of Asia are not embracing an alien creed. They are asserting their dignity as human beings.

I believe that history is on the side of freedom. There is a powerful trend toward open markets and open societies. Economic development depends upon the free flow of information; computers are the new vehicles of political expression. The software of freedom will, ultimately, prevail over the hardware of repression.

Asia, today, is in the midst of a remarkable transformation. There is a growing network of constructive relations among most of the region's key states; explosive economic growth; expanding human freedom; and new efforts to foster cooperation on economic and security issues. These achievements can be attributed to the skill, industry, and determination of the peoples of the region. But American engagement can make an even brighter future possible. Our involvement is essential to regional peace, prosperity, and the promotion of freedom. Our forward-deployed military presence is crucial to a stable regional balance of power. Our lack of imperial ambition makes us a trusted partner. Our technology, capital, and huge market make us a magnet for Asia's economies. And the universal values we embody—freedom, democracy, and the rule of law—make us a beacon for all the peoples of the region.

Virtually all Asian countries welcome and urge our active involvement. They understand that the failure of the United States to remain engaged could threaten these bright prospects, harming their interests and our own. On three immediate issues, urgent engagement by the United States is clearly central: China's evolution, North Korea's nuclear program, and improving our economic relations with Japan. How each question is resolved will directly affect the security and prosperity of the United States.

As much as any other single factor, China's political, economic, and social transformation will determine whether Asia fulfills its great promise. As you know, the President announced yesterday that the United States will renew China's most-favored-nation trading status while pursuing a broad strategy to promote human rights in China.

The President's decision reflects a comprehensive U.S. strategy of engagement and leadership in the Asia-Pacific. It aims to integrate China into the global community, and not to shut it out. It encourages Chinese cooperation in building a new regional and international order based upon peace and security. And it supports the peaceful development of a more democratic and humane society. Our relationship with China is important to all Americans. China possesses the world's largest army, a nuclear arsenal, and, not insignificantly, a veto in the UN Security Council. The United States and China share a compelling interest in a stable and secure Asia and a nuclear-free Korean Peninsula. China can contribute significantly and responsibly to global issues such as environmental protection and drug trafficking. China has the world's fastest-growing and third-largest economy. More than 150,000 American jobs are supported by U.S. exports to China, a figure that will grow in the years ahead.

When President Clinton took office, the broad consensus on our China policy that had prevailed for nearly two decades no longer existed. Last year, the President restored that consensus with an executive order that enjoyed solid bipartisan support. Since then, we have placed human rights firmly on the agenda with China, while working constructively to address other shared concerns.

The executive order and our strategy of diplomatic engagement have achieved positive results. We have established a genuine human rights dialogue with China. And China has fulfilled the mandatory conditions for MFN renewal, namely those relating to emigration and prison labor exports.

With respect to the executive order's five other criteria, the gains China has made did not constitute the "overall significant progress" contemplated by the order. Months ago I pledged that in making my recommendation to the President, I would neither invent nor inflate China's performance. I have not. Although there have been some gains, serious human rights abuses continue in China. These include the arrest and detention of those who peacefully voice their opinions, restrictions on religious freedom, and religious and cultural repression in Tibet.

The President made the correct decision last year in issuing the executive order. A number of Chinese dissidents are free today in part because of the pressure we have exerted. But as the President said yesterday, linking human rights to MFN has taken us as far as it can. It is not likely to yield more progress on human rights.

China is no longer an isolated nation. Today, millions of Chinese are exposed to Western radio and television. Millions are engaged in trade with other nations in a growing and dynamic private sector. This is a trend that must be encouraged. Few believe that a complete revocation of MFN would improve China's human rights record. We must intensify and broaden our engagement with China if we want to promote change.

Let me make clear that we are not relying on the invisible hand of economics alone to bring about human rights progress. Economic freedom may promote political freedom, but it is not by itself sufficient. That is why the President announced a vigorous new program to advance human rights and democracy in China.

We will work with U.S. business leaders to develop voluntary principles to improve working conditions. We will expand international broadcasting to China through the Voice of America and Radio Free Asia. We will make it a practice to meet with a broad spectrum of Chinese citizens, and to support and work with emerging non-governmental organizations. We will engage other nations and the UN in our efforts to advance human rights. We will maintain the economic sanctions we imposed after the Tiananmen massacre. And we will ban import of munitions from China because of the absence of "overall significant progress" on human rights. Almost a million cheap, semiautomatic rifles came into the United States last year from China. The President's policy will keep them out. We have focused a brighter spotlight on human rights practices in China. That scrutiny will continue, and our human rights dialogue with China will intensify.

Repression is not a cure for instability. In the long run, political democracy—what Wei Jingsheng has referred to as China's "Fifth Modernization"—must accompany economic democracy if China's great experiment is to succeed.

I am convinced our strategy of comprehensive engagement offers the best chance to influence China's development. In that way, we will advance our security, our prosperity, and our values.

The Asia-Pacific's most urgent security problem—and one on which we are working with the Chinese Government—is the North Korean nuclear program. Pyongyang's quest for nuclear weapons poses multiple dangers: It directly threatens the security of key U.S. allies; it dramatically increases the likelihood of a destabilizing nuclear arms race in Asia; and it raises the specter of the spread of nuclear materials to rogue regimes like Iran.

Working with the international community, our objective has been to halt and reverse North Korea's nuclear program and create the conditions for a stable North East Asia in the years ahead. Together with our South Korean and Japanese allies, and with the support of China and other countries of the region, we have proposed that North Korea join us in a broad and thorough discussion of outstanding issues between us. These discussions would offer the prospect of resolving the nuclear issue as part of a process of improving economic and political contacts and moving us to a more normal bilateral relationship. We have developed a strong consensus behind our efforts to achieve a peaceful settlement of the nuclear issue. If North Korea rejects these negotiations, our consensus-building strategy will strengthen our ability to mobilize the international community to take sterner measures if we have to move down that road. That path—international sanctions—condemns North Korea to continued isolation, economic hardship, and pariah status. That would prevent the people of North Korea from reaping the benefits of the dramatic economic progress underway in Asia.

Meanwhile, U.S. forces stand shoulder-to-shoulder with those of our ally, South Korea, to deter and defeat any aggression by the North. Confrontation is emphatically not our preferred path. If North Korea renounces a nuclear future and does not otherwise undermine peace in Northeast Asia, it has nothing to fear from us or from South Korea. Indeed, it has much to gain from participation in the community of nations.

Our efforts on North Korea underscore once again how critical U.S.-

Japan relations remain for ensuring stability and security in the Asia-Pacific region. Our partnership formed the core of U.S. efforts to combat Soviet expansionism in Asia during the Cold War. Today, that partnership also stands at the center of our efforts to address the challenges and dangers of the post–Cold War era.

Our military alliance is stronger than ever. We have worked together to build democracy in Cambodia. We are cooperating to expand economic linkages across the region through APEC. And we have reached bold new agreements on global issues such as the environment and AIDS.

Our economic bonds with Japan must become just as strong as the rest of our relationship. Earlier this week we agreed to resume negotiations under the U.S.-Japan Framework for Economic Partnership. We are again moving forward to improve this relationship.

As the world's second-largest economy, Japan has a vital role to play in promoting regional and global prosperity. The Framework calls for Japan to widen access to its market and take steps to increase its domestic growth. In committing to clear goals for agreements negotiated under the Framework, the United States and Japan have unblocked the road to progress.

Now we must move down this road by concluding solid agreements on specific industrial sectors and issues. I gained respect for Prime Minister Hata when we served together as Foreign Ministers. My first meeting with Foreign Minister Kakizawa indicated he is determined to take a constructive approach to resolving our economic differences. Against the backdrop of our fundamentally strong relationship, we look forward to working with Japan to promote economic growth for our peoples and the world.

Today, developments in Beijing, Pyongyang, and Tokyo dominate our headlines. These events carry profound consequences for America, the Asia-Pacific region, and, indeed, the world. In each of these areas, the Clinton Administration is pursuing a multifaceted strategy of engagement that will most effectively advance the full range of U.S. interests.

At the same time, away from this week's headlines, we continue to pursue a long-term agenda throughout the Pacific region. In July, I travel to Bangkok for the ASEAN Post-Ministerial Conference, to further strengthen our ties with Southeast Asia. I will also participate in regional security dialogues at the ASEAN Regional Forum, an important exercise in preventive diplomacy. And this fall, the ministers and leaders of

APEC will convene again, this time in Indonesia, to chart the course for expanding economic linkages across the Asia-Pacific region.

American leadership can help build a more hopeful future for all the peoples of the Asia-Pacific. It can help reduce the prospect of war and the proliferation of nuclear weapons. It can help ensure that America shares fully in the region's prosperity, and that the people of Asia share fully in the global movement to freedom.

ELEVEN

Revitalizing the OECD

With the Cold War's end, the Clinton Administration faced a situation similar to that which American leaders confronted at the end of World War II. At that time, the United States led the effort to enhance cooperation and integration through international institutions. Statesmen like Harry Truman, George Marshall, and Dean Acheson were instrumental in conceptualizing and designing this new architecture. Throughout the Cold War, organizations such as NATO, the United Nations, and the GATT helped keep the peace, manage crises, and promote economic prosperity.

Renewing these great international institutions for the post–Cold War era emerged as a dominant theme of our foreign policy agenda. The institutions needed to reflect new realities if they were to continue to reinforce American interests. This was the driving logic behind our policy to expand NATO, for example, and we saw a similar opportunity regarding the Organization for Economic Cooperation and Development (OECD).

The OECD is a Paris-based international organization that monitors and analyzes the economic performance of the industrialized world. Originally formed in 1948 as the Organization for European Economic Cooperation to support the Marshall Plan, in 1961 the group began to take on non-European members, ultimately including Japan, Australia, and New Zealand. It has produced impressive economic analyses but has never had a high profile. At the State Department, interest in the OECD waned during the 1980s. Secretary Baker did not attend any of the organization's annual ministerials, while Secretary George Shultz, himself an economist, attended only one.

The June 1994 OECD ministerial meeting in Paris, wedged between events in France honoring the 50th anniversary of the Normandy landing and a NATO meeting in Istanbul, provided a chance for its members to reenergize the institution and define its post–Cold War direction. The Administration viewed this ministerial as an opportunity to fulfill multiple goals. First, because the OECD was considering the admission of Poland, Hungary, the Czech Republic, and Slovakia, my presence and remarks in Paris would demonstrate U.S. leadership in urging that nations previously under Soviet control be brought into the democratic, free market family of nations—essentially into the West. Second, the OECD had forged a cooperation agreement with Russia, and I could reaffirm our support for closer ties between the West and Russia by joining Foreign Minister Kozyrev at the formal signing ceremony.[1] Finally, by articulating our interest in revitalizing the OECD to play a more prominent role in the post–Cold War era, I would have yet another opportunity to affirm the increasing importance of economic interests to foreign policy.

My remarks before the OECD ministerial built on each of these points. I explained that the OECD could be an important model for wider European integration. There was no reason why Western institutions should end at the old Iron Curtain. One line captured this sentiment: "We must now extend to the East the benefits—and obligations—of the same liberal trading and security order that have been pillars of strength for the West."[2] The use of the word "obligations" was purpose-

---

[1]The cooperation agreement did not make Russia an OECD member, but it did allow the organization to provide Moscow with Western expertise on such topics as foreign investment rules and regulations, economic laws, banking procedures, and strategies for privatizing state enterprises.

[2]At the next day's Istanbul NATO meeting, I reiterated the interrelationship between the eastward expansion of the West's economic institutions and that of its security architecture. "The quest for security in Europe cannot rely on security institutions alone," I said. "It also must rely on the political and economic reconstruction of newly democratic nations. . . . By widening the reach of NATO and of organizations like the OECD, the EU, and GATT, we will strengthen the prosperity of an undivided Europe and bolster the security that this Alliance continues to preserve."

ful. Insisting that new members meet OECD's criteria would bolster reform in the East and enhance the integration of East and West. The criteria included requirements that potential members be committed to democratic government and adhere to free market principles.

While concentrating primarily on European integration, I also made the case that the OECD should assume a larger role globally. We did not believe the OECD should be a universal organization like the UN, but we did think it should become more inclusive and less Eurocentric in nature. Indeed, the organization's global outlook was already evolving. Mexico had become its 25th member shortly before the Paris meeting, a development I welcomed in the speech. I called for the OECD to begin the process of including South Korea and to open a dialogue with other countries in Latin America and Asia. "The community of market democracies is not a closed club," I said in a line picked up by the press. "It is open to open societies. It is open to open markets. It is open to freedom everywhere."

In terms of specific issues, my OECD address made a firm statement on the bribery of foreign officials in international transactions. American companies are barred from such conduct by our Foreign Corrupt Practices Act, and they are understandably frustrated when they lose contracts because their foreign competitors are not so restricted. During the Carter Administration, I had urged the international community to act to level this aspect of the playing field. In this speech, I hailed the commitment of the OECD to take "concrete and meaningful" steps to curb such international bribery. The antibribery theme was one I reiterated on numerous occasions throughout the rest of my tenure. By the end of my term, I could point to a commitment by OECD members not to allow a tax deduction for amounts paid for bribery, as well as their firmly expressed intention to negotiate a treaty prohibiting the payment of bribes altogether.[3] In addition, the Organization of American States has adopted a convention on corruption in this hemisphere.

---

[3]At the end of 1997, the OECD members and five other nations took a major step in this direction by entering a convention in which each nation agreed to make it a criminal offense to bribe a foreign official for a business-related purpose.

Toward a More Integrated World

Statement at the Organization for Economic Cooperation and
Development Ministerial Meeting, Paris, June 8, 1994

It is a pleasure to be the first American Secretary of State to attend an OECD ministerial in more than a decade, and a pleasure to join Secretary Brown in today's proceedings. Let me take this opportunity to express my government's appreciation for Secretary General Paye's many contributions to the OECD over the past decade. He has earned our gratitude. I am especially pleased to be here today as the OECD welcomes its first new member nation in more than 20 years. By doing so, it reaffirms its scope as a truly global organization. I want to congratulate my neighbor and friend, Foreign Minister Tello. Mexico's commitment to economic reform and free trade have earned it the respect of the world. Now it can assume new responsibilities as a contributor to the OECD's important work.

Today, this organization is taking historic steps almost unimaginable five years ago. We have agreed to start membership negotiations with four of the new democracies to the East: Poland, Hungary, the Czech Republic, and Slovakia, and with South Korea as well. We hope that these five nations will attain full membership as soon as possible. And today we also will sign a cooperation agreement with the Russian Federation to extend the OECD's unique expertise to the great task of building a market economy in Russia.

With these actions, the OECD renews the purpose that inspired Jean Monnet, George Marshall, and other post-war leaders of long vision and strong will: to build a democratic and integrated Europe, and a more peaceful and prosperous world. Today, these goals are within sight.

We are gathered this morning at a historic site. It was here, after the Second World War, that the challenge of building peace and reconciliation was addressed. The United States and Western Europe understood, as George Marshall expressed it, that a "working economy" had to be revived "to permit the emergence of political and social conditions in which free institutions can exist."

The OECD evolved from that effort. Its predecessor, the Organization for European Economic Cooperation, helped coordinate post-war reconstruction under the Marshall Plan. As the first European institution dedicated to economic cooperation, the OEEC was a catalyst for economic recovery and integration on the western half of this continent. In the words of its first Secretary-General, Robert Marjolin, our predecessors were "convinced that the different European countries were indissolubly linked in their destinies."

That we can meet today in a vibrant city, in a prosperous Western Europe at peace, is a tribute to the success of their work. But to the east, the scourges that George Marshall described almost 50 years ago, "hunger, poverty, despotism, and chaos," still are vivid in the memory of nations that never had the chance to share our prosperity. These scourges are especially vivid in the former Yugoslavia. And they threaten the nations that emerged from the former Soviet Union. Marshall's vision, and Monnet's, encompassed all of Europe, but the reality of their time could not. The Eastern European nations were invited to join the Marshall Plan, but Soviet leaders would not allow it. The benefits of Western European reconstruction and integration were denied by the absolute divisions of the Cold War.

With the end of the Cold War, we cannot allow new divisions to arise. Europe must not be split into zones of prosperity and poverty, stability and insecurity. We must now extend to the East the benefits—and obligations—of the same liberal trading and security order that have been pillars of strength for the West.

Tomorrow, many of us will meet in the North Atlantic Council in Istanbul to review our progress in renewing NATO, especially through the Partnership for Peace. In Istanbul, we will continue to develop the important network of relationships with our new partners to the East. By widening the reach of NATO, and of organizations like the OECD, we will strengthen the security and prosperity of an undivided, democratic Europe.

I believe that the OECD, with its unique capabilities, can be a model and an instrument of wider integration in the post–Cold War world— just as its predecessor was during the early Cold War years in Western

Europe. The OECD can perform its core function as a forum for policy analysis and coordination at a time of accelerating economic change. And it can help complete the unfinished business of post-war reconstruction, in a new era and on a wider scale, by helping more countries throughout the world enter the community of advanced industrial nations.

Last January in Prague, President Clinton announced that the United States supported early entry into the OECD for the Visegrad countries, four nations that, in his words, have "confounded skeptics and surprised even the optimists." By undertaking the process leading to membership, they will push market reform further and ultimately lift economic growth and the living standards of their people. The United States has strongly supported the OECD's Center for Economies in Transition and its efforts to forge closer links with other nations in Eastern Europe and the New Independent States. As we learned in the years after the Second World War, economic cooperation is the best way to promote stability.

Five years ago, the countries of Eastern Europe won their freedom and helped cement ours. If we no longer fear a Third World War, if we can envision a Europe no longer riven by repression or conflict, we owe it in part to the struggles of men and women in Gdansk and Vilnius and Prague and Sofia. The Visegrad states have the potential to form one of the world's fastest-growing economic regions. Poland, for example, already has one of the highest growth rates in Europe, a budget deficit lower than the European average, and declining inflation. But expectations in the East have outpaced living standards. Market reforms have caused short-term pain. It continues to be in the interest of the world's advanced industrial democracies to help ensure that dislocation does not lead to disillusionment with democratic institutions and free markets. That is why the United States has provided more than $8 billion to support reform efforts in Central and Eastern Europe since 1989.

But economic assistance is not enough. We all must urge these countries to build legal, tax, and regulatory structures that will attract additional private capital to the region. These steps will complement the difficult actions already taken to privatize factories, reduce subsidies, and lower tariffs.

If the countries of Central and Eastern Europe have the courage to take these painful but necessary steps, we must be prepared to do our part. As President Clinton has said, "it will make little sense for us to applaud their market reforms on the one hand while offering only selective access to our markets on the other." We must lower the remaining trade barriers that limit their nations' exports and potential for development. Market access is not just an economic issue. At stake are the prospects for democracy and stability across Europe.

There is no reason why our institutions or our aspirations should stop at old frontiers of the Cold War. I believe that encouraging Russia's integration with the West is the best investment we can make in our security, and in the security of all the peoples of Europe. Integration will bring benefits to Russia—not only expanded trade and investment, but participation in military arrangements with NATO and political discussions with the G-7 nations. Integration also will require Russia to accept the obligations we all share: to pursue sound economic policies; to uphold democracy; to respect the rights of other countries. It is, of course, Russia's choice whether to take the path of integration. But we must do everything we can to encourage it to choose that path. Russia's recent agreement with the IMF is evidence that its government, under the leadership of President Yeltsin and Prime Minister Chernomyrdin, continues to make progress in stabilizing its economy. Substantial progress already has been made in privatization and decentralization—the twin reform objectives at the center of our assistance efforts. As a result, an increasing amount of Russian economic life is no longer controlled by the rigid hand of the state.

The agreement the OECD will conclude today with Russia is a welcome step. It will allow the OECD to provide expertise on structural reform and to carry out in-depth analyses of the Russian economy—just as it does each year, with such integrity and objectivity, for its members.

Our response to Russia's reforms, and to those of its neighbors, should be based on a simple proposition. The community of market democracies is not a closed club. It is open to open societies. It is open to open markets. It is open to freedom everywhere. The OECD had its origins in Europe; its initial membership was transatlantic. But with Japan a member for three decades and Australia and New Zealand for more than two, and with Mexico joining this year, the time has come for the OECD to evolve further as a global organization. It must create new and flexible relationships with non-member nations of growing economic importance. An open, creative, and dynamic OECD can help enlarge the community of free and prosperous nations throughout the world. The opportunity is there. South Africa has emerged as a source of healing and hope—and a potential catalyst for economic development in Southern Africa. In Asia, we have seen dramatic growth, ranging from India to China to South Korea. In Latin America, liberalization is opening markets, cutting tariffs, and creating jobs.

The United States welcomes the OECD's dialogue with dynamic economies in Asia and Latin America. We hope that South Korea will follow Mexico as a full member. The OECD can also assume a new importance in the architecture of the global economy, as a bridge between Atlantic and Pacific industrial economies. Just as European integration began with economic cooperation, so must the challenge of global integration. Implementation of the Uruguay Round is a critical task for us all. The world's advanced industrial democracies share a responsibility to sustain and strengthen the liberal world trading system that has allowed our economies to grow and our peoples to prosper. Now we must meet that great responsibility. Cordell Hull, a distinguished predecessor of mine who served Franklin D. Roosevelt as Secretary of State, did more than any statesman of his time to make America a champion of the liberal world trading system. He knew that open trade was good economics. He also knew, as he put it, that "when goods move, soldiers don't." President Clinton is committed to passing legislation to implement the Uruguay Round in this calendar year. The legislation will be submitted to our Congress this summer, and I am confident that it will be approved. This agreement is in the overriding interest of America and the world. Each of our nations must approve the Uruguay Round this year to ensure that the most far-reaching trade agreement in history takes effect by January 1, 1995. By approving the Round, we will open markets, boost confidence, spur growth, and create jobs. We will help new market democracies carry out difficult economic reform. We will help ensure that the post–Cold War world is not divided into new blocs: not North against South; not rich against poor; not North America against Europe or Asia.

We also must move ahead with a strong World Trade Organization to set the stage for a new century of prosperity. The WTO can strengthen the multilateral trading system through new rules and disciplines. The OECD can help it address the next generation of trade issues: the intersection of trade with investment, labor standards, and the environment.

New rules are also needed in other areas to make trade more efficient and equitable. Our nations will not have open competition unless we have clean competition. Our ability to advance economic development will be undermined as long as bribery distorts the allocation of resources, saps accountable government, and subverts the rule of law.

The United States has long sought to build an international consensus against the bribery of foreign officials in international business transactions. Last October, I proposed on my country's behalf an initiative to advance this vital objective. Now OECD member nations have committed themselves to take "concrete and meaningful" steps to stop illicit payments by their firms. We must mount a sustained campaign against bribery. With endorsement of the agreement at this ministerial meeting today, we can move from the discussion phase to the action phase of this campaign. The campaign against illicit payments is a prime example of the OECD's new, more activist role. The agreements we have reached with the Visegrad states and with Russia show that the OECD is playing its part in integrating Europe. The accession of Mexico, and the likelihood that South Korea will join soon, demonstrate the OECD's global reach.

The United States sees a broader role for the OECD but it also encourages its reform. The OECD must live within its means and streamline its operations and decision-making. It must focus its priorities on areas where it has a comparative advantage, such as structural analysis. A recent example is the seminal Growth and Employment Study that is helping our nations tackle the central task of job creation. That the OECD is changing and growing is a mark of progress not only for the institution but for the world. It means that the sphere of advanced, industrial democracies is growing. It means that economic cooperation is enlarging the circle of prosperity. As Jean Monnet once said, "Nothing is lasting without institutions." The gains of freedom will endure only if we have the foresight to extend to new nations the institutions that have served us so well for so long. Let us summon the confidence and the sense of common purpose that guided us through the last half century. Let us gain inspiration from the vision of Marshall and Monnet. Now that we can, let us strengthen our security by extending to others the blessings our predecessors secured for us.

Restoring Democracy to Haiti

Since the days of the Monroe Doctrine, promoting U.S. interests in Latin America and the Caribbean has been at the core of U.S. foreign policy. Almost every recent American President has faced a foreign policy challenge in that region—the Bay of Pigs in 1961, the Cuban Missile Crisis in 1962, the civil war in the Dominican Republic in 1965, the conflict between the Sandinistas and the contras in Nicaragua in the 1980s, and the invasion of Panama in 1989 stand out as dramatic examples. Events during President Clinton's first term proved no exception, as our attention turned to the ongoing problems in Haiti.

During the 1980s, a wave of democratization had swept through Latin America. Once ruled by the iron fists of military dictatorships, countries like Chile, Argentina, Nicaragua, and Guatemala had turned to democracy. This trend finally reached Haiti in December 1990. Under strong pressure from the United States and other nations, Haiti held free and fair elections. Jean-Bertrand Aristide was overwhelmingly elected President, with over 90% of Haitians voting.

Aristide soon ran into trouble with the military and the wealthy elite, and in September 1991, he was overthrown in a coup engineered by Lieutenant General Raoul Cedras. Aristide sought refuge in the United States, taking up residence in Washington just a few blocks from the White House. The Bush Administration withdrew all assistance from Haiti, and Secretary of State Baker announced that the United States would treat the Haitian regime as a pariah until it permitted Aristide to return to power. By imposing these economic sanctions, the Administration hoped to restore democracy to Haiti. There was widespread international support for this policy, and for the first time ever, the Organization of American States (OAS) endorsed a trade embargo against coup leaders. The Clinton Administration entered office supporting the policy of using sanctions as the primary leverage against Cedras and his cohorts. However, we doubted that sanctions alone would be sufficient.

During the 1992 presidential campaign, Governor Clinton had criticized the Bush Administration's policy of restricting the number of Haitian people trying to flee the Cedras regime who were allowed to enter the United States. Shortly before President Clinton took office, U.S. intelligence agencies warned that as many as 200,000 Haitians might take to the seas in anticipation of a U.S. policy change. Given that such an exodus not only would be dangerous for these refugees (most of whom would attempt to cross the treacherous channel in makeshift, overcrowded boats), but would also spark an immigration crisis for the United States, Clinton decided to continue the Bush Administration's restrictive approach. At the same time, however, the President pledged that he would dramatically step up our efforts to negotiate a peaceful return for Aristide.

Early Attempts to Resolve the Crisis

In the spring of 1993, we brokered an agreement between the military and Aristide to restore democracy to Haiti. Concluded in a July 1993 meeting on Governors Island off New York City, this accord outlined a series of sequential steps to return Aristide to power. The Governors Island Agreement was to be fully implemented by October 30, 1993.

The implementation of the Agreement soon foundered on the cynicism and brutality of the Haitian rulers. It became clear that despite their commitments, Cedras and his junta had no intention of adhering to its provisions. For them, it was just a play for time, which they hoped would weaken the international community's will to maintain sanctions. We worked hard to find a brokered solution to save the Agreement, but many of us began to understand that no matter what Cedras said, he would never leave power until forced to do so.

In October 1993, an already difficult situation was complicated by a troubling episode. Pursuant to the Governors Island Agreement, the Pentagon had ordered 200 army engineers and trainers to Haiti to help in construction projects and in retraining the Haitian military. They expected to be welcomed into a friendly environment. However, as they approached the Port-au-Prince harbor, the Cedras regime suddenly prevented the docking of their landing ship, the *Harlan County*. In addition, a mob apparently directed by the Haitian military engaged in a raucous demonstration that threatened the U.S. and UN diplomats who had come to greet the soldiers.

The ship was not equipped or prepared to be part of an invasion force or to enter a hostile environment. After spending two days anchored a mile offshore in the blazing sun, it returned to the U.S. naval base at Guantanamo Bay. In narrow terms, that seemed a prudent decision. But in diplomacy, images matter. In retrospect, it seems clear enough that the *Harlan County* should have been accompanied by fighting ships and well-armed personnel that would have ensured a peaceful arrival. Taken together with the reverses we suffered in Somalia that fall (see Chapter 32), the *Harlan County* incident created a perception of lack of resolve that took us some time to shake off. A few days later, with the peace process foundering, the UN reimposed an oil and gas embargo on Haiti that had been lifted earlier under the terms of the Governors Island Agreement.

Also complicating our efforts to restore democracy to Haiti was the rise in suspicion and criticism of Aristide by some in the United States. During 1994, his opponents, including some powerful voices in the U.S. Congress, spread rumors that he was a murderer, drug user, and crypto-dictator. To support their case, these critics leaked to the press intelligence reports that were a tangle of falsehoods, half-truths, and unsubstantiated rumors. Much of the information and innuendo was later proven erroneous, but as is often the case, the facts never fully caught up with the allegations in the public mind.

The basic point behind such criticisms was that the United States should never risk lives or dollars to return a "flawed" leader like Aristide to power; instead, we should support a compromise leader more acceptable to the junta. I strongly resisted these calls to dump Aristide. It seemed to me the ultimate in hypocrisy for the United States to claim that it supported democracy and not work to restore to office a man who had been elected with nearly 70% of the vote.

When I first met Aristide in 1993, during his long exile in the United States, the 40-year-old Haitian President was far different from the person portrayed by his critics. I found him shrewd and well educated; he not only was fluent in French, English, Spanish, and Creole, but also spoke Hebrew. Diminutive, balding, and bespectacled, Aristide had a quiet, soft-spoken manner. Beneath the surface shyness was a compelling, highly articulate, stubborn man of many dimensions, a man dedicated to "liberation theology" and to the poor people of Haiti who had elected him. With crowds, he became pyrotechnic and charismatic, verging on the demagogic. Over time, Aristide and I became quite well acquainted, as I contacted him to discuss developments or to ask his support on specific issues. National Security Adviser Anthony Lake devoted long hours to developing a relationship with him and seemed to earn his confidence. But the person in the Administration who had the most influence with him was President Clinton, who could persuade him on key points when the rest of us struck out.

Tightening the Screws

By the spring of 1994, our policy of trying to restore Aristide by using political leverage and economic sanctions to pressure Cedras was becoming untenable. Cedras and his cohorts shrugged off the prospect of stiffened sanctions. The military and wealthy elite in Haiti found ways to circumvent the sanctions and even to profit from them, while the poor suffered under the shortage of gasoline and other necessities. In May 1994, the UN imposed a total trade embargo on Haiti, but the pattern of repression and terror continued. Quite simply, as we had feared, the initial premise that the United States could restore democracy to Haiti through sanctions was turning out to be wrong.

The outflow of Haitian refugees trying to enter the United States aggravated our problems. The refugee crisis had become particularly acute by summer 1994. During July 3 and 4 alone, the U.S. Coast Guard intercepted over 6,000 boat people headed for American shores. In response to this problem, the Administration began negotiating with other

Caribbean countries to establish temporary safe havens for refugees fleeing from Haiti. Despite these efforts, this situation was unsustainable.

The media subjected our policy to intense criticism, much of it directed against our refusal to permit fleeing Haitians to enter the United
States. They paid great attention to Randall Robinson, a prominent
African American leader who went on a highly publicized hunger strike
to try to change our policy. Inside the Administration, we were all growing increasingly frustrated with our lack of success and the effect this was
having on public opinion, both within the United States and around the
world. All of these factors pressured us to cauterize the source of the
problem—Cedras and his repressive regime.

The use of U.S. military force to restore democracy in Haiti had always been considered the last resort on the continuum of our policy options. President Bush and Secretary Baker had judged that the national
interest did not justify the use of force in Haiti.[1] Remembering the long
and frustrating occupation by the marines earlier in the century and concerned about Aristide's commitment to democratic reform, our military
leaders were reluctant to get involved. Congressional and public opinion
reinforced this reluctance. Nevertheless, as the situation continued to
deteriorate that summer, with waves of refugees trying to leave the island, we began to explore the options relating to the threat and use of
military force.

One of the fundamental tenets of diplomacy is that for a threat of force
to have any coercive effect, it must be credible. A key component of a
credible threat in this case was the rallying of international support.
First, we worked with the OAS to forge a hemispheric agreement endorsing the use of force against Cedras. At a May 1994 OAS meeting in
Brazil, Strobe Talbott, who had been elevated to Deputy Secretary, and
Bill Gray, an able former Congressman who had been appointed as our
special envoy to Haiti, steered through a resolution in favor of UN intervention to restore the legitimate, democratic government of Haiti.
This unprecedented OAS resolution proved vital during the debate in
the UN Security Council two months later. On July 31, the Security
Council approved Resolution 940, authorizing the United States and its
allies in a coalition of the willing to use "all necessary means" to depose

[1]For Baker's brief account of the Bush Administration's handling of the Haitian
crisis, see *The Politics of Diplomacy*, pp. 601–2 (New York: G. P. Putnam's Sons, 1995).

Cedras and his military cronies.[2] This was the first time the UN had authorized using all necessary means expressly for the purpose of defending democracy, a result achieved through outstanding advocacy by then–UN Ambassador Madeleine Albright.

While working to build this international coalition, we also continued to plan our immediate diplomatic and military strategy. As the Administration assessed the range of options for dealing with the crisis, a consensus quickly emerged around the ultimatum option, whereby we would use the threat of force to try to induce the Cedras regime to leave. If the regime ignored or rejected the ultimatum, we would respond with a military invasion. In meetings in the late summer, I urged my colleagues to set a deadline for the use of force, so that the reliance on non-military options did not drift on aimlessly.

In early September, we agreed on a detailed plan for implementing the ultimatum strategy. A critical element of that plan was building support for the strategy at home. Accordingly, we began to focus public attention on the Haiti situation. Senior Administration officials fanned out across the nation to articulate our policy to newspaper editorial boards and local audiences.

We also began extensive consultations with Capitol Hill, where support for our troops would be vital. Assistant Secretary Wendy Sherman, an exceptionally valued adviser, led the Administration's effort to work with Congress. We faced an uphill battle there. It was an election season, and every aspect of the debate on the Hill was tinged with campaign politics. American public opinion usually opposes military intervention abroad, at least until our troops land. This was decidedly the case with Haiti, and congressional attitudes reflected this view. Congress made the customary claim that we had not consulted them enough, even though members of the Administration had participated in over 75 meetings

[2]The UN Security Council sometimes authorizes a coalition of the willing to carry out the mission identified in a UN resolution. For example, the Security Council authorized a U.S.-led coalition to perform the mission of repelling Iraq from Kuwait in 1991. The costs of such a mission are divided among the members of the coalition, upon whatever basis they may agree to. In contrast, the costs of a UN peacekeeping mission are covered by special UN assessments. In Haiti, the landing and initial operations to restore law and order were carried out by a coalition of the willing, which was replaced by a UN peacekeeping force after a safe environment had been created. The last UN peacekeeping contingent was withdrawn in 1997, though an international police training unit remains.

with subcommittees, groups of Members, and individual Members on the issue in 1994 alone. In an attempt to tie the President's hands, some on Capitol Hill argued that the Administration needed to seek congressional approval before any military action. We rejected this view, judging that the President was well within his constitutional authority as Commander in Chief to deploy force, but we realized that we had to do more to build a domestic consensus behind our policy.

The Presidential Ultimatum

The most important component of our public strategy was the President's address to the nation on September 15. I had recommended that he make such an address, advising him, "In the end, your leadership will be key to our success." Our ultimatum strategy would place American men and women in harm's way, and I felt that only the President could convince their families and the American people that this was justified. Speaking at 9:00 P.M. from the Oval Office, the President made the case for intervention. "The nations of the world have tried every possible way to restore Haiti's democratic government peacefully," he said. "The dictators have rejected every possible solution. The terror, the desperation, and the instability will not end until they leave." His address also bluntly delivered our ultimatum: "The message of the United States to the Haitian dictators is clear. Your time is up. Leave now or we will force you from power."

By this point, the President had already alerted U.S. military forces, including 1,600 reservists, to prepare for action. Along with wielding this stick, we also set forth the carrot, offering the Haitian leaders one last chance to depart voluntarily and arrange for the peaceful introduction of our military force. Before ordering troops in, the President wanted to make a final effort to achieve this result by sending an emissary to meet with Cedras. Coincidentally, former President Jimmy Carter had been contacted by Cedras, who had asked him to help broker a settlement. When Carter called to inform us of Cedras's offer, Clinton decided that he would be the right emissary. Carter had had past contacts with Cedras, and we hoped that he would be able to use his influence to persuade him to give up power peacefully. To show that both the military and Congress endorsed our policy, retired General Colin Powell and Senator Sam Nunn of Georgia joined Carter on this mission. Their task was to inform Cedras that if he didn't leave voluntarily, U.S. forces would invade Haiti to remove him from office.

When Carter, Powell, and Nunn arrived in Port-au-Prince on Saturday, September 17, to deliver the ultimatum, they worked under a deadline set by President Clinton: if, by noon on September 18, Cedras and his cohorts had not agreed to leave, the U.S.-led military invasion would commence. As the emissaries offered Cedras this last chance, 15,000 U.S. troops prepared for invasion. President Clinton had ordered paratroopers from the 82d Airborne Division at Fort Bragg, North Carolina, to board planes and be ready to depart for Haiti when the noon deadline passed. As I followed events with the President and others in the Oval Office, General Shalikashvili received minute-by-minute reports of the deployments. Carter called several times urgently asking for an extension of the noon deadline, saying that they were close to reaching an agreement. President Clinton reluctantly extended the deadline an hour at a time. Late in the afternoon, General Powell called to say that they had come to terms. An aide faxed us a copy of the proposed agreement, which provided that the junta members were not obligated to leave Haiti until the Haitian parliament approved an amnesty for them. We immediately concluded that such a plan was unacceptable because the condition for departure was subject to Cedras's control; he would be able to delay parliamentary action almost indefinitely by haggling over the terms of the amnesty. I stressed that it was essential to fix a specific and unconditional date for the departure of the military leaders, and the President approved October 15 as that date.

With the U.S. invasion aircraft already airborne from Fort Bragg, President Clinton finally had to give an unequivocal order for the emissaries to depart within 30 minutes, lest they be caught in Haiti after the invasion began. "You've got to get out," he told Carter. A few minutes later, Carter reported that Cedras and his allies had agreed to leave by October 15, and that Aristide would return to power on that date. The U.S. troops, with others from the coalition, entered Haiti without opposition, starting at 2:00 the following morning, September 19. Their mission was to ensure that Cedras lived up to his end of the deal and to create a peaceful environment for the restoration of the democratically elected government. Cedras soon fled to Panama.

Coming only 10 days after our forces entered Haiti, my speech before the United Nations Security Council recapped the key points of our diplomacy and framed the choices we had made in a larger context. Indeed, the strategy President Clinton pursued with respect to Haiti brought together many of the most important strands of U.S. foreign policy in the post–Cold War world. In Haiti, we sought to consolidate the gains of democracy, not simply for the people of the island, but throughout the hemisphere and the world. Our action sent a signal intended to help prevent the erosion of democracy in Latin America and other key regions.

The action had other positive results as well. Because it was successful and virtually casualty-free, it helped our military build up its confidence and enhanced its willingness to take on preventative and peacekeeping challenges. Moreover, by finally resolving the refugee problem in a humane and sustainable way, it demonstrated our ability to handle the increasingly frequent problems that have both domestic and international dimensions. As my speech emphasized, the Haiti intervention also highlighted the benefits of harnessing the resources of the international community on behalf of an important U.S. interest.

The approach used in Haiti can be useful in dealing with the kinds of antidemocratic threats that have become all too prominent around the globe. The key step was the authorization of a coalition of the willing by the UN Security Council. In the Haiti case, the coalition involved a diverse collection of 28 nations. Commanded by U.S. General Hugh Shelton (who later became Chairman of the Joint Chiefs of Staff), the coalition forces in Haiti showed the advantage of careful planning and operated with high efficiency. After these forces established a safe environment, the next step, as I said in the speech, was for the follow-on UN peacekeeping mission to take up its responsibilities.

On October 15, 1994, I accompanied Jean-Bertrand Aristide on his triumphant return to Haiti after three years in exile. I vividly recall sitting in a military aircraft with him and sharing his strong emotion when the plane touched down in Port-au-Prince. We traveled by helicopter to the Presidential Palace, which had been hastily repainted and spruced up for his return but still lacked air-conditioning and many other amenities. I joined Aristide and other dignitaries on the second-floor balcony of the mansion for speeches to the throngs of ecstatic Haitians in the square below. Aristide's considerable oratorical skills were on full display as he alternated among French, English, and Creole. He stirred the crowd to repeat after him: "No to violence!" "No to vengeance!" and "Yes to reconciliation!" The huge crowd responded to every phrase with enthusiasm and affection.

My UN speech notes that during one of his visits to the State Department, Aristide had observed that the true test of a new democracy is not its first election, but its second. I was struck by the wisdom of that statement and was reassured when Aristide kept his commitment to follow the Haitian constitution by not seeking reelection in 1995. With Aristide's support, Rene Preval won the election. However, because of his immense popularity among the masses, Aristide continues to wield significant influence in Haiti. At times, unfortunately, that influence has proved troublesome. For example, his opposition to privatization stymied Preval's efforts to reform the backward Haitian economy.

The United States–led initiative restored democracy and gave the Haitians an opportunity to succeed. Now, although the international community continues to offer material support, the responsibility for their future lies primarily with the Haitians themselves.

Restoring Democracy to Haiti

Address to the United Nations Security Council,

New York City, September 29, 1994

Mr. President, distinguished members of the Security Council, colleagues, and friends: I am pleased to have the opportunity to review with you the status of our efforts in Haiti. This Council continues to play a vital role in giving Haiti's people a chance to take back their destiny. Our shared determination is to deliver tangible results. The Haitian military leaders will step down. Legitimate government will be restored. The people of Haiti will have a chance to rebuild their country on a stable foundation of democracy and respect for human rights.

The multinational coalition is the culmination of three years of intensive, coordinated efforts by the United Nations, the Organization of American States, and the friends and neighbors of Haiti. Since the 1991 coup, this Council has viewed the overthrow of democracy in Haiti as a threat to regional security and to international norms. We recognized our responsibility to stand together for stability and the restoration of democratic government in the Western Hemisphere. Together, we explored every avenue to achieve a peaceful resolution. We negotiated in good faith. We imposed and then strengthened sanctions. We made plain to the military leaders that their tyranny in Haiti was neither tolerable nor tenable.

For almost three years, they met our efforts with defiance and disdain. In July 1993, General Cedras signed the Governors Island Agreement, which had been negotiated under UN auspices. But he refused to implement the accord. Instead, widespread atrocities continued. Three months ago, the military leaders expelled the monitors sent by the UN and the OAS to encourage respect for human rights. This Council then determined that the time had come to take decisive action. UN Security Council Resolution 940 and the multinational coalition it authorized are an expression of our collective resolve. An expanding coalition of 28 nations—as geographically diverse as Bangladesh, Benin, and Bolivia—has been forged in pursuit of a common cause.

This coalition is in the best tradition of the United Nations. It is grounded in principled diplomacy, and it is backed by the determination to use force if necessary. Our willingness to exercise military might, pursuant to Resolution 940, allowed us to reach an agreement for the peaceful restoration of democracy that has made the mission safer for our coalition and the Haitian people. It is enabling us to implement our common goals: the departure from power of the de facto leaders, the restoration of Haiti's legitimate government, and the return of President Aristide. It is allowing us to establish a safe and secure environment more quickly than otherwise would have been possible.

As leader of the multinational coalition in Haiti, the United States values and depends on close consultation with other member states. To that end, let me report to you on our progress. As you know, the first 3,000 soldiers stepped off their helicopters and landing craft on September 19. Since then, their ranks have grown to almost 16,000. The coalition has taken swift and important steps toward establishing a secure and stable environment.

One of the immediate priorities was to secure the airport in Port-au-Prince and seaports around the country. With the transportation hubs under control, we have moved nearly 42,000 tons of supplies into Haiti.

Another important element of promoting security is to reduce the number of guns on the streets. The coalition is taking a variety of measures to achieve that goal. Finally, hundreds of coalition personnel are in training in Puerto Rico, on their way to oversee and monitor the police in Haiti. The first group of international police monitors will arrive in Haiti in the next few days.

With the coalition's deployment, the time has come to prepare for the resumption of normal economic activity in Haiti. The United States and Haiti have introduced—with President Aristide's support—a resolution in the Council to lift completely UN sanctions when President Aristide returns. By passing this resolution, we will reinforce Haitian democracy. And we will signal our readiness to support Haiti's recovery when democratic government is restored.

As President Clinton announced on Monday, we will act expeditiously, consistent with Resolutions 917 and 940, to allow goods essential to the coalition's efforts to enter Haiti. In addition, the United States will lift all unilateral sanctions on Haiti except those targeted on the coup leaders and their named supporters. We urge other nations to do the same.

Part of the coalition's task is to create conditions in which refugees can return safely. Hundreds of Haitians, reassured that they can walk their streets, speak their minds, and sleep in their homes without fear, have voluntarily left Guantanamo for Haiti since September 26. We are confident that, with President Aristide's restoration, many more will want to go back to their homeland.

I believe that political developments in Haiti are also cause for optimism. Two weeks ago, President Aristide eloquently demonstrated his commitment to democracy when he said that the true test of a democracy is its second free election. He has called repeatedly for a spirit of reconciliation, and he is making frequent radio statements urging the people of Haiti to remain calm and to avoid disrupting a peaceful transition.

President Aristide has also called the Haitian Parliament into session, with an amnesty law as its first order of business. As you know, the parliament began its deliberations yesterday. Only two weeks ago, many Haitian parliamentarians were in hiding—fearful for their lives—or in exile. Now the presence of coalition forces permits them to emerge and to represent the Haitian people in safety. Another hopeful step forward is occurring today. Mayor Evans Paul, barred from City Hall by armed thugs last year, will reclaim his rightful office.

We should all be proud of the superb efforts of the coalition force in Haiti. We should remember that two weeks ago, elements of the Haitian security forces and the attaches were free to intimidate the public with impunity. Today, coalition forces allow Haitians to enjoy their first respite from terror in three years. The compassion and the competence of these troops have inspired the confidence of the Haitian people.

We all know that in Haiti, the international community has taken on a serious challenge. Our courageous troops will face difficult and sometimes dangerous situations. There will be risks, even setbacks, and we must be ready for them. Our hard work and commitment are essential, but we have the plans and the determination to move ahead.

A top priority for the coalition is to enable the UN Mission to enter Haiti promptly under conditions that will allow it to assume its full responsibilities. The United States will do its part to ensure an early and smooth transfer of authority. Twelve observers from UNMIH are in Haiti to coordinate with the coalition. They are working closely with General Shelton. Just as the coalition is fulfilling its mandate, so the UN Mission in Haiti must be ready to assume responsibility when a safe environment has been restored. Most of the nations participating in the coalition, including the United States, have indicated they also will participate in UNMIH. A number of other states have expressed an interest in joining. Clearly, the continued support of the Council, member states, and the Secretary General will be essential to ensure that the transition is seamless and effective.

Our mission in Haiti reminds us once again of the importance of effective UN peace operations. The United States is providing $1.2 billion for peace-keeping this year—a major step toward meeting our obligations. We also have proposed reforms to improve the way in which operations are financed, equipped, and organized. When we ask the UN to act, as we have in Haiti, we must provide it with the means for mounting successful missions in a timely manner.

The coalition will establish and the UN mission will help maintain a secure environment in Haiti. But the broader international community must provide Haiti with the economic, humanitarian, and technical aid that will spur development and consolidate democracy. An extensive humanitarian assistance program is already under way. Food, medicine, and medical supplies are being distributed. Sanitation is being improved. Engineering teams are helping to restore electricity. Last month, a World Bank meeting of many countries represented here today favorably reviewed President Aristide's economic recovery program. The United States has already committed $100 million and is ready to provide additional aid. But our effort must be part of a much larger undertaking. We look to other nations and the international financial institutions to respond rapidly and generously. The importance of supporting Haiti's recovery and reconstruction in the first months cannot be overstated. Assistance will be essential to provide balance-of-payment support and to clear arrears—an effort that will begin in earnest with a support group meeting our Treasury is hosting October 7.

On behalf of the United States, I strongly urge the members of this Council and other nations to do everything possible now to set Haiti's economy on the road to recovery. Haiti is the poorest country in the Western Hemisphere and one of the poorest in the world. But Haiti is not a state without institutions. It is a state with an elected government, an elected parliament, and a democratic constitution—all of which were shoved aside in 1991 by the de facto regime. The coalition's mission is not to invent new institutions but to create conditions that will allow Haiti's legitimate institutions to return.

All of us know that the coalition, UNMIH, and our economic assistance cannot and should not be a substitute for determined efforts by Haiti's Government and people to build a democratic and prosperous society. The hard work of rebuilding Haiti rests with them, and Haiti's democratic leaders fully understand that. Haiti has an opportunity to supplant the rule of fear with the rule of law; to take its rightful place in the growing community of democratic states; to work with the international community to solve the transnational problems we all face; and to become an inspiration to other nations—not an outcast.

In closing, I want to reaffirm the indispensable role that the international community has played in bringing Haiti to this hopeful point. By joining together in strength, the burden each of us must bear is reduced, and the prospect for success is increased. Our nations understand that the best way to achieve our goals is by acting together. That is what we did when we approved Resolution 940; that is what we are doing today; and that is what we will continue to do in the months ahead.

THIRTEEN

The Promise of Peace in the Middle East

Sometimes a Secretary of State uses a speech to build a foundation for an upcoming trip abroad, whether his or her own or the President's. A pre-trip speech can provide the strategic context for the places to be visited and the messages to be delivered. It can foreshadow for the American people and the traveling press the anticipated highlights of the trip—what policies will be emphasized and what outcomes should be expected. The speech I gave at Georgetown University in October 1994 was intended in large part to fulfill these purposes regarding President Clinton's upcoming trip to the Middle East.

As I look back now, it appears that the Georgetown speech came at a high point in our hopes for a comprehensive Middle East peace. After four decades of struggle, Jordan and Israel were about to sign a peace treaty. On the Israeli-Palestinian track, the key points laid down in the Declaration of Principles (see Chapter 4) were being carried out, despite terrorist opposition. On the Israeli-Syrian track, the parties were seriously engaged on the toughest issues. When President Clinton took off for his first official trip to the Middle East only 24 hours after the Georgetown speech, it was a moment of great promise. Some of this promise would be fulfilled, but some of it would not.

The President's first stop was the Arava Crossing, on the desolate border between Jordan and Israel near the Gulf of Aqaba, where King Hussein and Prime Minister Rabin would sign the peace treaty. After a non-stop overnight flight, we arrived in Arava on a blistering day. The temperature hovered around 100 degrees in the shade—and shade was hard to find, except in a large black tent erected to provide temporary relief from the mid-day sun prior to the ceremony.

Not all of the region's leaders were present at the Arava event. One stark Middle East reality is that while generally the Arabs have been aligned against Israel, they are just as often at odds with each other. The absences from the ceremony of President Hosni Mubarak of Egypt and PLO Chairman Arafat were cases in point. Neither had been invited to attend. Mubarak had an on-again, off-again relationship with King Hussein and did not hide his feeling that Egypt should have had a major role in any negotiations toward a comprehensive settlement. Arafat's problem was more specific: he was upset over the peace treaty's recognition of a historic role for Jordan as guardian of the holy sites in Jerusalem.

King Hussein, Prime Minister Yitzhak Rabin, and the President all made eloquent speeches. For Hussein and Rabin, two aging leaders who had come to like and respect each other during the secret negotiations leading up to the treaty, the moment was a poignant one. For Rabin, it was a chance to create a "warm" peace with a neighbor, in contrast to the "cold" peace with Egypt that had lasted 15 years. For Hussein, it marked his return to the good graces of the United States, after the estrangement and harsh criticism he had weathered for not opposing Iraq in the Gulf War. It also evoked the legacy of his grandfather Abdullah, who had dared to pursue the possibility of peace with Israel and who had been assassinated before Hussein's eyes for that reason. As a reflection of the rapprochement, President Clinton went from Arava to Amman, where he spoke to the Jordanian parliament, assuring his fascinated audience that "we know our people, our faiths, our cultures can live in harmony with each other."

After visiting Amman, Clinton continued on to Damascus. He was the first American President to travel to Syria since Nixon in 1974, and this visit provoked sharp controversy in the United States. Some objected to his going there while Syria remained on the State Department's list of countries that support terrorism, as well as on another list of countries failing to cooperate in combating drug trafficking. Other critics might have accepted a presidential visit to conclude an agreement between Syria and Israel, but objected to one that had no guarantee of success.

One of the specific purposes of my Georgetown speech had been to provide a context for this stop in Damascus. I stressed that the Syrian-

Israeli negotiations had "undergone important changes in the last year," that Syria had made a strategic choice to pursue peace with Israel, that the parties were engaged in serious discussions, but that "important gaps" remained that could be overcome only by a more active approach. The President hoped that his visit would embolden Syria's leader, President Assad, as well as Prime Minister Rabin, and open the way for a comprehensive peace. It was these circumstances, I argued, that justified the risks inherent in the Damascus stop.

The Clinton-Assad meeting took place in a massive hilltop palace overlooking Damascus in which I met with Assad more than 20 times. President Clinton pronounced himself satisfied by his three-hour session with Assad, but the press conference that followed was mainly notable for the opportunities Assad missed. For example, he failed to condemn or even indicate regret for the terrorist bombing of a Tel Aviv bus a week earlier that had cost 22 lives, even though he had expressed such regret in private. And when asked about a possible visit to Jerusalem in a manner that invited a conciliatory response, Assad gave a churlish reply, saying that adversaries should "not put conditions for achieving peace that one party should visit the other."

It is my judgment that in 1994–95 Assad missed the chance of his lifetime to recover the Golan Heights, which have been occupied by the Israelis since the 1967 war. Rabin was prepared to bargain, but Assad seemed immobilized by profound mistrust and a determination to get a better deal from the Israelis than Egypt's Anwar Sadat had. When Rabin was assassinated on November 4, 1995, the window of opportunity began closing. President Clinton had done his best to coax Assad to make a positive gesture for peace, but Assad wasn't willing to do so.[1]

Nevertheless, I am convinced that both President Clinton's efforts and my many visits to Damascus and meetings with President Assad were sound investments in the search for peace, for many reasons. First, persistence and tenacity are vital in that search. Breakthroughs come at unexpected moments, frequently after long effort, and it is rarely possible to

[1]Syria's self-imposed isolation has exacted a heavy toll on its already backward economy. In trying to encourage Assad to be forthcoming, I pointed out that Syria's per capita income is only a small fraction of that of Israel. He understood the point, but nothing changed. See John Lancaster, "Stalled Peace Talks Take Toll on Syrian Economy," *Washington Post*, January 29, 1998, p. A26.

make a valid cost-benefit assessment of any one visit or series of visits. Second, trying to achieve a settlement with Assad justified considerable effort in terms of both time and energy. A peace agreement between Israel and Syria would have great strategic importance for Israel, and hence for the United States. It would remove an important threat to Israel, help bring peace on its border with Lebanon, and free the rest of the Arab world to normalize relations with it. My own involvement in the Israel-Syria track was necessary because Assad refused to permit direct high-level negotiations between his nation and Israel—and because the Israeli Prime Ministers asked me to be an active intermediary.

Finally, there were collateral strategic benefits from the Damascus visits. Maintaining a strong effort with Syria was conducive to progress on the other peace process tracks and tended to keep Assad from closer ties with Iran and Iraq. Ignoring Damascus might have jeopardized both of these important interests. The relationships established in Damascus also helped the United States obtain Syrian cooperation in limiting the Katusha shelling of northern Israel at several tense moments during my term in office. In addition, my shuttling between Damascus and Jerusalem in April 1996 helped to bring an end to the Israeli "Grapes of Wrath" operation in Lebanon. These meetings led to creation of the Israel-Lebanon Monitoring Group, which continues to serve a useful purpose in forestalling the targeting of civilians in northern Israel and southern Lebanon. This group is now the only regular point of contact between Israel and her northern neighbors.

In the concluding portions of the Georgetown speech, I turned to a discussion of Iran and Iraq, which I described as "the region's most dangerous actors."

Journalists have speculated that my hostility to Iran stemmed from my prolonged negotiations in 1980–81 to free the 52 American hostages imprisoned in Tehran for more than 14 months. One can never know, I suppose, all the wellsprings of one's views, but contemporary events provided an ample basis for my attitude, without any need to go back 15 years. During 1993–97 Iran overtly sought to undermine the Middle East peace process and covertly was the most significant state sponsor of terrorism, not only in the Middle East, but in the world. Its determined efforts to acquire weapons of mass destruction—nuclear, chemical, and biological—stood as stark warnings of its longer-term intentions.

The attitude of many of our allies toward Iran frustrated us then, as it does now. I described the international community as "far too tolerant of Iran's outlaw behavior," a view to which I continue to adhere. Our allies' nuclear cooperation with, preferential economic treatment of, and large-scale investments in Iran only make it easier for that nation to promote terrorism and thwart the peace process.

Iraq also continued to threaten stability in the region. Even though soundly defeated during the 1991 Gulf War, Iraq remained a constant menace. Its violation of UN resolutions had caused President Bush to mount an air assault on Iraqi missile positions only a week before he left office, on the first day of my confirmation hearing. Three months later, the Kuwaitis had foiled a crude plan to assassinate former President Bush and other senior officials when they were visiting Kuwait. The Kuwaitis arrested 11 Iraqi citizens and charged them with plotting the assassination.

In mid-June 1993, the Clinton Administration began to get the results of the exhaustive investigation conducted by the CIA and the FBI as to responsibility for the plot against Bush. Initially, the amateurishness of the plan and allegations that the Kuwaiti investigators had engaged in torture made our intelligence specialists skeptical of confessions by the Iraqi suspects. However, when FBI agents interrogated the suspects, they not only repeated their confessions but provided an impressive level of detail on the plot, which they said was hatched by the Iraqi intelligence agency. Comparison of the intended bombs with devices used on other occasions by that agency removed all doubt as to high-level Iraqi complicity. To avoid leaks, our national security team met secretly with the President in his residence at night to review the results of the investigation and consider appropriate retaliation. The President decided to launch a retributive cruise missile attack against the headquarters of Iraqi intelligence in Baghdad.[2]

Even though this attack was postponed a day so that it would not fall

[2]After President Clinton had alerted former President Bush of the impending raid, I flew to Bush's summer home in Kennebunkport, Maine, to give him a run-down on the results of the investigation as well as the retaliation. The former President and Mrs. Bush received me warmly and gave me a tour of their oceanfront residence, which had been handsomely restored after extensive storm damage. While I was there, the Associated Press called Bush for a comment on the raid, and I was amused when he responded courteously but firmly, "I am not in the interview business anymore."

on the Muslim Sabbath, the decision to make it did not leak. The President ordered the missiles launched to reach their targets in Baghdad at around 1:00 A.M. so as to minimize loss of life to innocent civilians. Many of the missiles scored direct hits on their targets and caused significant, though not permanent, damage to Iraqi intelligence headquarters. In announcing the raid, the President said the plot to assassinate Bush for actions he took as President was "an attack against our country and all Americans."

Saddam Hussein threatened Kuwait again in early October 1994, only two weeks before my speech at Georgetown. At the outset, it looked like a rerun of the 1990 invasion. Saddam sent from 10,000 to 15,000 of his Republican Guard forces into positions close to the Kuwaiti border, and other Iraqi troops were also on the move. On October 9, President Clinton announced he was deploying 36,000 troops and some of our most potent aircraft to the region to respond to the Iraqi buildup. I was just then leaving on a trip to the Middle East and immediately revised my plans to include a stop in Kuwait.

During my visit to the troops in Kuwait on October 12, I saw the tremendous value of our policy of pre-positioning equipment on the territory of our threatened allies. Our service personnel could fly in, marry up with their equipment, and be on their way to the threatened border areas within 12 hours. Without pre-positioned equipment, it could have taken weeks to reach the same result. When I met with our troops at Camp Doha in Kuwait, I told them, "The message that you men represent seems to be getting through . . . some of his forces seem to be turning around and going north."

This Iraqi military thrust soon ended, but all through my years in office Saddam continued to harass UN weapons inspectors who were assessing compliance with UN resolutions. When the inspectors revealed that Iraq had developed a major biological weapons capability and had deployed biological weapons during the 1990 invasion of Kuwait, the world gained a fuller appreciation of the danger posed by Saddam Hussein.

The Georgetown speech is a good reminder of the hopes and aspirations, as well as the frustrations and disappointments, of the search for peace in the Middle East. I remain convinced that this search represents the pursuit of a vital interest for the United States, and that during President Clinton's first term we made great progress toward peace.

Maintaining the Momentum for Peace in the Middle East

Address at Georgetown University, Washington, D.C., October 24, 1994

Father O'Donovan, ladies and gentlemen: Thank you, Dean Krogh, for that introduction. Few institutions have done more to train and test the future leaders of our foreign policy than Georgetown. There is, of course, President Clinton. Only in America could one go on from the high office of undergraduate Chairman of the Georgetown Food Service Investigation Committee to become Commander-in-Chief. Georgetown also provided a home for Professor Madeleine Albright, our superb ambassador to the UN. It has sharpened the minds of countless other past, present, and future ambassadors and other diplomats.

Much has changed in the world since the cruel divisions of the Cold War disappeared. Containment of the Soviet Union need no longer be the focal point of American diplomacy. The United States has a new opportunity to build a more secure and integrated world of open societies and open markets.

But some things do not change. Four decades ago, in his final State of the Union address, President Truman captured the abiding nature of our national purpose: Circumstances change, and current questions take on different forms, new complications, year by year. But underneath, the great issues remain the same—prosperity, welfare, human rights, effective democracy, and above all, peace.

The extraordinary events of the last few weeks remind us once again that our nation's enduring interests do not shift with the times. And neither does our obligation to pursue those interests through persistent and steady diplomacy, backed by a willingness to use force when necessary. That kind of diplomacy does not seek immediate results at the expense of long-term goals. As we have seen so far in this remarkable autumn, the payoff comes over time.

In Haiti, President Aristide's triumphant return capped a three-year commitment to restore democratic government. When every avenue for a peaceful resolution was exhausted, we mobilized military action. Our willingness to back our commitments with force allowed us to meet our initial goals with maximum speed and minimum bloodshed. The coup leaders are gone. The legitimate government is back in place. Refugees are returning. We have sent a powerful message to would-be coup plotters: Democracy, the key to stability in the Americas, cannot be overturned with impunity and cannot be stolen from the people. In Haiti, as elsewhere, we must not be complacent. But we have made great strides.

Our determined diplomacy on the North Korean nuclear issue has yielded an agreed framework that advances long-standing American objectives. As implemented, it will lift the specter of a nuclear arms race from northeast Asia. Over 16 months of negotiations, we consulted closely with South Korea, Japan, and the International Atomic Energy Agency. We worked with China, Russia, and the other Security Council members and made real the threat of economic sanctions. The result is a broadly supported, verifiable agreement that preserves peace and stability in a region vital to our interests.

The recent achievements in Haiti and on the North Korean nuclear issue were the direct result of sustained American leadership, coalition-building, and diplomacy backed by force. That same consistent purpose and engagement have been the hallmark of this Administration's policy toward the Middle East. Today, I would like to focus on the dramatic changes that are occurring in this vital region. The Arab-Israeli conflict is coming to an end, with American leadership playing a critical role. What I want to do is to set the scene for the President's trip to the Middle East, which begins tomorrow morning.

The day after his election, almost two years ago, President Clinton reaffirmed America's enduring interest in the Middle East. He vowed to make the pursuit of Arab-Israeli peace one of his top priorities. And he put in place a comprehensive strategy to accelerate progress.

Diplomatically, the United States has helped to energize and sustain negotiations launched in Madrid and based upon UN Security Council Resolutions 242 and 338. Economically, we have marshalled international support for the Israeli-PLO Declaration of Principles. We have established the U.S.-Israel-Jordan Economic Commission. And we have pressed for an end to the Arab boycott. Strategically, we have strengthened our security ties with Israel and our key Arab friends, and thus formed a bulwark against aggression by the region's rogue regimes, especially Iraq and Iran.

Today, this strategy is producing historic results. In 24 hours, the President will embark on a trip that will reinforce every element of the basic approach he laid down almost two years ago.

First, to advance the peace process, he will witness Jordan become only the second Arab state to sign a full peace treaty with Israel. In Damascus, he will seek to build on this momentum by pressing for progress in negotiations between Israel and Syria.

Second, in his meetings in Israel, Jordan, Egypt, and Saudi Arabia, the President will preview next week's economic conference in Casablanca. There, 900 chief executive officers and senior executives from Israel, the Arab states, and around the world will explore the opportunities being created by the transformation of the Middle East and North Africa.

Finally, in Kuwait, the President will visit with American soldiers— part of the force he deployed there two weeks ago to turn back Saddam Hussein's threat to his neighbors. Throughout his trip, the President will deliver an unmistakable message: The United States will do everything in its power to advance the opportunity that exists to build a new future for the Middle East. We cannot allow the terrorists of Hamas and Hezbollah or the rogue regimes of Iraq and Iran to kill the prospects for peace. Standing shoulder-to-shoulder with Israel and our Arab partners, the United States will stay the course to ensure that the forces of the future triumph over the forces of the past.

This is also the message that Jordan and Israel will send at their signing ceremony on Wednesday. King Hussein and Prime Minister Rabin are committed to building a "warm" peace. These two courageous leaders are determined that their border will become a gateway rather than a barrier. Already, there are ads in Israeli papers for tours of Jordan's great historical sites in Petra and Jerash. Through the work of the U.S.-Jordan-Israel Trilateral Commission, plans are underway to develop joint economic projects, to share water resources, and to develop the Jordan Rift Valley. These projects will build bonds of human contact and common interest. They will cement an enduring peace.

Over the last year, the Middle East has begun a broad transformation that I believe is fundamental. The changes have been so rapid and constant that, today, we take for granted developments that two years ago seemed fantastic.

The Israeli-PLO Declaration of Principles is giving more than 800,000 Palestinians in Gaza and Jericho control over their lives. An agreement has been reached on early empowerment for the West Bank, and negotiations have begun for Palestinian elections. Of course, great difficulties remain. But Prime Minister Rabin, Foreign Minister Peres, and Chairman Arafat are determined to make peace a reality. Economic development is essential to the Palestinians' success. Palestinians need proof that peace will improve their lives. That is why the United States has mobilized the donor community to support Palestinian self-government. That is why we have worked so closely with Chairman Arafat to allow aid projects to begin in Gaza and Jericho. But more must be done to facilitate the flow of assistance and maximize its effect so it can be felt by people on the ground.

If the Palestinians' greatest need is economic development—and it is—the greatest threat they confront is Hamas terror. As surely as last week's bus massacre was targeted at Israelis, it was also aimed at destroying Palestinian aspirations. If peace brings nothing but more terror, the process of reconciliation surely will not succeed. Palestinians, more than anyone, will suffer. It is imperative that Chairman Arafat fulfill his responsibility to root out terror in the areas he controls. The same courage he has demonstrated in making peace must now be shown in fighting the enemies of peace.

The Israeli-Syrian negotiating track also has undergone important changes in the last year. For the first time, these once bitter enemies are engaged in serious negotiations to end their conflict. I have spent dozens of hours in intensive discussions with President Assad and Prime Minister Rabin. I can tell you that both men are deeply engaged in addressing the central issues of a settlement. We have succeeded in narrowing differences, but important gaps remain.

In my view, the time is fast approaching when some very difficult decisions must be made. If these talks are to succeed, if they are to produce the "peace of the brave" of which President Assad speaks, then the deliberate pace of the current negotiations must give way to a bolder approach.

We understand the risks and costs involved. For Syria, peace requires overcoming decades of suspicion and ending policies geared to confrontation. In an environment of genuine and comprehensive peace, in which there will be no place for terrorists on Israel's borders, we can look to the day when relations between Syria and the United States will improve. For Israel, peace with Syria will require difficult decisions. But the promise of peace is powerful: an end to the Arab-Israeli conflict, an end to the threat of war, and Israel's full integration into the political and economic life of the Middle East.

There are stern tests for peace between Israel and Syria. First, it must be a real peace that reflects an active commitment to reconciliation. It is significant that President Assad has said that Syria has made a strategic choice for peace with Israel and is prepared to meet its objective requirements. The requirements of real peace are clear to all: Agreed-upon withdrawal, full diplomatic relations, borders that facilitate the movement of people and goods, and a commitment never to threaten each other again.

Second, peace between Israel and Syria must provide security for both sides. After decades of hostility, each side needs to be sensitive to the security concerns of the other. If requested, the United States stands ready to participate, in an appropriate form, in the security arrangements negotiated between the parties. Let there be no doubt on this point: America's strategic commitment to Israel's security is unshakable. We will maintain Israel's qualitative military edge and its ability to defend itself by itself. As President Clinton has pledged, the United States will do all it can to help Israel minimize the risks it takes for peace.

Finally, peace between Israel and Syria must open the way to a comprehensive peace. An Israeli-Syrian agreement will inevitably widen the circle of Arab states making peace with Israel. And it will build the confidence of all that peace will endure. This is why we say an agreement between Israel and Syria is a key to a comprehensive peace. Our vision is simple: on the one hand, an Israel that is secure and at peace with every Arab and Islamic state of goodwill; on the other hand, an Arab world liberated from conflict, able to devote its resources to economic development and the needs of its people.

We are making dramatic progress toward a comprehensive peace. In just the last month, with American encouragement, Morocco and Tunisia established official ties with Israel. And in a meeting with me at the UN a very short time ago, Saudi Arabia and the other states of the Gulf Cooperation Council announced an end to the secondary and tertiary boycott of companies that deal with Israel. This opens enormous trade and investment opportunities both for Israel and American business. Very soon, we hope to see the entire boycott relegated, as it must be, to the history books.

Next week in Casablanca, the Middle East's progress toward a new future will take a leap forward when Morocco's King Hassan convenes the Middle East/North Africa Economic Summit Conference. Just as the Madrid conference shattered the taboo on political contacts between Israel and the Arabs, so too will Casablanca shatter the taboo on private sector cooperation.

Our message there will be powerful: The Middle East is open for business. Through investment, trade, and joint ventures, private commerce can build the ties that will transform peace between governments into peace between peoples. Only a vibrant private sector can generate the growth and integration needed to undergird an enduring peace. I am pleased that American companies will be well represented at Casablanca, and that they are poised to take advantage of tremendous new opportunities in the Middle East and North Africa. Governments, too, must do their part. They must reduce economic barriers and help build the infrastructure that joins the Middle East by road, air, fax, and microchip.

Redefining the Middle East from a zone of continuing conflict to one of expanding reconciliation is the opportunity that we must seize now. And that is the opportunity that we must protect from the enemies of peace. The recent wave of terror against Israel has been undertaken by desperate forces who know that their extremism has no future in a region moving toward peace. Their only hope is to fight a rearguard action of violence designed to return the Middle East to a tragic past of fear and conflict. We will not let them succeed.

The international community must reject the terrorism of Hamas, Hezbollah, and other extremists. Strong condemnation of terror, especially from Israel's Arab partners, is an essential starting point. But condemnation is not enough. A real penalty must be imposed. We must join together to turn off all foreign sources of funding for terrorism, both public and private. Front organizations based abroad that are linked to terrorism must be shut down. And the perpetrators and organizers of terror must be punished.

That is the course we are urging upon governments in the Middle East and around the world. And that is the course we are pursuing. We will do everything we can—and seek legislation where necessary—to ensure that Hamas and other terrorists do not get support from inside the United States. Of course, radical groups could not continue their atrocities without the support of rejectionist states. Iran and Iraq remain the region's most dangerous actors. Through our policy of dual containment, the United States is leading the world in combating the threat they pose.

Iran is the world's most significant state sponsor of terrorism and the most ardent opponent of the Middle East peace process. The international community has been far too tolerant of Iran's outlaw behavior. Arms sales and preferential economic treatment, which make it easier for Iran to divert resources to terrorism, should be terminated. The evidence is overwhelming: Iran is intent on projecting terror and extremism across the Middle East and beyond. Only a concerted international effort can stop it.

In recent days, the rogue state of Iraq has tested our resolve, and we have met the test. In a scenario chillingly like that preceding the 1990 invasion of Kuwait, Saddam Hussein moved troops to the Kuwaiti border. Within hours, President Clinton deployed U.S. forces to Kuwait. Saddam got the message, stopped dead in his tracks, and pulled back. The UN Security Council—acting under U.S. leadership—passed a unanimous resolution demanding that Saddam withdraw the forces he had moved to the south. It barred him from taking any actions in the future to enhance his military forces there. And it warned Saddam never again to threaten his neighbors or UN operations in Iraq.

Saddam has shown himself to be a repeat offender, trusted neither by the international community nor by the Arab world. We have put him on notice that any repetition of his recent threats will be met by all means necessary, including military force.

The Iraqi people should understand that Saddam's brutal regime bears full responsibility for their suffering. Saddam has continued to waste Iraq's resources on military ventures. He has refused to take advantage of UN resolutions that would permit humanitarian needs to be met. I assure you that Saddam will not intimidate the UN into lifting sanctions. He knows that sanctions can only be eased after Iraq complies in full with all relevant Security Council resolutions. Not surprisingly, that is the only approach he has not tried.

Saddam's continued aggression and Hamas' recent campaign of terror underscore that forces of hatred and extremism still stalk the Middle East. But we will not allow their violence to blind us to the broader sweep of history at work in the region. Amazing change is under way. As this century draws to a close, Arabs and Israelis stand on the threshold of a new future—one of hope and peace, not despair and war. American leadership, power, and diplomacy, through Administrations of both parties, has been indispensable in bringing us to this moment of promise. If the United States had not stepped forward, Iraqi forces might today be back in Kuwait City, North Korea would be proceeding to build nuclear weapons, and Haitians would still be suffering under military dictators. Our recent achievements remind us that only the United States has the strategic vision and the global capabilities to lead.

Now more than ever, American leadership is critical to ensure that the promise of peace becomes a reality. We cannot—we will not—allow the forces of the past to destroy this historic opportunity. The momentum for peace must be maintained.

Thank you very much.

FOURTEEN

The Middle East Opens for Business

The name "Casablanca" is magical for the American people. It symbolizes glamour, mystery, and intrigue, due in large part to the fame of its
namesake motion picture. In 1994, the city of Casablanca played a more
mundane but no less important role: it was the site of a major development in the economic dimension of the Middle East peace process.[1]

For a year after the historic handshake on the South Lawn of the
White House on September 13, 1993, the peace process had proceeded
at a dramatic pace. The year had brought many accomplishments, each
one of which was more than any of us had thought possible back in January 1993: Jordan and Israel had concluded a peace treaty; the Interim
Agreement that created the Palestinian Authority and produced Israeli
redeployment from Gaza and Jericho had been concluded in May 1994;
progress had been made, albeit slowly, in implementing the Israeli-PLO
Declaration of Principles; on the Israeli-Syrian track, the parties were
engaged in serious negotiations facilitated by my shuttle diplomacy; two
Arab states, Morocco and Tunisia, had joined Egypt and Jordan to establish ties with Israel; and the Arab world had begun to take steps to
end its boycott of Israel. It appeared that the peace process had come far

---

[1] I concluded my opening remarks at the 1994 Casablanca conference by para-
phrasing the famous Humphrey Bogart line: "This conference could be the beginning of a beautiful friendship." Although slightly delayed, the applause and smiles
from the audience made it clear that the film is a classic not only in America.

enough for us to bring the parties together to pursue its economic dimension.

Casablanca was chosen to host the meeting because it was one of the few Arab cities in which a large delegation of Israeli business leaders could expect a hospitable reception. This was a tribute to the tolerance and farsightedness of King Hassan II of Morocco, coupled with an important Jewish presence in Morocco. The conference brought together not only public officials but also nearly 1,000 private sector leaders, including 150 from the United States, to discuss everything from building common economic institutions to forging ties between individual businesses. The event proved to be a practical first step toward laying the economic foundations for future stability in the region, and symbolically it meant, as I said, that the Middle East was "now open for business."[2]

The logic behind the Casablanca gathering was quite simple: for lasting peace to take hold, there had to be more than just paper agreements between governments. A true peace process must engender confidence and trust between societies. Peace has to be tangible, something people can observe, understand, and embrace every day. It has to improve the quality of life and provide some hope for the future. In this sense, the prospects for strengthening and consolidating peace significantly depended on making both Arab and Israeli societies more prosperous, more confident, and more secure. We believed that rather than simply being a result of peace, improving commercial relations could help drive the process.

We first began to brainstorm about organizing an economic conference in the autumn of 1993, shortly after the Israeli-PLO signing. It grew out of an idea that Israeli Foreign Minister Shimon Peres had advanced. He had long believed that economic development would help foster political and social reconciliation; he often spoke in sweeping terms about his vision for close economic ties between Arabs and Israelis.

The specifics of a regional economic summit began to take shape by

---

[2]The Casablanca conference immediately followed President Clinton's first visit to the Middle East (see Chapter 13). Although the press coverage of that trip somewhat overshadowed that of Casablanca, the President's visit inspired enthusiasm throughout the region and provided a welcome boost for the conference.

the summer of 1994. The situation required more than a rerun of the conference we had hosted in October 1993 to mobilize assistance for the Palestinians. We needed to go beyond aid to promote investment and trade in the region. In this sense, the purpose of the conference was to create a supportive environment in which government and business leaders could meet and discuss ways to cooperate. During the conference, I vividly remember looking down into the courtyard of the convention hall to see the stunning sight of Israeli businessmen in dark suits and Arabs in their traditional white robes exchanging ideas and business cards. This remarkable scene captured what we were trying to accomplish in Casablanca.

To assure vigorous support from the Western private sector, we worked closely with Les Gelb of the Council on Foreign Relations and Klaus Schwab of the World Economic Forum. These organizations co-sponsored the conference, and the skillful and determined efforts of Gelb and Schwab proved invaluable. They were particularly influential in developing the concept of using the private sector as an instrument of diplomacy—not only to create regional prosperity, but to build a business constituency for the peace process. Along with the support of our host, King Hassan, their enthusiasm and dedication were major reasons the conferenc went so well. From within the Department, Joan Spero, the skilled Under Secretary for Economic Affairs, took the lead in ensuring participation by U.S. business, and Ambassador Dennis Ross played his usual vital role in dealing with the regional parties.

My October 30 address opening the conference outlined two basic themes. First, with a focus on facilitating private partnerships for trade and investment, Casablanca represented an effort to "transform the peace being made between governments into a peace between peoples." Second, to create the right environment for economic prosperity, many nations needed to retool their long-stagnant (and still largely statist and protectionist) economies. Although the Middle East has considerable riches, most of its capital is invested abroad rather than at home. To reverse this disturbing trend, I argued, governments had to undertake serious economic reform—whether through privatization, investing in infrastructure, or empowering their workers. Such efforts would also enhance international confidence about investing further in the region. I made the point that the Middle East, like every other region, had to compete in an increasingly global economy. Despite its recent economic success, the Middle East had no monopoly on the world's attention, goodwill, or, more to the point, investment capital. It would have to earn these through reform.

To demonstrate the U.S. commitment to establishing the economic foundation for peace, we came to Casablanca prepared to offer several substantial initiatives. I outlined all of these in my speech, which was designed to drive the conference's substantive agenda. They included establishing a $75 million investment fund through the Overseas Private Investment Corporation (OPIC) and pushing for the creation of a regional tourism board, which we considered a quick way to generate hard currency revenues. Perhaps most important to us was our commitment to lead the effort to create a Middle East and North Africa Bank for Cooperation and Development. Such a bank could provide private projects and regional public projects with funds that might not be available from other sources. The bank was opposed by several Western European governments because they felt that the World Bank was the proper institution to direct such funding and that support for it would be eroded by another bank. Although the bank initiative was controversial, it was consistently advocated by President Clinton, and many hailed it as the most concrete accomplishment of the Casablanca summit. The bank was finally chartered in 1996 with headquarters in Cairo, but it has not yet been funded by Congress, and other nations are waiting for us to take the lead.

I hoped that the Casablanca conference, commencing three years to the day after Arab and Israeli leaders sat face-to-face for the first time in Madrid, would one day be remembered as the economic corollary to that pathbreaking 1991 gathering. With a few years' hindsight, it is clear that the Casablanca meeting was indeed a historic event. Three follow-on conferences—in Amman, Cairo, and Doha—have taken place. Even though the political environment has soured between Israel's new Netanyahu government and the Arab world, and some Arab nations boycotted the 1997 Doha gathering (see Chapter 34), the conferences have continued to highlight the economic dimension of peace and have brought material benefits to the countries attending them.

Building the Structures of Peace and Prosperity in the New Middle East

Remarks at the Royal Palace, Casablanca, October 30, 1994

Excellencies, ladies and gentlemen: On behalf of President Clinton and the American people, I am delighted to attend this historic Middle East/ North Africa Economic Summit. We all owe King Hassan our deepest gratitude for hosting this unique event. Building on his vision of Middle East peace, the King has brought us together to remove walls and build bridges between the peoples of the Middle East and the world.

President Clinton and the United States are pleased to be co-sponsoring this summit together with President Yeltsin and the Russian Federation. Let me express our appreciation to Les Gelb and the Council on Foreign Relations and to Klaus Schwab and the World Economic Forum for their outstanding efforts to structure and organize this important gathering.

This summit convenes at an extraordinary time. I have just accompanied President Clinton on his recent trip to the Middle East. Let me share with you our assessment. The Middle East is undergoing a remarkable transformation:

Jordan and Israel have signed a peace treaty;

The Israeli-PLO Declaration is being implemented;

Morocco and Tunisia have established ties with Israel;

Israel and Syria are engaged in serious negotiations; and

Arab nations are taking steps to end the boycott of Israel.

These monumental events mean that the Arab-Israeli conflict is coming to an end. The forces of the future can, they must, they will succeed. The peacemakers will prevail.

Securing the future is what brings us here today. Our mission is clear: We must transform the peace being made between governments into a peace between peoples. Governments can make the peace. Governments can create the climate for economic growth. But only the people of the private sector can marshall the resources necessary for sustained growth and development. Only the private sector can produce a peace that will endure.

Three years ago to the day, nations gathered in Madrid for a conference whose significance grows with each passing month. As we realize now, Madrid opened the pathway to peace. Here, this week, let us declare that the Casablanca conference will open the pathway to economic ties and growth. Madrid shattered taboos on political contacts between Israel and its Arab neighbors. Let us ensure that Casablanca shatters taboos on private sector cooperation.

Let this summit send a message to the world: The Middle East and North Africa are now open for business.

Over the course of the 20th century, the world has learned a powerful lesson: Peace cannot be sustained when there is widespread suffering and misery. Following World War II, wise leaders applied this lesson to the reconstruction and integration of Western Europe. They built structures of cooperation, beginning with economic ties, to lessen the likelihood of conflict among nations. Our purpose in Casablanca is to apply that same lesson to this region, as we work to create a more peaceful and secure Middle East.

On Wednesday night in Jordan, President Clinton became the first American President to address an Arab parliament. There, he underscored the importance of generating the economic benefits of peace. As he said:

> If people do not feel these benefits, if poverty persists in breeding despair and killing hope, then the purveyors of fear will find fertile ground. Our goal must be to spread prosperity and security to all.

The Madrid conference of 1991 started us on the way. It not only launched a series of bilateral negotiations to resolve the region's political disputes. It also created a framework of meaningful multilateral talks among some 40 nations to promote Arab-Israeli cooperation on a region-wide scale. Joint projects are already underway to check the spread of the desert, to quench the region's thirst for water, and to protect the environment from oil spills. Under the leadership of the European Union, the working group on economic development has drawn up a list identifying priority sectors for economic cooperation.

Israel, Jordan, and the United States are working together to create opportunities for private sector investment in areas that were unthinkable only months ago. An ambitious master plan for the development of the Jordan Rift Valley has been completed. Joint efforts to promote tourism in the Red Sea ports of Aqaba and Eilat are already attracting millions of dollars of investment in hotels, infrastructure, and tourist facilities.

Progress toward Arab-Israeli peace has opened the door to economic cooperation in support of peace. Now, together, we must take a bold step through that door. We must form a public sector-private sector partnership for government and business to bring their political and economic power jointly to bear.

I have seen the situation from both sides—from the private sector, where I have spent most of my career, and from the public sector during my three tours in government. I have also been heavily involved in the affairs of the Middle East for the past two years. Let me offer a challenge and a prediction: If the forces of peace prevail and if governments here adopt free market reforms, the Middle East and North Africa will enjoy an era of economic growth that exceeds anything they have seen in this century. There is no reason why the economic miracles that are transforming parts of Asia, Eastern Europe, and Latin America cannot also transform this region. I can foresee a day when the 300 million people of the Middle East and North Africa, so long held back by strife and hatred, can finally join the mainstream of international commerce.

The presence here in Casablanca of almost 1,000 of the world's business leaders is proof that you understand the vast potential of this region. I salute your vision. But I also know that you are hard-nosed realists. The new Middle East holds no monopoly on attracting your attention or your capital.

That is why the Middle East, even a Middle East at peace, cannot be complacent; it must compete. The world must know that the Middle East is not only at peace but committed to long-term reform if world-class companies are to invest in this region.

Almost 150 American firms are here in Casablanca. They are well-poised to take advantage of the opportunities this region presents. American companies don't fear risk; they thrive on it. But like serious companies everywhere, they need confidence—confidence in a business environment that makes it possible to do business.

To create a climate for economic growth and development, we need commitment and action by governments inside the region as well as those outside. For decades, governments dominated economic development here, building infrastructure and national industries. In the process, they incurred massive foreign debts. Since 1970, the countries of the Middle East have borrowed more than $90 billion from abroad. Over 90% of this borrowing was absorbed by the public sector, where it was too often steered toward the military or inefficient state enterprises.

Not surprisingly, private capital and the private entrepreneurs that went with it fled the region. In the last 20 years, capital outflows from the Middle East and North Africa have exceeded $180 billion. This capital flight has had enormous practical consequences.

We must work to reverse this destructive trend. It is time for the region's private sectors to invest in their nations, in their peoples, and in their futures. They must bring their capital home. But if they are to do so, governments must take steps to create a favorable economic environment. How can you expect foreigners to invest here when citizens of the Middle East do not invest?

Governments here must undertake serious economic reform. Morocco has begun that process. Privatization is proceeding, stock market capitalization is rising, foreign investment is expanding, and growth is taking off. Other countries in the region, such as Tunisia, Israel, Egypt, and Jordan, have also begun to take similar steps.

But more must be done. Governments need to end trade restrictions and overcome other barriers to trade and investment. They must reform and modernize their tax systems and commercial dispute mechanisms. They need to ensure predictable, transparent, and fair legal systems and business practices. They need private financial markets. And they must lift the heavy hand of government regulation that stifles entrepreneurs.

An important political step to make the region's environment more attractive to global companies must be taken as well. The last remnants of the boycott aimed against Israel must be eliminated. Last month, Saudi Arabia and its partners in the Gulf Cooperation Council announced an end to the secondary and tertiary boycotts. This means enormous opportunities for investment and trade. Now it is time for other Arab leaders to follow the GCC's example. Indeed, it is time for the Arab League to dismantle the boycott entirely.

Governments outside the Middle East and North Africa must also do their part to create a climate conducive to economic growth. They can take steps to encourage their companies to invest in the joint ventures that will become the stuff of Middle East peace. They can provide incentives and reduce risks for foreign investors. They can encourage trade by reducing barriers. They can create the financial mechanisms that will help mobilize capital for regional projects.

The United States is already taking concrete steps in all these areas:

> Through our Overseas Private Investment Corporation, we have established a $75 million Regional Investment Fund to encourage investment in regional projects like those envisaged in the Jordan Rift Valley development plan.

> We have also used OPIC guarantees to help a group of American business leaders from the Arab and Jewish communities foster Palestinian economic development. These Builders for Peace have already launched five OPIC-backed private sector projects in the West Bank and Gaza.

> We are exploring practical means of expanding trade and investment opportunities, including initiatives to lessen barriers to trade and bilateral investment treaties.

> And, President Clinton, in consultation with interested governments, has decided that the U.S. will take the lead in supporting a Middle East and North Africa Bank for Cooperation and Development.

Other governments outside the region are engaged in similar efforts to support the involvement of their private sectors in the development of the Middle East and North Africa. But we all need to do more. This is the opportunity presented by the Casablanca Summit. We must seize it.

Here in Casablanca, our focus must be practical. Our work must not be limited to exhortation. We must generate specific outcomes, with mechanisms to act on our proposals.

Specifically, in this conference the United States will call for the following:

First, adoption of principles leading to the free movement of goods, capital, ideas, and labor across the borders of the Middle East and North Africa.

Second, the establishment of a Middle East and North Africa Bank for Cooperation and Development. A bank, properly structured, can serve as a financing mechanism for viable regional projects. It should be available for the private sector as well as the public sector, and should facilitate a regional economic dialogue.

Third, the creation of a regional tourism board. Tourism is one of the clearest and quickest ways to generate hard currency revenues. The Middle East and North Africa abound with incredible archeological and religious sites. Millions of tourists will flock to visit as package tours across previously closed borders become available.

Fourth, the development of a regional business council—a chamber of commerce, if you will. This entity will promote intraregional trade relations and commercial opportunities.

To move expeditiously on each of these proposals, this conference must establish two on-going bodies: first, a steering committee, to meet within one month; second, an executive secretariat, located in Morocco, that will serve as a clearing house of information. It will be an "address" for the private sector by sharing data, promoting contracts, and furnishing project information.

Finally, the United States will call for a follow-on conference in Amman in 1995. Casablanca represents the launching of a process to promote regional economic development and cooperation. Amman will represent the next milestone and point all of us to seeking very tangible accomplishments by the 1995 conference.

In a golden age over a millennium ago, the Middle East was the commercial and cultural crossroads of the world. Harkening back to the glorious economic and cultural history of the old Middle East, this summit heralds a new Middle East in the heart of the global economy once again. We have the opportunity—and the responsibility—to build a more peaceful, more prosperous, and more integrated Middle East and world. Working together in a public-private endeavor, let us dedicate ourselves to making that vision a reality.

If I may borrow the famous Humphrey Bogart line, this conference could be the beginning of a beautiful friendship.

Thank you very much.

FIFTEEN

Averting a Nuclear Threat in Korea

Of all the foreign policy challenges the Clinton Administration faced upon taking office, none was more immediately dangerous than North Korea. This remote communist nation, one of the most isolated and repressive on the planet, is caught in a time warp. Its economy is in shambles, with starvation rampant, but nonetheless the risk of a desperation strike at the South by its million-man army cannot be ignored. The South Korean capital of Seoul is well within North Korean artillery range, and North Korea's troops, heavily deployed along the Demilitarized Zone (DMZ) between the two nations, could quickly inflict serious damage. The United States has roughly 37,000 troops stationed along the DMZ, and we have extended our nuclear deterrent umbrella to the peninsula in support of our commitment to defend South Korea. Although every report I reviewed concluded that our forces would ultimately overcome an attack from the North, South Korea and indeed our own troops would sustain severe losses in the process.

Right from the start, our Administration placed Korea among its highest strategic priorities. On his first presidential trip overseas in July 1993, Clinton traveled to South Korea following the G-7 summit in Tokyo. He delivered a major policy address in Seoul and visited our troops along the DMZ. I accompanied him and was struck by the bleakness of the landscape and the stark reality of the hostile North Korean forces mobilized just across the line.

North Korea's aggressive effort to develop a nuclear weapons program destabilized matters further. When President Clinton came into office, the situation was frankly alarming. North Korea had signed the Non-Proliferation Treaty (NPT) in 1985. By entering into a nuclear safeguards agreement with the IAEA that same year, it had committed to opening its nuclear sites to inspections. But now it was refusing to allow IAEA inspectors to enter its nuclear complex at Yongbyon, where there was good reason to believe weapons-grade plutonium was stored. Substantial evidence also existed that North Korea was in the process of building another, larger nuclear reactor, potentially providing the capability to produce enough plutonium for 10 to 12 nuclear bombs a year. After several months during which the IAEA unsuccessfully sought access to the Yongbyon site, North Korea upped the ante by threatening to withdraw from the NPT. By the spring of 1994, the stalemate had become a crisis.

After intense deliberations, our Administration decided, in cooperation with South Korea and other key allies, to push the UN Security Council to approve economic sanctions against North Korea. We would continue to seek a diplomatic solution, but we had to make clear to North Korea that our patience had run out. Given Pyongyang's threats that it would consider the imposition of sanctions an act of war, we also began to augment our military capability in the region. A Patriot antimissile battalion and a group of Apache attack helicopters were among the assets the Pentagon deployed to the DMZ.

In June 1994, our effort to bring a diplomatic end to the crisis received an unexpected boost from former President Jimmy Carter. The North Koreans had asked Carter to visit Pyongyang, and he informed President Clinton that he wished to accept. Carter had long taken an interest in the Korean conflict. During 1993–94, Carter had been outspoken about our Korean policy, criticizing our push toward sanctions. He also had a significant personal connection to the region—our Ambassador to South Korea, James T. Laney, had previously been the President of Emory University and was closely associated with the Carter Center in Atlanta.

On June 16, Carter called from Pyongyang to report a breakthrough. The North Koreans, he said, had agreed to halt their nuclear program in order for negotiations to begin. While Carter's statement that the crisis was over was somewhat premature, the commitments he gained did provide a basis for negotiations. Carter had persuaded the North Koreans to state that they would leave the Yongbyon complex open for IAEA inspectors and suspend their efforts to obtain weapons-grade plutonium. In further discussions with a U.S. government team resulting in a one-page letter "formalizing" the commitments made to Carter and setting the stage for negotiations, the North Koreans also agreed not to refuel the Yongbyon reactor and not to reprocess any more used nuclear fuel to make plutonium. While welcome, these commitments did nothing to curb what North Korea could do with plutonium it already had, nor did they provide the international community with any way to gauge how far North Korea's nuclear program had developed.

Given this opening, however, I sent Ambassador Robert Gallucci, a capable career civil servant, to lead negotiations with the North Koreans. As the Assistant Secretary of State for Political-Military Affairs who had worked to investigate Iraq's nuclear program after the Gulf War, Gallucci had knowledge of these complex issues. Because of the nuclear dimension and global ramifications of the negotiations, the United States took the lead in them. But we kept the South Koreans—as well as the Chinese, Japanese, and Russians—closely informed. Just as negotiations began in July 1994, North Korean President Kim Il Sung died. To our surprise, the "Great Leader's" death seemed only a minor setback; Gallucci was still able to obtain some initial commitments by early August.

On October 21, after three months of tough, often heated negotiations with the notoriously obdurate North Koreans, Gallucci concluded a deal in Geneva. This "Agreed Framework" stipulated that North Korea would adhere to the NPT and permit IAEA inspections, and outlined specific steps for it to freeze, and later dismantle, its nuclear program. Further, North Korea committed to restarting its dialogue with South Korea regarding reconciliation. As an incentive to carry out this highly detailed agreement, which contained a series of sequential steps, the United States pledged to enable the North Koreans to obtain modern light-water nuclear reactors, which would provide power but have much less capability to provide plutonium for nuclear weapons. To organize and fund the project, the United States would create a multinational consortium known as the Korean Energy Development Organization (KEDO).

The visit I made to Seoul in November 1994 provided an important opportunity to convey a message of reassurance and support to our South Korean allies. Although the Agreed Framework was an important achievement—reducing the threat of nuclear conflict and laying the foundation for a gradual relaxation of tensions—many South Koreans remained uneasy about the accord. Moreover, they were frustrated, and in some cases suspicious, that the negotiations had taken place between us and Pyongyang. History has been cruel to the South Koreans, and many doubted that any deal acceptable to North Korea could be acceptable to them. The Pyongyang regime was indeed duplicitous and brutal. North Korea had invaded the South in 1950, attempted to raid the South Korean President's quarters (known as the "Blue House") in 1968, killed the wife of South Korean President Park in 1974, and assassinated members of the South Korean cabinet in Rangoon in 1983. Given such a legacy of danger from the North, the South Korean public feared the possibility that the United States would withdraw its security commitment prematurely or move ahead precipitously in forging ties with Pyongyang at their expense.

South Korea's hesitance concerned me for two main reasons. First, we could not even come close to implementing the complex Framework without its full cooperation. Along with Japan, South Korea would have to play a major role in financing and leading KEDO. Second, although our own contribution to implementing the agreement would be relatively modest (around $25 million annually), many in Congress, particularly on the Republican side, criticized the agreement and made it clear that we would have trouble getting the money. Without active and vocal South Korean support, we had no chance of convincing the skeptics to back our initiative.

In my private discussions and public statements in Seoul, I sought to explain the virtues of the agreement, encouraging the South Koreans to set aside their wariness and support it. With President Kim Young Sam, I reiterated the strength and value of our bilateral relationship and urged him to try to build public support for our efforts.[1] If anything, I told him, the U.S.–South Korean relationship was sounder and stronger after having been tested by the arduous negotiations in Geneva. I also reiterated that direct South-North dialogue and negotiations were central to the future of the peninsula.

I stressed the same points with my counterpart, Foreign Minister Han Sung Joo. An intelligent moderate who had pushed for South Korea to abandon its "zero-sum" approach toward the North, Han had been in-

[1]In five days, President Kim would meet with President Clinton at the second APEC Leaders' Meeting in Jakarta, and all of these themes would be reiterated.

dispensable during the Geneva negotiations. With full knowledge of the political risks to his own position, he had pressed Kim to endorse the Agreed Framework.[2] We now needed him to exhibit the same leadership on implementing it. He was ready to help us, suggesting some ways to ease President Kim's worries and reassure the South Koreans of our firm support.

In a November 9 speech before an audience dominated by Korean business leaders, I sought to explain the Agreed Framework in the clearest possible terms, reassuring them that the deal was in their best interests and that our commitment to their security was as strong as ever. This speech was the first full statement of what the complex deal meant and why it was important. I emphasized that the agreement was based not on faith and trust, but rather on verification of compliance via defined checkpoints. Our assistance to North Korea was entirely contingent on its satisfying the conditions of the agreement. Finally, I used the speech to frame the agreement, and our relations with South Korea generally, in the context of our strong engagement and wider goals in Asia.

While the speech was intended to sell the virtues of the Agreed Framework to various audiences, it was somewhat overshadowed by an event taking place in the United States—the 1994 mid-term congressional elections. I was stunned to find that the Democrats had lost not just one but both Houses of Congress. I found myself in the awkward position of trying to rally support in a foreign country on a tough and controversial issue just as our political coalition at home was falling apart.

As the dimensions of the Democratic Party's loss became apparent in Asia, I recognized both an opportunity and a responsibility to make a statement reaffirming our commitments around the world. This was important not only because of our objective of sending a specific message of reassurance to the South Koreans, but also because of the need to make the exact same point to our allies around the globe. To the new Republican majority, I also wanted immediately to communicate a sense of bipartisanship and cooperation. To that end, my colleagues and I made last-minute revisions in the final section of my speech. The changes stressed the tradition of continuity in American foreign policy and stated

[2]Foreign Minister Han was forced out of office in a cabinet reshuffle in early 1996.

that we would be "steadfast in our commitments around the world," including those on the Korean Peninsula. I also expressed my confidence that I could work effectively with the Republican leaders in a spirit of bipartisanship.

As I look back, the Agreed Framework stands out as one of the major achievements of our foreign policy. Perhaps because of its complexity, perhaps because it never became the subject of intense national debate, its importance has never been fully recognized. Yet it stopped and eventually will dismantle a dangerous nuclear program that, in the hands of such a reckless and ruthless adversary, could have gravely threatened the entire region's security and stability. This was an occasion on which the United States rose to the challenge of its indispensable leadership role.

●

Ensuring Peace and Stability on the Korean Peninsula

Remarks to the Korea-America Friendship Society,

Seoul, November 9, 1994

It gives me great pleasure to be the first Secretary of State to address the Korea-America Friendship Society. You certainly have deepened our appreciation of the heritage of Korean-Americans, who have made such remarkable contributions to our nation. Let me also commend your efforts to improve tolerance and understanding between peoples of quite different backgrounds, a mission that is extremely important at this critical time.

Earlier today, I met with President Kim, Foreign Minister Han, and their colleagues. In these meetings, I commended the President on his announcement that the Republic of Korea is willing to take step-by-step measures to encourage economic cooperation with the North. And I hope that North Korea will respond positively and promptly.

I am here this afternoon to reaffirm the enduring commitment of the United States to the security of the Republic of Korea and to peace and stability on the Korean peninsula. As President Clinton said when we were together here in Seoul last year, "geography has placed our nations far apart, but history has drawn us close together." Our friendship was sealed when our troops fought and died together to defend this soil against aggression. It broadened as we took full advantage of the peace that followed to build commercial ties. It matured as the "second miracle on the Han"—Korea's democratic miracle—strengthened our common bonds. Now our friendship and our alliance have been proven once again in the crucible of a common challenge. By working together, we produced an agreement on the nuclear situation in North Korea that will assure a more secure Republic of Korea and a more secure Asia.

The development of our alliance reflects America's engagement in the Asia-Pacific region. America is and will remain a Pacific power. We will stand by our security commitments, we will maintain our forward military presence, and we will sustain our non-proliferation efforts. We will promote integration and growth through the Asia-Pacific Economic Cooperation forum, and through relations with the region's key economic powers. And we will continue to support political freedom and human rights—for these are the ultimate guarantors of security and prosperity. We are working to achieve a Pacific future where our allies and partners are free from the fear of war; where nations are made prosperous by the free exchange of goods and ideas; and where citizens can participate in the decisions that affect their lives. These elements of our comprehensive Asia-Pacific strategy—security, prosperity, and democracy—are mutually reinforcing. That strategy has produced significant results in recent months:

A nuclear agreement that can lead to a more secure Korean peninsula;

The launching of an historic regional security dialogue in the Asia-Pacific;

Agreements with Japan to open key domestic markets to foreign competition;

Improved ties with Vietnam resulting from the fuller accounting they have given us for our POW/MIAs;

A reinvigorated relationship with China, with movement on both arms control and human rights.

These achievements advance not just America's interests, but those of our Asian allies and friends as well. But as President Clinton told your National Assembly last year, "we must always remember that security comes first." Over the past decade, the United States has been working with you to halt North Korea's development of nuclear weapons. Almost two years ago, North Korea's announcement of its intentions to withdraw from the Nuclear Non-Proliferation Treaty threatened to plunge the region into crisis, if not into war.

Now, our determined diplomacy—made possible by America's unshakable partnership with the Republic of Korea—has put the nuclear issue on the road to resolution. The Agreed Framework will achieve the central strategic objectives shared by our two countries. It pulls us back from the brink of a crisis that could have spiraled into armed conflict, it lifts the specter of a nuclear arms race from Northeast Asia, and it bolsters a nonproliferation regime that is so essential to stability in this region and the world.

We achieved the Agreed Framework by maintaining clear and consistent objectives and priorities, and by making it plain to the North Koreans that our negotiating positions reflected the unified views of the United States and the Republic of Korea. President Kim was an active partner every step of the way. And I assure you that without our partnership, the negotiations could not have succeeded and there would have been no agreement.

Let me outline what the framework requires, and why it is good for the Republic of Korea, the United States, Asia, and the world.

First, the agreement immediately freezes the North Korean nuclear program. The North has agreed not to restart its 5 megawatt reactor. It will seal its reprocessing facility and not operate it again. It will not reprocess the spent fuel from the 5 megawatt reactor and will ship that fuel out of the country in due course. In short, North Korea's current capacity to separate or produce plutonium—the raw material for nuclear weapons and the most toxic substance on earth—will come to an end. And all of these steps will take place with the oversight of the International Atomic Energy Agency, and with the careful scrutiny of the international community.

Second, the North has agreed to freeze construction of its 50 and 200 megawatt reactors and of its reprocessing plant. Ultimately, these large nuclear facilities will be dismantled, along with related facilities in North Korea. Absent this agreement, the two large reactors, once completed, would have been capable of producing enough plutonium for not just one or two bombs, but dozens of bombs each year. Within a decade, the Republic of Korea, the United States, this region, and the world could have faced the greatest threat to international security since the Cuban missile crisis.

Third, under the Agreed Framework, North Korea must fully disclose its past nuclear activities. The IAEA is to have access to the information it needs. North Korea is obligated to cooperate with the measures the IAEA deems necessary—including special inspections—to resolve questions about its past activities. Implementation will take place over a period of time. But the safeguards agreement must be implemented fully before any significant nuclear components of the first light-water reactor are delivered to North Korea—and that is very significant.

Finally, North Korea will remain a party to the Nuclear Non-Proliferation Treaty, and must also fulfill additional obligations that go well beyond it. These are technical, but they are important. These include an end to plutonium separation, the shipment of spent fuel containing plutonium out of the country, and the dismantlement of the entire gas graphite reactor system.

These are the elements of the agreement. Each is very important. But the signing of the agreement brings a new challenge for the United States and the Republic of Korea. This is an important moment. We are moving to a second and critical phase in resolving the North Korea nuclear issue. We are moving from negotiation to implementation, from words to deeds. In the coming weeks, we will be taking five concrete steps toward implementation:

> First, together with the Republic of Korea and Japan, we will establish the Korean Energy Development Organization. This consortium of many countries will provide South Korea-type light-water reactors and alternative energy to the North. South Korean companies will play a central role in the provision of the reactors, just as the Republic of Korea will play a central role in the management of KEDO. The United States, the ROK, and Japan will meet this month to prepare for a KEDO conference we plan to hold before the new year.

Second, American representatives will meet with North Korea this weekend in Pyongyang to discuss safe storage of the spent fuel under IAEA scrutiny until it is shipped out of the country at a later time.

Third, later this month in Beijing, the United States and North Korea will begin to discuss the light-water reactor project.

Fourth, the IAEA will soon meet with the North to agree how to monitor the freeze of the North's nuclear program.

Finally, in early December, we will meet with the North Koreans in Washington to discuss establishing liaison offices in our two capitals. President Kim has also made it clear that the Republic of Korea is determined to move forward. As the President indicated, the agreement has provided a basis for lifting your country's ban on business contacts with North Korea. As the framework is implemented, these links can demonstrate to the North the concrete benefits of ending its isolation. It really can mark the beginning of a better future for all Koreans.

The United States and the Republic of Korea are determined that North Korea's commitments be fully implemented. This agreement, like any good agreement, rests on compliance and verification—not on good faith and not on trust.

The path to full implementation has defined checkpoints. If at any checkpoint North Korea fails to fulfill its obligations, it will lose the benefits of compliance that it so clearly desires. If it reneges, it will remain isolated. And throughout the process, as I assured President Kim this morning, we will always take the steps necessary to assure the security of the Republic of Korea and the region.

In implementing every phase of the Agreed Framework, we will continue to work with the Republic of Korea. Our collective effort will open the door to a new and productive dialogue between the Koreas. We share the conviction that the agreement cannot be fully implemented unless that dialogue moves forward. Let there be no doubt that we share serious concerns with the Republic of Korea about other aspects of North Korea's behavior—including the forward deployment of its conventional forces, missile proliferation, past support for terrorism, and disregard for human rights. These concerns must be resolved if North Korea is to be brought fully into the family of civilized nations.

We recognize that, at times, our resolve and our mettle will be tested. But I am convinced our common efforts will raise the possibility that the last bitter legacy of the Cold War, the division of the Korean peninsula, can finally be overcome.

As we go down this untraveled road together, I want to make a pledge to you on behalf of President Clinton and the American people: The United States will stand by you. We will remain unshakably committed to your defense.

We know that North Korea continues to present both a nuclear and conventional threat. Accordingly, American soldiers, at the existing force level of approximately 37,000 troops, will continue to stand watch with the ROK armed forces over the most fortified frontier in the world. As President Clinton has pledged, "our troops will stay here as long as the Korean people want and need us here."

The bedrock of our security commitment to the region will remain our forward military presence, supported by our treaty alliances with not only the ROK but also with Japan, Australia, the Philippines, and Thailand. We now have nearly the same number of troops in Asia as in Europe. We will maintain our force levels and their military readiness in Korea and elsewhere in this vital region. In Asia, just as in Europe and the Middle East, the future is being shaped by a central geostrategic fact: No great power now views another as an immediate military threat. The end of the Cold War means that we and our allies can now work with China and Russia to resolve common security concerns in the Asia-Pacific region. That is why we are encouraging new regional security dialogues among past and potential adversaries. In this respect, we welcomed the inauguration of the ASEAN Regional Forum last July, and we applaud the important role that the Republic of Korea has played in its creation. The inclusion of China, Russia, and Vietnam in the forum reflects the enormous changes and opportunities transforming the Asia-Pacific region. The Northeast Asian security dialogue also provides a valuable forum for advancing our common interest in regional stability, and we encourage that dialogue to continue.

We seek to turn enmity to understanding, and suspicion to cooperation. For example, we are encouraging Chinese leaders to allay the concerns of their neighbors by being more open about their defense planning. We have also been working with China to advance important non-proliferation goals. Last month, we agreed to work for a global ban on producing fissile materials for nuclear weapons. And Beijing pledged not to export missiles that fall under the Missile Technology Control Regime. These agreements are the most recent example of the ways in which our engagement with China is producing positive results for the region and the world.

The United States' commitment to security and stability in the Asia-Pacific region safeguards our nation's enduring stake in the region's remarkable prosperity. Expanding trade and investment with the world's fastest growing region is vital to our economic security. Asia's markets now support 2.5 million American jobs. Through APEC, GATT, and our bilateral dialogues, the United States is working to widen our opportunities to participate in Asia's economic boom.

Last year in Seattle, President Clinton convened the historic first meeting of leaders from the APEC members. Later this week, I will be in Jakarta, along with Foreign Minister Han, for this year's APEC Ministerial meeting, and the President will soon arrive for the Leaders' Meeting. With the help of the Republic of Korea and other APEC members, we hope to fuel the momentum for liberalization and cooperation generated last year. We fully support the ambitious agenda of President Soeharto, this year's APEC chairman, to establish the goal of free and open trade in the region by a set date. I thought that President Kim had it exactly right when he told me this morning that last year the APEC leaders had a vision when they met in Seattle. This year, in Indonesia, they can begin to turn that vision into reality.

Ratifying the GATT Uruguay Round agreement is another critical step in opening markets and spurring growth. As you know, the President is committed to GATT ratification and open trade. I trust that all our Pacific partners—including Korea—will show similar resolve in ratifying the Round now.

The United States and the Republic of Korea share a growing stake in the economic dynamism of the Asia-Pacific region, and in an open world trading system. The Korean people have made their economy the 13th largest in the world. We are your largest export market; you are our seventh largest. The Dialogue for Economic Cooperation (DEC) initiated in July 1993 by President Kim and President Clinton is an example of the new maturity of our bilateral and economic relationship. Now we must build on the progress we made through the DEC to overcome the barriers that remain to imports in important sectors like agriculture and autos.

Under President Kim, Korea is integrating its economy into the world trading system. It is driving an ambitious regional trade liberalization effort through its leadership of APEC's Trade and Investment committee. And in its bid to become a member of the OECD—a bid strongly backed by the United States—it is signaling its willingness to assume the leadership responsibilities of a developed nation. Once a recipient of foreign aid, the Republic of Korea is now an aid donor. As a successful democratic nation, Korea has many lessons to share. Korea has demonstrated that a developing market economy flourishes best alongside robust political competition and free trade unions. And it has shown that sustained economic development is more likely where government is accountable to the people, where the rule of law protects property and contracts, and where people have access to uncensored media.

No one needs to tell the Korean people that democracy is not a Western export. Indeed, you have reminded us that the yearning for freedom is based on a fundamental respect for human dignity that is common to all cultures. As President Kim has said: "Respect for human dignity, plural democracy, and free market economics have firmly taken root as universal values." And let me add that our alliance is so much stronger than ever because that conviction enunciated by President Kim has prevailed here in the Republic of Korea.

Presidents Clinton and Kim have strengthened the ties between our two nations. Each is committed to reform and economic renewal. Each is committed to our solemn alliance. I know that President Clinton especially admires President Kim's personal courage and dedication to democracy. The common aspirations peoples have brought us to this hopeful point. The future holds even greater promise: a Korean peninsula finally liberated from the ever-present fear of conflict; an open door to the resolution of Korea's greatest tragedy, the division of its people; and our two nations working together in partnership for a more secure, prosperous, and democratic Asia.

On the eve of the next century, the United States and the Republic of Korea face this future in a spirit of confidence and cooperation.

Let me conclude by commenting briefly on yesterday's mid-term Congressional elections in the United States. It is an almost unbroken tradition that the party that holds the presidency—currently the Democrats—loses seats in the Congress in the mid-term elections. History tells us that the President's party will suffer losses at mid-term. Tonight in America, that is certainly the case. But it is also a tradition that whatever the outcome of the mid-term elections, there is a strong continuity in American foreign policy. Just before coming down here, I spoke to President Clinton. I want to assure this international audience that we intend to go forward in the spirit of bipartisanship and continuity. We will remain strong and steadfast in our commitments around the world.

Our policy toward Asia and particularly toward Korea has strong bipartisan support. I am confident that there will be continuity in our unshakable commitment to the security of the Republic of Korea, and to the maintenance of our troop levels here in the ROK.

I am also confident that the Agreed Framework, which puts the North Korea nuclear issue on the road to resolution, will command strong bipartisan support. That agreement, and the North-South dialogue, are in the best interest of the United States, the Republic of Korea, and indeed all the nations in the region, and as such, they merit unswerving support.

Our partners in the global economy should know that there will also be continuity in our Administration's approach to international economic policy and our commitment to open trade.

As Secretary of State, I have devoted considerable time to close consultation with our Congress, both with Democrats and Republicans. The major elements of our foreign policy have had bipartisan support, and I look forward to working with the new Congress to forge a bipartisan foreign policy.

Thank you very much.

SIXTEEN

NATO Expansion

The December 1994 ministerial meeting at NATO headquarters in Brussels was a major turning point in our effort to expand the Alliance. The decision to pursue expansion had been taken during the autumn of 1993 and publicly launched by the President's statement at the January 1994 NATO summit (see Chapter 8). However, most of the serious work on implementation remained. My presentations at the December meeting represented the real beginning of the process that, in July 1997, resulted in the invitation to Poland, Hungary, and the Czech Republic to join NATO.

As President Clinton publicly stated after a January 1994 meeting with Central European leaders in Prague, the Partnership for Peace was not designed as a "permanent holding room" in lieu of admission to NATO. "The question," he said, "is no longer *whether* NATO will take on new members, but *when* and *how*." Nevertheless, our policy still faced major obstacles.

First, both the Administration and our European allies spent most of the year preoccupied with the war in Bosnia. In early 1994, that war took several ugly turns, including a brutal attack on a Sarajevo marketplace which, in full view of CNN cameras, killed scores of innocent civilians. Not only did this conflict occupy much of our time and energy, but psychologically we found it exceedingly difficult to focus on expansion while NATO groped for a way to stop the bloodshed in southern Europe.

Moreover, I was surprised to find that in the spring of 1994 considerable resistance to our NATO strategy lingered in our own bureaucracy. Some U.S. officials, particularly in the Defense Department, were quite unenthusiastic about taking on the task of integrating out-of-date militaries into NATO and about assuming new Alliance defense commitments. Some preferred to regard the Partnership for Peace as an end in itself rather than a means to a larger goal. Finally, after months of haggling, an internal consensus coalesced in the fall of 1994.[1]

Another major challenge to our strategy was Russia. From the very beginning, we understood that we had to be sensitive to Moscow's concerns about NATO expansion. The Kremlin leadership remained worried that immediate expansion would feed common Russian fears about Western ambitions and would inflame nationalist sentiments. We recognized that for many Russians, NATO was an unpleasant reminder of their embarrassment in the Cold War. This was why, for example, I made a special effort to reassure Yeltsin about the Partnership for Peace program during our meeting at his hunting lodge outside Moscow in October 1993 (see Chapter 5). While we made clear to Russia that NATO expansion would move forward—I said this in almost every meeting I had with Kozyrev, and the President did the same in his meetings with Yeltsin—we pledged that expansion would proceed gradually and openly.

Throughout the fall of 1994, we confronted a Russian elite and political leadership that were becoming increasingly skeptical about NATO expansion, if not hostile to it. Although we sought to reassure them at every step, stressing that Russia could join the Partnership or possibly even NATO itself, the Russians began to develop a neurosis about expansion.

Up to the December 1994 meeting, consultations with Russia appeared to go smoothly. Deputy Secretary Strobe Talbott took the lead and opened a productive dialogue with his counterparts in the Kremlin, keeping them well informed of our strategy and plans for NATO expansion and for the meeting itself. There would be no surprises, but there would be no delay and no veto, either. The Russians seemed to

---

[1]To help steer the expansion policy through the bureaucratic process, I asked Richard Holbrooke, who had recently returned from his post as Ambassador to Germany to take over as Assistant Secretary for European Affairs, to head an interagency group on NATO. It was at this level that many of our internal battles were fought. Once a consensus was reached, this group led the preparations for my participation in the 1994 NATO ministerial.

be satisfied and signaled an intention that Russia itself would join the Partnership.

All of these considerations were reflected in my two statements before the December 1, 1994, NATO meeting. Together, these statements represented the transition from the conceptual decision of late 1993 to pursue expansion to a concrete effort to set the process in motion without delay. The statements formally established the Partnership as the path to NATO membership and stressed that the process must remain open and inclusive. I proposed setting a firm timeline for decision-making, calling for NATO Allies to brief members of the Partnership on the requirements and responsibilities of Alliance membership during 1995.

After I made these statements, the Russians pulled a troubling surprise. At the request of Russian Foreign Minister Kozyrev, a special session of the North Atlantic Council had been scheduled for late in the afternoon of December 1 so that Russia could join the Partnership for Peace with appropriate ceremony. Without any warning, however, Kozyrev came into the meeting and announced that he would not sign. He indulged in this unwelcome bit of grandstanding on instructions from Yeltsin, whose advisers had apparently told him, incorrectly and perhaps mischievously, that NATO was "accelerating" enlargement.

Two days later, Yeltsin one-upped Kozyrev's petulance in a speech at a summit meeting of the Conference on Security and Cooperation in Europe in Budapest. With Clinton and other heads of government in attendance, Yeltsin complained bitterly about the U.S. policy on NATO, ominously warning that a "cold peace" could be on the horizon. Once again, this came out of the blue.

This double surprise was undoubtedly the low point of U.S.-Russian relations during the first Clinton term. As they proceeded with difficult political and economic reform at home, the Russian leadership clearly felt that the United States and other Western nations did not give them the respect they deserved. Strobe Talbott privately referred to this as Russia's "Rodney Dangerfield syndrome." Although in the following weeks the Russians backpedaled from the confrontational stance they had taken in Brussels and Budapest,[2] these shots across the bow were not

---

[2]Russia finally signed the Partnership documents in March 1995.

soon forgotten. Talbott and I spent a great deal of time during early 1995 working to impress upon the Russians the fundamentals—the "red lines" and "bottom lines," as we put it—of our position and to engage them in an open and candid dialogue, identifying issues on which we agreed and ways to manage those on which we did not.

In the course of my December 1 opening statement at the NATO meeting, I made an effort to delink Bosnia from NATO, as I feared that Bosnia would undermine our goals for expansion. However, I came to recognize that there was a triangular relationship among NATO, Bosnia, and Russia that could not be ignored. The continued fighting in Bosnia left NATO looking impotent and irrelevant, and Bosnia was a constant source of friction between the United States and Russia, as evidenced by my long, unpleasant wrangling with the Russian delegation to Contact Group meetings.[3]

Ironically enough, we came to see that just as Bosnia had led to these problems, so it could provide an antidote to them. When the NATO sustained-bombing campaign in September 1995 finally brought the Serbs to the bargaining table, morale at NATO improved enormously. And when, thanks to the skillful efforts of Secretary of Defense William Perry and General Shalikashvili, an appropriate role was found for Russian troops in the NATO Implementation Force in Bosnia, relations with Russia over Bosnia were decisively mended. In broader terms, the eventually cooperative relationship between NATO and Russia in Bosnia was no doubt a vital factor in the later Russian acquiescence to NATO expansion and in the adoption of the NATO-Russia Founding Act that provides for regular consultation between NATO and Russia. The experience of NATO and Russia working together to achieve common goals proves a point we constantly stressed to the Moscow leadership: expanding the NATO security umbrella is not "anti-Russian." These positive developments can be traced back to the firm position we took in the statements that follow.

[3]Germany, France, the United Kingdom, Russia, and the United States, together with representatives of the United Nations and the European Union, were members of a Contact Group that met informally to coordinate efforts to resolve the Bosnia conflict.

A Time of Historic Challenge for NATO

Beginning the Process of NATO Expansion: Opening Statement
at the Meeting of the North Atlantic Council, NATO Headquarters,
Brussels, December 1, 1994

Mr. Secretary General, distinguished colleagues, and friends: I am privileged to serve as your President d'Honneur at our first formal meeting since we selected Willy Claes to succeed the brilliant and dedicated Manfred Woerner. Secretary General Claes has taken charge at a time of historic opportunity and challenge for the alliance. As we build European security for the 21st century, we are fortunate to have this statesman of strength and experience at NATO's helm.

The two greatest struggles of the 20th century—the battles against fascism and communism—are over. The fallen Iron Curtain has revealed a window of opportunity for open societies and open markets to prevail across a continent at peace.

It is important to recall that NATO played an essential role in bringing us to this hopeful point. For more than four decades it kept the peace, preserved our freedom, kindled hope in oppressed peoples, and, finally, helped bring the Cold War to an end—a victory for all who love freedom.

For half a century, NATO also provided the foundation on which our nations built the greatest community of peace and prosperity the world has ever seen. It cemented close relations among former adversaries in Western Europe. It formed the core of our transatlantic community—forging links that can never be broken. The ideals embodied in the Treaty of Washington—democracy, liberty, and the rule of law—proved no less powerful than the arsenals of this alliance. Dean Acheson said it best.

The importance of NATO in the long run goes far beyond the creation of military strength. . . . Future hope lies in the development of a community of free peoples. . . .

But NATO is not just about yesterday. It is about today and tomorrow—about Dean Acheson's "future hope." First, let me be clear about my own nation's conviction. American power and purpose are here in Europe to stay. This alliance will continue to be the anchor of American engagement in Europe, the linchpin of transatlantic security. Through more than four decades, under Democratic and Republican administrations, we have maintained a bipartisan commitment to a free, stable, secure, and prosperous Europe. Today, we are committed to keep 100,000 American troops on European soil as part of our continuing engagement.

As we meet today to continue to adapt this great alliance, we are keenly aware that the end of the Cold War has brought not only opportunities, but serious challenges. The terrible conflict in Bosnia continues to resist resolution. It has challenged NATO and all the institutions that have dealt with it. Frankly, when this conflict emerged from the ashes of the Cold War, the international community was insufficiently prepared. The world ultimately turned to the United Nations to shoulder the principal responsibility.

For its part, NATO has done whatever has been asked of it by the United Nations. It has established a no-fly zone and prevented the conflict from becoming an air war. It has maintained the sanctions pressure, and it has been instrumental in preventing the spread of the conflict. Contrary to some reports, NATO has not ruled out the use of air power. NATO stands ready to use air power, when requested, pursuant to United Nations resolutions. Now our task continues to be to seek a peaceful, negotiated end to the conflict, one that will preserve Bosnia's territorial integrity. We should renew our efforts to seek an immediate cease-fire and general cessation of hostilities. We should pursue with the parties the terms for a settlement, building on the Contact Group plan.

Let me stress one important fact: The crisis in Bosnia is about Bosnia and the former Yugoslavia; it does not diminish NATO's enduring importance. The allies remain committed to NATO's irreplaceable role as the key to European security. There is no disagreement among us on this point.

The tragedy of the war and bloodshed in Bosnia does not diminish our responsibility to build a comprehensive European security architecture that consolidates stability, addresses today's conflicts, and prevents others from happening in the future. On the contrary, the tragedy in the former Yugoslavia underscores the urgency of that task. Central to building a comprehensive security architecture for Europe is a measured process of NATO expansion, along with continued European integration and a determination to strengthen the Conference on Security and Cooperation in Europe. Yesterday's NATO helped to reconcile old adversaries, to embed free countries in strong and solid institutions, and to create an enduring sense of shared purpose in one another's security. Today's NATO must do the same—with new countries but with an enduring purpose. This alliance must preserve its core defensive role and adapt its military forces to meet the new demands of crisis management and peace-keeping. It must also help new partners learn Western standards of cooperation and draw them into NATO's practical work of providing stability in Europe.

Last January, at the NATO summit, the alliance committed itself to deepen its ties with Europe's emerging democracies when it approved President Clinton's proposal for a Partnership for Peace. In less than a year, the partnership has come to life. Twenty-three nations, including Russia, have joined. Belarus has just announced its intention to become our 24th partner. Tonight, NATO and Russia will agree on broad possibilities for cooperation, including Russia's program for the Partnership for Peace. And troops that for half a century faced each other in the Cold War are now coming together in joint military exercises. Our leaders also declared last January that the alliance is open to new members. Today, we take an important step in the process that will lead to NATO expansion. I urge that we agree to begin now our internal deliberations on expansion and, in 1995, to discuss with partners the obligations and implications of membership.

This process will be steady, deliberate, and transparent. I want to stress that expansion must not and will not dilute NATO. But NATO must, over time, be ready to include nations that are willing and able to assume the necessary alliance obligations and commitments and whose membership advances the goals of the alliance and broader European security. Expansion, when it comes, will occur in a manner that increases stability for all of Europe—for members and non-members alike.

As we pursue NATO expansion, we must also strengthen other structures of security cooperation. No single institution has the mandate or the capability to meet every challenge in Europe. Our NATO alliance must be complemented by other institutions that can address the full range of challenges facing Europe's future. We recognize an important role for European integration, supported by the European Union. There is also an important institution with untapped potential: the Conference on Security and Cooperation in Europe. We must build on its unique strengths as a structure for conflict resolution and prevention and as an institution that embodies the ideal of an undivided Europe.

Speaking as your Président d'Honneur, I say with confidence that the alliance is prepared to take up both the challenges of the moment and the future. And speaking as a representative of President Clinton and the American people, I say with equal confidence that as we do so, the commitment of the United States to participate actively in maintaining the security, prosperity, and freedom of Europe remains unshakable.

Developing the New European Security Architecture

Intervention at the Meeting of the North Atlantic Council,

NATO Headquarters, Brussels, December 1, 1994

Mr. Secretary General, distinguished colleagues, and friends: I am pleased to join you at this very important meeting of the North Atlantic Council. Allow me also to salute once again our new Secretary General. He assumes his responsibilities at a defining moment in the history of NATO and of Europe. These are times of great change in Europe. But America's interests in Europe have not changed. Neither have the basic principles guiding our engagement—principles that have long commanded bipartisan support.

The first principle is that NATO is and will remain the anchor of America's engagement in Europe and the core of transatlantic security. The United States has enduring political, military, economic, and cultural links to Europe that must and will be preserved.

A second core principle of American engagement remains our support for European integration and our partnership with the European Union. The United States has supported European integration from its inception. The EU remains a vital partner in trade, diplomacy, and, increasingly, in security, where we cooperate to combat weapons proliferation and terrorism. A capable European defense identity and effective cooperation between NATO and the Western European Union are critical elements of this relationship.

Fortifying the European pillar of the alliance contributes to European stability and to transatlantic burden-sharing. And it improves our collective capacity to act. I welcome the November 14 call by WEU ministers to accelerate work on the Combined Joint Task Force concept. CJTF offers a practical vehicle for making NATO assets and capabilities available to the WEU under certain circumstances. A moment ago, I noted that America's interests in Europe have not changed. What has changed in the last few years is that the sphere of political and economic freedom in Europe is wider than ever before. This leads me to the third core principle of our engagement: Breaking down the barriers that divide West from East will serve our collective interest in wider European stability. Our alliance of democracies can help consolidate democracy across an undivided Europe at peace. We can help design a comprehensive and inclusive architecture that enhances security and freedom for all. Our strategy of integration offers tangible rewards. It will help promote stability in Europe's eastern half—the region where two world wars and the Cold War began. It will strengthen the hand of forces committed to political, military, and economic reform. And it will help assure that no part of Europe will revert to a zone of great power competition or a sphere of influence and that no nation is left hanging in isolation.

The challenge we face today is not unlike the one we faced—and met—in Western Europe 50 years ago. After World War II, President Truman and Secretaries of State Marshall and Acheson understood that security and economic cooperation were essential to the defense of democracy. Within five years of D-Day, America and its Allies had launched the Marshall Plan, established NATO and the GATT, and laid the foundations for what became the EU and the OECD. These institutions helped us produce unparalleled peace and prosperity for half a century—but only for half a continent. Now, five years have passed since the Berlin Wall fell. We must build a security community of all democratic nations in the Euro-Atlantic region—one that endures where the Congress of Vienna, the Concert of Europe, and Versailles ultimately failed, and one that builds on the strength of our post-war success in Western Europe.

Developing the new European security architecture begins with reinforcing its foundation—the alliance that has preserved our liberty and prosperity for half a century. NATO has always been far more than a transitory response to a temporary threat; it has been a guarantor of European democracy and a force for European stability. The core values it champions—democracy, liberty, and the rule of law—are now ascendant around the world. For all these reasons, NATO's benefits are clear to Europe's new democracies. Since the NATO summit last January, we have taken remarkable strides to renew and invigorate the alliance. We have achieved our historic goal of deepening ties with the new democracies to the east. In less than a year, the Partnership for Peace has evolved from a bare idea to a bold reality. The United States considers the Partnership for Peace an integral and lasting part of the new European security architecture. That is why President Clinton indicated in July that he will ask Congress to designate $100 million in the coming fiscal year to advance the partnership's goals. I am pleased to say that Congress has already authorized an additional $30 million to strengthen the partnership's joint exercise program over the next year. I hope that other NATO members will soon announce comparable contributions and that we can coordinate our efforts to maximize the impact. But, of course, it will fall mainly to partners to ensure that the partnership realizes its full potential.

The United States is seeking agreement on additional measures for next year. First, we urge putting exercise programs for 1995 and beyond on a five-year planning cycle and building toward progressively more complex and diverse training scenarios. Second, NATO must ensure sufficient funding for the alliance's partnership-related costs. Finally, we should strive to have a partnership defense-planning process established and operational by early 1995.

The partnership is a critical tool in its own right. It is also the best path to membership for countries wishing to join the alliance. As both President Clinton and Vice President Gore have emphasized, NATO must be open to expansion. An exclusionary policy would risk maintaining old lines of division across Europe—or creating arbitrary new ones. The United States believes that Europe's institutional arrangements should be determined by the objective demands of the present, not by the tragedies of Europe's past. The United States believes it is time to begin the process—to begin deliberate consideration of the practical requirements for adding new members to the alliance. It is imperative that we agree, as an alliance, on our aims and our purpose in this historic evolution. The Washington Treaty is not a paper guarantee. New members will assume solemn obligations and responsibilities, just as we will extend our solemn commitments to them. This will require careful consideration and preparation. We are deciding today that the alliance begin its internal deliberations on expansion. A process has begun. It is also essential that we begin to present our views to interested partners during 1995. I expect the next several months to be particularly intense as we formulate a joint allied presentation. We have already provided your governments with our initial thinking, and we would propose building on that to develop allied consensus. I am personally committed to moving forward on this matter.

Our presentation to the partners should explain the practical implications and obligations of NATO membership. Let us be clear: These initial exchanges are not intended to be the beginning of accession negotiations. Neither will they indicate that any partner is necessarily a candidate for admission. But they will reflect our determination that the process for expansion be open and inclusive from the start.

The process of expansion should be steady, deliberate, and transparent. Each nation should be considered individually. No country outside of NATO will have a veto over any other. In our view, there are, however, certain fundamental requirements for membership that are reflected in the Washington Treaty. New members must be market democracies committed to responsible security policies and able to make a contribution to the alliance. As I noted earlier this morning, we cannot pursue NATO expansion in isolation. The new security architecture for Europe's future must be supported by other strong pillars. No single institution has the mandate or the capability to meet every challenge in Europe. The Conference on Security and Cooperation in Europe—the CSCE—has proven experience and untapped potential as an organization that can help ease tensions and prevent future conflicts. With its comprehensive membership and unique experience in preventive diplomacy, human rights protection, and dispute resolution, the CSCE can complement NATO's essential role. To make it more effective, however, we need to refine its mission. At the CSCE summit in Budapest next week, the United States will work with our allies and partners to enhance the CSCE's capabilities. President Clinton will urge his colleagues to approve his proposal to strengthen the role and structure of the organization. We hope to clarify the CSCE's role in the European security architecture and improve its ability to prevent future Yugoslavias.

Our economic and security institutions are gradually breaking down the outdated frontiers of the Cold War. The security and prosperity of all of Europe is inextricably linked to the stable development of Europe's emerging democracies in the East.

Our goal is the successful transformation of post-communist Europe into a community of sovereign, democratic states. A key component is the development of a democratic, market-oriented Russia. No less vital is the emergence of a stable, democratic, non-nuclear Ukraine and the realization of the promise of greater security embodied in the START I and START II agreements. In Budapest, we will take a significant step forward when President Clinton joins President Yeltsin and Prime Minister Major in receiving Ukraine's accession to the Non-Proliferation Treaty and signs security assurances for Ukraine, Belarus, and Kazakhstan. This action will pave the way for START I to enter into force. We welcome democratic Russia in assuming a full role in the common effort of building new structures. We welcome the agreement we will sign tonight on the NATO-Russia Individual Partnership Program. It sends an unmistakable signal of our alliance's desire to include Russia in a cooperative approach to security in Europe. At the same time, we will continue to pursue avenues for cooperation between NATO and Russia outside the Partnership for Peace. The United States welcomed the first meeting between an alliance working group and Russia on the question of nuclear weapons dismantlement. We also support intensifying Russia's cooperation with the G-7. And we are sponsoring Russia's membership in the GATT and its successor, the World Trade Organization. Integration will enhance Russia's security in a wider Europe and expand Russia's access to markets and capital. But it also carries obligations that all Western nations share. GATT membership will make Russia's trade practices consistent with world standards. Expanded ties with NATO and the EU, along with strengthened CSCE principles, will strengthen Russian democracy and promote respect for the sovereignty of its neighbors. Our support for Russian policies that adhere to these core principles will serve our vital interests and Europe's—especially the nations that so recently broke free from communist rule. By the same token, expanding Western institutions to Central Europe will benefit Russia.

In taking the steps I have outlined today, we will advance our shared interest in building a democratic, prosperous, integrated Europe at peace. These steps reflect the core principles of our engagement in Europe—our unwavering commitment to NATO, our continued support for European integration, and our determination to enhance security and stability in the East. The United States understands that our leadership remains indispensable if we are to achieve these goals. And we are determined to provide it.

SEVENTEEN

Principles and Priorities

November and December of 1994 were rough months for the President and the Administration.[1] Whereas we had been ebullient after the 1992 presidential election, we were deeply unsettled by the 1994 loss of both the Senate and the House of Representatives to the Republicans. No one was blaming the defeat on our foreign policy, but nevertheless, I identified strongly with the President in this situation. As I watched him struggle to adjust his course when we met in Indonesia for the APEC leaders' conference the week after the November election, I groped for some way to help him. I felt that he had been an effective foreign policy President, despite some early setbacks, and deserved more credit than he had received. I also thought that he should have maximum flexibility in laying out a new path for the second half of his first term, and before leaving for California for Christmas, I told him that I was prepared to resign. When I returned after New Year's Day, the President indicated he wanted me to stay on, instructing spokesman Mike Mc-

---

[1]The Administration lost one of its most talented and experienced officials when my senior cabinet colleague, Secretary of the Treasury (and former Senator) Lloyd Bentsen, resigned on December 6, 1994, to return to Texas. He had contributed significantly during the first two years of the Administration, especially to the passage of the Deficit Reduction Act of 1993, which was the foundation of continuing economic prosperity. He was succeeded by the talented Robert Rubin, who was immediately plunged into coping with the Mexican peso crisis (see Chapter 25).

Curry to tell the press that I would continue indefinitely as Secretary of State.[2]

I was buoyed by the vote of confidence. A therapeutic Christmas week at our beach house in California had left me refreshed and ready to start anew in January. To begin the new year, I decided to issue a comprehensive statement of the principles and priorities that would guide our foreign policy over the next two years. One of my goals in doing this was to project to the new Congress, as well as to our allies and adversaries, a new sense of confidence, a sense that the United States and the Clinton Administration remained determined to lead.

The John F. Kennedy School of Government at Harvard had many attractions for me as the site of these remarks. It was a serious forum, and the presence of both undergraduate and graduate students promised an attentive audience and lively questioning. On a personal note, our older son, Scott, was a graduate of the school.

In the first two years, we had dealt with several specific problems, particularly in North Korea, Haiti, and the Middle East. My public statements, too, had tended to focus on specific areas—whether supporting reform in Russia, revitalizing the European security architecture, fostering the Middle East peace process, or strengthening our ties to the Asia-Pacific region. Although many of those statements had also aimed to articulate our overall objectives, I felt, looking back, that I had not done enough to show how meeting such diverse challenges was linked to a core set of American interests and to the constancy of American leadership. The Harvard forum gave me the right opportunity to step back and outline the broader rationale driving our policy.

The Kennedy School address exemplified the "spoken essay" style and tone common to many of my foreign policy speeches. Indeed, that spring I published an expanded version of this statement in the international affairs journal *Foreign Policy*.[3] It was undoubtedly one of the most complex speeches I gave as Secretary, as well as one of the longest.

---

[2]McCurry, whom I had fortunately chosen as the State Department's spokesman in January 1993, was recruited to become the President's chief spokesman in late 1994. The bipartisan view in Washington is that McCurry ranks as one of the best in the long line of prominent presidential press secretaries.

[3]See "America's Leadership, America's Opportunity," *Foreign Policy* (spring 1995).

The conceptual spine of the speech was my explanation of four principles guiding our policy and five priorities for the coming year. My intent was not to outline anything particularly new, but rather to demonstrate how the differing parts of our foreign policy fit together as a whole. The four core principles—maintaining American leadership, strengthening relations with the other great powers, revitalizing institutions to promote cooperation, and supporting democracy and human rights—would shape our approach toward the five policy priorities. Identifying those priorities helped set an agenda, both inside the Administration and with our interlocutors abroad. In both establishing such a broad framework and setting specific goals, I intended the speech to be analogous to a presidential State of the Union address.

This speech did not satisfy the critics who complained about our lack of strategic vision and nostalgically looked for an overarching grand strategy that could be expressed in a single word or phrase, such as "containment." As I had indicated at my confirmation hearing in 1993, I was not inclined to attempt to fit our policy into a neatly tailored doctrinal straightjacket.[4] However, I did seek to make the concepts underlying our policy more explicit.

While the speech touched on nearly every critical foreign policy issue we faced at the time, my remarks about Russia were the most immediately sensitive. During the prior month, U.S.-Russian relations had soured abruptly. The downward turn had begun at the December meetings in Brussels and Budapest, with Yeltsin's and Kozyrev's unexpected and strident criticism of our intention to enlarge NATO (see Chapter 16).

Russia's internal situation had also deteriorated. Yeltsin, who had spent most of December in the hospital, seemed increasingly detached from those advisers who advocated reform, instead surrounding himself with a small group of hard-liners. On December 11, the Russian military had launched a vicious assault on Chechnya, a small, largely Muslim republic located in the Caucasus, in Russia's far southwest. Chechnya had become dominated by a violent nationalist group led by Dzokhar Dudayev and had been threatening to secede from Russia. The ragtag army

[4]Ambassador George Kennan, who is credited with having originated the notion of containment nearly 50 years before, strongly counseled me against searching for such a single grand concept when I hosted a dinner in his honor in October 1994.

of Chechens had put up strong resistance, and soon Moscow had a full-scale war on its hands. The ineffective Russian performance would soon reveal the extent to which Russia's military forces had declined.

From the first days of the Chechnya struggle, our Administration had criticized the violent character of the Russian response, but we had concentrated our efforts on urging the parties to seek a negotiated settlement. In early January, when the war escalated considerably, we decided to turn up the heat. Appearing on NBC's *Meet the Press* on January 15, I described Russia's invasion of Chechnya as "very harmful" and added that it had been "ill conceived and ill executed." In a meeting with Kozyrev three days later in Geneva, I pressed this point, explaining to him that U.S. support for Russia, both political and economic, would be jeopardized as long as the fighting continued. Kozyrev himself described the Chechnya conflict as a disaster and acknowledged that Russia was being severely damaged by it.

My statement regarding Chechnya at the Kennedy School two days later was noticeably blunt and garnered considerable attention in the media. Some had accused the Administration of being too easy on the Russians, and this was my first formal opportunity to speak out on Chechnya. I explained that Russia's "excessive" actions threatened to "have a corrosive effect" on the future of democratic reform. I also deliberately used the word "quagmire" to describe the situation, signaling to Moscow our concern that Chechnya could become a disaster for Russia, as Vietnam had been for the United States and Afghanistan had been for the Soviet Union. This statement foreshadowed the Administration's use of a tougher, more realistic tone when dealing with the Russians, a shift marked by my speech in Bloomington, Indiana, two months later.

However firm such statements were, I still believed that our best policy was to support Yeltsin and his reform allies. The cliché "tough love" aptly describes our attitude at the time, and since. After my Geneva meetings with Kozyrev, I noted to the President that our strong support for Yeltsin, Kozyrev, and company was a fairly high-risk wager, but one that had paid off before. In any event, I argued, we had no decent alternatives at that time.

One of the specific goals identified in the speech—non-proliferation—deserves special mention. It is rarely recognized how much progress we were able to make in stopping the spread of weapons of mass destruction. Several of the main elements of our strategy as outlined in this speech were achieved by the end of the President's first term: the "indefinite and unconditional extension" of the Non-Proliferation Treaty, negotiation of a Comprehensive Test Ban Treaty, U.S. ratification of START II, and the first steps in implementation of the Agreed Framework to freeze and ultimately dismantle North Korea's nuclear program.[5]

This is the first speech in which I singled out global problems such as crime, terrorism, and drugs for separate and special treatment. To me the tremendous impact of these and other transnational issues stood out as one of the major developments of the post–Cold War period. Perhaps the noise of the East-West conflict had simply drowned them out in earlier years, but I am inclined to think that their emergence reflects the new ease and speed of communications and transportation. I was particularly sensitive to the tendencies of these global threats to undermine stability and accountability in fledgling and fragile democracies around the world. In any event, I would give them more and more attention in the next two years.

I ended the speech with a plea for bipartisanship that was widely noted. The change in the political balance of power resulting from the mid-term elections was not, I said, "a license to lose sight of our nation's global interests or to walk away from our commitments in the world." With the help of moderate Republicans, we were able to maintain an effective foreign policy, though handicapped by the difficulty we encountered in obtaining the resources necessary to do so (see Chapters 22, 33, and 36).

Principles and Opportunities for American Foreign Policy

Address Before the John F. Kennedy School of Government, Harvard

University, Cambridge, Massachusetts, January 20, 1995

America stands today at the threshold of a new century and faces a challenge that recalls the opportunities and dangers that confronted us at the

---

[5]The Chemical Weapons Convention got caught in the 1996 campaign cross fire when Republican presidential candidate Senator Robert Dole withdrew his support for it, but it was eventually ratified in April 1997.

end of the First and Second World Wars. Then, as now, two distinct paths lay before us: either to claim victory and withdraw, or to provide American leadership to build a more peaceful, free, and prosperous world. After World War I, our leaders chose the first path and we and the world paid a terrible price. No one will dispute that after the Second World War, Harry Truman, George Marshall, Dean Acheson, Arthur Vandenberg—and, most of all, the American people—wisely chose the other path. That same farsighted commitment to American leadership and engagement must guide our foreign policy today. The Soviet empire is gone. No great power views any other as an immediate military threat. And the triumph of democracy and free markets is transforming countries from Europe to Latin America and from Asia to Africa. We now have a remarkable opportunity to shape a world conducive to American interests and consistent with American values—a world of open societies and open markets.

In the past year, we helped persuade Ukraine, Kazakhstan, and Belarus to give up nuclear weapons on their territory. Nuclear warheads and missiles from these states and Russia are being dismantled. Russian troops are out of the Baltic States and Germany. We have begun to build a new European security architecture. We helped to launch regional security dialogues in Asia. We negotiated an Agreed Framework with North Korea that freezes and will ultimately eliminate its nuclear weapons program. We reached an agreement with China that will sharply limit its missile exports. And we stopped Iraqi aggression against Kuwait dead in its tracks. We also contributed to historic progress in resolving conflict, backing democracy, and promoting development in countries around the world. We fostered agreements between Israel and the PLO, and the peace treaty between Israel and Jordan. We restored the democratically elected government in Haiti—and we are going to do our part to make sure that achievement endures. In long-troubled regions like Northern Ireland, South Africa, and Cambodia, the United States contributed to extraordinary advances toward peace and reconciliation. And at the historic Cairo Conference, we restored American leadership on the critical issues of population and development. Finally, we have taken giant steps to build the open trading system of the next century, with America at its hub. We won bipartisan support for the GATT agreement and led the way for its approval around the world. We helped to forge commitments to eliminate trade barriers in the Asia-Pacific region by 2020 and to negotiate free trade in our own hemisphere by 2005. And we made important progress in widening access to Japan's markets.

These are significant accomplishments. But we must not rest on our laurels. Aggression, tyranny, and intolerance still undermine political stability and economic development in vital regions of the world. Americans face growing threats from the proliferation of weapons of mass destruction, terrorism, and international crime. And a number of problems that once seemed quite distant, such as environmental degradation, unsustainable population growth, and mass movements of refugees, now pose immediate threats to emerging democracies and to global prosperity.

In meeting these opportunities and dealing with these dangers, our foreign policy is driven by several principles.

First, America must continue to engage and to lead.

Second, we must maintain and strengthen our cooperative relationships with the world's most powerful nations.

Third, it is essential that we adapt and build institutions that will promote economic and security cooperation.

Fourth, we must continue to support democracy and human rights because it serves our interests and our ideals.

The imperative of American leadership, the first principle of our strategy, is a central lesson of this century. It is sobering to imagine what the world would have been like without it in the last two years alone. We might now have four nuclear states in the former Soviet Union instead of one. We might have a full-throttle nuclear program in North Korea. We might have no GATT agreement or NAFTA. We might have brutal dictators still terrorizing Haiti. And we might very well have Iraqi troops back in Kuwait.

As a global power with global interests, the United States must not retreat from its leadership role. It is our responsibility to ensure that the post–Cold War momentum toward greater freedom and prosperity is not reversed by neglect or by short-sighted indifference. Only the United States has the vision and the capacity to consolidate these gains. As our recent accomplishments suggest, American leadership requires that we be ready to back our diplomacy with credible threats of force. And to this end, President Clinton is determined that the U.S. military will remain the most powerful and effective fighting force in the world—as it certainly is right now. When our vital interests are at stake, we must be prepared to act alone. Our willingness to do so is often the key to effective joint action. The recent debate between the proponents of unilateral and multilateral action assumes a false choice. Multilateralism is a means, not an end. Sometimes, by mobilizing the support of other nations, by leveraging our power and leading through alliances and institutions, we will achieve better results at lower cost in human life and national treasure. That is a sensible bargain I know the American people support.

Leadership also means focusing international attention on emerging global problems. That is why we have given new and enhanced attention to global issues such as the environment, population, and sustainable development. They deserve a prominent place on our foreign policy agenda, and as long as I am Secretary of State, they will have it.

Just as our nation must always maintain its military readiness, so we must be ready to advance our political and economic interests around the world through diplomacy. That requires highly trained men and women. It requires modern communications technology. And it requires adequate resources.

The second tenet of our strategy is the central importance of constructive relations with the world's most powerful nations: our Western European allies, Japan, China, and Russia. These nations possess the political, economic, or military capability to affect—for good or for ill—the well-being of every American. The relatively cooperative relations that these countries now have with each other is unprecedented in this century, but it is not irreversible.

Our strategy toward the great powers begins with Western Europe and Japan. We must revitalize our alliances with this democratic core. We must also seize the opportunities to build constructive relations with China and Russia, countries that were not too long ago our fiercest adversaries. Both are undergoing momentous, though very different, transformations that will directly affect American interests.

Our partnership with Japan is the linchpin of our policy toward Asia, the world's most dynamic region. This Administration has placed Asia at the core of our long-term foreign policy approach. Realizing President

Clinton's vision of a stable and prosperous Pacific Community will continue to be a top priority. Asia figures prominently in many of our central areas of emphasis for 1995.

It is also imperative that we reinforce our security and political ties with Japan—as well as with South Korea and our other treaty allies in the Pacific. It is equally essential that the strength of our economic ties with Japan matches the overall strength of our relationship. During this year that marks the fiftieth anniversary of the end of World War II, we will highlight and heighten our close cooperation on regional and global issues—while continuing to press for greater access to Japanese markets.

Our success in Asia also requires pursuing constructive relations with China, consistent with our overall interests. We welcome China's participation in regional security and economic organizations. We support its accession to the World Trade Organization on proper terms. And we will work hard to gain its cooperation with global non-proliferation regimes. In China's own interest, and consistent with its increasing role in the world community, it needs to demonstrate greater respect for human rights and the rule of law. China's recent crackdown on dissent is disturbing and incompatible with realizing the full potential of our bilateral relations.

Our relationship with Russia is central to America's security. It has been a key foreign policy issue for this Administration. Its importance is reflected in my meetings in Geneva this week with Andrei Kozyrev, where for more than eight hours we discussed a broad array of common challenges and concerns. The United States has an enormous stake in the outcome of Russia's continuing transformation. A stable, democratic Russia is vital to a secure Europe, to resolve regional conflicts, and to fight proliferation. An unstable Russia that reverts to authoritarianism or slides into chaos would be a disaster—an immediate threat to its neighbors and, with its huge nuclear stockpile, once again a strategic threat to the United States.

That is why the Clinton Administration has been unwavering in its support for Russian reform. Despite the setbacks that we knew Russia might encounter during this historic and difficult transition, our steady policy of engagement and cooperation has paid off for every American— from reducing the nuclear threat to advancing peace in the Middle East. That is why President Clinton reaffirmed last week in Cleveland his determination to maintain our substantial assistance for democratic and economic reform in Russia.

We are deeply concerned about the conflict in Chechnya. It is a terrible human tragedy. The way Russia has used military force there has been excessive and it threatens to have a corrosive effect on the future of Russian democracy. That is why I emphasized so strongly to Foreign Minister Kozyrev this week that the conflict must end and that a process of reconciliation must begin, taking into account the views of the people of Chechnya and the need to provide them with humanitarian assistance. What we do not want to see is a Russia in a military quagmire that erodes reform and tends to isolate it in the international community.

The third principle of our strategy is that if the historic movement toward open societies and open markets is to endure, we must adapt and revitalize the institutions of global and regional cooperation. After World War II, the generation of Truman, Marshall, and Acheson built the great institutions that gave structure and strength to the common enterprise of Western democracies: promoting peace and economic growth. Our challenge now is to modernize and to revitalize those great institutions—NATO, the UN, the IMF and the World Bank, and the OECD, among others. And we must extend their benefits and obligations to new democracies and market economies, particularly in Central and Eastern Europe.

At the President's initiative, our G-7 partners agreed that in Halifax next July, we will chart a strategy to adapt the post-war economic institutions to a more integrated post–Cold War period. We are also helping regional institutions and structures such as the Organization of American States, ASEAN, and the Organization of African Unity to promote peace and democratic development. As we go forward into the next century, we will find ourselves relying more and more on these regional institutions.

As a fourth principle, this Administration recognizes the importance of democracy and human rights as a fundamental part of our foreign policy. Our commitment is consistent with American ideals. It also rests on a sober assessment of our long-term interest in a world where stability is reinforced by accountability and disputes are mediated by dialogue; a world where information flows freely and the rule of law protects not only political rights but the essential elements of free market economies.

In the new year—in 1995—as we follow these basic underlying principles, I intend to focus on five key areas that offer particularly significant opportunities: advancing the most open global trading system in history; developing a new European security order; helping achieve a comprehensive peace in the Middle East; combating the spread of weapons of mass destruction; and fighting international crime, narcotics, and terrorism.

Open Trade

First, we must sustain the momentum we have generated toward the more open global and regional trade that is so vital to American exports and good jobs for Americans. A core premise of our domestic and foreign policies is that our economic strength at home and abroad are mutually reinforcing. I believe that history will judge this emphasis to be a distinctive imprint and a lasting legacy of the Clinton Administration.

We will implement the Uruguay Round and ensure that the new World Trade Organization upholds vital trade rules and disciplines. We will work with Japan and our other APEC partners to develop a blueprint for achieving open trade and investment in the Asia-Pacific region. We will begin to implement the Summit of the Americas Action Plan. And we will also begin to negotiate Chile's accession to NAFTA.

Let me add a word about something on all our minds today: Mexico, and our effort to address the economic crisis of confidence in that country. The President has demonstrated vision and leadership in assembling the package of support necessary to help Mexico get back on track. The package of loan guarantees has the backing not only of the Administration, but the bipartisan Congressional leadership and the Chairman of the Federal Reserve Board, as well as the international financial institutions. This package contains tough but fair conditions to protect U.S. interests and to ensure the guarantees are used wisely and well. As the President has said, we should resist the temptation to load up this package with conditions unrelated to the economic thrust of our effort. Let me say this to the Congress and the American people: This package is in the overriding interest of the United States. It should be acted upon quickly and favorably.

European Security Architecture

In our second area of opportunity, we will take concrete steps to build a new European security architecture. We understand that deep political, military, economic, and cultural ties make Europe's security and prosperity essential to ours. It has been so for at least half a century. Our efforts will focus on maintaining strong relations with Western Europe, consolidating the new democracies of Central Europe and the former Soviet Union, and engaging Russia as a responsible partner.

NATO remains the anchor of American engagement in Europe and the linchpin of transatlantic security. NATO has always been far more than a transitory response to a temporary threat. It has been a guarantor of European democracy and a force for European stability. That is why its mission has endured, and that is why its benefits are so attractive to Europe's new democracies. In earlier years, NATO welcomed new members who shared its purposes and who could add to its strength. Under American leadership, the alliance agreed last December to begin a steady, deliberate process that will lead to further expansion. We have already begun to examine with our allies the process and objectives of expansion. We intend to share our conclusions with the members of the Partnership for Peace by the end of this year.

As we move toward NATO expansion, we will also bolster other key elements of the new European security architecture: a vigorous program for the Partnership for Peace, which now includes 24 nations; a strengthened Organization for Security and Cooperation in Europe; and a process for enhancing the NATO-Russia relationship. The tragic war in Bosnia underscores the importance of building an effective new architecture for conflict prevention and resolution in Europe. Together with our partners in the Contact Group, we are seeking a negotiated solution in Bosnia because only a negotiated solution has any chance of lasting and of preventing a wider war. What we must not do is make the situation worse by unilaterally lifting the arms embargo. We have always believed that the embargo is unfair. But going it alone would lead to the withdrawal of UNPROFOR and an escalation of violence. It would Americanize the conflict and lead others to abandon the sanctions on Serbia. It would undermine the authority of all UN Security Council Resolutions, including resolutions that impose sanctions on Iraq and Libya.

Middle East Peace and Security

Our third area of opportunity is advancing peace and security in the Middle East. We have witnessed a profound transformation in the landscape of the Arab-Israeli conflict—one that would simply not have been imaginable just a few years ago. Of course, there are still many difficulties. But despite those difficulties, we must not let this remarkable opportunity slip away. On the Israeli-Palestinian track, we must continue to make progress in the implementation of the Declaration of Principles. I was encouraged by yesterday's meeting between Prime Minister Rabin and Chairman Arafat and by the serious efforts both sides are making to work out the complex issues in the next phase, where there will be self-government for the West Bank. Each side must see the benefits of peace. Israelis must gain security. Palestinians must achieve genuine control over the political and economic decisions that affect their lives. Each must build the trust and confidence of the other—especially at a time when those opposed to peace seek to destroy mutual confidence.

The negotiations between Israel and Syria are entering a very crucial phase. The parties are serious and some progress has been made in narrowing the gaps. If a breakthrough is to be achieved in the next few months, critical decisions must be made and the process must be accelerated. I assure you that President Clinton and I will do all we can to support these efforts.

As we promote peace in the Middle East, we must also deal with the enemies of peace. Iraq's massing of troops at the Kuwaiti border last October underscored the danger Iraq poses to regional security and peace. It is my conviction, and that of all the leaders with whom I have talked in the Middle East, that Saddam Hussein's regime cannot be trusted. Full compliance with all relevant UN obligations is the only possible basis on which to consider any relaxation of sanctions.

Another rogue state, Iran, now leads rejectionist efforts to kill the chances for peace. It directs and materially supports the operations of Hezbollah, Hamas, and others who commit atrocities in places such as Tel Aviv and Buenos Aires. It sows terror and subversion across the Arab world. Those industrialized nations that continue to provide concessionary credits to Iran cannot escape the consequences of their actions: They make it easier for Iran to use its resources to sponsor terrorism and undermine the prospects for peace.

Today Iran is engaged in a crash effort to develop nuclear weapons. We are deeply concerned that some nations are prepared to cooperate with Iran in the nuclear field. I will not mince words: These efforts risk the security of the entire Middle East. The United States places the highest priority on denying Iran a nuclear weapons capability. We expect the members of the Security Council, who have special responsibilities in this area, to join with us.

Non-proliferation

Our fourth area of emphasis for 1995 is to take specific steps to stop the spread of weapons of mass destruction and their means of delivery. With the demise of the Soviet Union, the proliferation of these weapons poses the principal direct threat to the survival of the United States and our key allies. Our global and regional strategies for 1995 comprise the most ambitious non-proliferation agenda in history.

The centerpiece of our global strategy is the indefinite and unconditional extension of the Non-Proliferation Treaty (NPT), which is up for renewal this year. The treaty's greatest achievement is invisible—weapons not built and material not diverted. But the impact of the treaty is clear: The nightmare of a profusion of nuclear weapons states has not come to pass. I think that history will record that the NPT is one of the most important treaties of all time.

Our global strategy also includes a moratorium on nuclear testing as we negotiate a Comprehensive Test Ban Treaty; a global ban on the production of fissile materials for building nuclear weapons; ratification of the Chemical Weapons Convention; and strengthening the Biological Weapons Convention. With the agreements President Clinton signed last December in Budapest, we can now begin to implement the START I nuclear reduction treaty. Later this month, I will be the Administration's lead witness in urging the Senate to promptly ratify START II. Finally, we will continue to support the Nunn-Lugar program, which has been so important in providing the funds to help dismantle former Soviet nuclear weapons and which counters would-be nuclear smugglers by improving security at vulnerable facilities.

When this Administration took office, North Korea had an active nuclear program. Left unchallenged, it was poised to produce hundreds of kilograms of plutonium that could be used in nuclear weapons. The stage was being set for a crisis that would imperil security throughout Northeast Asia and undermine our entire global non-proliferation effort. Last fall, the United States concluded an Agreed Framework with North Korea that freezes its nuclear program, provides for its dismantlement, and puts the whole issue on the road to resolution. The framework has the strong support of Japan and South Korea—key allies whose security it will protect and who will finance most of its implementation. Of course, we are under no illusions about North Korea. Implementation of the framework will be based upon verification, not trust. We are determined to ensure that North Korea fulfills every obligation at every step of the way. Those who oppose the framework with North Korea have a heavy responsibility to offer an effective alternative that protects our interests and the interests of our allies in Northeast Asia. They have not done so.

We also have an aggressive strategy with respect to conventional arms and missiles. We will seek to broaden the Missile Technology Control Regime. We will push for a global agreement to control the export of antipersonnel landmines—one of the real scourges of the world—and work bilaterally to remove the millions of mines still in place. We are also seeking to establish a COCOM successor regime, which will restrain trade in arms and sensitive technologies to the pariah states.

Crime, Terrorism, and Drugs

Turning to our fifth area of emphasis, international terrorists, criminals, and drug traffickers pose direct threats to our people and to our nation's interests. They ruin countless lives, destroy property, and siphon away productive resources. They sap the strength of industrialized societies and threaten the survival of emerging democracies.

That is why in 1995 we plan to implement a comprehensive strategy to combat these threats. The State Department is working on this plan in close and urgent cooperation with the Departments of Justice and Treasury and other law enforcement agencies. The strategy on international crime and terrorism will include several vital steps:

First, we will insist that other countries fulfill their obligations either to extradite or prosecute international fugitives and ensure that convicted criminals serve tough sentences;

Second, we will work with other governments to develop and implement tough asset-forfeiture and money laundering laws to attack international criminals in a vulnerable place—their pocketbook. Unfortunately, many countries have very weak laws as far as asset forfeiture and money laundering go.

Third, we will toughen standards for obtaining U.S. visas to make it more difficult for international criminals to gain entry to this country;

Fourth, we will propose legislation to combat alien smuggling and immigration fraud by providing increased penalties and more effective investigative tools; and,

Fifth, the Clinton Administration is planning new steps to expand the use of U.S. law against terrorists and against funding for their worldwide activities.

I have discussed five key areas of opportunity for American foreign policy in 1995. I also want to underscore that our foreign policy will continue to address a whole range of issues important to our interests, such as promoting stability and democracy in Asia, Latin America, and Africa; meeting humanitarian needs around the world; fighting environmental degradation; and addressing rapid population growth.

As I conclude, let me note that since my first week in office, I have consulted closely with both parties in Congress on every important issue on our agenda. We have gained bipartisan backing for key objectives of our foreign policy, including our approach on the Middle East peace process; our landmark trade agreements, such as NAFTA, GATT, and APEC; and denuclearization in the former Soviet Union.

The recent elections changed the balance of power between the parties. But they did not change—indeed they enhanced—our responsibility to cooperate on a bipartisan basis in foreign affairs. The election was not a license to lose sight of our nation's global interests or to walk away from our commitments in the world. Leaders of both parties understand that well, and I am glad to tell you that my extensive meetings with the new Republican leadership give me great confidence that we will be able to sustain the bipartisan foreign policy that is America's tradition. Bipartisan cooperation has always been grounded in the conviction that our nation's enduring interests do not vary with the times. President Harry Truman had it right 40 years ago: "Circumstances change," he said, "but the great issues remain the same—prosperity, welfare, human rights, effective democracy, and above all, peace."

With the Cold War behind us, the United States has a chance to build a more secure and integrated world of open societies and open markets. We are the world's largest military and economic power. Our nation's founding principles still inspire people all over the world. We are blessed with great resources and resolve. We will continue to use them with wisdom, with strength, and with the backing of the American people.

EIGHTEEN

A Sober Approach Toward the Former Soviet States

By late March 1995, the Administration had weathered four months that marked the roughest period in U.S.-Russian relations since the fall of the Soviet Union. Our problems had begun in December 1994 with the high-profile sparring over NATO expansion. The Russians had backtracked a bit from their troubling Brussels-Budapest performances, but they still sought to scuttle expansion.

Further friction had been caused by the war in Russia's breakaway region of Chechnya. The local secessionists had resisted Moscow's attempts to reassert control, and the central government had responded with an all-out assault that had killed as many as 25,000 civilians and, within a matter of days, obliterated the Chechen capital of Grozny. The episode was damaging to Russia as well as devastating for Chechnya; the brutality of Russia's conduct further alienated the Chechens, subjected the Russian army to scorn and condemnation, and lowered the standing of the Yeltsin government in the eyes of both its citizens and the world.

We also had significant difficulties with Russia in the security arena. Moscow was threatening to scuttle the 1990 treaty limiting conventional forces in Europe, and it showed little inclination to ratify the START II pact limiting strategic nuclear weapons. Moreover, reports surfaced that Russia was preparing broad-ranging assistance to Iran in the nuclear field. The Kremlin claimed that it would only build "safe" reactors—comparing its plan with the U.S.-backed agreement to provide lightwater reactors to North Korea—and justified the deal as a way to make money. Given that the planned cooperation went far beyond construction of civilian reactors, we were greatly concerned. Nuclear cooperation with Iran, a rogue state bent on developing weapons of mass destruction, was squarely against U.S. interests and would certainly evoke strong opposition in Congress.

These concerns were serious enough to cause considerable internal debate in March and April over whether President Clinton should attend ceremonies in Moscow in May commemorating the end of World War II in Europe. Some believed that he should condition his attendance on Russia's cooperation on such issues as Chechnya and Iran, while others argued that his skipping the event would have dire consequences for our relationship. In the end, the President decided, with my strong support, that the chances of moderating Russia's behavior would be better if he attended. Considering the enormous sacrifices of the Russian people in the war—over 20 million casualties—I felt that the President's absence on the 50th anniversary of the victory would never be understood in Moscow.

Our troubles over NATO, Chechnya, and Iran were exacerbated by the general sense that reform efforts in Russia were waning. Without a doubt, 1994 had been a tough year for Russian reformers. Key leaders like Yegor Gaidar had already left the government, and corruption, chaos, and crime threatened to undermine fledgling civil and political institutions. Yeltsin had become increasingly isolated, retreating into a small circle of advisers, many of whom were suspected of preferring authoritarian leadership to democracy. In all, little had happened to fulfill the hope and optimism that had characterized my earlier public statements—and U.S.-Russian relations generally.

It was time to articulate publicly our reaction to these disturbing developments. As Strobe Talbott put it, we needed a speech to "present to the world a way of thinking about Russia, what's going on there, and how we should try to affect it so as to protect and advance our own interests." Such an address was essential not only to send an unambiguous message to the Russians, laying the groundwork for several high-level meetings in May and June 1995, but to explain our policy to the American people.

Just as, in my 1993 speeches in Chicago and Minneapolis, I had sought to detail the importance of engaging and supporting Russia, I now needed to explain how the relationship had changed, what we expected from Moscow, and what we planned to do about it. For a venue, I decided to return to America's heartland: Bloomington, the home of Indiana University and its prestigious Russian and East European Institute. The Institute had been founded by renowned former Indiana University President Herman Wells, who at age 93 was present for the speech and greeted me warmly. The combination of the Institute and the Indiana setting promised to provide an informed audience that was not preoccupied by politics inside the Washington Beltway.

In this speech I aimed to signal that while the substantive core of our relationship with Russia remained the same—fostering democracy, supporting economic liberalization, and strengthening security—its tone had indeed changed. We still had a fundamental stake in supporting Russian reform and pursuing denuclearization, but we could not let these interests override other legitimate concerns, such as dealing with the Iranian nuclear threat. Russia had to behave responsibly in order for our relationship to evolve in a positive way. Rather than expressing uncritical support, the speech stressed our basic, pragmatic intent to "cooperate where our interests coincide, and to manage our differences constructively and candidly." We had to remain firm, encouraging Russia to move in the direction of domestic reform and international responsibility. To borrow a metaphor from Talbott, I believed that the United States needed to man a "lighthouse" that Russian reformers could steer toward, but that the decision to set the course toward it was fundamentally Russia's. This message, the bottom line of my speech, was captured in a formulation first used by President Clinton: "The plain truth is that Russia has a choice. It can define itself in terms of the past or in terms of a better future."

The Bloomington speech was also important for its emphasis on the other states of the former Soviet Union. We had a strong interest in strengthening ties with these nations and supporting reform throughout the region. The United States had worked successfully with Ukraine, Kazakhstan, and Belarus on denuclearization, and, as I explained in the speech, two-thirds of our 1995 economic assistance to the former Soviet Union went to non-Russian states. This explanation of our "region-wide approach" was mainly intended to reassure the Newly Independent States that we would stand by them with political and economic support. But it also served as a response to critics who claimed that our policy was too "Russiacentric."

On our three greatest foreign policy differences with Russia—Chechnya, Iran, and NATO—I minced few words. "Russia's conduct in Chechnya has been tragically wrong," I said bluntly. I called the destruction of Grozny a "serious mistake" and stressed that Russia was paying a heavy price for Chechnya, both at home and abroad.

I had had a firm discussion with Russian Foreign Minister Kozyrev on the subject of Iran the week before in Geneva, and my statement in Bloomington reiterated the points I had made to him. I called attention to the fact that dealing with Iran undermined Russia's own security interests. There was little doubt that a nuclear-equipped regime in Tehran would present a threat to Russia, a neighbor of Iran. My Chief of Staff, Tom Donilon, supplied the most quoted line of the speech: "[Russia] will rue the day it cooperated with this terrorist state if Iran builds nuclear weapons with the benefit of Russian expertise and equipment." I explained that no major Western ally cooperates with Iran on nuclear matters; they recognize that "it is simply too dangerous to be permitted."

On NATO expansion, I reasserted our position that the process would continue along the course I had outlined in Brussels in December 1994. I made clear that decisions on the issue would be made by NATO only (thus dousing any ideas about a Russian veto), and stressed that it remained "in Russia's interest to participate constructively in the process of European integration." Again, the emphasis was on Russia's opportunity: it could choose either to be a part of the new European architecture, or to be isolated.

In broader terms, the speech made an essential statement that I thought oftentimes went overlooked. The Cold War had ended, the Soviet Union had disintegrated, and Russia and the Newly Independent States were on the road to reform. Because of these events, and notwithstanding some setbacks, the American people were more secure than at any time since the end of World War II. Inevitably, differences in our views would emerge: we had complex, multifaceted, and broad agendas with all of these states. We had to keep an eye on our broader interests and not allow any of our relationships to be held hostage to a single issue. This was why, even with the ugliness of Chechnya, the President had decided to go to Moscow on V-E Day. We had a better chance of success through engagement than through isolation.[1]

---

[1] In early 1997, Russian and Chechen leaders reached a settlement giving Chechnya something close to de facto independence.

Along these lines, I repeated a point that I had frequently made over the previous four months: it would have been very easy to list the areas where we had differences, where the Russians pursued policies we didn't like—and walk away. But such a take-it-or-leave-it approach was a luxury we did not have. As Secretary of State, my responsibility was to try to manage the differences and advance our interests. The Bloomington speech outlined areas in which we disagreed with Russia, but it also made a strong case for resolving these differences through active leadership and engagement.

U.S. Policy Toward the New Independent States: A Pragmatic Strategy Grounded in America's Fundamental Interests

Remarks at Indiana University, Bloomington, March 29, 1995

Good afternoon. I would like to thank President Brand for that warm welcome, and Indiana University for inviting me to speak today. I am pleased to be here with Robert Orr, former Indiana Governor and former Ambassador to Singapore. Four decades ago, Indiana President Herman Wells showed foresight in founding the Russian and East European Institute. Today, the institute is among the country's most respected centers of regional study. Many of its graduates have forged distinguished careers in this field, including Jim Collins, my special advisor for the New Independent States.

Your state's political leaders have played a crucial role in shaping our policy toward the former Soviet Union. When I called Senator Lugar to ask if he could join me here today, he said he really needed to be in Washington shepherding the ratification of our START II Treaty with Russia through the Senate. Under these circumstances, I reconsidered my invitation. And I will always be indebted to your highly respected Congressman, Lee Hamilton, for his counsel and support. You should be proud that Indiana has produced two such outstanding leaders of both parties.

Since his first day in office, President Clinton has pursued a pragmatic policy of engagement with Russia and the other New Independent States as the best investment we can make in our nation's security and prosperity. Our approach is to cooperate where our interests coincide, and to manage our differences constructively and candidly where they do not. We support reform because, in the long run, its success benefits not only the people of the region, but the American people as well. We understand that Russia and the other new states face a tumultuous future. For that reason, our policy is focused on the long haul. In sum, our approach is realistic and grounded in America's strategic interests.

The successful transformation of the former Soviet Union into a region of sovereign, democratic states is a matter of fundamental importance to the United States. These 12 nations cover one-sixth of the world's surface. Their territory is home to tens of thousands of nuclear weapons. Their people and resources give them vast economic potential.

Twice in this century, political events in this region have remade the world—profoundly for the worse in 1917, and profoundly for the better in 1991. The events of 1991 set in motion two historic transformations, both of which have served our fundamental interests and those of the people of the region. The first is the disappearance of a hostile totalitarian empire, and its replacement by 12 newly independent states. The second is the collapse of communist dictatorship, and the movement toward democratic institutions and free markets.

These transformations have presented us with a remarkable opportunity to encourage stability in the region and enhance the security of the American people. We have taken advantage of that opportunity in ways that have paid enormous dividends. Indeed, our engagement with Russia, Ukraine, and their neighbors has made America safer than at any time since the end of World War II. Thousands of nuclear warheads, built to destroy America, are themselves being destroyed. Those that remain no longer target our cities and homes.

Last year, President Clinton negotiated a trilateral understanding with Russia and Ukraine that sets Ukraine on the path to becoming a non-nuclear power. In so doing, Ukraine joined Kazakhstan and Belarus in agreeing to give up nuclear weapons. We are leading efforts to dismantle their weapons and safeguard nuclear materials under a bipartisan program sponsored by Senator Nunn and Senator Lugar. In Defense Secretary Perry's words, it literally "removes the threat—missile by missile, warhead by warhead, factory by factory."

Last December, President Clinton and the leaders of the region's nuclear states brought the START I agreement into force and paved the way for implementing START II. Together, these important treaties will cut strategic nuclear forces in Russia and the United States by almost two-thirds.

Our diplomacy has also made Europe more secure. After patient but firm efforts by President Bush and President Clinton, Russian troops completed their withdrawal last August from Germany and the Baltic states. Now, for the first time since World War II, the people of Central Europe are free of occupying forces. Despite the progress that has been made, we have no illusions about how difficult the region's transformation will be, or how long it will take to overcome centuries of empire and autocracy. Ultimately, only the peoples of the region can assure their success.

From the outset, our approach has been focused on the entire region of the former Soviet Union, in part because the futures of all these countries are so closely linked. I am convinced that the success of reform in each of these countries will have a positive impact on success in the others.

Our region-wide approach can be seen in the emphasis we have placed on financial support to the non-Russian states—which in 1995 will represent two-thirds of our assistance to the New Independent States. Increasingly, we are supporting private sector trade and investment. American firms have signed multi-billion-dollar energy deals in Kazakhstan and in Azerbaijan—the latter country so rich in oil that its capital was described in the 12th century as "blazing like a fire all night." Last year, our Overseas Private Investment Corporation provided almost $1 billion in financing for projects in the region. These programs will generate new exports and jobs for Americans.

The Clinton Administration has been steadfast in support of the sovereignty and territorial integrity of all the New Independent States. The region's history of imperial conquest underscores how important it is that all these countries scrupulously respect international law and the rights of their neighbors.

Of course, some states of the former Soviet Union command particular attention because of their potential to influence the future of the region. Ukraine is critical. With its size and its position, juxtaposed between Russia and Central Europe, it is a linchpin of European security.

An independent, non-nuclear, and reforming Ukraine is also vital to the success of reform in the other New Independent States. That is why the United States has joined Britain and Russia in providing security assurances for Ukraine. The United States has consistently led the international effort to support economic reform in Ukraine. Last year, we convinced the G-7 to pledge over $4 billion for that country. In October, Ukraine's government launched a courageous program of market reform under newly inaugurated President Kuchma. We responded by increasing our assistance for 1994 by $250 million, to a total commitment of $900 million. Ukraine is now the fourth-largest recipient of U.S. assistance after Israel, Egypt, and Russia. It is important that the Ukrainian Rada fully support President Kuchma's economic reform program.

Of course, the future of Ukraine and every other state in the region will be profoundly affected by the outcome of Russia's new revolution. That is why the deliberations of Russia's parliament and the fate of the ruble are on everyone's mind, not just in Moscow, St. Petersburg, and Vladivostok, but also in Kiev, Almaty, and Baku.

In May, President Clinton will travel to Moscow to meet President Yeltsin for the seventh time. This summit comes at an important moment. Reform in Russia is under strain. The war in Chechnya continues. We have differences with Russia in foreign policy.

But whatever the problems, we must not lose sight of the breathtaking changes we have witnessed since the breakup of the Soviet Union. Ten years ago, almost 400 million people from the Baltic to the Bering Seas were subject to totalitarian dictatorship and hemmed in by minefields and barbed wire. Today, Vilnius, Warsaw, and Kiev are free. Moscow is alive with political debate. Siberia is becoming a synonym for opportunity, not oblivion.

Perspective and a sense of history are also important. Not long ago, a severe disagreement between the United States and the Soviet Union could have threatened a nuclear confrontation. Today, we do not always agree, and there are obviously new challenges in our relationship. But every difference is not a crisis. We can address our differences constructively, without threatening to blow up the world.

Today, the real question is not whether we should engage with Russia, but how. We reject policies that reflect short-term political pressures, but undermine the long-term interests of the United States. We are determined to continue to work with Russia where our interests coincide. We will not hold our relationship hostage to any one issue. But we will remain ready to speak openly and act appropriately when Russian actions run counter to our interests.

Our policy toward Russia has been and will continue to be based on a clear-eyed understanding of the facts on the ground. As President Clinton has stressed, we reject the superficial caricature of Russia that suggests it is predestined to aggression, predisposed to dictatorship, or predetermined to economic failure. At the same time, we are under no illusion that success is assured.

The plain truth is that Russia has a choice. It can define itself in terms of its past or in terms of a better future. In many areas Russia is courageously making the right choices. It has a freely elected president and parliament and a democratic constitution. It has an independent press, which often criticizes central government policies. Debate in the parliament is vigorous and open.

Economic reform is continuing. The government has acted boldly to bring inflation down. An ambitious privatization program has altered Russia's economic landscape. The private sector now acccounts for 50% of Russia's GDP.

Two weeks ago, Russia initialed a $6.4 billion agreement with the IMF, which requires Russia to continue its fight against inflation, implement an austere budget, liberalize the energy sector, and free more prices from state control. This agreement is a significant landmark on the hard march to a stable market economy.

These positive changes are all the more notable in light of the ruinous legacy that Russian reformers are having to overcome. After 75 years of communism, much of the old elite remains entrenched in government and industry. Trust in democratic institutions is fragile—and so are the institutions themselves. The rule of law is in its infancy. Crime and corruption are rampant. These problems could undermine democracy if they are not dealt with effectively.

The economic legacy is also difficult. The new Russia inherited from the Soviet Union a decrepit industrial base that has wasted natural resources and produced a string of environmental disasters—from Chernobyl, to chemical pollution in the Urals, to the drying up of the Aral Sea.

Then there is the legacy of empire. Some 150 ethnic groups live within Russia's 11 time zones. During the Soviet period, borders between the internal regions and republics of the empire were changed by communist leaders over 90 times to suit their particular purposes. The central government of Russia has made progress in improving relations with the diverse people within the Russian Federation. But its actions in Chechnya today threaten its ability to emerge as a democratic, multiethnic state. The Chechnya crisis began as Russia sought to deal with a complex problem with deep historical roots. Now a city and many villages have been destroyed, tens of thousands have died, and the tensions that led to the fighting have surely been exacerbated. Russia's conduct in Chechnya has been tragically wrong. Its decision to escalate fighting there in the last week is a serious mistake.

That is why I have urged the Russian Government to end the carnage, to accept a permanent mission from the Organization for Security and Cooperation in Europe, to provide humanitarian relief, and, above all, to reach a peaceful political settlement. It is patently clear that the Russian Government is paying a very high price both at home and abroad for the Chechnya adventure.

It is easy enough to enumerate our differences with Russia, or with other states of the former Soviet Union. But I do not have the luxury of making a list and walking away. My job is to build areas of agreement, to develop policies to manage our differences, and always to advance our nation's interests. Let me describe the five key goals of our strategy for the coming year, as they relate to all the states of the former Soviet Union.

First, we aim to resolve a number of important security issues vital to every American. In 1995, we are pursuing the most ambitious arms control agenda in history. President Clinton and I have urged the Senate to ratify START II before the U.S.-Russian summit in May. The Russian parliament should act promptly to do the same. We are working closely with Russia to achieve the indefinite extension of the Non-Proliferation Treaty. We will also press to conclude a Comprehensive Test Ban Treaty—thereby realizing the vision set forth three decades ago by President Kennedy.

We are also determined to combat the growing threat posed by nuclear smuggling. We must prevent rogue states and terrorists from acquiring nuclear weapons and materials. Nunn-Lugar programs will help us achieve this goal by dismantling nuclear weapons in the former Soviet Union and safeguarding the resulting nuclear materials. Full funding for

Nunn-Lugar is vital to our nation's security—and I hope Congress will receive that message loud and clear.

Because of the importance we attach to fighting the spread of nuclear weapons, we are firmly opposed to Russia's nuclear cooperation with Iran. Russia is a neighbor of Iran. It will rue the day it cooperated with this terrorist state if Iran builds nuclear weapons with the benefit of Russian expertise and equipment. Russia should take note that no major industrial democracy cooperates with Iran on nuclear matters. It is simply too dangerous to be permitted. For this reason, it is important that, in our meeting last week, Foreign Minister Kozyrev and I agreed to set up a working group to examine non-proliferation issues, particularly including the consequences of nuclear cooperation with Iran.

A second goal for 1995 will be to cooperate on a newer set of global or transnational issues, including crime, energy, the environment, and space. During the Cold War, such cooperation was impossible. Today it is essential. International crime is a growing threat to the lives and livelihoods of countless Americans, and to the prospects for reform in the former Soviet Union. I have made the fight against global crime a top priority of U.S. foreign policy. FBI Director Louis Freeh and I have worked together to set up an FBI office in Moscow—to work with the Russians to combat organized crime, corruption, and drug trafficking.

Vice President Gore and Prime Minister Chernomyrdin are spearheading efforts to improve the efficiency of the Russian oil and gas sector, thereby raising productivity and reducing that industry's high levels of pollution. They are also strengthening our cooperation with Russia in space—symbolized today by the space station Mir, with its first American crew member on board. Our cooperation on these issues is not limited to Russia. We will continue to work with Ukraine and our G-7 partners to overcome the dangerous aftermath of Chernobyl. We are also helping Kazakhstan to manage its enormous energy resources in economically sound and environmentally safe ways.

Third, we will continue carefully targeted assistance programs that increase our security, expand our prosperity, and promote our interest in democratic reform. Nunn-Lugar monies will continue to advance our strategic interest in dismantling nuclear weapons. Our assistance will also continue to support the vital elements of a working democracy and civil society, including a free press and jury trials. By supporting privatization and small business development, it will encourage free markets and open new opportunities for American companies. Most of our assistance will go to private organizations and local governments outside Moscow.

Assistance has put America on the right side of the struggle for change in Russia. Some people say we should end these programs to punish Russia when it does something we oppose. I am all for maximizing our leverage in every way we can. But I have personally reviewed our assistance programs and concluded that cutting them back now would simply not make sense. It would not be in the interest of the American people. The critics of those programs need to ask themselves some tough questions. Would they stop the funding necessary to dismantle the nuclear weapons that once targeted American cities? Would they cut off support for privatization and free elections—wiping out programs that strengthen the very forces in Russian society that share our interests and values? I believe that when they understand these choices, the American people will adopt the only course that makes sense: that is, to make the necessary investments now to make our nation more secure and prosperous for generations to come. I call on both the House and Senate to fund fully our request for assistance to the New Independent States.

The fundamental basis of the assistance program is to encourage all of the New Independent States to move forward with market and democratic reform. Free elections are especially vital. President Nazarbayev's recent effort to extend his term unilaterally is, I am sorry to say, a step backward for Kazakhstan. We call on him to renew his commitment to hold timely parliamentary elections, followed by scheduled presidential elections in 1996. At the same time, we applaud President Yeltsin's commitment to hold parliamentary elections at the end of this year and presidential elections next year. When President Clinton goes to Moscow in May, you can be sure he will underscore the importance we attach to that commitment. In meeting with President Yeltsin, President Clinton will be dealing with the first freely elected leader of Russia. But he will also talk directly to the Russian people and meet a cross-section of Russian society—especially those who are committed to reform. The United States will continue to cultivate strong ties with a wide range of leaders and institutions in and out of the Russian Government. To encourage pluralism in Russia, we will deal with Russia as a pluralistic society.

Fourth, we will reinforce the independence of Russia's neighbors and support their further development as market democracies. We will also use our good offices to help resolve conflicts in the region. Last December, we persuaded Russia that an OSCE-led peace-keeping mission in Nagorno-Karabakh was preferable to unilateral action. If a settlement is reached between the parties to that dispute, such a mission would set a powerful precedent for conflict resolution in the New Independent States. It is vital that Russia continue to cooperate with the OSCE to ensure its success.

Fifth, we will advance the President's comprehensive strategy for building a stable, peaceful, and integrated Europe. Just as we had in Western Europe after World War II, we now have a rare and historic opportunity to build a new security architecture—this time for all of Europe—that will last for generations. President Clinton's vision includes several important elements. The OSCE will have a larger and more operational role. NATO's Partnership for Peace will strengthen its ties to Central Europe and to the New Independent States. NATO will move forward with its steady and deliberate process to accept new members, following the approach laid out by the NATO ministers last December. And we will seek a stronger relationship between NATO and Russia in parallel with NATO expansion.

In the process of NATO expansion, each potential member will be judged individually, according to its capabilities and its commitment to the principles of the NATO treaty. The fundamental decisions will be made by NATO, in consultation with potential members. The process will be transparent to all and there will be no vetos by third parties.

As I emphasized to Foreign Minister Kozyrev last week, it is in Russia's interest to participate constructively in the process of European integration. Russia has an enormous stake in a stable and peaceful Europe. No country has suffered more when Europe has not been at peace. Russia's path to deeper involvement in Europe is open. It should not choose to isolate itself from this effort.

Building a new security architecture in Europe is part of a larger strategy of integrating the new democracies of the former Soviet Union into the major institutions of the West, including the European Union, the World Trade Organization, the OECD, and the G-7. These institutions give structure, legitimacy, and strength to the common enterprise of the Western democracies—namely, promoting peace and economic growth. It will serve our interests to extend the benefits of integration—as well as its considerable obligations—to Europe's new democracies, including the New Independent States.

The pace of integration in Europe, however, will depend on the extent to which the nations of the former Soviet Union continue on the reform path and adhere to international norms. WTO membership, for example, is only possible for nations that adopt trade and investment rules consistent with world standards. Likewise, the evolution of Russia's participation in Western institutions will be affected by the world's judgment of its conduct in Chechnya and by its respect for international norms.

The United States will continue to pursue a realistic and pragmatic course toward all the New Independent States—a course that has already produced concrete benefits for Americans. We will not take for granted the success of the historic transformations now under way in the former Soviet Union. But we will continue to work to bring about the best possible outcome. Our enduring interests demand that we stay engaged. Our policy is rooted in American interests. We will protect our security, our welfare, and our values.

As we travel this difficult yet promising path, we will call upon the same qualities that have sustained American leadership in the past: steadiness, consistency, and reliability in pursuing our interests and upholding our commitments. These are the qualities that have kept America strong and free. These are the qualities that must guide us now as we build the more secure and integrated world that is in the fundamental interest of the American people.

Thank you very much.

With President-elect Bill Clinton and Vice President-elect Al Gore at the Arkansas Governor's Mansion in Little Rock, November 1992. *Photo courtesy of Associated Press.*

(*above*) At the signing of the Palestinian-Israeli peace accord, Washington, D.C., September 13, 1993. *Clockwise from bottom:* Shimon Peres, Andrei Kozyrev, Prime Minister Rabin, President Clinton, Chairman Arafat, Palestinian senior adviser Abu Masin, author.

(*below*) Being greeted by President Yeltsin outside Moscow, October 1993. *Photo courtesy of the White House.*

With Marie in photo taken for State Department Magazine, 1993.

(*above*) With troops in Kuwait, 1994. *Photo courtesy of Associated Press.*

(*below*) With Norwegian Prime Minister Gro Brundtland in Oslo, January 1994.

(*above*) With President and Mrs. Clinton and Ambassador and Mrs. Pickering in Moscow, 1994.

(*below*) With U.S. Air Force squadron members in Korea, 1994.

(*above*) A Sunday meeting outside the Oval Office during a tense moment when troops were landing in Haiti, September 1994. *From left*: President Clinton, Betty Currie (*the President's secretary*), Leon Fuerth (*the Vice President's National Security Adviser*), Secretary Perry, General Shalikashvili, Leon Panetta, Strobe Talbott (*kneeling*), author.

(*below*) With President Clinton on the President's patio outside his private dining room adjacent to the Oval Office, 1995.

(*above*) With Prime Minister Yitzhak Rabin during a reflective moment in the Cabinet Room, looking out to the Rose Garden on a snowy day, 1995.

(*below*) In Red Square in Moscow, May 1995. *Photo courtesy of Bob McNeely, the White House.*

(*above*) Flag-raising ceremony at U.S. embassy in Hanoi, August 1995.

(*below*) Going over Bosnia maps in Dayton. *From left*, Chris Hill, author, Dick Holbrooke, President Izetbegovic, and President Milosevic, November 1995.

At Fort Myers, Virginia, immediately after Bob Frasure's funeral, 1995. *Clockwise from President Clinton, seated:* Anthony Lake, General Wes Clark, Samuel (Sandy) Berger, author, John Deutch, Dick Holbrooke, William Perry, Madeleine Albright, General John Shalikashvili. *Clockwise from left, standing:* Leon Fuerth, Chris Hill, General Don Kerrick, James Pardew.

(*above*) At Yitzhak Rabin's grave in Jerusalem, 1995.

(*below*) With some members of the foreign policy team in the Cabinet Room, March 1996. *From left:* Coit Blacker (*Special Assistant to the President for National Security Affairs*), Samuel (Sandy) Berger, John Deutch, Anthony Lake, author, Strobe Talbott, James Collins (*Ambassador-at-Large*). *Photo courtesy of Bob McNeely, the White House.*

With British Foreign Secretary Malcolm Rifkind (*above*) and German Foreign Minister Klaus Kinkel (*below*) at meeting on implementation of the Dayton accords, Paris, 1996.

(*above*) With Russian Foreign Minister Yevgeny Primakov, Helsinki, 1996.

(*below*) With King Hussein in the Oval Office (*President Clinton in background*), 1996.

(*above*) The Christophers viewing the Meeting of the Waters, where two large rivers join to form the mighty Amazon, Brazil, March 1996.

(*below*) With Peace Corps members in Mali, October 1996.

(*above*) In South Africa with President Mandela, October 1996.

(*below*) With President Clinton after announcing return to private life, November 1996.

(*above*) In Beijing with Foreign Minister Qian, November 1996.

(*below*) Author in Cabinet chair presented to him by his staff with, *from left*, Peter Tarnoff, William Burns (*State Department's Executive Secretary*), Dennis Ross, Lynn Davis, Joan Spero, Madeleine Albright, Strobe Talbott, Barbara Larkin, December 1996.

(*above*) With Marie, saying farewell to Chief Justice William Rehnquist, Inauguration Day, 1997.

(*below*) With President Jiang Zemin of China during his state visit to the United States, Los Angeles, November 1997. *Photo courtesy of Mike Guastella.*

NINETEEN

A New Transatlantic Agenda

By 1995, the Clinton Administration had made great strides in moving economic issues toward the center of American diplomacy. We had focused specifically on building trade and investment ties with Asia and Latin America, as exemplified by the strengthening of APEC and the ratification of NAFTA. Yet there was growing anxiety that our economic and political relations with Europe were languishing. We had paid a great deal of attention to Europe on the security front, establishing the Partnership for Peace and moving forward with NATO expansion. And in December 1993, we had come together with the European Union (EU) to conclude the GATT Uruguay Round, the most sweeping trade agreement ever. But I was still concerned that we were not doing enough to cement our overall relationship with Europe.

This concern was fueled in part by public comments in the first months of 1995 from many of my European counterparts, who worried aloud about the durability of the transatlantic partnership. Because the Clinton Administration had focused so much attention on Asia, Latin America, and the Middle East, some thought it was "abandoning" Europe. Undoubtedly, other stresses exacerbated such sentiments. Our effort to cope with Bosnia was a source of great tension that spilled over into every other area of our relations. Moreover, our European allies were struggling to establish a new, unified European identity through the EU. Plagued by internal divisions and a bitter fight over passage of the Maastricht Treaty, the EU remained in the midst of an uncertain transition.

Quite apart from these aggravating factors, however, some of the European concerns were understandable. We had spent significant time developing a long-term agenda in Asia and Latin America, building new architectures for regional cooperation and establishing goals for further economic integration. The Administration had not yet articulated a similarly concrete set of goals for the future of U.S.-European relations, except for NATO expansion. In previous decades, the Cold War had provided a natural strategic imperative drawing the United States and Europe together. Absent this impetus, we needed to intensify our search for a common purpose and vision. This was especially important as a new generation of leaders, largely untempered by a shared historical experience, began coming to power on both sides of the Atlantic. In short, there was a distinct need to build a "New Atlantic Community."

Our strategy to strengthen our political and economic ties with Europe was influenced significantly by Stuart Eizenstat, our Ambassador to the European Union in Brussels, who later became Under Secretary of State for Economic Affairs. Throughout the spring of 1995, Eizenstat laid out his recommendations to us in a series of cables and phone discussions. He quickly convinced me that the transatlantic relationship needed an ambitious vision that would help maintain public support as well as reinforce our efforts to reshape European security architecture. "At a time when Europeans are questioning our commitment to their enterprises," Eizenstat observed, "it is important to augment our NATO relationship with deeper political and economic ties which are suited to the post–Cold War era." I decided to act on this view, using a June 2, 1995, speech in Madrid to launch the effort.[1]

This address, given at Madrid's Casa de America, was a classic "agenda-setting" speech. It was longer than most of my major policy statements, reflecting the breadth of its goals. I took a comprehensive approach, offering both broad strategic concepts and specific policy initiatives. By es-

---

[1]The Madrid visit enabled me to strengthen my personal relationship with Spanish Foreign Minister Javier Solana. Shortly thereafter, I recommended him to the President and our Allies as NATO Secretary General to succeed Willy Claes, who had resigned because of allegations of his involvement in a fund-raising scandal in Belgium. It took firm U.S. leadership to persuade the other NATO countries to agree to Solana instead of another candidate whom they initially preferred, but he has more than met our highest expectations.

tablishing an ambitious agenda, I hoped the speech might help breathe some life into the U.S.-EU summit planned for December 1995 in Madrid, and into the overall partnership.[2] This effort would be augmented by circumstance: the Spanish, who had signaled their desire to advance the transatlantic agenda and deepen U.S.-European ties, would soon assume the EU presidency. I wanted to use this window of opportunity to establish clear goals for the summit, and at the end of the speech, I made our expectations explicit. As we had done in preparing for the November 1993 APEC Leaders' Meeting in Seattle, we deliberately used the upcoming U.S.-EU summit as a deadline to spark the policy process, both in Washington and in foreign capitals.

The speech quietly but explicitly reaffirmed our role in Europe and corrected any perception of American retreat. It not only placed our relationship with Europe in historical context, making the case for continuing cooperation based on shared interests, but mapped out new areas in which that relationship could develop.

After reiterating our security commitment to Europe and vowing to make the next 50 years "as great as the last," I moved into the core of the speech—the economic dimension of U.S.-European relations. I stressed that the Administration was committed to bringing the same energy and creativity to strengthening economic relations with Europe that we had brought to Latin America through NAFTA, and to Asia through APEC. The long-term objective, I emphasized, was "the integration of the economies of North America and Europe, consistent with the principles of the WTO [World Trade Organization]."

The most sensitive economic issue I discussed was the potential pursuit of a transatlantic free trade agreement, which some began to refer to as a "TAFTA." Many key Europeans (British Foreign Secretary Malcolm Rifkind, German Foreign Minister Klaus Kinkel, and EU Commissioner Leon Brittan) supported such an initiative, and I believed it was a prospect worth exploring. Within the Administration, I was per-

---

[2]Past U.S.-EU summits had had a sterile quality to them. This was due, in part, to the EU's system of rotating its presidency; each of its 16 members holds the office for six months at a time. This not only interrupts momentum but requires the full-time European Commission located in Brussels to share power with countries trying to use their six months in the presidency to the hilt. Lack of coordination and competition between the rotating presidency and the Commission often seem to handicap effective advance planning for summits.

haps the strongest proponent of such exploration. U.S. Trade Representative Mickey Kantor and some other U.S. economic officials were skeptical. Some felt that a bold new initiative might cause further strains among constituencies already unhappy over NAFTA. There was also a concern that it would undermine the WTO and create difficulties for U.S. industries, especially the agricultural sector. I disputed this view, stating in the speech that rather than undermining the WTO, the alignment of U.S. and European economies would promote global economic integration and "reinforce the open global trading system to the benefit of all nations." I signaled our interest in pursuing some sort of TAFTA, announcing that we intended to "give it the serious study it deserves."

With TAFTA only a long-term prospect, I outlined some topics we could address immediately. By taking such steps as developing more consistent investment rules, establishing uniform product standards and testing, and negotiating aviation agreements to ease transatlantic travel, we could create some momentum to tackle the tougher issues.

While economic interests should be at the core of the transatlantic agenda, I explained that U.S.-European cooperation also remained essential in the diplomatic realm. This was true regarding not only important regional issues—for example, Iraq and the Middle East peace process—but also new global challenges like weapons proliferation, terrorism, international crime, and environmental degradation. Although I had been calling attention to the importance of such challenges since taking office, this speech was one of the first times I framed them in a U.S.-European context.

Six months later, at the U.S.-EU summit in Madrid, President Clinton joined Spanish Prime Minister Felipe Gonzalez and EU President Jacques Santer to announce formally the New Transatlantic Agenda I had called for in June.[3] Since then, we had developed with the Europeans a specific Framework for Action calling for cooperation in areas as varied as supporting Bosnian reconstruction; exploring possibilities

---

[3]The President stopped in Ireland en route to Madrid to pursue U.S. efforts to help achieve an agreement ending the prolonged strife in Northern Ireland, which had claimed more than 3,000 lives in the last 28 years. From the beginning of his first term, Clinton had urged the British and Irish governments, as well as Ulster's main political parties and the Irish Republican Army (IRA), to resolve the conflict. He named former Senate Majority Leader George Mitchell as his special representative

for opening trade, possibly through a TAFTA; and coordinating efforts to fight international crime, drug trafficking, and infectious disease. The results reflected the fine work of Peter Tarnoff and Joan Spero, the Under Secretary for Economic Affairs, who led U.S. efforts in these negotiations.

Although progress remains slow and other strains have emerged in our relations, I remain convinced that there is enormous potential for U.S.-EU cooperation in both the diplomatic and the economic areas. It will be especially important to improve this relationship as the process of European integration continues and the EU looms larger as a cohesive counterpart to the United States.

●

Charting a Transatlantic Agenda for the 21st Century

Address at Casa de America, Madrid, June 2, 1995

Thank you, Director Remiro, for that kind introduction. Since its founding several years ago, CERI has already established itself as a leader in foreign policy research. I also want to thank Ambassador Garrigues and the Casa de America for co-hosting this event. I feel at home here—not only because of the name and purpose of this respected institution, but because the Ambassador served as Spain's Consul General in my home city of Los Angeles.

There is no more appropriate place to discuss the transatlantic partnership than Spain—a true Atlantic nation. As a member of both NATO and the European Union, you have placed your future in the vibrant mainstream of Europe and the transatlantic community of democracies. The spirit of renewal so evident here in Madrid is a tribute to King Juan

---

to the talks, and the parties ultimately asked Mitchell to serve as Chairman. As a way of encouraging the IRA to participate in the talks, the President authorized a visa for Gerry Adams, the leader of the political wing of the IRA (Sinn Fein), to visit the United States. The election of Tony Blair as Prime Minister of the United Kingdom in 1997 gave strong impetus to the negotiations, in which the parties are now considering a new Anglo-Irish peace plan.

Carlos, to Spain's democratic leadership, and to the determination of the Spanish people.

For half a century, the transatlantic partnership between the United States and Europe has been the leading force for peace and prosperity, not only in our countries, but around the globe. Together, the Old World and the New World have created a better world. Together we helped transform former adversaries into allies and dictatorships into democracies. We built the institutions that ensured our security and economic strength—most important, NATO and the EU. We created the great institutions of global cooperation—the UN, the IMF and the World Bank, the OECD, the GATT, and now the WTO. By standing steadfast through the Cold War, we have brought a democratic, undivided Europe within reach.

These are truly epic achievements. But at the threshold of the new century, there is another new world to shape—with challenges no less critical than those faced by our counterparts half a century ago. Terrorism, international crime, aggressive nationalism, and the proliferation of weapons of mass destruction threaten our security. Global problems like environmental degradation, unsustainable population growth, and mass movements of refugees undermine emerging democracies and the prosperity of all nations.

The new global economy offers great prospects for growth but also brings wrenching dislocation as our industries and workers seek to adapt. Although the world remains a dangerous place, our opportunities are enormous. Open societies and open markets are on the march. We have the opportunity to reduce the threat of nuclear weapons, enhance our prosperity, and, for the first time in history, build an integrated, undivided, peaceful Europe.

Nevertheless, there are those who question whether Europe and the United States have the will to maintain our partnership to meet these new dangers and seize these opportunities. In the absence of a single unifying threat, and at a time of understandable focus on domestic concerns, some argue that the ties that bind us are fraying and that America and Europe will inevitably drift apart.

I reject that view. From World War II to our strong support for German unification, the United States and Europe have shared a common destiny. But we must not take this relationship for granted. It cannot be sustained by nostalgia. Every generation must renew the partnership by adapting it to meet the challenges of its time. It is our responsibility to build the partnership that will ensure that, by working together, our next 50 years will be as great as the last. To achieve this goal, we must widen our horizons and lift our aspirations.

I believe this goal is shared on both sides of the Atlantic. In recent months, a number of European leaders have set forth their ideas on this very theme. President Clinton and Prime Minister Major discussed this issue when they met earlier this spring.

I have come to Madrid, on behalf of the President, to say that the United States welcomes this transatlantic dialogue. It is timely. It is constructive. And it should be intensified—to reaffirm our common purpose, to advance a common vision, and to forge a common transatlantic agenda for the 21st century. Today I want to suggest goals for our common agenda and how we might strengthen our ability to achieve them together.

A Comprehensive Strategy for European Security

In this year in which we commemorate the 50th anniversary of V-E Day, we cannot forget that security comes first. It is the bedrock of our partnership and the guarantor of our freedom. That is why President Clinton is pursuing a comprehensive strategy for European security based on America's continuing commitment to remain engaged on the continent.

That strategy has five key elements: adapting and enlarging NATO; strengthening the Organization for Security and Cooperation in Europe; supporting Europe's integration and EU enlargement; enhancing a European security and defense identity complementary to NATO; and engaging Russia in Europe's security structures.

NATO remains the central security pillar for Europe and the core institution for linking the security of North America to Europe. In the last five years, NATO has undertaken sweeping changes to match the sweep of Europe's transformation. I have just come from the NATO ministerial meeting in the Netherlands, where we took important steps to advance these goals. Russia's decision at that meeting to cross the threshold into active engagement with NATO puts into place an important element of our comprehensive strategy. We also reviewed the great progress made in just a year-and-a-half by the Partnership for Peace—NATO's mechanism to deepen cooperation with Europe's new democracies. And we reaffirmed that the alliance remains on a steady course toward enlargement.

These efforts are strengthening the security pillar of the transatlantic relationship to meet the challenges of the post–Cold War world. But for our partnership to thrive, it must be comprehensive. That means taking specific steps in the economic and political arenas that will complement and reinforce our security relationship.

The Economic Dimension

Deepening our economic relationship is central to this agenda; it undergirds not only our prosperity, but also our security. Although our ties have expanded with the Asia-Pacific region and Latin America, it is important to recall that the United States and Europe enjoy the largest combined external trade and investment relationship in the world today.

American exports to EU countries and European investment in the United States support over 7 million American workers. All told, Europe accounts for almost half the foreign revenues of American firms. Our investment in Europe alone roughly equals that in the rest of the world put together. And since the Berlin Wall fell, the United States has become the top foreign investor in Central and Eastern Europe.

Together, the United States and Europe have led the world toward open markets and greater prosperity. Our cooperation made possible every global trade agreement from the Kennedy Round to the Uruguay Round. Through the G-7, we work to stimulate global growth. And at the OECD, we are developing strategies to overcome structural unemployment and adapt to demographic change.

A hallmark of the Clinton presidency is its focus on global economic growth and expanding trade. Indeed, President Clinton is advancing the most ambitious international economic agenda of any American President in half a century.

In addition to implementing the North American Free Trade Agreement, his efforts include leading the way to the Miami agreement to complete negotiations on a free trade area in the Americas by the year

2005. He also helped forge APEC's decision to achieve free and open trade and investment in the Asia-Pacific region by 2020. None of these efforts will raise barriers to nonparticipants or exclude any economic sector. And they will meet the requirements of the new World Trade Organization.

Our vision for the economic relationship between Europe and the United States must be no less ambitious. The long-term objective is the integration of the economies of North America and Europe, consistent with the principles of the WTO.

We should undertake a transatlantic economic initiative to multiply trade and investment and create new, high-paying jobs on both sides of the Atlantic. It will make us an even more powerful engine of the global economy. It will align our efforts to promote transatlantic integration with the forces of integration around the world. And it will, like our other efforts, reinforce the open global trading system to the benefit of all nations. Thoughtful observers from Europe, Canada, and the United States have proposed that we seek a Transatlantic Free Trade Agreement. EU Commissioner Leon Brittan has launched a study of this proposal, and we, too, intend to give it the serious study it deserves, with its considerable potential to form an element of our overall strategy. There are, of course, important issues that need to be addressed. For example, any free trade agreement must advance our overriding objective of global trade liberalization, be consistent with an effective WTO, and not disadvantage less-developed countries.

Even as we undertake these studies, there are concrete measures that we can take in the near term to eliminate trade barriers progressively and deepen our integration, building on the momentum we achieved in the Uruguay Round.

First, we can create a comprehensive investment regime. The vast region from Honolulu to Helsinki is essentially a common investment area without common ground rules. We should promptly negotiate a Multilateral Agreement on Investment as agreed by OECD ministers last month.

Second, the United States and the EU need to develop more flexible rules to widen market access and spur innovation in information technology fields. At stake is open competition in one of the most dynamic sectors of the global economy.

Third, the United States and the EU should work to eliminate barriers to trade that result from differences in product standards and testing systems—and do so without compromising health or safety. Incompatible standards inhibit billions of dollars in new trade.

Fourth, we should open our skies. The aviation agreements we will soon complete with nine European countries will make transatlantic travel easier and cheaper and will spur trade and investment.

The United States and the EU should also work together to complete the unfinished business of the Uruguay Round. We must move forward to reach agreements to liberalize financial services within the next month—and telecommunications within the next year. And we must work to overcome our differences in key sectors such as audiovisual products and services. Trade means competition—and vigorous competition is healthy for our relationship and for our economies as well. But that competition must be fair. American businesses operate under the appropriate constraints of legislation barring bribery of foreign officials. Our nations made a commitment to address this problem multilaterally through the OECD last year. We must make progress now.

The private sector is the driving force in our economic relationship, and its leaders should have a larger voice in shaping our agenda. The Pacific Business Forum has helped propel the APEC process; the Transatlantic Business Dialogue launched by Commerce Secretary Ron Brown and Commissioners Bangemann and Brittan can do the same for transatlantic economic integration. I know that this is a special interest of Foreign Minister Solana, with whom I discussed this issue last night.

Global Political Cooperation

The United States and Europe are partners not only for prosperity, but in promoting stability, human dignity, and opportunity around the world. We share common interests and a common responsibility to lead. The political dimension of our proposed agenda will allow us to shape a world more conducive to our interests and consistent with our ideals.

First, we must intensify our efforts to halt the spread of weapons of mass destruction and their delivery systems. The indefinite extension of the Non-Proliferation Treaty last month would not have happened without the leadership of the United States and our European partners. The same leadership will be needed to achieve a Comprehensive Test Ban Treaty and a global ban on the production of fissile materials; to bring the Chemical Weapons Convention into force; and to strengthen the Biological Weapons Convention. We must also bolster our common support for dismantling nuclear weapons and safeguarding nuclear materials in the former Soviet states.

Second, we must strengthen our cooperation against international crime, terrorism, and narcotics trafficking. The United States and Europe have collaborated to combat money laundering through the Financial Action Task Force. Regular meetings of top American and European anti-narcotics officials could strengthen our arsenal in the fight against drugs. Those who traffic in weapons, narcotics, and human lives recognize no national borders. We must make sure they have nowhere to hide.

Third, we must coordinate our humanitarian and development assistance more effectively. Ninety percent of all global humanitarian assistance is provided by the United States, the European Commission, and the member states of the EU. We need to build on our successful joint experience, providing food relief to the Caucasus and technical assistance to Central Europe to develop a common strategy and to coordinate priorities, especially at a time when we all face financial constraints. More generally, we need to broaden our cooperation to address a range of emerging global problems. Our joint efforts in Cairo made the International Conference on Population and Development a success. And our annual high-level environmental dialogue has helped pave the way for multilateral initiatives like the Berlin Climate Conference and major agreements such as the Montreal Protocol. The joint program for cooperation between the United States and Japan—"the Common Agenda" embracing issues ranging from population to health, the environment, science and technology—provides a model of the concrete and high-impact opportunities for collaboration. I hope we can forge a comparable common agenda in the transatlantic area. Human rights, too, is an area where, working together, we can enhance our impact. We can maximize our effectiveness by cooperating closely.

Fourth, we must bolster our cooperation in regions where the United States and Europe share common interests and historic ties—for example, the Middle East. With EU support, the 1991 Madrid Conference launched the most promising opportunity for Arab-Israeli peace in two generations. Now is the time to make that promise real by more effectively coordinating our economic assistance and working together to bring into being the Middle East Development Bank proposed by Egypt, Jordan, Israel, and the PLO. And at the Amman summit this October, together we can build on the start we made in Casablanca last year to generate the private investment that is so essential to lasting peace and prosperity in the region.

We should also expand our cooperation in the Mediterranean, an area of vital interest to the EU and the United States. Spain has played a key role in advancing the EU's initiative on this important region, and we look forward to cooperating with you as the Barcelona Conference approaches. We can also explore new ways to work together to sustain democracy in the Americas, an area where Spain is an especially valuable partner.

Cooperation in Europe

Of course, nowhere is our regional cooperation more important than meeting the new challenges and opportunities facing Europe itself. We in the United States know too well that our security is at risk when Europe's is imperiled. And we have a common interest in assuring that the historic transformations now underway in Central Europe and the former Soviet Union are consolidated—and that these countries become integrated into our transatlantic community.

We have worked closely together to coordinate our assistance through the G-24, the World Bank, and the IMF. Our financial and technical assistance is helping countries like Russia, Ukraine, and Poland to free prices, privatize industry, and ease the pain of dislocation. Our economic assistance efforts are complemented by our support for durable democratic institutions throughout Central and Eastern Europe and the New Independent States. Together, the European Union and the United States are a vital force for stability in the region. We are also advancing European integration by extending our economic and security relations to the east. Our steady program for enlarging NATO is reinforced by the steps being taken by the EU. The prospects for stability in Europe's new democracies are unmistakably linked to their potential for prosperity—and to our willingness to open our markets to their goods.

The EU does more than open its markets to the new economies of the region, however. It provides incentive and shelter for the development of civil societies that are the surest guarantee for stability and security. And it encourages the resolution of ancient enmities, today in Central Europe as after World War II between France and Germany.

As we look to the future, the United States and the EU should work together to develop new areas for common action aimed at assisting the new democracies of Central Europe. For example:

We could help these states to cope better with the scourge of organized crime through efforts such as the International Law Enforcement Academy in Budapest;

We could promote the development of citizens groups and NGOs that can help build democratic societies from the ground up; and

We could refocus our technical assistance to ensure that the basic structures of a modern market economy are fully in place as the Central European countries make the transition from aid to trade.

The United States and the EU also have a special interest in supporting a democratic Turkey, integrated into the transatlantic community. Turkey is at the strategic crossroads of the Balkans, the Middle East, and the former Soviet states. We hope that the European Parliament will ratify the critically important customs union agreement between the EU and Turkey. At the same time, we strongly encourage Turkey to move ahead with democratic reform and strengthen the protection of human rights. We are also redoubling our efforts to achieve a political settlement—long overdue—in Cyprus prior to the start of EU accession talks.

The terrible conflict in Bosnia remains the single greatest threat to our vision of an integrated Europe at peace. The United States and Europe are working together, although it is clear to all that we have not achieved the results we seek. We have sought to contain the conflict, to alleviate suffering, and find a lasting peaceful settlement to the war. On behalf of the American people, I want to thank our European allies, Spain among them, who have put their troops and personnel in harm's way to help the people of the former Yugoslavia and to uphold the principles of the international community. We believe that a strengthened UNPROFOR is the best insurance against an even worse humanitarian disaster that would follow its withdrawal. That is why this week, the Contact Group and others have undertaken efforts to reinforce UN-PROFOR's ability to carry out its mission safely and effectively. The United States will continue to coordinate closely, through NATO, the United Nations, and the Contact Group.

One of the few bright spots in the midst of the Bosnian tragedy has been the agreement of the Muslim and Croat communities to end their conflict and establish a bicommunal federation. The United States and the EU have joined forces to help support this enterprise through the Friends of the Federation—helping to keep alive hopes for preserving a multi-ethnic society in Bosnia. This is a model for the joint initiatives that we should develop for the future.

The Way Ahead

To achieve the ambitious agenda I have set forth today, we must enhance our ability to work together more effectively. This will require commitment on three fronts.

First, the United States and Europe must remain engaged in the world, on our own and as partners. Our nations have the unique capacity to provide global leadership. We must resist the siren songs heard in so many capitals of isolation and withdrawal.

Second, the United States looks to Europe to be a strong partner for the United States and a capable actor on the world stage. Of course, the choice of mechanisms is for EU members themselves to decide. But the United States has a clear interest in Europe's continued integration and its enhanced ability in foreign and security policy. And the EU should move ahead with its historic process of enlargement. Forty years ago today, six European foreign ministers gathered in a monastery in Messina to launch a process that ultimately led to the Treaty of Rome and the establishment of the European Communities. Tomorrow, history will be made in Messina once again, as the EU under Spanish Chairmanship meets to plan the ambitious Intergovernmental Conference. The objective, as President Truman's Under Secretary of State Robert Lovett said in 1948, "should continue to be the progressively closer integration, both economic and political, of presently free Europe, and eventually of as much of Europe as becomes free."

Finally, we must strengthen the mechanisms of our cooperation. We must take advantage of immediate opportunities, such as the upcoming summit between President Clinton and Presidents Chirac and Santer, to define common goals and to advance them more systematically. In the next six months, the United States looks forward to working closely with the Spanish presidency of the European Union to develop more fully our common agenda. By the end of the year, we should have developed a broad-ranging transatlantic agenda for the new century—an agenda for common economic and political action to expand democracy, prosperity, and stability. Between now and the end of the year, we are prepared to engage seriously with representatives of the EU to forge this agenda. Closer government ties are essential, but in a time of generational change on both sides of the Atlantic, we need to deepen our interaction at every level. We should call on business leaders to tell us what must be done to tear down barriers to trade and investment in Central and Eastern Europe and between North America and Western Europe. We should encourage our elected representatives to intensify their contacts, from parliamentary exchanges to sister cities. We should broaden the academic and cultural exchanges to enrich our deepest ties of all—those between our people.

We must act now, for as President Kennedy told a European audience in 1963, "time and the world do not stand still. Change is the law of life. And those who look only to the past are certain to miss the future." I know that the partnership that brought us to this hopeful point in history will continue to shape the future as boldly as it shaped the past.

Thank you very much.

Engagement with China

Although U.S.-Chinese tensions had cooled after our 1994 decision to renew MFN, they returned to the boiling point in May 1995. This time, the issue was Taiwan, historically perhaps the most sensitive topic in U.S.-Chinese relations. Upon taking office, the Clinton Administration had chosen not to alter fundamentally the one-China policy followed since 1972. We would continue to have only "unofficial" relations with Taiwan and to insist that its status be determined peacefully by China and Taiwan. We had also decided early on, however, that our China-Taiwan policy should be modestly adjusted to reflect Taiwan's increased economic strength and movement toward democracy. These adjustments resulted in several U.S. cabinet-level visits to Taiwan, as well as facilitation of Taiwan's admission into international organizations that, unlike the United Nations, do not require statehood for membership.

Although we had realized that even such limited shifts would push the envelope with Beijing, the situation took an especially sour turn in early 1995. Taiwan's President, Lee Teng-hui, applied for entry into the United States to attend a reunion at his alma mater, Cornell University, in Ithaca, New York. Although we had previously permitted transit stops, this would be the first visit by a Taiwanese leader. But as we reflected further and observed overwhelming congressional support for the visit (fanned by a very aggressive lobbying campaign by Taiwan), we decided to allow it under carefully circumscribed conditions. We stipulated that Lee's visit would be entirely private and non-political; he would not meet with any Administration officials, and he would only be allowed to travel directly to and from Ithaca. All of us who conferred on this decision—Bill Perry, Tony Lake, Sandy Berger (the Deputy National Security Adviser), Winston Lord, and I—felt that we were justified in recommending a visa on that basis. In part, we felt that permitting the visit would help forestall congressional action that would do more damage to the U.S.-China relationship. There was no doubt that the Chinese would squawk about the trip, but we calculated that as long as we kept it private and non-political, relations would not suffer unduly.

Unfortunately, Lee's "private" visit to Cornell that summer went out of bounds, assumed a very political tone, and sent our relations with China into a tailspin. We had been told that his reunion address would be essentially non-substantive, but in fact it had a strong political flavor and was quite provocative. Tweaking the Chinese, Lee invoked the title "Republic of China on Taiwan" numerous times.[1] The Chinese were enraged, claiming that the visit and speech signified a fundamental shift in our one-China approach.

The problem was aggravated by a misunderstanding I had with Vice Premier and Foreign Minister Qian. I had told him when I met with him in April 1995 that we did not intend to make any change in our fundamental policy of only "unofficial" relations with Taiwan, but I had also warned him that overwhelming congressional support for the Lee visit (reflected by the 97–1 and 360–0 votes in the Senate and House on resolutions endorsing the visit) could not be ignored. This warning was intended to alert Qian that a visa might be issued. But he heard only the first half of my statement, and I was told that he was personally embarrassed when Lee was permitted to go to Ithaca.[2]

In the wake of the Lee contretemps, we conveyed private and public reassurances to the Chinese about our adherence to a one-China policy and our continued commitment to engagement rather than containment. I sent a letter to Foreign Minister Qian, and the President took the unusual step of meeting privately with the Chinese Ambassador at

---

[1] The Beijing Chinese regarded Taiwan as a province of China and reacted adversely to any assertion of independence by Taiwan.

[2] It can often be difficult for foreign leaders, especially in dictatorships, to recognize the importance of the legislative and judicial branches in our constitutionally ordained separation of powers. It may have seemed presumptuous to explain our system to them, but I often found it necessary to do so, and sometimes regretted it when I did not.

the White House. Nevertheless, Beijing reacted strongly, seeking to put us on the defensive and claiming that Lee's visit constituted a mortal sin. They canceled or postponed almost all meetings and visits with U.S. officials, withdrew their Ambassador, rounded up more dissidents, and detained American citizen Harry Wu,[3] all the while lambasting us publicly. They intended to send a message to the United States and the world about their sensitivity regarding Taiwan.

I believed that we had to respond firmly to these moves. In my view, the Chinese would respect us only if, rather than panicking, we projected a certain severity while still conveying our conviction that positive relations would further mutual interests. I advised the President that our message to China should be simple and brief: "We have not changed our policies on Taiwan or engagement; we have offered the means to restore momentum in our relations; it is up to you to respond in your own national interest; we are ready to engage anytime, but meanwhile we will go about our geopolitical business with confidence and strategic purpose."

The remarks I made to the National Press Club in Washington in July amplified this message to Beijing. Five days later, I would see Foreign Minister Qian in Brunei at the annual meeting of the ASEAN Regional Forum (ARF), and I wanted to signal our intentions and set a firm but positive tone. Although I did stress the need to confront our differences over human rights matters (such as the imprisonment of Harry Wu) and weapons proliferation, I also sought to reassure. I addressed Chinese concerns about the Lee visit directly, explaining that it did not constitute a shift in our policy toward Taiwan and China. Then I restated our adherence to the so-called three communiques, reciting the policy chapter and verse.[4] I said, "We have no intention of advocating or supporting a policy of 'two Chinas' or 'one China, one Taiwan.'"

Delivered on a Friday in Washington's sweltering summer, the speech received little attention in the U.S. press. However, as I discovered five

---

[3]Harry Wu, a photojournalist who had exposed grim conditions and forced labor in Chinese prisons, was taken into custody trying to enter China through a remote western province. A few months later, he was released and deported.

[4]The three communiques, which have been the foundation of U.S.-China relations since 1972, are the Shanghai Communique of 1972, the 1979 communique establishing diplomatic relations, and the 1982 communique on arms sales.

days later in Brunei, the Chinese, and many others in Asia, followed my remarks closely. Of all the speeches I delivered as Secretary, this one seemed to have the most immediate effect.

I anticipated that my meeting with Qian in Brunei would be one of the most important—and most difficult—in years. Our Beijing embassy warned me to prepare for a tough time. "You can expect Qian's mood to be somber—professional, but definitely cool," the embassy reported. I expected to be put on the defensive personally, and told President Clinton that the encounter would be the "most complex and problematic event" of my trip.

To my surprise, however, the meeting opened on a conciliatory note. Qian commented favorably on my National Press Club address, which he said he had not only read carefully but watched on videotape. He was pleased by our restatement of the one-China policy, although he did make the point that "words must be followed by deeds." I sought to make the most of this opening by reiterating the substance and tone of my Press Club remarks.[5] "Although this is a contentious period in U.S.-PRC relations," I told Qian, "I want to focus on common ground in addressing our differences." I detailed our policy on Taiwan, explaining that the United States would not agree to official relations or support an official role for Taiwan in the international community. I told Qian candidly that we would not rule out future visits by Lee or other senior Taipei leaders, but that we would permit them only if they were personal, private, unofficial, non-political—and rare. I stressed our desire to resume a dialogue with China on important bilateral issues, such as nonproliferation, arms control, and regional security, and asked to send Under Secretary Peter Tarnoff to Beijing to facilitate this effort. Finally, I conveyed the President's hope that President Jiang would be able to visit the United States in the near future. Qian seemed to be pleased with my presentation. He welcomed Tarnoff's proposed visit and reciprocated our hope for a presidential summit.

Given my dour expectations, the meeting with Qian was about as pos-

---

[5] I also gave Qian a three-page letter from President Clinton to President Jiang, which reiterated Clinton's personal commitment to improving relations and addressed Chinese concerns about Taiwan and the Lee visit, repeating in detail our one-China policy.

itive as could reasonably have been hoped. As I told the President the next day, "the tone was good; the chill I had anticipated was not present." As I looked ahead to future relations with China, I thought the meeting would prove to have been a positive turning point—a development helped in no small way by my Press Club speech. "We are in a position to regain the momentum that we had lost in our relationship," I cabled the President. "I sense that after the train wreck, we are both struggling to put the cars back on track, one by one, but it will clearly take time and effort. . . . The relationship may have bottomed-out, and will be on the mend unless there is some additional provocation."

In the remaining 16 months of my term, I worked closely with Qian to stabilize and improve U.S.-China relations. Our relationship had always been "correct," but now I began to sense a mutuality in our purpose. In all, I met with him 14 times during my four years, and I found him the most sophisticated and worldly of the Chinese leaders. He could, however, be very tough. Once, early in our relationship, I complained about China's criticism of the United States, saying that it only provided fuel for American critics of China. He shot back, "I hope you will conduct yourself in the future so that it won't be necessary for us to criticize." At the same time, he was highly professional and generally had a pleasant demeanor. He had become Foreign Minister shortly after the Tiananmen Square massacre, and he patiently led the Chinese back from pariah status.

All in all, the roller-coaster ride with China revealed to me the lasting importance of engagement—and of American leadership in Asia. "The meeting here in Brunei," I wrote President Clinton, "reminds me how much the other nations in the region depend on the U.S. to manage the U.S.-China relationship—and to help insure stability by maintaining its presence in the region."

My Press Club remarks also pointed out several areas in which the strategy of American engagement with the rest of Asia had produced positive results since my May 1994 speech before the Asia Society. After a rough spring and summer of 1994—marked by difficult trade negotiations with Japan, rising concerns about North Korea's nuclear ambitions, and tensions with China over MFN—our relations with Asia had finally begun to turn the corner. One positive development that the Press Club speech noted was the strengthening of our relations with our core regional ally, Japan. We had moved beyond the tensions of the spring of 1994. To be sure, bargaining remained tough and hot rhetoric lingered, but we had begun to move in the right direction. Through the U.S.-Japan Economic Framework negotiations, we had already reached 16 agreements that increased access to Japanese markets. We had also opened a dialogue with Japan to improve military ties, continuing a process launched during my March 1994 trip to Tokyo. The Press Club address, which contrasted significantly with the tough tone of the speech I gave during that 1994 trip (Chapter 9), mentioned these encouraging developments and called the American partnership with Japan the "cornerstone of our engagement" in the region.

We had also succeeded in freezing North Korea's nuclear ambitions. By July 1995, we had begun to implement the commitments under the 1994 Agreed Framework, and the Korean Energy Development Organization was up and running. Despite these accomplishments, however, significant work remained. In the Press Club speech, I stressed that only through the "resumption of a broader dialogue" between the two Koreas could lasting peace take hold.

In addition to addressing the important regional challenges posed by Japan and Korea, engagement had also helped us normalize relations with Vietnam and build regional security and economic institutions (see Chapter 21). We had made important strides toward creating the same strong institutional architecture in Asia that we had built in Europe after World War II. To broaden our security cooperation in Southeast Asia, we had aided in the formation of the ARF; in addition, we had continued to build on the spirit of Seattle by strengthening economic ties through APEC. In November 1994 in Indonesia, the second APEC Leaders' Meeting had taken a significant step in this direction by committing to achieve regional free trade by 2020.

As I had explained in my Asia Society speech, an engagement strategy is not a quick fix. It is a long-term approach, aiming to work through diplomatic differences, not walk away from them. By the time of my Press Club speech, the value of this approach had become apparent.

●

America's Strategy for a Peaceful and Prosperous Asia-Pacific

Address to the National Press Club, Washington, D.C., July 28, 1995

Tomorrow, I depart on my sixth trip to Asia as Secretary of State. First, I will go to Brunei for our annual meetings with the Association of Southeast Asian Nations—ASEAN. I will visit Malaysia to strengthen ties with that increasingly important regional partner. In Cambodia, where I will be the first Secretary of State to visit since John Foster Dulles in 1955, I will reaffirm our support for the efforts of its people to overcome their tragic past. In Vietnam, where I will be the first Secretary of State to visit since William Rogers in 1970, I will carry out President Clinton's far-sighted decision to normalize relations and continue to pursue progress on the fullest possible accounting for our POWs and MIAs.

Over the past half-century, I have personally witnessed many of the historic changes that have swept the Pacific. As a teenager, I moved to Los Angeles and watched California build new links between the far west and the Far East. As a young ensign in the U.S. Navy, I saw an Asia-Pacific region devastated by four years of war. As a young negotiator in textile talks with Japan in the early 1960s, I saw a region poised for rapid economic growth. Now, as a still young Secretary of State, I see a region with extraordinary potential for stability, prosperity, and democracy. This hopeful turn of events would not have come to pass without the indispensable role of the United States.

After the Second World War, America's leaders understood that a secure and prosperous Asia was vital to our national interest. Our military presence promoted stability and gave nations in the region the chance to build thriving economies for the benefit of all. The transformation of the Asia-Pacific region is truly breathtaking. In the space of half a century, nations that were among the oldest outposts of colonialism are now on the newest frontiers of capitalism. Underdeveloped, largely rural societies are giving way to dynamic modern economies offering broad opportunities to their people. These economic miracles are increasingly associated with the spread of political freedoms and vibrant civil societies.

As a result, we are turning the seas and skies that once divided us into channels for communication and cooperation.

The trade and investment dollars that stream between America and Asia create jobs and propel economic growth. Our nation has also been enriched by millions of Asian-Americans imbued with the values of education, hard work, and family—values as American as they are Asian.

On the 50th anniversary of the end of the Second World War, American leadership in Asia remains as essential to our security and prosperity as ever before. With the end of the Cold War, the political landscape in Asia is undergoing profound changes. Nowhere is this more apparent than in Asia's largest powers—Russia, China, and Japan. In this time of uncertainty, a stable U.S. presence is especially important. That is why President Clinton has renewed and reinforced our commitment to remain a Pacific power.

Our strategy in the region recognizes the new opportunities and challenges posed by the post–Cold War world. The region is now remarkably free of conflict. But while no major power views any other as an immediate military threat, there is a danger that age-old rivalries could be rekindled. Dynamic economic growth is spurring integration, yet competition for resources and markets is creating new tensions. And with that growth and new technology have come the spread of weapons of mass destruction, the emergence of narcotics networks, and severe pressures on the environment.

No nation in the Asia-Pacific can confront these complex challenges on its own. They can only be met by a community of nations acting together—a diverse community, to be sure, but one linked increasingly by shared interests and values. The leadership of the United States will be essential to bring that community to life.

To ensure a peaceful and prosperous Asia-Pacific for the 21st century, we have adopted a four-part strategy. First, we will maintain and invigorate our core alliances with Japan, Korea, Australia, the Philippines, and Thailand. Second, we are pursuing a policy of engagement with the other leading countries in the region, including former Cold War adversaries. Third, we are building a regional architecture that will sustain economic growth, promote integration, and assure stability over the long term. And fourth, we are supporting democracy and human rights which serve our ideals as well as our interests.

Our strategy starts with our core alliances because we understand that security must always come first. Our military presence remains the foundation for stability and prosperity in a region where the interests of four major powers intersect. That presence is our first line of defense. It safeguards our allies. It protects our economic interests. And it reassures a region still troubled by historical antagonisms. That is why our security presence in the Asia-Pacific is broadly welcomed.

The Clinton Administration's Bottom Up review of U.S. defense policy in 1993 confirmed the continuing need for our forward-deployed military presence. Hence, the United States is committed to maintaining approximately 100,000 troops in the Pacific—roughly equivalent to the level in Europe.

American policy in Asia begins with Japan. The U.S.-Japan partnership is the cornerstone of our engagement in the Asia-Pacific region. Fifty years ago, the United States made a strategic choice to help Japan rebuild. Today, our alliance with a democratic and prosperous Japan is one of the great successes of the post-war era. Our challenge is to ensure that the next five decades of the alliance are as successful as the last have been.

I am struck by how few Americans know that we maintain 47,000 U.S. troops in Japan—in addition to the men and women of the Seventh Fleet. Their presence is no "Cold War anachronism" as some commentators have claimed. These American troops stationed in Japan are a wise investment in future security for the entire region. They provide a stabilizing presence for all the nations of Asia.

Last November, the United States and Japan launched a dialogue to renew and enhance our security ties. The defense and foreign ministers of our two countries are examining issues such as improving the interoperability of our forces, which is facilitated by Japan's purchase of U.S. weapons systems. We are cooperating on Host Nation Support, under which Japan provides 70% of the cost of the U.S. military presence. And we are deepening our global cooperation, which has grown with Japan's valuable peacekeeping role in Cambodia, Mozambique, and Rwanda.

In the post–Cold War world, Japan is in a position to take on even greater responsibilities. That is why we support Japan's bid to become a permanent member of the UN Security Council. Together we are already supporting reform in Russia, peace in the Middle East, and stability in Haiti. And together we are addressing complex global issues such as unsustainable population growth, AIDS, and pollution through our ambitious Common Agenda.

As the world's two largest economies, America and Japan also share a responsibility to uphold the goal of open trade and to support the international financial system. The Clinton Administration has consistently sought to open Japanese markets, which will benefit American business and American workers, Japanese consumers, and the rest of the world. Under the U.S.-Japan Economic Framework, we have reached 16 agreements that expand access to Japan's markets. Last month, we concluded an important agreement with Japan that will widen access to Japan's market for autos and auto parts. Last week, we resolved a dispute over air cargo. While these agreements are an important accomplishment, we must work together to ensure that they are implemented. Ours is a rich, multifaceted partnership. It will achieve its broadest potential when all of its elements are strong—strategic and military, diplomatic and economic.

It is a tribute to the Republic of Korea's remarkable achievements that our long-standing security alliance is fast becoming a mature and complete partnership. Yesterday, President Clinton and President Kim Young Sam unveiled a Korean War Memorial that pays tribute to the shared sacrifice that sealed our alliance more than 40 years ago. Now that South Korea is a vibrant democracy, a valued trading partner, and a trusted comrade-in-arms, our relationship is stronger than ever. The U.S. security commitment to South Korea, demonstrated by the 37,000 American troops stationed there, remains unshakable. Over the last two years, our determined diplomacy has put the North Korean nuclear issue on the road to resolution. The Agreed Framework has already frozen North Korea's nuclear program. When fully implemented, the Framework will eliminate it entirely.

As North Korea carries out its obligations under the Framework, it can begin to develop more normal relations with the United States and other nations in the region. But any major improvement in our relations with the North can only come with progress in relations between the two Koreas. In this context, recent North-South talks on supplying needed rice to Pyongyang are a hopeful development. The resumption of a broader dialogue between North and South—especially on the issue of a nuclear-free peninsula—offers the only meaningful hope for reduced tensions and ultimate reconciliation.

The second element of our Pacific strategy is our policy of engagement with the other leading powers in the region, including former Cold War adversaries.

Few nations are poised to play as large a role in shaping the future of Asia than China. With its vast population, its geographic reach, its rich history of cultural influence across Asia, its growing military power, and its new economic dynamism, China is unique. As the United States shapes its policy and conducts its diplomacy with China, we must not allow short-term calculations to divert us from pursuing our long-term interests.

I need not tell this audience that we are now experiencing a period of difficulty in this important relationship. One immediate cause is China's concern that the recent private visit of Taiwan's leader Lee Teng-hui to his alma mater Cornell University represents a shift in our approach to China. This concern is unwarranted. The private visit by Lee Teng-hui was a special situation and a courtesy, consistent with American values and opinion. It did not constitute a shift in our policy toward Taiwan and China.

The United States has not and does not intend to change its long-standing one-China policy. In this period of difficulty, it is more important than ever for China, for Taiwan, and for the United States to focus and reflect on the shared interest we have in maintaining the continuity of this policy. It is a policy that is emphatically in the overwhelming interest of all of us. Over 20 years ago, the United States and China made the strategic decision to end more than two decades of confrontation. Since then, six American presidents, Democrat and Republican alike, have pursued a policy of engagement with China that has served the enduring interests of the United States and everyone in the region. That policy of engagement reflects the fundamental understanding that our ability to pursue significant common interests and to manage significant differences would not be served by a policy of isolation or containment.

The wisdom of that historic judgment two decades ago has been demonstrated time and again by our ability to work together on key challenges of regional and global importance, including China's recent support on the North Korea nuclear issue and on the indefinite extension of the Nuclear Non-Proliferation Treaty. And it has been demonstrated by the benefits of our success in Cambodia and the launching of new regional security dialogues.

Since 1972, the basis for our engagement has been our one-China policy. We have consistently followed basic principles developed in the Shanghai Communique of 1972, the 1979 communique establishing diplomatic relations, and the 1982 U.S.-P.R.C. Communique on arms sales: Pursuant to these documents, we recognize the Government of the P.R.C. as the sole legal government of China. We acknowledge the Chinese position that there is but one China and that Taiwan is part of China. We reaffirm that we have no intention of advocating or supporting a policy of "two Chinas" or "one China, one Taiwan."

This policy has produced enormous benefits for the United States, as well as for China and Taiwan. It has helped keep the peace and fuel prosperity on both sides of the Strait—and it has helped propel Taiwan's flourishing democracy. And just as we look to the continued strengthening of U.S.-China relations, we expect that the unofficial ties between Americans and the people of Taiwan, pursuant to the Taiwan Relations Act of 1979, will also thrive. The United States, China, and Taiwan share the responsibility to pursue policies that foster continued stability in the region.

Managing our differences with China on Taiwan and other issues does not mean downplaying their importance. On human rights, for example, we still have profound disagreements. We will continue to promote universally recognized human rights in China, as elsewhere.

We have serious concerns with respect to the proliferation of weapons of mass destruction. Today, such weapons and their delivery systems pose the greatest threat to global security. As a nuclear power, China—just as the United States does—has special responsibilities in this regard. Since the outset of this Administration, we have made the case to China that curbing proliferation is in our overriding mutual interest. We are especially concerned about arms transfers to volatile regions like South Asia and to rogue regimes such as Iran. The best way to resolve these concerns is through dialogue, which is why I urge China to resume our discussions on non-proliferation.

Just as we have a mutual interest in halting the spread of weapons of mass destruction, we share an interest in assuring regional stability. As China seeks to modernize its military forces, greater transparency about its military capabilities and intentions could do much to reassure its neighbors. Our differences with China are an argument for engagement, not for containment or isolation. Neither the United States nor China can afford the luxury of walking away from our responsibility to manage our differences. China has as much interest in maintaining constructive relations as we do. China can take an immediate step to help restore a more positive atmosphere with the immediate release of American citizen Harry Wu.

I look forward to my meeting with Foreign Minister Qian in Brunei on August 1. I intend to discuss with him the fundamentals of the U.S.-China relationship, to reiterate the continuity of our policy, to address candidly our areas of agreement and disagreement, and to seek to restore the positive momentum in our relations. A strong, stable, open, and prosperous China can be a valuable partner for the United States and a responsible leader of the international community.

A week from tomorrow, I will arrive in Hanoi. Since taking office, the President has made his top priority with respect to Vietnam the fullest possible accounting of our prisoners of war and missing in action. We have been encouraged by the results of Hanoi's cooperation. We are convinced that normalizing relations is the best way to keep up the momentum and achieve further results. That is why, after a decade of war and two decades of estrangement, President Clinton made the courageous decision to establish diplomatic relations between our two countries. Let me add that I have been inspired by working with elected leaders of both parties, including Senator John McCain, Senator John Kerry, Senator Robert Kerrey, and Representative Pete Peterson to help close a bitter chapter in our nation's history.

Closer engagement with Vietnam is in America's interest. We can work together to promote economic reform; to focus on the rule of law, human rights, regional peace, and stability; and to pursue areas of common interest like the fight against narcotics trafficking. Similarly, engagement with the other leading nations of Asia is crucial to our interests. Indonesia, Malaysia, and Singapore are examples of dynamic economic partners which can also make important contributions to regional stability.

In the long run, we need to build mechanisms of cooperation to assure that the current favorable environment will endure. Thus, the third element of our strategy is to build a sound architecture for regional cooperation. The creation of the ASEAN Regional Forum is an important initial step in this process. The Forum reflects what might be called the ASEAN way: consultation, consensus, and cooperation. We see the Forum and the emerging security dialogue in Northeast Asia as crucial supplements to our alliances and forward military presence.

Next week in Brunei, I will join my colleagues from 16 Asia-Pacific nations and the European Union for the second meeting of the ASEAN Regional Forum. We will discuss security challenges such as the North Korean nuclear issue and freedom of navigation. We have consistently urged claimants to the resources of the Spratly Islands in the South China Sea to solve their differences through dialogue, not military confrontation.

These nascent efforts to build mechanisms for security cooperation complement the remarkable economic integration our nations are achieving through APEC. These significant accomplishments are attributable in no small part to President Clinton's vision and leadership in convening the first-ever APEC Leaders' Meeting two years ago in Seattle. Last year in Bogor, Indonesia, the leaders committed to achieve free trade in the region by 2020. This year in Osaka, APEC leaders will turn their historic vision into a blueprint for action. That blueprint should set forth shared principles, specific goals, and a process for achieving them.

The fourth and final element of our strategy is our steadfast support for human rights and democracy. Just as open markets and open sea lanes promote prosperity and security in the Pacific, so do open societies. Business people in Shanghai and San Francisco may speak different languages, but they agree that enterprise thrives when ideas and information are exchanged freely. The experiences of the many democracies across the region tell us that accountable government and the rule of law are the bedrock of stability and prosperity. The experiences of countries like Burma and North Korea tell us that repression entrenches poverty.

Open societies also make better neighbors. History shows that the greatest threats to security in the Asia-Pacific region have come from governments that flout the rule of law at home and reject it abroad. Each nation will find its own way consistent with its history and culture. But all have a responsibility to meet international obligations and to respect the standards of the Universal Declaration of Human Rights. America will continue to champion human rights and the movement toward more open societies. We will do so without arrogance, but also without apology. And we will continue to assist countries that are embracing democracy, such as Cambodia and Mongolia, by encouraging the development of political parties and political institutions.

In Burma, the efforts of the United States and the international community helped lead to the recent release of imprisoned opposition leader and Nobel Prize winner Aung San Suu Kyi. We welcome this step, but believe its true significance depends on whether it represents real move-ment toward the restoration of democratic government. We have a par-ticular interest in encouraging accountable government in a country that is the world's largest supplier of heroin.

In sum, my trip to the region will advance the four key elements of our Asia-Pacific strategy—reaffirmation of our alliances, engagement with Asia's leading powers, the construction of enduring mechanisms for regional cooperation, and support for human rights and democracy. Taken together, these elements will advance our broad-ranging interests in a region that remains essential to our security and prosperity. To-gether we have traveled an enormous distance since the end of the war in the Pacific half a century ago. American leadership and engagement were essential on that great journey. They will be no less so as we seek to shrink the distances that separate us, and to create a promising Pacific fu-ture that all of us can share.

Thank you very much.

TWENTY-ONE

Opening Relations with Vietnam

The war in Vietnam had a profound effect on America for almost two decades, the 1960s and the 1970s. Of course, it affected most deeply those families whose loved ones served in Vietnam, but the entire population was involved in ways both direct and subtle. Having served in World War II, I am a bit too old to have been part of the Vietnam generation, but nevertheless the war touched my life in many ways.[1]

Violent protest against the war was often an important element in the urban riots and demonstrations that brought our country to the edge of chaos in 1967 and 1968. My role as Vice Chairman of the Governor's Commission on the 1965 Watts riots in Los Angeles had been an important factor in my selection as Deputy Attorney General in 1967. Vietnam had a powerful influence on my duties in that position. Shortly after I was confirmed, I was on my way to Detroit to serve as deputy to Cyrus Vance, then President Johnson's representative during the July 1967 riots there.

Whether in Washington or at the scene of the disturbance, as Deputy Attorney General I was responsible for helping to mediate the dispute and contain the violence, and for recommending the deployment of fed-

---

[1]An early instance came during the bilateral textile talks that I conducted in Tokyo in 1963. The Japanese delegation launched a sharp criticism of the U.S. role in Vietnam. I reacted by adjourning the meeting to protest the gratuitous digression from the agenda and refused to resume until given assurance that we would stick to the subject under discussion.

eral troops if that should become necessary. In 1968, when thousands of angry antiwar demonstrators attempted to shut down the Pentagon, I joined Secretary of Defense Robert McNamara to try to protect government operations, but also to ensure that the government's response minimized the risk of bloodshed and respected our constitutional traditions.[2] Because of concern over antiwar demonstrations, President Johnson designated me as law enforcement representative at the 1968 Democratic convention in Chicago. From my observation point on the second floor of the Hilton Hotel, I watched the police lose control and lash out indiscriminately against the demonstrators. Ultimately, I recommended that federal troops be deployed, as much to restrain the police as to control the demonstrators. I also watched the war take its physical and political toll on Johnson and ultimately lead to his decision not to seek reelection.[3]

Since the Clinton Administration had taken office, our strategy toward Vietnam had been best described as incremental engagement. We were essentially following the carefully calibrated road map that President Bush and Secretary Baker had laid down in 1991. After a half century of war and poverty, Vietnam was poised to join its neighbors in the region's economic and political transformation. We wanted to support this effort, because it was entirely consistent with our larger goal of creating a New Pacific Community. But in view of the excruciating legacy of the war and many legitimate sensitivities at home, we had to move slowly. Most importantly, we had to have cooperation from the Vietnamese on the POW/MIA issue.

Given these concerns, we steered a middle course, rather than either pursuing a "great leap forward" by immediately opening full relations (thus squandering any leverage we might have and rousing strong domestic opposition) or holding the line until we had complete cooperation (thus providing Hanoi little incentive to work with us). At the same time, we worked hard to shore up domestic support for strengthening ties to Vietnam, reaching out to such key leaders (and distinguished Vietnam

[2]Robert S. McNamara, *In Retrospect*, pp. 303–5 (New York: Times Books, 1995).
[3]The Vietnam War was still a central topic when I returned to Washington as Cyrus Vance's Deputy Secretary in 1977. I recall the extensive discussions that preceded Vance's decision to describe the Vietnam War as a "mistake" in his confirmation testimony that year.

veterans) as Senators John McCain, Robert Kerrey, and John Kerry, and Congressman Pete Peterson. National Security Adviser Tony Lake and Assistant Secretary Winston Lord spent an enormous amount of time and energy explaining our approach to veterans' groups and to organized POW/MIA support groups.[4]

We planned to proceed with a graduated, four-tier policy as an incentive to broaden relations; we would move through the tiers only if Hanoi continued to cooperate on the POW/MIA question. First, the United States would encourage international financial support, such as International Monetary Fund (IMF) loans or OPIC investment, for Vietnamese reform (which we did in 1993); second, the Administration would lift the bilateral trade embargo (which we did in 1994); third, we would establish liaison offices (also accomplished in 1994); and fourth, we would establish full diplomatic relations (which happened in July 1995). By moving through these four steps, we received more information on POW/MIAs than had any previous Administration, and we improved ties with Hanoi that served political and economic interests as well.

By the summer of 1995 the American public seemed ready to move beyond the war. Nevertheless, the President's decision to normalize relations with Vietnam, which he announced from the White House on July 11, 1995, stands out as one of the most difficult foreign policy decisions he made during his first term. Twenty years after the gripping image of the last helicopter lifting off from the Saigon embassy, Vietnam remained an agonizing chord in the nation's memory. For President Clinton, whose opposition to the war had become an issue during the 1992 campaign, the decision to normalize was not only politically sensitive, but personally courageous. I urged him to make it and was pleased that he did.

Despite the progress that had been made in improving relations, painful memories of the Vietnam War dominated my thinking as I embarked on a 10-day trip to Asia in late July 1995. Hanoi was to be our final stop, and it was that visit that had captured the attention of our traveling party, especially the unusually large press corps. But first we would

---

[4]Winston Lord also played a critical role in developing the U.S.-Vietnam relationship through his participation in several special presidential missions to Hanoi. These trips, which he co-led with Hershel Gober, the Deputy Secretary of Veterans Affairs, were instrumental in paving the way for normalization and my trip to Hanoi.

visit Brunei for the annual ASEAN meetings, then travel to Malaysia, a prosperous regional hub that provided a glimpse of the future of Southeast Asia, and next to the newly peaceful but very fragile Cambodia, which was slowly emerging from decades of war and strife. In Malaysia, I witnessed business deals that highlighted our burgeoning commercial ties and also pressed the oftentimes prickly Malaysian leadership to join us in a bolder and more productive dialogue on security and regional issues.

In Cambodia, which I was the first Secretary of State to visit in 40 years, I found a country devastated by war, with little or no infrastructure and a shortage of skilled people. It was not uncommon to meet Cambodians who had lost their entire families in the Khmer Rouge massacres. I recall in particular a searing conversation I had with a woman who had lost all four of her brothers. "I compromised," she said, and broke into tears.

During my brief stay in Phnom Penh I visited a museum built to memorialize those who had perished, and I gave an award to American soldiers who were working to remove the millions of land mines that littered the Cambodian landscape.[5] My official meetings with First Prime Minister Ranariddh and Second Prime Minister Hun Sen underlined our continuing support for consolidating Cambodia's hard-won democracy and overcoming its tragic past. Unfortunately, it was all too apparent even then that the two leaders had an uneasy relationship and that only a miracle could enable the coalition to survive. In July 1997, Hun Sen ousted Ranariddh in a military coup. Although Hun Sen promised early elections, the coup was a devastating setback for the country's nascent democracy and economic reconstruction.

Landing in Hanoi on August 5, 1995, was an emotional experience. Upon leaving my airplane, I immediately participated in a somber ceremony to return the fragmentary remains of four U.S. servicemen who had been missing in action. Standing against the background of "Thud

---

[5]In contrast to these gripping events, that night Marie and I attended a glittering dinner at the palace of Cambodian King Sihanouk. Despite his country's desperate poverty, Sihanouk still enjoyed all of the trappings of royalty. An engaging raconteur, the King entertained us with colorful stories from his more than four decades in the international spotlight. He recounted his relationships with Charles de Gaulle and John Foster Dulles, and described his prolonged exile during the Khmer Rouge terror.

Ridge," a mountain range where many American planes had been shot down en route to bomb Hanoi, I read my opening statement. "A generation ago, the trauma of war bound together the history of our nations for all time," I said. "Let us now lay our past of conflict to rest, and dedicate ourselves to a future of productive cooperation." Because I was the first Secretary of State ever to set foot in Hanoi,[6] my meetings and activities there symbolized the end of an emotional and difficult chapter in American history and the beginning of a new one for relations with Vietnam and the Asia-Pacific region.

My schedule was designed to address both the past and the future of those relations. The first day, highlighted by the airport repatriation ceremony and a briefing by the U.S. team residing in Hanoi to investigate POW/MIA reports, was intended to pay tribute to past sacrifices. In my meetings with Vietnamese officials that day, I noted their past cooperation on POW/MIAs but pressed them for further collaboration to solve pending cases. I also sketched the mutual interests we had in strengthening our ties. For Hanoi the strongest incentives were economic development and creation of a quiet counterweight to the looming Chinese presence in the north. We were careful not to portray our new approach toward Vietnam as being explicitly related to China. On the other hand, we didn't mind if both Beijing and Hanoi considered this factor.

The second day looked to the future. In addition to meeting again with Vietnamese officials, I met with U.S. business representatives and raised the U.S. flag over our embassy in Hanoi. The centerpiece of the day was my address before a group of Vietnamese University students.[7] With three-fifths of its population under the age of 25, Vietnam is a young nation. The entire country, it seemed, was in transition. "The older generation speaks French, the middle-agers speak Russian, and the young speak English," an elder Vietnamese general commented to me approvingly. English classes in Hanoi were oversubscribed, while French lessons went begging. Communist ideology seemed on the way out; in our two days of meetings, my interlocutors steered clear of the standard ideological histrionics. They preferred to talk market economics. Ironi-

---

[6]Henry Kissinger visited Hanoi as National Security Adviser. The last Secretary of State to visit Vietnam was William Rogers, who traveled to Saigon in 1970.

[7]Remembering our failed attempt in October 1993 to address a young audience in Moscow, my advance staff made sure that this crowd was suitably youthful.

cally, in several of these meetings, busts of Ho Chi Minh, the "great" communist liberator, loomed behind them while they welcomed our new relationship.

My speech was aimed directly at the young people who would inherit the future. Rather than being a detailed policy statement, it struck a broader, more thematic tone. I needed to tell the audience that the United States no longer considered Vietnam a pawn in a global rivalry: "With the Cold War over, we view Vietnam as the product of its own history and the master of its own destiny." Long isolated politically, economically, and strategically, Vietnam was slowly integrating into Southeast Asia by joining ASEAN, expanding trade ties, and participating in the ASEAN Regional Security Forum. In a subtle way, I also wanted to frame for my audience the stakes in this new world they were entering. Vietnam would have to open and liberalize to thrive. While I did not criticize any of its policies specifically, I stressed unmistakably that Vietnam needed to transform into an open society and open market.

Vietnam's tough, aging communist leaders had given me little reason to think that they would soon embrace political freedom. They were struggling to maintain a repressive and closed system, even though modern Vietnam was moving into a world characterized by CNN, fax machines, the Internet, and an influx of traders and investors. The old guard's resistance to change would be bound to put a damper on Vietnam's progress. Given this fact, I stressed to my student audience that "each of you ought to have the right to help shape your country's destiny, as well as your own."

The visit I made to Vietnam was perhaps the most fascinating of any I took as Secretary. Vibrant Hanoi stood in startling contrast to Phnom Penh and was much more attractive than I had imagined. The Metropole Hotel, where we stayed, had been handsomely restored. Classic French architecture remained prominent on tree-lined streets. I was struck by the city's vitality—there was an active nightlife, with stores open late and shopkeepers sporting wads of hundred-dollar bills. The Vietnamese capital did, however, appear to be on the cusp of becoming another Bangkok, choked by traffic jams and pollution. The streets were a wild mix of rickshaws, bicycles, and motorbikes, but it was easy to imagine their becoming clogged by cars when they became affordable.

What most impressed me about my visit was the complete lack of acrimony toward us. Despite the troubled history between our nations, the

Vietnamese people were eager to put the past behind them. From the students in my audience to the local employees in our embassy, the Vietnamese reached out to welcome us. One moment in particular stands out in my mind. As our party left a Vietnamese temple we had been touring, an elderly policeman snapped a sharp salute to Lt. General Dan Christman, a Vietnam veteran and the Joint Chiefs' representative on my delegation, who was dressed in his full military uniform. Christman returned the salute. As our car pulled away, the policeman blew our motorcade a kiss. That night I telephoned Senators McCain, Kerry, and Kerrey, as well as Congressman Peterson (now Ambassador to Vietnam), to share with them the joy of the reconciliation they had done so much to help achieve.

I found much reason for hope in Hanoi. Although Vietnam still had a long distance to travel before it could even approach the prosperity of its Southeast Asian neighbors, it was clearly heading in the right direction. I cabled the President that if we were wise, we would "get on the economic bandwagon that is Southeast Asia, rather than getting steamrollered by it. Your decision to start the [1993 APEC] Leaders' Meetings in Seattle will loom more important as the years pass. Right now, everyone [in the region] wants the U.S. to maintain its Pacific presence, and if we handle ourselves skillfully, we can keep it that way."[8]

U.S.-Vietnam Relations: A New Chapter

Address to the Youth of Vietnam, Institute for International

Relations, Hanoi, August 6, 1995

Thank you, Director-General Ngoc, for that kind introduction. It is a pleasure to be here with Vice Minister Le Mai and other distinguished

---

[8]A *New York Times* editorial said my trip was "an important step in the painful process of reconciliation" and that it had "set just the right tone." Quoting several lines from my speech, the editorial stated that the trip had "gotten [U.S.-Vietnamese relations] off to a sound and principled start." "Journey to Hanoi," Aug. 9, 1995.

guests. I am grateful to the Institute for International Relations for helping to organize this event. The staff and students of the Institute are playing an important part in charting a broader role for Vietnam as it continues to integrate itself into Asia and the world.

I have come to Vietnam on behalf of President Clinton and the American people to begin a new chapter in the relationship between our nations. And I have come here this afternoon to speak directly to the people of Vietnam about the future that I hope we can share together.

I am especially pleased to be able to address an audience that includes so many students and young people. One of the startling facts about Vietnam is that three-fifths of your countrymen and women are under 25 years of age. Vietnam is an old country, but a young nation. Its future, and its evolving place in the community of nations, are yours to shape.

This is the first generation of Vietnamese students in many decades to enter adulthood informed by the memory of war, but inspired by the promise of peace. This is what I know you call the "peace generation"— the first that can devote all its energies to renovation at home, and to cooperation with your neighbors and the world. Without forgetting the past, or abandoning tradition, you have a chance to help your country move forward with greater freedom and greater prosperity.

The ties between the United States and Vietnam reach back further than you might think: Way back in 1787, Thomas Jefferson, a champion of liberty, as well as a man of science, tried to obtain rice seed from Vietnam for his farm in Virginia. Fifteen years later, when Jefferson was President of the United States, the first American merchant ship sailed into a Vietnamese port. Almost 150 years later, Jefferson's words that "all men are created equal" were echoed in Vietnam's own declaration of independence.

Because of the war American troops fought on your soil, I have no doubt that American history books will always include a chapter on Vietnam—just as Vietnamese history books will surely include a chapter on America. Today, our people are still scarred by the war. But let us remember that history is a work in progress. That bitter past has also planted the seeds for a better future.

More than 3 million Americans served in Vietnam. Even amidst the death and destruction of war, many came to appreciate the culture of your people and the beauty of this land.

We have other bonds as well. The 1 million people of Vietnamese origin who now live in the United States can also be a bridge for reconciliation and cooperation between our two countries. Just south of my home city of Los Angeles, California, there is a place called "Little Saigon," where Buddhist temples and neighborhood groceries selling *rau muong* co-exist with the freeways and shopping malls of southern California. And when I look out my window from the State Department in Washington, I can see across the river to Arlington, Virginia—a historic old American community and also a vibrant new center of Vietnamese culture and commerce. Indeed, the United States has been enriched by our Vietnamese-Americans, one of the most successful immigrant groups in our recent history.

Yet apart from visits by returning veterans and family members, there has been little direct contact between our two countries over the last 20 years. I know these have been difficult years for Vietnam—years of economic hardship and until recently, years of conflict. But we have now reached a time of promise and a time of change. We still have history to make, a new chapter to write in the history we share.

A month ago, President Clinton decided the time had come to normalize diplomatic relations between the United States and Vietnam. He was supported in this decision by a majority of the American people and by an important group of American veterans who had served here during the war and who now serve in the United States Congress. The President believes, as do they, that closer ties are in the interest of both our nations. The diplomatic relations we initiated yesterday will help us to fully account for those who sacrificed in the past, and will also allow our countries to work together on behalf of regional prosperity and regional security.

Our most important priority in restoring ties with Vietnam is to determine the fate of each American who did not return from the war. Each soldier who was lost remains cherished, with a name, a family, and a nation that cares. There should be the fullest possible accounting for each one. This is a solemn pledge my government has made to the American people. Fulfilling it remains the key to a closer relationship between our two countries.

I want to thank the Vietnamese officials, veterans, and citizens who have helped us find answers, by sharing their memories of the war and by leading us to crash sites and burial grounds. They have come forward time and again to help Americans ease our sense of loss. I know that the people of Vietnam have endured great losses as well. That is why the

United States has released thousands of documents to help the Vietnamese authorities search for those of your countrymen who are still missing in action. And that is why we have funded humanitarian projects for war victims.

Of course, we cannot heal every wound or settle every debate from the past. We will leave that to students of history and to future generations. This moment belongs to the families looking for answers about lost loved ones and to the Vietnamese villagers who have given them a helping hand. It belongs to the American veterans who have returned to this country to provide prosthetics to victims of the war and to the Vietnamese veterans who welcome them as friends. It belongs to the entrepreneurs who are rebuilding this country, now that it is finally at peace. It belongs to the students such as you who question old assumptions and embrace new ways of thinking. As the great Vietnamese poet and statesman Nguyen Trai put it 500 years ago: "After so many years of war, only life remains."

After so many years of war and turmoil, Vietnam is turning its face to a changed world. Colonial empires have vanished, and the age of independence struggles is over. In the last two decades, 45 more sovereign countries have emerged. But it is not only new nations that have been born and maps that have been redrawn. A powerful revolution of ideas has swept the world. Indeed, the main story of the late 20th century is the ascendancy of open societies and open markets in country after country, which has the effect of lifting the lives of hundreds of millions of people.

Today in the Western Hemisphere, for example, every nation but one has a freely elected government and a market economy. After decades of struggle, South Africa is now a multiracial democracy. The former Soviet Union has also been transformed. In Europe, the fastest-growing economies are those Eastern nations that moved most decisively toward economic and political reform.

Communications technology is pushing the expansion of freedom for the individual at the same time as it is shrinking the distances between nations. This speech, for example, will be broadcast back to the United States by satellite. Through the Internet, it will be available to almost anyone in the world with a computer and a phone line. Governments cannot control the movement of ideas in this Information Age, even if they want to.

Consider how much Southeast Asia has changed as well. New civilian governments have been freely elected in Thailand, Cambodia, and the Philippines. Nations such as Malaysia, Thailand, and Indonesia are 10 to 20 times wealthier today than they were in 1965. My visit this last week to Kuala Lumpur underscored for me the enormous scale and dynamism of this region's transformation.

Because of these remarkable changes, America's relationship with the nations of Southeast Asia has been transformed as well. Twenty-five years ago, the largest American communities in the region revolved around military bases. The United States has vital military alliances and a substantial military presence in the region that are widely welcomed. Our security presence will continue to provide the stability and reassurance necessary for sustained economic growth. But today, American communities in the region also revolve around Chambers of Commerce and universities. The most common interaction across the Pacific takes place today among private citizens—among business people, scholars, and tourists. I believe that these currents of culture and commerce are bringing us closer to a New Pacific Community stretching from Los Angeles to Kuala Lumpur.

Vietnam is now moving rapidly into the mainstream of Southeast Asia. Last year, your country became a founding member of the ASEAN Regional Forum, the region's first multinational dialogue on security issues. This year, Vietnam has joined ASEAN itself. As its economy opens further and its laws governing trade and investment develop, Vietnam will be in a position to join its Southeast Asian neighbors in the Asia-Pacific Economic Cooperation forum and the new World Trade Organization. We want Vietnam to enjoy the benefits and to assume the obligations that go with belonging to these important international institutions.

With the Cold War over, we view Vietnam as the product of its own history and the master of its own destiny. As many in your country and ours have urged, we look on Vietnam "as a country, not a war." We view it as a nation with immense potential as a partner in trade and in diplomacy.

The process of establishing normal economic ties with the United States will take time. But we are prepared to move forward. We will do so in consultation with our Congress and consistent with our laws. The first step, the first building-block, in expanding our commercial relations is to negotiate a bilateral trade agreement that will provide for most-favored-nation trading status. Our goal is to develop with Vietnam the same full range of economic relationships that we enjoy with your Southeast Asian neighbors.

I hope that many more Americans will join companies such as Ford, Coca-Cola, and Baskin-Robbins in betting on Vietnam's future. I also hope that more private American organizations will join groups such as the Ford Foundation and World Vision in supporting Vietnam's development. I hope that more Vietnamese students will come to study in the United States, to join the 66 already participating in the Fulbright scholarship program.

There is a great deal our governments can do together. Through the ASEAN Regional Forum, for example, we can strive with others to assure stability in Southeast Asia. One of the key issues is the South China Sea, a vital sea lane through which one-quarter of the world's ocean freight passes. The United States will continue to urge countries with competing claims to resources there to resolve their disputes through dialogue.

Together, the United States, Vietnam, and its neighbors have an interest in cooperating to fight narcotics trafficking. Southeast Asia is the biggest source of heroin arriving on American shores. This deadly drug is ruining lives in the countries through which it passes, including Vietnam.

We have also started and will continue having a dialogue with Vietnam on human rights issues that are of great importance to the American people. Progress in this dialogue will enable our two nations to further deepen our ties.

This is a time of great possibility for our relations with Vietnam, for your country's continued growth and its integration in the region. But while further progress is possible, it is not guaranteed. If Vietnam is to find an important place in the community of nations and to attract additional investment, it should move beyond just opening its doors. The key to success in this rapidly changing world is the freedom to own, to buy, and to sell; and the freedom to participate in the decisions that affect our lives.

As your nation and leaders have recognized, free market reform is a necessary start. All over the world, courageous reformers have understood that command economies cannot bring prosperity to their people. Experience teaches that command economies cannot be dismantled piecemeal. I would ask you to look at economic reform as a passage over a ravine: You cannot do it by taking several little steps; only one giant leap will get you across.

There are many different models of market economies. But whether you go to New York, or Tokyo, or Bangkok, you will find most of the fundamentals are the same. All these places have private property rights, protected by an independent judiciary, and with ownership clearly defined by law. In each, one can borrow capital, buy insurance, and freely exchange information. In each, efficiency, hard work, and imagination are rewarded, not discouraged.

Vietnam has made great progress in creating these conditions, and the result has been stunning economic growth and a range of new opportunities. The policy of Doi Moi has been a tremendous success. But there is still much to be done to create an institutional framework in which a free market can flourish. Vietnamese entrepreneurs and foreign investors alike need a stronger system of private banking, and above all, less red tape and more transparency.

In Vietnam, as everywhere, a free market is the basic precondition for a productive business environment. But I believe sustained economic development is more likely where additional factors are present—where courts provide due process, where newspapers are free to expose corruption, and where businesspeople can make decisions with free access to accurate information. The foundation of market economies—rights that protect contracts, property, and patents—can only be fully guaranteed by the rule of law. Indeed, the reality of Japan, Hong Kong, South Korea, and Thailand tells us that the rule of law and accountable government are the bedrock of stability and prosperity. The reality of Burma and North Korea tells us that repression entrenches poverty.

Our conviction—that freedom is both practical and just—is neither Western nor Eastern. Most would agree with the 16th century Vietnamese poet who said that "the people are the roots of the nation."

Each nation must find its own way consistent with its history and culture. The people of Vietnam, especially its young people, will choose their way. But that is just the point. For when you hear Americans talk about freedom and human rights, this is what we mean: Each of you ought to have the right to help shape your country's destiny, as well as your own.

Today, the United States is embarking on a new relationship with your country, and most important, a new relationship with your people. There are issues on which we no doubt will disagree. But we have, I believe, a common vision of Vietnam taking its rightful place in a community of Southeast Asian nations—a community that is more open, more prosperous, and more secure than ever before. For the first time in many years, we will have a normal relationship in which each of our nations can advance its interests in a climate of cooperation and in an age of peace.

"Heaven has ushered in an era of renewal," says an inscription on Hanoi's Temple of Literature. Let us do all that we can together to seize this moment and to bring those immortal words to life.

Thank you very much.

Obtaining the Resources to Lead

During my last two years in office, I increasingly focused on fighting to get the State Department enough money to do its job. Indeed, I came to believe that the resources crunch we faced had become one of the most pressing foreign policy threats, endangering American leadership in the world. In the wake of the 1994 congressional elections and the so-called Gingrich Revolution, we had to work harder not only to maintain a bi-partisan consensus on the substance of American foreign policy, but, no less important, to prevent a shortage of resources from undermining our very ability to carry out diplomacy.

Securing enough funds for foreign affairs has never been easy. Jealously guarding its constitutional power of the purse, Congress reviews Administration requests item by item, line by line, and with a skeptical eye. After the 1994 elections, the money allocated to foreign affairs came under especially heavy attack. The congressional Republicans came into leadership positions determined to slash the federal budget, and resources for foreign affairs proved a tempting target. The new Chairman of one of our budget subcommittees, Congressman Sonny Callahan of Alabama, told me that he felt committed to his constituents to reduce his subcommittee's portion of the foreign affairs budget by one billion dollars a year, without regard to the merits of our arguments.

The political attractiveness of such a position is readily understood. With so many identifiable problems here at home, spending money abroad is never popular. But carried to its logical end, that attitude would have devastating consequences, and I was determined to defend the foreign affairs budget against the assault launched by the new Congress. This required not only working intensively on Capitol Hill, but taking the case directly to the American people as well. After November 1994, I spent about as much time protecting our resources from congressional cutbacks as I did handling any other single issue.

"Organizational flowcharts" and "budget outlays" are not terms most people associate with the duties of the Secretary of State. Yet, as I first learned as Deputy Secretary under Cyrus Vance, effective departmental management is essential to successful diplomacy.[1] The State Department is like a large corporation, with about 25,000 employees in Washington and in its embassies and consulates abroad. If it is not well organized and managed, the policy-making process becomes unduly attenuated, and U.S. interests suffer.

When I returned to Washington in January 1993, I found a Department badly in need of repair. It was still organized around the principles of the Cold War, and it had an infrastructure better suited to World War II. The communications systems were out of date and the computers so antique that spare parts could not be obtained. Decisions were stymied by requirements for multiple reviews and clearances, sometimes as many as 14 for a single document. Like international institutions such as NATO and the UN, our government's foreign affairs infrastructure needed to be reformed for the post–Cold War era. Accordingly, we undertook a major study called the Strategic Management Initiative pursuant to Vice President Gore's program to "reinvent government."[2]

The initiative produced many short- and long-term recommendations that I strongly endorsed. These included, among many others, (1) estab-

---

[1]By the time I became Secretary, I had also gained an acute sense of the importance of rigorous management from over a decade at the helm of my law firm, O'Melveny & Myers, which has more than 1,400 employees and 10 offices in the United States and abroad.

[2]The relationship between the State Department and other foreign affairs agencies also presented an opportunity for reform. In late 1994, I explored with the White House a plan to consolidate several of these entities, but ran into heavy opposition, especially from agencies that would be brought within the Department. After several fits and starts, in 1997 the Administration and congressional leaders finally agreed on a reorganization plan. Most importantly, this plan will integrate two independent agencies—the Arms Control and Disarmament Agency (ACDA) and the

lishing special teams to deal with urgent matters such as the Middle East peace process; (2) streamlining the upper echelon of the Department, "the Seventh Floor," to eliminate multiple high-level reviews and clearances and to give greater responsibility to the Assistant Secretaries and Office Directors; (3) reducing the number of Deputy Assistant Secretaries and other mid-level managers; (4) modernizing the outdated information system; and (5) reviewing domestic and overseas posts to ensure that they met current needs rather than reflecting Cold War priorities. I vigorously launched the implementation of the reforms in late 1994 but recognized that this would be a long-term process (indeed, there is still much to be done).[3]

In my view, however, the most serious problem was the discontinuity between our foreign policy goals and the resources we had to spend on them. I made it a personal objective to bridge this policy-resources gap and asked Craig Johnstone, a former career Foreign Service Officer with high-level experience in the private sector, to head the office advising me on the matter. Working alongside policy officials to create a Strategic Plan for International Affairs, by the end of 1994 Johnstone and his team had made great strides toward matching foreign policy objectives with budgetary realities.

Following the 1994 congressional elections, protecting our budget from draconian reductions became a central task. The budget process began within the Administration, because it is a Washington reality that the State Department budget will never rise above the President's request levels.[4] In consultation with Johnstone, Wendy Sherman (my chief

---

U.S. Information Agency (USIA)—under the State Department's umbrella, and will consolidate the administrative functions of the Agency for International Development (AID) with those of the State Department. My judgment is that these changes, if enacted into law, will save money and improve policy coherence.

[3]Two troubling class action lawsuits, charging discrimination against African American and female Foreign Service Officers, were pending when we took office in 1993. With skillful efforts from Legal Adviser Conrad Harper and his colleagues, both cases had been substantially resolved through consent decrees by the end of my term.

[4]In a frustrating contrast, Congress has repeatedly given the Department of Defense more than it has requested, adding millions for new programs and equipment never sought by the armed services, in a budget already more than 10 times that allocated to international affairs.

congressional adviser), and Tom Donilon, I developed a comprehensive briefing for the President and his senior budget advisers, explaining the rationale for maintaining the foreign policy budget and outlining our strategy for winning congressional support. At a Cabinet Room meeting with the President, I displayed numerous charts depicting the relative modesty of the resources devoted to international affairs. One pie chart showed that only a tiny sliver—1%—of the federal budget was allocated to foreign policy, in stark contrast to the 15% spent on grants to the states and localities, the 18% devoted to national defense, and the 48% funding direct benefit payments.[5] Another chart showed the rapid decline of the foreign affairs budget in real-dollar terms in the last decade (a decline of over 50%, by one reckoning). Both the President and the Vice President were impressed with our presentation and pledged to support our fight. Leon Panetta, the Chief of Staff and former Budget Director, pulled me aside to assure me that the President had heard my message.

The next struggles would be with Congress and the public. Once the President had made his decisions, as the Secretary I was responsible for defending not only the operating budget of roughly $2.5 billion that he proposed for the State Department, but his entire foreign affairs budget (about $20 billion), including economic assistance abroad. The headline writers lumped all of this together under the pejorative heading of "foreign aid," but it also funded such things as embassy operations, worldwide communications, nuclear weapons reduction overseas, invaluable international agencies such as the IAEA, and business promotion abroad. In seeking to protect this budget, I gave many formal testimonies on Capitol Hill and regularly lobbied individual Members of Congress, either by phone or in person. Johnstone and Sherman provided strong support for this effort.

The lack of public support for our budget stemmed in no small way from some serious misperceptions. For example, a University of Maryland poll showed that, on average, Americans believe the government spends 18% of its budget on "foreign aid."[6] Such an answer would have

---

[5] For this meeting I wore a small button that simply read "1%." The President liked the button and asked to have it, and I gladly handed it over.

[6] Ironically, the same poll showed that respondents believed that figure *should* be 6%, about five times as much money as actually provided by Congress.

been more appropriate in the days following World War II, when, during the Marshall Plan and the onset of the Cold War in Europe, the United States spent as much as 16% of its budget on foreign affairs. I sought to correct the public's misconceptions in a series of statements on resources and foreign policy. My September 1995 address before the Council on Foreign Relations was the first comprehensive effort in this vein outside a congressional hearing. Unlike the standard foreign affairs speech, which is marked by conceptual observations and somewhat esoteric policy points, this address has a simple message: without the necessary resources, all of our efforts to reassert American leadership abroad will be for naught.

Of all the public statements I delivered as Secretary, this one reads the most like a stump speech. Written with the assistance of Tom Malinowski and Bennett Freeman, its rhetoric is sharp. Early on, I pointed to the importance of continuing American leadership in two cases then dominating the front pages: Bosnia and the Middle East. I called recent legislative trends "an unprecedented assault on the country's ability to carry out an effective foreign policy." The cuts some Republican leaders desired would result in "the largest single reduction in foreign affairs spending in American history" and would deny us even the minimum resources needed to fulfill our existing commitments. I starkly pushed the question back to those who wanted cuts: where in the world should we start retreating?

The Council on Foreign Relations venue was deliberately chosen. Normally accustomed to so-called high-toned policy statements, the Council elite may have thought that coming to hear a Secretary of State talk about budgets was strange, if not downright boring. But that was exactly the point. I wanted to show that the resources issue is one of the transcendent *foreign policy* questions of the post–Cold War era. "Whatever disagreements we may have on specific policy issues," I said, "I ask you to consider this: If these cuts are made, in a few years we may not have the resources to conduct a foreign policy that is worth arguing about." This was a theme I returned to frequently during my remaining 16 months in office.

Resources for Leadership

Statement at the Council on Foreign Relations,

Washington, D.C., September 20, 1995

Thank you, Pete [Peterson], for that kind introduction. I want to say that I have great admiration for you and the many contributions you have made in your public and private sector careers. In the last decade, no one has done more to alert the country to the urgency of tackling the federal budget deficit. I had the honor of serving under you as Vice Chairman of the Council—but our real affinity, of course, comes from our shared prairie roots—Pete's from Nebraska and mine from North Dakota. Even though we both ended up in tall buildings in big cities, there were certain advantages to growing up in the wide open spaces on the spine of America.

As you know, I originally planned to talk tonight about the links between economics and our foreign policy. But this evening I have something much more immediate on my mind: the importance of American leadership and the need to have adequate resources to maintain it. Two areas that have been filling my hours this week—the former Yugoslavia and the Middle East—illustrate this need. Let me begin with a brief comment on each, before moving on to my central theme.

As we all painfully know, a peaceful resolution to the conflict in the former Yugoslavia has eluded the international community for more than three years. But now—thanks to President Clinton's leadership and a renewed determination by the international community—we are moving forward on a diplomatic and military track that seems to be genuinely promising. Two months ago in London, we persuaded our allies that Serb attacks on safe areas would be met by substantial and decisive air strikes. Since then, you have seen our highly effective NATO action implementing that decision. Two weeks ago our negotiating team, headed by Dick Holbrooke, helped to convince the parties to accept the continuation of Bosnia as a single state within its current internationally recognized borders.

Just 2 1/2 hours ago, the deadline for the Bosnian Serbs to move their heavy weapons from Sarajevo passed. Based upon conversations that I had earlier today with our military authorities and very recent information, I confidently expect that commanders in the field will say within just a few minutes that they have concluded that the Serbs have met that commitment. This means that the NATO bombing campaign can be suspended but only suspended so long as there is no threat to Sarajevo or other safe areas.

Our negotiating team returned to Washington early this morning for consultations and instructions. In the next few days, they will resume their intensive shuttle diplomacy, seeking sufficient agreement on key issues to allow direct negotiations on a final settlement to begin very soon. Without our military capacity and the will to use it, we would still be facing a stalemate in Bosnia. At the same time, without diplomacy, military strength alone does not create the conditions that make lasting peace possible. Diplomacy and force, we are reminded again, are indivisible instruments of American power, whether in Europe or elsewhere around the globe. In the Middle East, American diplomacy has been indispensable to the success of Arab-Israeli negotiations. In recent days and weeks, we have been intensively involved behind the scenes in an effort to help Israel and the Palestinians reach agreement on the implementation of the second phase of the Declaration of Principles signed in Washington just over two years ago.

The negotiations on the implementation of the second phase of the Declaration of Principles are an enormously complex undertaking involving redeployment of Israeli troops, security arrangements, elections, and the transfer of authority to the Palestinians on the West Bank. Little wonder that it has taken a little extra time to negotiate this agreement. The wonder is that the parties are overcoming such difficult issues and are close to an agreement. This agreement will reflect Israel's understandable security requirements and, for the first time, enable Palestinians throughout the West Bank to achieve control over the most fundamental aspects of their daily lives. Once again, the parties will look to us to play a central role in providing the support that can make real the promise of peace.

Bosnia and the Middle East are just two examples of the complex conflicts we continue to face in the post–Cold War world. The progress made over the last few weeks carries a clear lesson: When the world faces tough challenges, very little can be accomplished without American leadership, and American leadership cannot be sustained on the cheap.

As all of you know, the Council was founded seven decades ago to make the case for American leadership. In the wake of World War I and our retreat into isolationism, the first generation of Council members began to address one of the great challenges in our democracy: It began to construct a durable consensus for the proposition that commitments must be made and resources must be spent on behalf of a strong America and a better world.

Now, with the end of the Cold War, we have unparalleled opportunities to advance our interests and our values. Everywhere I go around the world, America is called upon to provide direction and leadership. Open markets and open societies are ascendant on every continent, giving us great opportunities to enhance prosperity and stability. But this promising state of affairs will endure only as long as we work to sustain it and to build on it. We cannot wish into being the world we seek.

Indeed, I believe that the importance of American leadership is a central lesson of this century. As a global power with global interests, retreat is not a responsible option for the United States. This remains a dangerous world. In the last few years, we have seen half a dozen armed conflicts in the former Soviet Union, territory that is still home to thousands of nuclear weapons. We have to be constantly vigilant to make sure that countries like Iraq and North Korea are denied weapons of mass destruction and prevented from menacing their neighbors. This imperative is underscored by the recent and clear confirmation that Saddam has sought to hide a massive biological weapons program. Terrorism and organized crime also threaten our safety, as well as the survival of new democracies.

As we look at today's world, the President and I have great hopes but no illusions. Our budget reflects our understanding of the opportunities and threats we face, and it seeks the resources America needs to meet them. In a world without dangers, the recent congressional attempts to deny these resources might be more comprehensible. But in the real world, these actions would weaken America at a time when we must remain strong. As Pete Peterson has so often reminded us, our nation faces no greater challenge than to get our own economic house in order. Since the early eighties, the deficit has constrained our ability to act and weakened our credibility with our allies and trading partners. In that vein, I view the President's deficit-cutting package of 1993 as one of our most important foreign policy achievements—one that has made us stronger around the world. The State Department has not been and should not be exempt from budget cuts. In fact, our international affairs spending has been reduced by 45% in real terms in the last decade. Under my direction, we have cut 1,300 jobs and reduced administrative expenses by 5% in two years.

The American people rightly demand that we apply the most rigorous standards when we decide how to spend their tax dollars. At the same time, they have a fundamental expectation that their government will do what it must to protect America's security and prosperity. The President and I have therefore drawn a line: We will fight budgetary strictures so radical that they would damage our nation's interests and cripple our ability to lead.

Regrettably, too many Members of the current Congress appear set on crossing that line. At every opportunity, the leaders of the new Congress call for American leadership. Yet, many would deny us the minimum resources that any administration would need to get the job done. If the Senate follows the levels approved by the Commerce, Justice, and State Appropriations Subcommittee, the State Department budget would be cut in one year by 20%—the largest single reduction in foreign affairs spending in American history. If these cuts remain, I will have no alternative but to recommend to the President that he veto the bill. Last November, on the day after the Congressional mid-term elections, I was in Seoul, Korea, on the first leg of a long trip through Asia. I believed then, as I do now, that the election was not a license to lose sight of our global interests, or of the need for bipartisanship in foreign policy. I therefore pledged that the United States would remain strong and steadfast in our commitments around the world.

The bipartisan consensus on behalf of American engagement in the world has been a vital source of America's strength. Five decades ago, that consensus enabled Democrats like Truman and Republicans like Vandenberg to come together to launch NATO and the Marshall Plan. A few years later, Dwight Eisenhower ran for President in part to put the Republican Party firmly—and he hoped permanently—on the side of global engagement.

In the last two years, that bipartisan consensus withstood the forces of isolationism and protectionism to pass NAFTA and GATT, and it has sustained our support for reform in the former Soviet Union and for the Middle East peace process. I was heartened to see former President Bush's statement yesterday warning against "the voices of isolation," and New York Mayor Giuliani's criticism of "the potent strain of isolationism that once again is infecting our political discourse." I still hope that their view will ultimately prevail in the Congress.

Bipartisanship has never precluded disagreement on matters of policy. But it does require agreement that we cannot protect our interests if we do not marshal the resources to stand by our commitments. We cannot have it both ways. Those who say they want a strong America have a duty to help keep America strong. And diplomatic readiness is our first line of defense—in large part so that we are not compelled to put our men and women in uniform in harm's way. Morale, equipment, and communications are no less important to our diplomats than to our soldiers. Regrettably, in the last few months, both Houses of Congress have put forward drastic proposals to slash the foreign affairs budget. The recent actions of the Senate Appropriations Committee pose perhaps the most immediate threat to our nation's interests.

For example, the Senate appropriators would cut the State Department's basic operating budget by almost $300 million. This could force us to close some 50 embassies and consulates—the equivalent of every post in Asia or Africa. It could force us to consider widespread furloughs and layoffs, closing passport offices, and halting the modernization of our communications system that is so long overdue. One casualty would be the principle of universality in our representation abroad—the principle that there should be a U.S. mission in virtually every country. Universal representation was invaluable earlier this year, when more than 170 countries in the world from Albania to Zambia had an equal say in the extension of the Nuclear Non-Proliferation Treaty and an equal need to be persuaded by American diplomacy. It is also essential when a crisis erupts in an unexpected place—whether in Burundi or Belarus—and when American citizens get into trouble abroad—and they do get into trouble in the darnedest places.

Day in and day out, our ability to meet these challenges depends on our people in the field. They are the ones responsible for the arms control agreements in Ukraine and Russia. They are the ones who worked out the details of our intellectual property rights agreement with China, and who must ensure that it is enforced. They are the ones who have to convince the parties in Bosnia to choose peace—at grave risk, as we have seen, to their own lives. That's why I get so angry when I hear disparaging comments about diplomats in long coats, high hats, and limousines.

Last year, the people at our posts abroad responded to almost 2 million requests for service from Americans overseas. We issued over 6 million passports—a record number. In the last few years, our people have helped American companies win billions of dollars in contracts. Our posts are also the operating platform for more than 38 other agencies, including the Defense, Commerce, and Agriculture Departments, the FBI, and the DEA. When Congress mandates deep and devastating cuts, I often wonder if they have given any thought to where in the world we should start retreating. Should we pull people from our embassies in the Middle East, at a critical time for the peace process? Should we close posts in Asia, the most dynamic market for our exports in the world? Should we prepare less for the next Western Hemispheric summit, ignoring the most dramatic march to democracy in the world? Had reductions of this magnitude been approved a few years ago, I wonder where the people on Capitol Hill would have chosen to cut back—from Haiti, from the Balkans, from Northeast Asia?

One of the primary tasks of our diplomats is to prevent crises that would otherwise cost us dearly. Our Agreed Framework with North Korea, for example, which has frozen its nuclear program, is also saving us hundreds of millions of dollars right now. Without it, we would have been compelled to increase dramatically our forces in Northeast Asia. Yet, we are having a hard time getting Congress to approve $20 million to help implement the agreement, as our modest contribution alongside the billions, not millions, that South Korea and Japan are prepared to contribute.

I am also determined to resist the drastic cuts that have been proposed in our obligations to international institutions. The Senate appropriators would slash our assessed contributions to international organizations by almost $400 million. These measures could affect our obligations to NATO. They would force us to cut support for the International Atomic Energy Agency, which is critical to our effort to ensure that countries like Iraq and North Korea do not become nuclear weapons states. They would hurt the World Health Organization, which is leading the fight against diseases like AIDS and Ebola.

Our peacekeeping contributions would be limited to only $250 million. This would force the withdrawal of peacekeepers and monitors from vital trouble spots, including the Middle East. We recognize that peacekeeping has not always achieved its intended purpose. But just as surely, it has allowed us to advance our interests without forcing our troops to take all the risks or our taxpayers to foot all the bills. Without peacekeeping as a tool, we would be left with an unacceptable choice each time a crisis arose: a choice between acting alone and doing nothing.

When we fail to pay our peacekeeping dues, we also compromise our ability to push for reform at the United Nations and other institutions. Far-reaching change is clearly needed. But we will not convince our allies to support our proposals if they think we are using reform as an excuse to avoid our obligations. We cannot reform and retreat at the same time.

The Senate appropriators have also voted to cut the Arms Control and Disarmament Agency by more than 50%. As you know, we are at the verge of major breakthroughs in this area, including a Comprehensive Test Ban. Why would we choose this moment to decimate the resources we need to negotiate and verify such vital and complex arms control agreements? The Senate would also slash funding for the USIA and for international broadcasting, the voice of our values and one of the most cost-effective ways we have to project our influence. Let me add that these agencies—ACDA, USIA, as well as the Agency for International Development—have distinct missions that should be maintained. The issue here is resources, not reorganization.

The cuts I have already described are compounded by other Congressional proposals, which, if enacted, would slash foreign assistance by almost $3 billion. This would devastate funding for multilateral development banks and for bilateral aid. I do not believe that President Eisenhower was wrong in calling foreign assistance America's "best investment." I do not think that every Congress elected since World War II was wrong in providing steady support to American diplomats in the field. I do not believe that every administration since the days of F.D.R. was wrong about the vital importance of international organizations.

The budgetary proposals we have seen reveal, in my view, how short our historical memory is. They reflect a troubling lack of appreciation for what the United States has accomplished in the world in the last 50 years—and how we have accomplished it. Very simply, cuts of the magnitude we face would represent a fundamental break with America's tradition of leadership. They are not responsible. The ability of this and every future President to protect American interests is at risk.

In addition to the budget cuts, I should add that the Senate Foreign Relations Committee is at this moment holding up 30 ambassadorial nominations. It is also refusing to permit a vote on two treaties—START II and the Chemical Weapons Convention—on which there is virtually unanimous agreement in the Congress. Taken together, the actions I have described this evening represent an unprecedented assault on the country's ability to carry out an effective foreign policy.

I value the Council as a place for lively discussion and for healthy debate. But whatever disagreements we may have on specific policy issues, I ask you to consider this: If these cuts are made, in a few years we may not have the resources to conduct a foreign policy that is worth arguing about. And that would be a tragedy for the United States and for the world as well.

Today, time is short. Each of us has to do a better job in defending the continuing need for American leadership. If we succeed, I hope we can get back to the debate we ought to be having—the debate about how to use America's strength, instead of whether we should be strong.

Thank you.

TWENTY-THREE

Reforming the United Nations

For many of us who came of age during World War II and its immediate aftermath, support for the United Nations has been an article of faith. We had lived through a catastrophic war that stemmed in large part from the failure of the League of Nations. Many ascribed that failure to the retreat of the United States into isolationism and its consequent unwillingness to join the League. To avoid a repetition of that tragic sequence of events, the United States took the lead in the international negotiations that led to the creation of the United Nations.

First President Roosevelt, then President Truman pressed his counterparts in the Allied nations to establish a strong and effective new international body. The United Nations was born at a conference in San Francisco in the spring of 1945, when its Charter was vigorously debated over a two-month period and finally agreed upon in a historic ceremony attended by a great congregation of world leaders.[1] New York was chosen as its headquarters, symbolizing the enormous stake that the United States had in the new world body.

Since the early 1950s, the UN has played a central role in interna-

---

[1] By coincidence, I was peripherally "present at the creation" of the UN. At 19, as an ensign in the Navy, I was ordered to San Francisco to await my ship. Assigned to the St. Francis Hotel—where the top floors had been converted to naval bachelor officers' quarters, and the lower floors housed the delegates to the UN Conference—I had my first chance to rub shoulders with the world's diplomats. My ship, the USS *Tomahawk*, soon arrived, however, and was diverted to Portland, Oregon, to repair damage from a collision, so my stay in San Francisco was brief.

tional politics. It has provided an essential forum for the creation of international coalitions to challenge aggression—including the forces fighting in Korea in the early 1950s and the coalition to expel Saddam Hussein from Kuwait in 1991. Specialized UN agencies such as the World Health Organization and UNICEF have become renowned for their humanitarian achievements. The UN Security Council and General Assembly have emerged as often indispensable forums for consideration of the world's problems.

By the 1990s, however, a litany of complaints had built up against the UN. Critics called it an ill-managed, wasteful bureaucracy. Favoritism and logrolling were said to be rampant. Every nation felt entitled to be represented on its staff, which made it extremely difficult to reduce personnel. Allegations of fraud and corruption regularly surfaced. Impressive television documentaries recounted stories of waste, fraud, and abuse in a manner calculated to undermine public confidence in the organization.

These allegations were compounded, especially during the Reagan Administration, by charges that UN agencies infringed on U.S. sovereignty. In addition, UN expenses had skyrocketed, with peacekeeping costs heading the list. During 1991–92 alone, eight new peacekeeping missions were authorized by the UN Security Council, with U.S. approval. Almost one-third of their cost (which had mushroomed fourfold to $2.8 billion) would have to be borne by the United States under the applicable formula, but no budgetary planning had been done in Washington to support these increasingly expensive operations. The UN was in danger of losing its constituency, especially in Congress. During the Reagan and Bush years, Congress protested what it saw as flaws in the UN by holding back on payments to it. Presidents Reagan and Bush proposed plans to bring our accounts current, but Congress resisted, to the point that the United States was over $1 billion in arrears when the Clinton Administration took office. In addition, UN mismanagement of the Somalia and Bosnia peacekeeping missions had undermined the organization's image among the American people.

The UN's 50th anniversary in October 1995 provided an excellent opportunity to address these problems. From the standpoint of public perception, waste and mismanagement cried loudest for attention. Substantively, the UN needed to update its focus to reflect the changing challenges of the post–Cold War era. Organizationally, it needed to be reformed to reflect new diplomatic realities. The Clinton Administration believed that the Security Council should be expanded to include such vital countries as Germany and Japan. Major developing nations like Brazil and India also clamored for membership in the Security Council. But any changes would be meaningless unless the UN began to address its major management problems. To maintain its effectiveness, its massive bureaucracy of almost 15,000 employees had to be reorganized and streamlined, its budget trimmed, and its organizational structure revamped.

My September 1995 address before the General Assembly pressed our case for reform. Standing in for President Clinton—who would address the Assembly a month later at the 50th-anniversary celebration—I spelled out the key themes of U.S. policy toward the UN and laid out a specific, four-part agenda for organizational change. I emphasized the importance of the UN taking on such new security challenges as weapons proliferation, terrorism, international crime, narcotics, and damage to the environment.

This address was consciously aimed at two audiences. First, to those sitting before me in the General Assembly, I reiterated that the best way to overcome the decline in U.S. support was through reform. "Tangible progress [in reform] will help us win the battle for UN support," I explained. Indeed, without immediate reform, there was no chance we could sustain domestic support for the UN, particularly in the Republican Congress. To my second audience—the American people—I wanted to make the point that to have any hope to revitalize the UN, we had to stay engaged with it. We could not reform it and retreat from it at the same time.

We realized that the reform we called for would be impossible without the right leadership. In many ways, deciding who would lead the UN was the first step in accelerating reform. This question assumed center stage in 1996, when selecting a new Secretary General for a five-year term commencing in January 1997 became one of our biggest foreign policy headaches.

The Secretary General serving at the time, Boutros Boutros-Ghali, was a diplomat of the old school, a sophisticated operator who had all the moves. An Egyptian who was not a Muslim but a Coptic Christian, Boutros-Ghali had been an adviser to Anwar Sadat and had been instrumental in the Camp David talks that resulted in the historic rapprochement between Egypt and Israel. He knew how to maneuver between the

"Perm Five" nations (the U.K., France, Russia, China, and the United States) that had veto power in the Security Council and the developing nations that dominated the General Assembly. When a stalemate had developed in the race for Secretary General in 1991, Boutros-Ghali had been offered as a compromise candidate, and the United States had supported him. During the 1991 election period, he had announced publicly that because of his age, 69, he would serve only one term. In lending its support, the United States and other leading nations had noted this statement. By the middle of his term, however, he had recanted it, and he ultimately indicated that he would seek a second term.

In the first months of 1996, the Clinton Administration gave intense consideration to whether the United States would support a second term for Boutros-Ghali. Our foreign policy team met several times, first among ourselves and then with the President, to consider the question. UN Ambassador Madeleine Albright was a vital member of that team and participated fully in all our discussions. She joined Perry, Lake, Shalikashvili, CIA Director John Deutch, and me for an informal breakfast meeting every Wednesday, and she regularly came down from New York when the foreign policy principals met to consider recommendations to the President.

Because of our long friendship, I felt comfortable giving Albright a unique degree of authority and flexibility in carrying out her UN duties. She responded by making a striking record, regularly performing miracles of persuasion in gathering votes in the Security Council. A key element in her success was her unusual capacity for friendship, which enabled her to establish a good rapport not just with the Ambassadors from traditional allies, but also with those from developing countries around the world. She was a highly effective spokesperson for our policies, not only at the UN but also on television and in speeches.

The decision on Boutros-Ghali was a tough call. Many of us in the Administration had cordial personal relations with him. Although some of our allies were lukewarm about a second term, none of them was prepared to oppose him openly, and it became apparent that the United States could block him only by casting a veto in the Security Council. It was bound to be a bruising struggle, which we hesitated to ask the President to undertake in the midst of his campaign for reelection.

Among UN critics, however, Boutros-Ghali's name was synonymous with everything that was wrong with the organization. Rightly or wrongly, many perceived him as a symbol of a bloated and impotent United Nations. Although he had taken some valuable steps—like appointing Joe Connor, a former Chairman of Price Waterhouse, as Under Secretary General for Management—he usually seemed to be reacting to pressure rather than leading from conviction. We believed that he would never accomplish the broad-scale reforms that we deemed essential.

In addition, over the previous four years Boutros-Ghali had made a series of controversial policy decisions that troubled the United States. For example, it had been on his watch that the UN mission to Somalia was disastrously broadened to include disarming the local warlords and capturing the clan leader Mohammed Aideed. In Bosnia, Boutros-Ghali had consistently hesitated to allow UN military commanders to turn the UN's "key" for NATO airstrikes on the Bosnian Serbs when they overran UN-designated safe areas. Even after the July 1995 London conference, in which the Allies had decided that NATO should be empowered to conduct substantial and effective airstrikes if another safe area were threatened, Boutros-Ghali had continued to resist and had acquiesced only after I made two tough telephone calls urging him to relinquish the UN key.

After a final review with his foreign policy team, President Clinton concluded in March 1996 that the UN needed new leadership. Without it, he believed that the organization could not achieve the support of the American people or of Congress, and that support was essential for its success. The President's decision was based on what was needed for the future of the UN, and it was firm.

While we had decided that Boutros-Ghali must go, we wanted to give him an opportunity to do so gracefully. To this end, I asked for the help of two close friends, former Secretary of State Cyrus Vance and David Hamburg, President of the Carnegie Corporation. Vance and Hamburg had been active with the UN and had a good rapport with Boutros-Ghali. I hoped that by enlisting them we might reduce the awkwardness of the Secretary General's situation. In a private meeting on April 11 at New York's Waldorf-Astoria Hotel, I asked them to approach Boutros-Ghali to inform him of the President's decision and see if he was prepared to work with us on a dignified exit, which might include his being named to a prestigious academic position. They met with him three days later, and their initial reaction was that he understood the firmness of the U.S. position and might be prepared to cooperate on a departure with dignity. However, he asked to meet with me to plead his case.

Our meeting at his residence in New York on May 13 was civil but uncomfortable. He insisted that I give him a bill of particulars as to our problems with his performance. I was reluctant to do so, believing it would only produce a harsh debate and minimize the chance for a friendly outcome. He also argued that all of his predecessors had served two terms, and he asked if the President would be willing to agree to his reelection with the informal understanding that he would step down in two and a half or three years. I told him that this proposal would not fly. However, it occurred to me that he might accept an extension of his term for approximately one year, which would enable him to state that he was stepping down on his 75th birthday in November 1997. He rejected this compromise and pressed me to go back to the President to ask for the longer extension, but I told him there was no point in doing so.

Boutros-Ghali then began to lobby key allies around the world for a two-and-a-half-year term. To all who would listen, he argued that the President's position was a campaign ploy and would change after the November election. To clear the air as to the U.S. position, I rescinded our one-year compromise offer and let it be known publicly that we did not intend to support Boutros-Ghali and would soon begin consultations to select a new Secretary General.[2]

The Boutros-Ghali saga thus continued throughout the rest of 1996. Despite our announced intention to veto a second term, he fought vigorously. He rallied the French to his side, and they engaged in a public exchange with us over his reappointment. Shortly after the President's reelection on November 5, he reaffirmed his opposition. Boutros-Ghali insisted on pressing for a vote in the Security Council and, on November 19, we finally had to exercise our veto.

Boutros-Ghali's term as Secretary General ended on December 31, 1996. In his place, Kofi Annan of Ghana, the candidate we supported, became the UN's seventh Secretary General. In the voting in the Secu-

---

[2]Privately, I began to make calls to a number of Foreign Ministers to outline our position and ask for support. Publicly, I provided the story on background to the *New York Times*, which gave our decision front-page attention. Steven Erlanger, "U.S. Will Oppose Move to Re-Elect Top UN Official," June 20, 1996.

rity Council in December, Annan's support had increased with each ballot. The threat that Boutros-Ghali's supporters would oppose any candidate we endorsed never materialized. As the first Secretary General from sub-Saharan Africa, Annan was also the first career UN official to rise through the ranks to the organization's top position. His experience gives him an acute understanding of the UN's management problems and needs. As the former Under Secretary General for Peacekeeping, he also is well aware of the UN's opportunities and limits in the post–Cold War era. When President Clinton's second term began, the challenges set forth in my September 1995 speech remained, but the UN had strong new leadership to confront them.

The United Nations: The Momentum for Reform Must Accelerate

Address at the 50th Session of the UN General Assembly,

New York City, September 25, 1995

Mr. President, Mr. Secretary-General, excellencies, distinguished guests: It is a privilege to speak to you today on behalf of the United States. A half-century ago, the General Assembly first met in New York—across the river in a converted skating rink at Flushing Meadows. In those modest surroundings, our predecessors began to put into place an ambitious framework they hoped would keep the peace as successfully as they had prosecuted the war.

In the years since, the United Nations has helped to bring peace, prosperity, and hope to countless people around the world. Technological change has brought nations closer together than the UN's founders could possibly have foreseen. The United Nations itself has been challenged in unforeseen ways. It has had to manage complex humanitarian emergencies, from civil wars to the mass movement of refugees to health epidemics. This evolution has placed great strains on the organization and revealed the necessity for far-reaching change in how it is run.

The Clinton Administration has vigorously made the case to our Congress and our people for continued American leadership at the UN.

The United States made a commitment to the UN Charter 50 years ago. We are determined to keep our commitment, including our financial obligations. We will always remember that for millions of people around the world, the UN is far from a faceless institution: It is, as Harry Truman once said, "a case of food or a box of school books; it is a doctor who vaccinates their children; it is an expert who shows them how to raise more rice, or more wheat." To millions more, it is the difference between peace and war.

Economic and social development, as well as protection of human rights, remain central to the UN's mission. But the UN must change to meet these needs more effectively. When money is wasted in New York, Geneva, or Vienna, and when time is lost to bureaucratic inertia, the people who pay the price are those most vulnerable to famine, disease, and violence. It is time to recognize that the UN must direct its limited resources to the world's highest priorities, focusing on the tasks that it performs best. The UN's bureaucracy should be smaller, with a clear organizational structure and sharp lines of responsibility. Each program must be held to a simple standard—that is, it must make a tangible contribution to the freedom, security, and well-being of real people in the real world.

In the last two years, under the leadership of Secretary General Boutros-Ghali, the groundwork for substantial change has been laid. The UN has an office with the functions of an inspector general and a mandate to crack down on waste and fraud. Under Secretary General Joe Connor has embarked on an aggressive campaign to improve the UN's management culture, and we fully support his work. The UN Secretariat has moved in the right direction by submitting a budget that begins to restrain spending. Now the momentum for reform must accelerate. Let me propose a concrete agenda.

First, we must end UN programs that have achieved their purpose, and consolidate programs that overlap, especially in the economic and social agencies. The UN has more than a dozen organizations responsible for development, emergency response, and statistical reporting. We should consider establishing a single agency for each of these functions. We should downsize the UN's regional economic commissions. We should ensure that the functions of the UN Conference on Trade and Development do not duplicate the new WTO. And we should adopt a moratorium on big UN conferences once the present series is completed, concentrating instead on meeting the commitments of those we have held.

Second, we need to streamline the UN Secretariat to make it more efficient, accountable, and transparent. Each part of the UN system should be subject to the scrutiny of an inspector general. The UN must not tolerate ethical or financial abuses and its managers should be appointed and promoted on the basis of merit.

Third, we should rigorously scrutinize proposals for new and extended peacekeeping missions and we should improve the UN's ability to respond rapidly when new missions are approved. We must agree on an equitable scale of peacekeeping assessments that reflects today's economic realities. And we should have a unified budget for peacekeeping operations.

Finally, we must maintain the effectiveness of the Security Council. Germany and Japan should become permanent members. We should ensure that all the world's regions are fairly represented, without making the Council unwieldy.

We welcome the formation of the high-level group on reform, initiated under the leadership of outgoing General Assembly President Essy. Our goal must be that a feasible blueprint for UN reform will be adopted before the General Assembly's 50th session finishes work next fall. The way forward is clear: We have already seen countless studies and reports. The time has come to act on the best proposals.

As you know, in my country there have been serious efforts to curtail our support for the United Nations. President Clinton and I and the entire Administration believe it would be reckless to turn away from an organization that helps mobilize the support of other nations for goals that are consistent with American and global interests. But to sustain support for the UN among the American people and the people of other nations, it is not enough that we defend the institution. The best argument against retreat is further reform. Tangible progress will help us win the battle for UN support that we are waging in the United States.

The United Nations must emerge from the reform process better able to meet its fundamental goals, including the preservation of peace and security. From Korea, to the Persian Gulf, to Haiti, the UN has provided a mandate to its members as they carried out this responsibility. The UN's own blue helmets have helped nations create the basic conditions of peace in some of the most difficult situations imaginable, even though they have not always achieved their intended purpose. Recently, a young Haitian father was asked what peacekeeping forces had achieved in his country. "We walk freely," he answered. "We sleep quietly. There are no men who come for us in the night." In Haiti, as for example in Cambodia, Mozambique, and El Salvador, the UN has shown that peacekeeping, for all its limitations, has been an enormously useful instrument. One region where UN forces and the international community have played a critical role is the Middle East.

Another historic milestone will be marked this Thursday in Washington when Israel and the Palestinians sign their agreement to implement phase two of the Declaration of Principles. That agreement will bring to life a goal first set in the Camp David accords—that is, to protect Israel's security and to give Palestinians throughout the West Bank control over their daily lives. The international community and the UN must continue to support this process politically and economically.

Without a doubt, the UN has never undertaken a mission more difficult than the one in the former Yugoslavia. The limitations of that mission are well known. But we must also recognize that it has provided relief for hundreds of thousands of people and saved thousands of lives. Today, with diplomacy backed by force, the United States and the international community are moving forward on a track that is producing genuinely hopeful results. The United Nations and NATO are working together effectively to bring peace to the region. On September 8 in Geneva, the parties to the conflict accepted the fundamental goal the Security Council has often expressed—namely, the continuation of Bosnia-Herzegovina as a single state within its current internationally recognized borders. I will be meeting with the foreign ministers of Bosnia, Croatia, and Serbia later today and I will urge them to maintain momentum toward peace and to establish constitutional structures for Bosnia.

The framers of the UN Charter created this institution to meet threats to peace and security posed by aggression and armed conflict. These threats are still very much with us. But the world also faces a set of new security challenges, including proliferation, terrorism, international crime, and narcotics, as well as the far-reaching consequences of damage to the environment. These have assumed a new and dangerous scope in a more interdependent world. As President Clinton said in San Francisco in June, the "new forces of integration carry within them the seeds of disintegration and destruction." While new technologies have brought us closer together, they have also made it easier for terrorists, drug dealers, and other international criminals to acquire weapons of mass destruction, to set up cocaine cartels, and to hide their ill-gotten gains. The collapse of communism has shattered dictatorships to be sure. But it has also left the political and legal institutions of newly liberated nations even more vulnerable to those who seek to subvert them.

Although these threats are sometimes sponsored by states, they increasingly follow no flag. Each of us must vigorously fight these enemies on our own. But we will never be truly secure until we effectively fight them together. That is the new security challenge for the global community. It must be the new security mission of the UN.

There is no area where the UN can make a more significant contribution than in non-proliferation. Fifty years ago, the United States was the only country capable of making a nuclear bomb. Today, many countries have the technology that would enable them to turn a fist-sized chunk of plutonium into a bomb as small as a suitcase. That is one reason why more than 170 countries agreed last May to extend for all time the Nuclear Non-Proliferation Treaty. That is an achievement that we must build on. Let me outline some steps.

First, we should have a Comprehensive Test Ban Treaty ready for signature by the time we meet here next year. As President Clinton announced last month, the United States is committed to a true zero-yield test ban. We urge other nations to join us in that commitment.

Second, we should immediately start negotiations on a Fissile Material Cutoff Treaty. Those who have been most vocal in calling for nuclear disarmament should recognize that it is essential to ban future production of fissile material for nuclear weapons.

Third, we should push forward with the historic reductions of the nuclear arsenals of the United States and the countries of the former Soviet Union. I call on the U.S. Senate, as well as the Russian Duma, to approve the START II Treaty so that we can lock in deep cuts in our strategic nuclear arsenals. In addition, Presidents Clinton and Yeltsin are working together to ensure the safety, transparency, and irreversibility of nuclear arms reductions. As part of this process, President Yeltsin will host a Nuclear Safety and Security Summit in Moscow next spring. This summit should have a very ambitious agenda, including a declaration of principles on nuclear reactor safety. We look to the summit to address the worldwide problem of nuclear waste management, including ocean dumping. The summit should also promote a plan of action to safeguard nuclear materials—a plan which should include new measures to prevent criminals and terrorists from acquiring nuclear material for use in weapons.

Finally, we should push for the earliest possible entry-into-force of the Chemical Weapons Convention. President Clinton has urged the U.S. Senate to act promptly on its ratification, and to stop holding it and the START II Treaty hostage to unrelated issues. The world has witnessed the effect of poison gas too many times in this century—on European battlefields during World War I, in Ethiopia and Manchuria during the 1930s, and against Iranian soldiers and innocent Kurdish civilians in the 1980s. The Chemical Weapons Convention will make every nation safer, and we need it now.

The UN is also playing an invaluable role in focusing attention on pressing regional proliferation problems. In Iraq, UNSCOM and its chairman Rolf Ekeus continue to uncover horrific details about Saddam Hussein's weapons of mass destruction. Under Saddam Hussein, Iraq developed a deadly biological weapons capacity hidden from view. It was conducting research to turn some of the most toxic substances known to man into weapons of war. We know that Saddam succeeded in putting anthrax and botulism in bombs and missile warheads. In December 1990, he deployed these weapons with every intent of using them against the international coalition and innocent civilians. He was dissuaded only by the steadfast determination of the United States and the international community.

In light of what Ambassador Ekeus has uncovered, we can only conclude that for the last 4 1/2 years Saddam Hussein has lied about the full scope of Iraq's weapons programs. There should be no easing of the sanctions regime until the Iraqi Government complies with the demands of the Security Council and demonstrates that it has changed its ways.

The UN should also promote responsibility and restraint in the transfer of conventional weapons. Last year at the General Assembly, President Clinton proposed, and the Assembly approved, the eventual elimination of antipersonnel landmines. On my recent trip to Cambodia, I saw the terrible damage these hidden killers can do. This year, we will again call on other countries to join us in ending the export of landmines. Two years ago, President Clinton called on the international community to devise a true international system that governs transfers of conventional weapons and sensitive dual-use technologies. I am pleased that the Russian Federation has joined with the United States and 26 other countries to agree on common principles to control the build-up of dangerous conventional arms. We hope to activate this global regime, called the New Forum, by the end of this year.

The proliferation of weapons has added a disturbing dimension to another threat we all face: international terrorism. Indeed, this year's sarin gas attack in Tokyo is a grim warning of what can happen when terrorists acquire weapons of mass destruction. More nations are joining the fight against those individuals and those groups who attack civilians for political ends. The United Nations has supported this effort in important ways. The UN Security Council recognized the importance of countering state-sponsored terrorism by imposing sanctions against Libya for the bombing of Pan Am 103 and UTA 772. Terrorists should be treated as criminals and there must be no place where they can hide from the consequences of their acts. States that sponsor terrorists should feel the full weight of sanctions that can be imposed by the international community. Let us not deceive ourselves: Every dollar that goes into the government coffers of a state sponsor of terrorism such as Iran helps pay for a terrorist's bullets or bombs. Iran's role as the foremost state sponsor of terrorism makes its secret quest for weapons of mass destruction even more alarming. We must stand together to prevent Iran from acquiring such threatening capabilities.

The United States has taken a leading role in meeting the international terrorist threat. We have intensified our sanctions against Iran. Last January, President Clinton also issued an Executive Order prohibiting financial transactions with terrorist groups and individuals who threaten the Middle East peace process. We are urging our Congress to tighten our immigration and criminal laws to keep terrorists on the run or put them behind bars.

The United States strongly supports the counter-terrorism measures the G-7 and Russia announced at the Halifax Summit, and we expect the P-8 Ministerial Meeting on Terrorism in Ottawa to produce a concrete action plan to implement these measures. Other kinds of international crime also threaten the safety of our citizens and the fabric of our societies. And globalization brings new and frightening dimensions to crime. The threat of crime is a particular menace to young democracies. It weakens confidence in institutions, preys on the most vulnerable, and undermines free market reform.

Of course, every country must take its own measures to combat these threats. The Clinton Administration is now completing a review of our approach to transnational crime that will lead to a stronger, more coordinated attack on this problem. To help other states deal with criminal threats, the United States and Hungary have created the International Law Enforcement Academy in Budapest to train police officers and law enforcement officials from Central Europe and the states of the former Soviet Union. We are providing similar help bilaterally and through the UN Drug Control Program to countries whose laws are challenged by drug cartels.

A particularly insidious form of crime and corruption is money laundering. All nations should implement recommendations by the OECD to attack money laundering. The nations of this hemisphere should also advance the anti-money laundering initiative introduced at last December's Summit of the Americas. Together, we must squeeze the dirty money out of our global financial system.

Through the UN's conventions on drugs and crime, the international community has set strong standards that we must now enforce. We call on UN member states who have not already joined the 1988 UN Drug Convention to do so. Those countries who have approved the convention should move quickly to implement its key provisions.

We are increasingly aware that damage to the environment and unsustainable population growth threaten the security of our nations and the well-being of our people. Their harmful effects are evident in famines, infant mortality rates, refugee crises, and ozone depletion. In places like Rwanda and Somalia, they contribute to civil wars and emergencies that can only be resolved by costly international intervention. We must carry out the commitments we made at last year's Cairo Conference, and the Rio Conference three years ago.

Never have our problems been more complex. Nor has it ever been more evident that these problems affect all nations—developed and developing alike. Only by working together can we effectively deal with the new threats we all face.

That is why, in this 50th anniversary year, we must shape the UN's agenda as if we were creating the institution anew. Just as the UN's founders devised a new framework to deter aggression and armed conflict, the United Nations, in particular the Security Council, must now assign the same priority to combating the threat posed by proliferation, terrorism, international crime, narcotics, and environmental pollution. We should dedicate our efforts in the UN and elsewhere to turning our global consensus against these threats into concrete action. We must renew and reform the United Nations not for its sake, but for our own.

Thank you very much.

TWENTY-FOUR

Bringing Peace to Bosnia

From the day I took office as Secretary of State, the war in Bosnia cast a dark shadow over our foreign policy. In 1991, Yugoslavia, once a strong, unified, multi-ethnic state, had become one of Europe's most troubled nations, as its six constituent republics—Serbia, Slovenia, Croatia, Montenegro, Macedonia, and Bosnia-Herzegovina—began to splinter. The primary cause of the separation was nationalism, stoked more by cynical, power-hungry leaders than by ancient ethnic hatreds. Yugoslavia's disintegration spiraled into violence in July 1991, when Yugoslav National Army forces, largely controlled by Serbia and its President, Slobodan Milosevic, began attacking the breakaway republics.

The most multi-ethnic of those republics, Bosnia-Herzegovina (hereinafter "Bosnia"), was home to large numbers of ethnic Muslims, Croats, and Serbs. The tensions among these three groups within Bosnia came to a boil in early 1992. A controversial referendum narrowly approved an independent Bosnian state, but the Bosnian Serbs, who preferred to unite with the Serbian republic just to the east, had boycotted the voting. War broke out in April 1992, shortly after the international community recognized Bosnia. Bosnian Serb paramilitaries, aided by Yugoslav National troops, began routing Bosnian Muslim and Croat civilians from their homes in an effort to create a "Greater Serbia." The term "ethnic cleansing" will forever be associated with the Serbs' atrocious conduct.

Although the primary aggressors were the Bosnian Serbs, violent tensions also escalated between the Bosnian Croats and Muslims, and by the end of the year, Bosnia had descended into a confusing, horrific three-way war. In September 1992, the United Nations had deployed peace-keeping troops (known as the United Nations Protection Force, or UNPROFOR), but there was little peace to keep. When I entered office in January 1993, the conflict had already become the bloodiest in Europe since the Second World War. There was no doubt that the deadly struggle was, as I would later characterize it, a "problem from Hell."

Early Efforts to Resolve the Crisis

At White House meetings during early February 1993, the Administration's senior foreign policy officials debated about how to react to the festering crisis in Bosnia. In particular, we considered what our response should be to the peace plan then being offered by Lord David Owen, the former British Foreign Secretary, and my good friend Cyrus Vance, who were leading a joint UN–European Community effort to negotiate a settlement. After a series of long meetings, we decided to bolster our overall negotiating position by stiffening economic sanctions against Serbia and calling on the UN to authorize a no-fly zone over Bosnia. We also agreed to step up humanitarian relief. In cooperation with our allies, we implemented these decisions. While we were not prepared to use military force to coerce acceptance of the Vance-Owen plan,[1] we decided that if the parties reached a negotiated settlement, we would join the UN, NATO, and other allies in deploying military forces to help implement and enforce it. This was a major commitment that had long-term ramifications.

I announced these decisions on February 10, tying the Bosnian conflict directly to U.S. interests and explaining why we could not afford to ignore it. In rather sweeping prose, I said that Bosnia "tests our ability to adopt new approaches to foreign policy in a world that has fundamentally changed. It tests our commitment to nurturing democracy. . . . It tests our willingness to help our institutions of collective security, such as

---

[1]The Vance-Owen plan divided Bosnia into 10 enclaves with various combinations of Muslim, Serb, and Croat governing structures. While admiring the Vance-Owen effort, we thought the plan too complex to be implemented.

NATO, evolve in ways that can meet the demands of a new age. It tests what wisdom we have gathered from this bloody century, and it measures our resolve to take early, concerted action against systematic ethnic persecution. . . . We cannot afford to miss any further opportunities to help pursue a resolution to this conflict."

This rhetoric proved to be well ahead of our policy. Despite the steps we were taking with our allies, the war in Bosnia raged on. In mid-April we began another intense round of White House meetings. We were all frustrated that we had failed to stop the bloodshed, but we realized that our options were limited. The Pentagon advised that air power alone could not prevail in the Balkan terrain, and no one had enthusiasm for commitment of U.S. ground troops to force a settlement; many, including myself, were concerned that American public opinion would not support a prolonged and risky deployment for such a purpose. General Colin Powell, then completing his term as Chairman of the Joint Chiefs and a formidable presence in these sessions, was particularly pointed in noting the risks of military intervention.

In late April, President Clinton decided to propose that the UN lift the arms embargo that had operated so unfairly against the Bosnian Muslims. This would level the military playing field between Muslims and Serbs; once the Muslims had better means to defend themselves, the logic went, there would be less need for outside intervention. However, we were well aware that in the short term, lifting the embargo might cause the Serb Army to take advantage of the existing disparity in weaponry and go all-out on the ground before the Bosnian Muslims could rearm. Therefore, President Clinton also decided that NATO airstrikes might be necessary to protect the Muslim forces during this transition period.

The May 1993 Trip

The President recognized that the United States could not unilaterally implement this policy, soon referred to simply as "lift and strike." While we could design the policy and take the lead in effecting it, lift and strike would require both NATO and UN support. The President therefore decided that I should leave immediately to present the lift and strike proposal to our key allies in Europe. Since we knew many Europeans were skeptical about raising the stakes in Bosnia, we decided not to frame the President's plan as a fait accompli. My instructions were to take a more conciliatory approach, laying the proposal before our allies, describing it as the only complete option on the table, and asking for their support.

This effort ran into trouble from the moment I landed in Europe on May 2. Our central concept of lifting the arms embargo was adamantly opposed at several key stops, especially London, Paris, and Moscow. British Prime Minister John Major told me that although he wanted to help us, his government would fall if he tried to muster parliamentary support for lifting the embargo. French President François Mitterrand said that while he recognized the "morality" of our proposal, France could not support it; Serb retaliation would pose too great a danger to the French troops serving in the UN force in the region. And Russian President Yeltsin and Foreign Minister Kozyrev strongly opposed our idea, partly because they thought negotiations were on the brink of a breakthrough.[2] The Germans and Italians were only slightly less negative.

I returned to Washington sobered but still hopeful that lift and strike could be salvaged. Briefing the President, the Vice President, and the national security team at a Saturday-morning meeting in the White House immediately after I returned, I urged that we stay the course and try to bring the Europeans along. My trip had convinced me that they would not follow us based solely on the merits of our plan. "They will only be persuaded by the raw power approach," my report to the President said. "That is, we have to tell them that we have firmly decided to go ahead with our preferred option and that we expect them to support us." In determining whether to pursue this policy, we had to assess whether it was feasible to assemble the votes in the UN Security Council to lift the arms embargo, and whether the diplomatic and political costs of doing

---

[2]My trip was complicated by false hopes raised during a meeting that week in Athens. On May 2, under pressure from Vance and Owen, the Bosnian Muslims and Bosnian Serbs announced their agreement to a negotiated settlement. Although many claimed this was a genuine breakthrough, we were suspicious of the Serbs' true position. Within days, our skepticism proved correct. On May 5, the Bosnian Serb parliament rejected the agreement, and 10 days later, the Bosnian Serb people followed suit in a referendum.

so were acceptable. The effort would require the President to make personal appeals to his counterparts, confront them publicly, and make a strong case to Congress and the American people. "You are not publicly committed to a particular option," my report said, "and hence you are free to consider other options, although none seems attractive. In view of your public posture, what you may not be free to do is to follow the Bush strategy of doing nothing and waiting for the parties to wear themselves out."[3]

As I made my presentation, however, it became evident that there had been a sea change in attitudes during the week I had been away. No one else argued in support of pursuing the lift and strike option with our allies. Enthusiasm for a bold stroke that might draw us into a Balkan quagmire had evaporated. The President reportedly had been reading books on Balkan history that presented a grim picture of prospects for reconciliation, especially Robert Kaplan's *Balkan Ghosts*. Memories of Vietnam caused many, especially those in the military, to resist a commitment to a dangerous and uncertain mission in a confusing and complicated conflict. This viewpoint, always present, had once again become ascendant. The European opposition strengthened the arguments of those skeptical about U.S. intervention. To them, the costs seemed too high to act. So although lift and strike remained formally on the table, attention turned to how we could keep the conflict from spreading and deal with the humanitarian problems it had created.

These early attempts to grapple with Bosnia affected the course and content of our diplomacy there over the next two years. Throughout 1993–95, that diplomacy proceeded fitfully. We often believed we were on the cusp of a peaceful settlement, only to see violence return. In developing U.S. positions over those years, we kept coming back to core questions about acceptable risks and political will. Ultimately, in mid-1995, the President decided that the United States should take a stronger hand, diplomatically and militarily.

[3]The Bush Administration, grappling with changes in the Soviet Union and heavily engaged in seeking new approaches to Middle East peace, had concluded that our national interests did not justify U.S. military intervention in the Bosnian conflict. Indeed, Secretary Baker had declared that the United States "didn't have a dog" in that fight. For more detailed accounts, see James A. Baker, *The Politics of Diplomacy*, pp. 648–51 (New York: G. P. Putnam's Sons, 1995), and Warren Zimmerman, *Origins of a Catastrophe* (New York: Times Books, 1996).

The 1995 Diplomatic Initiative

By the summer of 1995, the crisis in Bosnia had reached its culminating stage. The British and the French, whose troops were the backbone of the UN force there, began to signal that they would leave the region by the end of the year. Moreover, in response to "pinprick" NATO airstrikes in May 1995, the Bosnian Serb Army had taken some UN personnel hostage and chained them to possible air targets. Many of us feared that these acts would be the last straw, and that the UN would decide to withdraw. If this happened, the United States was committed to contributing ground troops to a NATO force that would help ensure a safe withdrawal. I felt that this would be an embarrassing as well as perilous use of American forces, but, on the other hand, failure to keep our commitment would undermine our credibility as the leader of the Alliance.

As we debated our diplomatic options, the military situation deteriorated. In July, the Bosnian Serb Army overran two UN safe areas, Srebrenica and Zepa. The massacre in Srebrenica was devastating, and we realized that something had to be done. The UN safe area at Gorazde, the last Muslim enclave in eastern Bosnia, appeared to be the next target.

To determine the international response to these attacks, John Major called an emergency meeting of Allied and other interested Foreign Ministers in London on July 20. I led the U.S. delegation, which included Secretary Perry and General Shalikashvili. At the meeting we decided that there could be no more half measures; we could not permit the loss of the beleaguered town of Gorazde. NATO had to present the Bosnian Serbs with a clear and unambiguous warning to leave Gorazde alone. During a day of tough negotiations in the sweltering heat of London's Lancaster House, and with a major assist from the new British Foreign Secretary, Malcolm Rifkind, we persuaded the Allies to agree that an attack on Gorazde would be met by the "substantial and decisive" use of air power. For this reason, the meeting was a vital turning point in our approach toward Bosnia: we finally committed to put some real muscle behind our rhetoric.

The London conferees also agreed to streamline the decision-making process on airstrikes, eliminating the so-called dual key system, which had foiled previous attempts to deploy substantial air power because UN civilian officials had refused to approve NATO missions. In succeeding days, however, despite having been present at the conference, UN Secretary General Boutros-Ghali attempted to backtrack and preserve his "key." On July 26, I intervened with Boutros-Ghali, and after two firm phone conversations, he finally relented. In a meeting in Brussels a few days after the London conference, NATO agreed with the U.S. position that the new "London rules" should apply to all safe areas, including not only Gorazde but Bihac and Sarajevo as well.

With these key decisions made, in August we launched a major diplomatic initiative to bring peace to Bosnia. Tony Lake and the NSC staff took the lead in preparing an approach to our European allies and effectively managed the interagency deliberations. After weeks of internal planning, concluding with meetings with the President, we decided to push a peace initiative largely based on an earlier recommendation calling for a 51–49% territorial split between the Muslim-Croat Federation and the Bosnian Serbs. Under this plan, we would not only seek a stable cease-fire but work to establish local structures that would begin rebuilding Bosnia's government and society. We all believed this was the last chance for negotiations before the UN withdrew, so we decided to leave no doubt as to the firmness of the U.S. position. If our allies were unwilling to follow our lead this time, we were prepared to lift the arms embargo unilaterally. However, we did not want to take that path if we could avoid it.

In mid-August, Tony Lake and Peter Tarnoff set off to inform our key European partners of the substance and form of our initiative, and they gained strong expressions of support at every stop. Europe was finally ready to respond to unequivocal U.S. leadership. To follow up, I asked Richard Holbrooke to lead an interagency team to negotiate with the regional parties in the Balkans. As Assistant Secretary of State for European Affairs, Holbrooke was the natural choice for this role. I had known him since we served together in the Carter State Department, and I valued him as an aggressive and creative negotiator, just right for dealing with the complex issues and tough personalities we faced in the Balkans.

To maximize U.S. negotiating flexibility, I felt that Holbrooke and his team had to be allowed to shape the specifics of an agreement. I remembered my efforts 15 years before in Algiers to secure release of the American hostages in Iran, when President Carter and Secretary of State Edmund Muskie allowed me wide bargaining flexibility. From this experience, I knew how essential such latitude would be in Bosnia. I trusted the

Holbrooke team to stay within the red lines of our policy, such as preserving the territorial integrity of Bosnia and adhering to the 51–49% territorial breakdown between the Muslim-Croat Federation and the Serbs. The team gave us updates, often several times a day, about their progress and key decisions. Holbrooke and I also consulted frequently on the best ways to use my leverage as Secretary of State, which we both agreed should be husbanded carefully for maximum impact.

During the first leg of their trip, the Holbrooke team suffered a tragic setback. While crossing Mount Igman en route to Sarajevo, one of their vehicles slipped off the narrow road, rolling several hundred yards down the mountain's steep side. Three U.S. diplomats were killed—Samuel Nelson Drew of the National Security Council, Joseph Kruzel of the Pentagon, and Robert Frasure, our special envoy to the Contact Group and Holbrooke's chief deputy at State. I immediately flew back from a vacation in California to attend the funerals and to help reconstitute the team.

The deaths were a tremendous emotional blow to all of us who knew these fine men as colleagues, but the terrible accident only stiffened our resolve to push forward. After a brief return to Washington to mourn and regroup, Holbrooke and Lieutenant General Wesley K. Clark of the Joint Chiefs of Staff resumed their shuttle diplomacy. To replace their fallen comrades, we added to the delegation Brigadier General Donald Kerrick of the NSC, James Pardew of the Pentagon, Chris Hill of the State Department, and Roberts Owen, legal adviser to Secretary Vance and a longtime friend of mine.

While Holbrooke and his team were in the Balkans, the Bosnian Serbs launched a brutal mortar attack upon a Sarajevo marketplace, killing 37 people. Following the new London rules, on August 30 NATO began to bomb Bosnian Serb positions in retaliation. For the first time, negotiators worked in the region with the full fury of NATO military power behind them. After weeks of intense shuttling between the Balkan capitals, Holbrooke's team achieved several breakthroughs.[4] They negotiated an agreement for a country-wide cease-fire and got the parties to

---

[4]As the team hopscotched among the countries, it drew heavily on the thinly stretched resources of our embassies in Sarajevo, Zagreb, and Belgrade. These embassies not only provided vital logistical support, but also gave advice on the changing moods of the principal players, and frequently had to follow through and clarify issues after the traveling party had moved on to the next stop.

sign on to a set of broad political principles. It was particularly impressive that they had achieved these results without providing the sanctions relief that Serbian President Milosevic had been demanding.

By early October, we believed that the time was ripe to convene peace talks. After vigorous debate within the Administration, we concluded that the best venue would be a secluded location in the United States, as Holbrooke had recommended. Assistant Secretary Pat Kennedy surveyed various sites, and we ultimately chose Wright-Patterson Air Force Base outside Dayton, Ohio. It was a perfect choice. Each delegation had its own hastily refurbished building for working and sleeping, but the structures were arrayed around a central courtyard so that the parties could easily go back and forth to communicate with one another. A conference center provided accommodations for larger meetings, and a central dining facility brought the participants into close contact at mealtimes. The military authorities provided security and helped us limit access by the press.[5] Finally, the airport facilities on the base simplified arrivals and departures.

During the 21 days that the Dayton negotiations lasted, I visited Wright-Patterson four times, and I participated continuously during the last four days. The four statements presented below provide a glimpse of the critical aspects of the negotiations, although they by no means give an exhaustive account.

Dayton: Opening Remarks

The three Balkan Presidents who would determine the fate of Bosnia had all agreed to attend the Dayton talks. They were a strange trio. Milosevic, 55, a tough, aggressive, hard-drinking former bank president, had bulldozed his way to power in Serbia in 1989. Seeking to extend his influence, he had been supplying military equipment to the Bosnian

---

[5]Under the Dayton ground rules, the only reports about the progress of the talks would come from our capable State Department spokesman, Nicholas Burns. The three Dayton events described herein were the only ones the media were allowed to attend. Otherwise, there was a generally effective communications blackout that had the beneficial effect of keeping the parties focused on the negotiations rather than on "spinning" the press.

Serbs. Though unscrupulous and suspected of war crimes, Milosevic has a rough charm, and he appealed to some Western European leaders as a bulwark against an Islamic tide. A good tactician but a poor strategist, he had been weakened by the recent military setbacks of the Bosnian Serbs and the drastic effect of the UN sanctions on the Serbian economy. Yet he had somehow coerced the Bosnian Serbs into giving him authority to negotiate in Dayton on their behalf.

Alija Izetbegovic, 71, Milosevic's principal interlocutor, was a different type. He came across as an ascetic intellectual, misplaced among the hard-bitten political pragmatists who surrounded him. Earlier in his career, the Yugoslav government had jailed him twice for Islamic activism, the first time after World War II for three years, the second time in 1980 for five years for writing a book on the status of Bosnia's Muslims. Entering into politics at age 65, he founded the Bosnian Muslim Democratic Action Party, led his country to independence, and became its first President in 1992. Tougher than he appeared on first impression, friendly to the United States but a hesitant leader, he had been strengthened by recent Croat-Muslim victories over the Bosnian Serbs in northern Bosnia.

Franjo Tudjman, 74, the acknowledged strongman of Croatia, arrived in Dayton riding high; his forces had just driven the Serbs out of the Krajina area of Croatia, which borders Bosnia on the north. Not as centrally involved in the negotiations as the other two Presidents, he nevertheless had important goals, including ensuring a Serb withdrawal from Eastern Slavonia (a sector of Croatia adjacent to Serbia) and looking after the interests of the Bosnian Croats. As a youth, Tudjman had joined the resistance movement led by Josip Broz (Marshal Tito) against the pro-Nazi Ustache government of Croatia. After a military career that saw him rise to the rank of general, he became a history professor with a highly nationalistic outlook. When Croatia gained independence in 1990, Tudjman's reputation as the "most Croat" of all the candidates brought him the presidency. Although Tito had jailed him for two years in the 1970s, he nevertheless seemed to regard himself as Tito's rightful heir. He often posed, Tito-like, resplendent in a white military uniform, with carefully pompadoured gray hair.

When the conference opened on November 1, I joined the key players at a circular table placed in the middle of the B-29 Room of Wright-Patterson's conference center. The densely crowded room, decorated like any other hotel convention hall in middle America, was bright with fluorescent lights. Seated across from me were Tudjman, Izetbegovic, and Milosevic.[6] The other members of the European Contact Group— Carl Bildt, the European Union's special envoy; Pauline Neville-Jones of Great Britain; Jacques Blot of France; Igor Ivanov of Russia; and Wolfgang Ischinger of Germany—all took their places around the table. Richard Holbrooke took the seat on my right.

In my opening remarks, I tried to set a tone that was at once urgent and optimistic: this was our best and perhaps our last chance for peace, and we had to seize it. I also emphasized that success in Dayton was required by broader Western interests in preventing the conflict from spreading further, ensuring the viability of the Atlantic Alliance, and stopping the worst atrocities Europe had witnessed since World War II. In addition, my brief statement established some explicit terms for the negotiations, all of which the President had stressed privately in a White House meeting with the U.S. delegation the previous day: Bosnia had to remain a single state within its internationally recognized boundaries; Sarajevo's "special history" had to be taken into account, which was an only slightly veiled requirement that the city remain unified; the agreement had to guarantee human rights and assure that those who committed atrocities would be held accountable; and the talks had to resolve the situation in Eastern Slavonia, the sliver of Croatian territory the Serbs had held since 1991. Finally, I reiterated our commitment to participate, through NATO, in implementing the agreement once it was reached. At the outset of what promised to be tough negotiations, it was important to reassure the parties that we would stand behind them in the risks they would all have to take.

The Federation Signing

One of our early goals at Dayton was to negotiate a follow-on agreement between the Bosnian Muslims and Croats to solidify and strengthen their

---

[6]Before my opening statement, I walked around the table to these three, encouraging them to shake hands. Although they had done so before, I believed that such an act—like the Rabin-Arafat handshake on the White House's South Lawn—would provide an important boost symbolically, not only for the delegates in Dayton, but for the millions watching around the world.

governing Federation. The very existence of the Muslim-Croat Federation—and the significant problems with it—exemplifies how complicated the Dayton negotiations were. The Federation was an essential but tenuous alliance. Throughout 1993, the Bosnian Muslims and Croats battled each other in fighting as fierce as any in the four-year conflict. In late 1993 we encouraged them to set aside their differences and join forces, politically and militarily. From our perspective, the two sides needed to turn their energies against the stronger and more threatening adversary, the Bosnian Serbs. The result of this effort was a U.S.-mediated Federation Agreement establishing a formal Muslim-Croat political partnership and governing structure. Tudjman and Izetbegovic signed this agreement at a March 1994 ceremony hosted by President Clinton at the White House.

Despite our success in establishing the Federation on paper, no serious effort was made to implement its political elements until the Dayton meetings. The alliance was successful militarily—the Croats and Muslims worked together throughout the autumn of 1995 to retake nearly 20% of Bosnian territory from the Serbs—but political structures that would make it a viable governing entity had yet to be created.[7] Institutions handling such common functions as law enforcement, taxing, and education had been slow to form, and such basic rights as freedom of movement for refugees remained illusory. In a meeting with President Clinton a week before the Dayton talks, both Tudjman and Izetbegovic complained about the Federation's weakness and, blaming each other, claimed that the United States had to intervene to make it function.

In my own bilateral meetings on the first day of the Dayton sessions, I made clear to both Izetbegovic and Tudjman that they had to work together to solve these problems. If we couldn't strengthen the Federation, I said, whatever peace we concluded at Dayton would have little hope for success. The two leaders seemed to get my message, and they set out to draft a document establishing mechanisms for implementing the Federation Agreement.

---

[7]Under the proposed Bosnian constitutional structure, Bosnia would remain a whole state composed of two constituent "entities"—the Muslim-Croat Federation and the Bosnian Serbs' Republika Srpska. Therefore, assuring that the Federation became a functioning, enduring political body would be essential to the success of the Dayton talks.

When I arrived in Dayton for my second visit on November 10, this document was about 90% complete. Along with Dick Holbrooke, I worked to mediate some of the final disputes between the parties, and we returned to the B-29 Room for a public ceremony to sign the Implementing Agreement for the Federation. Although these Federation negotiations undoubtedly slowed our efforts on other fronts, Holbrooke and I hoped that the agreement and signing ceremony might give the talks some valuable momentum. My statement at the ceremony both reflected this hope and stressed the importance of turning the parties' commitments into reality. Unfortunately, I proved all too correct in saying, "It will not be easy." The Federation continues to take shape slowly, and its fragility remains one of the weaknesses of the Dayton agreements even today.

The Dayton Endgame

After leaving Dayton the evening of November 10, I returned to the talks twice more—on November 14, en route to Osaka for the APEC meetings, and on November 18, when I returned from those meetings. I had originally planned to stay in Japan to join the President for an official state visit in Tokyo. However, after my one-day stop in Dayton on November 14 showed me how far we had left to go, I decided to cut short the Asian trip and return there.[8]

Two weeks into the Dayton conference, many critical disputes still remained to be resolved. Unfortunately, these included the two most contentious, the territorial division of Bosnia and the future of Sarajevo. These subjects were so sensitive that to continue to make progress in other areas, such as political arrangements, Holbrooke had decided to defer them until the end. Otherwise, the talks would have bogged down in screaming matches. My return to Dayton on November 18 was designed to help resolve these outstanding matters. After Holbrooke carried an issue as far as he could, he would bring me in as the "closer." He

---

[8]It happened that the President also canceled his trip to Tokyo, instead staying in Washington to continue the difficult budget negotiations with Congress. Vice President Gore went to Japan in his place.

thought that my position as Secretary of State would calm the parties and help induce them to accept our suggestions.

By this point the parties had been at Dayton for longer than they (or we) would have liked, and were making threats to leave. Their restlessness created strong pressure to complete the talks quickly. For the three days after my return from Japan, negotiations proceeded around the clock. Although ragged after my 72-hour round trip to Asia, I was energized by the determination of our delegation. At several points we thought we had come to a final agreement, only to see the parties backtrack.[9] The Muslims were especially difficult to pin down, and remained so until the very last minute. At midnight on the night before agreement was reached, I had an uncharacteristically loud confrontation with Izetbegovic during which I pointed out that we had achieved all that he demanded, and he still wouldn't say yes. This reflected his profound ambivalence about agreeing to any territorial division or, indeed, any deal with the Serbs. At another crisis point, when the Croatians held out, we arranged for President Clinton to call Tudjman and press him to be helpful. In the end, he was.

Although we were pulling out all the stops, we recognized the very real possibility that the talks would end without resolution, and began to think about next steps. Indeed, we prepared two closing statements—a "failure" statement, in which we outlined our disappointment but pledged to support continuing negotiations and possibly further shuttle diplomacy, and a "success" statement. During the last few hours at Dayton, the principal drafter of both of these statements, Tom Malinowski, became something of a weather vane. Some members of our delegation took their cues about how the talks were going based on which statement Holbrooke and I were pressing Malinowski to finalize.

At last an agreement was reached incorporating all the goals outlined in my November 1 remarks. The success statement that I gave from the dais of the B-29 Room at the initialing of the agreement paid tribute to the dedicated efforts of all the parties, and especially the Holbrooke

---

[9]For example, shortly after 4:00 A.M. on November 20, we thought we had an agreement, and I called for a bottle of wine. Our celebration lasted only 37 minutes, ending abruptly when the Croatian delegation examined the maps and denounced the territorial exchange. I went back to my room, showered, changed clothes, and returned to start another day of negotiations.

team, throughout these difficult negotiations.[10] It highlighted what the Dayton accords could accomplish but also, like my November 10 remarks, reminded all sides that hard work remained: the commitments now on paper had to be put into practice. The statement concluded on an upbeat note, one in which I tried to capture the essence of those 21 days in Dayton.

Building Public Support

The Dayton accords provided a strong foundation for peace, but the true test would come in their implementation. Mutual distrust and hostility still ran deep among all the Balkan parties. The Clinton Administration, along with our European allies, had played a central role in getting those parties to Dayton, and we would have to remain engaged for a lasting peace to take hold. The Administration had pledged to deploy 20,000 U.S. troops as part of a NATO-led force to implement the accords and to take the necessary steps to achieve military stabilization between the opposing forces in Bosnia. We had also agreed to supply economic assistance for reconstruction.

All of these commitments had significant opposition in Congress and among the American people, and we set out to overcome it. We embarked on an Administration-wide effort to make the case for active American leadership in implementing the accords. President Clinton asked the American people for support directly in a prime-time television address, and Perry, Shalikashvili, Holbrooke, and I joined in an all-out offensive to get Congress to back our commitments. As part of this effort, on December 1, I testified before the Senate Foreign Relations Committee on this "acid test of American leadership." My statement reviewed the history of our national interest in finding a peaceful solution to the Bosnian conflict, described how completely we had achieved the goals set forth in my November 1 statement, and outlined the consequences that were likely if we failed to support implementation. Finally, it directly ad-

---

[10]By previous arrangement with the Europeans, the Dayton Agreement was only initialed in Dayton. It was formally signed three weeks later at a ceremony in Paris.

dressed many of the Senators' concerns, particularly their hesitation about the U.S. role in the military Implementation Force (IFOR).

The Broader Implications of Dayton

Four days after my Senate testimony, Secretary Perry and I attended an unprecedented meeting in Brussels of the Defense and Foreign Ministers of all 16 NATO members. I reported to the President that for several reasons, this meeting would long be remembered as one of the most important steps in building a post–Cold War security system for Europe. First, our discussions showcased the Alliance's unity of purpose on the eve of the Bosnia deployment. Second, the involvement of Russia and Central European countries in the Implementation Force demonstrated that NATO and former Warsaw Pact nations could work together toward mutual interests. Third, we continued our steady progress on NATO expansion by launching a second phase of the process. We outlined a plan to begin intensive consultations in 1996 with those states most interested in joining NATO, and took steps to strengthen the Partnership for Peace. Finally, the meeting welcomed Javier Solana, an impressive former Spanish Foreign Minister with a powerful appreciation of America's role in the Alliance, as NATO's new Secretary General.

The importance of the Administration's success in forging a peace in Bosnia was apparent in all of my discussions at NATO that week. The Dayton Agreement not only brought peace to Bosnia, but also reinforced the central role of NATO in Europe's security architecture. Only a few months before, many in Europe as well as in the United States had questioned whether NATO had a role to play in the post–Cold War era. Now, with the Alliance's recent success in bolstering diplomacy with force and with its current responsibility to implement the Dayton Agreement, NATO's continuing importance was universally acknowledged. Among our Allies, I reported to the President, there was a palpable feeling of relief that impotence had been replaced by determination, and that the divisions that had haunted us from the beginning of the war in the former Yugoslavia had been replaced by unity.

Moreover, by providing a basis for a partnership between NATO and Russia in the Implementation Force, the Bosnian settlement was a major step toward building a broader cooperative relationship between former military adversaries. Proof that NATO and Russia could successfully work side by side in IFOR would be critical to allaying Russian concerns about NATO expansion.

Finally, the success at Dayton reaffirmed the imperative of American leadership. Some Europeans grumbled about how we had dominated the Dayton process, but as I noted to President Clinton, they really knew that without us, the settlement would not have happened. Coupled with the President's trips to Northern Ireland to discuss peace and to Madrid to inaugurate the New Transatlantic Agenda (see Chapter 19), our discussions at NATO concluded what I called a "watershed week" for American leadership.

As I write this two years after the Dayton talks, I remain hopeful about the prospects for lasting peace in Bosnia. In many ways, the Dayton agreements have succeeded: the war has truly ended, and we are no longer careening from cease-fire to cease-fire. NATO military implementation has proceeded more smoothly than anyone expected, and thankfully with very little loss of life. With major help from IFOR, national elections were successfully carried out throughout Bosnia in September 1996. Governing structures have taken root, albeit less deeply than we had hoped. Most important, perhaps, a semblance of normalcy has returned to a people who, for the better part of four years, knew little more than the bloody realities of war.

Yet the greater promise of Dayton remains unfulfilled. NATO military leaders have narrowly interpreted their role in Bosnia, though this situation has improved with the appointment of General Wesley Clark as the Supreme Commander of NATO. Many fundamental aspects of the accords—such as securing freedom of movement, ensuring refugee return, creating a viable Federation, and bringing war criminals to justice—remain to be fully achieved. Republika Srpska is a shambles, both politically and economically.

As we look ahead, it remains true that, as I wrote to the President in February 1996, after my first post-Dayton visit to Bosnia,

> the U.S. leadership role in implementation is as essential as it was in reaching the Dayton accords. No other country has the confidence of all the parties, and the leverage to get this difficult job done. . . . We have a great deal invested in making sure that our efforts to date are not squandered by inadequate follow through, a message we will need to take to the Congress and the American people as well as the parties to the conflict.

●

The Promise of This Moment Must Be Fulfilled

Statement at the Opening of the Balkan Proximity Peace Talks,
Wright-Patterson Air Force Base, Dayton, Ohio, November 1, 1995

Good afternoon. President Izetbegovic, President Tudjman, President Milosevic, Prime Minister Bildt, Deputy Minister Ivanov, honored colleagues: On behalf of President Clinton and the American people, I welcome you to the United States for the start of these historic proximity peace talks. My special thanks go to the people of Dayton, Ohio, and Wright-Patterson Air Force Base for their magnificent support.

We have an urgent and important purpose today. We are here to give Bosnia-Herzegovina a chance to be a country at peace, not a killing field—a place where people can sleep in their homes, walk to work, and worship in their churches, mosques, and synagogues without fear of violence or death. We are here to prevent a wider war that would undermine the security of Europe at a time when the whole continent should finally be at peace.

The talks that begin here today offer the best chance to achieve peace since this war began four years ago. If we fail, the war will resume, and future generations will surely hold us accountable for the consequences that would follow. The lights so recently lit in Sarajevo would once again be extinguished. Death and starvation would once again spread across the Balkans, threatening to engulf the region and possibly Europe itself.

To the three presidents, I say that it is within your power to chart a better future for the people of the former Yugoslavia. The United States, the European Union, Russia, and others in the international community will help you succeed. But while the world can and will help you make peace, only you can ensure that this process will succeed. And you must begin today.

As President Clinton said yesterday, the "whole world is watching." We must persevere until an agreement is reached and the promise of this hopeful moment is fulfilled.

There are some who say these talks can only end in failure. They have written off the Balkans as a region cursed by its past to a future of endless hatred and retribution. I have heard those arguments before—in the Middle East, where Arabs and Israelis are now ending an armed conflict that has lasted 10 times as long as the one in the former Yugoslavia. I have heard the same arguments applied to Northern Ireland, where a centuries-old conflict may be nearing resolution. I have heard them applied to South Africa, where former enemies have abandoned apartheid to build a multi-ethnic democracy. I know that negotiations can work when people have the courage and patience to make them work.

We have reached this moment because the international community took firm measures to enforce its mandate in Bosnia-Herzegovina and because, for the first time, all sides have agreed to a cease-fire, to constitutional principles, and to a common set of institutions for a single Bosnian state. We must all resolve to stay on the path that brought us here. For each of us, the stakes are enormous.

For the people of Bosnia-Herzegovina, whatever their heritage, the success of our efforts can mean an end to the killing and the beginning of hope for a normal life. The people of Bosnia deserve a chance to live as they once did—in harmony with their neighbors in a country at peace.

For the nations at war, the stakes are clear as well. They have a choice between two futures—a future of peace and integration or a future of violence, poverty, and isolation from Europe and the world. We must always remember: As this region is engulfed in flames and violence, a new Europe is being built around it. Some of the fastest-growing economies in Europe today are found in this region. The new democracies of Central Europe are resolving disputes with their neighbors and earning the right to be considered for membership in NATO and the European Union.

When the Cold War ended, nobody imagined that once-vibrant cities such as Sarajevo, Mostar, and Vukovar would be set so tragically apart from Europe by the sight of tanks and the sound of gunfire. The door to Europe and the West is still open to the nations of the region—if you end this war peacefully and respect the human rights of your people. You alone can choose your destiny.

The United States and the international community also have a vital stake in sustaining progress toward peace. If war in the Balkans is reunited, it could spark a wider conflict like those that drew American soldiers in huge numbers into two European wars in this century. If this conflict continues—and certainly if it spreads—it would jeopardize our efforts to promote stability and security in Europe as a whole. It would threaten the viability of NATO, which has been the bedrock of European security for 50 years. If the conflict continues, so would the worst atrocities Europe has seen since World War II. As President Clinton has said, the "only way to stop these horrors is to make peace." We must and we will stay engaged to advance our interests and to uphold our values.

The United States and its Contact Group partners will make every effort to help you reach an agreement that will settle outstanding questions over territory, constitutional arrangements, elections, and the return of refugees. We have worked hard to create the right atmosphere for progress at this site. And I know that Ambassador Holbrooke, Prime Minister Bildt, and Deputy Minister Ivanov will continue to provide the most effective and evenhanded mediation that is possible.

If peace is to endure, we must do more than separate the military forces. For a peace to last, several key conditions must be met:

First, Bosnia-Herzegovina must continue as a single state within its internationally recognized borders and with a single international personality. The principles to which the parties have agreed provide a firm foundation for achieving that goal.

Second, the settlement must take into account the special history and significance of Sarajevo and its environs. Sarajevo was the city where the first of this century's two bloody world wars began. But 10 years ago, it was also the city where the world came together to celebrate the Olympics—a city of many communities living, working, and prospering together in peace. It must have a chance to become that wonderful city again. It deserves that chance.

Third, any agreement must guarantee that the human rights of all the citizens of the region are respected. This terrible war has uprooted people from every ethnic community. All must be able to return home or to receive just compensation. And it is vital that all those who have committed atrocities are held accountable. Full investigation of all such charges, regardless of where they occurred, must be undertaken swiftly and firmly, and responsibility must be assigned.

Finally, we also believe that these talks must establish a process of normalizing the status of Eastern Slavonia, as a part of Croatia and in a peaceful manner.

If and when a formal agreement is reached—but only then—the United States and its partners, including Russia, will provide military personnel to help implement the peace. NATO is the only organization with the resources and capacity to perform this task. It already has begun planning for a robust peace implementation force.

For each nation participating in the implementation force, deploying soldiers is a difficult and solemn choice. The American people and the United States Congress are asking serious and appropriate questions about U.S. participation in the Implementation Force. They will watch very closely for signs that the parties are finally ready to lay down their arms and begin a lasting, stable peace.

The United States will not send troops where there is no peace to keep. Before we deploy, the parties must reach a peace agreement. They must be prepared to stick to it. They must use the time when our troops are on the ground to consolidate it. And the Implementation Force must have a clear exit strategy.

The international community is also determined to help the people of the region rebuild their institutions, their economies, and their lives. The Organization for Security and Cooperation in Europe will help organize and supervise elections in Bosnia-Herzegovina—which ought to come at the earliest possible date—to ensure that they are free and fair. Under the leadership of the EU, a major effort to support the reconstruction of Bosnia-Herzegovina will be launched. Lasting security will depend on bringing the region's economy back to life.

In other words, once an agreement is signed, a multi-dimensional effort will begin, to help ensure its success. It will be backed by soldiers, diplomats, bankers, and engineers; by governments; and by private organizations from countries around the world.

We know that Bosnia-Herzegovina will not easily recover from four years of ethnic cleansing and destruction. Nothing we do will erase our memory of the violence or bring back its victims. But if we succeed, we can make it possible for the sons and daughters of those who have died to live without fear. If we succeed, we can ensure that the sons and daughters of America and Europe do not have to fight again in a larger, more terrible war. If we succeed, we may yet realize our vision of a Europe at peace, united, prosperous, and free. We must rise to the challenge.

This will be a long journey. But it all starts here. Let us get to work, and let us reaffirm our pledge to make it work.

The Federation: An Essential Building Block of Peace in Bosnia and Herzegovina

Statement at the Signing of the Agreement Implementing the Federation of Bosnia and Herzegovina, Wright-Patterson Air Force Base, Dayton, Ohio, November 10, 1995

Thank you. Let me say a few words about what has been achieved here today.

The Federation is an essential building block of peace in Bosnia and Herzegovina as a whole. In the peace agreement we are discussing, the Federation will be one of Bosnia's two constituent parts. For a settlement to endure, the Federation must be functioning and strong.

A year and a half ago, the United States helped to mediate the agreement that created the Federation. That agreement saved countless lives by ending the fighting between the Bosniac and Croat communities of Bosnia and Herzegovina. Until today, however, many serious obstacles to implementation remained, including the slow development of common institutions, restrictions on the freedom of movement within the Federation, and the continued division of Mostar. Today, the parties have adopted a plan to resolve each of these problems.

As it is implemented, today's agreement will bring the Federation to life. It will create common political and economic institutions that will unite the two communities. It will be a model for inter-ethnic cooperation and renewed trust in a country that is sorely in need of both.

This agreement was negotiated under the auspices of the U.S. and German delegations in Dayton. It certainly could not have been reached without the determination of President Izetbegovic and of President Tudjman.

The Contact Group and the European Union were also our full partners. Like the United States, the EU is dedicated to the idea that one community can be forged from many disparate parts. We share the conviction that Europe's post–Cold War peace must be based on the principle of multi-ethnic democracy.

The agreement finally gives the Federation the authority to govern effectively. The central government of Bosnia and Herzegovina will keep the powers it needs to preserve the country's sovereignty, including foreign affairs, trade, and monetary policy. It will transfer most of its other responsibilities, including police, courts, tax collection, health, and education to the Federation. The new structures the agreement creates will replace all of the separate, local Croat and Muslim authorities on Federation territory.

The agreement commits the Federation to respect the human rights of all who live within it regardless of their ethnic background and to allow them to move about its territory freely. Federation authorities will develop and implement a comprehensive plan to permit refugees and displaced persons to return to their homes.

The agreement provides for the sharing of revenues and a joint customs administration. Internal customs checkpoints, which had marred the Federation before, will be removed. Finally, the parties have agreed to the reunification of the city of Mostar under a single administration.

Of course, the true test of this agreement will lie in the way it is carried out. The parties have agreed to report to the United States, Germany and the EU every two weeks on the progress they are making. We will monitor that progress carefully, and stand ready to help them however we can.

It will not be easy. But today, we can celebrate another moment of hope in this long, hard process of building the Federation. The parties have understood that peace means more than the absence of war. It requires practical cooperation and the mutual recognition of shared interests. In the case of Bosnia-Herzegovina, the ugly alternative is starkly symbolized by the shattered bridge that once united the city of Mostar.

It is certainly harder to build bridges than it is to tear them down. And some people, of course, still believe that the conflict between Muslims, Croats, and Serbs is insoluble. By making the Federation work, the communities this agreement unites are showing that view to be cynical and false. After all, until recently, the peoples of Bosnia-Herzegovina lived together in peace. They deserve a chance to do so again.

If the Federation can succeed as a multi-ethnic democracy, then so can Bosnia-Herzegovina as a whole. A comprehensive peace remains our fundamental challenge here in Dayton. The agreement we signed today is an important first step and a sign that progress is possible when the parties are determined to achieve it.

The Dayton Peace Agreement: Building Peace with Justice

Remarks at the Initialing of the Dayton Peace Agreement,

Wright-Patterson Air Force Base, Dayton, Ohio, November 21, 1995

President Izetbegovic, President Milosevic, President Tudjman, Mr. Bildt, Deputy Minister Ivanov, General Shalikashvili, Deputy Secretary White, honored colleagues and guests: We have reached a day many believed would never come. After three weeks of intensive negotiations in Dayton, the leaders of Bosnia-Herzegovina, Croatia, and Serbia have agreed to end the war in the former Yugoslavia. They have agreed that four years of destruction is enough. The time has come to build peace with justice.

Today's agreement would not have come without the vision and leadership of President Clinton. The diplomatic and military strategy that he launched this summer has borne fruit. I am gratified at the result and determined to see that it is implemented.

We have come to this hopeful moment because the parties made the fundamental choices that lasting peace will require. And we are here because our international negotiating team successfully led the parties to agreement. Assistant Secretary Holbrooke and his team took on a hard, exhausting task and succeeded in a way that will long be remembered and admired. I also want to recognize the tireless efforts of my friend and colleague, National Security Adviser Tony Lake. The European Union and the members of the Contact Group—Germany, France, the United Kingdom, and Russia—were with us every critical step of the way.

No one thought these negotiations would be easy, and all of us on this stage can tell you they were not. What we wanted was a comprehensive settlement, and that is what we have achieved. The hard-won commitments we will initial today address the wrenching and fundamental issues over which the war was fought.

Today's agreement assures the continuity of a single state of Bosnia-Herzegovina, with effective federal institutions, a single currency, and full respect by its neighbors for its sovereignty. The city of Sarajevo, which has gripped the world's attention for the last four years, will no longer be divided. It will be reunified under the Federation of Bosnia and Herzegovina. Checkpoints and closed bridges will no longer divide its families. All Bosnia's people will have the right to move freely throughout the country. Refugees and displaced persons will have the right to return home or to obtain just compensation. Free and democratic elections will be held next year.

The agreement contains strong human rights protections. It confirms the parties' obligation to cooperate fully in the investigation and prosecution of war crimes. It excludes indicted war criminals from military or government office.

The agreement requires the parties to withdraw their forces to agreed positions and provides for important confidence-building measures among them. The parties have pledged to cooperate fully with a NATO-led peace implementation force and to ensure the safety of its personnel. And it sets the stage for a comprehensive program of economic reconstruction.

Today's agreement certainly does not erase memories of what has come before, or guarantee that the fabric of Bosnia's society will easily be restored. But still, it is a victory for us all. The agreement is a victory for people of every heritage in the former Yugoslavia. It offers tangible hope that there will be no more days of dodging bullets, no more winters of freshly dug graves, and no more years of isolation from the outside world.

The agreement is a victory for all those who believe in a multi-ethnic democracy in Bosnia-Herzegovina. Securing that goal will require an immense effort in the days ahead. But that effort can now begin as the war that has torn Bosnia apart finally comes to an end.

The agreement is a victory for all those in the world who believed that with determination, a principled peace is possible. That conviction was shared by the three brave American diplomats who gave their lives in pursuit of peace in Bosnia—Bob Frasure, Joe Kruzel, and Nelson Drew. We honor their memories. I am so pleased that their families are with us today.

But this victory will not be secure unless we all get to work to ensure that the promise of this moment is realized. The parties have put a solemn set of commitments on paper. In the coming days and weeks, they will have to put them into practice—extending them to every mayor, every soldier, every police officer in their territory. The United

States and the international community will continue to help them succeed. It is profoundly in our self-interest to do so.

As we move forward, we must be realistic and clear-eyed. We should not assume that the people of the former Yugoslavia have resolved all their differences. But we should also remember that we can now begin to leave behind the horrors of the last four years. This war was waged against civilians; it is they who are the real winners today.

The American people should be proud of that achievement. The war in Bosnia has been a challenge to our interests and our values. By our leadership here, we have upheld both.

I trust that one day, people will look back on Dayton and say: This is the place where the fundamental choices were made; this is where the parties chose peace over war, dialogue over destruction, and reason over revenge; this is where each of us accepted the challenge to make those choices meaningful and to make them endure.

Thank you.

●

Bringing the Agreement to NATO

At Sixteen-Plus-Sixteen Meeting of NATO Foreign and

Defense Ministers on Bosnia, in Brussels, December 5, 1995

Mr. Acting Secretary-General, distinguished colleagues: It is a great privilege for Secretary Perry and me to speak with you today on behalf of the United States and President Clinton. For the first time in NATO's history, all 16 of our foreign ministers and all 16 of our defense ministers are meeting together. As we prepare to launch this historic mission in Bosnia, our alliance has never been more united.

We are united because our mission is deeply rooted in NATO's fundamental purpose: to combine our strength in the defense of peace. That purpose was conceived by NATO's founders a half century ago in the wake of the two most destructive wars in human history. They created this permanent alliance to ensure that we would never have to fight a third great war.

In its first half century, our alliance met its greatest test. As a result, we have reached the most hopeful period in the modern history of Europe. Thanks to NATO, Western Europe emerged from the Cold War more secure and united than ever before. Thanks to NATO, Central Europe was able to win its freedom, and the barbed wire that once divided this continent has been discarded for good. Thanks to NATO, the partnership between the United States and Europe is indissoluble, and we can pursue our shared interests and values effectively together.

The Cold War is over, but we still have great challenges to meet. Such a challenge is clearly posed by the war in the former Yugoslavia. In the first shots that rang out in Sarajevo, we heard an ominous echo of the origins of World War I. In the killing fields and concentration camps of Bosnia we have seen our most terrible memories of World War II come to life again in the heart of Europe.

This summer, the war in Bosnia reached a point of crisis. NATO faced the prospect of withdrawing UN troops from Bosnia under fire. But in these terrible events, we saw a chance to change the course of the war. Together, we agreed to take decisive action to protect Bosnia's remaining safe areas.

Without NATO's determined use of force, our diplomacy could not have brought the parties to the table. Without the prospect of a NATO implementation force, the parties would not have had the confidence to reach—and to implement—a comprehensive settlement. Without NATO, there would be no peace and no hope in Bosnia.

The Dayton Peace Agreement has given us our best hope to achieve a lasting peace. We wanted an agreement that addressed all the fundamental issues that divided the parties, with no short cuts or ambiguities, and that is what we obtained. We wanted Bosnia to remain a single state, and it will. We did not want Sarajevo to be divided as Berlin once was, and it will not be.

As we negotiated, we constantly insisted on an agreement that our troops could implement and enforce safely and effectively. Each part of the agreement was carefully constructed to take the needs of our armed forces into account. The three Balkan presidents have provided formal assurances for the safety of our troops. We expect them to take the necessary steps to ensure that this and every other commitment made at Dayton is fully honored.

NATO has approved a detailed operational plan to implement the agreement. This plan meets two tests that President Clinton laid out in his address last week to the American people. First, the mission is "precisely defined—with clear, realistic goals that can be achieved in a finite period of time." NATO can provide a respite from fear and a chance to start rebuilding, but only the people of Bosnia can finish the job. Second, our troops will have the strength and authority to protect themselves and to fulfill their mission. I am confident this plan will have the support of the American people and our Congress.

For each of our nations, deploying troops is always a difficult and solemn choice. But President Clinton has made clear that the United States is determined to carry out the responsibilities of leadership. Meeting that responsibility is profoundly in the interest of our nation and the world.

Last weekend in Ireland, President Clinton reminded us that European soldiers have stood shoulder to shoulder with America far from European shores, most recently in the Persian Gulf and in Haiti. Nowhere is it more important that we stand together than in Europe, where our common security interests are so great. We designed NATO to secure these interests effectively and to share the risks of our collective effort.

Our 16 nations will form the critical core of the NATO force in Bosnia. But equally important, we will be joined by our new partners from Central Europe and the New Independent States, who will serve side by side with NATO troops for the very first time.

The breadth of this coalition is not unique just in NATO's history. In all of modern European history, this is the first time that soldiers from every European power will serve together in a common military operation. Think of it: soldiers from France and Germany, Britain and Spain, Greece and Turkey, Poland and Sweden, Russia and the United States all sharing the same risks on the same soil, under the same banner, at the same time. Never before could we say with such conviction that our only remaining enemy is war itself.

We are closer than ever to fulfilling the dream that Harry Truman expressed upon the signing of the North Atlantic Treaty. "If there is anything inevitable in the future," he said, "it is the will of the people of the world for freedom and peace."

Because of the mission we launch today and because of our strategy of integration, the entire continent can one day share the blessings of peace that unite our community of free nations. As we strive with our partners to overcome the division of Bosnia, we can also help overcome the remaining division of Europe. Bosnia, once the symbol of Europe's post–Cold War disintegration, can be the proving ground for a broader and deeper transatlantic community.

These are goals that the United States and Europe can and will achieve as allies, as partners, and as friends. Winston Churchill's immortal words remain our guidepost: "Let us move forward together."

Thank you.

TWENTY-FIVE

New Momentum for American Diplomacy

As 1996 began, my mood was more buoyant than it had been a year earlier. By almost any measure, we had had a good year. Around the globe, the impact of American leadership was evident. In Asia, we had steered through a difficult period with China and had begun to establish a new tone in our relations. We had also continued to implement the Agreed Framework with North Korea and achieved a historic breakthrough by opening relations with Vietnam. In Latin America, we had averted an international financial crisis by helping Mexico stabilize the peso.[1] In the Middle East, we had acted to solidify the Oslo agreements and pursue Israeli negotiations with Syria, and after the tragic assassination of Yitzhak Rabin in November, we had helped keep the peace process moving. In Europe, we had moved forward with NATO expansion in partnership with our Allies and in consultation with Russia. And most critically, our diplomacy had brought an end to the bloodshed in Bosnia. When I re-

---

[1]In December 1994, the Mexican peso plunged precipitously, Mexican banks tottered on the edge of insolvency, and the Mexican economy was near collapse because of overexpansion and mismanagement. The IMF did not have sufficient reserves to handle this crisis, and it took a joint IMF-U.S. effort to assemble a $48 billion stabilization fund. President Clinton initially sought bipartisan support for the U.S. effort, but when the congressional Republicans refused to follow the lead of Majority Leader Dole and Speaker Newt Gingrich, Clinton had to go it alone for the U.S. share. With the help of the stabilization fund, the Mexican economy recovered, and the loans from the United States and others have now been repaid with interest. The outcome is a tribute to the President's courage and the sagacious advice of Treasury Secretary Rubin.

turned to Harvard in January 1996 for a second "State of the Union" foreign policy address, I therefore began by assessing what I called a "remarkable period of achievement in American diplomacy." This line is
more self-congratulatory than I usually allow, but it was one I could utter without much exaggeration or embarrassment.

I have long believed that when it comes to U.S. leadership, there is a
great "spillover effect" among issues, positive and negative. Diplomacy
cannot be compartmentalized, and credibility is not divisible. Our ability
to manage one important challenge enhances our ability to handle others. No 1995 event demonstrated this spillover effect more dramatically
than our success in ending the war in Bosnia. Bosnia not only had
haunted U.S. policy for nearly three years, but had strained our relations
with Europe and sullied the credibility of both the UN and NATO. It
was easy to see that our frustrations there had damaged our ability to
lead in other areas. During 1995, assertive U.S. diplomacy, coupled with
decisive NATO air power, at last enabled us to bring peace to Bosnia (see
Chapter 24). This achievement reinforced both the reality and the perception of American leadership. Together with other accomplishments,
the Dayton success inspired a new confidence in America's role in the
world, a confidence felt not only within the Administration but also
abroad.

Ironically, although we had just shown the great power and potential
of American diplomacy, Congress still wanted to slash our foreign affairs
budget. Despite our vigorous efforts to emphasize the need for adequate
resources, the Administration plainly faced an uphill battle with the Republican Congress.

This speech took a tough line on the resources issue. I was upset by
Republican proposals that would force the Administration to cut personnel, close important embassies, and renege on international commitments. We could not, I said flatly, maintain our strength "on the cheap."
I had no doubt that the presence of our embassies in Sarajevo, Belgrade,
and Zagreb had been essential to our success in Dayton. Yet the closing
or merger of such diplomatic missions is exactly the type of "efficiency"
that would be required by further budget reductions.

If I was upset by the proposed cutbacks, I was truly incensed by the
recent government shutdowns (lasting a total of 27 days) that the Republicans had forced upon us by holding the budget hostage to their po-

litical agenda. From my travels and vantage as Secretary of State, I could see what a tremendous impact this had had on our foreign relations. My counterparts abroad could not believe that we had let this great country close up shop. The shutdown was also a crushing blow to morale at the State Department, both within the foreign and civil services and among the dedicated foreign nationals who served in our embassies. Reports poured in from our posts abroad that American employees, some of them facing hardships themselves, had taken up collections to ease the suffering of the foreign national employees. Three lines in the speech summed up my indignation: "For leaders and ordinary citizens in many parts of the world, it seemed as if the most powerful nation in the world was closing for business. Our failure to pay our bills and our employees was conduct not worthy of a great nation. It must not happen again."

This speech touched on almost every key topic to which I would return in the coming year, while reaffirming the guiding principles laid down a year earlier. I identified three priorities for American foreign policy in 1996: "pursuing peace in regions of vital interest to the United States" (Bosnia and the Middle East), promoting open markets and open societies (by implementing the far-reaching agreements achieved in the three preceding years), and "confronting the new transnational security threats."

This last goal was becoming increasingly important. I had raised the topic of global security threats in my 1995 Kennedy School address. Since then we had made significant conceptual strides in treating these threats as vital matters of foreign policy. President Clinton had made a major statement along these lines in an October 1995 speech before the UN General Assembly, in which he outlined the challenge of transnational threats in an interdependent world. I had also returned to the topic frequently in public statements and congressional testimony. And we had begun to address issues like terrorism, international corruption, crime, narcotics, and environmental degradation more thoroughly in our bilateral discussions in every region of the world.

My remarks foreshadowed an even more vigorous treatment of global subjects in the coming year. I gave full-dress speeches on such issues as the environment and terrorism, and highlighted these subjects during trips to Latin America and Africa. This emphasis reflected my judgment that such global opportunities and threats would be defining issues for future American foreign policy.

Looking ahead, I was also acutely aware that 1996 was an election year. Frequently foreign policy has become a focal point in presidential campaigns. During the last year of the Carter Administration, for example, the crisis involving the American hostages in Iran and the consequences of an international contraction in oil supplies, including long gas lines and high inflation, took center stage. Many attributed President Carter's reelection defeat to these problems.

Although I was intensely loyal to President Clinton I felt I would serve both him and the national interest best by keeping an even keel in the international arena in the months ahead. I wanted to avoid subjecting foreign policy to the vagaries of the political season. With primary campaigning already well under way, this meant taking the high road and not firing back whenever one of the candidates attacked our foreign policy in search of a headline. As a bit of preventive medicine, I used this speech to stress to "every candidate who aspires to the Presidency" the importance of our involvement in the world and the need for America to be a "reliable and principled leader."

Leadership for the Next American Century

Address Before the John F. Kennedy School of Government, Harvard

University, Cambridge, Massachusetts, January 18, 1996

Let me begin by thanking Joe Nye not only for giving me that warm introduction, but for laying to rest one persistent canard about this fine institution. It used to be said in some circles that the Kennedy School was a plot to infiltrate the federal government. Joe Nye's appointment proves that the opposite is true: The federal government is in fact a plot to infiltrate the Kennedy School.

A year ago, I met with you to explain the guiding principles of this Administration's foreign policy and our priorities for 1995. I am here today to assess a remarkable period of achievement for American diplomacy and to discuss our main objectives for 1996. The end of the Cold War has given us an unprecedented opportunity to shape a more secure world of open societies and open markets—a world in which American interests and ideals can thrive. But we also face serious threats from which no border can shield us—terrorism, proliferation, crime, and damage to the environment.

This is not the end of history, but history in fast-forward. Eight decades ago, when this century's first Balkan war ended, it took an international commission to piece together what had happened. Now, images of violence in Sarajevo are beamed instantly around the world. Six decades ago, it took several years for the Great Depression to become a global disaster. Now, an economic crisis in Mexico can disrupt the global economy in the blink of an eye.

In this time of accelerated change, American leadership must remain constant. We must be clear-eyed and vigilant in pursuit of our interests. Above all, we must recognize that only the United States has the vision and strength to consolidate the gains of the last few years and to build an even better world.

Six years after the fall of the Berlin Wall, some still think that we can escape the problems of the world by building walls around America. But the evidence of the last three years should settle the debate about America's role in the world. Because President Clinton has rejected the path of retreat, we have forged a record that proves the enduring value of American leadership and American engagement.

The President, with help from internationalists in both parties, has made the United States the world's driving force for peace. Think of it. Had we not led, the war in Bosnia would continue today, wasting innocent lives, threatening a wider war, and eroding the NATO alliance. Had we not led, there would not be the prospect of comprehensive peace in the Middle East. And there would be scant hope for reconciliation in Northern Ireland. Without American leadership, thugs would still rule in Haiti, and thousands of Haitian refugees would be trying to reach our shores. The Mexican economy would be in free-fall, threatening our prosperity and harming emerging markets and the global economy. We would not have made the kind of progress on the fullest possible accounting of American POWs and MIAs that allowed us to recognize Vietnam. We would not have gained the indefinite extension of the nuclear Non-Proliferation Treaty—the most important barrier against the spread of nuclear weapons. And North Korea could be building nuclear bombs.

The lesson is clear. If we lead, we can sustain the momentum that defeated communism, freed us from the danger of nuclear war, and unfurled freedom's flag around the world. Our strength is a blessing, not a burden. President Clinton is determined to use it wisely and decisively.

Our strength simply cannot be maintained on the cheap. And yet for a year now, the President and I have been fighting those forces in Congress who would cut our foreign affairs budget so deeply that we would have to draw back from our leadership—closing important embassies, shutting down peacekeeping, and self-destructively slashing our international programs. These are not responsible proposals. They would weaken America precisely when we must remain strong, precisely when other nations are looking to us for leadership. They betray a lack of appreciation for what America has accomplished in the last 50 years and a lack of confidence that our great nation can shape the future.

The recent shutdown of the U.S. Government was particularly troubling to me because it eroded our international reputation for reliability and integrity. In my recent travels abroad, I have been struck by the far-reaching consequences of the shutdown. For leaders and ordinary citizens in many parts of the world, it seemed as if the most powerful nation in the world was closing for business. Our failure to pay our bills and our employees was conduct not worthy of a great nation. It must not happen again.

Three weeks ago, I was described in the pages of Newsweek as a "true believer that America must be involved in the world." I plead guilty. I came of age after World War II, in the years when our leaders made the investments whose benefits all of us are reaping today. I am not a politician. But I do have a bias: for the kind of foreign policy that makes America a reliable and principled leader—a bias for a foreign policy that projects America's unique purpose and strength. I hope that every candidate who aspires to the Presidency will keep these important guideposts in mind.

Our commitment to provide leadership is the first of the central principles guiding our foreign policy that I outlined here last year. A second principle I enunciated then is the need to strengthen the institutions that provide an enduring basis for global peace and prosperity. These institutions, such as the United Nations, NATO, and the World Bank, help us share the burdens and costs of leadership. This year, a top priority will be working with Congress to meet our financial obligations to the UN as it undertakes an essential program of reform.

A third principle is that support for democracy and human rights reflects our ideals and reinforces our interests. Our dedication to universal values is a vital source of America's authority and credibility. We simply cannot lead without it. Our interests are most secure in a world where accountable government strengthens stability and where the rule of law protects both political rights and free market economies. That is why we have provided such strong support for courageous reforms in nations such as South Africa, Mexico, and the new democracies of Central Europe. That is why we are so pleased that there have been 16 inaugurations following free elections in this hemisphere in the three years we have been in office. This year, another important goal will be to help the War Crimes Tribunals establish accountability in the former Yugoslavia and Rwanda for two of the greatest tragedies of this decade.

A fourth principle is the critical importance of constructive relations with the great powers. These nations—our allies in Europe and Japan, as well as Russia and China—have the greatest ability to affect our security and prosperity.

In the last few years, some have said that the United States and Europe would inevitably drift apart. We have proved them wrong. Our common action in Bosnia has dramatically reinforced the transatlantic alliance and has opened new prospects for lasting European security cooperation. And the New Transatlantic Agenda agreed by the United States and the European Union in Madrid last month will not only expand our economic ties but enhance coordination on political and security challenges around the world.

With Japan, we are also putting each pillar of our alliance—security, economic, and political—on a sound basis. A year-long review of our relationship, which Joe Nye led with Assistant Secretary Winston Lord, has revitalized our security ties. We have reached 20 market access agreements, which have contributed to the recent sharp decline in our bilateral trade deficit.

We have also pursued our interest in strengthening our cooperation with Russia and China, at a time when both countries are undergoing difficult transitions. From the beginning of his Administration, President

Clinton has recognized that only by engaging with Russia could we protect our national interests. Our strategy has produced concrete benefits for the security of the American people. We have achieved massive reductions in nuclear arsenals and made nuclear materials more secure. By working with Russia, we have advanced our goals of peace in Bosnia and the Middle East.

Of course, it is easy to enumerate our differences with Russia, such as on nuclear cooperation with Iran and the war in Chechnya. This week's events provide more evidence that the current military approach in Chechnya will only deepen that war. The cycle of violence can end only through negotiations. But as I have said before, I do not have the luxury of making a list of differences with Russia and then walking away. My job is to build areas of agreement and to develop policies to manage our differences.

Back in 1993 in my first major speech as Secretary of State, I observed that Russia's struggle to transform itself would be long and hard and that success was by no means assured. That remains my judgment today. On the plus side, four years into the post-Soviet period, Russia's economy is increasingly governed by market principles. Free elections, unthinkable a few years ago, are becoming a fact of life. But Russia has not yet overcome the ruinous legacy of seven decades of communism—a legacy visible in crime, corruption, and poverty.

Recent events reflect troubling signs of Russian reform under strain. The Russian people face an important choice in the June presidential election. In the final analysis, only they can choose their leaders and determine their future. Our obligation—the American obligation—is to promote democratic values and democratic institutions and to pursue our national interests at all times.

When I meet with new Russian Foreign Minister Primakov, I will tell him that the United States is determined to continue working with Russia on the many common challenges we face. I will, however, make it clear that Russia's integration with the institutions of the West, which is in our mutual interest, depends on Russia's willingness to abide by international norms and to stay on the path of reform.

Turning to China, we also have a profound stake in helping to ensure that that powerful nation pursues its modernization in ways that contribute to the overall security and prosperity of the region—for our own sake and in the interest of our key allies and friends. That is why we are pursuing a strategy of engagement. It is designed to integrate China into the international community and to enhance our cooperation on such common problems as the North Korean nuclear program, drug trafficking, and alien smuggling.

We continue to have important differences with China on such issues as human rights, proliferation, and trade. In recent months, we have come through a rocky period in our relations with China. The United States is ready to restore positive momentum to our relationship. We have reaffirmed our "one-China" policy, and we reject the short-sighted counsel of those who seek to isolate or contain China. China's President has said that his country, too, seeks a positive relationship. Let me be clear: The United States will do its part, but if we are to build a lasting, productive relationship, China has a responsibility to take meaningful steps to address areas of our concern and to respect internationally accepted principles.

In the coming year, we will give special emphasis to three main objectives: first, pursuing peace in regions of vital interest to the United States; second, confronting the new transnational security threats; and third, promoting open markets and prosperity.

A year ago, the war in Bosnia was the greatest unresolved problem we faced. Nothing is yet assured in Bosnia, of course. But by joining the use of force to diplomacy, we have transformed a situation some considered hopeless into one in which rebuilding, reconciliation, and justice are all possible. The President's visit to our troops last week reminded us again of the uncommon spirit and confidence they bring to their mission.

The peace agreement we forged in Dayton means that we can look beyond four years of horror—the concentration camps, the ethnic cleansing, the hunger and death. In 1996, our immediate challenge is to implement the military and civilian aspects of the Dayton Agreement. We expect all parties to comply fully with their obligations under that carefully negotiated agreement. It is important to recognize that success in Bosnia will also have broad implications for our goal of an integrated Europe at peace. Our actions in Bosnia have proven that NATO is here to stay as the guarantor of transatlantic security. Without NATO's action, it is clear this war would continue today.

The very nature of the coalition we have forged and are leading in Bosnia has historic implications. This is the first time that soldiers from every power and region of Europe will serve in the same military operation. Russians and Lithuanians; Greeks and Turks; Poles and Ukrainians; British, Germans, and French have joined with Americans and Canadians to share the same risks under the same flag to achieve the same noble goal. As we help overcome the divisions of Bosnia, we also help overcome the division of Europe itself.

The mission in Bosnia will give some of our new partners in the Partnership for Peace a chance to show that they can meet the challenges of membership in an enlarged NATO alliance. The process of enlargement is already making NATO a force for stability and democracy in the east. We have made it clear to our partners that to gain NATO membership, they must consolidate democratic reforms, place their armed forces under firm civilian control, and resolve disputes with their neighbors.

It is in Central and Eastern Europe that the greatest threats to European security—ethnic conflict, proliferation, and poverty—must be faced. That is why it would be irresponsible to lock out half of Europe from the structures that ensure security and prosperity on the continent. That is why the European Union is moving forward with its own plans to add members. NATO enlargement should proceed on roughly a parallel track.

We recognize that as Russia redefines its international role, NATO enlargement must proceed in a gradual, deliberate, and transparent way. But Russia should understand that the alliance with which it is working so closely in Bosnia does not threaten its security. Indeed, we continue to encourage Russia to construct a long-term, special relationship with NATO. In the Middle East, American leadership is also indispensable. Today, for the first time in half a century, we stand on the threshold of ending the Arab-Israeli conflict. A comprehensive peace between Israel and its immediate neighbors and, indeed, with the entire Arab world, is no longer a dream, but a realistic possibility.

I have just returned from my 16th trip to the region. Last week I was with King Hussein of Jordan on the day he dedicated a trauma unit to the late Prime Minister Rabin; it's hard to believe, but that was in a hospital in Tel Aviv. Few events more vividly capture how much the landscape of the region has changed. What is more, in just two days, almost 1 million Palestinians will vote in the first free elections in the West Bank and Gaza.

Now we must work to complete the circle of peace in the Middle East. The key lies in achieving a breakthrough between Israel and Syria.

Both sides believe the United States is critical to this effort. Under our auspices, Israel and Syria are now holding intensive negotiations on Maryland's eastern shore. Although there is much work still to be done, we are crossing important thresholds and we seek an agreement in 1996. The United States is determined to help complete this historic task.

We will also continue our efforts to resolve conflicts and build security in other regions. We will pursue initiatives in places such as Northern Ireland, Haiti, Cyprus, Angola, Burundi, Peru, and Ecuador. We will strengthen the foundations of peace and security in the Asia-Pacific region by deepening our security cooperation with our treaty allies, and through our participation in the very promising ASEAN Regional Forum. And in this hemisphere, we will build on the new level of political cooperation we achieved at the Summit of the Americas in Miami.

Our second major area of focus this year is to continue to take on new challenges to global security. As the President emphasized in a landmark UN speech last October, transnational threats such as proliferation, terrorism, international crime, drugs, and environmental damage threaten all of us in our interdependent world.

We will continue working to stop the spread of weapons of mass destruction—the gravest potential threat to the United States and our allies. Thirty-three years ago, the nuclear powers took what President Kennedy called a "step backward from the shadows of war" by signing the Limited Test Ban Treaty. Now we must complete a comprehensive test ban treaty in time to sign it this year. And this year we must ratify the Chemical Weapons Convention.

We must also lock in deep reductions in the nuclear arsenals of the United States and the countries of the former Soviet Union. I urge the Senate and the Russian Duma to ratify the START II Treaty, which will remove an additional 5,000 warheads from the arsenals of our two countries.

Our regional non-proliferation efforts are also vital. It is critical that North Korea's nuclear program stays shut down and on the way to the scrap heap. And pariah states such as Iraq, Iran, and Libya must be stopped in their efforts to acquire weapons of mass destruction. The information that UN inspectors have uncovered on Iraq's biological program is chilling. It is now clear that Saddam Hussein possessed biological weapons and was on the verge of using them against civilians in the

Gulf War. These revelations are an urgent reminder that Saddam remains a menace and that sanctions against Iraq must be maintained.

President Clinton has also put the fight against international criminals, terrorists, and drug traffickers at the center of our foreign policy. We are determined to continue our drive to put such international predators out of business. We have taken unprecedented steps against the Cali cartel, and many of its leaders are now behind bars. We will continue to deny terrorists and drug kingpins access to their assets; we will put decisive pressure on governments that tolerate such organizations; and we will step up operations attacking crime and drugs at their source.

Protecting our fragile environment also has profound long-range importance for our country, and in 1996 we will strive to fully integrate our environmental goals into our diplomacy—something that has never been done before. We will seek further reductions in greenhouse gases and press for Senate approval of conventions on biodiversity and the Law of the Sea. Working closely with the Vice President, I have also focused on how we can make greater use of environmental initiatives to promote larger strategic and economic goals. That means, for example, encouraging joint water projects in the Middle East, increasing environmental cooperation with our global partners, and helping our environmental industries capture a larger share of a $400-billion global market.

The third element of our agenda is to build on the economic achievements that will be a lasting legacy of the Clinton Administration. President Clinton's personal leadership on NAFTA, the Uruguay Round, APEC, and the Summit of the Americas has made the United States the hub of an increasingly open global trading system. This year, our watchword is implementation—making sure that the trade commitments and agreements we have reached produce concrete opportunities so that American companies and workers can compete abroad on a level playing field. In the Asia-Pacific region through APEC, with the European Union through the transatlantic marketplace, and in this hemisphere through the Miami process, we are removing barriers to trade and investment and opening markets for U.S. exports. We also remain committed to obtaining fast-track authority to negotiate Chile's accession to NAFTA. As this presidential election year begins, we are hearing once again from those who preach the dangerous gospel of protection and isolation. America and the world went down that road in 1930s, and our mistake fueled the Great Depression and helped set the stage for the Second World War. Shutting America off from the world would be just as reckless today as it was six decades ago. As President Clinton said at the beginning of his Administration, "we must compete, not retreat."

Ladies and gentlemen, everywhere I go, I find that the nations of the world look to America as a source of principled and reliable leadership. They see American soldiers bridging rivers and moving mountains to help peace take hold in Bosnia. They see us working for peace in the Middle East and for security in Korea. They see us negotiating trade agreements so that every nation can find reward in emerging markets. They see the most powerful nation on earth standing up for persecuted peoples everywhere, because we believe it is right and because those who struggle for freedom represent the future.

The world sees us as an optimistic people, motivated by a broad view of our interests and driven by a long view of our potential. They follow us because they understand that America's fight for peace and freedom is the world's fight. At the end of the American century, President Clinton is determined that we continue to act in the highest traditions of our nation and our people.

The President's answer to the voices of isolationism is clear. We can no more isolate our nation from the world than we can isolate our families from our neighborhoods, or our neighborhoods from our cities. As a global power with global interests, retreat is not a responsible option for the United States. We must continue to lead. If we do, the end of this millennium can mark the start of a second American century.

Thank you very much.

TWENTY-SIX

A New Era for the Americas

The transformation of Latin America by the mid-1990s was almost as profound and sweeping as that of Eastern Europe. No longer was the region known for military dictatorships, civil strife, and economic despair. Democracy had truly taken root, peace prevailed, and economic reform was the rule of the day. This transformation had occurred quietly, without much fanfare and without a dramatic event like the collapse of the Berlin Wall. It had been made possible by the failure of the authoritarian regimes to deal with economic and political issues, and by the growing intolerance of human rights abuses.

The December 1994 Summit of the Americas in Miami symbolized the enormous political and economic progress that had been made. Hosted by President Clinton, it brought together all 34 democratic heads of state in the hemisphere in an effort to consolidate that progress and sustain the momentum. The leaders developed an action plan to enhance cooperation and made commitments to 23 policy goals, from furthering open trade to stemming crime and reducing corruption. However, what was perhaps the summit's greatest accomplishment was less tangible: it fundamentally transformed the way the United States and other nations approached hemispheric relations. Old ideological arguments and recriminations were replaced by a spirit of cooperation and partnership. Indeed, the goals agreed upon were so ambitious and comprehensive that subsequent letdowns and disappointments were almost inevitable. The hesitation of Congress in renewing President Clinton's "fast track" authority was among these disappointments.[1] Nevertheless, the overall mood of inter-American relations has continued to be upbeat.

I understood firsthand how significant this new "spirit of Miami" was. My first foray to the region as Deputy Secretary of State in the Carter Administration had reflected the considerable scratchiness that then characterized our hemispheric relations. In March 1977, I sought to dissuade the Brazilians from signing a major deal with West Germany to construct nuclear reactors in Brazil. We were concerned that Brazil might use this technology to build nuclear weapons, but we also regarded the deal as commercially impractical. In meetings in Brasilia, I found the Brazilians highly suspicious, at times even hostile. It seemed that regardless of its merits, any advice the "Big Brother" of the North might give would be viewed as U.S. heavy-handedness. The Brazilians went ahead with the agreement, but the costs were enormous and the delays lengthy.

A weeklong visit I made to Latin America in 1996 aimed to bring the hemisphere's dramatic transformation into sharper focus and to symbolize our commitment to the region. It had been eight years since a Secretary of State had visited South America, and I was anxious to show our appreciation for the progress that had been made. Though the trip's primary purpose was not to negotiate any specific issues or offer any new initiatives, it did give us a chance to build on the momentum of the Miami summit by working with the Latin American leaders to bolster regional stability, economic reform, and democratic institutions. Together with Thomas F. ("Mack") McLarty, the former White House Chief of Staff who had become the President's Special Adviser for Latin America and had played a major role in Miami, I visited five success stories—El Salvador, Chile, Argentina, Brazil, and Trinidad and Tobago.

The day before I began my trip, an outrageous incident occurred that, ironically, furthered our goals of highlighting the region's transformation and promoting cooperation. On February 24, Cuba shot down two small U.S. civilian planes, resulting in four deaths. The planes were operated

---

[1]Fast track authority, granted to every President since Gerald Ford, authorizes the President to negotiate trade agreements with other nations on the understanding that Congress must accept or reject those agreements without amending or attaching conditions to them.

by Brothers to the Rescue, a group of anti-Castro Cubans living in Miami. The flights were intended to boost the morale of those in Cuba who opposed the repressive rule of President Fidel Castro, to seek help for refugees fleeing Cuba by boat, and occasionally to drop leaflets on Havana. Because the planes were over international waters and unarmed when attacked, they presented no threat to Cuban security, and the attack blatantly violated international law. President Clinton strongly condemned it, citing it as "further evidence that Havana has become more desperate in its efforts to deny freedom to the people of Cuba."[2]

In a White House meeting the day I left for the region, we decided that one of my main tasks would be to rally our Latin American colleagues to condemn Cuba. The timing of the incident could not have been worse for Castro. His flagrant act gave us the perfect opening to strengthen the regional consensus against his regime.

The Cuba situation dominated my public and private discussions during the first few days of the trip, which got off to a good start at a mini-summit in El Salvador.[3] This conference was originally intended as an opportunity for us to discuss economic and political issues with the Central American Presidents, but instead those attending focused much attention on Cuba. Our Cuban policy has never been popular in the hemisphere as a whole, and some of the leaders were initially hesitant to condemn Castro publicly. However, El Salvadoran President Armado Calderon Sol did a superb job in helping me persuade his colleagues to condemn the unwarranted shootdown. At the press conference after the meeting, he made a strong statement on behalf of the assembled leaders, supporting our position without qualification or equivocation. This meeting was also notable for candid discussions of the scourge of international crime and

[2]This incident dashed our hopes for a comprehensive dialogue with the Cuban government. In 1995, we had been slightly encouraged by hints that the Castro regime might be moderating its repressive policies, especially in the economic field. And, thanks to skillful diplomacy by Peter Tarnoff, we had worked out a migration agreement under which 20,000 Cubans could legally emigrate to the United States each year, and the Cuban government would discourage others from attempting to make the dangerous boat trip to the mainland. We even came to the point of discussing a speech proposing a broader dialogue. But the shooting down of the unarmed plane and other new repressive steps made this a speech that was never given.

[3]Attending this gathering were Honduran President Roberto Reina, Belizean Prime Minister Manuel Amadeo Esquivel, Costa Rican President Jose Maria Figueres, and Guatemalan Minister of Government Rodolfo Mendoza.

of the problems created by the historic antiextradition attitudes of many Latin American countries.

My bilateral meeting with Calderon Sol highlighted the remarkable distance El Salvador had traveled since the end of its 12-year civil war in 1992. The war had ravaged the country, claimed tens of thousands of lives, and produced grotesque atrocities. While all of the countries in the region had made significant progress in strengthening democracy and human rights, El Salvador deserved special credit for overcoming its recent past and embarking on a program of reconstruction, in which the United States had invested $300 million. I found Calderon Sol a courageous leader, willing to challenge old orthodoxies and dedicated to moving his country beyond simply implementing the peace to focusing on economic growth and development.

The positive momentum continued in Santiago, Chile, where I met with President Eduardo Frei and Foreign Minister Jose Miguel Insulza. The Chileans, who had recently normalized relations with Havana, were chagrined about Castro's action and supported our condemnation of it. On the bilateral agenda, our meetings focused on economics and expanding NAFTA. The NAFTA issue had dominated U.S.-Chilean relations since the Miami summit. We had been unable to obtain fast track authority from Congress to include Chile in a NAFTA-like arrangement, despite the fact that, as I cabled President Clinton, Chile "is confident and robust, reflecting a series of economic miracles and solid . . . steady progress toward democracy." The Chileans were upset that we still had no free trade agreement with them. Having been politically exposed by relying on U.S. statements about early inclusion of Chile in a NAFTA-like agreement, President Frei felt somewhat burned. I reiterated our commitment to seek fast track authority in 1997, but accepted the Chileans' judgment that public reference to specific deadlines or timetables would be greeted with great skepticism and hence should be avoided.

Stops in Argentina and Brazil—once two of our major detractors and now two of our closest friends—were the focal points of the trip. My meetings with Presidents Carlos Menem in Buenos Aires, Fernando Henrique Cardoso in Brasilia, and their senior ministers made it clear that these men were talented leaders who had chosen able cabinet members. Their governments created the basis for solid economic growth and bolstered cooperation on such multilateral issues as international peacekeeping and environmental protection. Menem and Cardoso, both of whom had been persecuted by military regimes, exemplified the dramatic transformation of Latin America and offered a refreshing contrast to the leaders with whom I had met in 1977.

In Buenos Aires, Menem expressed "solidarity" with us on the Cuba issue and told me to convey to President Clinton that Argentina would always be on the U.S. side. We also discussed UN peacekeeping, nuclear proliferation, our support for Argentina's membership in the OECD, and cooperation in space (NASA Chief Daniel Goldin joined us for these meetings). Without hesitation, Menem said we could count on him to supply troops for UN peacekeeping missions, including police for Bosnia. Later, to underscore U.S.-Argentinean economic ties, the respected Economic Minister, Domingo Cavallo, and I visited the massive new Wal-Mart store in Buenos Aires. Open for less than a year, this had already become one of the most popular retail outlets in the country, doing as much as $1 million a day in sales and using locally made products whenever feasible.[4]

My two days in Brazil were a firm reminder to me that given its size and strength, Brazil is *the* critical regional player. It is the world's fifth-largest country, with a population greater than that of the rest of South America combined, and its tenth-largest economy, with more U.S. investment than any other country in Latin America. Clearly we could not build the kind of hemisphere envisioned in Miami without Brazil's active involvement.

Under Cardoso's leadership, Brazil had abandoned the confrontational non-aligned attitude I had witnessed in 1977. Cardoso had traveled extensively, exuding confidence and vision, steering Brazil toward closer ties with the West, and encouraging it to play a greater role in the UN. Thanks to his efforts, U.S.-Brazilian relations were at an all-time high. He sought to work with us on several matters on which we had often disagreed in the past—environmental protection, non-proliferation,

---

[4]This Wal-Mart visit was also intended to send a signal to the American people about the importance of remaining engaged in the global economy. The 1996 presidential campaign was under way at home, and Republicans like Pat Buchanan were stirring up anxieties about open trade and foreign investments. In a statement at the Wal-Mart, I said, "We're hearing again from those who say the United States should erect walls and shut off from the world. Let me assure you that we will not do that. As President Clinton has said, 'we must reach out and not retreat.'"

counternarcotics, and space technology. My personal relationship with Brazil's able Foreign Minister, Luis Felipe Lampreia, was among the closest I developed during my tenure, and we worked constructively together on many issues.

The speech I gave on March 2 before the American Chamber of Commerce in Sao Paulo aimed to capture the spirit of my trip generally and the importance we attached to Brazil specifically. I wanted to reiterate our commitment to the Miami process and regional cooperation, and to emphasize the hopefulness with which we approached the Americas. I touched on all of the important issues I had addressed privately throughout the week—condemning Cuba, expanding economic relations, promoting free trade, and cooperating on transnational challenges. And, repeating something President Cardoso had said to me, I called Brazil "a natural partner of the United States."[5]

My stop in Brazil, especially a fascinating visit to the National Institute for Amazon Research in Manaus, on the Amazon River, brought home to me the importance of protecting the South American environment. The river and its surrounding rainforest harbor an astounding array of flora and fauna, exemplifying the biodiversity vital to its ecosystems.[6] My remarks at the Institute, Brazil's premier center for scientific research on Amazon ecology, stressed our commitment to carrying out the October 1995 U.S.-Brazil Common Agenda on the Environment. My exchanges there generated some of the ideas I would outline in a speech the following month at Stanford University on the relationship between our national interests and the environment.

After a brief stop in Trinidad and Tobago, where I emphasized cooperation on drug enforcement by turning two speedboats over to Trinida-

---

[5]I spoke before a crowd of more than 700 on a Saturday—one executive observed that "anybody who is anybody in Sao Paulo is here today"—and my remarks were warmly received. The occasion was spiced by a loud protest by two pro-Cuba demonstrators, who somehow got into the long dining room and unfurled banners about thirty feet from my podium. They were booed loudly by the crowd and were quickly escorted out.

[6]Seeing the Amazon was a truly remarkable experience. I was particularly impressed by the famous "Meeting of the Waters," where the clear black waters of the Rio Negro join the murky brown Solimoes River to form the Amazon itself.

dian officials to use in catching drug runners, I returned to Washington.[7] Overall, the contrast between this trip and my first official venture to Latin America in 1977 could not have been more stark. Hemispheric unity was taking shape. I went home convinced that our Summit of the Americas initiative was alive and well, but that, like every new effort, it required constant and careful nurturing.[8] Sometimes nations, like individuals, fail to pay attention to the opportunities closest at hand. While the Administration had justifiably spent much of its time during the last three years dealing with front-burner issues like China, Bosnia, and the Middle East, the trip reminded me of the enormous opportunity in the Americas. One lesson learned, I told President Clinton, was that "we should never forget to pay attention to our savvy and powerful friends in the hemisphere as well as the trouble spots in the world."

Shaping a New World: U.S. and Brazilian Leadership in a Democratic, Prosperous Hemisphere

Address Before the American Chamber of Commerce,

Sao Paulo, March 2, 1996

In the mid-19th century, the famous English explorer Sir Richard Francis Burton wrote that "Hospitality is the greatest delay in Brazilian travel . . . you may do what you like; you may stay for a month, but not for a day." I decided to take his advice. That is why I am spending two days in Brazil.

I am delighted to be in Sao Paulo, the largest city in South America— "the city that can't stop." Millions of Americans would feel right at home here in a city that has the scale of my home city of Los Angeles, the

[7]My visit to Port of Spain, Trinidad, was cut short by a few hours because of a terrorist bombing in Tel Aviv. Given the symbolic importance of the Trinidad stop, I resisted suggestions to skip it entirely; however, after morning sessions with leaders there, I flew back to Washington to attend a White House emergency meeting on the Middle East.

[8]The second Summit of the Americas is being held in Santiago, Chile, in April 1998.

power of Chicago, the pace of New York, and the beat—perhaps I should also say the heat—of Miami. The industrious people and innovative businesses of Sao Paulo are driving this country and this continent to the forefront of the global economy.

It is an honor to address the American Chamber of Commerce of Sao Paulo. You have helped level the playing field for foreign investors and helped build a more open economy. You are giving back something of value to the people of Brazil. Your "Quality in Teaching" project in this city's poor neighborhoods is a model for those trying to expand opportunity everywhere.

I have come to Latin America at a defining moment in our shared history. Never before has this hemisphere been more free or more prosperous. Where once country after country was subjected to military rule, today our hemisphere proudly counts 34 democracies among its 35 nations. Where once economy after economy was caught in the grip of closed markets, choking debt, and hyperinflation, today Latin America and the Caribbean is the second fastest-growing region in the world. Never before have so many of its people enjoyed the liberties and opportunities of democracy.

Fifteen months ago at the Summit of the Americas in Miami, we inaugurated a new era. Already the spirit of Miami has become shorthand for the new relationship based on cooperation and mutual respect between the United States and its Latin American and Caribbean neighbors. We simply must sustain our momentum. That is why the United States supports holding a second Summit of the Americas in late 1997 or early 1998.

At Miami, our leaders charted a bold path to the future. Together, we are strengthening the democratic values and institutions that form the bedrock of our new hemispheric community. We are aiming to narrow inequality and expand opportunity. We are protecting the environment. And we are setting our sights on an ambitious goal: negotiating a Free Trade Area of the Americas by the year 2005.

Since the Miami summit, a series of events threatened our progress and tested our resolve. A little more than one year later, we can say that we are passing the test with flying colors.

When Mexico was plunged into a financial crisis, President Zedillo acted boldly to stabilize the economy without reverting to the discredited policies of the past. President Clinton moved courageously when he mobilized the United States and the international financial institutions to stand by Mexico in its time of need. Here in Brazil and in Argentina, President Cardoso and President Menem reacted to Mexico's crisis by staying the course of economic reform.

When armed conflict broke out between Peru and Ecuador, Brazil acted quickly with Argentina, Chile, and the United States to help end the fighting and preserve the remarkable peace of our hemisphere. In Haiti, despite the skeptics' doubts, free and fair elections went forward for both the parliament and the presidency.

In short, 1995 was a year that proved the durability, not the fragility, of positive change in the Americas. But we still have important work to do together. Today, our hemisphere faces a dual challenge. Within our nations, our task is to strengthen the foundations of democracy and open markets. Among our nations, our task is to harness the collective power of our shared values to meet the new challenges that transcend the borders of this region and reach around the world. Critical to this effort is a dynamic, democratic Brazil. Few nations face the future with greater opportunities or greater responsibilities.

Together, Brazil and the United States share a special ability to help meet the challenges within and among our nations. We are the largest democracies in the New World. We are two of its three largest economies. Our countries embrace immense resources, mighty rivers, and vast lands. We have a common interest in opening markets and expanding the benefits of growth. We have a common stake in resolving conflicts, in preventing the spread of weapons of mass destruction, and in protecting the environment.

These common goals are rooted in our history and shared values. The promise of boundless opportunity has brought immigrants of every color and creed to our shores from every corner of the globe. We share a commitment to safeguarding human rights, ensuring the rule of law, and extending liberty. As President Cardoso has said, today Brazil is "a natural partner of the United States." Perhaps we have not been as close to one another as we should have been, but that is changing. Now we have the chance to combine our strength and form a strategic partnership.

Of course, Brazil's first obligation is to its people, and its greatest recent achievement has been to return democracy to its citizens. Now Brazil is demonstrating that democracy works—that good governance can support economic stability and advance social justice.

President Cardoso has used his office to advance his life-long commitment to the cause of human rights. By compensating the families of those who "disappeared" during the long years of military rule, Brazil is redressing injustices of the past. Honoring those who fight for human rights sends a powerful message as well. In the examples of Cardinal Arns and the movement to protect street children, Brazilians and South Americans can find hope for the future.

As President Clinton has said, "when historians look back on our times, they will marvel at the speed with which democracy has swept across the entire Americas." Through collective action in Haiti, we demonstrated that we are prepared to take forceful steps to preserve democracy in the hemisphere. Democracy is ascendant across the region except in Cuba, where in the past week the regime in Havana has once again shown its true colors.

After traveling across Latin America this past week, let me say this to the leaders of Cuba: In defending your brutal and illegal actions of last Saturday, you are alone; in refusing to allow the Cuban people the democracy and human rights they desire and deserve, you are alone. I am confident that one day soon the people of Cuba will join the irresistible tide to freedom and prosperity that has swept our hemisphere.

We thank Brazil and the other democratic nations of our hemisphere, as well as the members of the UN Security Council, for their support in deploring the shootdown of the two defenseless American aircraft. Today the family and friends of the victims are traveling to the site of the tragedy for a commemorative ceremony. My government is doing all it can to see that the memorial service is peaceful and safe—and Cuba must do the same. Be assured that the United States will act to protect the rights and liberties of its citizens. We will not allow the reckless actions of one country to threaten peace in our neighborhood.

Just as we must stand together against the enemies of democracy, we must join together to meet the new challenges that threaten us. The Summit of the Americas recognized that threats such as weapons proliferation, terrorism, international crime, and narcotics trafficking have grown more dangerous in a world grown closer. As President Clinton said in his UN General Assembly speech last fall, "These forces jeopardize the global trend toward peace and freedom, undermine fragile new democracies, sap the strength from developing countries, and threaten our efforts to build a safer, more prosperous world."

No country can afford to sit on the sidelines, and no country can meet these challenges on its own. Now we have a new weapon with which to confront them. The weapon is unity. Brazil can play a leadership role in galvanizing that unity in this hemisphere and around the globe.

A decade ago, Brazil and Argentina were pursuing programs that increased the risk of nuclear proliferation. The decision to turn away from this dangerous course stands as a powerful rejection of those who think that the spread of weapons of mass destruction is somehow inevitable. This year we will work with Brazil to complete a comprehensive test ban treaty. And I urge Brazil, in the same vein, to sign the nuclear Non-Proliferation Treaty.

Brazil and Argentina are helping to stabilize the region by their prudent approach to modernizing their armed forces and avoiding a conventional arms race. By maintaining peaceful borders with its 10 neighbors, Brazil has long been a force for peace and security on this continent. Brazil and the United States are working together with the other Rio guarantors to help finally achieve a lasting settlement between Peru and Ecuador. Ending this dispute will take us toward the important goal proposed at last year's defense ministerial meeting: resolving all remaining border disputes in the Americas.

Brazil and the other nations of the Americas are helping to extend the benefits of peace to regions beyond our hemisphere. Two days ago in Buenos Aires, I was honored to review Argentine peacekeepers bound for duty in the former Yugoslavia. From Brazilian soldiers in Mozambique and Angola to Uruguayan forces in Cambodia, to Chilean participation in Northern Iraq and Bosnia, we in the Americas are doing our part.

Closer to home, we are bringing new force to the hemisphere's fight against terrorism. Next month in Lima, the members of the Organization of American States will convene to adopt the first hemisphere-wide plan of action to combat it.

We have scored important victories in the continuing fight against another scourge—the drug traffickers. The United States is cooperating closely with our summit partners to implement a comprehensive counternarcotics campaign strategy as we agreed in Miami. As a result of the meeting last year in Buenos Aires, we are changing laws to prevent criminals and drug traffickers from laundering their ill-gotten gains.

President Clinton has placed a high priority on attacking the menace of drugs. In this fight, we value the cooperation of friends like Brazil and Mexico. And by identifying those who fail to meet their responsibility, we seek to create incentives to do better in the future. That is what the certification process and the certification decisions made by the President yesterday are all about.

President Clinton's appointment of Gen. Barry McCaffrey to spearhead our counternarcotics campaign reinforces our determination to cooperate with all the nations of Latin America and the Caribbean. As the former U.S. Commander in this region, General McCaffrey is well-positioned to lead my country's fight. And we will intensify the pressure against narcotics use at home where our fight against drugs must also be won.

In all of these areas—stemming proliferation, maintaining security, and combating drugs and terrorism—Brazil has a critical role to play. But there is no area in which Brazil has greater opportunities or responsibilities for leadership than in harnessing the full weight of this economy to achieve hemispheric prosperity. You have the chance to do this because of President Cardoso's commitment to economic reform. Brazil, like Argentina and Chile, is privatizing and decentralizing. It has stabilized its currency and reduced inflation, cut its debt and restored growth, and expanded its trade and welcomed foreign investment.

The economic transformation of Latin America and the Caribbean has caught the imagination of the world. Achieving this hemisphere's economic promise requires a new generation of leaders determined to bring the benefits of integration and growth home to their people. These leaders are men and women who understand the future, who embrace change, and who know that the private sector and open markets are the engines of growth. There are few better examples than Presidents Cardoso and Clinton: This region is blessed with many such leaders, several of whom hosted me on this trip—President Menem of Argentina, President Frei of Chile, and President Calderon Sol of El Salvador.

From the day he took office, President Clinton has placed job creation, open markets, and fair trade at the center of our economic strategy. He fought to enact NAFTA and to complete the GATT Uruguay Round. He brought together the leaders of the Asia-Pacific region to forge a bold commitment to open trade. He and the leaders of the European Union have committed to build a new Transatlantic Marketplace. At the Miami summit, he helped forge a hemisphere-wide consensus to negotiate a Free Trade Area of the Americas that will create a $12-trillion market of 850 million consumers. His aim is clear: to make this hemisphere an even more dynamic hub of the global economy and to open markets, create jobs, and lift living standards.

With this task ahead, the great nations of the Americas must step forward. Brazil has already demonstrated leadership in the movement toward integration through the MERCOSUR customs union, an important building block toward our goal of region-wide open trade. Now Brazil should join us in energizing the effort to achieve a Free Trade Area of the Americas by 2005. All the Summit nations need to agree on a plan that will enable us to begin genuine negotiations to reach that goal. That plan should be comprehensive, and it should include the new priority areas of government procurement, services, competition policy, and intellectual property rights.

As you well know, intellectual property rights are among the essential rules of the road in an open and competitive global economy. The passage this week of modern patent legislation by the Brazilian Senate will help attract investment. Each summit partner must do its part.

At home in the United States, we are hearing from those who would shut us off from the rest of the world. Let there be no doubt: The Clinton Administration will continue to engage the world. We will fight for open and fair trade and for the jobs it produces. The United States, as the President said last week, will continue to "reach out, not retreat . . . to break down walls, not build them up." The next century offers us the spectacular panorama of growth as we break down barriers across the Americas, across the Pacific, and across the Atlantic. Our responsibilities have never been greater. We will meet them.

All of you know that the private sector must play an essential role in making real this vision of growth and integration. Your investment decisions, marketing strategies, and technological innovations together break down barriers between our economies every day. We appreciate and need your advice and support to ensure that every step we take has practical, concrete relevance to business. Without your intensive involvement in the Miami process, we will not be able to meet our goals on the road to 2005.

To do your part, you need a stable and open business environment. When you enter a new market, you have a right to know that the law is the law, and it will be upheld. We welcome the progress underway throughout the hemisphere to remove the stain of bribery and corruption in all its dastardly forms.

Economic growth cannot be blind to the needs of our people or our planet. "Growth," as President Cardoso has said, cannot be sustained "without social justice or if it destroys the balance with nature."

Across the continent, your nations are realizing that no group should have a monopoly on the benefits of growth. Over the last five years, hundreds of thousands of Chileans have risen from poverty with the help of programs designed to create microenterprises and jobs. Here in Brazil, President Cardoso's commitment to investing in education holds the promise of a brighter future for this country's children.

Next year marks the fifth anniversary of the Rio Earth Summit. This is an appropriate time to rededicate ourselves to achieving the summit's essential goals for sustainable development.

We know that we cannot sustain economic growth if we deplete our finite resources. But as President Clinton has said, we do not have to accept "the false choice between development and protecting the environment." Last Tuesday in San Salvador, I met with a dedicated group of business people who are helping to solve the global problem of greenhouse gases. Their theory is simple: A better environment for the world is also a better environment for business.

Here in Sao Paulo, the public and private sectors are beginning to work together to reduce air and water pollution. Tomorrow, I will fly to Manaus on the edge of the world's largest rainforest. My visit reflects two critical imperatives that underlie our commitment: first, safeguarding precious natural resources; second, ensuring that these resources benefit our people.

In his inaugural address, President Cardoso gave voice to an abiding faith that Brazilians and Americans share. He spoke of belonging to "a generation that grew up cherishing the dream of building a Brazil that would be both democratic and developed, free and just."

Here in Brazil and across this hemisphere, that dream of the Americas is coming true. As we enter a new millennium, the New World is new once again. Together we are building that better world in which free market democracies lift the lives of their people, peacefully resolve conflicts, and work together to address daunting global threats.

In facing these challenges, the United States and Brazil have much to gain and important responsibility to bear. But I am confident that we will rise to this challenge and leave to the children of the Americas a safer, freer, and more prosperous hemisphere and world.

TWENTY-SEVEN

A Democratic and Undivided Europe

In the spring of 1996, I gave a speech laying out the Administration's vision of an undivided Europe with an expanded NATO at its heart.[1] Speaking to a Central European audience, precisely the people we wished to include in NATO, I tried to place our case in the broadest historical, moral, and strategic context. The speech marked a turning point in our policy: after it there was no doubt in Central Europe, among our allies, or in Russia that NATO expansion would take place. The decision to make this statement reflected the Administration's belief that clarity and firmness concerning the U.S. position were our best assets in managing Russia's lingering opposition to that expansion.

I delivered the speech during a trip that took me from the Middle East to cities in Europe, with a final stop in Moscow. I felt that giving the speech just before the Moscow stop would be the most forceful way to get the message across, and we considered both Prague and Warsaw as venues. The argument for Warsaw was that Poland was really at the core of the debate about NATO expansion; of the main candidates for admission, it had the most compelling claim, and Russia's angst was focused on it. Choosing Prague would also be a powerful signal, but a less provocative one. If we were going to get into an argument with

---

[1] This address established a conceptual framework for our policy in Europe, while a subsequent speech given in Stuttgart was more programmatic, drawing a road map for the months ahead (see Chapter 31).

Russia, I wanted it to be about substance, not symbols, and so we chose Prague.[2]

As it turned out, the setting was just right for our message. Because it escaped destruction in World War II, Prague has two advantages over some other Central European capitals: it is stunningly beautiful and amazingly resilient after the long Soviet occupation. In more ways than one, it is closer to Paris than to Moscow. Seeing the obvious distance that Prague was putting between its democratic present and its communist past, it was easy for us and for our traveling press to imagine the Czechs as allies and hard to imagine why this plainly European nation should be kept out of an integrated Europe.

The first part of the speech described the conflicting strains in the history of modern-day Central Europe. Nations such as the Czech Republic had been both "battlegrounds and burial grounds for Europe's great powers." But they had no less a claim than Western Europe to the traditions of democracy and tolerance that defined our transatlantic community. This portion of the speech sought to rebut the superficial argument that the whole region was mired in ancient ethnic hatreds and thus not ready for membership in Western institutions.

Next, I made the case for American involvement in Europe, drawing a contrast to British Prime Minister Neville Chamberlain's infamous dismissal of Hitler's invasion of Czechoslovakia as "a quarrel in a far-away country between people of whom we know nothing." Much of the analogy had to be implied, but I wanted the audience to consider this comment in the context of Bosnia. I made the point that American intervention in this European war was indispensable, because even the "far-away" countries matter.

Most fundamentally, the speech was a call for reuniting Europe, with NATO expansion playing a vital role. I rejected the idea of buffer zones and spheres of influence in Central Europe, an implied criticism of Russia's objections to Central European membership in Western institutions. At the same time, I reminded the more advanced Central European countries that their quest for such membership could not be a race to escape their poorer neighbors. For the first time, I suggested that the

---

[2]Being in Prague also gave me an opportunity to refer to Madeleine Albright as a "Czech woman who learned to cherish freedom in her youth and who now defends it as America's ambassador to the United Nations."

first wave of NATO expansion would not be the last, a crucial point that was to move to the center of the Administration's message after Poland, Hungary, and the Czech Republic were invited to join in July 1997.

Only a short section of the speech focused on NATO expansion itself, but this section got the most press. "Enlargement is on track, and it will happen" was the most quoted line of the speech. The point was to say clearly and forcefully that the outcome of the process was no longer in doubt. In fact, on the morning of the speech we toyed with using the word "inevitable," but decided it had a ring of arrogance about it. "Will happen" made the point just fine.

The Russia section also received considerable attention. A few days before the speech, the Duma had voted to reconstitute the Soviet Union, an action that dominated our discussions in Kiev. My remarks condemned the Duma resolution, while giving Yeltsin credit for refusing to follow it. I emphasized that although we wanted a close relationship between Russia and NATO, the ball was in Russia's court. As I had explained a year before in Bloomington, we would not isolate Russia, but it was also up to Russia not to isolate itself. NATO expansion, I stressed, would "neither determine, nor be determined, by events in Russia." Unlike some of our critics, we did not believe that NATO's actions would have a decisive impact on the future of Russian democracy, for that was up to the Russians themselves. At the same time, we made it clear that Russia would have no veto on expansion.

Predictably, the Central Europeans responded positively to the speech, but I expected a chillier reception in Moscow. Indeed, shortly after arriving there on March 21, I had a rough dinner with Russia's new Foreign Minister, Yevgeny Primakov. Having just been publicly rebuked by Yeltsin for being too "soft" on Javier Solana (the Secretary General of NATO, who had taken the lead in negotiations for a charter between Russia and NATO), Primakov complained bitterly to me about the Prague speech and intimated that it somehow represented a change in U.S. policy. I firmly responded that I had not been freelancing in the speech; it reflected the Administration's long-standing plans for NATO expansion. I took Primakov through the speech point by point, showing him our balanced approach to European integration. I had the sense, however, that regardless of what I said he was under strict instructions to criticize the speech, and he really let me have it.

I had first met Primakov in Helsinki in February 1996, soon after he had replaced Kozyrev as Russian Foreign Minister. Primakov is shrewd, pragmatic, and professional. He is a survivor at 66, with a career spanning those of Soviet and Russian leaders from Leonid Brezhnev to Boris Yeltsin. Before becoming Foreign Minister, Primakov headed the KGB. A Middle East specialist, he is perhaps most notorious for his meddlesome and unprincipled efforts to negotiate a settlement with Saddam Hussein before the Persian Gulf War began in 1991.[3] I found Primakov at ease, well prepared in discussing a comprehensive foreign policy agenda, and confident of his new position in the Yeltsin government.

Despite many of my colleagues' deep suspicions about Primakov, I nevertheless hoped to develop a constructive relationship with him. We both recognized that the personal rapport between Presidents Clinton and Yeltsin had been vital to managing overall relations, and we agreed to try to develop a similar relationship with one another. In Helsinki, we spent some time together developing five principles to observe in doing business. These were: avoiding surprises (he agreed that the December 1994 Budapest incident should not be repeated); continuing regular consultations; providing advance warning of initiatives that would affect each other's interests; fulfilling all existing commitments; and resolving differences without confrontation. That diplomats should adhere to such principles may seem basic, even obvious. However, by explicitly committing ourselves to them, Primakov and I hoped to get our relationship off on the right foot. We had many tense encounters in 1996, but I developed a grudging respect for him. I was not surprised to hear that, no doubt acting under Yeltsin's instructions, he was somewhat helpful in effecting the agreement between NATO and Russia in May 1997.

My hour-long discussion the next day with Yeltsin in the Kremlin was one of the best we had during my term as Secretary. The Russian President was clearly playing "good cop" to Primakov's "bad cop." Despite rumors of his health problems, I found Yeltsin alert, positive, and vigorous. Totally immersed in his current electoral campaign, he seemed hy-

---

[3]See Michael Beschloss and Strobe Talbott, *At the Highest Levels*, pp. 268–80 (Boston: Little, Brown, 1993); Baker, *The Politics of Diplomacy*, pp. 396–400 (New York: G. P. Putnam's Sons, 1995).

persensitive about any hint that we might be hedging on his chances. I assured him that there had been no change in President Clinton's position. However, reacting to reports that Yeltsin was considering canceling the elections scheduled for July 1996, I told him flatly that such a decision would be received negatively in the United States.

NATO expansion came up only as we walked out of our meeting. Yeltsin lightly said that I had been wise not to raise the issue. I responded that I had not done so because Primakov had provided a full statement of Russia's view the night before. My Prague speech, I told Yeltsin, was the official U.S. position.

I left Moscow with my original expectations confirmed: Russian opposition to NATO expansion was a given. To manage the issue, we had to be candid about our intentions and firm about our timetable. With the elections pending, it seemed clear that the domestic political scene would preoccupy Yeltsin and provide the context for all his policy decisions, including those on NATO.

Our firm approach on NATO enlargement was vindicated by subsequent events. Only when the Russian leaders understood that they could not derail expansion did they give serious attention to building a constructive relationship with NATO. Our success in working together in Bosnia clearly helped Russia feel confident that it could forge a satisfactory relationship with NATO. Ultimately, that relationship was codified by the Founding Act signed by NATO and Russia in May 1997. The outcome had been well foreshadowed in the Prague speech.

A Democratic and Undivided Europe in Our Time

Address at Cernin Palace, Prague, March 20, 1996

Foreign Minister Zieleniec, fellow foreign ministers, ladies and gentlemen: I would like to speak with you today about what we must do to fulfill the promise of our time—an undivided Europe of free nations stretching from Russia in the east to the Atlantic in the west, with this beautiful Czech capital, once again, at its heart.

Yesterday I was flying to Prague from Kiev, and I was reminded of this region's painful past of conflict and shifting frontiers. Below me, I could see towns and villages that, in this century alone, have been Russian, Austrian, Soviet, German, Czechoslovak, Polish, and now Ukrainian, Slovak, and Czech. These borderlands have been battlegrounds and burial grounds for Europe's great powers. It was here that this century's two great wars—and the Cold War—began. Today, it is here in this region that the greatest threats to European security must be faced.

Yet, it is also here that our century's most inspiring victories for freedom have unfolded. These hopeful events also have roots in the long history of this region: They are part of a tradition that includes the Polish Constitution of 1791, Europe's first written constitution. They harken back to the Ukrainian Rada of 1917, the first representative voice of an independent Ukraine. They have strong roots right here in Prague, where democracy flourished after World War I as fascism rose in the west and where freedom flickered ever so briefly after World War II as Stalinism was imposed from the east.

That era in Prague was epitomized by Thomas Masaryk, the elected president who believed that "for all the evils that may arise from political liberty, there is one tried remedy: more liberty." It also produced a Czech woman who learned to cherish freedom in her youth and who now defends it as America's ambassador to the United Nations: my esteemed colleague, Madeleine Korbel Albright. That democratic spirit endured the demoralizing years of communism. It inspired the Prague Spring and the Velvet Revolution. It animated coalminers and students, playwrights and electricians from the Berlin Wall to the walls of the Kremlin, and it gave them the power to overcome a totalitarian system that some thought could never be changed from within. Now, thanks to elected leaders like Vaclav Klaus and his counterparts, this region is home to the fastest-growing economies in Europe. Many nations are resolving old ethnic and border disputes. All now have their first real chance to enjoy independence and stability at the same time.

Europe's fears and hopes have met in the former Yugoslavia. From the first shots that rang out in Sarajevo to the destruction of Vukovar to the killing fields of Srebrenica, Europe relived the worst horrors of the First and Second World Wars. On the other hand, if we look at Bosnia today, we will see something that has never been seen before: soldiers from the United States and Russia, from Poland and Lithuania, from the Czech

Republic and Germany, and from 26 other countries joined in a mission of peace, justice, and reconciliation. This broad participation in IFOR is taking NATO's Partnership for Peace to new heights. It is showing the world how far the nations of Central and Eastern Europe have come and how much they have to contribute as our partners to European security.

Europe's future will be shaped by one of two very different paths: either by the divisive intolerance that left Bosnia in ruins or by the democratic integration to which most nations in this region aspire. For the right choice to prevail, there is a challenge you must meet, a challenge the United States must meet, and a challenge we must meet together.

The first challenge is that each nation in this region must take responsibility for building democratic stability from within. Free elections and free markets are only the first steps. Building a true democratic culture requires not just tolerance but respect for human rights and minority views and a willingness to come to terms with painful episodes from the past. It requires a free press, free trade unions, and a network of private organizations outside government control. Likewise, sustaining economic growth requires completing market reforms. It calls for privatization and a stable legal framework for investment. It requires accountable institutions that effectively confront problems like poverty, corruption, crime, and environmental damage.

This first challenge falls to a new generation in the new democracies—to the students, the young entrepreneurs, the young mayors, the young teachers who are building their nations anew. Their parents and grandparents struggled for many years to give them this opportunity. With the power to control their destiny, they have a responsibility to safeguard freedom and to use it with wisdom and justice for the common good.

The second challenge is for the United States: We must continue to engage and to lead in Europe. The Cold War may be over, but American leadership is still critical to transatlantic peace, security, and democracy. America's efforts helped make possible the smooth unification of Germany, the withdrawal of Russian forces from the Baltics, Ukraine's decision to give up nuclear weapons, and now the end of the war in Bosnia. There are isolationists in my country who would weaken our vital historic ties to the continent, but I assure you we will not heed them. It is a central lesson of this century that America must remain a European power.

The United States has a particular interest in assuring the success of Europe's new democracies. We have an interest in your liberty, because when you won your freedom, we were liberated from the Cold War. We have an interest in your security, because we wish to avoid the instability that drew over 5 million Americans to fight in two deadly world wars in Europe. We have an interest in your prosperity, because our own prosperity depends upon a Europe that is open to our exports, our investment, and our ideas.

We know we have an interest in your success, because standing here in Prague, we cannot fail to remember history. In 1938, as Hitler threatened to conquer Czechoslovakia, many Americans saw his aggression as a European problem. Yet no European state would intervene at that time in what Neville Chamberlain dismissed as "a quarrel in a far-away country between people of whom we know nothing." The world paid the price for that dangerous short-sightedness. A half-century later, a war in Bosnia threatened peace and security throughout Europe. And, again, it was the United States working together with Europe that made peace possible. President Clinton understood that only America—the leader of NATO—could step in and make a decisive difference.

That is why we went all out for peace at Dayton. That is why I was in Bosnia at D-plus-45, the 45th day of the NATO enforcement mission, and that is why I met with the three Balkan leaders this week in Geneva. Yesterday was D-plus-90, and it is clear that our troops have met their first critical challenge. The killing has ended. The armies have withdrawn. And in Geneva, the parties agreed to a series of concrete steps to pave the way for our next critical test: holding free elections this summer. Our work in Geneva provides the foundation for our Contact Group meeting to be held at the ministerial level on Saturday in Moscow. This series of meetings reflects the fact that much remains to be done, that we must stay with the process in Bosnia, stick with it day-in and day-out. Only that way will lasting peace be achieved.

In this region, the United States will remain a leader in support of democracy and free markets. Total American assistance to Central Europe has already topped $10 billion in this post–Cold War period. Our 12 enterprise funds have capitalized thousands of small businesses. We have helped rewrite commercial codes, as we did in Latvia, to create stock exchanges, as we did in Hungary, and to prepare the way for foreign investment throughout the region.

We are ready to meet a third challenge: the one we must meet together. That challenge is to reunite this continent, to erase the outdated boundaries of the Cold War. At long last, we must become equal partners, with equal responsibilities. Fifty years ago, when we emerged from World War II, the United States forged a permanent alliance with Europe's democratic states. Together, we created institutions that gave the West a half-century of peace and prosperity. That alliance kept Soviet armies at bay. It also brought France and Germany together. It integrated Italy and eventually Spain into our community of democracies. It gave shattered economies confidence to recover, and they did recover. This alliance remains a force for transatlantic unity.

Today, our goal is to extend eastward the same structure of values and institutions that enabled Western Europe to overcome its own legacy of conflict and division. These institutions—NATO and the European Union among them—are not ends in themselves. But history teaches that they create the conditions that allow democracy and free markets to flourish. For Europe's new democracies, integration will bring a new era. With the struggle for independence won, we are now able to work together to meet the responsibilities that Western nations share. That is what we are doing now in Bosnia and what many of you will do as you ultimately become full members of NATO and the European Union.

Together, we can build lasting security. We can build a true transatlantic marketplace that will deepen America's ties with a broader Europe. We can fight terrorism, organized crime, and proliferation, and we can protect the environment. We can keep working together in peacekeeping missions. We can speak and act together in support of freedom around the world, just as others stood with you during the long years of communist rule.

We are determined to keep faith with the nations of this region, to open the door that Stalin shut when he said "no" to the Marshall Plan. No nation in Europe should ever again be consigned to a buffer zone between great powers or relegated to another nation's sphere of influence.

To achieve that end, President Clinton has advanced a broad-ranging strategy for European security. It includes a revitalized NATO, ready for the missions and roles of the next century. It includes support for deeper and broader European integration. It includes a strong and productive relationship with Russia. The President's approach is comprehensive. It is far-sighted. And it is working.

We began to put this strategy into place two years ago when President Clinton proposed the Partnership for Peace—a Partnership that has been an extraordinary success, a Partnership that has established habits of cooperation that made the effective operation of IFOR possible. It will remain a permanent feature of security cooperation in Europe, and we are determined to strengthen it further.

Last weekend, I visited NATO's Supreme Headquarters in Mons. Paradoxically enough, in a building where the Allies once planned to defend Berlin against Soviet attack, Russian officers now work alongside NATO's members, alongside former neutral countries, and alongside the nations of central and eastern Europe. In the main hall of that building, 43 flags fly in alphabetical order, recognizing no artificial distinctions between countries. That is our vision for the new Europe come to life.

For some nations, the Partnership will also prepare the way to NATO membership. NATO enlargement is not a step we will take lightly. It involves the most solemn commitments that one nation can make to another. New allies will be full members of NATO, with all the benefits that entails. But they must be ready to assume the full risks, costs, and responsibilities that come with membership.

This year, NATO has entered the second phase of a process that has been gradual, deliberate, and transparent. NATO has begun intensive consultations with interested partners to determine what they must do— and what NATO must do—to prepare for enlargement. Based on the results, we will decide on next steps in December. We are determined to move forward. NATO has made a commitment to take in new members, and it must not and will not keep new democracies in the waiting room forever. NATO enlargement is on track, and it will happen.

By extending NATO's guarantees to strong, new democracies, we will extend the area where conflicts are deterred. This will make it less likely that America will ever again have to send its troops to fight in this region. Enlargement will help us erase a Cold War-dividing line drawn solely by the accident of where the Red Army stopped in 1945. The prospect of enlargement has also given every potential member of NATO an incentive to maintain democracy and good relations with their neighbors. In this way, enlargement will benefit members and non-members alike.

Indeed, by encouraging the peaceful resolution of disputes between countries like Hungary and Slovakia, NATO has already become a force for conflict prevention in this region. The United States and every

NATO ally looks forward to Slovakia's ratification of its treaty with Hungary, and we hope that Hungary and Romania will reach a similar agreement soon. NATO is the linchpin of European security, but other institutions are also critical. The OSCE is vital because true stability depends on the standards it promotes: respect for an open society and for the rule of law. This year, the OSCE will test its new operational role as it supervises elections in Bosnia. The Chairman in Office of the OSCE at the present time is Switzerland, stepping forward to take new responsibilities in a Europe moving toward integration.

The enlargement of the European Union is just as critical to the future of central and eastern Europe as is the enlargement of NATO. It will tear down what Lech Walesa called the "Silk Curtain"—the artificial economic barrier that still divides Europe between east and west. The standards the EU establishes will lock in democratic and market reforms and give this region's courageous entrepreneurs a fair chance to compete in a single European market. The EU must maintain its momentum toward enlargement, just as NATO is doing.

Let me make one final, critical comment about our strategy of integration. The process will be inclusive. It will not build new walls across this continent. It will not recognize any fundamental divide among the Catholic, Orthodox, and Islamic parts of Europe. That kind of thinking fueled the killing in the former Yugoslavia, and it must have no place in the Europe that we are building.

The enlargement of Western institutions will naturally begin with the strongest candidates for membership: If it did not start with them, it would not start at all. But our goal is not to help these nations "escape" from central and eastern Europe at the expense of their neighbors. On the contrary, those who are first have an obligation to ensure that their membership keeps the door open for others. Ukraine's integration with Europe is especially important to stability and security in this region. That is why we value Ukraine's participation in the Partnership for Peace, why we want NATO and Ukraine to build a strong relationship, and why we will participate in a major military exercise in Ukraine this summer. Yesterday in Kiev, I reaffirmed America's commitment to Ukraine's freedom, independence, and prosperity.

It is also critical that Russia take its rightful place in the new Europe. Nowhere is it more important that democracy take root than in Russia. Russia's reform efforts are under strain, and success is far from assured.

But we support reform because, in the long run, its success benefits not only the Russian people, but Europe and America as well.

One of the central issues in the future of Europe will be Russia's relationship with its newly independent neighbors. Last week, we were confronted with a dark vision of that future when the Russian Duma voted in favor of reconstituting the U.S.S.R. Five years ago, millions of former Soviet citizens freely chose independence, and the United States will continue to support its right and determination to keep it. I applaud President Yeltsin for opposing the Duma resolution. He and most Russians understand that Russia's interests lie in treating all its neighbors as equals, as sovereign partners in an integrated Europe.

On Friday, I will be meeting with President Yeltsin and Foreign Minister Primakov in Moscow to discuss our common interest in the safety of nuclear weapons and nuclear reactors and to prepare for the April nuclear summit. We will review our efforts on arms control, including our goal of a comprehensive nuclear test ban. And we will discuss the positive contribution Russia can make to European security. Russia can and should develop a cooperative relationship with NATO, in and beyond the Partnership for Peace, building on the excellent cooperation between Russia and NATO, as well as Russia and the United States, in Bosnia.

We must avoid the danger of three Europes: a prosperous, stable west; a center on its way to NATO and the EU; and an east consigned to isolation and crisis. Central Europe's integration will neither determine, nor be determined, by events in Russia. But we have an equal interest in integrating, not isolating, Russia. Of course, Russia must not isolate itself. Its integration, like that of central Europe, will depend on the choices its leaders and its people make. Integration depends on adherence to international norms at home and abroad.

Today, every nation in this region can make the choices that lead to an undivided Europe—a Europe whose eastern frontiers are determined by shared values, not by geography or history. As President Clinton said right here in Prague: "Freedom's boundaries now should be defined by new behavior, not old history." The West itself must be open to open societies and open markets everywhere. Europe's new democracies were born in a peaceful struggle for dignity.

That struggle committed millions of Czechs, Slovaks, Poles, Romanians, Russians, and others to the highest standards of solidarity, civility, and courage. It created a generation that, in the words of Pope John Paul II, "called good and evil by their name, and did not blur the picture." That special history gives you a special role to play, in partnership with the United States, in Europe's future. For each of us, that role must live up to what President Havel has called "the politics of responsibility." We must accept the responsibility to uphold the ideals that set us free.

So let us rededicate ourselves to an old goal. Let us build a Europe of sovereign, equal democracies, united with each other and America by shared values and institutions. Let us build a Europe where you can always count on us, and we can always count on you. Let us make this vision a reality in our time, not in our children's time.

Thank you very much.

TWENTY-EIGHT

Diplomacy and the Environment

As I entered my fourth year as Secretary, I wanted to find a way to underscore emphatically that environmental protection must be fully integrated into the mainstream of American foreign policy. Although I had frequently mentioned environmental challenges in public statements (see, e.g., Chapters 19 and 23), neither I nor any other Secretary of State had ever given a full-length speech on these concerns. I decided that doing so would demonstrate the depth of my conviction and spark a conversation not only in the Washington policy community, but throughout the United States and the world. Thus, the fact that I delivered the speech at all was as important as any particular initiative announced in it.

My awareness of the importance of environmental protection had built up over time. Growing up in North Dakota, I had seen the devastating effects of soil erosion, caused by prolonged drought and mammoth dust storms, during the Great Depression of the 1930s. (Indeed, until studying economics in college, I thought all depressions were caused by droughts, windstorms, and crop rust.) A later influence on me was Senator Edmund Muskie, a congressional leader on environmental issues who spent eight months as Secretary of State in 1980–81, when I was Deputy Secretary. Later, when I served as Chairman of the Stanford University Board of Trustees in the mid-1980s, I often had eye-opening conversations about worldwide environmental deterioration with Dr. Donald Kennedy, a distinguished biologist and then Stanford's President. Another strong influence was Vice President Al Gore, whose best-selling book, *Earth in the Balance*, reflects his thorough understanding of and deep commitment to environmental issues. In our regular meetings, we often discussed environmental problems such as climate change, and he inspired me to address these through our foreign policy.

Environmental matters had long been considered primarily the domain of such domestic agencies as the Environmental Protection Agency and the Department of the Interior. The State Department had an Oceans, Environment and Sciences Bureau (OES), but it was a kind of organizational orphan, often seemingly lost in the bureaucracy. One of my first steps as Secretary was to ensure high-level attention for critical transnational issues, including the environment, by establishing the office of Under Secretary of State for Global Affairs. On my recommendation, President Clinton named Tim Wirth, a former Democratic Senator from Colorado and a committed environmental activist, as the first Under Secretary. Wirth elevated the profile of OES, which now reported to him, and ensured that a steady flow of information concerning the environment crossed my desk and those of other Seventh Floor policy makers. Wirth also formed powerful alliances with non-governmental organizations (NGO's) devoted to environmental causes, and he organized some useful breakfasts and other meetings at which I could exchange views with the NGO leaders.

This organizational change had a profound effect, but I wanted to do more to integrate environmental concerns into bureau and overseas mission planning, resource allocation, and public diplomacy. In early 1996, I sent all Under and Assistant Secretaries a six-page memorandum outlining my thoughts about environmental matters and specific steps I wanted every bureau to take to address them. These steps were to include (1) incorporating appropriate environmental and population goals into program plans; (2) on my overseas trips, arranging events designed to highlight the importance of environmental issues; (3) including these issues in talking points, to be used not only for my own bilateral meetings, but for those of the President and other senior officials; and (4) including the State Department's environmental specialists in the planning meetings preceding important negotiations, conferences, and meetings. I asked Jim Steinberg, the Director of Policy Planning and a committed environmentalist, and Eileen Claussen, the knowledgeable Assistant Secretary of OES, to oversee the Department's effort to accomplish these tasks.

This initiative immediately produced tangible results. For example, on my trips to Latin America in March 1996 and Africa in October 1996, environmental issues were prominent on the agendas of my bilateral meetings and were the focus of several of my other activities. And throughout the Department, I sensed a new recognition of the importance of environmental concerns.

But working within the government to address these concerns was only part of our task. To ensure that they secured a place on America's diplomatic agenda, we had to persuade the American people that a healthy environment is critical to national security. We needed to foster a conceptual transformation, showing how what some considered to be a "soft" issue had a place in U.S. diplomacy alongside the more traditional "hard" foreign policy concerns. Such conceptual change was the core goal of my speech at Stanford University in the spring of 1996.

Working with speechwriter James Gibney, I spent an unusual amount of time drafting and redrafting portions of the speech to explain the logical relationship between environmental protection and national security as clearly as possible. We also chose our venue with care. The address was aimed primarily at the American people, so I wanted to deliver it in the United States, preferably in a place that could amplify the importance we attached to the subject. Northern California's strong commitment to the environment, my own personal ties to Stanford, and Don Kennedy's presence combined to make the University the ideal host.

The speech outlined our foreign policy approach toward the environment from three perspectives: global, regional, and bilateral. In the first few paragraphs, I summarized the core reasons that the world's environmental conditions have profound direct and indirect impacts on our national interests. The direct effects occur when environmental forces transcend borders and threaten "the health, prosperity and jobs of American citizens." As an example, I mentioned the potential damage caused in this country by the release of greenhouse gases worldwide.

The indirect effects arise when environmental problems influence political and economic stability in regions vital to the United States. In the Middle East, for example, many of my diplomatic missions brought to light serious problems of water scarcity, overpopulation, and poverty that needed to be addressed as part of the peace process. In Africa, Rwanda and Burundi stood out as tragic cases in which environmental degradation exacerbated political unrest, causing massive human suffering.

Closer to home, Haiti's environmental devastation—including the loss of almost all of its forests and half its topsoil—created instability that enormously complicated that tragic nation's political problems. Looking to the future, the speech described the alarming environmental challenges facing China, where 22% of the world's population is supported by only "7% of its fresh water and cropland, 3% of its forests, and 2% of its oil."

While the speech's main focus was conceptual, I also mentioned several specific initiatives that highlighted our commitment to the issue. The two most important were establishing Environmental Hubs and issuing an annual "Report on Global Environmental Challenges." The Environmental Hubs proposal called for us to concentrate environmental specialists and related resources in key embassies, one in each region.[1] These Hubs would be responsible for advancing environmental priorities in their regions, cooperating not only with the host governments but with U.S. firms doing business there. The Global Environmental Challenges Reports were designed to bring the same attention to environmental issues that the annual Human Rights Reports have brought to human rights since the Carter Administration. The first report, issued on Earth Day 1997, was well conceived and executed, and gained wide public attention.

In terms of drawing attention to environmental protection as a key element of our foreign policy, the Stanford speech more than fulfilled our expectations. The extensive press coverage accurately described it as evidence of an effort to reshape America's diplomatic agenda. The concepts expressed still reverberate in policy discussions today, and in environmental circles, the "Stanford speech" is regarded as something of a watershed. The distinguished Stanford biologist Paul Ehrlich commented, "I never thought I would live long enough to hear a Secretary of State express so many concerns of the world's scientific community and say

---

[1]In August 1996, I followed up on the Stanford speech by hosting a breakfast meeting with over 30 environmental, foreign policy, and business leaders to discuss the Department's efforts to integrate environmental matters into foreign policy. At the meeting, I announced the first two of a dozen embassies to be designated as Hubs: those in Amman, Jordan, where the focus is on water and natural resource issues arising from the Middle East peace process, and in San Jose, Costa Rica, where we are following up on the sustainable development goals launched at the 1994 Summit of the Americas.

that if we don't address these issues we are going to be in deep, deep trouble." A lead *Boston Globe* editorial succinctly conveyed the message the speech aimed to send: "The subcontext of [the] link between national interests and environmental stability is that all the missiles and smart bombs in the U.S. arsenal will not be able to protect Americans from rising oceans and the northward movement of mosquito-borne diseases such as malaria and dengue fever."[2] In short, this is a prime example of how speeches can be used as instruments of policy. The challenge now is to translate our concerns into action.

●

American Diplomacy and the Global Environmental Challenges of the 21st Century

Address to the Alumni and Faculty of Stanford University,

Stanford, California, April 9, 1996

Thank you very much for that kind introduction. I am especially honored to be introduced by Gerhard, whom I have known and admired in his various incarnations, especially his current one. Even putting aside my personal ties, I can think of no better venue for my remarks today on global environmental issues than this university. From the founding of the Sierra Club in 1892 to the first Earth Day in 1970, Stanford faculty and alumni have led efforts to preserve our country's natural resources for future generations. Your centers for Conservation Biology and Global Ecosystem Function have done pioneering work. Let me also say that I am personally grateful for the continuing work of Coach Montgomery and Coach Willingham to keep the California Bear population under control.

With strong leadership from President Clinton and Vice President Gore, our Administration has recognized from the beginning that our ability to advance our global interests is inextricably linked to how we

[2]"Ecological Diplomacy," Apr. 14, 1996.

manage the Earth's natural resources. That is why we are determined to put environmental issues where they belong: in the mainstream of American foreign policy. I appreciate and value this opportunity to outline our far-reaching agenda to integrate fully environmental objectives into our diplomacy and to set forth our priorities for the future.

The environment has a profound impact on our national interests in two ways: First, environmental forces transcend borders and oceans to threaten directly the health, prosperity, and jobs of American citizens.

Second, addressing natural resource issues is frequently critical to achieving political and economic stability and to pursuing our strategic goals around the world.

The United States is providing the leadership to promote global peace and prosperity. We must also lead in safeguarding the global environment on which that prosperity and peace ultimately depend.

In 1946, when I came to Stanford as a law student, the connection between the environment and foreign policy was not so readily apparent. At home, Americans were entering a period of unprecedented prosperity fueled by seemingly infinite resources. Abroad, we were beginning to focus on the struggle between the United States and the Soviet Union. And I was trying to master the intricacies of contracts, torts, and something called remedies, taught by Stanford's version of John Houseman. I was also trying to measure up to the high standards set by a new young Dean, Carl Spaeth, who had just come to Stanford from a very promising career at the State Department and who first stimulated my interest in the work in which I am now engaged full time.

But since 1946, population growth, economic progress, and technological breakthroughs have combined to fundamentally reshape our world. It took more than 10,000 generations to reach a world population of just over 2 billion. In just my lifetime—a period that may seem like an eternity to many of the students in the audience—the world's population has nearly tripled to more than 5 1/2 billion.

These changes are putting staggering pressures on global resources. From 1960 to 1990, the world's forests shrank by an amount equivalent to one-half the land area of the United States. Countless species of animals and plants are being wiped out, including many with potential value for agriculture and medicine. Pollution of our air and water endangers our health and our future.

In carrying out America's foreign policy, we will, of course, use our diplomacy backed by strong military forces to meet traditional and continuing threats to our security, as well as to meet new threats such as terrorism, weapons proliferation, drug trafficking, and international crime. But we must also contend with the vast new dangers posed to our national interests by damage to the environment and resulting global and regional instability.

As the flagship institution of American foreign policy, the State Department must spearhead a government-wide effort to meet these environmental challenges. Together with other government agencies, we are pursuing our environmental priorities—globally, regionally, bilaterally, and in partnership with business and non-governmental organizations. Each of these four dimensions is essential to the success of our overall strategy.

First, our approach to these problems must be global because pollution respects no boundaries, and the growing demand for finite resources in any part of the world inevitably puts pressure on the resources in all others.

Across the United States, Americans suffer the consequences of damage to the environment far beyond our borders. Greenhouse gases released around the globe by power plants, automobiles, and burning forests affect our health and our climate, potentially causing many billions of dollars in damage from rising sea levels and changing storm patterns. Dangerous chemicals such as PCBs and DDT that are banned here but still used elsewhere travel long distances through the air and water. Overfishing of the world's oceans has put thousands of Americans out of work. A foreign policy that failed to address such problems would be ignoring the needs of the American people.

Each nation must take steps on its own to combat these environmental threats, but we will not succeed until we can effectively fight them together. That realization inspired the path-breaking efforts of the United Nations at the Stockholm Conference on the Human Environment 25 years ago and at the historic Rio Summit on Environment and Development four years ago. There, the international community forged a new global commitment to "preserve, protect, and restore . . . the Earth's ecosystem" and to promote economic development in ways that also preserve our natural resources.

Since Rio, the United States has intensified our global efforts. We led the way to an agreement to phase out the remaining substances that damage the ozone layer, to ban the ocean dumping of low-level radioactive waste, and to achieve a new consensus in Cairo on stabilizing global population growth.

We are working to reform and strengthen the UN's key environmental and sustainable development programs. We have joined forces with the World Bank to incorporate sound environmental policies in lending programs and to fund projects through the Global Environment Facility that directly benefit our health and prosperity. We are striving through the new World Trade Organization to reconcile the complex tensions between promoting trade and protecting the environment—and to ensure that neither comes at the expense of the other.

This year, we will begin negotiating agreements with the potential to make 1997 the most important year for the global environment since the Rio Summit. We will seek agreement on further cuts in greenhouse gases to minimize the effects of climate change. We will help lead an international process to address the problems caused by toxic chemicals that can seep into our land and water, poisoning them for generations. We will develop a strategy for the sustainable management of the world's forests—a resource that every great civilization has discovered is "indispensable for carrying on life," as the Roman historian Pliny once wrote. We will work with Congress to ratify the Biodiversity Convention, which holds benefits for American agriculture and business. We will also seek ratification of the Law of the Sea Treaty, which safeguards our access to ocean resources. We will provide the leadership needed to ensure that this June's UN summit in Istanbul effectively confronts the pressing problems associated with the explosive growth of cities in the developing world. Finally, by the end of 1997, the State Department will host a conference on strategies to improve our compliance with international environmental agreements—to ensure that those agreements yield lasting results, not just promises.

This is a daunting global agenda. Achieving these goals will take time and perseverance. But I often remember Don Kennedy's advice to graduates to set a "standard higher than you can comfortably reach."

The second element of our strategy—the regional element—is to confront pollution and the scarcity of resources in key areas where they dramatically increase tensions within and among nations. Nowhere is this more evident than in the parched valleys of the Middle East, where the struggle for water has a direct impact on security and stability. In my many trips to the region, I have seen how rapid population growth and pollution can raise the stakes in water disputes as ancient as the "Old Testament." As Shimon Peres once remarked to me, "The Jordan River has more history in it than water." We are helping the parties in the Middle East peace process to manage the region's water resources—to turn a source of conflict into a force for peace.

There can be no doubt that building stable market democracies in the former Soviet Union and Central Europe will reinforce our own security. However, for these new nations to succeed, we must help them overcome the poisonous factories, soot-filled skies, and ruined rivers that are one of the bitter legacies of communism. The experience of this region demonstrates that governments that abuse their citizens too often have a similar contempt for the environment.

Three weeks ago in Kiev, I walked through the wards of a children's hospital that treats the victims of Chernobyl. I saw first-hand the terrible damage that this 10-year-old catastrophe still inflicts on the region's people. We are helping Ukraine to ensure that there will be no more Chernobyls. In Central Asia, we are helping nations recover from Soviet irrigation practices that turned much of the Aral Sea into an ocean of sand. Our Regional Environment Center in Budapest supports the civic groups in Central Europe that are essential to a healthy democracy and to a healthy environment.

The United States also has an enormous stake in consolidating democratic institutions and open markets in our own hemisphere. To deepen the remarkable transformation that is taking place across Latin America and the Caribbean, we are advancing the agenda for sustainable development that our 34 democracies adopted at the Miami Summit of the Americas. To help democracy succeed, for example, we must ease the pressures of deforestation and rapid population growth that I have seen at work in the bare hills and crowded city streets of Haiti. To sustain our prosperity, we must work to preserve the rich diversity of life that I saw in the Amazon rainforest. To help heal the wounds of old conflicts, we must reverse the environmental damage that has narrowed economic opportunities and fueled illegal immigration from El Salvador. And to help combat drug trafficking and crime, we are encouraging sustainable agriculture as an alternative to the slash-and-burn cultivation of opium poppies and coca from Guatemala to Colombia. These goals will be high on our agenda at the Sustainable Development Summit this December in Bolivia.

In Africa, we are pursuing environmental efforts designed to save tens of thousands of lives, prevent armed conflict, and avert the need for costly international intervention. Our Greater Horn of Africa Initiative, for example, addresses the root causes of environmental problems that can turn droughts into famines and famines into civil wars. We must not forget the hard lessons of Rwanda, where depleted resources and swollen populations exacerbated the political and economic pressures that exploded into one of this decade's greatest tragedies. We also have a national interest in helping the nations of the region address the AIDS crisis, which is decimating a whole generation of young Africans and wasting the economic resources that African nations so desperately need to build stable governments and a brighter economic future.

To intensify our regional environmental efforts, we will establish environmental hubs in our embassies in key countries. These will address pressing regional natural resource issues, advance sustainable development goals, and help U.S. businesses to sell their leading-edge environmental technology.

The third element of our strategy is to work bilaterally with key partners around the world—beginning, of course, with our next-door neighbors. Whether it is fishing on the Georges Bank or in the Gulf of Mexico, or clean drinking water from the Great Lakes or the Rio Grande, we cannot separate our environmental interests from those of Canada or Mexico.

We are extending our century-old cooperation with Canada on behalf of clean water and flood control in the Great Lakes region. We are improving conservation in our adjoining national park lands. Through the U.S.-Canada Joint Commission, we are protecting human health and natural habitats. And with all our Arctic neighbors, we are establishing a partnership to protect that fragile region.

Our joint efforts with Mexico have grown in importance since NAFTA took effect just over two years ago. Under the NAFTA side agreements on the environment, we have set up new institutions to help communities on both sides of the border safeguard the natural resources they share. Later this spring, we will launch an innovative program that will enable business and government leaders from Texas, New Mexico, and Ciudad Juarez to reduce some of the region's worst air pollution. When our two nations' cabinets meet in Mexico City next month, I will emphasize the importance of Mexico continuing to strengthen its environmental standards.

Through our Common Agenda with Japan, the world's two largest economies are pooling their resources and expertise to stabilize population growth, to eradicate polio, to fight AIDS, and to develop new "green" technology.

Our New Transatlantic Agenda with the European Union will spur global efforts on such issues as climate change and toxic chemicals. Together, we are already advancing our environmental goals in Central Europe and the New Independent States.

Russia and China are both confronting major environmental problems that will have a profound effect on their future—and on ours. In Russia, the fate of democracy may depend on its ability to offer the Russian people better living standards and to reverse a shocking decline in life expectancy. From Murmansk to Vladivostok, poorly stored nuclear waste poses a threat to human life for centuries to come. Economic reforms will not meet their potential if one-sixth of the Russian land mass remains so polluted that it is unfit even for industrial use and if Russian children are handicapped by the poisons they breathe and drink.

We are cooperating with Russia to meet these challenges. Ten days from now, President Clinton will join President Yeltsin and other leaders at a Nuclear Safety Summit in Moscow, which will promote the safe operation of nuclear reactors and the appropriate storage of nuclear materials. Vice President Gore and Prime Minister Chernomyrdin are spearheading joint initiatives to preserve the Arctic environment, reduce greenhouse gases, and promote the management of key natural resources. We are even taking the satellite imagery once used to spot missiles and tanks and using it to help clean up military bases and track ocean pollution.

As we discussed this morning at your Institute for International Studies, the environmental challenges that China faces are truly sobering. With 22% of the world's population, China has only 7% of its fresh water and cropland, 3% of its forests, and 2% of its oil. The combination of China's rapid economic growth and surging population is compounding the enormous environmental pressures it already faces. That is one of the many reasons why our policy of engagement with China encompasses the environment. Later this month, Vice President Gore will launch an initiative that will expand U.S.-China cooperation on sustainable development, including elements such as energy policy and agriculture.

In our other bilateral relationships, we have created partnerships that strengthen our ties while moving beyond the outdated thinking that once predicted an inevitable struggle between North and South. Under the Common Agenda for the Environment we signed last year with India, for example, we are cooperating on a broad range of shared interests from investing in environmental technologies to controlling pesticides and toxic chemicals. During my trip to Brazil last month, we strengthened a similar Common Agenda with agreements on cooperation in space that will widen our knowledge about climate change and improve management of forest resources.

The fourth and final element of our strategy reinforces these diplomatic approaches by building partnerships with private businesses and non-governmental organizations.

American businesses know that a healthy global environment is essential to our prosperity. Increasingly, they recognize that pitting economic growth against environmental protection is what President Clinton has called "a false choice." Both are necessary, and both are closely linked.

Protecting the environment also opens new business opportunities. We are committed to helping U.S. companies expand their already commanding share of a $400-billion market for environmental technologies. This effort was one of many championed by my late colleague and friend, Commerce Secretary Ron Brown. His last mission to Africa helped an American firm win a contract that will protect fisheries and fresh water supplies for 30 million people in Uganda, Tanzania, and Kenya. On my recent visit to El Salvador, I met with U.S. firms, non-governmental organizations, and their Central American partners who are pioneering the use of solar and wind power stations.

Non-governmental organizations working with USAID have played a crucial role in advancing our environmental objectives overseas. For many years, for example, the Sierra Club has been deeply engaged in international population efforts, and it made an important contribution to the Cairo Conference. As part of these joint efforts, the World Wildlife Fund is helping to conserve biodiversity in more than 40 countries, the World Resources Institute is confronting deforestation in Africa, and the Nature Conservancy is protecting wildlife preserves across Latin America. Through the State Department's new "Partnership for Environment and Foreign Policy," we will bring together environmental organizations, business leaders, and foreign policy specialists to enhance our cooperation in meeting environmental challenges.

It is the responsibility of the State Department to lead in ensuring the success of each one of the four elements of the strategy that I have discussed today—global, regional, bilateral, and partnerships with business and NGOs. Working closely with the President and the Vice President, I have instructed our bureaus and our embassies to improve the way we use our diplomacy to advance our environmental objectives. We will raise these issues on every occasion where our influence may be useful. We will bolster our ability to blend diplomacy and science and to negotiate global agreements that protect our health and well-being. We will reinforce the role of the Office of Under Secretary for Global Affairs, which was created at the beginning of our Administration to address transnational issues. We will strengthen our efforts with USAID to promote sustainable development through effective environment and family planning assistance. And we will reinforce the environmental partnerships that we have formed with the EPA and the Departments of Defense, Energy, Commerce, Interior, and Agriculture.

In addition, I am announcing today that starting on Earth Day 1997, the Department will issue an annual report on Global Environmental Challenges. This report will be an essential tool of our environmental diplomacy, bringing together an assessment of global environmental trends, international policy developments, and U.S. priorities for the coming year.

I will continue to work with the Congress to ensure the success of our environmental efforts. The current Congress has slashed critical funding for needed environmental programs at home and abroad. We will press Congress to provide the necessary resources to get the job done.

Our strength as a nation has always been to harness our democracy to meet new threats to our security and prosperity. Our creed as a people has always been to make tomorrow better for ourselves and for our children. Drawing on the same ideals and interests that have led Americans from Teddy Roosevelt to Ed Muskie to put a priority on preserving our land, our skies, and our waters at home, we must meet the challenge of making global environmental issues a vital part of our foreign policy. For the sake of future generations, we must succeed.

Thank you very much.

TWENTY-NINE

Standing Firm with China

For several months following my August 1995 meeting with Chinese Foreign Minister Qian in Brunei, our efforts to stabilize bilateral relations with China bore some fruit. The Chinese released American citizen Harry Wu from custody, and Under Secretary Peter Tarnoff had productive talks with his counterparts in Beijing. Despite these steps forward, however, we knew that significant challenges loomed ahead. Indeed, I believed that our relations with China would lead to the most difficult policy questions we would confront in 1996. As Winston Lord noted to me at the start of the year, we faced with China a series of "minefields, not milestones."

Most troublesome among the minefields was the escalating hostility between China and Taiwan. After my National Press Club speech and Brunei meeting with Qian (see Chapter 20), the Chinese seemed reasonably confident of the U.S. commitment to "one China."[1] The problem now was with Taiwan itself. Its first direct presidential election was scheduled for March 23, 1996, and President Lee Teng-hui, running on the Nationalist Party ticket, was the clear front-runner. Lee's efforts to carve out an independent image for Taiwan agitated the Chinese, who

---

[1]Our reassurances did not prevent the Chinese from continuing to press us on the Taiwan issue, however. In the fall of 1995, they proposed that we negotiate a "fourth communique" putting on paper a formula I had outlined orally—that any Taiwanese leaders' visits to the United States would be personal, non-political, unofficial, and rare. The idea of a fourth communique was a non-starter with us, and the Chinese quickly backed off.

were still smarting from his Cornell visit. China was concerned that a democratically elected Lee would be even more vocal about independence and would encourage other nations to recognize Taiwan or invite him for official visits. These fears were not entirely unfounded; some in the U.S. Congress were already saying that if elected, Lee would be invited to address a joint session of Congress (a proposal aggressively advocated by the well-organized Taiwan lobby). Although the Administration remained adamantly and publicly opposed to this idea, it complicated our efforts to overcome the chill in our relations with China.

The other challenges our relationship faced in 1996 were most-favored-nation trade treatment, weapons proliferation, Chinese piracy of U.S. entertainment products and computer software, and human rights concerns. Early in the year, I led a quiet effort to plan a comprehensive strategy to help us navigate through these difficult topics, as well as attempt to move forward on a positive agenda (which included, for example, environmental protection and the fight against narcotics and crime). To this end I hosted several meetings in my office; these were attended by my senior aides as well as the Deputy National Security Adviser, Sandy Berger, who was a consistently constructive influence on U.S.-China policy. These consultations served us well as the challenges we had anticipated—along with several we had not—emerged over the course of the year.

As the Taiwanese elections approached, Chinese rhetoric and actions toward the island became more blustery and reckless. In early January, we received warnings from both official and private sources that the Chinese had plans on the shelf for a possible military attack against Taiwan. Although the existence of such plans was hardly surprising, this saber rattling was clearly an effort to intimidate Taiwan's population and leadership before the election. In response, the Taiwanese raised the ante, publicizing the passage of an American aircraft carrier, the *USS Nimitz*, through the 125-mile-wide Taiwan Strait, an international waterway, in late December 1995. Though the publicity made it sound as if this passage had been specially timed, in fact U.S. ships make such transits through international waterways routinely and without fanfare, as quiet but firm affirmations of our presence and international rights.

The tit-for-tat exchanges continued. The Chinese announced plans to conduct a massive military exercise in the Taiwan Strait. Soon afterward, they test-fired missiles that bracketed the island, with those on the northern end reportedly passing over Taiwan's territory. Although neither we nor the Taiwanese leadership believed that these actions were precursors to invasion, they were dangerously provocative. In a tense environment of mutual hostility and deep distrust, the Administration was concerned that a simple miscalculation or misstep could lead to unintended war. Because Asian and Pacific nations looked to the United States to preserve stability in the region, we had to take action to calm the situation.

In early March, acting on the wise suggestion of Secretary Perry, President Clinton ordered a second Navy aircraft carrier group to join one already in international waters near Taiwan. Although we remained publicly guarded about what these ships would do in the event of hostilities—I said on NBC's *Meet the Press* that we wanted them "in a position to be helpful if they need to be"—their mere presence put both Taipei and Beijing on notice of our commitment to keeping the peace. We also conveyed our concerns privately to each side.[2] While our actions and rhetoric were unmistakably firm toward Beijing and reassuring to Taipei, we also affirmed our one-China policy and counseled Taiwan against unnecessary provocations that could ignite conflict.

In response, China loudly criticized us for "interfering" in the "internal affair" of Taiwan. In rhetoric as hot as any since the Chinese shelling of Quemoy and Matsu in 1955, China boasted that it would easily "bury" us if armed conflict occurred. But Beijing got the message, as did our friends in Asia, most of whom welcomed our carrier moves as a demonstration of U.S. commitment to the region. (Most of their supportive comments were made in private.)

After the March 23 election, which Lee won with 54% of the vote, the China-Taiwan situation calmed rapidly. Beijing's effort to influence the outcome through intimidation had backfired badly in Taiwan, and in Asia generally, and China stepped back from the brink.

Several problems persisted between us, however. One of the most sensitive was China's sale of a sensitive nuclear technology, "ring magnets,"

---

[2]During March, a senior Chinese official met with a U.S. delegation led by National Security Adviser Anthony Lake for lengthy and valuable consultations at Ambassador Pamela Harriman's farm in Virginia. A few days later, Sandy Berger and Peter Tarnoff secretly met with the Taiwanese National Security Adviser in New York City. This was the highest-level meeting we had had with Taiwanese officials since severing formal diplomatic ties with Taiwan in 1979.

to Pakistan.[3] We had threatened to impose economic sanctions on China if those sales continued.

I raised the ring magnets issue during a four-hour meeting with Qian Qichen on April 19 at The Hague. This was my first meeting with Qian since the Taiwan Strait crisis had subsided, and I wanted to resume our dialogue on several key topics. We covered a range of issues—Russia, human rights, North Korea—but ring magnets emerged as the most time-consuming and contentious of them. I had previously told Qian that we would not pursue the threatened sanctions if China ruled out any future assistance, including the sale of ring magnets, to unsafeguarded nuclear facilities in Pakistan or elsewhere. After extensive discussion, Qian finally agreed, but he continued to oppose my suggestion that we convene "expert talks" to discuss China's nuclear export policy. "China's non-proliferation export policy is China's policy," Qian told me flatly. "We have no need to discuss it with the U.S. government." I left The Hague without final agreement on this last remaining issue, but a month later, the Chinese accepted our proposal for further steps to strengthen their nuclear export controls, and the troublesome ring magnets episode ended on a positive note.[4]

A speech I gave on May 17, 1996, at the Council on Foreign Relations in Washington, D.C., provided a chance to reflect on the rocky past few months with China and to reassert our interests and goals. I drew on the lessons of the Taiwan Strait crisis, the ring magnets problem, and the industrial piracy negotiations to assess our relations and develop a policy template for the future. Significantly, this was the Administration's first full-dress speech devoted solely to China, although that nation had often emerged as the most important topic of previous speeches on Asia.

I approached the speech with a sense of realism and confidence.

---

[3]A Chinese company had sold nearly $70,000 worth of ring magnets to the Pakistani organization responsible for producing the highly enriched uranium used in the country's nuclear weapons program. Ring magnets are essential although unsophisticated components of the centrifuge machines Pakistan uses to enrich the uranium.

[4]Another very sensitive topic at this time was Chinese piracy of U.S. computer software, movies, and compact discs. USTR took the lead on dealing with this issue. After several months of arduous negotiations, marked by the threat of U.S. trade sanctions, the Chinese finally committed to curb this piracy. The Acting U.S. Trade Representative, Charlene Barshefsky, deserves much credit for her skillful handling of these marathon negotiations.

Whereas a year earlier, the United States had needed to mend strains in the relationship stemming from Lee's visit to Cornell, we stood on firmer ground following the Taiwan Strait crisis. China had overstepped, the Beijing leadership knew it, and I did not hesitate to point out the new balance in our relationship. Both sides have legitimate interests, I explained, and both are responsible for solving mutual problems. "We do not have any illusions about the difficulty of managing our relations," I said. "On some critical issues, we have deep differences. Our focus must be on the long term, and we must seek to resolve our differences through engagement, not confrontation. We will do our part, but China, too, must do its part."

Because 1996 was a presidential election year, the domestic political environment was particularly charged regarding many matters, including China.[5] This speech aimed to provide a sober counterweight. Recently, some critics had argued that rather than engage the Chinese, we should isolate or contain them, as we had the Soviets during the Cold War. I believed that such an approach was foolhardy, and bluntly said so. "Demonizing China is as dangerously misleading as romanticizing it," I argued in a sentence picked up by the press. The next line summed up the logic of engagement: "American policy toward China has been most successful when we have acknowledged that country's great complexity, recognized that change requires patience as well as persistence, and respected China's sovereignty while standing up for our own values and interests."

The speech outlined three core elements of our China policy: encouraging the development of an open and secure China; supporting Chinese integration into the international community, with all the responsibilities this entailed; and managing differences through engagement. Although these approaches were not particularly new to the Clinton Administration's policy, their formulation in the speech provided the strategic clarity, context, and organization that they had theretofore lacked.

Of the specific issues I raised, MFN renewal was the most immediately important. We were relatively confident that we would obtain con-

---

[5]In a speech given a little over a week before mine, Senator Bob Dole, the presumptive Republican presidential nominee, claimed that the Clinton Administration "lack[ed] a strategic policy toward China" and that this was "erod[ing] American power and purpose in the Pacific." Despite Senator Dole's sweeping statements, the specific policy positions he outlined, including support for continuing MFN for China, closely resembled our own, which the press duly noted.

gressional approval for the renewal. However, with partisan politics in Washington even more sour than usual, we could not take anything for granted. We saw the more moderate Senate as likelier to support MFN; thus my remarks were primarily aimed at the House of Representatives, where sentiments for "containing" or "isolating" China were more pronounced. (In the end, the House upheld the President's renewal of MFN by a wide margin, 286–141.)

Finally, I used the speech to set in motion a proposal that we hoped to unfold over the next several months: arranging for high-level visits between Washington and Beijing. Given the tense state of recent relations, this was the element of my speech that attracted the most attention in the U.S. press. Although I had first raised the issue with Qian in Brunei 10 months earlier, it had been put on hold while we addressed our differences. With our relationship now on the mend, I thought the time was right to get the process moving again. By instituting high-level exchanges, we hoped to develop a forum to iron out our inevitable problems as well as expand the positive agenda we had started to pursue in late 1995. The Administration had not yet decided exactly what visits to push for. My speech left the issue open, calling for a "more regular dialogue" and "periodic cabinet-level consultations." I privately hoped to be able to arrange for home-and-home visits between President Clinton and President Jiang Zemin.

Two months later, on July 24, Foreign Minister Qian and I met for the fourteenth time—in Jakarta, on the margins of the ASEAN ministerial—and reaffirmed the positive trends in U.S.-Chinese relations. Beijing had received my May speech warmly, and the relationship had begun to move forward. We pinned down a series of cabinet-level visits that I had called for, including a trip by the Chinese Defense Minister and National Security Adviser to Washington to meet with William Perry and Anthony Lake, and discussed a possible China trip by Vice President Gore in 1997. I accepted China's long-standing invitation to visit Beijing again and told Qian I would come in November.

The rest of my 90-minute conversation with Qian exemplified both the challenge and the promise of engaging China. I pressed him on weapons proliferation and human rights, and he repeated a condensed version of his boilerplate on Taiwan. But we also discussed our common interests, including our joint approach toward facilitating armistice talks between North and South Korea and our concern about Hong Kong's future.[6] As I told the President, the meeting "illustrated once again that conducting this relationship will be one of our most complex international challenges. We have stabilized our dealings and charted our future course. But prickly nationalism, leadership succession maneuvering, Middle Kingdom smugness and suspicions of the world's only superpower will make Beijing one of the most difficult leading actors on the world stage."

●

American Interests and the U.S.-China Relationship

Address Before Council on Foreign Relations,

Washington, D.C., May 17, 1996

Thank you for that very kind introduction. It is a great pleasure to see Les Gelb and Barber Conable again. I want to thank the Council on Foreign Relations, the National Committee on United States-China Relations, the Asia Society, and Business Week for hosting me. I am very pleased to have the chance to speak with you today about the United States and China.

There can be no doubt that the stakes in our relationship with China are tremendous. China's future will have a profound impact on the security and prosperity of the Asia-Pacific region and the world. As Secretary of State, I have an important responsibility to develop our relationship in

[6]With its scheduled transition to China in July 1997, Hong Kong would become a major issue as the year went on. We had regularly raised this subject with the Chinese, trying to convince them that a prosperous and secure Hong Kong was as much in their interest as ours. During my April 19 meeting with Qian at The Hague, I had asked him several specific questions about the details of the transition, telling him that I had developed a personal interest in the Hong Kong issue and, as a private citizen in 1984, had delivered a speech on the subject. In that speech, as I explained to Qian, I had made the point that the manner in which China dealt with Hong Kong would have an important psychological effect on Taiwan. Qian agreed that Taiwan would watch Hong Kong closely.

ways that will benefit the United States, as well as China and our allies and friends.

To reach this goal, we strongly support China's development as a secure, open, and successful nation that is taking its place as a world leader. China has an important and constructive role to play in the coming century, and we welcome it. The United States and China share many interests that can only be served when our two countries deal constructively and openly with each other. By deepening China's integration into the international system, we can best ensure that China's development as a strong and responsible member of the international community promotes our interests as well as its own.

We do not have any illusions about the difficulty of managing our relations during this period of dramatic change and transition in China. On some critical issues, we have deep differences. Our focus must be on the long term, and we must seek to resolve our differences through engagement, not confrontation. We will do our part, but China, too, must do its part. Here at home, we must mend the consensus, frayed since Tiananmen, that has supported a constructive approach to China for almost a quarter-of-a-century—an approach that has profoundly served our national interest.

I have had the privilege of witnessing many of the remarkable changes that have shaped America's role as a Pacific power. As a young officer in the U.S. Navy, I was present in Tokyo Bay at the time of Japan's surrender in 1945. As a trade negotiator with Japan during the 1960s in the Kennedy Administration, I saw the beginnings of that nation's dramatic rise. As Deputy Secretary of State during the 1970s, I helped achieve the normalization of our ties with China. And as Secretary of State, I joined President Clinton in uniting the leaders of the Asia-Pacific region behind a bold vision of economic growth and integration.

The roots of that vision for the Asia-Pacific region reach back almost two centuries. From the days of the China Clippers carrying merchants and missionaries, to Admiral Nimitz's armadas, the United States has had enduring interests across the Pacific. Over the last half-century, our military presence—and our generous assistance—have promoted stability and given Asian nations the chance to build thriving economies and strong democracies.

President Clinton recognizes that Asia is more important to our interests now than ever before. During the last three years, we have pursued a comprehensive strategy in Asia that has produced concrete benefits for each and every American. Today, Americans are more secure because we have invigorated our core alliances in Asia and maintained 100,000 troops in a region where we have fought three wars in the past half-century. We are more prosperous because we have opened markets among the fastest-growing economies in the world. Our trade with Asia has almost doubled since 1990. And we face a brighter future because we are cooperating with former enemies to build new ties across the Pacific.

China's evolution will play a central role in shaping that future. From North Korea to the Spratly Islands, China can tip the balance in Asia between stability and conflict. Its booming economy holds a key to Asia's continued prosperity and, increasingly, to our own. Its cooperation is essential to combating threats ranging from the spread of nuclear weapons to alien smuggling and global environmental damage.

China's people have made dramatic progress in building a market economy and a more vibrant society. In roughly two decades, China has managed to quadruple its economic output—a monumental achievement by any measure. Millions of Chinese consumers have moved well beyond the "four musts"—a bicycle, a radio, a watch, and a sewing machine—and now often own cellular phones and personal computers. The most revolutionary slogan of the last decade has been Deng Xiaoping's injunction that "to get rich is glorious." Party propagandists and the People's Daily compete now for attention with radio call-in shows, satellite dishes, and the Internet.

But these changes have also generated what historian Jonathan Spence calls "internal pressures that the rest of us can only guess at." Rising incomes and an easing of social controls have raised expectations. Economic advances have brought improved living standards for many but left millions behind. Farmers flock to cities in search of better jobs—a restive "floating population" that numbers as many as 100 million people. Population growth and pollution strain China's natural resources. China's leaders face these complex challenges at a time of political transition. Confronted with the worldwide collapse of communism and the passing of the Deng Xiaoping era, they are turning to nationalism to rally their country and to legitimate their hold on power. This, in turn, has prompted fears that an increasingly nationalistic China might exert its power and influence in ways that challenge the security and prosperity of its Asian neighbors.

These changes have opened important new opportunities for U.S.-China cooperation on a broad range of shared interests, including non-proliferation, peace on the Korean Peninsula, and the fight against narcotics trafficking. But the same changes in China have also created serious strains in our relationship. In the wake of China's crackdown following the Tiananmen Square demonstrations, some Americans see China's growing power, and our differences on such issues as trade and human rights, as proof that China represents a fundamental threat to our interests. Some Chinese contend that despite our public assurances, the United States really seeks to contain and weaken China.

Both views are fundamentally flawed. We reject the counsel of those who seek to contain or isolate China. That course would harm our national interests, not protect them. Demonizing China is as dangerously misleading as romanticizing it. American policy toward China has been most successful when we have acknowledged that country's great complexity, recognized that change requires patience as well as persistence, and respected China's sovereignty while standing up for our own values and interests.

Since 1972, the foundation for deepening engagement between our nations has been the "one China" policy that is embodied in the three joint communiques between the United States and the People's Republic of China. This policy is good for the United States, the P.R.C., for Taiwan, and the entire region. It has helped keep the peace on both sides of the Taiwan Strait. And under its umbrella, Taiwan's democracy and prosperity have flourished.

The United States strongly believes that a resolution of the issues between the P.R.C. and Taiwan must be peaceful. We were gravely concerned when China's military exercises two months ago raised tensions in the Taiwan Strait. Our naval deployment at that time was meant to avert any dangerous miscalculations between either party. We are encouraged that both sides have now taken steps to reduce tensions in the Taiwan Strait. On the eve of the inauguration next Monday of Taiwan's first democratically elected president, it is timely to reflect on the enduring value of our "one China" policy for both the P.R.C. and Taiwan—and on our common interest and responsibility to uphold it. I want to tell you publicly, today, what we have been saying privately to the leaders in Beijing and Taipei in recent weeks.

To the leadership in Beijing, we have reiterated our consistent position that the future relationship between Taiwan and the P.R.C. must be resolved directly between them. But we have reaffirmed that we have a strong interest in the region's continued peace and stability—that our "one China" policy is predicated on the P.R.C.'s pursuit of a peaceful resolution of issues between Taipei and Beijing.

To the leadership in Taiwan, we have reiterated our commitment to robust unofficial relations, including helping Taiwan maintain a sufficient self-defense capacity under the terms of the Taiwan Relations Act. We have stressed that Taiwan has prospered under the "one China" policy. And we have made clear our view that as Taiwan seeks an international role, it should pursue that objective in a way that is consistent with a "one China" policy.

We have emphasized most strongly to both sides the importance of avoiding provocative actions or unilateral measures that would alter the status quo or pose a threat to peaceful resolution of outstanding issues. And we have strongly urged both sides to resume the cross-Strait dialogue that was interrupted last summer.

The United States also has an important interest in ensuring a smooth transition in Hong Kong on July 1, 1997. We support the 1984 Sino-British Joint Declaration and its "one country, two systems" framework. Beijing's commitment to maintain Hong Kong's open economy, democratic government, distinct legal system, and civil liberties is crucial to Hong Kong's future prosperity—and to China's.

Building on our enduring "one China" policy, the Clinton Administration's approach to China is guided by three tenets. First, I said at the outset, we believe that China's development as a secure, open, and successful nation is profoundly in the interest of the United States. Second, we will support China's full integration and its active participation in the international community. And, third, while we seek dialogue and engagement to manage our differences with China, we will not hesitate to take the necessary action to protect our interests. Let me briefly explain each of these three elements.

First, the wisdom of encouraging a stable and thriving China is best shown by considering the dangerous consequences of its opposite. History demonstrates that an isolated China can produce harmful, even disastrous, results for the Chinese people, the region, and the world. The reforms that China has undertaken since the late 1970s have produced great benefits. As China meets the needs of its people, it will be more secure. And a secure China is likely to be more open to reform and to be a better neighbor. Our participation in China's internal economic development, for example, has helped to expand our commercial ties, with U.S. exports to China doubling in the first half of this decade. Our exchanges on the rule of law with China are contributing to legal reforms in China that strengthen accountable government and make it easier for American companies to do business.

The second element of our strategy is to support a China that not only abides by international rules but plays an active and responsible role in setting them. As China gains the benefits of this participation, it must assume commensurate obligations. China's full participation in the international community is essential to our ability to address the critical global and regional challenges of the next century. No area better illustrates the benefits of gaining China's deeper involvement in the international community than the fight against the spread of weapons of mass destruction.

A little over a decade ago, China stood outside of the world's major non-proliferation regimes. Today, China is a member of the International Atomic Energy Agency and a signatory to the nuclear Non-Proliferation Treaty and the Chemical Weapons Convention—a dramatic turnabout that our engagement helped to produce. The United States and China have worked together to achieve unconditional extension of the NPT, controls on ballistic missile exports, and the shutdown of North Korea's nuclear weapons program. With China's help, we hope to complete a comprehensive test ban treaty and have it ready for signature at the UN General Assembly this September.

We still face serious proliferation challenges with China. But we should not underestimate the significance of the steps that already have been taken. China's smooth integration into the global trading system is also in our interest. That is why the United States strongly supports China's accession to the World Trade Organization on commercially acceptable terms. We have worked with China to develop a roadmap of concrete steps to widen access to its markets and bring its trade practices in line with WTO rules.

Both our nations' interests are also served by China's full participation in new structures for regional security and economic cooperation. China's membership in the ASEAN Regional Forum is an important example. That membership encouraged China's statement last year that it would abide by international law to settle its claims in the Spratly Islands. And as a result of its membership in APEC, China is lowering its tariffs as part of its down-payment toward achieving open and fair trade in the region by the year 2020.

But the process of integration is incomplete, and there remain important areas of difference. To manage these differences, we seek engagement. And for engagement to be successful, we must be prepared to take actions necessary to protect our interests—the third element of our approach. Where we have differences, we will press our views and interests candidly and forcefully, with all the appropriate means at our disposal.

Our willingness to enforce U.S. law, for example, was critical to reaching an understanding last week with China on non-proliferation and nuclear-related exports. Following intensive discussions that I held last month with Vice Premier Qian, China has made a public commitment not to provide assistance to unsafeguarded nuclear facilities. And it has agreed to important consultations on export control policies and related issues. At the same time, we continue to have serious concerns about China's nuclear and military cooperation with Iran, and we will continue to press this issue with Chinese leaders. We have also stressed to China the importance of fully implementing the agreement to protect intellectual property rights that we reached in February 1995. The piracy of compact disks, videos, and software is growing, causing billions of dollars in losses to American companies. The President has made it clear that if the Chinese authorities do not act to curtail sharply this piracy, we will have no choice but to go ahead with carefully targeted sanctions that were announced this week.

We do not want a trade war with China. That would serve no one's interests. The sanctions lists issued this week should not be seen as the end of the process—but as a step that could lead to a successful outcome. That said, like any other nation, China must fulfill its agreements and meet its responsibilities as a leading trading nation. No one should doubt that we will protect our interests.

Trade and investment are helping to create a more open China. But we will not rely solely on the beneficial impact of increasing economic development to bring about progress in human rights. Recent economic and legal reforms have somewhat diminished the arbitrary power of the Chinese Government over the daily lives of its citizens. But grave human rights abuses continue, including the arrest of those who peacefully voice their opinions, including restrictions on religious freedom, as well as repression in Tibet.

The American people have a deep and abiding interest in the promotion of human rights in China and around the world. We will continue to speak out on behalf of those in China who defend universally recognized rights, as we did together with our European Union colleagues at the UN Human Rights Commission last month. We will continue to work with China to strengthen its judiciary. We know that change in China will take time—and that the most repressive periods in recent Chinese history have occurred when China was isolated from the world. That is one of the strong reasons why we continue to pursue engagement with China.

Our support for continuing most-favored-nation trading status for China should be seen in the context of the three elements of our policy. The MFN debate should not be a referendum on China's current political system or on whether we approve of the policies of the Chinese leadership. The issue at stake is whether renewing MFN unconditionally is the best way to advance American interests. The President and I are convinced that the answer is a resounding "yes"—a conclusion reached by every American president since 1979.

Revoking or conditioning MFN would not advance human rights in China, but it would damage our economy and jeopardize more than 200,000 American jobs. It would harm Hong Kong, which is why legislative leader Martin Lee and Gov. Chris Patten strongly support MFN's unconditional renewal—as they emphasized in Washington last week. It would hurt Taiwan, whose economy depends heavily on its commercial ties with the P.R.C. and U.S.-China trade. It could also undermine our ability to work with China on regional security issues, such as North Korea, and on any of the other important interests we share— from non-proliferation to the global environment. And it would weaken our influence throughout a region that still looks to America as a source and a force for stability and security.

The issues that I have discussed today only begin to reflect the breadth of our relationship with China. We have an extraordinarily diverse and demanding agenda with China.

Given the range of our interests and the importance of China to our future security and well-being, I believe the time has come to develop a more regular dialogue between our two countries. Holding periodic cabinet-level consultations in our capitals would facilitate a candid exchange of views. It would provide a more effective means for managing specific problems, and it would allow us to approach individual issues within a broader strategic framework.

I also believe that our nations' two leaders should hold regular summit meetings. I intend to discuss these ideas with Vice Premier Qian when we meet in Jakarta in July.

In the United States, we also face an immediate priority. If we are to sustain the advances that we have made with China since the historic opening in 1972, we must rebuild the bipartisan consensus that has guided our relations with China since then. Our interests demand it, and our allies and friends expect it. We must continue to have the full support of the American people to meet the difficult challenges that lie ahead.

Thank you very much.

THIRTY

The War Against Terrorism

Terrorism is as old as civilization, but it really struck home for Americans in the 1990s. Law enforcement officials charged international terrorists with several high-profile attacks: the 1992 bombing of Pan Am flight 103 over Lockerbie, Scotland, which killed 273 people; the 1993 New York World Trade Center bombing, which killed six and injured more than 1,000; and the 1993 gunning down of two CIA employees at the entrance to Agency headquarters near Washington, D.C. Domestic terrorists' 1995 bombing of the Oklahoma City federal building killed 168 people and gave the whole nation a collective sense of insecurity. The two 1997 trials stemming from this bombing brought the issue of terrorism into our homes, via television and radio, on a daily basis. Another horrifying development that year was the use of a biological weapon, nerve gas, in an attack in the Tokyo subway system that caused eight deaths and hundreds of injuries. The mobility provided by modern transportation and the power of the weapons now available to terrorists, coupled with the lightning speed at which information travels, have produced new levels of danger and concern.

Terrorism has had perhaps its strongest impact in the Middle East, where it has posed one of the greatest challenges to peace. From the hostage-takers at the 1972 Munich Olympics to the suicide bombers of the 1990s, Middle Eastern extremists have often resorted to destroying innocent lives to make political statements. As the peace process made startling progress in the 1990s, desperate opponents turned to terrorism in last-ditch efforts to thwart it.

Events in late 1995 and early 1996 demonstrated the potency of these efforts. The assassination of Prime Minister Yitzhak Rabin by a right-wing Israeli terrorist in November 1995 was a crippling blow to the peace process. Then, in a span of just two weeks in February and March 1996, four separate suicide bombings in Israel took 61 lives. Palestinian militants connected with the terrorist group Hamas were blamed for these attacks. Imagining the distress that such a series of bombings would create in the United States increased my admiration for the resilience of the Israeli people. Nevertheless, this campaign of terror brought the peace process to the verge of collapse.

In response to this crisis, President Clinton joined Egyptian President Hosni Mubarak and Israeli Prime Minister Shimon Peres in calling for a meeting of world leaders. This meeting, attended by President Clinton and the leaders of 26 nations in Europe and the Middle East, was held on March 13, 1996, in Sharm el-Sheikh, an Egyptian resort on the Sinai Peninsula at the tip of the Red Sea. The event had a surreal quality; as a brilliant sun beat down on the all-white buildings, the likes of German Chancellor Helmut Kohl, British Prime Minister John Major, and French President Jacques Chirac walked in dark suits among the scuba divers and sunbathers.

This "summit of the peacemakers" was a landmark event. Once it had been taboo for Arab spokesmen to acknowledge the reality of the state of Israel, let alone take joint action with its leaders. Yet at Sharm el-Sheikh, 14 Arab leaders stood side by side with the Israeli Prime Minister to denounce acts of terrorism in Israel, support the Israeli people, and bolster peace. The presence on short notice of these and so many other world leaders sent an unmistakable signal: the international community is united against terrorism and will not be deterred by extremists.[1]

The summit produced tangible as well as symbolic results. Those attending agreed to work together to prevent terrorist groups from operating. Leading the way, the Clinton Administration promised to promote

---

[1]After the summit, President Clinton flew to Israel as a further show of support. Because of the heightened terrorist threat, more than 10,000 Israeli policemen—over half of the nation's police force—mobilized to protect the President during his 24-hour visit. To accommodate his massive security entourage, most of Jerusalem's streets were closed, as well as the highway linking Tel Aviv to Jerusalem. Despite this disruption, Israeli media reported widespread appreciation of the President's visit.

legislation (which was subsequently enacted) giving U.S. law enforcement officials tools to stop terrorists before they can strike and to prosecute them if they do. We also worked with Congress to produce an executive order expanding legal restrictions on suspected terrorist groups. In the Middle East itself, Ambassador Dennis Ross chaired working sessions with Israeli and Palestinian officials to develop plans for cooperating against terrorism. This effort had been launched a few weeks before the Sharm el-Sheikh summit. A team of counterterrorism experts led by CIA Deputy Director (now Director) George Tenet had traveled to Israel and met with these officials to discuss how to combat terrorist acts, and to share such technical assets as satellite information and eavesdropping technology. President Clinton had earmarked $100 million to help upgrade Israeli anti-terrorism equipment.

Given these developments and the heightened concern about terrorism, I wanted to devote an entire speech to the subject. I did so in May 1996, speaking at the Washington Institute for Near East Policy. Like my Stanford speech on the environment (see Chapter 28), this address was an agenda-setting effort. It was intended to help develop the public's awareness of how this terrifying global phenomenon threatened American interests.

The speech reviewed the accomplishments of the Sharm el-Sheikh summit, explained its significance, and repeated its clear signal that the United States would not allow terrorist acts to temper its resolve in support of Middle East peace. "The United States is determined to ensure that the enemies of peace do not succeed," I said. "We will never give in to their terror."

One cannot address modern-day terrorism without discussing Iran. Iran is the world's most significant state sponsor of terrorism and the most ardent opponent of the Middle East peace process, as I emphasized in my 1994 Georgetown speech (see Chapter 13). Since coming into office, I had urged that the Administration take a very hard line against the Iranian regime. I believed Iran could not be moderated with words alone; only a determined combination of economic and political pressure could alter its behavior.

While the Administration remained committed to a tough stance against Iran, coordinating this policy with our European allies was a challenge. Lured by prospects of economic benefit, several of our key European partners, in particular France and Germany, continued to maintain friendly relations with Iran. We constantly prodded them to distance themselves from Iran and to suspend trade, as we had done. In private meetings, we shared with them evidence gathered by our intelligence agencies, showing Iran's links to such Middle East terrorist groups as Hamas and Hezbollah.

Our Administration also worked to build a public case against Iran. It was vital, I believed, that the world know exactly what that nation was doing. While preparing the Washington Institute speech, I pressed our intelligence agencies to allow me to release publicly the most up-to-date information on Iran. Along with mobilizing public opinion, which I hoped might inspire a change in European policy, I aimed to remind the Iranians that we knew what they were up to and had the capabilities to trace the supporters of terrorist acts. Thus, the speech noted that Iran provides approximately $100 million annually to Islamic terrorist groups, that a mortar in transit intercepted by Belgium came from Iran and was intended to be used against a Jewish target in Europe, and that an Iranian-backed group was the primary suspect in a recent drive-by shooting of an Israeli-American student on the West Bank. Although the audience at the Washington Institute was hardly surprised by these revelations, their public airing was an escalation of our efforts.

Unfortunately, the struggle to stop our allies from doing business with Iran has not yet succeeded. We have convinced them of Iran's terrorist intent, but we still differ on how best to deal with that rogue country. Although the United States usually prefers an engagement strategy of the kind pursued by the Europeans, the grossness of Iran's conduct warrants the unyielding U.S. position until that conduct changes. At the same time, the United States should not have permanent enemies and should be prepared to hold discussions that would emphasize our concerns and probe for openings justifying a change in our approach.

The speech also discussed Syria. Although the United States maintains diplomatic relations with Syria, it continually pressures Damascus to stop providing a haven for militant groups that engage in terrorism. Nevertheless, Syria remains on our list of nations that support terrorism, and I made clear to Assad during my visits to Damascus that Syria has no hope of enjoying a fully normal relationship with the United States until he drives the terrorist organizations from within his borders. Assad did not help his cause by refusing to attend the Sharm el-Sheikh summit, and we let him know it.

Despite these difficulties, the speech noted, Syria should not be grouped with Iran and other rogue states. Unlike those states, Syria says that it has made a strategic commitment to seeking peace, and it has pursued peace negotiations with Israel. In addition, it has shown some, though not enough, willingness to cooperate against terrorism. For example, in April 1996, as on several prior occasions, Syria was instrumental in ending Hezbollah's attacks against Israel in southern Lebanon. Moreover, after a week of my shuttling between the parties, Syria joined in an agreement to establish a monitoring group meant to prevent attacks on civilians in northern Israel and southern Lebanon.

A month after the Washington Institute speech, a horrifying event gave me a firsthand look at the consequences of terrorism. After meetings in Cairo on June 25, I was preparing to return to the United States when word came that a bomb had exploded at a U.S. military housing complex in Dhahran, Saudi Arabia. I diverted our aircraft to Dhahran and was the first high-level American civilian to reach the scene. An FBI team located in Saudi Arabia had already arrived and was commencing an investigation.

The huge bomb, which had left a crater 35 feet deep, had sheared the entire front off an eight-story apartment building, as if a giant knife had sliced down and laid bare the devastated interiors of the apartments. The explosive force and flying debris had killed 19 U.S. servicemen and wounded hundreds of Americans and Saudis living in that and adjacent buildings. The terrorists had driven a bomb-laden truck into an unguarded parking lot next to the apartment building, set the bomb to explode, and escaped in a waiting car.

When I visited the wounded in the nearby hospital, I learned that flying glass had caused most of the injuries, some of which were so extensive that the patients were almost completely swathed in bandages. Most of those wounds could have been prevented if the building had been equipped with shatterproof glass. The Pentagon and the press engaged in a wrenching debate on how high up the military chain of command blame should be affixed for failure to take this and other necessary precautions. Ultimately, the disaster brought an end to the military career of the base commander, Brigadier General Terry Swallier. Secretary of Defense William Perry later ordered most American military personnel in Saudi Arabia moved to a remote base in the central part of the country, where they could be more readily protected.

Saudi Foreign Minister Prince Saud al Faisal joined me at the bombing site and promised his government's full cooperation in investigating the attack and searching for those responsible. Prince Saud was a highly professional and experienced diplomat who was often helpful in concerting the views of the Persian Gulf states.[2] Conservative in outlook and operating within a rigid bureaucracy, Saud frequently appeared to have little flexibility in presenting the Saudi point of view, especially on peace process issues, but I felt that he was sympathetic and tried to be helpful when he could. Unfortunately, promises of cooperation in the bombing investigation melted down in the crosscurrents of royal family intrigue and Saudi secretiveness, and our investigators faced continual frustration. As of this writing, more than a year and a half after the blast, responsibility for it still has not been fixed.

The fight against terrorism will likely occupy U.S. foreign policy well into the 21st century. Despite the Sharm el-Sheikh summit and the policies outlined in the Washington Institute speech, terrorism is still a tragic part of Middle Eastern politics. In the summer of 1997, another wave of anti-Israeli violence swept the region, and the peace process again threatened to implode. Looking ahead, we should remember that ultimately the only way to defeat terrorism in the Middle East is to embrace the very future that the suicide bombers seek to shatter—a comprehensive, warm peace.

Fighting Terrorism: Challenges for Peacemakers

Address to the Washington Institute for Near East Policy
Annual Soref Symposium, Washington, D.C., May 21, 1996

[Introductory remarks deleted]

Thank you very much. I last spoke at the Institute in October 1993, soon after Prime Minister Rabin and Chairman Arafat shook hands on the White House lawn and forever changed the course of Middle East

---

[2]Tall, handsome, and completely fluent in English, Saud often spends part of the summer with his family in Beverly Hills.

history. Since then, much has happened. Israel and Jordan are at peace. Palestinians defied the Hamas call to boycott elections and in doing so gave their clear mandate for peace. Today, they govern themselves in Gaza and most cities in the West Bank. The Palestinian National Council voted overwhelmingly to make good on its commitment to cancel the egregious provisions of its charter. Economic summits have been held in Casablanca and Amman. Eight members of the Arab League have made official visits to Israel, and—with the exception of Libya, Iraq, and Sudan—every Arab League member has participated in some aspect of the peace process.

Had I predicted these events in 1993, you probably would have said that I needed a long rest. The scope and pace of change has truly been breathtaking. It has come so fast that what was previously unthinkable is now routine. In the face of difficult challenges, it is easy to forget how dramatically the peace process has already transformed the landscape of the Middle East. As we move forward, we must remember the enormous progress we have made.

None of the challenges we now face is more pressing than the fight against terrorism. Terrorism destroys innocent lives. It undermines a society's sense of security—and with it the very foundation upon which a lasting peace must be built. As such, terrorism is a threat to our national interests—not simply in the Middle East but around the world. President Clinton has rightly identified terrorism as one of the most important security challenges we face in the wake of the Cold War. As he said in his address to the United Nations last October, terrorism today is a worldwide phenomenon. No one is immune—certainly not Israel but also not Egypt or Japan or France, Britain or Germany or Turkey, Saudi Arabia, Argentina, or Algeria, and, unfortunately, not America, where terrorists have struck from lower Manhattan to Oklahoma City.

As if the threat is not already severe enough, we now face an even more alarming danger: the terrorist armed with weapons of mass destruction. Last year's nerve gas attack on the Tokyo subway system was a grim omen. It was also a wake-up call for the world. The threat is real. We must act now to meet it.

The United States is leading the way. Last month, the President signed into law landmark anti-terrorism legislation. This bill provides law enforcement with new tools to stop terrorists before they strike and to bring them to justice when they do. It strengthens our ability to prevent international terrorists from raising funds in the United States. And while ensuring legal safeguards, it allows us quickly to expel foreigners who provide support for terrorist activities.

The United States also has spearheaded efforts to combat terrorism on the global level. We have imposed strong sanctions against states that sponsor or harbor terrorists. We have intensified our counterterrorism cooperation with other countries, allowing us to apprehend key figures in attacks such as the World Trade Center bombing. Last December, with our partners in the G-7 and Russia, we convened a ministerial meeting in Ottawa to develop common strategies for fighting terror. In April, President Clinton joined President Yeltsin and other leaders in Moscow, where they agreed on new steps to prevent nuclear materials from falling into the wrong hands. Nowhere in the world has America's leadership in the fight against terror been more evident than in the Middle East. We have maintained UN sanctions against Libya for its role in the bombing of Pan Am flight 103. And we are working to increase pressure on Sudan for its support of last June's assassination attempt against Egypt's President Mubarak.

America's most critical role, however—and the one I want to focus on today—is defending the Middle East peace process and peacemakers against the vicious attacks of their enemies. Terrorists and their supporters are now engaged in a systematic assault on Israel and the peace process. Their goal is clear: They seek to kill the very possibility of peace by destroying every Israeli's sense of personal security. The enemies of peace are escalating their attacks for a very clear reason: The peace process is succeeding. With every step toward peace that Israel and its neighbors take, the enemies of peace grow more desperate and more determined to lash out. They must promote fear because they know that hope is their undoing.

The United States is determined to ensure that the enemies of peace do not succeed. We will never give in to their terror. We refuse to allow terrorists to undermine our resolve or divert us from our goal of a real, secure, and lasting peace for Israel and for all the people of the Middle East. When Israel was terrorized by a wave of suicide bombings in February and March, President Clinton responded by organizing the Sharm el-Sheikh summit. Literally overnight, leaders from around the world answered his call to join Israel—not to celebrate another breakthrough in the peace process but to defend the peace process at a moment of crisis. It was an unprecedented event that sent an unmistakable message: The enemies of peace are doomed. Their terror will only strengthen our resolve to complete the circle of peace and put them out of business for good.

Sharm el-Sheikh launched a process to expand joint efforts against terrorism throughout the region. Most recently, President Clinton and Prime Minister Peres signed a new antiterrorism accord that will strengthen cooperation between our two governments. In addition, the United States is providing Israel with more than $100 million in anti-terrorism equipment and training.

We also have begun to bolster the counterterrorism capabilities of the Palestinian Authority. With our support, Israeli and Palestinian security services are now cooperating in a joint campaign to root out the terrorist infrastructure in the West Bank and Gaza. Palestinian forces have intercepted many suicide bombers. They have uncovered explosives and arms caches. They have arrested, tried, and imprisoned perpetrators of terrorist acts, and they continue to hunt down others.

Chairman Arafat today clearly understands that he must give a 100% effort in the war on terror—and not just because his agreements with Israel require it. He is doing it because he knows that the bombs of Hamas and Islamic Jihad are trying to destroy Palestinian aspirations as much as they are Israeli lives. The United States will continue to insist that this increased Palestinian effort be sustained.

As with Hamas before it, Hezbollah's purpose in last month's attacks in Lebanon also was to kill the peace process. As hostilities escalated, America's responsibility and interests were clear: to use our influence to stop the suffering of innocent civilians, to end the crisis, and to create a new framework to limit the chances of it happening again.

The agreement that resulted from my shuttle mission achieved those objectives. Hundreds of thousands of Israelis and Lebanese have been able to return to their homes. New, written understandings have been reached to contain the dangers of any hostilities. An international effort will be mounted to assist in Lebanon's reconstruction. We are organizing a monitoring group in which Israel, Lebanon, and Syria are being brought together for the first time to help prevent another crisis. This recent campaign of violence has again shined the spotlight on a disturbing reality: When it comes to terrorism against the peace process, Iran is playing a leading role. Iran's leaders regularly use rhetoric that incites terrorism. President Rafsanjani called Prime Minister Rabin's assassination "divine vengeance." And just prior to the Hamas bombing spree, Iran's Supreme Leader, Khameini, preached that "The power of Islam will ultimately bring about the end of the rootless Zionist regime . . . which must be destroyed."

Iran has not stopped at rhetoric. It frequently meets with all the major terrorist groups—including Hezbollah, Hamas, Palestinian Islamic Jihad, and the PFL-PGC. It actively encourages these groups to use terror to destroy the peace process. It provides them with money—up to several million dollars a year in the case of Hamas, Islamic Jihad, and others and up to $100 million a year for Hezbollah. Iran also supplies them with arms and material support, training, and—in some cases—operational guidance. The evidence has grown in recent months. In advance of Israel's elections, Iranian-trained terrorists have been sent to infiltrate Israel and the Palestinian territories. Some have been intercepted. Others narrowly failed in carrying out their deadly activities. Still others have succeeded in their murderous missions. We believe that an Iranian-backed group was responsible for last week's drive-by shooting of an Israeli-American yeshiva student in the West Bank. In another case, Belgium intercepted a shipment containing a mortar, which came from Iran and was probably intended for an attack on a Jewish target in Europe.

There should no longer be any debate about Iran's involvement in terrorism against the peace process. German Foreign Minister Kinkel left no doubt about that in remarks he made here in Washington just two weeks ago. He said that Germany is "fully aware of the evil things that Iran has been doing and is still doing." He went on to say that

> [T]he Americans and the Germans agree as to the general assessment of what Iran means by way of terrorism . . . support of Hezbollah, Hamas, and Jihad.

While we and our allies now share a similar analysis of the facts, we differ when it comes to how best to deal with Iran. The United States believes that Iran will change its behavior only when the world makes it pay a sufficiently high political and economic price. We must deny Iran's leaders the resources to finance their dangerous policies.

That is why the President decided, last year, to impose a comprehensive embargo on U.S. trade with Iran. And that is why we have been working with Congress on legislation to further tighten economic restrictions on Iran. In contrast, some European nations continue to engage Iran in what they call a critical dialogue while maintaining normal trade. The Europeans themselves acknowledge that their policy has produced no significant change in Iranian behavior. We remain convinced that no amount of dialogue will alter Iran's policies unless it is coupled with real economic pressure. Let me stress one point: We do not oppose the EU policy because we oppose the principle of speaking with Iran. The United States has long said that we are ready to conduct an open dialogue with authoritative representatives of the Iranian Government, in which we could fully air our two major concerns: First, Iran's support for terrorism, especially against the peace process and, second, its efforts to acquire weapons of mass destruction. Iran, however, has never taken up this offer.

Our determination to contain Iran and to defeat the enemies of peace is clear. But so is our commitment to press ahead with negotiations on a comprehensive Arab-Israeli peace. Anything less would hand the terrorists the very victory they seek.

To close the circle of peace, agreements between Israel and Syria and between Israel and Lebanon are essential. Syria presents us with a unique challenge. On the one hand, we continue to have serious problems in our bilateral relationship with Syria. Syria remains on our narcotics list as well as on our terrorism list.

Both President Clinton and I have consistently pressed our concerns with President Assad and other senior Syrian officials. We will continue to do so and to make clear that these concerns must be met before the United States can build a mutually beneficial relationship with Syria.

Yet we recognize that Syria is different from Iran. Iran rejects the very notion of peace and has dedicated itself to Israel's destruction. By contrast, Syria has been negotiating directly with Israel to end their conflict. I have no illusions: Translating that willingness to negotiate into a peace agreement will be difficult. But the talks thus far have provided a solid foundation for progress when negotiations resume.

As long as we remain convinced that peace is possible, we must continue to work with the parties to achieve a breakthrough that would have far-reaching strategic consequences—not just for the Middle East but for America's vital interests. A comprehensive peace will dramatically reduce the risk of another Arab-Israeli war. It will remove the final constraints on Israel's having normal relations with the entire Arab and Muslim world.

Finally, and perhaps most importantly, ending the Arab-Israeli conflict will allow us and our friends to harness our resources to meet the common set of strategic challenges that threaten us all—especially the rise of extremist movements that use terrorism and violence and rogue states, such as Iran and Iraq, that possess weapons of mass destruction.

These are the real dangers that we and our friends will have to address in the coming years. In pursuit of our national interests, we are determined to do so. A critical part of our strategy must be a continued effort to seize the historic opportunity that now exists to achieve a secure and comprehensive peace.

Thank you.

THIRTY-ONE

A New Atlantic Community

The fall of 1996 seemed a good time to announce the specifics of the European strategy I had outlined in Prague that spring (see Chapter 27). In particular, we wanted to send another unmistakable signal that America has a continuing role in Europe and is committed to expanding NATO. And this time we wanted to give a timetable for that expansion. The resulting statement, made in Stuttgart, exemplifies how a speech can be both an instrument for America's leadership and a catalyst for coming to grips with issues that might otherwise have been postponed, such as the setting of a date for the next NATO summit.

President Clinton had considered making this statement himself, but in the thick of his reelection campaign, we were concerned that critics at home and abroad would view his announcement of NATO expansion as a political ploy. We hoped that my delivering the speech would help remove our policy from the context of presidential politics. This consideration also influenced our choice of venue: delivering the speech on European soil at a long-planned commemorative event would make it harder for critics to define it as a message crafted at the last minute for the U.S. electorate.

Early in 1996, Klaus Kinkel, the German Vice Chancellor and Foreign Minister, had urged me to speak in Stuttgart on the 50th anniversary of the famous "speech of hope" delivered there by Secretary of State James Byrnes. Byrnes's historic address reassured his wary German audience that the United States would remain engaged in Europe and would provide strong support for rebuilding Germany from the ruins of World

War II. I decided to accept the invitation out of personal regard for Kinkel and because I sensed that Stuttgart would be a good backdrop for the announcements I wanted to make.[1]

Stuttgart provided stirring reminders of the war era—and of all that had changed since that time. I spoke from the same stage in the State Theater that Secretary Byrnes had used in 1946. Before my remarks, a United States Air Force band played Glenn Miller music. It was a moving moment; I remembered dancing and listening to the Glenn Miller Orchestra during the war, a memory that much of the German audience seemed to share. I genuinely meant it when I told the overflow crowd, "More music, less talk. That's a motto that I can enthusiastically endorse." Stuttgart's popular Mayor, Manfred Rommel, the son of the famous World War II field marshal, preceded me to the rostrum, where he eloquently expressed his gratitude for America's support for Germany after the war.

In the "speech of hope," Secretary Byrnes had announced to a defeated and impoverished German public that the United States would be magnanimous in victory, working toward the political and economic unity of their nation and returning its government to them. Setting an equally ambitious agenda for post–Cold War Europe, I used my speech to envision development of a New Atlantic Community by the start of the next century. That community would include Russia and Central Europe, and would be anchored by an enlarged NATO and EU and by a partnership between the United States and Europe. And, like Byrnes, I sent an emphatic signal that the United States intended to stay involved in Europe.

Enlargement of NATO was crucial to the creation of the New Atlantic Community. Following our decision late in 1993 to pursue NATO

[1]Even in this era of computers and cyberspace, personal relationships continue to play a central role in the world of diplomacy and, in my judgment, always will. My decision to speak in Stuttgart rather than some other European city owed a great deal to my relationship with Klaus Kinkel. During my four years as Secretary, almost every major European foreign ministry changed hands at least once. Germany's proved the exception, and Kinkel was one of my most valued colleagues from the very outset. He frequently telephoned to alert me to European attitudes on key issues or to give candid appraisals of U.S. positions. He was a solid supporter of NATO expansion, our efforts to bring peace to Bosnia, and our New Transatlantic Agenda with the EU. Stuttgart is only a few miles from Kinkel's home city, and he added a personal touch by inviting me and a few colleagues to join him for dinner at the famous Cistercian abbey at Bebenhausen after the speech.

expansion, we had steadily pushed the process forward. We had also taken complementary steps to bolster the basic goal of the integration of Europe. These included developing the Partnership for Peace and the New Transatlantic Agenda, establishing a broader dialogue with Central European states and new security relationships with Russia and Ukraine, and, under NATO's leadership, implementing a Bosnia peace agreement. Those advances—most importantly, the success of the Dayton talks and of the NATO-led IFOR in Bosnia—had brought us to the point of making NATO expansion a reality. As we entered the final year of President Clinton's first term, I believed the time was ripe to make firm plans to invite new members to join the Alliance.

Accordingly, the Administration began to consider calling for a NATO summit to be held in mid-1997. In diplomacy, summits frequently become action-forcing events; preparing for them helps to energize the policy process not only abroad, but also within the U.S. government. We deliberately used two summits—January 1994 and July 1997—to drive NATO expansion.

The Stuttgart speech represented an important element in our effort to "tee up" the summit announcement so that it could be made at the December 1996 NATO ministerial meeting. After the usual last-minute negotiations with the White House and with other interested agencies (here the issues included the timing of the NATO expansion announcement and of the summit), I was authorized to say, "I would expect that our leaders will meet in the spring or early summer of 1997 at an extremely important summit," a summit at which the Alliance should invite several countries to begin negotiations to join it. In addition, the speech gave substance to our commitment that the first new members of NATO would not be the last by proposing that dialogue with other interested countries continue after the summit.

Before the Stuttgart speech, I traveled to London, Paris, and Bonn to preview the speech for the leaders of our core NATO Allies—Prime Minister Major, President Chirac, and Chancellor Kohl. They had no substantial objections to our plans regarding NATO expansion, though they did suggest some minor language changes to the speech, which I was glad to accept. All three agreed that a 1997 NATO summit would be an ideal occasion for taking historic steps on NATO enlargement, and also on a NATO-Russia charter.

The United States had long considered the possibility of an agreement outlining mutual understandings and defining areas for cooperation between NATO and Russia. We believed that such an agreement would not only allay Russia's concerns about NATO but further its integration into Europe. Russia's role in implementing the Dayton Agreement sharply improved the prospects for this kind of charter. Secretary of Defense Perry and my Deputy, Strobe Talbott, who were instrumental in securing Russian participation in the Bosnia force, believed that a direct line could be drawn from the present relationship between Russia and IFOR to a future one between Russia and NATO. I also believed that as NATO enlargement began to appear inevitable to the Russians, they would turn their attention away from derailing the process and toward securing their interest in constructive ties with the Alliance.

Perry, Talbott, and I had already begun to discuss such a charter privately with our Alliance and Russian counterparts. Now, in the context of our decision to call for a 1997 summit, we needed to move these negotiations front and center to keep them moving in parallel with Alliance expansion. I wanted to use the Stuttgart speech to energize our talks with the Russians, and my statement that "we seek a fundamentally new relationship between Russia and the new NATO" was the most direct message I had sent them yet. I also noted that an agreement should "create standing arrangements for consultation and joint action between Russia and the Alliance." These remarks gained the most media attention of any part of the speech; the press described them accurately as evidence of our effort to enter into a more cooperative relationship with Russia.

Three months later, in December 1996, I arrived in Brussels for my last meeting of NATO's governing council. Since my first such meeting in Athens in June 1993, when I had secured agreement to hold a NATO summit in January 1994, these semiannual events had proved essential to our effort to drive policy and transform NATO. At each meeting, my public statements and private discussions had inched the expansion process forward.

The December 1996 meeting was the capstone of these efforts. The NATO ministers unanimously called for a summit in Madrid in July 1997, to which those nations selected for accession negotiations would be invited. The ministers also agreed that the first new members would be admitted by 1999. Most gratifyingly, Russian Foreign Minister Primakov signaled a willingness to move forward with a NATO-Russia charter. We decided that while the U.S.-Russia channel would remain open, NATO Secretary General Solana would take the lead in negotiating this charter with Moscow. We achieved all of our goals and more at this meeting. I reported to President Clinton afterward, "All the elements of our strategy are now launched."

From the vantage of private life, I anxiously watched the NATO expansion strategy come to fruition in 1997. On May 27 in Paris, NATO and Russia signed a charter formally known as the Founding Act on Mutual Relations, Cooperation and Security between NATO and the Russian Federation. At the July 1997 NATO summit in Madrid, the 16 Alliance leaders invited the Czech Republic, Poland, and Hungary to begin discussions about entering NATO. Together, the Paris signing and the Madrid summit marked perhaps the most decisive development in European security policy since the fall of the Soviet empire. Undoubtedly, these events will prove critical in shaping the future of the New Atlantic Community that is described in the Stuttgart speech.

A New Atlantic Community for the 21st Century

Address at the State Theater, Stuttgart,

Germany, September 6, 1996

Minister-President Teufel, Foreign Minister Kinkel, Mayor Rommel, General Jamerson, Governor James, Congressman Roth, ladies and gentlemen: Before I begin today, let me pay a special tribute to my colleague Klaus Kinkel, who has meant so much to U.S.-German relations, who has been my close friend and confidant all through my 3 1/2 years as Secretary of State, and who invited me to come here today. I am very much indebted to you, Klaus. Thank you ever so much. I know that you'd all want me to thank the United States Air Force for playing music in the tradition of Glenn Miller and giving us so much pleasure here today. Let's give them a hand, too. When I finish my remarks today, I'm afraid there will be a new motto springing up from the audience, along the lines of more music, less talk. That's a motto that I can enthusiastically endorse.

As you know, I have come to commemorate with you the "speech of hope," which my predecessor, Secretary of State James Byrnes, gave here in Stuttgart 50 years ago on this very day, in this very auditorium. I have come to recall the half-century of progress we have achieved together since that speech and to discuss how we can assure a thriving partnership into the next century.

It will come as no surprise that Secretary Byrnes, like many public officials, had some help in preparing his speech. His principal helper was John Kenneth Galbraith, the famous economist, author, and U.S. Ambassador to India. When I called Professor Galbraith a few days ago to reminisce about the Byrnes speech, he commented, with a smile in his voice, "I have never listened to a speech with a greater sense of approval." Of course, all of Europe listened intently, for its future hung in the balance. The United States had joined with our Allies to win the war, because we knew America could not be free if Europe was not. But in 1946, we had not yet won the peace. Though the first American care packages began to arrive in August of that year, a German reporter who traveled to Stuttgart with Secretary Byrnes could look from the train window and describe "countless women with tattered knapsacks . . . a few men plodding homeward in the dusk" returning to homes where "the children have no shoes, daughter has no coat, the house has neither window glass nor fuel in the cellar. And winter approaches." Meanwhile, to the east, liberation brought not liberty but a new communist tyranny that would divide families, nations, and the world.

Secretary Byrnes' address came to be known as the "speech of hope," because it put America firmly on the side of those who believed in a better future for Germany and Europe. The principles he expressed in the speech laid the foundation for our successful post-war partnership. They formed the basis for what became a bipartisan American strategy, symbolized by Republican Senator Arthur Vandenberg, who was present at Secretary Byrnes' speech. The principles shaping our approach to Europe to this very day are the ones laid down by Secretary Byrnes.

First, Byrnes pledged that America would remain a political and military power in Europe. After World War I, we had withdrawn from European affairs and paid a terrible price. "We will not again make that mistake," Byrnes said. "We are staying here."

Second, Byrnes asserted that our support for democracy was the key to lasting peace and recovery in Germany and in Europe. "The American people want to return the government of Germany to the German people," he said. We were confident that a democratic Germany could emerge as our partner.

Finally, Byrnes expressed America's commitment to Germany's political and economic unity. The United States believed that Germany had to be united, democratic, and free if Europe as a whole was to achieve stability and integration. Byrnes' far-sighted approach set the stage for George Marshall, Konrad Adenauer, Jean Monnet, and the remarkable generation that led the recovery of Europe and gave us 50 years of peace and prosperity. Thanks to them, we realized the promise of the speech of hope. America maintained its engagement and its armed forces in Europe. The German people chose freedom and achieved unification. And together, we stayed the course of the Cold War. Today, Checkpoint Charlie is no more than a museum for tourists. And at NATO headquarters, where we once planned to defend Berlin and Stuttgart from Soviet attack, the flags of 43 European nations, including Russia, now fly.

In the last half-century, the United States and Germany have built a relationship deeper than even the ties forged by our soldiers and diplomats. We have a cultural and intellectual partnership, so well represented by the Fulbright program, the Goethe Institute, the German Marshall Fund, and many, many others. We have an economic partnership, too: America is the top foreign investor in Germany, and it is the primary beneficiary of German foreign investment abroad. We also have an environmental partnership. Together, for example, we are fighting toxic waste in eastern Germany, acid rain in Wisconsin, and deforestation in Brazil.

Fifty years ago, Secretary Byrnes said America wanted to "help the German people win their way back to an honorable place among the free and peace-loving nations of the world." Our shared achievement has been just plain breathtaking. Now this city and the land around it represent the Europe familiar to all of us: a place where democracy, prosperity, and peace have become a matter of course. Germany is the united heart of an increasingly united continent, and that continent now looks to Germany as a symbol and as a catalyst for the integration it is striving to achieve.

Yet for all the progress that we have made, we still have challenges to meet in Europe. The end of the Cold War did not bring an end to armed conflict on this continent. And while the division that resulted from the Cold War is fading, it has not been fully overcome. That division is still visible in the economic gulf between east and west. It is perceptible in the pollution that shortens lives from Ukraine to Silesia. Above all, it is tangible in the desire for greater security felt by citizens from the Baltic to the Black Sea, across a region where our century's two great wars as well as the Cold War began.

In just a few years, we will begin a new century. Let me share with you the vision that President Clinton and I have for the United States and Europe in the next century. It is a vision for a New Atlantic Community. This community will build on the institutions our predecessors created, but it will transcend the artificial boundaries of Cold War Europe. It will give North America a deeper partnership with a broader, more integrated Europe on this continent and around the world. It carries forward the principles that Secretary Byrnes set forth 50 years ago today.

As the next century dawns on this New Atlantic Community, our joint efforts will have made us confident that the democratic revolutions of 1989 will endure, confident that wars like the one in Bosnia can be prevented, and confident that every new democracy—large and small—can take its rightful place in a new Europe. In this New Atlantic Community, the United States will be fully engaged—in partnership with our friends and allies and in a more effective European Union that is taking in new members. In this Community, NATO will remain the central pillar of our security engagement. It will be a new NATO, adapted to meet emerging challenges, with the full participation of all current allies and several new members from the east. NATO's Partnership for Peace and the OSCE will give us the tools to prevent conflict and assure freedom for all of our citizens. In our vision for this New Atlantic Community, a democratic Russia will be our full partner. Our economies will be increasingly integrated and thriving. Europe and America will be taking joint action against the global threats we can only overcome by working together.

This is the kind of vision that gave our partnership strength and our people hope in the darkest, most dangerous days of this century. Ten years ago, it was still a dream. Ten years from now, the opportunity may be lost. But I believe we can realize it if we meet four challenges together in the final years of this century.

The first challenge is to build a secure and integrated Europe, to erase the Cold War's outdated frontiers forever. The new democracies of central Europe and the New Independent States want to be our partners. It is in our interest to help them assume our shared responsibilities. It is in our interest to extend to them the same structure of values and institutions that enabled Western Europe to overcome its own legacy of conflict and division. It is certainly in Germany's interest to work with us and our other allies in this task, for it can make Germany's eastern border what its western border has long been: a gateway, not a barrier.

At the January 1994 NATO summit, President Clinton proposed and our allies embraced a comprehensive strategy for European security. President Clinton believes that another summit is needed to complete the implementation of this comprehensive strategy. I would expect that our leaders will meet in the spring or early summer of 1997 at an extremely important summit. Their objective should be to agree on NATO's internal reforms, launch enlargement negotiations for NATO, and deepen NATO's partnership with Russia and other European states. The purpose of NATO reform is to ensure that NATO can meet new challenges in a Europe where no power poses a threat to any other. This year, my colleagues and I agreed on a historic program for building a new NATO. It will permit a more visible and capable European role in the alliance and add substance to the special European function of the Western European Union. It will improve NATO's ability to respond to emergencies and make it easier for our partners in Central Europe and the New Independent States to join us when we do. And it will preserve the qualities that have made NATO so effective. Our goal, ultimately, is a new NATO in which all of our allies, including France and Spain, will fully participate.

NATO enlargement, too, is on track, and it will happen. Right now, NATO is engaged in an intensive dialogue with interested countries to determine what they must do, and what NATO must do, to prepare for their accession. Based upon these discussions, at the 1997 summit we should invite several partners to begin accession negotiations. When the first new members pass through NATO's open door, it will stay open for all of those who demonstrate that they are willing and able to shoulder the responsibilities of membership. NATO should enter a new phase of intensified dialogue with all those who continue to seek membership after the first candidates are invited to join.

Enlargement will ensure that NATO's benefits do not stop at a line that lost its relevance when the Berlin Wall fell. The steps our partners are taking to prepare for membership—strengthening democracy and building trust with their neighbors—have already given central Europe greater stability than it has seen this century. Indeed, no alliance has ever been more effective in preventing conflict than NATO. That is why we created it. That is why our partners in the Partnership for Peace wish to join it. And that is why NATO is at the heart of our European strategy.

Of course, all of Europe's new democracies, whether they join NATO sooner, later, or not at all, deserve a full opportunity to help shape Europe's future. For this reason, we must expand the scope of NATO's Partnership for Peace. Thanks to the Partnership for Peace, we can now form the first truly European-wide military coalitions in which soldiers from Russia and America, Poland and Ukraine, Germany and Lithuania train side by side, ready to deploy at a moment's notice to protect our security.

To this end, we should expand the Partnership's mandate beyond its current missions. We should involve our partners in the Partnership for Peace in the planning as well as the execution of NATO's missions. We should give them a stronger voice by forming an Atlantic Partnership Council. In all of these ways, NATO gives us a foundation to build our New Atlantic Community—one in which all of Europe and North America work together to build lasting security.

The Organization for Security and Cooperation in Europe is essential to this evolving community. That is evident from its important and courageous missions in Bosnia, Chechnya, and the Baltics. The Helsinki principles—respect for an open society and the rule of law—provided the guidepost for all we accomplished in the last decade, and they also shape our vision for the future. At the OSCE summit this December in Lisbon, we should build on these principles to define our security coop-eration for the next century. In Lisbon, our leaders should take practical steps such as launching negotiations to adopt the CFE treaty to Europe's new security landscape. Closer political cooperation in the European Union, and its coming enlargement, will contribute to the security and prosperity of the New Atlantic Community and strengthen the partner-ship between Europe and the United States. President Clinton has been a strong supporter of deeper European integration, reaffirming the com-mitment made, in earlier years, by President John Kennedy.

A critical goal of the New Atlantic Community is to achieve Ukraine's integration with Europe. Ukraine has embraced market democracy and given up nuclear weapons. It is seeking strong ties with Russia and central Europe and a close partnership with Western nations and institutions. We want to help Ukraine consolidate its independence by overcoming its severe economic problems, by gaining access to critical markets in the West, and by developing an enhanced partnership with NATO.

The vision I have outlined here today for the New Atlantic Community can succeed only if we recognize Russia's vital role in the New Atlantic Community. For most of this century, fear, tyranny, and self-isolation kept Russia from the European mainstream. But now, new patterns of trust and cooperation are taking hold. The Russian people are building a new society on a foundation of democratic and free market ideals. Though their struggle is far from complete, as the assault on Chechnya has demonstrated, the Russian people have rejected a return to the past and vindicated our confidence in democracy—the same kind of confidence that Secretary Byrnes expressed from this platform 50 years ago. Now, an integrated, democratic Russia can participate in the construction of an integrated, democratic Europe.

Today, I want to say this to the Russian people: We welcome you as our full partners in building a new Europe that is free of tyranny, division, and war. We want to work with you to bring Russia into the family of market democracies. We want you to have a stake and a role in the institutions of European security and economic cooperation. That is why we seek a fundamentally new relationship between Russia and the new NATO.

Such a relationship, I am confident, is possible. It is important to all of us and we are determined to make it happen. Russia's cooperation with NATO should be expressed in a formal charter. This charter should create standing arrangements for consultation and joint action between Russia and the alliance. NATO and Russia need a charter because we share an interest in preventing armed conflict. We are equally threatened by proliferation, nuclear smuggling, and the specter of disasters like Chernobyl. The charter we seek should give us a permanent mechanism for crisis management so we can respond together immediately as these challenges arise. Our troops should train together for joint operations. The potential of our partnership is already on display in Bosnia, where our troops are shouldering common burdens and sharing common achievements. Let us, with Russia, take the next logical step.

Our efforts in Bosnia have demonstrated both the possibilities and the urgency of building a New Atlantic Community. In many ways, Bosnia today stands where Europe stood in 1946: Its city parks have been turned into cemeteries; its children have known terror and hunger, and they have seen the destructive power of hatred. Yet, it also stands on the threshold of a better future. The war is over, and the way forward is clear: It depends on democracy, justice, and integration. Last month, I was in Sarajevo, and I saw the tremendous progress made since the Dayton Accord opened the way to peace. Germany's diplomacy, its economic aid, and its military contributions have all been vital in providing that new possibility for Bosnia and for all the people of that tragic country.

In just a week from now, elections will be held to establish the institutions of a unified Bosnian state. Every party in Bosnia—both those in power now and the opposition—supports holding these elections on September 14. The Bosnian people clearly want to regain the voice the war denied them. Our task is to help them exercise that right under appropriate conditions. By postponing the municipal elections, the OSCE has already sent a clear signal that basic standards must be met. We must have confidence in the power of democratic choice in Bosnia. We must also remember that elections are but a first step. We will have to work hard together over the long term to hold Bosnia's leaders to the commitments they made at Dayton and to help all the nations of the former Yugoslavia as they seek to rejoin Europe. Our second challenge in building a New Atlantic Community is to promote prosperity among our nations and to extend it globally. The United States and Europe have built the largest economic relationship in the world. It supports over 14 million jobs on both sides of the Atlantic.

We must move toward a free and open Transatlantic Marketplace, as the United States and the EU foreshadowed in their summit meeting last December. As barriers fall and momentum builds, the boundaries of what seems feasible will certainly expand. We are already at a stage when we can realistically discuss the true integration of the economies of Europe and North America. We should now pursue practical steps toward even more visionary goals, such as reducing regulatory barriers.

Our vision for open trade and investment in the New Atlantic Community must be as broad as our vision of that community itself. In other words, it must extend to central Europe and the New Independent States, including Russia. President Yeltsin, for example, has made it a priority to open Russia to foreign investment, and President Clinton is personally committed to encourage that goal. We strongly support Russia's entry into the WTO on appropriate commercial terms. We understand that for Europe's new democracies, stability depends upon prosperity and on our willingness to open our markets to their products. That is one reason we strongly support an expansive program for the enlargement of the European Union. The prospect of EU membership will help lock in democratic and market reforms in central and eastern Europe. It sets the stage for a true single European market. We believe that it should move forward swiftly.

Together, we also have a responsibility to ensure that the international economic system and its institutions are fit and ready for the 21st century. We have already worked together to reform the International Monetary Fund and the World Bank. We completed the Uruguay Round and created the World Trade Organization. At the WTO's first ministerial meeting this December in Singapore, we should push to complete the Uruguay Round's unfinished business and begin to set priorities for the next century. We must also do our part to ensure that the world's poorest nations benefit from open markets. All this is a task for the United States and Europe.

Our New Atlantic Community will only be secure if we also work together to meet the threats that transcend our frontiers—threats like terrorism, nuclear proliferation, crime, drugs, disease, and damage to the environment. The danger posed by these threats is as great as any that we faced during the Cold War. Meeting these threats is our third challenge for the waning years of this century, and I want to discuss today just two elements of it: terrorism and the environment.

We must be united in confronting terrorism wherever it occurs. From the clubs of Berlin to the metros of Paris, from the sidewalks of London to the office towers of New York, lawless predators have turned our citizens into targets of opportunity and our public places into stalking grounds.

President Clinton has pledged to lead an international effort against this common foe of terrorism. The strategy against terrorism that the President unveiled at the UN General Assembly last fall was a clear sign of our determination in this regard, and the 25 specific measures adopted by the G-7 nations and Russia adopted two months ago in Paris are a blueprint for putting terrorists out of business and behind bars. I urge all nations to implement them as soon as possible.

Working together against state sponsors of terrorism is an imperative—not an option. It is a cause to which all nations should rally. Our principled commitment to free trade simply does not oblige us to do business with aggressive tyrannies like Iran and Libya. We must join forces on effective multilateral measures that deny these rogue regimes the resources that they crave and need for their deleterious acts around the world.

Iraq, too, is a sponsor of terror and, as we have seen, a continuing threat to peace in the Middle East. Let me express my deep appreciation to Chancellor Kohl, Foreign Minister Kinkel, and to Germany as a whole for supporting President Clinton's determined response to Saddam Hussein's new aggression. Environmental threats also respect no borders. They harm our economies and the health of our people. That is why President Clinton and I have acted to place environmental issues in the mainstream of American foreign policy. Here in Europe, our most urgent environmental challenge is to repair the ravages done by decades of communist misrule. From the abandoned villages around Chernobyl, to the depleted forests in Siberia, to the rusted hulks of factories in central Europe, environmental damage is among the most devastating legacies that Europe's new democracies must overcome.

Around the world, our cooperation can make 1997 the most important year for the global environment since the Rio summit five years ago. In this next year, we can provide leadership to achieve realistic, legally binding commitments to cut greenhouse gasses and their emissions. We can agree on sound management of the world's forests, a resource that Germans and Americans have always held so dear.

All the steps that I have suggested today will require our governments to work more closely together. But the strength of our relationship depends ultimately on the ties among our people. And that is the fourth and final challenge I wish to discuss today.

After World War II, Germany and the United States pioneered the people-to-people programs of cultural and academic exchange that have been so important, and continue to be so important, to Americans and Europeans. Because of our partnership in the Cold War period, and the many things we had to do together then, millions of Americans lived and worked in Germany and Europe, and we could take it almost for granted that our people knew each other well. But now the Cold War is over, and we need to forge a new set of links. We need to build on the bonds being formed each day by our companies, our universities, our parliamentarians, and our non-governmental organizations.

In November, the United States and the EU will convene a conference to strengthen transatlantic exchanges. I have one particular idea to suggest to that conference: Let us create a Fellowship of Hope—an exchange between the foreign affairs agencies of the United States, the EU, and its member states so that our young leaders can work together and learn from each other. Our private sector can also do more. Today, 500,000 Americans work for German firms, and 600,000 Germans work for American firms. Let us encourage all of our companies to follow the example some firms are already setting by expanding exchange programs for their employees.

I am confident that our peoples and our governments alike can deepen the partnership that we have so long enjoyed. After all, the principles underlying that partnership—the principles that Secretary Byrnes expressed here—are enduring principles. In the west, they withstood the trauma of World War II. In the east, they outlasted the purges and propaganda of communist rule. In the last decade, they inspired us to work together to unify Germany, to end the war in Bosnia, to support reform in Russia, and to forge the most open global trading system in history.

All this began right here, amidst the rubble and despair of 1946. And if our hopes are high today, it is because of what Germany has achieved with its partners since then. Because of what we have done together, my country can look forward to a future partnership with a new Germany in a new Europe—a Europe where frontiers unite rather than divide; a Europe with horizons wider than its borders.

We struggled with you to build this new Europe. And now, as my predecessor did 50 years ago, let me say on behalf of America: We are staying here. We can meet the challenges I have outlined. We can build a free, united, and prosperous New Atlantic Community. And when we do, people around the world will be inspired by the example that Europe and America have set, just as we have been inspired by the example that Germany has set.

Thank you very much.

THIRTY-TWO

A Changing Relationship with Africa

As the first post–Cold War Administration, we set out to give more attention to areas of the globe where other U.S. foreign policy interests had been overshadowed by the superpower rivalry. Africa was certainly such an area. When we had paid attention to Africa during the Cold War, we had seemed to choose our policies based more on our competition with Moscow than on their impact on the continent. An important exception was South Africa, where the salient issue for Americans had been apartheid. Now that the Cold War was history, we saw an opportunity to reshape U.S. policy to establish new relationships with regions like sub-Saharan Africa.

In a May 1993 speech before the African-American Institute in Washington, I set forth an agenda for our Africa policy during the next four years. That agenda was threefold: to bolster the movement toward democracy and free markets; to address the health, environmental, and population issues that threaten lives and imperil sustained development; and to help Africans build their capacity for preventive diplomacy and conflict resolution. In other words, we wanted to promote African solutions to African problems.

While we were generally able to pursue the course laid out in this speech, we also had to address two tragic crises in the region. In December 1992, President Bush had sent American troops to lead a UN peacekeeping mission designed to stop interclan fighting and combat starvation in Somalia. In 1993, in what came to be recognized as imprudent "mission creep," the UN forces extended their activities to rebuilding the shattered nation. In October of that year, 18 U.S. troops were killed while pursuing warlord Mohammed Aideed, who was obstructing the UN forces. This loss of life, combined with Somalia's continuing anarchy, soured the public on continued engagement there and on UN peacekeeping operations generally.

These graphic images were very much on people's minds when Rwanda also spiraled into a genocidal civil war. By July 1994, more than one million Rwandan refugees had fled into neighboring Zaire. Because their makeshift camps lacked adequate food and clean water, starvation and cholera were rampant, and the death toll reached over 5,000 refugees per day. Although earlier in the year the Administration had judged that our European partners with long involvement in the region should take the lead in the Rwandan peacekeeping effort, we now felt compelled to act.

To provide emergency assistance and to support UN relief forces already on the ground, President Clinton ordered 2,000 U.S. troops to Rwanda and Zaire in late July as part of Operation Support Hope. These forces facilitated a massive U.S. airlift of aid supplies, including food, medicine, and blankets, as well as water purification equipment. The shadow of Somalia loomed large over our internal planning, and Secretary Perry and General Shalikashvili were careful to heed its lessons and take steps to avoid mission creep. As a result, the Rwanda mission was limited to those tasks for which we had unique capabilities, such as the air transportation of heavy equipment. The incidence of cholera was sharply reduced by the end of September, and most of our forces left the region.

Although the challenges posed by such "failed states" as Somalia and Rwanda dominated the headlines throughout much of the term, we quietly made progress toward our broader goal of establishing a new relationship with Africa. Even apart from the two dire situations, the Clinton Administration devoted more high-level attention to Africa than any other Administration since President Carter's. Indeed, the problems in Somalia and Rwanda only bolstered our resolve to move forward on the three-part agenda I had outlined in May 1993, so as to prevent such disasters from recurring. An example of our efforts was the pioneering initiative in May 1994 by AID Administrator Brian Atwood to help East African states prevent another famine in the Horn of Africa. The following month, President Clinton brought together political leaders, academics, and businesspeople for a far-reaching White House Conference on Africa. This meeting was followed by several important diplomatic missions to the region, including those of Vice President Gore, Commerce Secretary Ron Brown, National Security Adviser Anthony Lake, UN Ambassador Madeleine Albright, and Deputy Secretary Strobe Talbott.

Lake, who had an abiding interest in Africa (he had written a book on Zimbabwe), played a central role in the development of the Administration's policy and kept all of us cognizant of Africa's importance. He worked closely with the Department's point man on the region, Assistant Secretary of State George Moose, an able and dedicated Foreign Service Officer who taxed his stamina to the utmost with constant trips to the area. Strobe Talbott, who frequently represented the United States abroad with great distinction, made one of his most useful trips in October 1994, visiting Burundi, Zimbabwe, Malawi, Zaire, Ghana, and the Ivory Coast. The purpose of his mission was to underscore American support for regional democracy-building efforts, such as those that Zimbabwe and Malawi were conducting in neighboring states, as well as regional peacekeeping of the kind that Ghana was leading in Liberia.

The high point of my personal involvement in our Africa policy was my weeklong visit to Mali, Ethiopia, Tanzania, South Africa, and Angola in October 1996. The trip provided an opportunity to recognize progress in political and economic reform as well as to continue our efforts to forge new ties with the region.

In significant ways, Africa was a study in contrasts. While many of its countries were rapidly integrating into the world economy, others were among the poorest on the planet. And while democracy had taken hold in several key areas, dictators still held sway in many nations. The five countries I visited represented the continuum of change in Africa, from the hopeful Mali and the impressive South Africa to the still–war-ravaged Angola. Symbolically, I sought to convey the message that the United States would support the nations of Africa in their continuing struggles for economic and political development. Substantively, I aimed to highlight the core elements of the strategy I had outlined in my 1993 speech. And specifically, we sought African cooperation on two important issues. We hoped to develop a multinational African Crisis Response Force (ACRF) to engage in intra-African peacekeeping and conflict prevention, and we sought understanding of our decision not to back

Boutros-Ghali, the putative "African candidate," for a second term as UN Secretary General (see Chapter 23).

The ACRF initiative, launched in September 1996, was a concerted effort to respond to a clearly expressed African desire to participate more effectively in both regional and international peacekeeping. In particular, African governments wished to assume greater responsibility for preventing and resolving conflicts and crises on their own continent. Under the ACRF plan, the United States and others in the international community would provide African forces with the necessary training, equipment, and financial support to enable them to perform these activities. This capacity, once developed, could be used in larger United Nations peacekeeping or humanitarian efforts in Africa or elsewhere. It might also enable the formation, when appropriate, of all-African forces to respond to humanitarian contingencies. The idea was to split the difference between the stark, either-or alternatives of "doing nothing" and "doing it all ourselves" when crises arose in Africa. Moreover, by responding to Africans' wish to assume greater control over their destiny, the ACRF initiative exemplified our policy of finding African solutions to African problems. During my trip I was to learn that almost all the African leaders looked favorably on the ACRF, at least in principle. However, each one stressed the importance of African "ownership" of the force, and the need to cement it to regional organizations such as the Organization of African Unity (OAU).

Mali

After a short stop in Israel on October 6 to reopen talks on implementing the languishing Oslo accords (see Chapter 34), I made the long trek to Bamako, Mali, a trip that crossed the widest part of Africa and was lengthened by the need to avoid Libyan airspace. My day in Bamako was inspiring; Mali is a country headed in the right direction. While it suffers from grave problems—including deep poverty, a scarcity of natural resources, and poor health conditions—it has made remarkable progress.

My day began with a meeting with General Amadou Toure, who had engineered a coup in 1991 but quickly stepped aside and in 1992 presided over an election in which Mali's current President, Alpha Konare, was victorious. Toure has stayed scrupulously out of politics since that election, despite his youthful vigor and enormous popularity. Because he is well informed and remains in touch with other African leaders, I was anxious to seek his advice on the deteriorating situation in Burundi, as well as to compare notes on Mali. I later met with President Konare, whom I found impressive. He pledged to participate in the ACRF and said he would support our decision concerning Boutros-Ghali, although he could not do so publicly at that time. He joked that he had much in common with President Clinton: "We are from the same generation, and he is the President of the world's richest country, and I am President of the world's poorest." Yet, despite Mali's evident shortcomings, Konare was leading it through democratic and market reform. "He is one of the bright lights of Africa and a strong exponent of human rights," I reported to President Clinton.[1]

I ended my visit to Mali by traveling about thirty miles from Bamako for a demonstration by Peace Corps volunteers of their work to protect water quality and to improve the productivity of mango trees. Several hundred villagers attended the demonstration. I later told President Clinton that the "American people would have been very proud to see these young men and women with their hands in the soil and mortar, helping to improve the lives of these very poor people, at virtually no cost except their own labor."

Ethiopia and Tanzania

During two days of talks in Addis Ababa, Ethiopia, and Arusha, Tanzania, I covered a wide range of bilateral and regional security issues. In Addis Ababa, I had an especially interesting session with Prime Minister Meles Zanawi, who struck me as one of the most promising of the new African leaders. When I questioned the limitations he had imposed on press freedom, he did not give a combative response, but engaged me in an extensive discussion of the role of the media in an emerging nation. I was much impressed by his inquiring tone, though hardly persuaded by his bottom line. While we spoke mostly of the progress Ethiopia is mak-

---

[1]Konare was reelected and paid a successful visit to the United States in 1997.

ing under his leadership, he also encouragingly foreshadowed the African reaction to our opposition to Boutros-Ghali, saying, "Wait and see what happens if you maintain your position after President Clinton's reelection."

Later that day, I met with the Secretary General of the OAU, Salim Salim. In disrepute since the 1970s, the OAU had begun to turn around under Salim's leadership. It had recently begun to assume a new mission of preventing or resolving African conflicts, and at the time of our meeting was taking the lead in dealing with the brewing crisis in Burundi.[2] The development of such leadership was a significant step in a region long without collective solutions to regional problems. The United States publicly supported the OAU's approach to the Burundi crisis, but I urged Salim to consider lifting some of its sanctions to reward positive steps taken by Burundi's leader, Pierre Buyoya.

Salim was prescient in expressing concern about "the danger spot nobody wants to talk about"—Zaire. With the end of Zairian President Mobutu Sese Seko's long reign looming, Salim said that maintaining civil stability and managing the transition to democracy would be great challenges. "If the transition goes wrong," he said, "there would be far-reaching consequences. Burundi and Rwanda would look like tea parties." Efforts by the United States and other nations to help produce a democratic transition in 1996 came to naught, and Laurent Kabila forcibly seized power in 1997. Considering conditions today, Salim's warning about the danger of the transition remains absolutely on target.

From Addis Ababa I flew to Arusha, where I met with Presidents Benjamin Mkapa of Tanzania, Daniel T. arap Moi of Kenya, and Yoweri Museveni of Uganda in the shadow of majestic Mount Kilimanjaro. I applauded their willingness to take collective responsibility for their close neighbor, Burundi. I urged them, too, to calibrate their sanctions on Buyoya, but found them reluctant to do so.[3] I had not seen Moi since I

---

[2]Tensions between extremists in Burundi's two historically hostile ethnic groups—Tutsis and Hutus—had been rising since 1993. In July 1996, the situation worsened with the overthrow of Burundi's Hutu President by Pierre Buyoya, a Tutsi. To pressure Buyoya to restore democratic political institutions and reopen negotiations with the Hutus, the OAU had placed economic sanctions on Burundi.

[3]This reluctance may have been due partly to their acknowledged inexperience with sanctions, which tended to lead to an "all or nothing" mindset about using them. Museveni told me that when they first took action against Burundi, they "didn't even understand the difference between sanctions and a blockade."

had welcomed him at the White House in 1979, and it was sad to see how much he had been slowed by age and how rigid his views had become.[4]

South Africa

My stop in South Africa, the engine of growth and development in the southern part of the continent, was the cornerstone of my trip. At 8:30 on a Saturday morning, I met with Nelson Mandela at his official residence in Cape Town. As always when I met with him, I felt I was in the presence of greatness. Although 78 years old and recovering from knee surgery, Mandela was engaging, gracious, and vigorous. Later, using no notes, he gave the press a calm, masterful summary of our one-hour meeting, putting the emphasis just where he wanted it.

When I told him we thought that at 74, Boutros-Ghali should not have another term as UN Secretary General, Mandela joked that such talk about old age made him feel self-conscious. Nevertheless, he promised to work with other African leaders to find a way out of the impasse. He also gave qualified support to the ACRF idea, but on this point he kept his cards close to the vest. He said that he liked the concept, that it would be preferable if such an initiative came from the United Nations rather than the United States, and that his government would study the proposal and consult with existing organizations on possible options.[5]

The public highlight of the trip was my October 12 address at University of the Witwatersrand in Johannesburg, one of South Africa's most

---

[4]In Arusha, I also had the opportunity to meet with Louise Arbour, the tough-minded Chief Prosecutor of the International War Crimes Tribunals for Rwanda and the former Yugoslavia. She argued for U.S. support in addressing the administrative and financial problems of the Rwandan prosecutions, as well as for an expanded role for NATO troops in apprehending indictees in Bosnia. I had supported the tribunals from the start and told her that I would try to be helpful on the two difficult issues she raised.

[5]Despite difficult questions about the ACRF's precise mission (which could probably only be determined on a case-by-case basis), I still believe that there are no insurmountable obstacles to moving ahead, at least with the initial phases of training and equipping the force. Most of the reservations expressed by Mandela and others are being successfully addressed through close consultation with African leaders, and the concept continues to build support.

prestigious educational institutions. That speech provided an opportunity to underline the main themes of our Africa strategy while also reinforcing the special importance of South Africa. The speech emphasized U.S. interests in Africa, and in that sense it was addressed as much to the American people as to the Africans. I felt that building an American constituency for our Africa policy was just as critical as engaging the Africans themselves. Particularly crucial would be support from the Republican Congress, whose desire to cut funds for international operations would otherwise have a disproportionate impact on Africa. "I cannot be here today and pretend to you that there is no debate in America about Africa's relative importance," I said. "But my travel to Africa this past week has only strengthened my conviction that America must remain engaged on this continent. . . . We cannot and we will not walk away from Africa."

The part of my speech that garnered the most international media attention was a reference to French-U.S. tensions over Africa. As I was beginning my trip several days earlier, a French minister had been widely quoted as saying that with the American election only three weeks away, our "new" interest in Africa was directly linked to presidential politics. Although reportedly cautioned by French President Chirac, the minister had nevertheless repeated his remarks with added emphasis, and he seemed to have considerable support within his government. The source of the French angst seemed to be a belief that my trip (particularly given its starting point in Mali, in the heart of French West Africa) was the leading edge of a U.S. effort to encroach on a "traditional" French diplomatic and commercial domain. Annoyed at the uncalled-for assertion that I was playing politics on this point, I reworked my speech to include an indirect response that no one could miss. "The time has passed when Africa could be carved into spheres of influence or when outside powers could view whole groups of states as their private domain," I said. "Today, Africa needs the support of all its many friends, not the exclusive patronage of a few."

Angola

I ended my trip with a troubling stop in war-ravaged Angola. Ever since the 1994 accords between the government of President Jose dos Santos and Jonas Savimbi, leader of the right-wing rebel group UNITA, Angola had been technically at peace after almost twenty years of civil war. The fighting, however, still continued sporadically, especially in southern Angola, where Savimbi's strength was concentrated. My brief stopover was intended to boost the lagging implementation of the accords and restart a dialogue between dos Santos and Savimbi. The Angolan government still had (and still has) some distance to go in complying with the military and political obligations of the accords, but dos Santos assured me it intended to do its part. UNITA was a larger problem; Savimbi had refused to move to Angola's capital, Luanda, to join the government, as anticipated in the accords. He even declined my invitation to meet in Luanda. I asked George Moose to stay behind, go down-country to see Savimbi, and remind him that new UN sanctions would be likely if he did not comply with the accords.[6]

The utter devastation in Angola resulting from two decades of warfare made a deep impression on me. During the Cold War, Angola became a battleground for a proxy war between the superpowers, with the United States backing the UNITA rebels against the then-Marxist government. Even though Angola has vast resources in oil and diamonds, not to mention a good climate and rich soil, its long preoccupation with war and weapons has left it in terrible condition. Luanda is rife with poverty, scarred by battered Soviet-era architecture, and reeking of uncollected garbage in the streets. Conditions are little better in the countryside.

I was shocked to learn that there are more land mines than people in Angola, and that more than 150 people a week are injured by explosions. To highlight the land mine scourge, I joined in a UN ceremony to recognize the work of teams removing mines. I returned to Washington with a renewed conviction that land mines should be outlawed.[7]

As I explained in Johannesburg, much of Africa is at a critical crossroads. Many nations are trying to adapt to democracy and free markets

---

[6]UNITA's foot-dragging continued, and the UN proposed new sanctions in September 1997.

[7]The debate on this subject intensified in 1997 after I left office. Following an international conference, 122 nations signed a treaty outlawing the manufacture and use of antipersonnel land mines. Although the United States attended the conference and moved a long distance toward supporting the total ban, the President held out for an exception in the dangerous border area between North and South Korea, and we did not sign the treaty.

after long periods of dictatorship and state control of the economy. These are not easy transitions, especially for nations with histories of poverty and violence. Yet this is exactly "the point at which good leadership, sound policies, and steady international support and engagement can make the greatest difference." The United States should not fail to do its part.

●

Africa at a Crossroads: American Interests and American Engagement

Address at the South African Institute of International Affairs,

University of the Witwatersrand, Johannesburg, October 12, 1996

Thank you for that warm welcome. Some of you may have heard that an unnamed American newspaper has questioned my ability to pronounce difficult African names during the course of this jet-lagged trip. Well, I took this as quite a challenge, so I decided to give this speech at the university in Africa with the most difficult, unpronounceable name. That's why I came here to the University of "Wits."

It is an honor to speak at a university known around the world for its principled opposition to apartheid and for its leading role in building the new South Africa. I want to thank the South African Institute for International Affairs for hosting me and for your work in raising awareness of global issues in this country.

For some time now, Americans have been coming to South Africa to celebrate with you the end of apartheid. That has been our great privilege, and it is mine, too. But now we have new work to do. The victory of freedom has opened new challenges for your people. It also has opened an opportunity that our nations must grasp: the opportunity to act together to advance common interests in Africa and around the world. That is why today I want to speak about America's engagement on this continent and to explain why peace, democracy, and prosperity in Africa matter so much to the United States.

I wanted to give this speech in South Africa because your example has inspired Americans and the world. Today, people look at South Africa and say: If this diverse, once-divided nation can be united by common values and aims, then so can any multi-ethnic nation in Africa and the world. If South Africa can forge a community of interest with the neighbors it once fought, then any region can come together. If South Africa can elect a former political prisoner to be its president, if it can tell the truth about its past and move forward, so can any nation striving to overcome a painful legacy.

When people say that South Africa is a leader, it is not just a testament to your size and your economic might. It is a tribute to the courage, patience, and tolerance that you have shown in your remarkable transition. It is a tribute to the optimism that you inspire in others, through Africa and around the world.

Today, all the nations of Africa have a chance to realize the potential that exists in their human and natural resources. This was impossible when Africa was divided by Cold War cleavages and superpower rivalries. It was impossible when most African nations stagnated under single-party rule, pursuing economic policies that were based upon ideology, not experience. It was impossible when South Africa stood in opposition to its neighbors, unable to exercise moral or political leadership.

It is possible today because all over the world, people are recognizing the truth that Robert Kennedy expressed here in South Africa 30 years ago: that our

essential humanity can only be protected and preserved where government must answer, not just to the wealthy, not just to those of a particular religion, or a particular race, but all its people.

The triumph of that democratic ideal ended the Cold War. It overcame apartheid. And in country after country, it is empowering Africans to shape their own destinies.

Of course, when we talk about Africa's renewed promise, we must not gloss over the tragic problems of those nations still in crisis. Nor can we underestimate the devastation caused by poverty, environmental neglect, excessive population growth, and disease. We also dare not overlook the persistence of human rights abuses or the continued existence of injustices such as slavery.

When we speak about Africa, we must of course recognize its great diversity. But many African nations have this in common: that they are at a crossroads. Many countries have ended violence but have not yet established conditions for lasting peace. Many have held elections but not yet solidified the rule of law. Many are freeing their economies from the shackles of state control but have not yet been able to free their people from poverty. In other words, much of Africa is at a fragile mid-point— the point at which good leadership, sound policies, and steady international support and engagement can make the greatest difference. That's where the opportunity lies.

All nations must cooperate, not compete, if we are going to make a positive difference in Africa's future. The time has passed when Africa could be carved into spheres of influence or when outside powers could view whole groups of states as their private domain. Today, Africa needs the support of all its many friends, not the exclusive patronage of a few.

The United States will do its part not only because it is right but because it is in our interest to help Africa succeed.

We need African partners in our effort to meet global challenges. African nations played a leading role in extending the Non-Proliferation Treaty. Without the support and help of democracies such as Benin and South Africa, we might have lost our most important barrier against the spread of nuclear weapons. Likewise, without the nearly unanimous support of African nations, we might not have gained the UN General Assembly's approval of the Comprehensive Test Ban Treaty last month.

We need African partners if we are to dismantle the global networks of crime, narcotics, and terror that, unhappily, are also gaining a foothold here. The health and prosperity of Americans depend on preserving the global environment, and we can only do so if we are fully engaged in Africa. America, like the whole world, has an interest in preserving Africa's tropical forests, which have given us effective treatments for leukemia and Hodgkin's Disease.

We clearly have an interest in helping Africa realize its immense and mostly untapped economic potential. As Africa's regions come together, as its nations become more stable and free, opportunities for investment and trade in Africa will only grow.

Our late Commerce Secretary, my friend Ron Brown, understood this. No one ever worked harder or with more success to broaden and diversify our trade and investment relationship with Africa, including southern Africa, which he named one of the 10 great emerging markets in the world. We are carrying on Ron's work. U.S. trade with sub-Saharan Africa grew by 12% last year. Our exports to Africa already exceed those to the entire former Soviet Union. Here in South Africa, our ambassador has told me that almost one new American company is starting or expanding its operations every week. I want to pay tribute to our ambassador, Jim Joseph, who is here with me today. He has done such a fine job in representing America in this country that he loves so much.

We also recognize our interest in helping Africa resolve the conflicts that stand in the way of a better future. Crisis after crisis has taught us that the cost of prevention is never as great as the price of neglect; that lifting lives is even more rewarding than saving lives. The American people have always responded with generosity when a humanitarian emergency sears our conscience. But if together we succeed in being peacemakers and democracy-builders, we will not be called upon to provide emergency relief nearly as often, and that is surely in our interest and Africa's as well.

For all these good reasons, President Clinton is determined to intensify American engagement in Africa. In the last four years, in a tough budgetary climate in the United States, he has sought to protect our assistance to Africa, even as aid to other regions declined sharply. We have provided $600 million to support South Africa's transition to democracy. We have helped nations such as Mali and Benin consolidate democracy. We launched an initiative to prevent conflict and achieve food security in the Greater Horn of Africa. We have been deeply engaged in support of peace in Mozambique and Angola. Our armed forces provided critical support for relief in Rwanda and they helped save hundreds of thousands of lives in Somalia. We are the world's leading supporter of eliminating landmines in Africa—a cause I think the world is finally awakening to.

I cannot be here today and pretend to you that there is no debate in America about Africa's relative importance. But my travel to Africa this past week has only strengthened my conviction that America must remain engaged on this continent. I intend to build on the experiences of this visit and to draw on its lessons to make that case to the American people. We cannot and we will not walk away from Africa.

Our approach to Africa is to promote democracy, to prevent conflict, to encourage economic prosperity and integration, and to support sustainable development. These fundamental elements are inseparable. Political freedom is the key to peace within nations. Economies perform best where people are free to shape their destiny. But democracy itself cannot thrive in nations divided by armed conflict or crippled by dwindling natural resources. Let me discuss each element of our approach in turn.

The first is to promote democratic government, human rights, and the rule of law. I can remember when apologists for colonialism argued that Africa was not developed enough to be "ready" for democracy. Sadly, many African leaders have used the same excuse to justify dictatorship. But now the tide is turning. Since 1989, more than 20 nations have embraced democratic government, rejecting what Mali's President Konare has condemned as "the logic of 'shut up and obey.'"

The rising tide of democracy means that Africans are finally gaining a chance to solve problems and to shape their future. In southern Africa, drought has not led to catastrophe in part because most governments in this region are held accountable by their voters and by a free press. Democracy makes it more likely that internal divisions will be settled peacefully at the ballot box. That has been possible in emerging democracies such as Mozambique and Namibia, and certainly it has been impossible in dictatorships such as Sudan. Democracy makes it more likely that business people will invest, because they have more confidence in a place where the rule of law will protect their investments.

Of course, democracy means more than elections. It depends on a free press, independent courts, and a public culture in which every person can participate fully in political and community life.

In the last four years, American assistance has helped women's groups get involved in politics, helped human rights advocates gain a voice, and defended independent journalists. We support institutions that establish accountability for past abuses, such as South Africa's Truth and Reconciliation Commission. This morning, I had the honor and pleasure to sign an agreement on behalf of the United States that will provide $400,000 for the commission's work, and I had the pleasure and inspiration of being with President Mandela and Archbishop Tutu. We are also the world's leading supporter of the Rwanda War Crimes Tribunal.

Former President Soglo of Benin certainly had it right when he said that Africa can't afford to be held to a lesser democratic standard by the world. Nigeria's oppressive rule is especially troubling at the moment. Nigeria should be a leader in Africa. But its rulers have squandered their nation's potential and made it the poorest oil-rich country on earth. The effects of corruption and drug trafficking in Nigeria can already be felt from South Africa to North America. The United States hopes that the

Nigerian Government will move forward with political and economic reform. We are open to dialogue with its leaders. But we are prepared to take appropriate steps if repression continues.

When democracy is threatened, its fate depends in part on the will of other nations to defend it. Already, many African leaders have recognized that national boundaries must not shield abuses that threaten whole regions. As I said at the OAU two days ago in Addis Ababa, by acting together African nations can effectively vindicate the principle that democracy must be safeguarded, that military coups are unacceptable, and that election results must be respected.

The second element of our approach is to work with African nations to resolve Africa's remaining armed conflicts and to prevent new ones. In Africa's Great Lakes region, the United States and South Africa are working with regional leaders to avert renewed genocide. I was in Arusha yesterday to support the efforts to achieve a negotiated solution to the crisis in Burundi. I had an opportunity to discuss this issue with President Mandela this morning and found that we fully share the goal of achieving an agreement that will restore democracy and protect minority rights. In Angola, which I will visit Monday, we also are working to resolve the war that has raged there for a generation.

Our experience in Angola has demonstrated the essential role the United Nations can play in resolving conflict. We are determined to meet our responsibilities to the UN. We are striving to improve its effectiveness and strengthen its leadership.

Like other parts of the world, Africa also needs strong regional and subregional organizations, such as SADC, that take responsibility, in partnership with Africa's friends abroad, at moments of crisis. It needs well-trained regional forces that can be deployed rapidly when and where they are needed for humanitarian and peacekeeping missions. It needs a mechanism that combines the experience of Africa's armed forces with the resources and capabilities of its non-African partners.

To meet this need, we are working with our partners in Africa and around the world to create what we are calling an African Crisis Response Force. This concept is not new, but it is certainly necessary. It allows us to realize a goal that the OAU has espoused and other nations have long shared: to build Africa's capacity for resolving conflict—just as we have done in many other regions of the world.

The crisis in Burundi adds urgency to the creation of such a force. But it could meet Africa's long-term needs as well. It can help ensure that neither my country nor any African nation will ever face a choice between acting alone at times of crisis or doing nothing. I am happy to say that a number of African nations already have expressed their willingness to contribute to such a force. Based on the results of my trip, I am increasingly confident that an African Crisis Response Force can and indeed will be created.

The third element of our approach is to help Africa realize its economic potential. Many countries in Africa have acted to reduce budget deficits, privatize enterprises, and deregulate economies. These are hard and sometimes painful steps—in Africa and everywhere else in the world. But they are the only path to sustained growth and rising living standards.

The United States strongly supports the efforts of the international financial institutions to help African nations succeed in traveling down this path, and President Clinton is seeking adequate funding for this work. We also helped forge the consensus that donor nations reached last month to relieve more of the debt owed by the world's poorest countries.

We applaud the World Bank's greater focus on education, because education is critical to economic development. There is no good reason why the donor community and African countries cannot work together to help every child in every country benefit from at least a full primary education by the year 2010. Development also depends on unleashing the talents of all of Africa's people. Africa's women, in particular, must gain full access to every school, clinic, and parliament if the continent is to succeed in tapping its full potential.

The United States also strongly supports the new measures that the World Bank and IMF will be taking against corruption around the world. The private sector can thrive only when ordinary citizens are not forced to pay bribes for basic services, when contracts are awarded fairly, and when foreign investors are not intimidated. Fighting this kind of corruption is a global challenge. It is also an African challenge. We are encouraged by the priority that African democracies such as Tanzania are giving to rooting out these corrosive practices.

We also should work together to help Africa become more integrated with the global economy. Thirty-two sub-Saharan African nations have joined the new World Trade Organization, and we are helping them share its benefits and meet its requirements. In this region, SADC is eliminating duties and non-tariff barriers. We encourage it to work with its counterparts in East and West Africa to liberalize trade throughout the continent.

The final element of our approach is to overcome the transnational problems that undermine democracy, peace and prosperity. African nations will prosper only if their economies grow faster than their population. Africa's economies will grow only if they manage wisely the forests, grasslands, waters, and wildlife that are fundamental to every industry from agriculture to tourism to manufacturing.

When some people look at the massive social and environmental pressures your continent faces, they predict anarchy and chaos. They think violence is the inevitable consequence of environmental decay, disease, and population growth. These forces are, to be sure, destructive. But I believe that human neglect and unaccountable government are the most important causes of the human disasters we have seen in countries such as Liberia. Genocide is not a natural disaster.

I am convinced, as President John Kennedy once said, that "problems created by man can be solved by man." During my trip this week, I have been inspired by the men and women I met who are struggling to meet Africa's greatest challenges and are succeeding. Thanks to them, infant survival rates, life expectancy, and literacy are steadily rising. Thanks to them, a higher proportion of Africa's lands are set aside for protection than anywhere in the world.

The United States stands with them. In Africa, the U.S. Agency for International Development is placing particular emphasis on sustainable development. When I was in Addis Ababa earlier this week, I visited a community where the U.S. is working with local people to pave streets, fix bridges, and create economic opportunity. When I was in Mali, I visited our young Peace Corps volunteers, who are working with villagers to plant trees and to keep drinking water safe. They are doing that in an area threatened by the desert, and this is fascinating and heroic work. Any American who saw what I saw this week would be proud of our country's role on this continent and just as determined as I am to preserve it.

The goals I have talked about here this afternoon—democracy, peace, prosperity, and sustainable development—are goals I know the United States and South Africa share. I also know that South Africa faces great challenges at home—from the old quest to assure justice and opportunity for all to the new urgency of fighting crime and narcotics. The most important thing South Africa can do for Africa and for the world is to ensure that its own transformation here at home succeeds. We remain optimistic about the future of the South African economy and its leadership. But I know you do not believe your responsibility ends here in South Africa.

South Africa has already made great progress in promoting regional cooperation and peace in southern Africa. SADC has been a tremendous success, and under President Mandela's leadership it will only grow stronger. But your national interest does not end even in this region. After all, no one wants the nations that we once called the "front line states" to find themselves on a new front line, facing instability and poverty to the north. That is why we applaud President Mandela's courageous leadership on human rights and South Africa's growing engagement in the OAU.

South Africa is an important global partner for the United States, too. Your nation has provided decisive leadership against nuclear proliferation, not once but many times. We share an interest in fighting terrorism, drugs, and crime, and in protecting the global environment. The Binational Commission chaired by Deputy President Mbeki and Vice President Gore already has put many of these practical issues on our common agenda and we're working together on these issues.

When I look around the world, I see very few countries with greater potential to help shape the 21st century than the new South Africa. I see few relationships as vital to advancing our common interests as the US.-South Africa relationship.

Our nations are linked by so much shared history, so many shared values, and so many shared common aspirations. You have struggled to become what Bishop Tutu calls "the rainbow people of God." In America, we have struggled, in the words of Martin Luther King, "to transform the jangling discords of our nation into a beautiful symphony of brotherhood." Despite all of our remaining problems, our examples still inspire the world. Nations look to us to exercise principled leadership. Let us continue to heed their call.

THIRTY-THREE

Military Force and Diplomatic Readiness

I began my term as Secretary of State with a strong conviction that diplomacy and force are closely related and mutually reinforcing. My experiences in office only deepened this conviction. Whether in protecting our interests on the Korean Peninsula, repelling Saddam Hussein's aggression in the Persian Gulf, bringing peace to Bosnia, or ousting the dictators from Haiti, both negotiating skill and military strength proved essential. In statecraft, force and diplomacy are indeed inseparable companions. I decided to use an October 1996 speech before the cadets at the U.S. Military Academy at West Point to develop this concept and emphasize its importance.

I had been wanting to find an opportunity to speak before one of the military academies, and enthusiastically accepted the invitation extended by Superintendent Dan Christman to come to West Point in October of 1996. I knew Christman well from his previous assignment. Like other Secretaries of State, I was regularly accompanied on my travels abroad by a representative of the Joint Chiefs of Staff, usually a three-star officer, who served as my military adviser. This assignment has consistently attracted some of the military's most successful officers. Indeed, a Chairman of the Joint Chiefs, General John Shalikashvili, had been one of Secretary Baker's military advisers. During my tenure, three terrific officers filled this role—Air Force Lieutenant General Mike Ryan, Army Lieutenant General Christman, and Air Force Lieutenant General Dick Myers. I formed close relationships with all three. I could always count on them to contribute substantively to our policy discussions and to project a sense of authority and seriousness in meetings with foreign leaders, and they often proved instrumental in coordinating policy with the Joint Chiefs. After their tours with me, they all went on to excellent assignments—Ryan became Air Force Chief of Staff, Myers Commander of the U.S. Air Force in the Pacific theater, and Christman Superintendent of West Point.

As a Californian whose visits to the Empire State had been mainly to New York City, I had fallen into the trap of overlooking the rest of the state. A trip to West Point on a sparkling October day was a good reminder of how beautiful the upstate area of New York is, and how many historic events have taken place there. As we flew up the Hudson Valley, the fall colors glistened, with the shades of red and orange becoming more dominant as we went north. When we arrived, General Christman conducted a walking tour of the many historical sites on and near "the Point." The Revolutionary War came alive as he described the fighting in the area and the heavy iron cable strung across the Hudson to prevent British warships from coming south. A luncheon in the historic Superintendent's House, where General John J. Pershing had once lived, preceded my talk to the cadets.

The speech's emphasis on the relationship between power and diplomacy was hardly novel. Over a century ago, Carl von Clausewitz observed that war is nothing more than "politics by other means." The strategist Thomas Schelling, in perhaps the most influential contemporary work about the relationship between military force and diplomacy, explained that military power—the threatened or actual use of force—is absolutely essential to diplomatic influence. "The power to hurt is bargaining power," he observed. "To exploit it is diplomacy—vicious diplomacy, but diplomacy."[1] While such ideas are often cited in the scholarly community, they are not commonly presented to a broader public audience. In the post–Cold War era, when the need for military power may seem less pressing and the relationship between force and diplomacy less obvious, I thought it important to rearticulate these concepts in a public address.

I used the speech to outline three principal ways force and diplomacy

---

[1]See Thomas Schelling, *Arms and Influence*, p. 2 (New Haven, Conn.: Yale University Press, 1966).

are combined in statecraft: defending against aggression, deterring potential adversaries, and securing and maintaining peace. By referring to examples from the previous four years—Korea, Kuwait, the Taiwan Strait, Bosnia, and Haiti—I hoped to show that such concepts have tangible consequences. This part of the speech responded to those critics who had charged that the Clinton Administration was reluctant to use force and did not appreciate the essential role of military power in statecraft.

To some, it may seem unusual that a Secretary of State traveled to a military academy to deliver a major speech on the use of force. However, by addressing this subject, particularly before the future officers upon whom would fall the burden of actually using force, I demonstrated that diplomats do understand the gravity—and, on occasion, the necessity—of a decision to deploy military power. Just as importantly, I could make a point that a soldier-statesman like George Marshall well understood: that diplomacy, too, is indispensable.

In addition to making a conceptual statement on the force-diplomacy relationship, the speech addressed an immediate policy challenge related to resources. Just as American statecraft needs resources to maintain superior military readiness, it needs them to maintain what I called diplomatic readiness. Citing Secretary Perry's comment that diplomacy is America's "first line of defense," I stressed the importance of being diplomatically pre-positioned by keeping embassies open and trained personnel posted around the world, maintaining a constructive relationship with the [other] great powers, playing a central role in international organizations, and assisting fledgling democracies. Put simply, maintaining diplomatic readiness would make it less likely that we would have to send U.S. forces into harm's way. "If we rely on our military strength alone," I said, "we will end up using our military all the time." For this reason, the speech was a call to rebuild the resource base for American foreign policy. I wanted to say quite bluntly that I did not believe diplomacy could carry its share of the load with constantly diminishing budgets.

This was a point I had made frequently in speeches and testimony before Congress since my appearance at the Council on Foreign Relations a year earlier (see Chapter 22). Indeed, "We cannot sustain our diplomacy on the cheap" had become something of a mantra since the November 1994 congressional elections. Nevertheless, our international affairs budget remained sorely underfunded. With each budget cycle, things only got worse. The State Department had already been forced to close 30 embassies and consulates abroad. Much of our vital communications equipment was obsolete, even antiquated, a condition no competitive American business would have tolerated. I appreciated the need to reduce spending and streamline the government, but I felt that the cuts for foreign affairs had gone too far. As I said at West Point, "We have long since cut through fat to muscle and bone."

It was especially frustrating that while Congress slashed funding for foreign policy, crippling our ability to solve problems through diplomacy, it consistently authorized the Pentagon to spend *more* money than it had requested. This always struck me as ironic, because many of the same people on Capitol Hill who gave the Pentagon more than it had asked for were reluctant actually to deploy military forces abroad, arguing that other nations should assume more of the burden.

With the presidential election only two weeks away, I wanted to keep my pledge of bipartisanship in foreign policy, despite my anger at congressional budget cuts. I was therefore careful to avoid any undertone of campaign rhetoric. The speech rarely referred to Congress and did not even mention the Republican Party. I made the point that the resources question would be critical whoever was elected President and whatever the composition of the Congress, and I urged a fundamental reassessment of our foreign affairs funding at the beginning of 1997: "It is time for our nation to commit itself to a new bipartisan consensus recognizing that diplomatic readiness remains fundamental to our national security and that we must—and we will—fulfill the responsibilities of leadership."

When we submitted the draft speech to other government agencies for "clearance," officials at the Office of Management and Budget (OMB) raised concerns about my aggressive stance. They were leery that a statement I proposed to make about the need "to reverse the decline" in foreign affairs spending would be read as an implicit criticism of the President's budget and would lock him into a position before negotiations began. Believing that a shortage of resources was one of our greatest foreign policy threats, I fought to keep the main thrust of the statement intact. After several rounds of negotiations with OMB (including one via telephone as I flew to West Point on the morning of the speech), I agreed to slight revisions that did not dilute the central message. For example, the statement about "reversing the decline" was replaced by, "I do not believe we can sustain our global leadership and protect our interests with constantly contracting resources. We must do better."

The media took note of these points about resources and diplomatic readiness. The *Los Angeles Times* seconded my call for a new bipartisan consensus on foreign affairs spending, explaining that "the world's most powerful nation is almost willfully abandoning its opportunities to spread its influence and deter crises." Writing in the *New York Times*, Tom Friedman called Congress's insistence on overfunding the Pentagon "insane" and wrote that in 1997, the President's first foreign affairs negotiation would have to be with the 105th Congress.[2] Starting such a dialogue became one of my final and most important missions as Secretary, and I returned to the theme of resources in my last major speech, in January 1997.

Force, Diplomacy, and the Resources We Need for American Leadership

Remarks to Cadets at the U.S. Military Academy,

West Point, New York, October 25, 1996

Today, I want to talk with you about combining diplomacy and force to advance America's interests and ideals. There could be few more appropriate places for such a discussion than West Point, with its tradition of eminent soldier-diplomats. This is a tradition to which your new Superintendent, General Christman, certainly belongs.

In his two years as my military adviser, General Christman's counsel was superb—especially on the many important trips we took together. As a Vietnam veteran, he contributed greatly to the success of my trip to normalize relations with Hanoi last year. Dan also succeeded in bringing together for the first time high-ranking general officers from Israel and Syria—even though the two countries remain technically at war.

---

[2]See "Imperiled Clout in Foreign Arena: Christopher Should Be Heeded on Diplomacy Funding Cutbacks," *Los Angeles Times*, Oct. 31, 1996; Friedman, "Your Mission, Should You Accept It," *New York Times*, Oct. 27, 1996.

Dan's assignment to West Point seems an ideal opportunity to return to the scene of his early achievements—he graduated first in the class of 1965. I understand he has already earned a nickname for himself up here—"Chief Rabble Rouser." Given how good he was at rousing the troops wherever we went together, I hope that he—and you—will give a demonstration right here and now.

West Point is very fortunate to have Dan at this moment in history, when so much has changed from the world we knew during nearly half a century of Cold War. Your instructors never imagined 10 years ago that their students would be going on joint patrols with Russian soldiers in Bosnia, or exercising with Baltic troops on the bayous of Louisiana.

But in the midst of these changes, the fundamentals have stayed the same. American leadership and strength are just as critical to our nation's security and prosperity now as they were 50 years ago.

Consider where we might be today if we had failed to lead over the last four years. Iraqi troops would be back in Kuwait. There would be not just one but four nuclear states on the territory of the former Soviet Union. North Korea would be well on the way to possessing nuclear weapons. War would still rage in Bosnia. Dictators would still rule Haiti. And there would be no framework for peace in the Middle East.

Where America is called upon to lead, often it is you who will be on the front lines. That is why President Clinton, with bipartisan support in Congress, has made sure that the United States has the best-trained, best-equipped and most ready forces in the world. And today, our military might is matched by the strength of our economy and by the powerful attraction of our ideals. Together with our diplomacy, they allow us to exercise our global leadership and to protect our interests.

In today's world, when American interests are more global than ever, our national security requires the wise use of force and diplomacy together. Diplomacy that is not backed by the credible threat or use of force can be hollow—and ultimately dangerous. But if we do not use diplomacy to promote our vital interests, we will surely find ourselves defending them on the battlefield. Today, in more places and more circumstances than ever before, we must get the balance right. To do the job properly, we must field and fund a world-class military. But we must also field and fund world-class diplomacy.

The Chairman of the Joint Chiefs, General Shalikashvili, understands well that defense and diplomacy must work hand in hand. As he says, "the walls have come down between our two institutions . . . the days when the military viewed diplomats as the striped pants set . . . are long gone." He has personally put that insight into action in recent missions like Operation Restore Democracy in Haiti and IFOR in Bosnia.

The lesson of our time is that we must combine force and diplomacy when our important interests are at stake. We are working together across a broad spectrum of circumstances. Let me discuss several of them today: defending against aggression, deterring potential adversaries, and securing peace in regions of vital interest.

It is the fundamental responsibility of the President to defend against attacks on our nation, our people, our allies, and our vital interests. The military role is critical—but our diplomacy is also indispensable. There is probably no better example than Desert Storm, when our diplomacy built a coalition to turn back Iraq's invasion of Kuwait. Since then, we have maintained strong partnerships with our friends in the Gulf. And we have kept robust forces available. As a result, we were ready when Saddam Hussein renewed his threats against Kuwait in 1994. Within hours, with the cooperation of our Gulf partners, the President was able to send Army tank units to the border and order an aircraft carrier group to the region, together with over 300 Air Force planes. Our resolve forced Saddam to stop in his tracks and pull back. Today in Iraq, we maintain our strategy of troop deployments, an expanded no-fly zone, and a tough sanctions regime.

There is no doubt that we will use force when we must. But our military can also provide deterrence to make it less likely that our service men and women will be sent into battle.

On the Korean Peninsula, our soldiers and diplomats together practice a textbook example of deterrence. Some 37,000 American troops still stand watch on the last fault line of the Cold War. There they deter an attack from the North. Our strong alliance with Seoul has allowed our two countries to stand shoulder-to-shoulder against aggression.

In recent years, North Korea has raised the stakes with its pursuit of nuclear weapons. We reinforced our troops and pursued tough but painstaking diplomacy to halt and reverse North Korea's nuclear program. Negotiations have brought important progress. But we have left no doubt that we are prepared to respond militarily in defense of our interests in this critical region.

In the Taiwan Strait, the timely combination of our military presence and our diplomacy helped to ensure the stability of the whole region at a moment of great tension last March. We demonstrated our resolve by sending two carrier groups into the waters around Taiwan. Diplomatically, we reiterated our adherence to the three communiques that have defined our long-standing China policy. And we pressed both sides to reduce tensions and resume their dialogue.

The combination of force and diplomacy is also essential to deal with the complex challenges of securing peace in many regions of vital interest to the United States.

In Bosnia, it took both American diplomatic initiative and intensive NATO airstrikes in the summer of 1995 to end four years of war that threatened the stability of Europe. Without overwhelming air power, we could not have brought the Serbs to the negotiating table. But without a dedicated negotiating team of both diplomats and soldiers, we could not have produced the Dayton Agreement.

We did this through the unprecedented involvement of the military members of our negotiating team, led by General Wes Clark—who, by the way, also was first in his class here in 1966. Their pivotal role in Dayton last fall ensured that IFOR's mission would be well-defined and appropriately limited—and that our soldiers would have the authority, and the rules of engagement, they needed to do their job. And let me also say that our 20,000 IFOR troops, led by another West Pointer, General William Nash, have performed superbly.

Only IFOR could create the secure environment in which a lasting peace can be built. But only civilians can rebuild a civil society in Bosnia. That is why our diplomatic efforts have emphasized elections, multi-ethnic institutions, and economic reconstruction.

Haiti was another example of careful advance cooperation to ensure that the civilian and military parts of the operation would work effectively together. Our troops gave Haitians the security they needed to hold free and fair elections resulting in the first peaceful, democratic transfer of power in Haiti's history. And our diplomats assembled the coalition we needed to convince Haiti's dictators to stand aside—allowing U.S. troops to come in peace and leave on time. Now we are working with the people of Haiti and the international community to support economic reconstruction and help build a strong future for democracy.

But, of course, we will serve the American people best of all if we can prevent the conflicts and emergencies that call for a military response. As

Secretary of State, it is my responsibility to marshal our resources to do just that. Secretary Perry calls our diplomacy our first line of defense. If we hold that line around the world, we are much less likely to have to send you and the troops you will command into harm's way.

Nowhere does the United States have more at stake than in Europe, where 5 million Americans were sent to fight this century. After World War II, we created NATO—perhaps the most successful example of military-diplomatic cooperation the world has ever seen. Today, NATO plays a central role in overcoming Europe's historic divisions and laying the foundations for a lasting peace. Now we are adapting and expanding the alliance—NATO should take in its first post–Cold War new members by 1999. They will be ready, both politically and militarily, "to share the risks and responsibilities of freedom," as President Clinton said on Tuesday. And as we consolidate the political gains of Europe's new democracies, we are making it less likely that we will ever again have to send American troops to fight a war or to keep the peace on the borderlands of central and eastern Europe. And we are working with all the nations of Europe, including Russia, to build an undivided and peaceful continent.

In Asia, President Clinton has renewed our commitment to remain a Pacific power with 100,000 forward-deployed troops. Alongside the deterrence our military presence provides, our diplomacy is building the cooperation that will keep the region stable. We have reinforced our core alliances with Japan, Korea, Australia, Thailand, and the Philippines, and we have promoted a new structure for regional security cooperation as well as dialogues among former adversaries.

In Africa, we are building a broad strategy to prevent the violence that threatens the future of many emerging democracies. Our diplomacy is helping to rebuild civil society in countries like Mozambique and to avert new conflicts. We are also prepared to help Africans respond to African crises. That is why we are working with our partners in Africa and Europe to create an African Crisis Response Force. African nations would provide the troops for such a force. The United States and other nations would make a substantial contribution of equipment, training, and logistical support—to help Africans build peace themselves.

Here at West Point, I doubt that I need to convince you of the need for this kind of diplomacy. You know the world is now more interdependent than ever, that the line between domestic and foreign policy has been erased, and that our security and economic interests are inseparable. The logic of these changes is that America must be more engaged in the world, not less.

Especially because you are future officers, you have a keen interest in a foreign policy that helps us avert costly conflict and crisis. It may sound like a paradox, but the history of this century teaches us that as America's engagement around the world increases, the likelihood that we will be drawn into conflict decreases. It is when we seek to escape the world's problems that we pay the greatest price.

Americans understand we need a strong military whose requirements are strongly supported. Because American diplomacy is also vital, I believe the national interest requires that we provide sufficient funding for both. Only by doing so will we be able to maintain and enhance our diplomatic readiness.

Just as military readiness requires maintaining forces and bases around the world, so diplomatic readiness requires keeping embassies open and trained personnel posted around the world.

Diplomatic readiness means maintaining constructive relations with the great powers. For example, we need a strong presence in Russia to manage relations with that country as it goes through a momentous transition. A presence in each of the Newly Independent States of the former Soviet Union is also decisively important.

Diplomatic readiness means reaping benefits for our own security and prosperity by playing a central role in international organizations. Our funding for the International Atomic Energy Agency, for example, supports inspections that help control the nuclear programs of such countries as North Korea and Iraq.

Diplomatic readiness means supporting American business overseas, so we can break down barriers to American exports in countries like Japan and Brazil. Business leaders often tell me how much they appreciate our support—and how they wish we had the resources to do more.

Diplomatic readiness means having adequate communications facilities. In today's 24-hour, fast-paced world, we cannot make do with information technology that is years out of date.

Diplomatic readiness also means providing targeted aid to struggling democracies—an investment in their future, and in ours. Earlier this month in the West African country of Mali, I saw firsthand how just a few hundred dollars of materials, and the labor of our Peace Corps volunteers, are helping farmers defend their land against the encroaching Sahara desert and build a better future for their families.

Today, our diplomacy is also essential to confront the new transnational threats to our security, such as international crime, drug trafficking, terrorism, proliferation, and environmental damage. These threats respect no borders. No nation—and no army—can defeat them alone. Without diplomatic representation in almost every country of the world, we could not have marshaled global support to renew the nuclear Non-Proliferation Treaty—or to adopt a Comprehensive Test Ban Treaty. Without law enforcement agents stationed around the world, we could not track down criminals and drug dealers to make sure they stand trial in the United States.

Simply put, we cannot sustain our diplomacy on the cheap—unless we want to shortchange the American people. But that is just what is happening. Since 1984, our international affairs spending has fallen by 51% in real terms—51%. The total amount the United States spends on international affairs now constitutes just 1.2% of the federal budget—a tiny fraction of the amount we must spend when foreign crises erupt into war.

I am constantly impressed by the ingenuity our people around the world show in doing more with less. But there comes a time when less is really just less. As President Clinton said last month, our international affairs budget "is well below what we need to assure that we can achieve our foreign policy objectives." This reflects the fact that the President has consistently sought greater resources than the Congress has provided.

We have long since cut through fat to muscle and bone. Since I became Secretary of State, budgetary pressures have forced us to close 30 embassies and consulates. We cannot advance American interests by lowering the American flag. Our global presence should be expanding, not contracting. We must find a way to continue to provide vital facilities and services to military attaches and personnel from other government agencies. And we must be able to provide essential services to American citizens.

In a world without dangers, these cuts in our diplomacy might be comprehensible. But in the real world, the failure to maintain diplomatic readiness will inevitably shift the burden to America's military. The President has made clear that we will use force when we must. But if we rely on our military strength alone, we will end up using our military all the time. That would impose too high a cost in lives and dollars.

I do not believe we can sustain our global leadership and protect our interests with constantly contracting resources. We must do better. Next January a new Congress will be sworn in. Whatever its composition and whoever is elected President, it will be high time to face up to the implications of the funding cuts of the last few years and the requirements of future budgets. In the context of the need for deficit reduction, I believe that we must renew our support for American diplomacy.

Our diplomacy and our military power must go hand-in-hand if our great nation is to fulfill its potential. It is time for our nation to commit itself to a new bipartisan consensus recognizing that diplomatic readiness remains fundamental to our national security and that we must—and we will—fulfill the responsibilities of leadership.

As President Clinton put it on Tuesday, "Wherever I go, whomever I talk with, the message to me is the same: We believe in America. We trust America. We want America to lead. And America must lead." With a new generation of leaders like you, I am confident that, working together, our military forces and our diplomats can meet that challenge of leadership today—and tomorrow.

Thank you.

THIRTY-FOUR

Bolstering a Flagging Peace Process

Cairo became a symbol to me of the ups and downs, the triumphs and setbacks, of the Middle East peace process. I had traveled there in February 1993 on my first trip abroad as Secretary of State, as part of our effort to restart that process.[1] Ultimately, I made 14 trips to Cairo, and so it was fitting that it should be my final stop in the region as Secretary.

Egypt, the most populous Arab country and the first to make peace with Israel, claims a proprietary interest in the peace process. In the wake of the 1997 Camp David accords, it has become the recipient of the second-largest amount of U.S. foreign aid ($2 billion annually, compared to $3 billion for Israel). It is a key regional ally, and the Israel-Egypt agreement remains the linchpin of peace in the region.

From the peace process standpoint, Egypt *is* its plainspoken and forceful President, Hosni Mubarak. When he took office after Anwar Sadat's assassination in October 1981, Middle East experts were betting that he wouldn't last a year, but he consolidated his power and took firm control. Egypt has the trappings of a parliamentary democracy, and the military remains an important source of power, but Mubarak is the unchallenged ruler.

Although he has claimed the mantle of Sadat, Mubarak is more con-

---

[1]On that trip, Marie and I paid an early-morning visit to the Pyramids and the Sphinx. A photographer got a picture of me with the Sphinx in the near background. Poking fun at my unsmiling face, newspapers in the United States ran the picture with the caption, "Which one is the Sphinx?"

servative than the great Egyptian peacemaker. In contrast to Sadat, whose 1977 trip to Jerusalem was a historic breakthrough for peace, Mubarak has made only one visit to Israel, to attend Yitzhak Rabin's funeral in 1995. Under Mubarak's leadership, there has never been more than a cold peace between Egypt and Israel.

Mubarak often seemed to be playing his two key foreign affairs advisers off against each other. Foreign Minister Amre Moussa, a suave and fluent diplomat, was hostile to Israel and advanced an aggressive pro-Arab line. When he spoke for Egypt, it often created problems for Israel and the United States. The other adviser, Osama el-Baz, an articulate, Harvard-trained intellectual, had long worked with U.S. officials on the peace process. When Mubarak deployed el-Baz, it usually meant that he wanted to find a way to resolve a problem. Although they often took different tacks, Moussa and el-Baz both helped Mubarak navigate the difficult terrain between the demands of militant Arabs in the region and Cairo's interest in supporting U.S. efforts to promote peace.

One source of Egypt's influence on the peace process was its relationship with PLO Chairman Arafat. In dark days, Arafat almost always turned to Egypt for advice and help. Mubarak provided him with a palace and often furnished him with helicopters and other logistical support. I occasionally met with Arafat in Cairo, sometimes with Mubarak, but also separately.

The Mubarak-Arafat relationship produced one of the most memorable and bizarre 24-hour periods of my four years in office. In May 1994, the Israelis and the Palestinians were on the verge of reaching an agreement giving the Palestinians self-governance authority in Gaza and Jericho, as envisioned in the Oslo agreement. Mubarak invited Prime Minister Rabin and Chairman Arafat to Cairo to resolve the remaining issues, such as the boundaries of Jericho and of the area within Gaza that would remain under Israeli control. I joined Mubarak in pressing them to agree, and after a time, he put them in a room next to his office to hammer out the final details, while he and I discussed ways to overcome the sticking points periodically reported to us by their aides. As the evening wore on, Mubarak ordered in stacks of traditional Egyptian bean sandwiches from a sidewalk vendor, asked Rabin and Arafat to come back into his office, and insisted that we all partake. Doing so violated a number of my rules on how to stay healthy in the Middle East, but under

Mubarak's watchful eye, I had no choice. Arafat was also reluctant to join in the feast, which did nothing to ease my concern. After the meal, it was back to the adjacent room for Arafat and Rabin.

When midnight came without an agreement having been reached, Mubarak and I joined them and helped to mediate the final differences. At one poignant moment, responding to laughter on the Israeli side, Arafat asked Rabin, "Are you laughing at me? Do you think I am a joke?" In his gravest manner and deepest voice, having quieted everyone in his delegation, Rabin replied, "No, we take you very seriously." The tension eased, and the final issues were resolved, or so we thought.

We finished around 2:30 A.M., and an elaborate signing ceremony was scheduled for the next afternoon. It was held in a large auditorium, with a considerable audience, many dignitaries on the stage, and heavy television coverage. But, astoundingly, when it came time for Arafat to sign, he simply refused to do so, saying that he wasn't satisfied with the maps depicting the transfer of territory to Palestinian control. I had never seen anything like the chaotic scene that followed. After half an hour of frantic scurrying around, we finally found a formula that would satisfy Arafat, and he signed the agreement.[2]

Starting in 1994, the annual Middle East / North Africa Economic Summits became crucial to our policy of providing a strong economic impetus to the Middle East peace process. As I said at the first meeting in Casablanca, we hoped to use these summits to build a framework for regional cooperation and to highlight the importance of pursuing market reform. These objectives, designed to provide the economic underpinning for peace, fit into what we called a triangular relationship among the international community, the regional states, and the private sector.

The 1995 summit, held in October in Amman, Jordan, built on the promise of Casablanca, underscoring the regional parties' growing self-confidence and commitment to working together toward common objectives. In Amman, we saw the face of the future. Over 1,500 participants from throughout the region and the world went there to do business, and the summit significantly increased the economic connections among them. In Casablanca, I had declared the Middle East "open for

---

[2]My satisfaction that we had achieved a resolution at last was mingled with relief that none of us had suffered any lasting ill effects from the previous night's feast.

business," but many private sector people had been drawn to the Casablanca conference largely by curiosity or U.S. encouragement. In Amman, I stressed that the region was now "doing business."[3]

For the Arab participants, that meant doing business with Israelis, with each other, and with Americans and Europeans. Over 160 U.S. companies were represented at the summit, a result of the vigorous work that Commerce Secretary Ron Brown and his people did in promoting it. Brown joined me at several events in Amman, events made successful partly by his flair and contagious enthusiasm.

The success of the summit was attributable in large part to Jordan's improving relations with Israel during the preceding year. Since signing a formal peace accord in October 1994, the two nations had moved closer to a warm peace. The Israeli and Jordanian air forces had conducted joint flight operations, and King Hussein, an accomplished pilot, had flown his aircraft through Israeli airspace. In our meeting the day before the summit, the King said he hoped that such taboo-shattering actions would help build bridges between the two peoples. I have great admiration for King Hussein and believe that he has been one of the most critical links in the peace process. Unlike several other of our Arab allies, he has been willing to take bold steps. "You have done more in one year to bring peace with Israel than the Egyptians had done in 17 years," I told him when we met in Amman.

This comment addressed a broader issue: the growing fissure among Arabs about how to approach the peace process. Unfortunately, this rift came into full display at the Amman summit. During the opening plenary session, Egyptian Foreign Minister Moussa stunned the audience with a downbeat speech calling for those in the region not to "rush" to normalize relations with the Israelis. In an impromptu response, King Hussein eloquently disagreed with Moussa, saying that if peace meant a better life for the region's people, "we are not just rushing but running." No other speaker supported Moussa's remarks. Egyptian businessmen openly criticized him and concluded some deals with Israelis. Moussa, seeing that he had gone too far and fearing that he might be jeopardizing Egypt's chances of hosting the 1996 economic summit, privately went to many at the Amman summit to say that he had been misunderstood. He

---

[3]In closing my remarks, I again borrowed a famous line from the movie *Casablanca*, saying, "Today, in Amman, it is time to play it again, Sam."

later apologized to King Hussein. Although the impact of this incident soon dissipated, it reflected a backpedaling trend in some Arab circles.

Sadly, the positive spirit shown in Amman was short-lived. Six days after the summit, Israeli Prime Minister Rabin was killed in the streets of Tel Aviv by a young right-wing Israeli assassin. Taking over as Labor Party leader and Prime Minister, Shimon Peres continued to pursue negotiations, but a series of terrorist bombings against Israeli civilians by Palestinian extremists during the spring of 1996 set back his efforts. Although the antiterrorism summit at Sharm el-Sheikh temporarily revived the peace process, much damage had been done (see Chapter 30). In an election in the summer of 1996, Peres narrowly lost his office to Likud Party leader Binyamin Netanyahu, a critic of the Oslo accord who had campaigned on the theme that the Labor Party's approach to the peace process endangered Israel's security.

That September, reports came in that the Israeli-Palestinian peace talks were on the verge of a complete collapse. Both sides had dug in and were doing little to fulfill either the spirit or the substance of Oslo. In particular, Netanyahu had opened a new entrance to the Hasmonean tunnel in a highly sensitive area of Jerusalem without consulting with Chairman Arafat. This had sparked gun battles in Gaza and the West Bank costing the lives of 70 Palestinians and 15 members of the Israeli Defense Force. This new provocation came on top of the Israelis' refusal to complete a promised partial troop withdrawal from Hebron, the last major West Bank city scheduled for return to Palestinian control, until new security arrangements could be agreed upon. Netanyahu's actions reflected a continuing tension between his ideological desires and his obligations under the Oslo peace agreement. Seeking to have it both ways, he was satisfying no one.

The President was deeply involved in his reelection campaign, but nonetheless I called him twice from New York, where I was attending the opening of the UN General Assembly, to discuss these anguishing developments. I felt we needed to act decisively to prevent the violence from spinning completely out of control. After conferring with my colleagues, I recommended that the President interrupt his campaigning to host a White House meeting of the key Middle East leaders on October 1–2. Netanyahu and Arafat had refused my suggestion that they meet in the Middle East, but I felt they would not decline an invitation from the

President. Clinton agreed without hesitation, even though it was a risky initiative and the meeting would come only a few days before the first presidential debate.

The parties did accept his invitation, but when the meeting convened, they were in a fractious mood. After bitter all-night negotiations yielded no progress, I had to bring their top aides together at the State Department the next morning in a last-ditch effort to find a basis for resuming talks in the region. Later that day, under the President's strong hand, and with a major push from Jordan's King Hussein, who was also in attendance, Netanyahu and Arafat agreed to have their negotiators resume discussions on implementation of the Oslo accords, with U.S. participation.

A few days later I flew to the Erez Checkpoint on the Gaza border to launch this new round of negotiations. Based on my discussions with Netanyahu and Arafat during my brief stay, I reported to President Clinton that my visit was worthwhile in carrying forward the fragile agreement he had negotiated in Washington. After my departure, a U.S. delegation led by Dennis Ross remained at Erez to facilitate these sensitive discussions, which focused on the redeployment of Israeli troops from Hebron.

These talks were still ongoing as we approached the Cairo economic summit, held in November 1996. The parties had come close to an agreement at the end of October, only to pull apart at the last minute. A settlement still seemed far off by early November, and overall, the prospect of a comprehensive peace seemed more remote than at any earlier time in President Clinton's first term.

In these difficult circumstances, we wanted the Cairo summit to provide some needed encouragement to the countries in the region. Our economic goals in Cairo were twofold: to make clear that America still believed that a vibrant public-private partnership could bolster integration of the regional states into the global economy, and to reaffirm the critical importance of the region's private sector as a core constituency of peace. On the political side, we hoped that the interaction of the leaders at the summit would restore some momentum to the peace negotiations.

Although there had been some discussion within the Administration about sending a less senior delegation to Cairo, I had argued that without our high-level participation, the summit would be almost certain to fail. Since I had already announced my intention to step down as Secretary of State, I anticipated that this trip would be my last to the region, as indeed it was. My participation thus became a personal appeal to all of the parties to recognize the benefits of peace, and to continue working to see it realized.

Unlike my Casablanca and Amman statements, which had concentrated primarily on the potential for regional prosperity, my remarks before the opening session of the Cairo conference stressed the broader purposes and benefits of pursuing a comprehensive peace. At a time of pessimism about the future, I believed it was important to remind the parties of all the accomplishments of the peace process. In the first half of the speech, I aimed to explain the gains made thus far, emphasizing that every step toward a comprehensive peace, from Camp David and Madrid to Oslo, the Jordanian accord, and Sharm el-Sheikh, had been fundamentally sound and beneficial for both Arabs and Israelis. These were gains on which the parties could build, but as I told them, there could be "no winners and no losers" in the peace process. Unless the parties stepped out of their tit-for-tat mindsets, the fruits of peace would never be realized.

Despite the downturn in the political environment, the economic news in the region was quite good, partly because many Arab states were undertaking economic reform measures that we had urged at Casablanca and Amman. As the business environment became more hospitable, investors began to see opportunities in the region. Significantly, more senior business representatives from around the world were in Cairo than had ever before gathered in one place in the Middle East. Nevertheless, the grim condition of the peace process cast a shadow of uncertainty over the summit.

I also used this final trip to the region to push on the most immediate issue under negotiation—the Israeli redeployment from Hebron. The night before the conference opened, I had my last meeting as Secretary of State with Chairman Arafat. This meeting exemplified the roller-coaster nature of negotiations in the Middle East. The primary source of recent headaches had been Netanyahu's precipitous actions, such as the opening of the Hasmonean tunnel. Now, Arafat's attitude was emerging as the principal roadblock. He had evidently sensed that Netanyahu was under great pressure to show progress, and was taking advantage of the situation by holding out for more. Although the parties kept talking, they were plagued by mutual mistrust. Just as one side seemed ready to deal, the other would pull away. In my late-night meeting with Arafat in

Cairo, I tried unsuccessfully to persuade him to accept a package deal combining Israeli commitments to withdraw from Hebron and PLO pledges to reach agreement on other outstanding issues. Arafat seemed in no special hurry to negotiate seriously, and it was not until January 1997 that he and Netanyahu agreed on a U.S.-sponsored plan for Israeli redeployment from much of Hebron.

The three Middle East economic summits held during my time in office clearly stimulated trade and investment within the region. I had hoped that this development would help sustain the peace process, and still believe that it will in the long run. At present, however, the cause-and-effect relationship seems to be working the other way: the stalemate in the peace process in 1997 caused many Arab nations to boycott the fourth economic conference, held in Doha, Qatar, on November 16, 1997, and other nations, including Israel, to downgrade their representation. It was especially disappointing that Egypt, which had elbowed others out of the way to host the 1996 conference, pulled out of the 1997 event.

○

Our Vision of a Prosperous Middle East at Peace

Remarks at the Cairo Economic Conference,

Cairo, November 12, 1996

Excellencies, ladies and gentlemen: On behalf of President Clinton, I want to express my deep gratitude to President Mubarak and to the people of Egypt for hosting this third annual economic conference. I also want to express my enormous appreciation to the more than 1,500 businesspeople, from over 70 countries, who are attending this conference. Their willingness to invest in a better future is what brings us together here today.

We have come to Cairo, to this city of greatness—ancient and modern—because we share a vision of a prosperous Middle East at peace. We share a conviction that if this vision is to be realized, the peace process must move forward in both its political and economic dimensions at the same time. And we share a commitment to deepen the partnership between governments and the private sector so that peace can endure and thrive.

Today, the world can look to Cairo, to this economic conference, as a vote of confidence in the peace process—a peace process that has already brought us so far. And we can once again thank President Mubarak for reminding the region and the world of the stake that we have in peace.

President Mubarak shares this great responsibility with other leaders of wisdom and good will. Two years ago, King Hassan convened the first Middle East and North Africa Economic Summit in Casablanca. There we opened up a whole new dimension of the peace process to complement the political negotiations launched in Madrid five years earlier. Last year, King Hussein brought us together in Amman to build new bridges of prosperity across old barriers of hostility.

It was also to the economic summit in Amman that Prime Minister Rabin made his last journey for peace. The Prime Minister spoke to the entire Middle East when he said this:

> So far we have invested much blood, much time, and much money in a product which may have been essential for our national existences but of little benefit for our citizens. We invested in war. Today, and from here on, we are committed to invest in peace.

Just one week later, sadly, tragically, the peace process lost one of its strongest champions.

There is no doubt that the peace process has been tested—tested severely—by the traumas in the last year since Prime Minister Rabin's assassination. But over the last year, and especially in recent weeks, the peace process has also demonstrated great resilience. Arabs and Israelis alike know what war means. They have already glimpsed the promise of peace. By looking back into the abyss, both Arabs and Israelis recognized the imperative of moving forward.

Both Palestinians and Israelis, like all the people of the region, have a fundamental self-interest in bringing this conflict to an end. They understand that this decades-long conflict can be resolved in phases over time. They remain committed to resolve this conflict through the structure of the negotiations that they have built together. And they are coming to accept that without peace there can be no security, and without security there can be no peace.

In the wake of the recent violence, Israel and the Palestinians have pledged to uphold the agreements they have negotiated and carry out the commitments they have made. The current negotiations have been intensive and, at times, frustrating. But I believe that a final set of very specific understandings on Hebron is close at hand. And once those negotiations finally succeed, I urge the parties to move ahead with the same urgency to implement the remainder of the Interim Agreement.

For these and future negotiations to succeed, each side must go the extra mile to understand the needs of the other—to take their requirements into account. Each side must accept that to succeed, there can be no winners and no losers. Each side must win and be seen to win—or both sides will lose. Each side must recognize that it is not possible to make peace without taking risks—but that maintaining the status quo poses even greater risks for their future. Each side should also know this: The United States will continue to help them take those risks and support them along the hard, long journey to peace.

Peace in the Middle East is a vital national interest of the United States. That is why President Clinton has made such a strong personal commitment to stand with the peacemakers at every step of the way over the last four years. That is why the newly reelected President and the next Secretary of State will continue to make the advancement of the Middle East peace process a top priority over the next four years.

There are historic gains to preserve, gains on which the parties can build. There are two landmark agreements between Israel and the Palestinians—and path-breaking cooperation to fight terrorism and violence. There is the peace treaty between Israel and Jordan—and a new set of diplomatic and commercial contacts between Israel and its Arab neighbors. There is the opportunity for a comprehensive peace that includes Syria and Lebanon—a peace that must finally be achieved if this region is to enjoy real security. And there is, of course, the founding pillar of peace still firmly in place—and that is the peace between Egypt and Israel.

We can see how far we have really come if we look at ourselves—if we look at this economic conference. Despite all the setbacks and uncertainties of recent months, more and higher-level business representatives from around the world are here in Cairo than have ever before assembled at one time in the region. You recognize opportunity amidst the risk, and you are attracted by the reforms that are making the Middle East and North Africa a more hospitable business environment.

Your profit strategies are perfectly complementary to our strategies for peace. Private sector capital is the most direct way to translate the abstract promise of peace into concrete benefits that can lift the lives and livelihoods of ordinary people. By giving individuals and communities a stake in peace, you can pave the way for true reconciliation among people and nations. By crisscrossing borders with new electrical grids, fiber optic cables, and gas pipelines, you can integrate the region's economies and make war ever less likely.

The process that we launched in Casablanca two years ago, and that we renew today, will reinforce our partnership for peace and prosperity. By bringing so many business people together, we are generating the contacts that can lead to contracts. We are showcasing opportunities available in our host country—Egypt—and the other countries participating here. And we are giving fresh impetus to the new institutions that will promote economic development and cooperation across the region.

The Middle East-Mediterranean Travel and Tourism Association is now established, with a secretariat in Tunis. It is working with the private sector to develop the enormous potential for tourism that these lands of miracles and monuments hold for us. And the Regional Business Council is poised to become an important forum for exchanging business information, publicizing investment opportunities, and developing ways to support the private sector.

We are make progress toward opening the flagship regional institution—the Middle East Development Bank. I am pleased to say that the United States will sign the Bank's Charter next week and we will send representatives to the bank's transition team to Cairo later this month. The bank's mission is to be a catalyst—to support key private sector projects and to focus on the region's growing infrastructure needs. The Clinton Administration will work with the new Congress to gain strong American backing for the bank so that it can become operational by the end of next year. I urge other nations to come forward now to support the bank's funding needs.

For too long, this region has been held back by the ravages of conflict and war—and by the inefficiencies of statist and protectionist economic policies. It faces a dual challenge if it is to prosper. To compete effectively, this region must not only make peace. It must reform. Two years ago in Casablanca and again last year in Amman, I called upon the governments of the Middle East and North Africa to meet this challenge—

to modernize their economies, open up their markets, crack down on corruption, and remove the bureaucratic bottlenecks and regulatory obstacles that have for too long scared off investors and drained away precious capital. Today, we can see encouraging progress across the region.

Here in Egypt, reform is brightening the prospects for growth and attracting the interest of foreign companies and investors, as President Mubarak so clearly outlined this morning. The government has already privatized over 100 companies. It has cut tariffs on capital goods and eased registration procedures for investors. The new standby arrangement with the IMF will help support Egypt as it consolidates these and other business-friendly reforms, such as restructuring the tax system. Egypt is also making important progress in strengthening its protection of intellectual property rights. That is one reason why Microsoft decided to open a regional office here in Cairo. Over 50 American companies now have manufacturing operations in Egypt, demonstrating confidence in the growing potential of this market—and that number will certainly grow. The United States will continue to develop our economic cooperation with Egypt through the partnership led by President Mubarak and Vice President Gore.

Jordan's recent reforms—from adopting a new investment law to lowering trade barriers—are also beginning to modernize its economy. The capitalization of its stock market is increasing rapidly. American companies, from Sheraton to Sprint, are seizing opportunities to help Jordan build its infrastructure. I am delighted to announce that only yesterday, the United States and Jordan signed an Open Skies agreement to fully liberalize commercial aviation between us. It is the first such agreement we have reached outside of Europe, and I hope that we can negotiate similar agreements with others in this region soon to make both business and tourist travel more efficient.

Israel is also carrying out important reforms that are giving its economy a new dynamism. Privatization is contributing to growth and attracting foreign investment. Israeli and Arab business people from virtually all the countries represented here today are forging links that were inconceivable just several years ago. I am very encouraged by Prime Minister Netanyahu's commitment to deepen economic reform. And I am confident that trade and investment between the United States and Israel and the other countries in this region will continue to expand.

Today, I want to encourage greater American economic engagement across the Middle East and North Africa—from the dynamic Gulf States to Morocco and Tunisia, two countries that are taking so many positive steps to encourage trade and foreign investment. I also want to salute the Israeli and Arab business people who have begun to build relationships to move forward. You are definitely pioneers for peace, and we need your courage and perseverance now more than ever.

But most urgently of all, I want to encourage you to invest in peace where it can make the greatest difference. Economic conditions in the West Bank and Gaza have not prospered as we had hoped. They must improve—and improve quickly—if we are to give Palestinians a full and tangible stake in peace. We must work together to help the Palestinians build a prosperous free market economy and overcome the barriers to the flow of goods, services, and people. President Clinton has recently signed legislation to grant duty-free access for Palestinian exports to the United States. We hope our major trading partners will take similar steps. We are also working to establish special industrial zones that can become magnets for investment, jobs, and especially for hope.

As Secretary of State, in my frequent travel to this region, I have spent the bulk of my time talking to government leaders and diplomats. One reason I value these economic conferences so much is that they give me a chance to speak to the business community so well represented here today. When I am with you, I feel I am also addressing the vast majority of the people in the region who speak the common language of commerce, and who share our vision of a better future. You are indeed the constituency for peace.

You have already waited too long to see this region's borders become open gateways—not fortified barriers—to trade and investment. You have an interest in pushing for progress in the peace process. And you have a responsibility to work with the governments of this region to wipe out the barriers and boycotts and prejudices and taboos that obstruct commerce and hold this region back.

We share a common purpose, and we have mutually supporting roles to play. We both understand that there can be no lasting peace for the Middle East without rising prosperity, and that there can be no lasting prosperity in this region without a deepening peace. If we build on the diplomatic and economic progress we have already made, a new millennium of peace and prosperity will soon dawn over these ancient lands.

Thank you very much.

THIRTY-FIVE

China: Setting a Course of Cooperation

Following the tense spring of 1996, U.S.-Chinese relations entered a new and more hopeful phase. Typically, the attention paid to China in the media and elsewhere focuses on the problems—Taiwan, human rights, weapons proliferation, intellectual property. My view, as outlined in the May speech at the Council on Foreign Relations (see Chapter 29), was that while the United States and China had to continue to manage these differences through active engagement, we also had to make progress on a positive agenda based on mutual interests. That speech established a reassuring but realistic context for our relationship, and we spent most of the summer and autumn moving forward on the positive agenda. In the late fall, having announced my intention to step down as Secretary of State, I wanted to set the relationship solidly on this new course for the President's second term. A trip I made to Beijing and Shanghai on November 20–21 was designed to boost this effort.

My 10 hours of meetings with Qian Qichen, Li Peng, and Jiang Zemin in Beijing on November 20 were valuable symbolically as well as substantively. In a way, the trip closed the circle that had opened with my difficult visit to China in March 1994. It not only enabled me to complete my tenure at State on a positive note, but also showed how far U.S.-Chinese relations had come in what had been an uneven and, at times, a rough four years.

The Chinese made a great effort to assure that my visit was perceived by all as cordial and productive. They seemed anxious to erase the memories of March 1994. All their leaders—even the typically sour Li Peng—were friendly, upbeat, and forthcoming. I found them gracious about my decision to leave office. "Happy is the man who is relieved of official duties," President Jiang reflected. Substantively, their comments on non-proliferation, Korea, and other regional topics were generally positive. My impression was that they genuinely wanted to improve ties. While we still had many deep-seated, persistent differences with Beijing, I told the President, "we made more progress on the trip than expected."

This China visit came on the eve of a meeting between President Clinton and Chinese President Jiang at the annual APEC summit in Manila. In Beijing, I sought to line up agreements that the Presidents would ratify at the Manila talks. The most important of these agreements related to arranging reciprocal summits between the two leaders. I believed that holding regular summits would be a way to improve overall relations. In separate meetings the summer before, Tony Lake and I, together with our Chinese counterparts, had developed the modalities of possible summits.[1] Throughout the autumn, there had been a series of cabinet- and subcabinet-level visits to and from China, and we were organizing for a trip by Vice President Gore in early 1997. Before my departure for Beijing, we decided I would tell the Chinese that in Manila, President Clinton would propose summit exchanges. The Chinese were obviously pleased with this message and agreed that the summit meetings should be discussed further by the two leaders.

Aside from preparing the ground for the summit announcement, my main objective on this trip was to proceed with our dialogue on the positive agenda of shared interests. "You will recall that at the end of our meeting last September [at the UN], I lamented that our short encounters seem to dwell almost exclusively on our bilateral differences," I said to Qian during our first session in Beijing. Qian responded positively. "I share your view that our common interests are greater than the issues which divide us," he said. "I cannot deny that there are significant differences, some avoidable perhaps, but China maintains that we should increase cooperation and reduce troubles, thereby increasing trust." We

---

[1] I met with Qian in Jakarta in July, and Lake participated in important talks in Beijing that month. After meeting with Chinese leaders, among them Jiang Zemin and Li Peng, Lake announced that he expected the Chinese and U.S. Presidents would exchange state visits.

then proceeded to have a constructive discussion on several global and regional issues. I found the Chinese very interested in cooperating more closely to address environmental problems, including climate change, pollution, and unsustainable development. The primary regional concern we discussed was the Korea situation. The Chinese confirmed they would participate with us in four-party talks to foster a dialogue between North and South Korea, and I pressed them to use their leverage to moderate Pyongyang's oftentimes outrageous behavior.[2]

Qian and I also had several frank exchanges about areas of difference, notably human rights and weapons proliferation. Our discussions were more productive on the latter subject. The Chinese had planned to provide a nuclear facility to Iran, but Qian said he considered it "impossible" that they would do so. He also reassured me that China intended to strengthen its nuclear export control regulations, a key demand of ours since the ring magnets episode earlier that year, and pledged that China would ratify the Chemical Weapons Convention by April 1997 (which it did).[3]

I raised human rights issues in all my meetings on this trip and presented a new Administration proposal on the subject that was limited in scope but left the door open for further discussion.[4] As expected, my exchange with Premier Li Peng on the issue was the most contentious that I had on the trip. In response to my comment that China needed to adhere to the Universal Declaration of Human Rights, Li Peng complained that America sought to "infringe" on China's sovereignty. I replied that we respected that sovereignty, but that for our nations to make progress

---

[2]The four-party talks finally got under way in 1997 with useful sessions in New York City and Geneva.

[3]Earlier, we had worked well together in achieving a renewal of the Non-Proliferation Treaty and adoption of a Comprehensive Test Ban Treaty.

[4]The proposal was that, in exchange for China's fulfilling four "expectations," the United States would privately commit not to sponsor, co-sponsor, or support a resolution against China at the 1997 meeting of the UN Human Rights Commission in Geneva. The "expectations" were the development of clear understandings that China would take positive steps on prisoner releases, adherence to international human rights covenants, resuming talks with the International Red Cross on prison visits, and setting up a joint U.S.-China forum on human rights. The Chinese response to our proposal fell well short of what we needed. As it had done in previous years, the United States sponsored a resolution criticizing China on human rights, which China was, as before, able to block on a procedural vote.

on our mutual agenda, we would need some convergence on this topic. "Our relationship," I told Li bluntly, "will never reach its highest level of fulfillment until we have a sound and meaningful dialogue on human rights."

I spent the next day in Shanghai, an energetic and vibrant city of 14 million people. Shanghai had undergone extraordinary economic growth, and it was progressively resuming its role as China's economic and financial capital. It represented the nation's enormous economic potential— Shanghai's GDP had risen by 14% over the past four years, and foreign investment had grown by 25% in that period.

A highlight of the day was a luncheon meeting hosted by Shanghai's ebullient Mayor, Xu Kuangdi. Mayor Xu was engaging, confident, and very much at ease with Westerners. We had quite a lively discussion of both the opportunities and the challenges confronting his city. Our meeting room high atop the Peace Hotel overlooked Shanghai's magnificent waterfront (known as the Bund) and gave us an impressive view across the harbor to Pudong Island, where scores of new skyscrapers rose from the horizon, including what would be the tallest building in China.[5] It looked as though an entire city were being built at once.

My speech later that day at Fudan University, one of Shanghai's most prestigious universities, was the public focus of the entire trip. I wanted to use this opportunity to speak directly to China's people, particularly its young citizens. My speech was not pathbreaking, but it explained the recent turn in U.S.-Chinese relations, summed up the bilateral agenda for President Clinton's second term, and laid out a strategic vision for the future. Its central message, which I had privately previewed for Qian the day before in Beijing, was that the United States and China have a mutual interest in cooperating on global affairs and ensuring regional stability and prosperity. I also reiterated that we must manage our differences, not "demagogue" them. This theme, which I had been building upon since my May 1994 speech before the Asia Society (see Chapter 10), had once been referred to widely as "engagement." However, we had learned from our Chinese counterparts that the word didn't translate

---

[5]Shanghai officials estimated that over 18% of the world's construction cranes were operating in the city. Although the figure seems extraordinary, I had no reason to doubt it, given the veritable forest of cranes I saw.

well—the nearest Chinese word is *jiechu*, which means "making contact." Since this can have negative as well as positive connotations, I decided to replace it with the term "dialogue." In the question-and-answer session following my remarks, one perceptive student asked me why I had stopped using "engagement."

Quite a lot of attention was paid to another word I decided not to use at Fudan—"partnership." In the speech's initial drafts, "partnership" was used to describe the new U.S.-China relationship. The original title was "Building a Partnership for the 21st Century," and my advance staff had made a large banner with this phrase on it to hang behind the podium. On the way to China, however, I began to have second thoughts. The term "partnership" described relations with our closest allies, states like Great Britain, Germany, and Japan. Although our relations with China had certainly improved—and I wanted to convey exactly that—"partnership" sounded a little too cozy. It was what we were aiming for, but we weren't there yet. "Cooperation" seemed a more apt term, and we changed the text (and the banner) the night before I gave the speech.[6]

Because of its size and strength, the Middle Kingdom will always warrant major attention—and as long as it retains its present form of government, it will pose challenges for American foreign policy. Some critics have claimed that the Clinton Administration, and I personally, somehow neglected relations with China in favor of other, less important matters. In particular, some assert that my tactical decision to visit Beijing only twice represented a lack of strategic focus. Such charges are unfounded. Along with Russia and the Middle East, China was always given a top priority in policy-making inside the State Department and the White House, and in our process of deciding which leaders to meet with abroad. Over my four years as Secretary, I met with Qian Qichen 14 times and wrote him numerous letters analyzing the state of our relations and identifying agendas for negotiation. Frequently, Qian and I were able to make more progress by meeting around the edges of other international gatherings, outside the glare of publicity that inevitably attended my visits to

---

[6]This last-minute alteration created a bit of a stir in the U.S. press. Both the *Washington Post* and the *New York Times* printed articles on it. Although this attention was a little excessive, it might have inadvertently helped us send a signal to the Beijing leaders: although relations were on the mend, we did not consider them full "partners" yet.

Beijing. I was also with President Clinton for each of his four meetings with Jiang Zemin. Overall, despite some rough spots, our diplomacy enabled us to preserve the U.S.-China relationship, and to raise it to a much higher level than that at which we had found it four years earlier.

In sum, our decision to reject calls for isolation and containment and instead to work with the Chinese, cooperating in areas of mutual interest and managing our differences, proved to be the right choice. With summit exchanges planned for 1997–98, I left office in January 1997 believing that our relationship was headed in the right direction.[7]

The United States and China: Building a New Era of Cooperation for a New Century

Address at Fudan University, Shanghai, November 21, 1996

Good morning. President Yang, thank you very much for that nice introduction. Vice Mayor Zhao, honored guests: I am delighted to be here today. It really gives me great pleasure to be at this center which has played such a valuable role in promoting the study of American history, culture, and foreign policy. I am honored to meet with the scholars and students of Fudan University, one of China's most distinguished institutions of intellectual achievement. Here in this city where East and West have long met and mixed, you are helping to shape a modern China with growing links to the wider world.

On behalf of President Clinton, I have come to this great city to speak to you about the challenges now facing our two nations. My message is clear: Now more than ever before, the American and Chinese peoples can and must work together to advance our interests. Like all great nations, we will no doubt at times have divergent views. But history has given our two countries a remarkable opportunity—the opportunity to build a new era of cooperation for a new century. It is an opportunity which we simply must seize.

[7]President Jiang paid a state visit to the United States in late October 1997, and President Clinton plans to return the visit in 1998.

The shape of the world is changing almost as dramatically as this city's skyline. Today, the Cold War is over, the risk of global nuclear conflict has been greatly reduced, and the free flow of goods and ideas is bringing to life the concept of a global village. But just as all nations can benefit from the promise of this new world, no nation is immune to its perils. We all have a great stake in building peace and prosperity and in confronting threats that respect no borders—threats such as terrorism and drug trafficking, disease, and environmental destruction.

To meet these challenges most effectively, China and the United States must act together—must act in concert. Some have argued that with the Cold War's end, the strategic importance of the United States-China relationship has somehow diminished. I believe they have it exactly backwards. As a new century begins, the importance of strengthening the ties between the United States and China will grow even stronger.

Last May, I proposed that we deepen our cooperation by developing a more regular dialogue, including meetings at the highest level. During the last few months, contact between our government officials has intensified across a broad range of issues—a healthy sign of maturing relations. Yesterday in Beijing, I had the opportunity to meet with President Jiang Zemin; Premier Li Peng; and my counterpart, Vice Premier Qian Qichen. And just three days from now, President Clinton and President Jiang will meet at the APEC Leaders' Meeting in the Philippines.

These meetings have one overriding purpose: to reach new understandings that will bring concrete benefits to the citizens of both countries and the citizens of the world. The United States is convinced that by expanding our cooperation at every level—global, regional, and bilateral—we will advance our shared interests. Let me outline briefly why.

First, I want to talk about the need for the United States and China to work together on the international stage in dealing with global events. Our great nations share a weighty, heavy responsibility: As nuclear powers, as permanent members of the UN Security Council, and as two of the world's biggest economies, we simply must lead. We have a common stake in building and upholding an international system that promotes peace and security and prosperity around the globe.

Nowhere has cooperation been more crucial than in our efforts to halt the spread of weapons of mass destruction. The last few years demonstrate just how much the U.S. and China can accomplish when we work together. Together, we helped ensure the indefinite and unconditional extension of the nuclear Non-Proliferation Treaty and together helped achieve one of the landmarks of this current period, namely the conclusion of the Comprehensive Test Ban Treaty. These two giant steps have made our citizens safer. Americans and Chinese will be even more secure if we can redouble our efforts to end the production of fissile material for nuclear bombs, if we can work together to join the global convention to ban chemical weapons and to strengthen the ability of the international community to detect and stop illicit nuclear programs.

While the United States and China have worked side by side to reach important understandings on non-proliferation, much remains to be done. Indeed, in my meetings yesterday in Beijing we advanced our work together toward this goal. The new regular dialogue that we will have between officials from the United States and China on non-proliferation and arms control issues will facilitate further progress. We have a shared interest in preventing the introduction of sensitive technologies into volatile regions such as South Asia and the Persian Gulf. Let me be particularly clear on one point: Countries such as Iran that sponsor terror and work against peace cannot be trusted to respect international norms or safeguards. Their attempts to acquire nuclear and chemical weapons and missile technology threaten the interests of both of our countries and, indeed, of all their neighbors. We must work together to stop them.

Both of our countries will also benefit from an effective global coalition against terrorists, international criminals, and drug traffickers. In his speech at the UN last September, President Clinton called on all nations to deny sanctuary to those global predators in the narcotics and terrorism field and to ratify the conventions that prevent and punish terrorism. In addition, China and the United States should forge strong ties between our law enforcement officials to fight common foes such as the drug lords in Burma whose traffic in heroin threatens citizens from Shanghai to San Francisco.

China and the United States have an immense stake in building an open global trading system for the 21st century. Together, our two nations account for almost one-third of the global trade and output. For both of our nations, exports are increasingly important to our economic growth. We can both profit by joining to establish and uphold rules that will open markets and will make trade fairer than it is now.

The United States actively supports China's entry into the World Trade Organization—WTO—on commercially meaningful terms. We welcome China's commitment not to introduce new laws or policies that would be inconsistent with its WTO obligations. We are prepared to negotiate intensively to achieve a WTO accession package on the basis of effective market access commitments by China and adherence to WTO rules.

Our economic growth and well-being are also dependent upon responsibly managing our natural resources. For the United States and China, choosing between economic growth and environmental protection is what President Clinton has called "a false choice, an unnecessary choice." Both are vitally important and both are mutually reinforcing.

Our nations must demonstrate global leadership on these critical environmental challenges; perhaps the most dangerous current one is climate change. The United States and China are leading producers of greenhouse gases. These gases threaten to raise sea levels, damage our crop production, and spread deadly disease. As two nations at different stages of development, we will shoulder our responsibilities in somewhat different ways, but we should agree to act together and to act now—globally, regionally, and bilaterally. That is why we are jointly promoting renewable energy sources and energy efficiency. Most important for the long term—and especially to great cities such as Shanghai—we are exploring new energy technologies that are less harmful to the world's atmosphere. On a wide range of environmental issues—saving fisheries, controlling toxic chemicals, preserving forests—our two countries have recently expanded our environmental dialogue. We do this to spur progress through the Sustainable Development Forum which is led by Vice President Gore and Premier Li Peng.

Let me now turn to the second broad area for cooperation between the United States and China, namely, the important regional interests that we share as great Pacific nations.

Across an ocean where terrible conflicts have given way now to more peaceful relations between nations, today's hard-earned security and prosperity depend upon maintaining and strengthening stability in this region. We have had significant successes. We have joined together to ensure a non-nuclear Korean Peninsula—and we are working with China to push forward four-party talks to try to ensure permanent peace on the Korean Peninsula. In Southeast Asia, our two countries have worked together with the United Nations to promote peace and reconciliation in Cambodia.

Throughout the Asia-Pacific region, America's continuing military presence makes a vital contribution to stability. Some in your country have suggested that our presence here in the Asia-Pacific region is designed to contain China. They are simply wrong about that. We believe that our security presence advances the interests not only of the United States, but of China and all the countries of the region. For this reason, the United States will remain a Pacific power in the next century no less than in the last century. In the wake of the Cold War, the United States has taken steps to reinvigorate our relationships across the Pacific. We believe that our five alliances in this region reinforce peace and benefit all nations—including China. So do broader contacts between the militaries of the United States and China. My nation looks forward to increased exchanges between our armed services, regular defense minister meetings such as the one that will take place between Minister Chi and my colleague Secretary Perry next month, and more port calls such as the one paid by the *USS Fort McHenry* to Shanghai last February. The United States and China also will gain from the success of new regional security dialogues such as the ASEAN Regional Forum. These dialogues encourage meaningful talks, they defuse tension, and they promote confidence-building measures.

The United States also is committed to working with China to promote regional economic growth and prosperity. When the original 12 members of APEC met in Canberra in 1989, they recognized that the best way to sustain Asia's dynamism was to ensure that the economies of the APEC countries would grow together. And now today's APEC members conduct almost 70% of their trade with each other. This week in the Philippines, the United States, China, and all the other APEC economies will set out plans that will lead to the elimination of all barriers to trade and investment in this region by the year 2020. We also will work on plans for economic and environmental cooperation throughout the region. China and the United States, as APEC's two largest members, have a special responsibility to turn these plans into forthright action.

Our ability to advance these regional and global goals ultimately rests on a strong US.-Chinese bilateral relationship—and that is the third matter that I want to touch on briefly today.

Here in Shanghai almost 25 years ago, the People's Republic of China and the United States of America—nations too long separated by mistrust and suspicion—took a historic step. We agreed to advance common strategic goals and broaden ties between our people. Since then, relations between our nations have been guided by the set of principles set out in the Shanghai Communique and the two communiques that followed in 1978 and 1982.

As I have said many times, the United States is firmly committed to expanding our relationship within the context of our "one China" policy as embodied in these three communiques. We believe that the P.R.C. and Taiwan must act to resolve their differences between themselves. At the same time, we have a strong interest in the peaceful resolution of the issues between Taipei and Beijing. We believe that the P.R.C. and Taiwan share that interest in a peaceful resolution of these issues. We have emphasized to both Taipei and Beijing the importance of avoiding provocative actions or unilateral measures that would alter the status quo or pose a threat to peaceful resolution of the outstanding issues. We are encouraged that both sides have taken steps to reduce tensions in the Taiwan Strait. We hope that the P.R.C. and Taiwan will soon resume a cross-Strait dialogue that can help build trust and settle differences.

Both China and the United States also have vital interests in a smooth and successful transition of Hong Kong from Britain to China. More than 40,000 U.S. citizens call Hong Kong home, and American investments total more than $13 billion in Hong Kong. We have welcomed China's pledge to maintain Hong Kong's unique autonomy, to allow its open economy to flourish, and to respect its traditions of law and individual freedoms. These guarantees are crucial to Hong Kong's continued dynamism—and to the prosperity of China as a whole. As that vital date approaches—as July 1, 1997 approaches—the world will look on with great interest and watch as China, we all hope, will respect its commitments to Hong Kong and to these important principles that will guide Hong Kong in the future.

China and the U.S. also stand to gain from the sustained economic growth that brings prosperity to every province of your nation. For two decades now, America's actions have reflected our deep interest in the success of China's efforts to lift the living standards of its people. The United States has supported multilateral assistance to help China meet basic human needs. American foundations have helped China promote education and health. And American universities have helped educate almost 200,000 Chinese students—some of whom, I'm sure, are here in the audience today.

Here in Shanghai, the economic benefits of our relationship are readily apparent. About 2,000 American companies have contracted to invest almost $4 billion in this city alone, more than anywhere else in China. From aerospace and computers to capital markets and life insurance, our businesses and workers are turning Shanghai into an engine of growth and innovation not just for China and the United States but for the world as a whole.

These economic links have already made America your largest export market and China one of our most important customers. Now we can expand those links by cooperating to meet future needs in agriculture, energy, and infrastructure—areas where American know-how is unrivaled. We must work together to widen market access in China and open new opportunities for consumers and workers. We must consolidate the gains that we have already made, by strengthening the protection of intellectual property. Economic piracy poses a threat not just to American businesses but to China's software, film, and music industries as well. By upholding its commitments to protect intellectual property, China will enhance its ability to attract foreign investment in the future.

Our work in these and other areas is bringing together our business representatives, scientists, legal experts, and scholars—in person and on the Internet. Last year, more than 400,000 Americans came to China. Speaking of Americans in China, I am very pleased and proud to have with me today Ambassador James Sasser and his wife, Mary. Ambassador Sasser was a leading U.S. senator for 18 years, a member of the President's party, and now is our ambassador to China. Please join me in giving a hand to Ambassador Sasser. The flow of visitors has grown in both directions, and last year more than 160,000 Chinese visited the United States. From the Chinese officials who visit America's small towns to the Hollywood producers who flock to the Shanghai Film Festival, we are building a human bridge across the Pacific, enriching our countries and cultures with new ideas and new products. Strengthening these links will deepen our understanding and our trust and will enable our ties of friendship to grow even stronger.

In all the areas that I have discussed today—global, regional, and bilateral—one lesson stands out: Containment and confrontation will hurt both of our nations; cooperation and dialogue on the other hand will best advance our mutual interests. It is that spirit of cooperation and commitment that infuses my country's approach to our relationship. Cooperation, of course, is a two-way street: If we are to produce concrete results, China must also do its part.

The United States and China will continue to face profound differences, some rooted in history, others in tradition and circumstance. During my meetings yesterday in Beijing, we discussed our disagreements quite openly and quite candidly. We have a responsibility to ourselves and to the world to manage those differences constructively and to approach them in ways that do not undermine our ability to achieve our important common goals.

In recent years, our nations have had divergent views about democracy and the freedoms enshrined in the Universal Declaration of Human Rights. The United States tries to live up to these principles by fighting injustice at home and speaking up for all those who are persecuted for seeking to exercise universal rights—wherever they may live. While we recognize that each nation must find its own path consistent with its own history, we believe that these ideals of the Universal Declaration reflect the values not just of the United States but of countries and cultures all over the world.

Americans promote individual freedoms and the rule of law not only because they reflect our ideals but because we believe they advance our common interest in security and prosperity. History shows that nations with accountable governments and open societies make better neighbors. Nations that respect the rule of law and encourage the free flow of information provide a stable, predictable, and efficient climate for investment. Those that give their people a greater stake in their future are more likely to enjoy economic growth over the long term. China's recent efforts to invest authority in its people through legal and administrative reforms and village elections are a positive step in that direction.

For more than two centuries, Americans and Chinese have reached out to each other across a wide geographic and cultural divide. Many of my country's finest entrepreneurs, architects, scientists, and artists have come from your shores to shape our society and drive our economy. At times, the results have been nothing short of brilliant. Americans, in turn, have made contributions to China, whether building factories that provide jobs or bringing ideas that open new opportunities. Yet too often in our history, distance and difference have blinded us to our common hopes and interests, creating distorted images of each other that drive us apart.

Each of us still has much to learn. But technology has shrunk the miles between us and given us new insight into one another's lives. We know each other better now than ever before. In a world where barriers are falling and borders are blurring, our nations are united by increasingly shared opportunities and challenges.

The United States strongly supports China's development as a secure, open, and successful nation. We welcome its emergence as a strong and responsible member of the international community. Now, on the brink of a new century, our nations have a chance to establish a broad and durable set of ties for the new era.

As we meet together in this city "above the ocean" that links our great lands, let us rededicate ourselves to advancing shared goals. If we unite ourselves in common purpose, we can create a new era of promise. History has given us this priceless opportunity, and we must and will meet the challenge.

A Final Call to Action

Before leaving office on Inauguration Day, 1997, I wanted to take one last opportunity to address the American people. At this time of transition, I wanted to reflect on the main themes of our foreign policy over the past four years, as well as the challenges ahead. My third trip to Harvard University's John F. Kennedy School of Government provided the ideal occasion for this statement.

During President Clinton's first term in office, we had dealt with the pressing problems that were on our plate when we arrived and had sought to establish a firm foundation for American diplomacy in the 21st century. In my confirmation statement, I had urged the American people to reject isolationism and had made the case for continuing U.S. leadership. Over the next four years, we had worked to demonstrate the essential value of American engagement around the globe. By the end of the term, "Should the United States lead?" was no longer a serious question. Whether in dealing with Russia or China, opening markets in Asia or Latin America, or working for peace in Bosnia, Haiti, or the Middle East, America had proven itself to be what President Clinton called "the indispensable nation." My third Kennedy School speech reviewed our accomplishments in key regions, highlighting how American leadership had been decisive in advancing our interests and ideals.

The most recent of these achievements was our securing of an agreement for Israel's redeployment from much of Hebron, the only city on the West Bank from which such redeployment had not taken place. The Netanyahu government's reluctance to redeploy was seen by the Pales-

524

tinians and the Arabs more generally as indicating that the Israelis had no intention of carrying out the Oslo agreement. Since jump-starting the peace process with the White House summit of October 1996 (see Chapter 34), the United States had concentrated its efforts on resolving the Hebron issue. Special Middle East Coordinator Dennis Ross had spent much of his time since the summit shuttling between the parties.[1]

Ross and I were in close touch, often several times a day, during the final Hebron negotiations. Because we felt that the peace process was in crisis, we went beyond our traditional intermediary role. With my endorsement, Ross put a U.S. proposal on the table, telling the parties how we thought their long stalemate should be resolved. We had hesitated to do this because we feared that the parties would become too reliant on us and not feel obligated to reach their own solutions in the future, or that we would incur the ill will of one or both. By this point, however, the risk seemed worth the gamble—and indeed, on the eve of my Harvard address, Ross finally brought the parties to an agreement that had been stimulated by our proposal.[2] Resolving a problem that had haunted our Middle East diplomacy for the better part of a year, the Hebron agreement enabled me to conclude my tenure on a positive note.

I hoped that the two sides would use the momentum from this agreement to move toward peace, and in my speech I explicitly called on them to do so. "Now that the parties have taken this difficult step," I explained, "they must not relax or step back in fatigue." Unfortunately, as 1997 unfolded, they did exactly that: Netanyahu and Arafat both pulled back, and the peace process stalled. Relations between Israel and the Palestini-

---

[1]Over the course of four years, Ross and I had become close friends. As head of the peace team, he had joined me on every Middle East trip. We frequently spent hours together driving between the Tel Aviv airport and Jerusalem, or to see Arafat in Gaza or the West Bank, as well as planning and conducting negotiations, particularly on the protracted Syrian track. Tall and athletic, Ross combines the attributes of very high intelligence with a fine temperament and a tireless dedication to the peace process. He is a consummate negotiator who can see glimmers of light on even the darkest days. My regard for Ross was such that I became furious when Arafat publicly charged in late 1996 that he was tilting toward the Israeli side. That was a strange reward for the hundreds of hours that Ross had spent trying to help the Palestinians carry out the Oslo agreement, and I did my best to let Arafat know that he was out of bounds.

[2]In an unusual tribute to Ross's evenhandedness, Arafat and Netanyahu asked him to speak for both of them in explaining the intricate agreement to the press.

ans have eroded alarmingly, amidst their leaders' mutual recriminations. Although there are rays of hope, produced mainly by U.S. diplomacy, the situation remains bleak.

To make progress in the future, Israelis and Palestinians must put aside the old mentality of the zero-sum game. A gain for one party need not be a loss for the other. Geography and history have given the two a common destiny, and it is not too much to ask that each look around the corner and weigh the consequences for its neighbors before acting.

My speech also explained that U.S. leadership was essential in addressing global dangers like weapons proliferation, international crime, terrorism, environmental degradation, and overpopulation. I had stressed global issues throughout my term, especially since my first Kennedy School speech two years earlier. On this occasion, I singled out the challenge of urban overpopulation. During travels in 1996, I had been troubled by the out-of-control growth of such megacities as Sao Paulo, Mexico City, Jakarta, and Cairo. The concentration of such massive numbers of people brought with it air pollution, water shortage, and disease. To me, these were perfect examples of problems not regularly regarded as foreign policy matters that we would have to confront in the coming years. Looking back to January 1993, when I first emphasized the importance of such global issues in the post–Cold War era, I was glad that we had taken many positive steps, both conceptual and organizational, toward treating them as mainstream U.S. foreign policy concerns. But these steps were, I knew, only a beginning, and the follow-up would be all-important.

Farewell addresses are frequently remembered for single, central points. History books will always refer to President George Washington's caution against "entangling alliances" and President Dwight Eisenhower's words about the "military-industrial complex." In a modest way, I wanted to follow such examples, and on leaving office reemphasize for the American people what I called the biggest crisis facing our foreign policy today—the need for adequate resources with which to conduct that policy. By describing the key lesson of my tenure as the imperative of American leadership on regional and global challenges, I established the context for this message on resources.

This was my third major statement about resources; the first two were my September 1995 remarks before the Council on Foreign Relations and my October 1996 address at West Point (Chapters 22 and 33). While all of these speeches made the same substantive argument, my rhetoric this time was more pointed. At West Point, for example, I had tried to speak apolitically; at the Kennedy School, I zeroed in on Congress as causing the resources problem.

I was particularly agitated by the desire of many on Capitol Hill to have it both ways. Congress tended to talk a lot about U.S. leadership but to shirk the hard decisions to provide the necessary resources for it. "Members of Congress do not call me to say close some embassies, lower the flag, and bring our diplomats home by Christmas," I said. "On the contrary, Congress calls to protest whenever we reluctantly decide that we must close a mission because Congress cut back our funding. What is more, while cutting our budget, Congress regularly calls on us to increase our global engagement." Given this gap between rhetoric and reality, I explained, our foreign policy was "endangered by a new form of isolationism that demands American leadership but deprives America of the capacity to lead."

One of the greatest dangers we faced was that the American people, and by extension Congress, tended to take day-to-day foreign policy for granted. That policy has been compared to the electricity: as long as it's on, you don't notice it, but when it goes out, you're reminded how vital it is. Our challenge was to explain that diplomacy is as much about maintaining embassies abroad, cultivating good relations with other major powers, and supporting international institutions as it is about dealing with crises. During my last year as Secretary, I spent considerable time articulating this theme and emphasizing that maintaining a global presence in these ways requires resources. My final Kennedy School speech was designed to be a call to action for both the American people and Congress. Secretary Albright built on this effort, announcing that her first diplomatic mission would be across town to Capitol Hill to lobby for increased support.

Reflecting on my public service over nearly four decades, I wanted to end my last address on a positive note. Although I had said much during the past four years about the great dangers of the world and the challenges faced by America, I remained confident about the future.

When I finished my military service at the end of World War II, the United States was a young country, new to the ways of power. We had become the world's strongest nation but had not fully grasped the consequences of that status. Two great oceans separated us from the intrigue and power politics that had gone on for centuries in Europe and Asia. There was a streak of isolationism in America as wide as the Middle West and as long as the Mississippi.

Yet for all our innocence and inexperience, the United States has done pretty well with its new leadership. We have averted a third world war for more than 50 years. The nuclear weapon has not been used since 1945. We have prevailed in the Cold War; Soviet communism has been tossed into the dustbin of history. And, as a nation, we have matured. Notwithstanding some awkward moves and downright mistakes, America now exercises its leadership with less arrogance and more assurance. The rich diversity of our population is proving more a strength than a weakness. In observing the political process from many perspectives for half a century, I have never lost confidence in the informed good sense of the American people.

The speech's closing paragraphs reflected these optimistic sentiments. As I happily headed back to private life, I had good reason to believe that in the last four years we had stayed on course for a peaceful and more prosperous future. And I felt confident that we would continue on that path.

●

Investing in American Leadership

Address at the John F. Kennedy School of Government,

Harvard University, Cambridge, Massachusetts,

January 15, 1997

I went to thank Joe Nye for that very generous introduction. It was a real privilege for me to serve in government with such an able official and such a distinguished scholar. Joe's contributions, along with those of so many other members of the Kennedy School faculty, are shining examples of the Kennedy School's commitment to public service, and I congratulate you for that today.

This is the third straight year I have had the opportunity to speak with you, and I also want to thank you for welcoming me so warmly again. A few years ago, I promised myself I would keep on coming up to Boston every January until the Patriots made it to the Super Bowl. Now that I've kept my promise, I'm ready to go home. But before I do, I want to reflect on the record of these last four years and to focus on the investments we must make to sustain American leadership and engagement in the world.

When our Administration took office in 1993, we faced an array of challenges that required urgent attention. Russia's democracy was in crisis; its economy was near collapse. The nuclear arsenal of the former Soviet Union was scattered among four new countries with few safeguards. The war in Bosnia was at the peak of its brutality and threatening to spread. North Korea was developing nuclear weapons. The Middle East peace process was stalemated; negotiations were stymied. Repression in Haiti was pushing refugees to our shores. NAFTA's passage was in serious doubt, threatening our relations with the entire hemisphere.

Not all at once but step by step, over the last four years, we have resolved these pressing questions and built an enduring basis for our engagement in a more secure and prosperous world. Indeed, it was in this period, with our leadership, that the world of the 21st century began to take shape. It is a world where no great power views any other as an immediate military threat, a world where the institutions we built after World War II are being adapted to meet new challenges, a world where open societies and open markets have a strong competitive advantage, and a world where America remains the indispensable nation.

A new and distinctive element of our strategy has been the priority we have attached to addressing emerging global issues like proliferation, terrorism, international crime, drug trafficking, and damage to the environment. These transnational issues cannot be adequately addressed by traditional country-to-country diplomacy or even on a regional basis. Global problems require global solutions.

We began to address these problems in 1993 by appointing an Under Secretary of State for Global Affairs to focus on many of these issues. I believe the progress we have made since will be seen as a principal legacy of the Clinton Presidency and, I hope, of my term as Secretary of State.

A central part of our global strategy has been to ensure that weapons of mass destruction do not threaten the American people. That is why we worked so hard to extend indefinitely the nuclear Non-Proliferation

Treaty and to secure the Comprehensive Test Ban Treaty. It is why we have a program in place to keep nuclear weapons in the former Soviet Union from falling in the hands of terrorists or rogue states. It is why we acted to freeze and eventually eliminate the North Korean nuclear program. It is why we have been determined to shut down Iraq's biological weapons program. And it is why, over the next several months, the President and our Administration will press hard for ratification of the Chemical Weapons Convention.

Just as important, we are confronting the new security threats that have emerged with such clarity since the Cold War ended. We have put the fight against terror, drugs, and crime at the top of the agenda of the G-7 and the United Nations. As a result, law enforcement cooperation among nations is stronger than ever, major terrorists have been caught, and many acts of terror have been prevented.

I have also made it a personal priority to integrate environmental issues into every aspect of our diplomacy. In my travels, I have been startled by the massive, bursting, overcrowded cities I have seen in many parts of the world—great cities like Sao Paulo and Mexico City, Jakarta and Manila and Cairo—cities where overpopulation and pollution threaten the health and welfare of nations and regions. In the Middle East, I've seen how the shortage of water is a source of conflict. In the New Independent States of the former Soviet Union, I've been struck by the ruinous impact of pollution on public health, on life expectancy, and on the prospect for economic recovery. A few years ago, these issues were barely on our screen. Now, they are in the mainstream of our diplomacy, and I believe they will become even more central in the next century.

I believe another lasting legacy of the President's first term will be the record we forged in advancing our economic interests. Thanks to the Uruguay Round and NAFTA, tariffs on U.S. exports are lower than ever before. Thanks to over 200 new market opening agreements, we have created 1.6 million American jobs. Thanks to the free trade commitments we forged in our hemisphere and across the Pacific, we have an opportunity to become the hub of a dynamic, open marketplace that stretches from Chile to Canada, from Australia to Korea. We simply must not squander that marvelous chance.

In every region in the world, our leadership has been decisive in advancing our interests and ideals. Across the Atlantic, we are on the verge of building a stable, democratic, and undivided Europe. American leadership ended the war in Bosnia, and it is winning the peace. We have led the reinvigoration and transformation of NATO. All of Europe's new democracies have joined the Partnership for Peace, and this year NATO will invite several to begin negotiations to join the most successful alliance in history. At critical moments, we stood by democracy in Russia, and we have opened the door for its integration, including a new charter with NATO.

Asia, too, is entering the next century prosperous, at peace, and with new structures of cooperation designed to keep it that way. Again, our leadership has been vital. We have provided stability by maintaining our military presence, strengthening our cornerstone alliance with Japan, and standing with South Korea against provocations from the North. We have provided vision by leading APEC to embrace open trade. We have worked with China to advance the vital interests we share, even as we address our very serious differences on issues like human rights.

In the Middle East, we are closer to realizing our goal of a comprehensive peace. Our diplomacy was vital in helping Israel reach agreements with the Palestinians and a peace treaty with Jordan. We helped open a new dimension of the peace process by galvanizing the economic summits at Casablanca, Amman, and Cairo and encouraging important steps toward normalized relations between Israel and its neighbors in the Middle East. While peace has faced many severe tests in recent months, the achievements are enduring. And we are determined to move forward.

The agreement on Hebron and other issues reached last night is really an extraordinary achievement. It demonstrates that there is a powerful logic to peace—an imperative powerful enough to overcome the setbacks and hesitations of recent months. The protocol on Hebron and the U.S.-drafted Note for the Record are a clear roadmap for the future of the peace negotiations. They set forth commitments and a timeframe for both Israel and the Palestinians to implement the agreements they have already reached. The Note also fixes a time for the commencement of the vital negotiations on the final status issues.

Now that the parties have taken this difficult step, they must not relax or step back in fatigue. They must use this new momentum to move ahead to build the peace that is in the common interest of Israelis and Palestinians alike. And we must remember that we were able to help the parties reach their agreement because of our leadership and engagement—and because we have had the resources to support those who took risks for peace.

In the Western Hemisphere, we have seen a dramatic movement toward open societies and open markets in a region that is the fastest-growing market for U.S. exports in the world. When the hemisphere's democratic trend was threatened by the dictatorship of thugs in Haiti, it was America's decisive action that restored legitimate government. When free markets were threatened by the financial crisis in Mexico, it took our leadership to restore confidence.

In Africa, we have been engaged on a continent that has now reached a crossroads—a point at which sound policies and steady international engagement can make the difference between war and peace, poverty and growth. That is why we have made a vigorous effort to encourage democracy, resolve conflicts, and promote trade and investment.

It is why we are working to create an African Crisis Response Force that would enable countries in the region to respond to emergencies with their own troops but with financial and logistical support from the United States and our allies.

In all these areas, the record we have forged is itself the best argument for a principled and robust policy of American engagement in the world. Because of our military and economic might, because we are trusted to uphold universal values, there are times when only the United States can lead. We must lead not because the exercise of leadership is an end in itself, but because it is necessary to advance the interests and ideals of our great nation.

I went through this summary of accomplishments deliberately, because I wanted to lay the basis for the case I want to make to you today: that we must sustain our leadership and back it up with sufficient resources. This is really the central lesson of our era. Because the United States led, a century that was never safe for democracy is ending with peace and freedom ascendant. The end of the Cold War has only strengthened the imperative of American leadership. As President Clinton has said: "This is the greatest age of human possibility in history and that gives us special opportunities, but it also imposes special responsibilities."

The need for American leadership is rarely questioned in our country. Yet, today, our ability to lead is open to question. Let me explain: No one in public life will stand up and say we can afford to retreat; we can ignore our commitments; we can build a wall around America. Members of Congress do not call me to say close some embassies, lower the flag, and bring our diplomats home by Christmas.

On the contrary, Congress calls to protest whenever we reluctantly decide that we must close a mission because Congress cut back our funding. What is more, while cutting our budget, Congress regularly calls on us to increase our global engagement—by enlarging NATO, supporting the independence of Russia's neighbors, promoting investment in Africa, and protecting workers' rights in Asia, to name just a few examples.

Of course, Congress is absolutely right to say we should do all these things. But our foreign policy will not be sustained by rhetoric or good intentions. Talk is cheap; leadership is not. Leadership in foreign policy requires resources: enough to keep our embassies open and our people trained; enough to maintain constructive relations with the world's great powers; enough to multiply our leverage through international institutions; enough to provide targeted aid to struggling democracies that can one day emerge as allies and export markets; enough to meet threats like terrorism and international crime.

As I said before, we would not have been able to achieve the Hebron agreement without constant leadership in the Middle East, without constant engagement in the peace process, and without the resources we provided over the years. There is just no free lunch. We simply have to make the investments to sustain our engagement.

The biggest crisis facing our foreign policy today is whether we will spend what we must to have an effective foreign policy. Since 1985, our spending on international affairs has been slashed by 50% in real terms—50%. Our budget for foreign affairs is now just over 1% of the overall federal budget.

The amazing thing is these cuts have not been accompanied by any serious congressional debate. They have not been motivated by any reassessment of our interests in the world. As I said, everyone is for U.S. leadership in principle. Some people just think we can have it without paying the price. As a result, we are endangered by a new form of isolationism that demands American leadership but deprives America of the capacity to lead.

One casualty of inadequate resources will be the principle of universality in our representation abroad—the principle that there should be a U.S. mission in virtually every country. Budget cuts have forced us to close over two dozen consulates and several embassies. If the hemor-rhaging continues, we will have no option but to close more facilities. In an unpredictable world, we need a voice in every nation. In the last few years, we have seen over and over again how vital our presence can be, often at unexpected times in unexpected places. Over 170 nations— from Albania to Zambia—had an equal say in extending the nuclear Non-Proliferation Treaty and approving the Comprehensive Test Ban Treaty. Each had an equal need to be persuaded by on-the-spot American diplo-macy, and I can tell you that it happened over and over again. We could not have negotiated the Dayton peace agreement had there not been em-bassies in each of the former Yugoslav republics. We needed people on the ground in every Balkan capital to gather information, to conduct ne-gotiations, to spotlight atrocities, to prepare the way for our troops, and, not least, to symbolize our commitment to that troubled region.

Likewise, we almost certainly could not have convinced Belarus, Ka-zakhstan, and Ukraine to give up nuclear weapons if we had not opened embassies in each of the New Independent States when the Soviet Union broke up. And yet, if we faced a situation like the break-up of the Soviet Union or Yugoslavia, I doubt if we could afford to open the necessary new facilities.

Budget cuts have also forced the people who serve our country abroad to work under intolerable conditions. Our diplomats in Beijing work with obsolete technology in decaying buildings. At our embassy in An-gola, which is a focal point of talks to end that country's civil war, our people work out of a makeshift trailer park. Our embassy in Tajikistan is run out of a Soviet-era hotel; utilities go off for days at a time, and our diplomats have to carry jugs of water up the stairs. These are the people we call on when Americans get into trouble, when our companies need help to crack new markets, when we need to track down terrorists and drug lords.

One of the principal tools of our diplomacy is foreign assistance. These programs give us the leverage our diplomacy needs to be effective. They help us prevent conflict and catastrophe. As crisis after crisis has shown, the cost of prevention is never as great as the price of neglect. We have already spent nearly as much money dealing with the short-term crisis in Rwanda and Burundi alone as we were able to spend last year to promote development and peace in all of Africa.

Our assistance programs have declined by 37% in real dollars in the last 10 years. Half of our bilateral aid now supports the Middle East peace process. These funds advance a vital interest and must be fully preserved. But aid to Israel, Egypt, and Jordan will inevitably come under pressure—possibly irresistible pressure—if our other assistance programs continue to be decimated and this imbalance grows.

Our diplomats also help America compete in the global economy. Indeed, in the last four years, we have achieved a major cultural change in our embassies. They are now aggressively supporting American companies in winning and carrying out contracts abroad. American business leaders have told me how much they have been helped by this aspect of our "America's Desk" effort. But now I am hearing another message. They say that our Ambassadors are striving mightily but that personnel cuts have left them stretched too thin to do what they want to do to be helpful.

Another casualty has been our support for international institutions, including the international financial institutions and the United Nations. For 50 years, the United States has led in the United Nations, because it is a valuable tool for advancing our interests. That is more true today than ever with the emergence of new global issues. But now we face stark alternatives. We can continue to meet global challenges through the UN, where we share the burden with over 180 nations, or we can meet them alone, forcing our soldiers to take all the risks and our taxpayers to foot all the bills. That is our choice.

In part because of U.S. arrears, the UN is hobbled in doing tasks of great importance to our interests—in peacekeeping, in refugee operations, in human rights, in world health, to take only a few examples. By failing to pay our dues, we also compromise our ability to shape a smaller, leaner, and more effective UN.

But our campaign for reform has begun to make progress. The UN has a new Secretary General, a leader with the ability and conviction to make the UN an effective institution for the next century. The UN must do its part. But now so must the United States. It is time to pay our dues and our debts. It is time to recognize that we cannot reform and retreat at the same time.

More broadly speaking, it is time to recognize that we have a vital national interest in adequately funding our international efforts. Just as we need to preserve our military readiness by maintaining forces and bases around the world, we need to preserve our diplomatic readiness by supporting the people and programs that help keep our soldiers out of war. In a world of real dangers, the failure to maintain diplomatic readiness will inevitably shift the burden of leadership to our military. The cost will be measured in lost opportunities and lost lives.

Our Defense Department has wisely designed a strategy to cope with two nearly simultaneous major regional conflicts. While our Defense Department has a two-crisis capability, the State Department is in danger of having a no-crisis budget.

We cannot respond to a crisis in one part of the world without taking funds from valuable programs in other regions. To support our deployment in Haiti, for example, we had to cut aid to Turkey. To monitor the cease-fire in Northern Iraq, we had to short-change the peace process in Guatemala. If a new crisis occurred today, we would have to make a painful choice: Which long-term interest—probably an already underfunded long-term interest—should be sacrificed to meet the short-term need?

I urgently and earnestly call on the Congress to reassess the erosion of our diplomatic readiness and to support, on a bipartisan basis, the President's international affairs budget. This is a challenge that must be met if we are to maintain our strength in the next century.

As I leave this wonderful office that I have been privileged to be in for the last four years, I have many reasons to be optimistic about the future. I know that time and again—from Haiti to Bosnia, to Mexico to Russia to China—President Clinton has made the tough and correct decisions that leadership requires, and I know he will continue to make them. I know that Ambassador Albright, too, will be an eloquent and effective advocate for America's tradition of global engagement. I know that with any reasonable support, the men and women of our Foreign and Civil Service will keep on advancing our interests in every part of the world, despite the hardship and danger they accept and endure.

I am optimistic because I know the American people stand with us. I have seen it as I have traveled around the country: Americans are proud we are the world's leading nation, and they know leadership carries responsibilities; they understand that better than the people in Washington. They see the evidence that isolationists miss: that the security of our nation depends on the readiness of our diplomats as our first line of defense; that the safety of our streets depends on our fight against drugs and terror abroad; that our jobs at home depend on the health of the global economy.

I am optimistic because my own career has spanned a very inspiring period in the history of America's involvement in the world. Unless we're all in for a big surprise, I will be the last Secretary of State who served in World War II. My memories of that time and my experience of the last 50 years teach me to have confidence in the choices Americans will make.

After I left law school in 1949, I went to work for Justice William O. Douglas. As I was ending my year with him, I asked him for some advice. He responded: "Get out in the stream of history and swim as fast as you can." I got out of it a bit further than I ever imagined I would, but let me tell you what I saw along the way.

I saw a whole generation of leaders of both parties who recognized our interest in helping Germany and Japan rebuild so they could become our strong allies and trading partners. I saw the American people make the investments that paid off in half a century of peace and prosperity and in freedom's victory in the Cold War. Now as Secretary of State, I have seen former political prisoners like Havel and Mandela lead their countries as Presidents. I've seen former adversary states on their way to become our allies. I've seen once-impoverished countries become our leading export markets. All over the world, people credit the United States for helping to achieve this transformation, and they look to us to continue to lead.

Today, as before, alliances mean peace; engagement means greater security; leadership brings friends to our side. And your generation has an even greater opportunity than mine: You have the key that unlocks the door to another American century. But you also have a responsibility to make the investments my generation made; the investments leadership demands; the investments that will make this an even safer, freer, better world.

Thank you very much.

THIRTY-SEVEN

Farewell

As I prepared to leave Washington at the end of my term, I pondered how best to say farewell to "the building." After four years as Deputy Secretary and now four more as Secretary, I had developed great respect and affection for the Foreign Service Officers and other civil servants in the Department. Although I am not fond of emotional good-byes, I certainly didn't want to leave without words of appreciation and farewell.

As a place to say good-bye, the Dean Acheson Auditorium, our largest facility, seemed a little too cold and formal. Since it was mid-January, an outdoor event would have been too cold in a different sense. My able Executive Assistant, Maura Harty, now Ambassador to Paraguay, remembered that Secretary George Shultz had made his farewell remarks in the large, flag-lined entrance lobby on C Street, and I decided to do the same. Since Inauguration Day, January 20, a government holiday, fell on a Monday, and I planned to depart immediately after that, the preceding Friday afternoon would be the right time for leave-taking.

I wrote the first draft of these remarks and sent it to Bennett Freeman, who was usually a compulsive reviser. He sent it back with a plea not to change a word. Ultimately, he and Jim Steinberg did help to revise a few lines, but the original draft remained largely unchanged.

When I went down to the lobby, I was startled to see it overflowing with cheering co-workers from every part of the Department. A Coast Guard jazz quintet was playing "California, Here I Come." Surrounded by Marie and my senior colleagues, I spoke from a stairway leading up to a second-floor alcove. The remarks speak for themselves, and there is no need for elaboration here.[1]

●

Farewell Remarks to State Department Employees

C Street Lobby, Department of State, January 17, 1997

Good afternoon, and thank you. This is the last time I'll have a chance to talk to you as Secretary of State. Usually I have spoken with a substantive purpose in mind, in the usual State Department mode—to lay out four principles, or five priorities, or six accomplishments. Today, Marie and I have a more personal purpose: to say Aloha.

When I leave Washington on Monday, I will have served in this Department almost exactly eight years—not to mention the time when I was here in the building as a part-time trade negotiator in the early 1960s. Even in the long span of my life, eight years is a substantial period of time. It gives me a sense of belonging here. Although many of you as I look out have been here much longer than I, I must say I don't feel like an outsider or an impostor.

During those 96 months, first in the Deputy's office, now in my wonderful study, I have had the pleasure of looking out over my southern exposure to see the Lincoln Memorial, and to be inspired by remembering what Lincoln meant to our country. Now my southern exposure takes in the Vietnam Memorial and the Korean War Memorial as well. On some days I walk down there to remind myself what it is we are striving to avoid.

On a nice day, whenever I can, I have stood out on the balcony of the eighth floor and let my eyes sweep 180 degrees from the Capitol over to

---

[1] I closed with what I thought was a quote from Huckleberry Finn when his voyage downriver ended. Alas, it was a paraphrase, not a quote. Thomas W. Lippman of the *Washington Post*, one of the most thoughtful reporters in town, corrected the quote in his story without noting my error. It should have read: "I reckon I got to light out for the territory ahead of the rest, because Aunt Sally she's going to adopt me and sivilize me, and I can't stand it. I been there before."

Arlington, pausing to think of old Jeff standing so straight and tall in his Memorial.

Since I have this sense of belonging, I have a flood of memories about you, my co-workers. You don't have time to hear more than a few, but I can't resist a few.

I have a memory about a young Foreign Service ambassador; I guess everybody seems young these days. This young ambassador accepted a $5,000 award, and used it not to flee his hardship post for a week in Paris, but rather divided it among his Foreign Service National employees, for whom, of course, the payments were a small bonanza.

I remember the Civil Service secretaries who, in the cold, bleak winter in one of the New Independent States of the former Soviet Union, had to work in heavy overcoats and heavy gloves and had to cross a muddy unpaved street if they wanted to wash their hands.

I remember the Foreign Service Officer, one of the American hostages in Iran, who told me that night in Algiers almost exactly sixteen years ago, that she had spent most of her 444 days, she said and now I'm quoting her, "in prayer and meditation, trying to remember that there were a lot of people in the world worse off than I."

I remember the Foreign Service Officer who, when confronted with an awful set of alternatives, said ruefully that we'd have to "decide which waterfall to go over," and then gave his life in pursuit of peace.

I was first inspired to the idea of public service by my law school dean, who had come to Stanford directly from the State Department. He was devoted to Dean Acheson, and soon made me a great devotee of Acheson's as well. That started me thinking about a combined career in law and diplomacy.

When Secretary Acheson made his farewell remarks 44 years and one day ago, he told the State Department's employees, "Yours is not an easy task, nor one that is much appreciated." Secretary Acheson went on to say that although what we do intimately affects the lives of every citizen of this country, we are dealing in what he called "an alien field of knowledge," one that is not easy for every citizen to understand. This remains true to some extent, but the public outreach program that has been started recently is designed to remedy that situation.

In fact, the Department is doing more now than ever before to reach out to our citizens—through television and radio interviews; our Website on the Internet; town hall meetings in every part of the country; and a new permanent exhibit of our diplomatic history. In fact, every desk here is what I call "the America desk." Making the case to the American people for our engagement in the world must be seen as part of the professional responsibility of everyone who is here. As you go back to your desks today, I ask you never to forget why it was you came here.

When I think about Dean Acheson, another point comes to mind: The post–Cold War period we've been through together the last four years is very much like the post-World War II period of the late 1940's. Acheson's generation built the great institutions like NATO, GATT, and the United Nations. We have been adapting them and extending them. His generation faced a crisis in Korea; we have averted one. They were present at the outset of the Middle East conflict; we've come closer than ever before to resolving it for good.

This is not to be a speech bugling about our accomplishments. But in these ways and so many others, our work together has made the American people safer, more secure, and a little more prosperous and it has advanced our basic values. Most of the pressing questions that we faced when we came together four years ago have been answered. Most important, I think we've settled beyond any reasonable doubt that America intends to stay true to its tradition of leadership.

When people look back on the progress that we've made in the last four years, they may try to explain it by pointing to big historic forces and trends. And of course, that will be partly right. But to get to the whole truth, they'll have to tell your story, and the story of the employees of this Department around the world. They'll have to tell the story of the men and the women of our Foreign and Civil Service, who have served our country without cavil or complaint, in Washington and around the world, despite the hardships and the dangers they endure.

When we are confronted by the conflicts and tragedies of a still-dangerous world, it seems to me that we can respond in one of three ways. We can choose the easy way, taking some satisfaction in taking sides and lashing out, "taking a bat to the beehive" as Bob Frasure liked to put it. Or we can choose to walk away and wash our hands. Or, we can make the choice that the people in this room make day in and day out: the choice to persevere until a solution is found.

It is that spirit of persistence and improvisation, that preference for negotiation over confrontation, that willingness to hold onto small gains and never to take no for a final answer, that exemplifies the profession we practice together. It's been the secret to our shared success over the last four years. That's why I leave office with such great respect, admiration, and appreciation for what you all do.

As I leave office, I have many, many reasons to be optimistic about the future. I know that those of you who remain will carry on in advancing American interests and American values around the world. All my experience and convictions tell me you will continue to do so superbly. I have great confidence in my successor Ambassador Albright and her team, and I know that the President will keep on making the tough choices that American leadership requires.

I'm optimistic also because I know the American people are proud that we are the world's leading nation and they know leadership carries with it responsibility for resources. I'm optimistic, too, because in my own career I've seen an inspiring time in our history of global involvement. I've seen the American people make the investments that paid off in freedom's victory around the world, and I have confidence in the choices they will make in the future.

Years ago, Secretary Marshall used to end many of his speeches with a simple peroration. "We have an acknowledged position of leadership in the world," he would say. "We have been spared the destruction of war which literally flattened Europe. We are enjoying a high degree of prosperity. These things being so, the character and strength of our leadership may well be decisive in the present situation of the world." Those spare words, those terse words of General Marshall, ring just as true today as they did in his time.

As long as our nation continues to make the investment that leadership demands, as long as we give you the support you need, America will be well served by you and your successors in the Department of State.

Next week I'll be back in California, no longer looking across the Mall to the Potomac, one of my favorite views, but instead looking out over the great and pacific ocean, where the sun sets in the proper direction. I'll be confident that our country's interests are in safe and steady hands, because I know they will be in your hands, the men and women with whom I've served, the men and women of the State Department.

And now, in the historic words of Huckleberry Finn when his voyage downriver ended, "I reckon I got to light out for the West Coast ahead of the rest. Otherwise those East Coast folks are going to try to civilize us. And we been there before."

Thank you all so much, and God bless you.

Epilogue

I deliberately planned a heavy schedule for the fall of 1996. As was traditional for Secretaries of State, I would take no part in the presidential campaign. I was determined, however, that we would maintain momentum in our foreign policy rather than putting it on hold for several months, as I had seen done during too many presidential campaigns.

As it turned out, there was no risk that international relations would move to the back burner this time. The fall was jammed with significant foreign policy events—including some that we had not planned on. Late August brought another fire drill over Iraq, this one caused by Saddam Hussein's attempt to reassert power over the Kurds in the north. Maintaining my perfect record of interrupting our late-August vacations in California, I quickly returned to Washington for White House meetings to decide how to respond to Saddam's move. Then, immediately after Labor Day, I headed to London, Paris, Bonn, and Stuttgart to discuss Bosnia (and, given the recent developments, Iraq) with allied leaders and to make a long-planned speech in Stuttgart (see Chapter 31). The remaining days of September were punctuated by my annual weeklong visit to New York for the opening of the United Nations General Assembly. Among the events that stood out for me that week were the approval of the Comprehensive Test Ban Treaty by all but three members of the UN,[1] and a

---

[1]The completion of the Treaty reflects the thoughtful contribution of John Holum, director of the U.S. Arms Control and Disarmament Agency. Unfortunately, India and Pakistan oppose the Treaty, which will prevent it from becoming international law unless they change their position.

contentious meeting with Syrian Foreign Minister Farouk Shara during which I tried unsuccessfully to find a basis for putting the Israel-Syria peace talks back on track. The UN meeting was followed by the emergency White House summit on the Middle East (see Chapter 34), and after that I left for a brief stop in Israel and a long-planned swing through Africa (see Chapter 32).

A Time to Go

With President Clinton maintaining a double-digit lead in the polls after Labor Day, intense speculation focused on the makeup of his second-term cabinet. The White House let it be known publicly that if the President was reelected, it would be up to me to decide whether to continue as Secretary. However, although I was careful not to turn myself into a lame duck by making a public statement prior to the election, I had no doubt that there should be a new Secretary of State for the second term.

There were several reasons for my decision, but the main one was my long-standing conviction that, generally speaking, four years in one of the top national security positions is long enough. The end of the first term was a natural time to leave, and if I stayed on, there might not be another until the end of the second.

I wanted to tell the President my intentions in person, and we arranged to meet in Little Rock on the afternoon of Election Day itself, one of those rare moments when a President is suspended between yesterday and tomorrow, with a little time on his hands. The first returns were not in when we met, but his reelection seemed assured; the only questions were the margin, and the makeup of the Congress.

The burdens and experiences of his first term had changed the President. He was more confident and more mature than he had been four years earlier. He had taken the measure of the world's leaders and knew that he belonged in their class. Indeed, if he was candid with himself, he knew that through a combination of his personal charm and his position, he could persuade other heads of government to follow his lead. I had observed this metamorphosis taking place and had witnessed his great capacity for international leadership.

We talked for almost two hours, largely without interruption, but got through the difficult part for me fairly quickly. I thanked the President for supporting me in good times and bad, saying that there was no way for me fully to express my gratitude. Nevertheless, I told him without any equivocation, it was time for me to return to private life. He responded with a number of generous comments, but accepted my decision. He knew how much Marie and I wanted to return to California, and he himself had expressed concern during the last year as to whether I was pushing myself beyond reasonable limits.

I was leaving for Cairo the next weekend and would be on the road almost continuously for the following month. So that speculation about my future would not dominate my travels, I wanted my decision announced promptly. The President agreed, after confirming that I did not think this would weaken me in dealing with foreign leaders. He asked me to stay on until my successor was in place; I agreed, of course, but emphasized that we had a lot of work to do together before Inauguration Day. I also promised to give him my thoughts on foreign policy issues in the second term, and I was reassured that he intended to maintain the main thrust of the foreign policy that we had developed in the first.

Most of our time together was spent discussing other cabinet-level changes he was considering. It was like old times at the Governor's Mansion four years earlier. The President was well aware of my reluctance to comment adversely on colleagues, but he also knew that I felt a responsibility to give him my best judgment if he asked a direct question. He commented that high national security positions are hard on those who "need to be loved." A smile then crossed his face, and he said, "People say that about me, but I certainly made a lot of enemies along the way for a guy who wants to be loved."

With my mission accomplished, I left for Washington in the early evening, without stopping at the victory celebration that was just beginning in Little Rock. I arrived at home at about 11 P.M. to celebrate quietly with Marie both the election returns and our anticipated return home to California.

On his flight to Washington, D.C., the next day, the victorious President talked informally to the press. He told them of my intentions, said our conversation in Little Rock had been a warm one, and observed, "We're very close and we have an unusual relationship. I have never known anyone quite like him." The following day, the President held a White House ceremony to announce my return to private life. Despite the short notice, virtually all of my senior colleagues from the State Department and many from the White House and elsewhere in government were present. The President began by joshing me about wearing Savile Row suits and being "the only man ever to eat presidential M&M's on Air Force One with a knife and fork." He then said some kind words about my work on the Middle East, Bosnia, and Haiti, and expressed the belief that my legacy, built behind the headlines, was laying the foundation for our future "in taking on new threats like terrorism, the spread of weapons of mass destruction and environment degradation."

Objectives for the Future

My four years as Secretary did not change my view that no single word or phrase can explain U.S. policy in all its complexity, or predict the future with all of its possibilities. I continue to believe that a bumper-sticker slogan describing our foreign policy is neither possible nor desirable. In the absence of an all-encompassing threat like Soviet communism, we must take a nuanced, pragmatic approach, firmly rooted in fundamental American interests. This is the policy that I tried to implement as Secretary and the strategy that the preceding speeches reflect. What follows are my views on the objectives to which we should give priority in the future.

AN INTEGRATED EUROPE

Our first objective should be to help build an integrated, peaceful, and democratic Europe that works in harmony with the United States. If that can be achieved, for the first time in history the tranquillity of Europe will not be endangered by hostile rivalries and threats of armed conflict across fortified borders—rivalries and threats that have resulted in two world wars in the twentieth century.

The heart of our European policy is strengthening NATO, already the greatest military alliance in history. Like other alliances, NATO serves internal as well as external purposes. It sets standards for behavior, encourages cooperation, and prevents conflict among its members. For example, the risks of war between Greece and Turkey would be much greater if they were not both Alliance members. NATO provides a regular forum for them to meet, and the advantages of membership are strong incentives for them to resolve their problems peacefully.

Throughout President Clinton's first term, we moved NATO expansion along steadily and openly. This effort culminated in NATO's welcoming Poland, Hungary, and the Czech Republic as potential new members in July 1997. After these three countries have been fully integrated, NATO should reach out to a second group of new members. In the meantime, it is essential that we employ the Partnership for Peace to provide meaningful and reassuring involvement for the 23 former Warsaw Pact members that did not make the first list.[1]

In the years ahead, the other great institutions of Western Europe should also be extended to Central and Eastern Europe. The European Union and its associated bodies, such as the European Parliament, have been too slow to reach eastward and include the new market democracies that were formerly members of the Warsaw Pact. The best way to ensure that such nations resist antidemocratic and anti–free market forces is to envelop them in Western institutions that can help provide better lives for their people, and to condition their membership in these institutions upon adherence to democratic and free market principles.

The integration of Russia into the West stands out as a special challenge. Ambassador George Kennan, the key architect of the containment policy that defined the Cold War, has observed that today's friendly relationship among the great powers is "without precedent in the history of recent centuries," and that "it is absolutely essential that it be cherished, nurtured and preserved into the future."[2] Kennan's observation has particular pertinence to Russia because of its inherent strength and vast nuclear arsenal. Managing U.S. relations with Russia was at the top of our agenda from the very beginning. President Clinton took a great interest in Russian policy and established strong personal ties with President Boris Yeltsin. The 1996 reelection of President Yeltsin marked a victory for democratic forces, and the economy has begun to stabilize, with production increasing at last. Russia appears to have chosen the path of in-

---

[1]Former Secretary of Defense William Perry and I outlined our views regarding the future mission and composition of NATO in an op-ed piece, "NATO's True Mission," in the *New York Times* on October 21, 1997. On January 16, 1998, the United States and the three Baltic states (Estonia, Latvia, and Lithuania) signed a Charter of Partnership that commits the United States to supporting their eventual membership in NATO but does not specify any timeframe.

[2]From a speech delivered by George F. Kennan at the Foreign Service Institute in Arlington, Virginia, on October 13, 1994.

tegration, not self-isolation. The NATO-Russia Founding Act, Russia's participation in Bosnian peacekeeping, and its membership in the Council of Europe and the ASEAN Regional Forum (ARF) are examples of this integration.

But much remains to be done to anchor Russia firmly in the West. Russia and NATO must find new ways to work together to implement the Founding Act. Russia's ambivalence toward the other former Soviet states should yield to an enlightened recognition that its security is not threatened anywhere along its extensive borders. The United States should press for Russia's full economic integration, including membership in the World Trade Organization and ultimately the European Union. And we must embrace those Russians—particularly those in the younger generation—who, in President Clinton's phrase, have the imagination to visualize a different future.

Economic ties between the United States and Europe also must be improved. GATT's Uruguay Round negotiations revealed tensions and hostilities that are unhealthy among close political and military allies. It is ironic that the United States has target dates for free trade with Asia and with Latin America, but not with Europe. The United States can most effectively address any dislocations resulting from liberalized trade during its present prosperity, and should move toward such trade without delay.

European integration is unfinished business, but the foundation for addressing the remaining issues was firmly laid in the first Clinton term. Reflecting the priorities and challenges we perceived, more of the speeches in this book addressed this group of issues than any other.[3]

AN ASIA-PACIFIC COMMUNITY

Our second objective should be to enhance our leadership role in the Asia-Pacific community, with special emphasis on maintaining a strong presence in the region and promoting good relations with China and Ja-

[3]United States leadership at each of the stages leading to NATO's expansion in July 1997 is described in Chapters 8, 16, and 27. The special problems of Russian integration into the West are treated in Chapters 2, 5, and 18. The broadening of OECD membership is discussed in Chapter 11. An agenda for relations between the United States and Europe in the next century is outlined in Chapters 19 and 31. Finally, the struggle to find peace in Bosnia, which reveals so much about the past and future of those relations, is summarized in Chapter 24.

pan. For several reasons, our national interests require that we give the Asia-Pacific region a prominence equal to that of Europe. The nations there have grown enormously in both power and potential. The region holds the bulk of the world's population and constitutes our largest trading partner. We have fought three wars in Asia in the last 55 years, and it is the central arena for the debate over human rights.

In the first Clinton term, we fostered the idea of an Asia-Pacific community. We should continue to build on this concept, which recognizes common interests in the region and ensures that regional institutions are transpacific rather than Asian only. A thriving Asia-Pacific community, whose members are doing well economically and have a strong multilateral community spirit, protects U.S. interests and anchors us in the region. It provides multilateral support for free trade and open investment, and it supplements but does not supplant our military presence and alliances.

There are a number of steps we should take to keep developing this community. First, we should seek to strengthen the emerging transpacific organizations. Through APEC, which we have sought to energize by annual Leaders' Meetings, we should continue to move toward open trade and investment. We should also extend APEC's agenda to emphasize environmental issues and expand the annual leaders' sessions to cover political as well as economic topics. On the security front, the ARF should promote meaningful confidence-building measures and encourage transparency regarding military forces. Over time, the ARF should also develop a conflict resolution capacity. In addition, it would be valuable to convert the unofficial Northeast Asia dialogue involving China, Japan, North Korea, South Korea, Russia, and the United States into a governmental forum. The United States and China should continue to sponsor and mediate peace talks between North and South Korea, taking care to keep Japan and Russia informed. And we should maintain our strong military presence in the region, at a level of about 100,000 troops, to promote stability and deter aggression.

We should also seek to ensure that the lessons of the current economic crises in Asia are heeded. These crises have underlined the importance of the international economic institutions. In exigent circumstances, the Asian dynamos had to turn for help to the International Monetary Fund, backed up by the United States and the other leading powers. In addition, the crises have demonstrated the need for democratic values, like openness and accountability, and for institutions, such as a free press to expose corruption and the rule of law to ensure remedies for wrongful practices. The crises have also revealed the need for more intensive oversight of securities trading and banking practices. Where reasonable, crisis aid should be conditioned on a commitment to adopt reforms along all these lines.

Besides addressing these regional issues, the United States must maintain its key bilateral relationships in Asia. Our partnership with Japan should remain the cornerstone of our policy there. That partnership, built on our security alliance, should encompass the entire range of mutually important issues; for example, we should support Japan's effort to obtain a permanent seat on the UN Security Council. Being good partners also means being able to air differences candidly. The United States should press Japan to solve its economic problems through deregulation and domestic stimulus, rather than by exacerbating our trade deficit.

China, of course, remains critical. The United States must work to strengthen its relationship with China and to promote bilateral interests as well as China's regional and global integration. Sustained engagement with Beijing should include regular summits and the broadening of our areas of cooperation, such as those relating to Korea, Cambodia, the environment, drugs, and smuggling. At the same time, we should press hard and skillfully on such difficult subjects as human rights, non-proliferation, and market access. Concurrently, we should diligently pursue bilateral relations with South Korea, Indonesia, Vietnam, and the other nations of Asia.

PEACEMAKING AND DEMOCRACY BUILDING

Our third objective should be to use our power and influence to bring about peace and democracy in situations where our national interests are involved. As the world's only remaining superpower, the United States has a unique status. Our ability to project our power great distances is unmatched, and when challenged, we can mobilize resources not available to others. These resources, both military and economic, give us enormous diplomatic leverage. Frequently we are the only nation capable of bringing peace to war-torn areas in remote parts of the globe. Our leadership in the Middle East peace process is a striking example of this indispensable role, carried out in pursuit of important national interests.

This unique capacity presents a dilemma for both policy makers and the American people. No nation, not even ours, has the resources to address all of the world's humanitarian crises and threats to peace and democracy. For example, the financial burden imposed upon the United States by the eight new UN missions authorized in 1991–92, quadrupling the budget, turned out to be more than our political system could absorb and caused a backlash in public attitudes toward the UN. On the other hand, there will be circumstances in which failing to exercise our power, out of caution or pressures to "come home," will be detrimental to our national interests. Over time, enough such failures will result in forfeiture of our global leadership.

Defining our national interest is a dynamic process, and efforts to formulate an all-inclusive, permanent definition have not proven very fruitful. In some situations, such as attacks on our own territory, our national interest is clear and unambiguous. In others, such as humanitarian crises abroad, it can be murky, and sometimes it becomes clear only after alternatives to our involvement have been tried and found wanting. If we decide to use force, it is preferable to do so as part of a multinational coalition. As we learned during 1993–97, U.S. leadership is almost always necessary to build such coalitions.

The experiences recounted in this book illuminate these points. In Haiti, we began in 1993 by seeking to use negotiations and escalating sanctions to oust the military junta that had overthrown the democratic government. When it became apparent that the junta would not leave unless forced to do so, the importance of restoring democracy in the Caribbean and coping with an intractable migration problem led the President to conclude in September 1994 that the national interest justified the commitment of American troops. The U.S.-led multinational effort was greatly facilitated by supporting resolutions by the UN and the Organization of American States, resolutions that we helped secure. Ultimately, responsibility was transferred to a UN mission, in which Canada later assumed the leading role. This precedent should be remembered as a possible model for future efforts.

In the tragic and vexing case of Bosnia, the international community tried for three frustrating years to achieve peace through an arms embargo, sanctions, and a UN peacekeeping mission, all led by the Europeans. These efforts failed. In 1995, the President decided humanitarian needs and the risks of a broader war in Europe warranted heavier U.S.

involvement. As described in Chapter 24, we thereafter employed two strategies that had not been adopted earlier, namely, sustained NATO bombing in response to threats to UN-proclaimed safe areas in Bosnia and determined U.S. leadership of the negotiations. This approach produced the Dayton accords, which the United States took the lead in implementing by committing 20,000 troops to an international force. Although our troop commitment has since been reduced, our presence was extended in 1996 and a consensus has emerged that our national interests are too much engaged to allow a total withdrawal in 1998.

The national interests involved in the deployment to Kuwait when Saddam Hussein threatened it in October 1994 were quite different in character. The reliance of our economy on oil supplies from the Middle East and our continuing opposition to naked aggression against friendly countries both came into play. Our commitment to the security of Israel provides an extra dimension to our national interest in securing peace in that volatile region.·

As we face new threats to peace and democracy in the future, we can benefit from understanding this recent history. We should always be mindful of our responsibilities of world leadership in answering these threats, but the analysis must include up-to-date evaluations of our national interests and a proper concern for the wise husbanding of our resources.

ECONOMIC DIPLOMACY

Our fourth objective should be to pursue vigorous economic statecraft. The high priority given to international economic issues is one of the hallmarks of the first Clinton term. In 1993, this emphasis produced the triple play consisting of organization of the first APEC Leaders' Meeting, ratification of NAFTA, and approval of the Uruguay Round of tariff cuts. The booming U.S. economy created 13.5 million new jobs in Clinton's first term, many in our flourishing export trade, resulting in the lowest unemployment rate in two decades.

When he took office, President Clinton recognized that American access to foreign markets was essential to our economic recovery. The world has become a single marketplace, with instantaneous communications and great mobility of capital. Two decades ago, many U.S. companies were content to compete solely in the more accessible and easily understood U.S. market. Now, with intense competition in that market, they know they must look abroad to prosper. Most major American companies, and many smaller ones as well, have turned to the global market to provide their margin of profit. The post–Cold War era also offers global economic opportunities that extend far beyond exports, important as they are. American capital is finding international investments that yield high returns. Imports provide not only critical materials but also consumer goods at prices that improve living standards and combat inflation. Severe shortages of personnel in the United States are sometimes remedied from labor markets abroad.

America is well positioned to compete in the global marketplace. We know more than any other country about the things that matter most in today's economy—technology, telecommunications, software, environmental science, and the management of great industrial enterprises. Our investors are shrewd and daring. Some version of the free market philosophy is triumphant almost everywhere on the globe, and America knows what works and what doesn't in a competitive environment. Indeed, we have a chance to expand our role as the principal force in the world economy, but we will not do so if we become complacent and fail to address the challenges of the new era.

For us to reap the full benefits of the global market, our foreign policy must be designed to increase our access to the markets of other countries. This means another round of tariff cuts through a negotiation comparable to the Uruguay Round. It means aggressive pursuit of the APEC goal of open trading in the Asia-Pacific region by 2010 for the industrialized nations and by 2020 for the other countries. It means meeting the Miami summit's goal of an open trading system in the Western Hemisphere by 2005.[4] And it means broadening the Transatlantic Agenda to include a commitment to free and open trade between the United States and Europe by an early date.

To achieve the market access that is essential for American businesses and workers, the President needs to have fast track authority on a worldwide basis. This authority is important not just for the expansion of NAFTA, but also to enable us to make desirable sectoral or bilateral

---

[4]Experience with NAFTA underscores the importance of including well-balanced provisions protecting the environment and workers' rights in subsequent free trade agreements.

arrangements any place on the globe. If Congress continues to refuse the President this authority, we will watch other nations or groups of nations step in and conclude trading arrangements that leave the United States at a disadvantage. Our friendly competitors around the world are all too ready to move in and take advantage of our hesitation.

The United States should also begin to see the World Trade Organization as an ally, not an obstacle. As the world's greatest trading nation, we benefit from rigorous enforcement of international rules and procedures, although that enforcement may be painful in some instances. If China and other non-members can be brought into the WTO without compromising its standards for admission, our leverage for requiring those countries to comply with the international regime will increase.

We have an enormous stake in the international economic system, and we should strengthen and protect it. The Mexican peso crisis of 1994–95 demonstrated how interconnected and fragile that system is, and how quickly the contagion of crisis can spread if the international community does not step in. The new emergency credit facility of the IMF deserves our strong support, in part because it can make it unnecessary for us to take the lead in future economic rescues. The failure of Congress to provide additional funds for this facility at the end of 1997 was extraordinarily shortsighted, especially in light of the spreading Asian currency crisis.

In addition to benefiting the U.S. economy, economic statecraft—frequently in the form of economic sanctions—can be used to induce others to alter their behavior. Indeed, when we face a crisis, economic sanctions are frequently the first instrument we deploy. Often, they fulfill the need for us to "do something" immediately while considering other options.

There is no doubt that, used properly, economic sanctions can hurt the target state's economy. Less clear, however, is how well they shape behavior. Frequently, the target country refuses to bend to the sanctions, and it may even use them to whip up morale. Moreover, economic sanctions are blunt instruments that frequently have unintended consequences. Sometimes they punish us more than they do the target country, which can usually obtain the sanctioned products elsewhere. United Nations sanctions, with which all members are obligated to comply, often harm neighboring nations more than the target country, because they prevent them from trading with or through that country. And often, it is only the poor people in the target country who are injured, while the elites manage to evade the sanctions or turn them to their advantage. In the future, sanctions, like drugs with powerful side effects, should be used only if they pass the most rigorous cost-benefit tests.

HANDLING GLOBAL DANGERS

Our fifth objective should be to address the growing family of global threats, which are now emerging as the greatest dangers to our security. These threats include proliferation of weapons of mass destruction, environmental damage, terrorism, narcotics trafficking, international crime, and information warfare.[5] They seldom appear alone, and they become more hazardous in combination. Many of them are not new but are aggravated or amplified by modern conditions.

Because these threats know no borders, they usually cannot be handled solely on a bilateral or even regional basis. They need to be addressed through the cooperative action of all nations; such action can perhaps be coordinated most effectively through international organizations. However, the appeal for joint and universal action is often handicapped by differing appraisals of threat, the uneven burdens of remediation, and the low priority that nations, including the United States, are sometimes inclined to accord to less tangible problems that do not immediately threaten their existence. On three global threats in particular—proliferation, environmental damage, and terrorism—my speeches sought to combat these sources of resistance, explaining the significance of the dangers and the need for U.S. leadership in responding to them.

---

[5]The newest addition to the roster of global threats is unauthorized invasion of our information systems, sometimes called information warfare (when the threat is to national security) or computer crime (when the threat is to private information systems). Amateur hackers from abroad have demonstrated the capacity to penetrate highly sensitive U.S. military and NASA computer files. Others have broken into our 911 emergency systems and rendered them temporarily useless. From overseas, still others have perpetrated massive frauds by invading our financial systems. In December 1997, when the Justice and Interior Ministers of the highly industrialized countries met in Washington to consider measures to deal with these cyber-criminals, Attorney General Janet Reno said, "Computers and networks are opening up a new frontier of crime. Criminals are no longer restricted by national borders." The Defense Science Board of the Defense Department has convened a task force of experts to develop defenses against threats to our national security that might result from hostile efforts to attack our information infrastructure.

Proliferation

The international framework is in place to prevent the further spread of dangerous weapons. Over 170 parties have signed the Non-Proliferation Treaty, thus agreeing to forgo forever the acquisition of nuclear weapons. In parallel, the nuclear powers decided in 1996 to ban their own testing of such weapons, and the United States and Russia are committed to significant reductions in their strategic nuclear arsenals. The Chemical Weapons Convention, which entered into force in 1997, and the 1992 Biological Weapons Convention offer global forums for responding to the dangers posed by the potential spread of chemical agents and deadly bacteria. And the Missile Technology Control Regime is structured to prevent transfers of long-range missiles and their related technologies.

But many critical non-proliferation tasks lie ahead. We must aggressively implement the agreements outlined above. We must ensure that the vast amounts of nuclear materials made available by the reduction of nuclear arsenals are safely stored and do not fall into the hands of terrorists or rogue states. We must complete the elimination of the North Korean nuclear program through steady implementation of the 1994 Agreed Framework. We must find ways to keep India and Pakistan from crossing the nuclear threshold and declaring themselves as nuclear powers. We must support the United Nations inspectors in their efforts to inspect all suspicious sites and to destroy all of Iraq's dangerous weapons, including its estimated 200 tons of nerve gas, theoretically enough to kill all the humans on earth. Working together with Russia and China, we must thwart continuing Iranian efforts to acquire not only weapons of mass destruction, but also long-range missiles and sophisticated conventional weapons. American leadership has been critical in putting the global non-proliferation framework into place, and we must continue to give non-proliferation a high priority.

Environmental Damage

My April 1996 speech at Stanford outlined my view that environmental protection is vital to our national security. Developments since that speech have only reinforced my conviction that environmental degradation is one of the most serious problems facing the United States and the international community.

The smoke and haze from forest fires that devastated vast areas in Southeast Asia affected much of that region for months in late 1997 and called attention to the severity of the pollution problem in Asia. The *New York Times* has reported that considerably more people die in Asia each year from the effects of pollution than died from the 1950s to the 1970s in the Indochina Wars.[6]

The worst pollution of air and water usually occurs in the early stages of industrialization. As a result, government officials in developing countries too often fall back on the false choice between economic growth and environmental protection. Japan has demonstrated that a nation can have both: it has maintained its industrial growth and still moved in three decades from being one of the most polluted to one of the least polluted countries on earth. This is a lesson that should be considered by every nation facing pollution problems. Even the recent downturn in the Asian economy is no reason for governments there to ignore the health needs of their people. We have technological know-how that can help identify and address these needs, and we should work with the nations of Asia to do so.[7]

Building on earlier international efforts, the conference on global warming in Kyoto, Japan, in December 1997 provided a further opportunity to find ways to limit emissions of heat-trapping greenhouse gases. The conference revealed sharp tensions between developed and developing nations. At Kyoto, the United States and other developed nations agreed on ambitious goals to be achieved by 2010, but no comparable agreement was reached involving such developing nations as China and India. It is unlikely that the necessary U.S. Senate ratification can be obtained without parallel requirements for the developing nations. Now that the United States is committed to expensive limitations on emis-

---

[6]The polluted, overpopulated megacities are heavily concentrated in Asia; 13 of the 15 cities with the worst air pollution in the world are located there. Despite the horrible urban conditions, people keep pouring into these megacities from the less polluted countryside, drawn by the bright lights and the hope of economic betterment. Nicholas D. Kristof, "Across Asia, a Pollution Disaster Hovers," *New York Times*, Nov. 28, 1997, p. 1.

[7]For example, it was previously claimed that the Indonesian air pollution problem was caused by burning by small landowners, aggravated by bad weather conditions. United States satellite technology has disclosed that the true sources of this pollution are huge ranches and industries.

sions, it is in a strong position to provide much-needed leadership to bring the developing nations into the regime.

Terrorism

Terrorism is perhaps the most frightening of the global phenomena that threaten U.S. foreign policy interests. In 1997, international terrorist attacks continued to fill the headlines. Suicide bombings in Israel dealt further blows to the faltering Middle East peace process. Islamic militants in Algeria continued their reign of terror, killing scores of residents, including defenseless women and children, in cities close to Algiers. In Luxor, Egypt, Islamic radicals gunned down 58 foreign tourists in a single attack, a crude attempt to undermine Egypt's secular government. And in Karachi, Pakistan, four American businessmen were slain, apparently in retaliation for the conviction of a Pakistani for his role in the 1993 New York World Trade Center bombing.

Modern technology has worsened the threat of international terrorism. Conventional bombs, the customary weapons of terrorists, are increasingly powerful and can cause immense damage, as we saw in New York and Oklahoma City. Reflecting the use of these crude but powerful bombs, the death toll from international terrorism rose from 163 in 1995 to 311 in 1996, even though the absolute number of incidents declined. Moreover, the threat of chemical terrorism is now a reality, as shown by a terrorist cult's 1995 sarin nerve gas attack in the Tokyo subway. Weapons of mass destruction that use biological agents, such as anthrax, present an even more horrifying threat. A planeload of anthrax spores released into the atmosphere would prove more deadly than any single nuclear weapon. Much easier to manufacture and deploy than nuclear weapons, biological weapons may become the arms of choice for those overwhelmed by the U.S. military's conventional superiority.[8]

The U.S. procedures for handling terrorism are basically sound, and we should advocate their adoption by other nations. Our policy of refusing to make deals with terrorists or submit to blackmail should become the international norm; acting otherwise only invites further terrorist

[8]The threat of terrorists' use of weapons of mass destruction is impressively discussed in Richard Betts, "The New Threat of Mass Destruction," *Foreign Affairs* 77, no. 1 (Jan.-Feb. 1998): 26–41. The author believes that we should consider building civilian defenses against these new threats.

acts. We are also correct to treat terrorists as criminals and to pursue them aggressively all around the world. Terrorism should never be confused with an expression of religious faith, a struggle for freedom, or any other legitimate act. We should continue to try to persuade our allies to have zero tolerance for nations that sponsor terrorism, and to join us in imposing strong sanctions on them. If we combine these firm policies with an enhanced exchange of intelligence data and the computerization of criminal records, we will be taking major steps in the fight against terrorism. New levels of international cooperation are plainly essential to deal with this alarming problem.

Each of the other global threats also needs to be vigorously addressed on an international basis. Narcotics trafficking, international crime, and information warfare are severe problems that threaten the stability and security of all nations and cannot be dealt with adequately by any one alone. They are particularly dangerous for new democracies. President Clinton has observed that for the first time in history, more people live under democracy than under dictatorship, but it is not inevitable that this trend will continue. In coming years, we may have to concentrate on preserving the progress we have made by defending fragile democracies against these global threats.

The Need for American Leadership

A common theme runs through the five objectives I have outlined: the imperative of American leadership. It is a basic feature of the post–Cold War world that this leadership is fundamental to efforts such as stopping wars, addressing humanitarian or financial problems, and strengthening international institutions. That is the lesson of every crisis of the past few years—Bosnia, Haiti, the Middle East, North Korea, the Taiwan Strait, the Mexican peso crash. It is also the lesson of every important international initiative of that period, from NATO expansion to the GATT Uruguay Round and the APEC Leaders' Meetings.

The main threat to our ability to lead is the risk that as a nation, we will turn inward, embracing a new form of isolationism. Perhaps because we are sheltered by two great oceans, or perhaps because of our pride in our success, some form of isolationism has long held a special lure for Americans. We indulged in it after World War I and paid the heavy price of World War II. Today, the reasons to reject isolation and embrace engagement with the world are not only strategic and political, but economic as well. Every business leader with sales abroad understands how important U.S. engagement is to the health and growth of the American economy.

But that engagement will not be sustained just by rhetoric or good intentions. Leadership requires resources and long-term commitments. Unfortunately, the 1994 election brought to Washington many new Members of Congress who did not understand this. In 1996, the trend toward congressional disdain for foreign affairs accelerated with the retirement of many internationally minded Members of both parties— people like Nancy Kassebaum, Mark Hatfield, Sam Nunn, Bill Bradley, and Claiborne Pell. The internationalism of Senator Dole will also be missed. Although no one in public life will stand up and say we should retreat—indeed, the calls for our leadership are still loud—many now are willing to starve our international affairs budget, thus depriving us of the resources necessary to lead.

During 1995–96, I made this issue one of my highest priorities. Three of my speeches in this book are largely devoted to the proposition that American leadership cannot be exercised unless Congress provides adequate financial resources.[9] From the vantage point of private life, I feel even more strongly about this. Realistically, for the necessary resources to be forthcoming, the relationship between the executive branch and Congress must improve. Thus, it seems fitting to close this book with some thoughts on how to accomplish this.

Relations with Congress

My relations with Congress generally were cordial and friendly. After a congenial hearing before the Senate Foreign Relations Committee, I was

---

[9]Perhaps all our efforts have finally begun to bear fruit. In 1997, with a strong push from the President, Congress reversed the sharp decline in funding for international affairs and appropriated $19 billion for the fiscal year beginning October 1997, slightly more than for the prior year.

unanimously confirmed on Inauguration Day in 1993. When the Republicans took control of both Houses in the mid-term election, existing relationships on both sides of the aisle enabled me to work relatively well with the new leadership. I liked most Members, and I admired their willingness to subject themselves to the rigors of running for office. For the most part, I enjoyed our meetings and looked upon them as valuable opportunities to learn how grassroots America regarded our foreign policy.

Over four years, I appeared in 48 open, formal hearings of congressional committees or subcommittees.[10] My senior State Department colleagues appeared 138 times, and I or one of my top advisers ordinarily reviewed their testimony in advance. In addition, I went to Capitol Hill scores of times to consult with Members and had literally hundreds of telephone calls to and from the Hill, sometimes more than 10 in a single day.

When we worked together in a bipartisan fashion, the executive and legislative branches achieved some remarkable results in foreign affairs. Under the leadership of Democratic Senator Sam Nunn of Georgia and Republican Senator Richard Lugar of Indiana, there was bipartisan support for funds to help dismantle the Soviet nuclear arsenal and to support Russian steps toward democracy and a market economy. Republican Senate Majority Leader Dole helped the Administration compile an impressive record in the international economic field, though sometimes, as in the Mexican peso crisis, he overestimated his ability to bring his Republican colleagues along. Republican Senator John McCain of Arizona understood the need for presidential authority in foreign affairs, even when he didn't agree with the President's actions. His help was crucial in normalizing relations with Vietnam in 1995 and in preventing Congress from overturning our Bosnia policy after the Dayton conference. When the Republicans took control of Congress, Senate Appropriations Chairman Hatfield and House Appropriations Chairman Robert Livingston

---

[10]The State Department's congressional relations staff was, I believe, among the best in the federal government. Headed by Wendy Sherman for the first three years and by Barbara Larkin the fourth year, the "H" staff, as it was known, consisted of talented, experienced women and men at all the key positions. They had high standards and took pride in getting me ready for every formal hearing, as well as for smaller meetings and phone calls. I prepared for each hearing as a lawyer would prepare for a short trial, usually spending at least a full day, and sometimes two, working with the staff.

were personally sympathetic and tried to be helpful within the budget parameters. And Republican Speaker Newt Gingrich talked like an internationalist, though sometimes his actions belied his words.

Yet the record as a whole was one of controversy and conflict between the branches. Republicans in Congress led repeated efforts to cut and then cut again the budget for international operations. Moreover, despite our constant contact with the Hill, Congress continually complained of a lack of communication. Why were these things so?

As I saw it, a significant part of the problem arose from some rather common misunderstandings about responsibilities. Some Members failed to distinguish among informational briefings, consultation, congressional oversight, and congressional decision-making. Too often Members believed that if they were told about something, they ought to get to make decisions about it. But Congress's power of the purse is not a right to micromanage every aspect of our foreign affairs. The Constitution wisely vests the conduct of our foreign policy in the executive branch, and no Administration should lightly surrender this important responsibility.

Paradoxically, congressional assertiveness about foreign policy is often combined these days with a kind of proud disinterest in it. The 1994 freshman class was noteworthy not only for its proclaimed disdain for foreign policy, but also for its unshakable conviction that the funds for carrying out that policy should be cut and that Congress should micromanage those few issues that it could not avoid. We tried countless times to schedule a foreign policy seminar for members of that class, but it never happened. The foreign affairs committees, once sought-after assignments, had to go begging for members. Committee attendance was often sparse, and when they came, many members only stayed long enough to make inflammatory statements designed not to further dialogue but to generate media coverage at home. Finally, congressional travel abroad became less frequent. Such travel is now such an easy target for criticism that it is difficult to blame Members for shying away from it.

The congressional role in the imposition of economic sanctions has been particularly abused. Often, a narrow coalition of Members, or perhaps a single powerful committee chairman, will conclude that a particular country should be punished for past behavior or coerced into changing its ways. Often the country that is the object of congressional ire is unpopular, weak, or both, and hence there is little to lose in imposing sanctions. Having chosen a target, the proponents select a vehicle for the sanctions provision, often a complex appropriations bill or other important piece of legislation. They then hold up the bill, through one artifice or another, until the sanctions provision is added to it. The scenario is repeated time after time, until there is a baffling network of sanctions, many of which overlap.

Fifteen years ago, shortly after I left the Carter Administration, I wrote an article urging a new "compact" between the executive branch and Congress based upon mutual respect, deference, and complementarity of roles.[11] I stand by that recommendation, but its attainment seems unrealistic in the present climate. Accordingly, at this time I recommend a series of smaller steps that could significantly improve interbranch relations, if undertaken by both parties in the context of an enhanced commitment to pursuit of the national interest.

First, the White House and Congress should agree on the form and process of consultation. In many instances, the national security team needs to consult with Congress on a proposed military operation or a significant new development in foreign affairs. It is obviously not practical to consult with all 535 Members, but at present, there is no agreement on the appropriate consultation forum or number of participants. At least four committees in each house—Armed Services, Foreign Relations, Intelligence, and Appropriations—can plausibly claim that they must be consulted. Congressional egos being what they are, the "guest list" becomes a major issue, and sometimes this results in the consultation being abandoned. During my tenure, our offers to consult were frequently not taken up by the Republican leadership, especially in the Senate, for reasons left obscure.

If the process and participants could be agreed upon in advance, both branches would benefit and many of the excuses for non-consultation would disappear. If the Majority and Minority Leaders of the two Houses do not feel empowered to settle such a matter, the congressional party caucuses should be able to resolve it. As to which Members should participate, I believe a two-tier approach would be useful: for top secret

[11]"Ceasefire Between the Branches: A Compact in Foreign Affairs," *Foreign Affairs* 60, no. 5 (summer 1982), p. 989.

matters, a small group of five (the Speaker of the House and the Majority and Minority Leaders from both Houses), and for confidential but slightly less sensitive matters, a larger group of 21 (those five plus the Chairmen and Ranking Members of the Armed Services, Foreign Relations, Intelligence, and Appropriations Committees). But these specifics are less important than simply having a structure in place, so that consultation does not break down at a crucial time because of a dispute over process or procrastination in selecting participants. On the Administration side, the President should be included whenever feasible, along with the Secretaries of State and Defense, the National Security Adviser, the Chairman of the Joint Chiefs of Staff, and from time to time, the UN Ambassador and the Director of Central Intelligence. Consultation should take place at regular intervals, as well as at times of crisis. Its value is likely to be directly proportional to the degree to which confidences are both given and respected.

Second, it is in everyone's interest to get the facts straight. The entire international affairs budget, including but by no means limited to foreign aid, is only a little more than 1% of our total budget—not 5%, 10%, or 20%, as surveys consistently show the public to believe. When Congress, possibly influenced by these inflated figures, makes deep cuts in foreign policy funding, we become less able to maintain diplomatic readiness. Inevitably, the burden of protecting our national interests then shifts to America's military. No one would deliberately put our servicemen and -women in harm's way more often than is necessary, and one good way to avoid doing that is for both political parties to cooperate in setting the record straight as to the relative size of the international affairs budget.

Third, Congress and the Administration need to develop guidelines that support and encourage congressional overseas travel while preventing abuses. With rare exceptions, such travel is not luxurious. Most overseas trips begin with overnight flights in overage military aircraft. And the schedules are often punishing; I have seen too many Members and their State Department escorts return bleary-eyed and exhausted to regard such trips as perks or boondoggles.

Congressional trips abroad serve vital educational purposes and are very much in the public interest. Without such travel, for example, there would have been no program to dismantle the nuclear arsenals in the former Soviet Union. Similarly, bipartisan congressional delegations, called "Codels," that took arduous trips to Bosnia kept Congress from undermining the policy that brought peace to that region. Because congressional travel is so open to caricature by cartoonists and columnists, it needs to be defended by those who recognize its importance. Carefully drawn guidelines, monitored by an appropriate body like the congressional accounting office, would go a long way toward encouraging the right kind of overseas travel.

Fourth, American business leaders and workers and both political parties should awaken to the importance of electing Members committed to global engagement. In recent times, there seems to have been a perceptual disconnect between our continued prosperity and the need for such Members. But if President Clinton's unofficial 1992 campaign slogan, "It's the economy, stupid," were understood to be relevant only within our borders, that would be a gross and dangerous distortion. In fact, it is essential for our nation to pursue economic policies that give American companies access to trade and investment opportunities abroad.

Those who recognize the importance of global engagement should make sure candidates for Congress discuss this subject. If candidates in recent congressional elections heard mainly from small local businesses with parochial interests, those businesses with a stake in overseas markets should now start making their voices heard. Once in Congress, Members who now avidly seek places on the Armed Services or Appropriations Committees to help their districts should be reminded that service on foreign affairs committees can help their constituents obtain the access abroad that is vital to continued national and local prosperity.

As these pages have shown, there is a constant need to explain and justify actions taken by the United States in the international sphere. Public diplomacy takes many forms, including press conferences, background briefings, appearances on television and radio programs, and now, even dialogues on the Internet. The State Department should use all the available forms of communication and be alert to promising new means of reaching the public. But no other statement (except occasionally a presidential speech) is as likely as a speech by the Secretary of State to present a reasoned, comprehensive outline of the Administration's positions on important policy issues. For the foreseeable future, studying such speeches and their contexts can give students, scholars, and members of the general public crucial insights into the making and the content of American foreign policy.

Reference Matter

Organizations and Acronyms

ACDA: Arms Control and Disarmament Agency

ACRF: African Crisis Response Force. Organization proposed in 1996 to be created and run by Africans, with international support, for the purposes of intra-African peacekeeping and conflict prevention

APEC: Asia Pacific Economic Cooperation. Forum established in 1989 for managing economic interdependence and facilitating cooperation among Asia-Pacific economies. Members as of 1998: Australia, Brunei, Canada, Chile, China, Hong Kong, Indonesia, Japan, Malaysia, Mexico, New Zealand, Papua New Guinea, Peru, the Philippines, Russia, Singapore, South Korea, Taiwan, Thailand, the United States, and Vietnam

ARF: ASEAN Regional Forum. Regional multinational forum for dialogue on security issues, established in July 1993. Members as of 1998: the ASEAN nations, plus Australia, Canada, China, Japan, Russia, South Korea, and the United States

ASEAN: Association of Southeast Asian Nations. Formed in 1967 to promote economic, social, and cultural cooperation among nations of Southeast Asia. Members as of 1998: Brunei, Cambodia, Indonesia, Laos, Malaysia, the Philippines, Singapore, Thailand, and Vietnam

CFE treaty: Treaty on Conventional Armed Forces in Europe

CJTF: Combined Joint Task Force. Concept designed to make NATO military assets available for wider operations. Approved at January 1994 NATO summit

COCOM: NATO's Coordinating Committee on Multilateral Export Controls. Formed to prevent sensitive materials from being sold to hostile nations

Contact Group: Established in 1994 to coordinate efforts to resolve the Bosnia conflict. Representation from the EU, France, Germany, Russia, the United Kingdom, the UN, and the United States

Council of Europe: Established in 1949 to coordinate European policy and maintain the basic principles of human rights, pluralist democracy, and the rule of law. 34 member countries

CSCE: Conference on Security and Cooperation in Europe. Established in 1972 by NATO and Warsaw Pact members to further East-West relations through a commitment to non-aggression, human rights, and cooperation. Name changed to OSCE in 1995. 54 member countries

DEA: Drug Enforcement Agency

EC: European Community. See EU

EU: European Union. Established in 1991 as the EC, this body is designed to coordinate European political, social, security, and economic policies. Members as of 1998: Austria, Belgium, Denmark, Finland, France, Germany, Greece, Ireland, Italy, Luxembourg, the Netherlands, Portugal, Spain, Sweden, and the United Kingdom. The principal EU institutions are the Commission, located in Brussels, and the Parliament, located in Strasbourg.

European Commission: See EU

European Parliament: See EU

European Security and Defense Identity: Proposed European security capability separate from but coordinated with NATO

Exim Bank: Export-Import Bank

G-7: Group of Seven leading industrialized nations, who meet annually to discuss world economic and other issues. Members: Canada, France, Germany, Japan, Italy, the United Kingdom, and the United States

G-7 Plus One: The G-7 nations plus Russia

GATT: General Agreement on Tariffs and Trade. Organized to promote reductions of tariff and trade barriers. Worldwide membership

GCC: Gulf Cooperation Council. A forum among Persian Gulf states for coordinating policies. Members as of 1998: Bahrain, Kuwait, Oman, Qatar, Saudi Arabia, and the United Arab Emirates

IAEA: International Atomic Energy Agency. Organization promoting safe and peaceful uses of atomic energy and monitoring violations of the Non-Proliferation Treaty

IFOR: Implementation Force. NATO military force implementing the November 1995 Dayton accords in Bosnia. In December 1996, became the Stabilization Force, or SFOR

IMF: International Monetary Fund. Promotes international monetary cooperation and currency stabilization

KEDO: Korean Energy Development Organization. Multinational consortium established in 1994 to organize and fund the provision of modern light-water reactors to North Korea

MERCOSUR: Mercado Comun del Sur. A South American free trade association. Members: Argentina, Brazil, Chile, Paraguay, and Uruguay

MFN: Most-favored-nation trading status, which is normal trade relationship between the United States and most other countries in the world

NAC: North Atlantic Council. NATO's governing body

NACC: North Atlantic Cooperation Council. Created in 1991 to promote cooperation between NATO and the states of Central and Eastern Europe and the former USSR, it holds meetings in conjunction with those of NAC

NAFTA: North American Free Trade Agreement. 1993 agreement liberalizing trading among Canada, Mexico, and the United States

NATO: North Atlantic Treaty Organization

NGOs: Non-governmental organizations

NPT: Nuclear Non-Proliferation Treaty

NSC: U.S. National Security Council

OAS: Organization of American States

OAU: Organization of African Unity

OECD: Organization for Economic Cooperation and Development. Multinational organization founded in 1948 that monitors and analyzes the economic performance of the industrialized world. 54 member countries

OEEC: Organization for European Economic Cooperation. Name of the OECD from 1948 until 1961

OMB: U.S. Office of Management and Budget

OPIC: Overseas Private Investment Corporation. Provides political risk insurance for overseas investments by U.S. companies

OSCE: Organization for Security and Cooperation in Europe. See CSCE

PFL-PGC: Terrorist group in the Middle East

PLO: Palestinian Liberation Organization

POW/MIAs: U.S. service personnel who were prisoners of war or missing in action during the Vietnam War, and are still unaccounted for

SADC: Southern African Development Community

SALT: Strategic Arms Limitation Treaty. Capped U.S. and Soviet nuclear arsenals

SCC: U.S.-Japan Security Consultative Committee. Ministerial-level committee that holds periodic meetings on security issues

START: Strategic Arms Reduction Treaty. Three-stage treaty between the United States and the Soviet Union reducing nuclear arsenals. START I has been ratified by both the U.S. Senate and the Duma. START II has been ratified by the U.S. Senate, but not yet by the Duma. Discussions in START III are pending.

TAFTA: Transatlantic Free Trade Agreement. Proposed NAFTA-like arrangement between the United States and the nations of Europe

UNHCR: UN High Commissioner for Refugees

UNITA: National Union for TOTAL Independence of Angola. Right-wing rebel group led by Jonas Savimbi; now technically at peace with Angolan government

UNMIH: UN Mission in Haiti

UNPROFOR: UN Protection Force. British- and French-led UN peace-keeping force deployed in Bosnia from September 1992 through 1995; succeeded by IFOR

UNSCOM: UN task force investigating Iraq's biochemical weapons program

Uruguay Round: Most recent round of GATT negotiations, completed in December 1993

USAID: U.S. Agency for International Development

USIA: U.S. Information Agency

USTR: U.S. Trade Representative

WTO: World Trade Organization

Index

Library of Congress Cataloging-in-Publication Data

Christopher, Warren.
  In the stream of history : shaping foreign policy for a new era /
Warren Christopher.
    p. cm.
Includes index.
ISBN 0-8047-3225-6 (cloth)
ISBN 0-8047-3468-2 (pb.)
  1. United States—Foreign relations—1993– 2. United States—
Foreign relations administration.   I. Title.
JZ1480.C48 1998
327.73'009'049—dc21   98-3772
                                       Rev.

∞ This book is printed on acid-free, recycled paper.

Original printing 1998

Last figure below indicates year of this printing:

06 05 04 03 02 01 00 99 98